Studies on Ibero-Romance Linguistics

Dedicated to RALPH PENNY

Juan de la Cuesta
Hispanic Monographs

Estudios lingüísticos, N° 7; *Homenajes* N° 24

FOUNDING EDITOR
Tom Lathrop
University of Delaware

EDITOR
Alexander R. Selimov
University of Delaware

EDITORIAL BOARD
Samuel G. Armistead
University of California, Davis

Annette G. Cash
Georgia State University

Alan Deyermond
Queen Mary and Westfield College of the University of London

Daniel Eisenberg
Excelsior College

John E. Keller
University of Kentucky

Steven D. Kirby
Eastern Michigan University

Joel Rini
University of Virginia

Donna M. Rogers
Middlebury College

Russell P. Sebold
Real Academia Española

Noël Valis
Yale University

Amy Williamsen
University of Arizona

Studies on Ibero-Romance Linguistics Dedicated to RALPH PENNY

Edited by
ROGER WRIGHT and PETER RICKETTS

Juan de la Cuesta
Newark, Delaware

Back cover photograph (center) of Ralph Penny © 2005 by Mercedes Quilis.

Copyright © 2005 by Juan de la Cuesta—Hispanic Monographs
270 Indian Road
Newark, Delaware 19711
(302) 453-8695
Fax: (302) 453-8601
www.JuandelaCuesta.com

MANUFACTURED IN THE UNITED STATES OF AMERICA

ISBN: 1-58871-072-6

Table of Contents

1. Introduction and Bibliography of Ralph Penny
   ROGER WRIGHT. 11

2. Representational Models vs. Operational Models of
   Literacy in Latin-Romance Legal Documents
   (with special reference to Latin-Portuguese texts)
   ANTÓNIO EMILIANO 17

3. On the Formation of the Present Indicative Paradigm of
   Spanish *ir* and the Origins of *vamos* and *vais*
   JOEL RINI 59

4. The Pronunciation of *h-* and *f-* in Bilingual Spanish/Arabic
   Treaties from the Thirteenth Century
   ROBERT BLAKE 75

5. Reflections on Dialect Mixing and
   Variation in Alfonsine Texts
   DONALD N. TUTEN 85

6. Some Phonological Features of Insular French:
   a Reconstruction
   MARTIN J. DUFFELL 103

7. Prayers in Medieval Occitan:
   Critical Edition, Translation and Notes
   PETER T. RICKETTS 127

8. *"Confundamus ibi linguam eorum"*:
   Some Accounts of the Tower of Babel
   in Medieval Castilian Literature
   ALAN DEYERMOND 153

9. The Count / Non-Count Distinction in Castilian:
   Evidence for its Place and Function
   in the Medieval Language
   RAY HARRIS-NORTHALL 167

10. Variation of the Spanish Demonstratives
    aqueste and *este*
    DIANA L. RANSON 187

11. Textual Evidence of the Development of
    the Sibilants of Peninsular Spain
    from the Eleventh to the Sixteenth Centuries
    DANA L. ALLEN 215

12. *Ingenio, Juicio, Prudencia*: the Linguistic Doctrine
    of Juan de Valdés
    THOMAS R. HART 233

13. Vowel Prosthesis and its Maintenance in Spanish:
    a Comparative Perspective
    RODNEY SAMPSON 241

14. *Ambiguitas* and the Secret Language of the Glossed *mote*
    IAN MACPHERSON 259

15. A Study of Intra-Personal Linguistic Variation
    in Cervantes (Grapho-Phonology)
    K. ANIPA 277

16. Analogical Feminines: Uniformity and
    Variety in Golden Age Spanish
    JOHN ENGLAND 299

17. Gender without Sex: the Semantic Exploitation
    of the Masculine/Feminine Opposition
    in the History of Spanish
    CHRISTOPHER J. POUNTAIN 329

18. Template Formation in Western Hispano-Romance
    DAVID PHARIES 349

19. From "Thinking" to "Caring":
    the Semantic Evolution of Lat. COGITARE
    and CURARE in Hispano-Romance
    STEVEN N. DWORKIN 363

20. Achievement Verbs in Medieval and Modern Spanish
    IAN MACKENZIE 375

21. La lengua, patria común: política lingüística,
    política exterior y el post-nacionalismo hispánico
    JOSÉ DEL VALLE 391

22. El atlas de Paraguay y la distinción [s] / [θ]
    FRANCISCO MORENO FERNÁNDEZ 417

23. A Forbidding Agenda: the Morphosyntax,
    Semantics and Pragmatics of Prohibition in Spanish
    JOHN N. GREEN 431

24. Convergence and Divergence in World Languages:
    Spanish, Latin and English
    ROGER WRIGHT 445

NOTES ON CONTRIBUTORS 459

TABULA GRATULATORIA 465

1
Introduction

RALPH PENNY IS A star. This volume celebrates his retirement in 2005 from the Chair of Spanish Linguistics at Queen Mary and Westfield College, at the age of 65, after many years of valuable service to the college, during which he has also become an internationally-known leader in the study of both Spanish Dialectology and the History of the Spanish Language.

His earliest research was carried out in the field of dialectology. He spent his time as a Ph.D. student travelling around Cantabria on a motorbike, investigating the speech of the Montes de Pas; the results were eventually published as *El habla pasiega: ensayo de dialectología montañesa*, in the series of *Támesis* publications in London. The care and detail manifested here in the analysis of the data, as well as the grasp of the relevant theoretical perspectives, has stood him in good stead ever since. He remained in the field of dialectology for his next major work, with an ever increasing awareness of its new companion discipline of sociolinguistics, while preparing his study on the speech of Tudanca; this was published in the most prestigious Romance Philology series of all, as an annex of the *Zeitschrift für Romanische Philologie*.

Ralph was becoming increasingly interested in historical questions, and began an ambitious project to prepare an up-to-date University handbook on the history of Spanish. Several articles which he published in the 1970s concentrated on thorny questions of Ibero-Romance diachrony, and their production accelerated through the 1980s. The eventual work of synthesis, *A History of the Spanish Language*, was published by Cambridge University Press in 1990, and immediately established him as a major authority in the field. His earlier expertise is built on skilfully; for example, the lengthy chapter on phonology gives great emphasis to metaphony, a notable feature of the Northern dialects, but not one that usually stars in most other accounts of the development of Spanish. The chapter on grammar follows a more recognizably Spanish academic line: Spanish linguists often use the compound noun *morfosintaxis*, showing more interest in morphology and less in syntax than most of their English-language counterparts, and Ralph calques that term as *Morpho-syntax* for the title of his chapter on grammatical developments. The book was so impressive that a Spanish translation came out very soon afterwards; this has been paid the great compliment of becoming a standard course textbook in many Spanish universities, such that his expert services have been much in demand in

Spain itself from this period onwards.

A second edition, carefully expanded and revised in many respects, came out in 2002. This edition is eighty pages longer, and almost every paragraph has been re-thought and altered. The book now ends with a brief but sensible new chapter on "Past, present and future," concluding that "The internal and external health of Spanish is reasonably assured for the foreseeable future" (p.321). Not many languages can claim that; and Ralph's textbook has helped ensure that the diachronic study of the language remains a vibrant and progressive field of academic activity, inspiring and intriguing students and colleagues alike.

The connections between his two areas of expertise, sociolinguistics and historical linguistics, have come to combine in splendid fruition in what is probably generally seen as his most important work, *Variation and Change in Spanish*, also published by Cambridge University Press. The greatest recent advances in the understanding of language change have come from the appreciation that the discoveries of sociolinguistics have relevance to the distant past as well as to the present; the merit of this book is that in it he considers from a sociolinguistic perspective the whole historical development of the language in the entire Spanish-speaking world. His acute understanding of the general processes involved in the formation of emigrant dialects and koines helps us understand, for example, why Ibero-Romance is less complex than the Romance of Italy (both internally and dialectologically), why *andaluz* is less complex than Castilian, and why parts of Latin America have simplified further; this was a train of thought which he adumbrated in his inaugural lecture of November 1986 (*Patterns of Language-Change in Spain*), the most exciting inaugural lecture I have ever heard. His conception of the dialect continuum is also entirely convincing; in linguistic reality there are no spatial frontiers between isolable "dialects," and insofar as clear isoglosses exist at all they do not naturally coincide. The picture is muddied by standardisation, of course, which has its own chapter at the end. This book is unlike the *History* in that he does not need to discuss those changes that have led to the same result all over the Spanish-speaking world; "these cases are inherently uninteresting" (p.79) from a variationist viewpoint. *Variation and Change in Spanish* will soon become an indispensable classic, written by probably the only expert with the necessary combination of talents. And it is so accessibly written, with clearly organized and self-contained sections, that the interested non-specialist will also be fascinated and intrigued. It is highly encouraging to know that a Spanish version of this work too is currently in Press.

Much of the inspiration for these two great works, and the reason for their unusual clarity of focus and presentation, comes from his ability and experience as a teacher. He much enjoys teaching, and his students appreciate that in turn. But he has contributed to the profession in a wide variety of ways. He edited the Linguistic volume of the Acts of the first ever Anglo-Spanish Hispanists Conference, held at Huelva in 1992 as part of the celebrations of the Quincentenary of Columbus's first voyage, where the Linguistic section which he ran was notably well organized and successful. He has been an assiduously active participant in conferences in many parts of the world, including as a member of the Organizing Committee of the triennial conferences of the International Association for the History of the Spanish Language. His influence and ideas will continue to have a wide resonance and arouse general admiration for decades to come.

So when we decided to organize a Festschrift volume in his honour, it was simple to find a large number of willing participants. Many of those invited to contribute expressed the view that few people have deserved this honour as much as Ralph does. The authors of these chapters include colleagues, and one doctoral student, from Queen Mary and Westfield College itself; but the majority are Hispanists working in a wide range of other Universities, who have gladly given of their time and expertise to honour the master. The result is this present collection, which covers many important aspects of the past, the present and even the future of the Ibero-Romance Languages (not just of Castilian), and, indeed, of Occitan, French and Insular (Anglo-) French as well. Nothing is definitive, because this is a fast-moving and exciting field in which to work, where new ideas, new analyses and new data are being examined and developed all the time; and that very progressiveness is part of the legacy which Ralph Penny has given us. We all wish him well in retirement, and hope and suspect that it will not really be retirement at all; with luck his ideas will be inspiring us for many years to come.

ROGER WRIGHT
Liverpool
April 2004

A select bibliography of the works of RALPH PENNY

1. BOOKS:

El habla pasiega: ensayo de dialectología montañesa, Támesis (Serie Monográfica A, no.13), London, 1969.
Estudio estructural del habla de Tudanca, Niemeyer (Beihefte zur Zeitschrift für Romanische Philologie, Band 167), Tübingen, 1978.
Patterns of Language Change in Spain, Westfield College, London, 1987.
A History of the Spanish Language, Cambridge University Press, 1991; second edition, 2002. Translation of 2nd ed., 2005.
Gramática histórica del español, Ariel, Barcelona (translated by José Ignacio Pérez Pascual), 1993.
Variation and Change in Spanish, Cambridge University Press, 2000. Spanish translation, 2005.
(with Lourdes García-Macho), *Historia de la lengua española, II: Morfosintaxis*, UNED, Madrid, 2001.

2. BOOKS EDITED:

Actas del Primer Congreso Anglo-Hispano, Tomo I, Lingüística, Castalia, Madrid and the Junta de Andalucía, 1993; (with Alan Deyermond) *Tomo II: Literatura*, 1994; (with Richard Hitchcock) *Tomo III: Historia*, 1994.
(With Ian Macpherson) *The Medieval Mind: Hispanic Studies in Honour of Alan Deyermond*, Támesis (Serie Monográfica A, no.170), London, 2000.

3. ARTICLES:

"Vowel harmony in the speech of the Montes de Pas (Santander)," *Orbis* 18, 1969, 148-66.
"Mass nouns and metaphony in the dialects of North-Western Spain," *Archivum Linguisticum* n.s.1, 1970, 21-30.
"The re-emergence of /f/ as a phoneme of Castilian," *Zeitschrift für Romanische Philologie* 78, 1972, 463-82.
"Verb-class as a determiner of stem-vowel in the historical morphology of Spanish verbs," *Revue de Linguistique Romane* 36, 1972, 343-59.
"The convergence of B, V, and -P- in the Peninsula: a reappraisal," in *Medieval Hispanic Studies presented to Rita Hamilton*, ed. Alan Deyermond, Tamesis, London, 1976, 149-60.
"The Northern transition area between Leonese and Castilian," *Revue de Linguistique Romane* 42, 1978, 44-52.
"Do Romance nouns descend from the accusative? Preliminaries to a reassessment of the noun morphology of Romance," *Romance Philology* 33, 1980, 501-09.
"El dialectalismo de *Peñas Arriba*," *Boletín de la Biblioteca Menéndez y Pelayo* 56,

1980, 377-86.

"The Peninsular expansion of Castilian," *Bulletin of Hispanic Studies* 60, 1983, 333-38.

"Secondary consonant groups in Castilian," *Journal of Hispanic Philology* 7, 1983, 135-40.

"Esbozo de un atlas lingüístico de Santander," *Lingüística Española Actual* 6, 1984, 123-81.

"Sandhi phenomena in Castilian and related dialects," in *Sandhi Phenomena in the Languages of Europe*, ed. Henning Andersen, Berlin, Mouton de Gruyter, 489-503.

"Derivation of abstracts in Alfonsine Spanish," *Romance Philology* 41, 1987, 1-23.

"The Old Spanish graphs 'i', 'j', 'g' and 'y' and the development of Latin $G^{e,i}$- and J-," *Bulletin of Hispanic Studies* 65, 1988, 337-51.

"The stage jargon of Juan del Encina and the castilianization of the Leonese dialect area," in *Golden Age Literature: studies in honour of John Varey by his colleagues and pupils*, ed. Charles Davis and Alan Deyermond, Queen Mary and Westfield College, London, 1990, 155-66.

"The Language of Christopher Columbus," in *Christopher Columbus: Journal of the First Voyage*, ed. Barry Ife, Aris and Phillips, Warminster, 1990, xxvii-xl.

"El origen asturleonés de algunos fenómenos andaluces y americanos," *Lletres Asturianes* 39, 1991, 33-40.

"Labiodental /f/, aspiration and /h/-dropping in Spanish: the evolving phonemic value of the graphs *f* and *h*," in: *Cultures in Contact in Medieval Spain: Historical and Literary Essays Presented to L. P. Harvey*, ed. David Hook and Barry Taylor, King's College, London, 1991, 157-82.

"La innovación fonológica del judeoespañol," in *Actas del II Congreso Internacional de Historia de la Lengua Española*, ed. Manuel Ariza et al., Pabellón de España, Madrid, 1992, Vol.II, 251-57.

"Dialect contact and social networks in Judeo-Spanish," *Romance Philology* 46, 1992, 125-40.

"Final /e/ in Asturian feminine singulars: another mass-noun marker?" *Journal of Hispanic Research* 1, 1992, 182-85.

"Neutralization of voice in Spanish and the outcome of the Old Spanish sibilants: a case of phonological change rooted in morphology?," in *Hispanic Linguistic Studies in Honour of F. W. Hodcroft*, ed. David Mackenzie and Ian Michael, Dolphin, Oxford, 1993, 75-88.

"The linguistic work of Menéndez Pidal," *Journal of Hispanic Research* 2, 1993, 134-35.

"Continuity and innovation in Romance: metaphony and mass noun reference in Spain and Italy," *Modern Language Review* 89, 1994, 273-81.

"Sobre el concepto del castellano como dialecto revolucionario," in *Historia de la Lengua Española en América y España*, ed. María Teresa Echenique Elizondo et al., Universidad de Valencia, 1995, 403-07.

"El árbol genealógico: ¿modelo lingüístico desfasado?," in *Actas del III Congreso Internacional de Historia de la Lengua Española*, ed. A. Alonso González et al., Arco Libros, Madrid, 1996, 827-39.

"Judeo-Spanish varieties before and after the expulsion," in *Acts of the Ninth British Conference on Judeo-Spanish Studies* (= Donaire 6), 1996, 54-58.

"The Language of Gonzalo de Berceo, in the context of peninsular dialectal variation," in *The Medieval Mind: Hispanic Studies in Honour of Alan Deyermond*, ed. by Ian

Macpherson and Ralph Penny, Támesis, London, 1997, 327-45.

"¿En qué consiste una historia del castellano?," in *Actas del IV Congreso Internacional de Historia de la Lengua Española*, ed. Claudio García Turza et al., Universidad de la Rioja, Logroño, 1998, II, 583-94.

"La grafía de los textos notariales castellanos de la Alta Edad Media: ¿sistema logográfico o fonológico?," in *Estudios de grafemática en el dominio hispano*, ed. José Manuel Blecua et al., Universidad de Salamanca, 1998, 211-23.

"Judeo-Spanish," "Mozarabic" and "Spanish," in *The Encyclopedia of the Languages of Europe*, ed. Glanville Price, Blackwell, Oxford, 1998, 277-78, 327 and 451-60.

"Standard vs. Dialect: linguistic (dis)continuity in the Iberian Peninsula," in *Essays in Hispanic Linguistics dedicated to Paul M. Lloyd*, ed. Robert J. Blake et al., Juan de la Cuesta, Newark, 1999, 43-55.

"Contacto de variedades y resolución de la variación: aspiración y pérdida de /h/ en el Madrid del s.XVI," in *Actas del V Congreso Internacional de Historia de la Lengua Española*, ed. María Teresa Echenique Elizondo et al., Gredos, Madrid, 2002, 397-406.

"Procesos de clasificación verbal española: polaridad de vocales radicales en los verbos en *-er* e *-ir*," in *Pulchre, Bene, Recte: Estudios en Homenaje al Prof. Fernando González Ollé*, ed. Carmen Saralegui Platero et al., Universidad de Navarra, Pamplona, 2002, 1053-70.

"Historical Romance Linguistics: a sociolinguistic perspective," *La Coronica* 31.2, 2003, 83-88.

"Ambigüedad grafemática: correspondencia entre fonemas y grafemas en los textos peninsulares anteriores al S.XIII," in *Lengua romance en textos latinos de la Edad Media*, ed. Hermógenes Perdiguero Villarreal, Universidad de Burgos, 2003, 221-28.

"Evolución lingüística en la Baja Edad Media: evoluciones en el plano fónico," in *Historia de la lengua española*, ed. Rafael Cano, Ariel, Barcelona, 2004, 593-612.

" 'Continuum Dialectal' y fronteras estatales: el caso del leonés medieval," in *Orígenes de las lenguas romances en el Reino de León; siglos IX-XII*, ed. José María Fernández Catón et al., Universidad de León, in press.

"The Spanish-speaking Caribbean," in *Sociolinguistics Handbook*, 2nd ed., ed. Peter Trudgill, Mouton de Gruyter. Amsterdam, in press.

2
Representational models vs. operational models of literacy in Latin-Romance legal documents (with special reference to Latin-Portuguese texts)

António Emiliano

INTRODUCTION

IN ORDER TO UNDERSTAND the emergence of Portuguese writing in the early thirteenth century, we must bear in mind that it was preceded by a Latin-Portuguese tradition, which was based on the Late Latin Visigothic tradition, which in turn was based on the tradition of Late Antiquity, and so on, with no intervening linguistic interruption: it is crucial that we ask ourselves what this textual tradition was, how it came about, how it evolved throughout several centuries of document production, and in particular how speakers of Old Portuguese communicated in writing by means of this tradition.

What it was, in terms of textual typology, and how it came about is the object of Diplomatics, and I will not go into that in this article. How it evolved is of tremendous importance for the History of the Portuguese Language, because in my view this tradition is *the* origin of Portuguese writing, and its texts are the first instances of the textualization of Portuguese. Many of the things discussed here in this respect apply also to other northern Ibero-Romance linguistic areas.

This earlier tradition of writing, which can be conveniently referred to as Latin-Romance, or Latin-Portuguese, was the only available means for writing legal Old Portuguese before the thirteenth century, and although the texts look Latinate in appearance, their latinity is a highly vulgarized one.

In the early thirteenth century people did not suddenly stop writing Latin, and begin writing Old Portuguese out of the blue; rather they began systematically to write Old Portuguese in a new way. This new way of writing, which would eventually evolve into modern Portuguese orthography, attained a high degree of stabilization in the Royal Chancery by 1214, and in many monastic and capitular centres across the realm scribes were developing and experimenting with a considerably 'de-latinized' or 'vulgarized' writing system throughout the twelfth century.

The Latin-Portuguese tradition was old and rich: the earliest original Latin-Portuguese charter that we know of dates from 882, but notarial documents were almost certainly written much earlier than that, and from the period between 882 and the end of the twelfth century there are about 3500-4000 known original charters. If we count the documents that were preserved in cartularies the figure of known Latin-Portuguese documents written before the thirteenth century increases three- or four-fold. Their importance for our knowledge of the early periods of the history of the Portuguese language is enormous and cannot be overstated.

The documents written before the thirteenth century have been referred to traditionally as *Latin*, because in a certain sense they look Latin, they have a certain Latin-like quality. However, close scrutiny of these texts shows that their latinity is peculiar, that it is very different from Classical Latin, and that it clearly deviates from the grammatical standards prescribed by the *artes grammaticæ* that were studied throughout the Middle Ages.

1. LATIN, ROMANCE AND LATIN-ROMANCE

Iberian notarial latinity, which was fairly homogeneous throughout the northern realms, was a special register of written communication, and the only available means for representing Ibero-Romance vernaculars before the thirteenth century. One must look at the Notarial Latin found in documents from Castile, León, Galicia, and Portugal before the thirteenth century as a special written code designed to meet specific communicative needs: the documents formed a particular textual and communicative domain or genre, which had specific traits and characteristics.

Notarial documents were, so to speak, a "scripto-linguistic laboratory," where for centuries scribes experimented with many of the graphemic solutions that would finally lead up to the development of autonomous Romance scriptographies in the early thirteenth century. But before the creation of these new spelling systems there was no other way of representing the Ibero-Romance vernaculars: in order to write Romance, before a Romance spelling system was available, scribes had to make do with the old Latin tradition. Romance was therefore written as if it were Latin, with some inflectional morphology, with some Latin lexis, and some Latin syntax. But when it was read aloud it sounded like Romance, because it was read with Romance phonetics.

Thus the study of notarial documents must take account of the complex relationship that existed between the several types and modes of communication in medieval societies. Both the Latin written tradition and the Romance vernaculars developed without any break or discontinuity from Antiquity through the Middle Ages. It has been systematically overlooked by Romanists and Latinists that the relationship between the written and spoken languages in Romania was therefore unbroken for centuries, until the Carolingian reforms, headed by Alcuin of York, introduced a completely new way of pronouncing Latin and new standards of orthographic correctness. Written Latin then became largely unintelligible to monolingual native Old French speakers. In the eleventh century a similar reform, known as the Gregorian Reform (or Cluniac Reform), which, among other things, introduced Medieval Latin into Iberia, paved the way for the distinction between Latin and Ibero-Romance as separate languages.

We can use the expression "Latin-Romance," coined by Roger Wright, to refer to the special written code of non-literary texts (documents, legal codes, proceedings of councils and synods, chronicles), before the thirteenth century: it looked like Latin, but Romance-speakers of the time must have regarded it as the written representation of a formal variety of the vernacular.

Wright actually coined the expression in Spanish, i.e. "lengua latino-romance," to comment on the expression "nostra lingua" used in the *Chronica Adefonsi Imperatoris* from the twelfth century:

> Me parece que con la frase *nostra lingua* se refiere el autor a lo que concebimos nosotros como dos lenguas pero que él concebía como una lengua, la lengua latino-romance. (Wright 1992:883)

"Lengua latino-romance" in Wright's phrase refers to the written representation of an Ibero-Romance vernacular by means of the traditional Latinate spelling, at a time where no Romance spelling system was available. The Portuguese historian Rui de Azevedo used the expression "latino-português," as an adjective referring to the oldest known original document in Portuguese territory (Azevedo 1932). It seems to mean simply "a Latin document written in Portugal." The Spanish latinist Maurilio Pérez González adopted the expression and attributed it to Wright in his article about the *Diploma Silonis regis* (Pérez González 1993a), but gave it a slightly different meaning, and I am not sure that Wright would subscribe to this use of his expression:

> ... una lengua que está a punto de perder su identidad en beneficio de las diferentes lenguas romances provenientes de ella misma. (Pérez González 1993a:126),

and

> Así pues, la lengua que se manifiesta en el diploma del rey Silo por medio de la pluma de un amanuense que no poseía un elevado nivel de educación lingüística, es decir, poco influido por la tradición escolar, no es latina ni romance, sino latino-romance. Y pensamos que dicha lengua sería comprendida tanto por los eruditos como por los iletrados; es decir,

aceptamos para el s.VIII la comunicación vertical, en expresión feliz de Banniard. (id., 138)

This use of "latino-romance" is comparable to the Portuguese expression "latim bárbaro" used by historians and philologists.

However, the expression "Latin-Romance" has already been used in English by the American latinist Ernst Pulgram (1975), but with a quite different meaning: Pulgram uses it to refer to the historical *continuum* between Latin and the Romance languages. In a review of this book (published in *Language* 55:698-701, 1979) Paul Lloyd explains Pulgram's use of the expression:

> P(ulgram) insists on his view of the diglossic situation under the late Republic and Empire because he feels it essential to combat the notion (still too widespread, unfortunately), that 'Classical Latin' developed into the ancestor of the Romance languages, whether called 'Vulgar Latin' (an extremely ambiguous term that he avoids completely) or 'Proto-Romance' or something else. One statement deserves particular emphasis: '...Classical Latin did not evolve into anything; it merely petered out as living idiom' (129). For this reason, P prefers to speak of Latin-Romance, a continuously developing tongue without any discrete breaks. (Lloyd 1979: 698)

Personally, I find that Proto-Romance is a much more efficient (and accurate) way of referring to the Latin/Romance continuum, because it dispenses with the term "Latin" altogether, which is indeed a great advantage, because of all the problems surrounding the precise linguistic meaning of the term Latin.

Notarial documents, no matter how "barbarous" their language may seem to post-Renaissance latinists, were valid communicative acts. Their language and spelling were accepted by their users as normal and adequate, and reflected a stable tradition of writing, which preceded for many centuries the development of Romance orthographies. Thus, any assessment of these texts which is based on a dysfunctional conception of scribal competence is not sufficient, for the simple reason that it is not grounded on solid evidence, and explains nothing.

For the historians and philologists that have written about the "barbarousness" of Notarial Latin the documents are nothing more than result of widespread and ingrained ignorance, and were written by poor semi-literate scribes, who were culturally isolated and backward, who did not know the *auctoritates* and the *litteræ*, who struggled to no avail to master the intricacies of Latin orthography and grammar, whose vernacular kept creeping up as they tried to write good Latin, and whose feeble attempts at writing good Latin would achieve nothing but a corrupt and garbled text.

This pessimistic and widespread perspective on medieval Iberian literacy and the early notaries of Spain, should now yield to a more enlightened view that takes account of important recent developments in several areas of research.

In discussing Latin-Portuguese documents we need now to use concepts such as discourse community, textual interpretability, pragmatic competence, scripto-linguistic competence, graphemic structure, lexical access, grapho-phonemic transcodification vs grapho-semantic transcodification, graphemic polymorphism and variation, and other concepts taken from research areas such as sociolinguistics, pragmatics, text linguistics, discourse analysis, psycholinguistics, scriptology, graphemics, cultural anthropology, social anthropology, etc.

It is also time to move on from a nineteenth-century perspective on these texts. Throughout the nineteenth and twentieth centuries Latin-Portuguese documents had the status of historical sources or records. Only seldom, and then in a biased way, were they seen as linguistic sources or records. Even the romanists, who saw in the vulgarized spellings the emergence or interference of the Romance vernaculars, could not help looking at the texts as a whole as corrupt and decadent.

2. REPRESENTATIONAL MODELS VS. OPERATIONAL MODELS IN THE LATIN-ROMANCE WRITTEN TRADITION

The interpretation of medieval literacy-related phenomena requires an adequate framework, which must rely on anthropological, cultural, linguistic and graphemic data.

First and foremost, it is crucial to keep in mind that reading and writing are not universal categories; on the contrary, they are manifestations of local knowledge, and as such, reading and writing are culturally conditioned practices and activities—they are not the same phenomena across different cultures. Therefore every text in every culture is based on a set of expectations shared by the textual community concerning what a text is and how it should look (or sound, if it was read aloud); every text must fit into an accepted model or genre of textual production; and medieval notarial texts were no exception. Their structure and their language fitted into what the textual community of the time considered adequate and expected to find. If we bear this in mind, we can avoid making anachronistic statements about the correctness of these texts, and avoid any perspective—linguistic, stylistic or cultural—that resorts to a handicapped view of medieval scribes and medieval documents; our aim should be to explain how a writing system worked for centuries for the people who used it. This means that we need to grasp the actual patterns of textual production that were learnt and used by medieval scribes, instead of applying our own conceptions of Latinity, correctness, grammar, style, composition, logic, literacy, etc.

Literacy, as many anthropologists and some linguists know, is not a universal category: there is no such thing as an autonomous or absolute concept of literacy. Literacy practices cannot be isolated from other practices of a given culture. Medieval literacy was not modern literacy. So we need to make the effort to integrate medieval literacy in the set of beliefs, knowledges, prejudices, and social and cultural practices that were functional at the time: it was according to that set of beliefs and standards, not according to our own, that the the texts of that age were received and accepted.

Michael Stubbs has stressed this notion of "relative literacy" in a fundamental book about language and literacy:

> *Functional literacy* is a term coined by Gray (1956), and is used particularly in connection with literacy programmes organized in developing countries by Unesco. It defines literacy as relative to the requirements of an individual within a particular society: it is the degree of literacy required for effective functioning in a particular community. Since a Brazilian peasant requires a different kind of literacy from an American urban dweller, *there is no single definition of functional literacy for all the world's population.* (Stubbs 1980:14; my emphasis)

The validity of a text (whether literary, scientific or legal, public or private), depends on the local criteria of acceptability which exist in the period and in the community where the text is produced. In the case of Latin-Romance notarial documents, as a body of texts with very specific characteristics, textual acceptability (1) presupposed diachronically the existence and permanence of a special *discourse tradition*, where contemporary scribal practices were rooted, and (2) depended synchronically on the *expectations of the textual community* concerning written communication acts. These expectations determined the form and modes of textual production, and the social structures and contexts in which the texts were received and perceived.

To phrase it in very simple terms: what the scribes and notaries wrote and what they thought they were writing may not be the same thing to an outside observer, due to the fact that the scribes considered themselves as part of an ancient discourse tradition, but at the same time were obliged to meet the textual and linguistic expectations of the textual community to which they belonged. That is to say that the development of the Latin-Portuguese notarial language was based on a balance between the need to write traditionally, and the need for communicative realism (what Francesco Sabatini called the "esigenze di realismo comunicativo": Sabatini 1965).

The analysis of the texts shows that Notarial Latin fits perfectly the picture suggested by Roger Wright: the written and the spoken language existed, not in a situation of diglossia, but in a situation of what he has called "complex monolingualism" (Wright 1993 and 2003). One of the aims of this article is to develop that notion by highlighting some of the complexities of the monolingual situation of the Old Portuguese linguistic community before the thirteenth century.

In modern language communities that have a complex social stratification, and where a standard language has been developed (which conditions or determines both the actual language usage and the attitudes towards language in the community), it has been found that there is not always an absolute coincidence between the judgments that speakers are able to make about their language use and the reality of their linguistic production. The distinction between what speakers and writers say that they say or write (or say that ought to be said or ought to be written) and what they *actually* say or write is an important aspect of the attitudes towards language in a complex community, and is one distinction that has important consequences for the overall evaluation of the patterns of language variation and change in any given community, as much modern sociolinguistic research of the Labovian type has shown.

This type of distinction is well known to anthropologists and sociologists, to whom the mythical or ideological—or simply, conceptual—framework of many daily aspects of community life and community structures is viewed as distinct from the pragmatic and concrete dimension of actual practice and behaviour. Many examples could be given from many types of societies, such as the conceptualization of territoriality or of time cycles, the boundaries of social mobility, the regulation of kinship and marriage systems, the internal stratification of the communities, the elaboration and content of genealogical narratives transmitted orally, cosmogonic or epic narratives transmitted both orally and in writing; or even—in modern urban western societies—the self-evaluation of individuals in polls regarding aspects such as political and social stability, consumer habits, economic status, voting intentions in national elections, attitudes towards language, feelings of urban safety, rights of citizenship, xenophobia, etc. In all these aspects what the subjects may report that they do, or are, or intend to do, or should be done, can sometimes be quite startlingly different from what is recorded by an external observer. Pre-election polls or stock-market predictions are perhaps the best example of such a distinction between conceptualization and behaviour: in many instances the results predicted by pollsters and analysts are proved wrong.

This notion that there is always a *mismatch* between implicit models (incorporated, inherited or imposed) and explicit practices is particularly important for the study of literacy acquisition and practice in different communities, cultures and periods.

What I am suggesting is that it is useful to adopt a uniformitarian perspective and apply certain types of knowledge or information that can be acquired by observing and analysing modern language communities to the study of language communities of the past.

* * *

The introduction and implementation of the Gregorian Reform in the Iberian Peninsula, especially after the Council of Burgos in 1080, had important consequences for the development of Hispanic written traditions (cf. Wright

1982 for a general overview). The changes which can be perceived in the texts after the Reform should be regarded as the result of a tendency towards a greater isomorphism between **models** of language correctness and scribal **practices**, especially in the area of spelling. The changes should not be perceived as indicating the occurrence of a sudden and generalized "restoration of latinity," as was proposed by Ramón Menéndez Pidal in *Orígenes del Español* where he expounded his theory of the two trends of vulgarization in the notarial language:

> Descubría así dos encontradas corrientes de vulgaridad en la lengua notarial: una que venía de los siglos antiguos y se extinguía en el curso de los dos primeros tercios del XI; otra que empezaba en el último tercio del XII y triunfaba con la adopción del lenguaje vulgar en el XIII. ¿Qué había ocurrido a fines del XI para detener la primera de estas dos corrientes? Pues *la reforma cluniacense que restauró la latinidad* y se alzó como barrera aisladora entre las dos direcciones reseñadas. Y ¿qué ocurrió a fines del siglo XII para iniciar la segunda corriente? Pues un movimiento general a toda la Romania que llevaba a secularizar la cultura, y por tanto a entronizar el romance como lengua oficial ordinaria, dejando el latín solamente como supletorio para los actos más solemnes. (Menéndez Pidal [1926] 1980[9]:viij; my emphasis)

The Portuguese historian José Mattoso, in a rare remark about language matters, referring to "a greater care in the use of the Latin language, even in legal acts" which he observed in texts written after the Reform, wrote in a similar vein:

> Com efeito, a partir dos anos 80 do século XI, diminui consideravelmente o uso das preposições com o caso universal (acusativo), melhora o emprego das declinações, abandona-se mais frequentemente a utilização de vocábulos da língua vulgar. O latim afasta-se, assim, das contaminações do *sermo vulgaris*. O fenómeno está, sem dúvida, relacionado com a melhor formação escolar dos monges e clérigos, mas esta, por sua vez, é sobretudo imposta pela necessidade de utilizar os novos livros litúrgicos, redigidos num latim mais clássico. (Mattoso [1983] 1985:379)

Had the restoration of Latinity happened in such a straightforward way or so abrupt a manner as is implied by both Pidal and Mattoso, it would have created immediately an unbridgeable gap between the written and oral Ibero-Romance codes at the end of the eleventh century, a hypothesis which is not supported by the evidence. Examination of the texts does not show such a break between written and oral communication, and so the changes that took place must be viewed as reflecting *an adjustment of the scribal tradition to a new cultural reality*; in other words, the Reform narrowed in some sense the gap between the models of scribal production and the grammatical and rhetorical models of the past, contained in the *artes grammaticæ*, the *auctoritates*, the Scriptures and the liturgy.

This adjustment brought about two developments which appear to be contradictory in nature:

1. on the one hand, the level of traditional correctness in the latinity of legal documents seems to have increased as regards some *scriptoria* and scribes;
2. on the other hand, the Reform seems to have heightened the graphophonemic awareness of many scribes, and as a result, many documents from the twelfth century show a high degree of vernacularization and de-latinization (which indeed paved the way for the emergence of Romance *scriptæ* in the early thirteenth century).

Throughout the Middle Ages scribes, clergy and monks in general had access to the old Latin grammatical tradition: they were taught to read and write according to that tradition, and they had books written in Latin. Models of correct Latinity ("old" Latinity) were available at all times to people who wrote documents. The people who wrote documents also copied books. So we may ask ourselves why there was this noticeable difference between the linguistic models and the scribes' practices before 1080.

This discrepancy between models and practices corresponds to a distinction made in cultural anthropology between *representational models* and *operational models*, which means that what a culture does and what it thinks it does, can be, and often are, from the point of view of an external observer, different things. In the 60's the American sociolinguist William Labov detected this type of discrepancy between what informants thought they said and what they actually said, especially regarding sociolinguistic variables associated with social prestige (Labov 1966).

What a culture thinks it does results from a representational model of their world, something that can be more or less articulate and can be even verbalized, and is framed by (or enshrined in) a vision of their past. This can be phrased as "we act the way we were taught to act" or "we do this the same way our forefathers or ancestors did." On the other hand, what a culture really does is based on implicit models which guide behaviour in certain situations and settings, and which are not necessarily conscious; i.e. they cannot or need not be verbalized (Holland and Quinn 1987:5-6).

This distinction between norms and actions is what the Finnish linguist Esa Itkonen aptly calls a distinction between "ought" (i.e. what ought to be done) and "is" (what is actually done) (Itkonen 1983: 55-56, 177-78). Itkonen, in a lengthy and fundamental discussion of the notion of causality in Linguistics, proposes a dichotomy between "normativity" and "spatiotemporality," a dichotomy which in my view can be adequately applied to the analysis of medieval literacy:

> In relation to actions the dimension of normativity is about what *ought* to be done, whereas the dimension of spatiotemporality is about what *is* done. (Notice, however, that actions done do not exemplify *mere* spatiotemporality, because the intentional element of actions cannot be defined in purely spatiotemporal terms.) The same distinction applies, somewhat less obviously, to what one ought to believe and what one believes in fact. As here understood, the use of 'ought' is either justified or unjustified, depending on whether it conforms to or conflicts with a standard or a *norm*. When a norm exists, its existence is a *fact*, but not a *spatiotemporal* fact like a man uttering a sentence or an apple falling to the ground. (It is true, of course, that norms are 'spatiotemporal' in the abstract and secondary sense that they are likely to differ in different times and/or places.) [...]
>
> It is a well-known philosophical principle that what ought to be can be neither derived from nor reduced to what is. (Itkonen 1983:55-56)

Texts *qua* physical embodiments of real language acts produced by real individuals in concrete locations and at concrete points in time are spatiotemporal entities. The norms that governed the production of medieval texts were shared knowledge, with a social and traditional dimension. If norms are "contingently nonempirical" as Itkonen (1983:60) puts it, they may vary and change with time, and may be different from culture to culture, even in genetically related cultures, but they are not empirically falsifiable.

The task of the medieval philologist is to make explicit the norms that were behind the production of texts, and to relate the actual texts to the assumed norms; this entails the consideration of two types of information: (1) the information directly supplied by primary sources, i.e. the texts themselves and their structural/linguistic content, and (2) the indirect information about the existence of textual and linguistic norms supplied by metalinguistic texts such as grammatical treatises which were known and read at the time when the primary sources were produced.

It can be safely assumed that at the representational level medieval notaries had as their goal the written representation of some form of Latinity, whereas their texts indicate that this Latinity was in fact the written expression of their vernacular language, albeit in a highly formal and stylized variety.

Itkonen also introduces in his characterization of the empirical status of norms ("norm-sentences") the distinction between "agent's knowledge" and "observer's knowledge":

> [...] the truth of norm-sentences is known because the norms are *learned*;

and for X to learn a norm means for X to learn to do *himself* that which is right, and which he (intuitively) *knows* to be right. By contrast, we can never 'learn' the physical, nothing-but-observable reality in the same way, simply because the physical reality (unlike our representation of it) contains no norms. Thus we ultimately come to see that *the age-old distinction between 'agent's knowledge' and 'observer's knowledge' lies at the core of the distinction between normative-non empirical and spatiotemporal-empirical.* (Itkonen 1983:60; my emphasis)

And also, in a previous work:

[...] our knowledge of events and regularities is observer's (or 'outsider's') knowledge, whereas our knowledge of actions and rules is agent's (or 'insider's') knowledge. [...] The basis for the peculiar nature of agent's knowledge can be seen in the fact that, [...], *man's relation to his actions is not empirical, but conceptual.* (Itkonen 1978:193-94; my emphasis)

When a culture declares "we act the way we were taught" what they actually do may be noticeably different from the behaviour they think they are replicating, because they perceive their actions in terms of a conceptual representation of those actions. An outside observer can detect the difference, but someone belonging to the culture, who is completely attuned to the culture's historical development, and has agent's knowledge of the inner workings of his culture, will not be able to notice any changes or differences: medieval scribal models of correctness belonged to a representational level of medieval culture, and had an ideological dimension, whereas the actual practices tended to meet the contemporary demands for communicative realism, and did not correspond isomorphically to the inherited models or norms.

In other words, to a medieval scribe who wrote legal documents each document was the result (or the embodiment) of an action which was carried out according to a set of internalized rules, models and norms. A medieval scribe had agent's knowledge of the texts *qua* language acts. This operational knowledge did not necessarily coincide with the traditional norms that were inherited from the Late Antiquity, although these norms, belonging to a representational or conceptual level of medieval literacy, were still regarded as valid and authoritative.

To a modern philologist or linguist looking at the same documents many centuries after they were written, with the intention of studying them as textual and linguistic artefacts of a long gone culture and society, the texts are "simply" events. Therefore the philologist's and linguist's knowledge of medieval documents can only be outsider's, observer's knowledge. Since this knowledge of medieval texts is empirical, a modern scholar is in a position to detect discrepancies between the norms that were in place at the time the documents were written and the actual behaviour of the scribes reflected in the scriptolinguistic contents of the documents.

To add to the complexitity of this issue, what a culture says about itself may change with time, as the culture changes, and again this will only be noticeable to an outside observer. Jack Goody and Ian Watt (1963) observed this phenomenon in the way certain elements of the past of illiterate communities, which had ceased to be relevant in the present, were discarded:

> The social function of memory—and of forgetting—can thus be seen as the final stage of what may be called the *homeostatic organization of the cultural tradition* in non-literate society. The language is developed in intimate association with the experience of the community, and it is learned by the individual in face-to-face contact with the other members. What continues to be of social relevance is stored in the memory while the rest is usually forgotten: and language—primarily vocabulary—is the effective medium of this crucial process of social digestion and elimination which may be regarded as analogous to the homeostatic organization of the human body by means of which it attempts to maintain its present condition of life. (Goody & Watt [1963] 1972:315; my emphasis)

and also:

> *One of the most important results of this homeostatic tendency is that the individual has little perception of the past except in terms of the present*; [...] Myth and history merge into one: the elements in the cultural heritage which cease to have a contemporary relevance tend to be soon forgotten or transformed; and as the individuals of each generation acquire their vocabulary, their genealogies, and their myths, they are unaware that various words, proper-names and stories have dropped out, or that others have changed their meanings or been replaced. (*id.*, 319; my emphasis)

The existence of this "homeostatic tendency" means that the vision that a community has of its past, of its history, and of its cultural structures is continually being restructured and reshaped according to their contemporary needs and demands. I have suggested elsewhere that this concept could be applied with success to the way Latin-Romance writing evolved "homeostatically" out of Late Latin writing (Emiliano 1995, Emiliano 2003).

It should not go unnoticed in this respect that almost 50 years ago Christine Mohrmann had used the expression "normativisme évolutif" (Mohrmann 1958:189 et passim) to refer to the dynamic balance between tradition and innovation shown by Medieval Latin texts in general (whose most extreme expression is probably the flexible Latinity of Merovingian and Leonese pre-Reform charters, with their striking combination of traditional elements and graphic innovations).

Given the importance of this perspective outlined by Goody and Watt, and bearing in mind the proviso that medieval Ibero-Romance societies were not illiterate but societies with restricted literacy, some of Goody and Watt's statements could be slightly re-phrased in order to fit perfectly the homeostatic development of notarial Latin. Such an exercise in explicit plagiarism is worth undertaking, since it does shed light on the process by which some elements and structures of the Latin tradition were gradually discarded or changed from within in the notarial language:

1. One of the most important results of this homeostatic tendency is that the individual has little perception of the past except in terms of the present. (319)

could be re-written as: One of the most important results of this homeostatic tendency of medieval writing is that the individual scribe or reader/hearer had little perception of the linguistic past (Latin) except in terms of the linguistic present (Romance).

2. The elements in the cultural heritage which cease to have a contemporary relevance tend to be soon forgotten or transformed; and as the individuals of each generation acquire their vocabulary, their genealogies, and their myths, they are unaware that various words, proper-names and stories have dropped out, or that others have changed their meanings or been replaced. (319)

could be re-written as: The graphemic elements in the scribal heritage which cease to have a contemporary relevance for writing notarial documents tend to be soon forgotten or re-interpreted; and as the scribes of each generation acquire their vocabulary, their grammar, their scribal competence, and their scribal models, they are unaware that various words, structures and constructions have dropped out of their texts, or that others have changed their meanings or been replaced.

3. The content of the cultural tradition grows continually, and in so far as it affects any particular individual he becomes a palimpsest composed of layers of beliefs and attitudes belonging to different stages in historical time (340)

could be re-written as: The content of the scribal tradition grows continually, and in so far as it affects any particular text it becomes a palimpsest composed of layers of spelling conventions and scribal practices belonging to different stages in the history of the written tradition.

This last altered quote, which accurately refers to the different strata of writing that coexisted in the notarial tradition, brings unavoidably to mind Pidal's "capas cronológicamente diversas," that according to him coexisted in conflict in tenth-century Leonese documents,[1] and Banniard's "couches successives."[2] Those strata were functional structures in their synchronic interrelation, but their representational status and legitimacy should be sought in their rapport with different and successive stages of language history in Iberia.

Goody and Watt's assessment of the way in which some cultures practice what John Arundel Barnes (1947:48-56) called "structural amnesia"[3] is so important for our area of studies (notarial documents having been in the past been consistently and notoriously abused and misused by traditional philologists) that I hope that, by borrowing their insights and adapting them slightly to meet the needs of the study of medieval documents, I am able to suggest how this "homeostatic" perspective can be instructive.

One of the interesting consequences of this homeostatic development, which is really a self-regulated state of equilibrium of a complex system, is that it is functionally, if not also formally, invisible to those affected by the changes. Latin-Portuguese notarial documents continued to be written after 1080 with a noticeable degree of vernacularization, as if the deviations from Latin spelling and grammar were invisible and irrelevant to the participants in the various stages of the process of composing, writing, validating, and copying a notarial document.

For example, it is impossible not to wonder how and why some scribes from the Chapter of the See of Braga (which was what some call a proto-chancery, a *de facto* chancery, the first in Portuguese territory) were allowed to write "incorrect Latin" after 1080 in documents that were witnessed and confirmed by people such as Archbishops St Gerald or Mauritius Burdinus (Frenchmen who were trained as Cluniac monks at Moissac and were renowned for their learning). The only explanation is, in my view, that the deviations that the documents presented were either functionally and homeostatically invisible, irrelevant, or normal, or a combination of the three. Even if the scribes and their contemporaries perceived the enormous differences that existed between the notarial language and, for example, the language of the Scriptures, nevertheless they would have no qualms about stating that what was being written in the

---

[1] "Sea lo que quiera, el hecho es que un estrato de formas latinas y tres de formas romances se sobreponían en la lengua escrita en León durante el siglo X. Un mismo individuo en un mismo documento podía mezclar voces pertenecientes a cualquiera de estas cuatro capas cronológicamente diversas." (Menéndez Pidal 1980^9:518)

[2] "les monuments écrits offrent l'aspect d'un massif homogène dans lequel il nous appartient de discerner des couches successives au moyen de repères philologiques précis." (Banniard 1992:522)

[3] Quoted from Goody and Watt [1963] 1972:317.

documents was Latin—Latin being simply a convenient label for written language in general.

What happened in the late eleventh century was not the sudden restoration of Latin as Menéndez Pidal thought, but merely a profound, and gradual, readjustment of the practices to the models, especially at the levels of spelling and (less so) morpho-syntax, a readjustment which would lead in time to a split between the written and the spoken languages (what Michel Banniard calls "la rupture de la communication verticale," Banniard 1992, passim). When Romance orthographies emerged in the early thirteenth century in Iberia a new conception of the relationship between written language and spoken language must have already been in place: so the conceptual distinction between Latin and Romance was first a distinction between written and oral modes of language, and only much later a full distinction between two separate languages.

We can say that the distinction between Latin and Romance as separate entities occurred at the representational level, changing the representational models, and conceptually separating de facto distinct but co-existing operational models, by assigning them to different languages—Medieval Latin and Romance—which explains why in the late twelfth and thirteenth centuries there was a need for new spelling systems for the Ibero-Romance languages; these were now perceived as different entities from Latin, and required their own special spelling systems.

As for the ancient trends of orthographical vulgarization, present in the earliest known charters; they were simply internal aspects of the homeostatic development of the Latin tradition, and so they affected the operational models but not the representational models of literacy. That is, they never did, and probably never could, bring about a conceptual distinction between Latin and Romance.

* * *

Post-Reform documents are indeed different from those of the earlier stages of document production, both in spelling and grammar. Nevertheless the fact remains that the improvement in the "correctness" of notarial documents never attained the levels of medieval scholastic or Renaissance Latin, and even the changes that happened took a long time to become generalized; and most of all (an issue which is outside the scope of this article), the vernacularization of the Latin tradition did not cease, i.e. documents continued to be written in a highly romanized way even after the Reform; probably, indeed, because of the Reform. This may seem paradoxical, but we must note that the Reform brought about a greater graphemic awareness, and so the notion that written Latin and spoken Romance were in fact different linguistic systems made possible the piecemeal development of autonomous Romance *scriptae*.

3. EXAMPLES FROM NOTARIAL DOCUMENTS FROM BRAGA

The functional invisibility of the spelling and grammatical deviations in notarial documents—*qua* deviations or errors with respect to Latin orthography and grammar—can be best demonstrated by looking at documents written before or shortly after 1080 which are preserved both in their original manuscripts and in copies produced significantly after 1080 by scribes who were no longer trained in Visigothic script. It is fair to assume that twelfth- and thirteenth-century scribes and notaries, who were still for the most part clerics and monks, must have possessed scribal skills based on standards of literacy which were different from those of their tenth- and eleventh-century predecessors.

Given this fact, one would expect to find extensive corrections in the copies of notarial documents, both in spelling (such as insertion of initial H, substitution of the correct vowel letters to hide the effects of several Romance vowel changes, substitution of the correct consonant letters to hide the effects of obstruent voicing in intervocalic position, etc.) and in morphosyntax (such as substitution of the correct case endings in nouns and pronouns governed by prepositions or verbs, substitution of the correct form of the relative pronoun QUIS, substitution of UT for QUE, etc.). The texts show that this was not the case: we do find corrections, i.e. insertion of correct Latin spellings, and correct case-forms in nouns and pronouns, but not on the scale one would expect had a full restoration of Latinity happened in post-Cluniac Iberia.

Documents from Braga in Northern Portugal provide good examples of this. The Gregorian Reform was introduced there during the term of office of Bishop Peter, between 1070 and 1091: he was an enterprising individual who, among other achievements, founded the first school on record in the Portuguese territory. The Canons of the See of Braga were trained there, and they must have been taught, along with other traditional subjects, to draft and write notarial documents. After an interregnum of seven years, that followed the demise of Peter, two Frenchmen ruled the See of Braga for about 20 years, Gerald of Moissac, from 1099 to 1108 (he was a Cluniac monk and the first Archbishop; he was canonized shortly after his death), and Mauritius Burdinus, from 1109 to 1118 (also a Cluniac monk, who became Antipope in 1118 under the name of Gregory VIII).

Braga was the most important Portuguese ecclesiastical centre for many centuries (the Archbishop of Braga bears to this day the title of *Arcebispo Primaz*), and it was the first to adopt and implement the Gregorian Reform in Portuguese territory. One would expect that the standards of literacy of the scribes and notaries hailing from Braga would reflect the implementation and spread of Gallo-Roman Medieval Latin, and that the documents produced in Braga after 1080 would bear different scriptolinguistic traits from the pre-Reform tradition of Latin-Portuguese document production.

Most of the documents produced in or around Braga, especially those pertaining directly or indirectly to the estate of the See of Braga, survive only in copies contained in the cartulary known as the *Liber Fidei*. This important cartulary was written between 1221 and 1254, and is formed by the combination of two pre-existing *libri testamentorum* (which did not survive) into a single bound volume. No attempts were made to harmonize the contents of the two *libri testamentorum*; so the documents were not sorted out before being included in the cartulary, and some were repeated. The *Liber Fidei* contains many notarial documents from the tenth and eleventh centuries, as well as some texts from the previous centuries. For a very few of the documents copied into the *Liber Fidei* we have the original charters, preserved today mostly in Braga (and some in Lisbon). Each document in the *Liber Fidei* is thus a copy of a copy, and we have no way of determining how many copying stages intervened between the original and the cartulary version, because we do not know whether the *Liber Fidei* is itself the copy of another cartulary which already contained the two *libri testamentorum*. So the copies in the *Liber Fidei* are second, third or fourth generation copies.

Comparing the few extant Braga originals with their copies in the *Liber Fidei* leads one to the conclusion that the copyists regarded the language of the originals as normal or acceptable, or else they would have corrected them extensively; cartularies were not made for scholarly research, they were compiled and written for very practical purposes, which means that the copies of the documents needed to be clearly understood and accepted by any party for whom these records were of importance.

1). The first example is taken from a long and solemn charter from 1025 (witnessed and confirmed by the King and Queen of León, court dignitaries, noblemen, bishops and abbots). Probably because of its solemnity and of its public nature the language does not show the overall "vulgarization" which is normal in private notarial documents from the tenth and early eleventh centuries. The document is a *carta de agnição*, a judicial document concerning a dispute about jurisdiction rights over Braga and its outcome. In view of the enormous political importance of the text, it is reasonable to suppose that the task of writing it down was handed to an experienced scribe: this means that the charter could well reflect the scriptolinguistic patterns of the previous century, because the scribe would not have been a young person but rather a mature and seasoned notary.

This document survives in two versions:

[A] Arquivo Distrital de Braga, Gaveta de Braga, n.° 67, the original, in cursive Visigothic script
[B] Arquivo Distrital de Braga, *Liber Fidei* (*Liber Testamentorum* I), doc. 22, ff. 12v-15r

One of the characteristics of the old Latin-Portuguese notarial tradition was the frequent loss of final T in 3rd person singular verb forms, the replacement of intervocalic T by D (with the frequent occurrence of hyper-correct forms, like *aput, set*), and the replacement of TI plus vowel by CI (representing the alveolar affricate /ts/, and sometimes also voiced /dz/). If we plot the different frequencies for final and intervocalic T followed by a consonant letter (vowel + T + vowel + consonant) to avoid interference from TI, and calculate their percentual weight against the total amount of T's in both versions, and of all cases of intervocalic D against the total amount of D's, we obtain the following results:

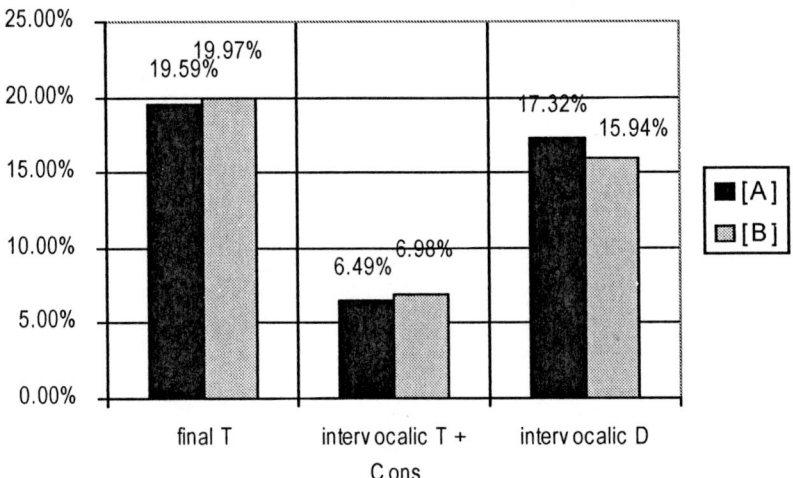

GRAPH 1

Graph 1 shows a very slight increase in final T, a very slight increase in intervocalic T, and a noticeable decrease of intervocalic D in [B]. This is compatible with the document having undergone some degree of correction or "Latinization" in its spelling, even though the difference is not very great.

If we now consider the frequencies of consonant letters P, T, and C in intervocalic position in each text, comparing them with B, D, and G in the same context a consistent pattern of change seems to emerge in Graph 2.

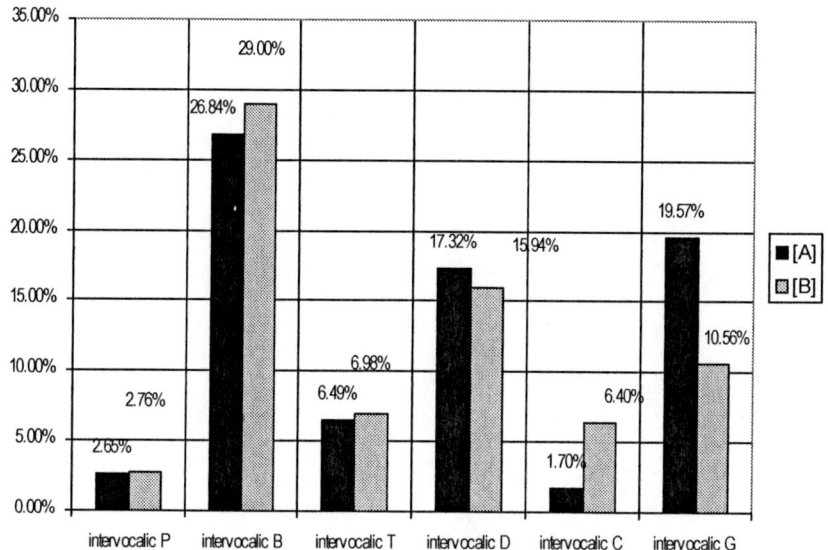

GRAPH 2

The percentages are calculated like this: the letter B for example has a combined total of 231 occurrences in the two texts. Version [A] has 62 occurrences of intervocalic B (=26.84% of 231) and [B] has 67 occurrences (=29.00% of 231). The values plotted in Graph 2 for intervocalic C and G are only before A/O/U (i.e. velar C and G), of intervocalic T only before vowel letter followed by consonant letter (to avoid the interference of TI plus vowel), and of intervocalic P with the exception of the lemma *episcopus*. All cases with intervening R after the consonant letter were also considered, since in the groups *muta cum liquida* the Latin obstruents also underwent voicing.

The pattern seems to be clear: an increase in the copy of intervocalic T and velar C, a decrease in the copy of intervocalic D and velar G. P shows only a slight increase in the copy.

As to B the results are inconclusive due to the fact that in version [A], U was used in many instances in place of B to represent the fricative /v/ from Latin /b/, and there are also reverse spellings of B for U, and in 13 instances version

[B] replaced U with B.[4] The alternation B ~ U clearly interfered in the pattern of the use of B for /b/ as the result of voicing of Latin /p/.

There is a marked change in the frequency of intervocalic C and G, and this is the only case where we can say that there were statistically significant changes in the spelling of the original text.

Differences in the voicing rates of the Latin voiceless obstruents were noted by Carmen Pensado in a study of voicing in tenth-century Leonese documents. She remarks:

> ...in some corpora there seems to be a preference for the voicing of -*k*-, and in others for -*t*-. There can be non-phonological factors for the high voicing rate of -*k*- in spite of its being much less frequent than -*t*-. First, orthographic rules involving /k/ and /g/ were intrinsically more complex due both to the existence of three symbols for /k/ (i.e. <k, c, qu>) and to the fact that <c, g> were also used for the outcomes of palatalization. (Pensado 1991:198)

The figures that Pensado gives for all the letter replacements indicating voicing show higher scores for the voicing of /k/, i.e. for the replacement of velar C by G. Variation in the voicing rates in the early texts could either reflect (in a fossilized manner) the order in which the Latin intervocalic obstruents were voiced, or, perhaps, more plausibly, it could reflect some degree of standardization, especially in very frequent words like *eglesia*, *sesiga*, *diagonus*, *monagus*, even *sigut*, among many others. Whatever the reason for the high score of G for C, later scribes would interpret this pattern, which would have stood out in the documents, as a symptom of vernacularization which should be suppressed in the copies. Apparently, this is what happened to the Charter from 1025 when it was copied, at least a century and a half later.

4	A	B
	aueatis	abeatis (twice)
	ligauiiem	ligabilem
	ouitum	obitum
	ouitum	obitum
	placiuile	placabile
	pleue	plebe (three times)
	prouationem	probationem
	rouorasent	roborassent
	rouorauerunt	roborauerunt
	rouorem	roborem

If we look at the actual variants we get a clearer picture of the spelling reformatting that occurred in version [B], which is clearly dominated by a desire for the avoidance of non-etymological intervocalic G:

VARIANTS WITH SUBSTITUTION OF T AND VELAR C
IN THE COPY FOR D AND VELAR G IN THE ORIGINAL

[A]	[B]	
bragala	bracara	2
bragalense	bracarense	1
bragalensem	bracarensem	1
digant	dicant	1
edifigauit	edificauit	1
eglesiaro	ecclesiario	1
eglesiaro	eclesiario	1
godiga	gotica	1
godiga	gotica	1
idem	item	4
iudigabit	iudicauit	1
iudigantes	iudicantes	1
iudigauerunt	iudicauerunt	1
iudigum	iudicum	1
leouegodo	leouegoto	1
pacifigam	pacificam	1
progul	procul	1
sagramento	sacramento	1
sigut	sicut	8
testifigamus	testificamus	2
testifigandi	testificandi	1
traugant	traucant	1

TABLE 1

All the hypercorrect spellings in the original involving deviation from the Latin norm were eliminated in the copy:

HYPERCORRECT SPELLINGS IN THE ORIGINAL CORRECTED IN THE COPY

[A]	[B]	
acnitio	agnitio	1
aput	apud	1
comez	gomez	1
hacnitionis	agnitionis	1

TABLE 2

REVERSE SPELLINGS IN THE ORIGINAL CORRECTED IN THE COPY

[A]	[B]	
adque	atque	2

TABLE 3

There is only one case of reverse spelling in the copy (in a proper name):

REVERSE SPELLINGS IN THE COPY

[A]	[B]	
tructemunda	trucdemunda	1

TABLE 4

And there is only one case of a hypercorrect spelling in the copy (also in a proper name):

HYPERCORRECT SPELLINGS IN THE COPY

[A]	[B]	
daudi	dauti	1

TABLE 5

However some forms in the original with representation of obstruent voicing were not corrected in the copy:

DEVIANT FORMS NOT CORRECTED IN THE COPY

A & B	
didagu	3
fromarigu	1
fromarigus	1
godiga	1
godiga	1
honorigo	1
honorigus	1
portugalense	1
semedipsos	1
ueridigas	1

TABLE 6

Out of a total of 2185 words in the *Liber Fidei* version of the text, only 42 words show spelling changes related to the voicing of obstruents, almost all corrected according to the norm. This is due to the fact that, at the start, the original was not a highly vulgarized text with respect to obstruent voicing. The copyist(s) did not feel the need to be thorough in his (their) corrections: this is particularly interesting in the context of the restoration of latinity that the Cluniac reform supposedly brought to medieval Spain and Portugal.

2). The second example is also taken from the 1025 Charter and concerns morphosyntax.

The prepositions AD and PER required the accusative case in their governed complements. In Iberian Latin-Romance documents the absence of the case ending -M in governed pronouns, nouns and adjectives is very common. For singular items, beside the occasional "correct" forms in -M, we find in most instances a general unmarked case-less singular form (ending in -A, -E ~ -I, or -O ~ -U), similar both to the Latin ablative form and to the uninflected Romance form; for plural items we find in most instances the unmarked case-less forms in -AS, -ES and -OS, which come directly from the Latin plural accusative, and hence look grammatically correct in the texts. In some cases we find nominative singular, and also genitive singular and ablative plural forms. The 1025 Charter is no exception to this general picture.

I give all occurrences of AD and PER with nominal and pronominal complements:

CASE ENDINGS WITH THE PREPOSITION AD IN THE 1025 CHARTER

[A]	[B]
a prestina seruitute	ad pristinam seruitutem
a seruitium	a seruitium
ad aserto	ad asserto
ad eos	ad eos
ad eos	ad eos
ad gundesaluo menindiz	ad gundisaluo menendiz
ad humilitatem	ad humilitatem
ad ille aepiscopo domno pelagio	ad ille episcopo domno pelagio
ad ille comite	ad ille comite
ad ille rex	ad ille rex
ad illos	ad illos
ad ipse conmite	ad ille comite
ad ipsum diem	ad ipsum diem
ad iudicem	ad ipse eyta fortuniz
ad iudicium prefinitum	ad iudicium prefinitum
ad iuramento	ad iuramento
ad lex	ad lex
ad misericordiam	ad misericordiam
ad obitum suum	ad obitum suum
ad prendendum uillas	ad prehendendum uillas
ad presura	ad presura
ad rex domno eremudo et conmite menindus	ad rex domno uermudo et comite menendus
ad sacramentum	ad sacramentum
ad suo concilio	ad suo concilio
appetitione tardenato	a petitione tardenato

TABLE 7

CASE ENDINGS WITH THE PREPOSITION PER IN THE 1025 CHARTER

[A]	[B]
per alphetena	per alfetena
per conditionem	per conditionem
per epistola	per epistolam
per hanc setentias	post hanc setentiam
per ligauilem placitum	per ligabilem placitum
per manu ipsi sagioni	per manu ipsi sagione
per multis temporibus	per multis temporibus
per sagioni annagia uermudiz	per sagioni annaya
per scripturas	per scripturas
per se senator gundiario	per se [...] gundiario
per semedipsos	per semedipsos
per suis terminis et agyacentiis suis	per suis terminis et aiacentiis suis
per suos colmellos et scripturas firmitatis	per suos colmellos et scripturas firmitatis
per uerifice ordine	per uerifice ordine annaya
per unasqueque sedes	per unasqueque sedes

TABLE 8

The correct Latin singular -M forms are rare in both versions, and only in two instances did the copy correct the original (*a prestinaØ seruituteØ* replaced by *ad pristinam seruitutem*, and *per epistolaØ* replaced by *per epistolam*). All the other forms were left untouched. In one noteworthy case the copyist had the opportunity to give a correct Latin solution, because he replaced the original text with something completely different (with the probable intention of making the context clearer): he replaced *ad iudicem* with *ad ipseØ eytaØ fortuniz*. He failed to add the case-ending to *ipse* and to the proper name *eyta*. I give the full context:

[A] pro id roboraberunt placitum ut in IIIo [...] ...gissent ad lex sub unus de amborum partibus **ad iudicem** que preelectus erat de ipse rex magnus et quod illis prebuisset eis accepissent

[B] pro id roborauerunt placitum ut in IIIo die pergissent ad lex sub unus **ad ipse eyta fortuniz** qui preelectus erat de ipse rex magnus et quod illos ordinasset eis accepissent

The hypothesis that the copyist replaced the original text in order to clarify the meaning is strengthened by the fact that he also replaced *prebuisset* by *ordinasset*, although this can hardly be claimed to be Latinization; on the contrary, the more Latin form would have been *ordinauisset*, and *ordino* carries in this context the Romance causative meaning of "to order something to someone," instead of the older meaning "to lay out something, to arrange."

In the same context referred to above, where he added the -M ending to *epistola*, he failed to mark the direct object of the verb in the same sentence, preferring the general unmarked case-less form, changing *–um* to *–o:*

[A] per epistola **testimonium** dicant
[B] per epistolam **testimonio** dicant

These data from morphosyntax are quantitatively different from the results shown above in relation to changes in spelling: the copyist(s) did not bother to correct the morphosyntax, and this can only be explained by the fact that, in spite of his (their) grammatical training, he (they) did not feel the need to do so.

3). The earliest stage of Iberian Latin-Romance document production (from the second half of the ninth century to the first half of the eleventh) presents many examples of the case-less (uninflected) and preposition-less genitive, a strange-looking construction which probably reflects a very old stage in the development of Ibero-Romance in which there was a two- or three-case system (cf. Pérez González 1991, 1993). In the 1025 Charter there are several instances of this construction. The copy preserves each and every one of them. I quote only a few of the examples below:

UNINFLECTED GENITIVE IN THE 1025 CHARTER

[A]	[B]
appetitione tardenato	a petitione tardenato
de parte tardenato	de parte tardenato
manu comite petrus uimaraniz	manu comite petrus uimaraniz
manu ipsi sagioni	manu ipsi sagione

TABLE 9

In these examples *petitione, manu* and *parte* are the heads of the noun-phrase whereas *tardenato, petrus uimaraniz*, and *ipsi sagioni* are the complements. One would expect in Notarial Latin something like:

a petitione de tardenato
de parte de tardenato
manu de comite petro uimaranici
manu de ipso sagione

or in old-fashioned Latin:

a petitione tardenati
ex parte tardenati
manu comitis petri uimaranici
manu ipsius sagionis

4). A fourth and final example from the morphosyntax of the 1025 Charter. The preposition DE in Latin-Romance documents, besides being used in different syntactic contexts from those of the original Latin preposition, governed noun phrases whose elements usually had the general unmarked form. There are also instances of the correct use of ablative plural forms after DE. Instances abound, however, of nouns and pronouns with other case endings. I give just the most deviant examples from the 1025 Charter.

CASE ENDINGS WITH PREPOSITION DE IN THE 1025 CHARTER

[A]	[B]
de aepiscoporum successorum uestrorum	de episcoporum successorum uestrorum
de amborum partibus	de amborum partibus
de amborum partibus	de amborum partibus
de domni pelagii aepiscopo	de domni pelagii episcopi
de durio	de durio
de ipsam sedem	de ipsam sedem
de ipsam sedem	de ipsam sedem
de ipsam sedem	de ipsam sedem
de ipse extirpe	de ipse stirpe
de ipse rex	de ipse rex
de ipse rex magnus	de ipse rex magnus
de ipsi omines	de ipsi homines
de ipsius arba	de ipsius arba
de ipsius auii que	de ipsius auii qui
de ipsius sedis	de ipsius sedis
de istius presentes	de istius presentes

de istius qui	de istis qui
de rex	de rex
de rex domno adefonso	de rex domno adefonso
de sancte marie	de sancte marie
de sancte marie	de sancte marie
de sedem sancte marie	de sede sancte marie
de seruitium	de seruitium regis
de seruitium	de seruitium
de seruitium	de seruitium domne marie
de seruitium sancta marie	de seruitium sancte marie
de uitus	de uitus

TABLE 10

There are only two cases of correction in [B] (*de sedem sancte marie* replaced with *de sedeØ sancte marie*, and *de istius qui* replaced with *de istis qui*) a fact which is quite astounding, especially in view of such remarkable uses as *de istius presentes* (instead of Latin *de istis presentibus* or *istorum presentium*), *de rex domno adefonso* (instead of Latin *de rege domino adefonso*, or *regis domini adefonsi*), and *de seruitium* (instead of Latin *de seruitio* or *seruitii*).

Many of these strange uses of case-endings had a "scripto-pragmatic" function; that is, they served as tokens of Latinization, given the formal nature of this style of written communication. In order to give a Latinate appearance to the text a scribe could use almost any nominal ending that he could think of: some endings did not always signal grammatical relationships, but were sometimes just there as markers of the formal nature of the discourse contained in the text; in other words, they served the purpose of giving the text a polished and official look.

The addition of a case ending in certain prepositional phrases to a dependent element (determiner, pronoun, noun, or adjective) was also a way to reinforce the grammatical function of the noun phrase governed by a preposition whose original Latin function had changed; hence we find DE governing NP's marked with genitive endings, and AD governing NP's marked with dative endings, although not in the 1025 Charter. A good example is *de ipsius sedis* above (left uncorrected in [B]), instead of just *de ipsa sede* or *ipsius sedis*. Rather than being labelled as instances of incorrect morphosyntax, constructions like these should be regarded as examples of redundant morphosyntax. This is not a trivial observation; the use of redundant morphosyntax reveals that the scribe had implicit knowledge of correct Latin morphosyntax, and, moreover, that he acknowledged that some prepositions had new non-Latin functions which were equivalent to the case endings in some Latin synthetic constructions.

The idea that these Latin-Romance morphosyntactic patterns would have seemed strange or unacceptable for someone trained in Medieval Latin grammar is probably not well founded. After all, both the eleventh-century original scribe and the thirteenth-century copyist knew their grammar, and neither of them had any problems writing these things in such an important and solemn document. For both men, the original scribe and the last copyist, the consistent restoration of Latinity seemed unnecessary or, more accurately, irrelevant.

So what do the variants of versions [A] and [B] of the Charter of 1025 tell us about the norms taught and learnt by the [A]-scribe and by the copyists that generated [B]? Are the graphemic and morphosyntactic differences between the two witnesses so significant as to indicate a change in representational models during the time interval that separates the original text from the copy? In my view the fact that [B] tends to eliminate some written reflexes of obstruent voicing should not make us overlook the fact that [A] did not substitute intervocalic B, D, and G for P, T, and C in all possible instances. The fact that he failed to do that crucially indicates that the [A]-scribe already possessed a model of written language where some instances of intervocalic /b,d,g/ (i.e. those that resulted from the voicing of Latin /p,t,k/), ought to be written as P, T, and C (or QU). The difference between [A] and [B] in this respect is then a statistical difference in the implementation of the same spelling norm. Therefore even if we must acknowledge that [B] corrected [A] in many instances, i.e. that [B] has in general a more correct spelling than [A], we must also accept the fact that in other cases there was no need to correct, because [A] presented the traditional spellings. Also, [B] did not correct all the incorrect forms present in [A]. This seems to point to a difference in the degree of possible graphemic variation, not to a difference between radically distinct spelling models. The same applies to morphosyntax, especially in the use of case endings.

To sum up: the differences between versions [A] and [B] of the 1025 Charter regarding certain aspects of spelling and morphosyntax seem to be located at the level of the operational models, i.e. of actions, not at the level of norms.

* * *

I turn now to another document from Braga from a later date, a charter containing a deed of gift on behalf of the Archbishop and the See of Braga, dated to 1110, during the office of the French Archbishop Mauritius Burdinus (Maurice Bourdin), which survived in three versions:

[A] Arquivo Distrital de Braga, Gaveta 2.ª das Propriedades do Cabido, n° 137

[B] Arquivo Distrital de Braga, *Liber Fidei* (*Liber Testamentorum* I), doc. 389, ff. 110r-110v
[C] Arquivo Distrital de Braga, *Liber Fidei* (*Liber Testamentorum* II), doc. 703, ff. 189r-189v

For ease of collation of the three versions I have divided the text into paragraphs referred to below as 'P' and I give a normalized transcription (with abbreviations expanded, etc.). The convention '[***]' indicates the absence of a sequence in one of the copies.

LINEATED COLLATION OF THE THREE VERSIONS OF THE CHARTER OF 1110 FROM BRAGA [5]

```
<P01>
A   in nomine sancte et diuidue trinitatis patris et filii et
B                       indiuidue
C                       indiuidue

A spiritus sancti cuius honor et gloria regnum et imperium manet
B
C

A per infinita tempora in domino deo eternam salutem amen
B                                      eterna   salute
C

<P02>
A mos quippe est omnibus seruientibus deo aliquid sue
B
C

A facultatibus tribuere propter deum unde clementer cum sanctis
B
C

A et electis porcionem accipiant commoda quoque sibi celestia
B            portionem           quomoda
C            portionem           quomoda

A adquirant
B
C
```

---

[5] This collation was automatically generated with the computer programme *Collate 2* written by Peter Robinson (Robinson 1994).

<P03>
A qua propter nos famulos dei didagus cresconici et uxor mea
B   cresconiz
C   cresconiz

A lupa pelagiz concedimus propter nomen domini dei nostri illi
B   pelaiz   [****** ***** ****** *** ******]
C   pelaiz

A eclesie sancte marie braccarense et uobis archiepiscopo
B ecclesie   bracarense
C ecclesie   bracarensis

A domno mauricio atque clericis ipsius sedis hereditatem
B
C

A nostram propriam que abemus in uilla radicata subtus monte
B   quam habemus
C   quam   radigata

A spino territorio braccarense discurrentibus aquis in riuum
B   bracarense   ad
C   bracarensi   ad

A cataui et locum in quo dicunt paretes
B
C

<P04>
A et uenit nobis ipsa hereditate de patre nostro pelagio fafilaz
B   hereditas   meo
C   hereditas

A tam de auolenga quam de ganantia siue de contramuda ipsius
B   contramutata
C

A hereditatis
B
C

<P05>
A concedimus uobis ipsas hereditates ad locum predestinatum sic
B
C

A concedimus et annuimus illic loco predicto sicut scriptura
B   predestinato
C

```
A docet et continet ut inde serui dei habeant
B                       in deo clerici
C

A stipendium et ego habeam inestimabile premium
B                 nos habamus
C                             inextimabile

<P06>
A neminem quidem permittimus qui ibidem uobis aliquam
B
C               permitimus

A conturbationem nec in modico faciat nec filii neque nepotes
B                                                 nec
C                                                 filium

A siue unus ex prosapia nostra aut extraneus
B
C

<P07>
A igitur si quis audaciter inuadendo surrexerit qui hunc factum
B                                                         nostrum
C

A nostrum infringere uoluerit sit excomunicatus et
B factum
C

A anathematizatus et maneat ab omni cetu catholicorum extraneus
B anatematizatus                         caholicorum
C

A et cum iuda domini traditore in eternalibus penis
B                    traditorem                sedibus
C

A supplicium paciatur et insuper det ipsam hereditatem in
B
C

A quadruplum et D solidos
B
C

<P08>
A est facta series testamenti IIIo kalendarum nouembrium era Ma
B
C

A Ca XLa VIIIa
B
C
```

```
<P09>
A ego didagus cresconiz et uxor mea lupa pelagiz
B                                          pelaiz in hac series
                                                         testamenti
C        didacus [*]                       pelaiz

A manus nostras roboramus
B
C

<P10>
A qui      uiderunt pelagio ts petro ts suarius ts gunsaluus ts
B porro    testes   pelagius   petrus
C                   pelagius   petrus   suerius

<P11>
A menendus diagonus notuit
B          diaconus
C          diaconus
```

If one takes a cursory look at the original it becomes apparent that the spelling and the grammar seem more correct, more Latin-like than in private documents from the ninth to eleventh centuries. The text is strikingly different from those documents, in spelling, morphology, syntax, lexis, and formulae. The hypercorrect form *braccarense* (P03, twice), the place-names *cataui* (P03), *paretes* (P03), and the proper-name *lupa* (P03, 09) reveal the special care of the scribe in avoiding the voicing of intervocalic obstruents. The word *Bracara* and its derived forms were pronounced with intervocalic /g/ in Old Portuguese, and thus were often written with G: the unusual CC spelling looks as if the scribe wanted to flag the form *braccarense* to prevent a native *lector* from using the Old Portuguese pronunciation [bɾaga'es], and to indicate instead the Reformed Latin pronunciation [bɾaka'rense] (or [bɾaka'rẽse]). This is perfectly consistent with the Gregorian Reform's aim of restoring the correct pronunciation of Latin, which was necessary for all sorts of public reading; it could also be an indication of some insecurity on the part of a native notary trying hard not to get his spelling wrong because of the new standards of correctness. Nevertheless a few forms escaped the scribe's attention, *didagus* (P03, 09), *contramuda* (P04), and in his own signature the scribe wrote *menendus diagonus notuit*, i.e. with *diagonus* (with the contracted form *dgnus*) instead of *diaconus* (the vernacular pronunciation would have been something like [di'agõo]). The pressure of the vernacular was too strong. Judging from his name *Menendus* was not French, and it would have been a daunting task systematically to devoice obstruents (in writing or in reading aloud) that were voiced in his own native Portuguese tongue, especially in common words, even if he had been thoroughly trained in the new standards of correctness of Gallo-Roman Medieval Latin. In spite of the high degree of correctness of this text the copyists of the *Liber Fidei* felt the need to make some corrections, and it is worth looking closely at some of the changes they made.

We find a few variants in the spelling of words. Some of the changes are well motivated in terms of the Latin norm, but as many are not:

SPELLING DEVIATIONS IN THE ORIGINAL
CORRECTED IN THE COPIES OF THE 1110 CHARTER

<P01>	diuidue	indiuidue B C
<P02>	porcionem	portionem B C
<P03>	eclesie	ecclesie B C
<P03>	braccarense	bracarense B, bracarensis C
<P03>	abemus	habemus B
<P03>	braccarense	bracarense B, bracarensi C
<P05>	inestimabile	inextimabile C
<P09>	didagus	didacus C
<P11>	diagonus	diaconus B C

TABLE 11

SPELLING DEVIATIONS INTRODUCED
BY THE COPIES OF THE 1110 CHARTER

<P02>	commoda	quomoda B C
<P03>	cresconici	cresconiz B C
<P03>	pelagiz	pelaiz B C
<P03>	radicata	radicata B, radigata C
<P04>	contramuda	contramutata B, contramuda C
<P05>	inde	in deo B, inde C
<P05>	ego habeam	nos habamus B, ego habeam C
<P06>	permittimus	permittimus B, permitimus C
<P07>	anathematizatus	anatematizatus B, anathematizatus C
<P07>	catholicorum	caholicorum B, catholicorum C
<P09>	pelagiz	pelaiz B C
<P10>	suarius	suarius B, suerius C

TABLE 12

SPELLING DEVIATIONS MAINTAINED
IN THE COPIES OF THE CHARTER FROM 1110

<P03>	didagus	didagus B C (pro 'didacus')
<P03>	illi	illi B C (pro 'illic')
<P03>	abemus	habemus B, id. C
<P05>	inestimabile	inestimabile B, inextimabile C
<P07>	paciatur	paciatur B C (pro 'patiatur')
<P09>	didagus	didagus B, didacus C
<P10>	gunsaluus	gunsaluus B C (pro 'gundisaluus')

TABLE 13

In morphosyntax there are also interesting variants. Both copyists corrected a few incorrect case-forms in the original, replacing them with the correct Latin ones:

<P04>	hereditate	hereditas B C
<P10>	pelagio	pelagius B C
<P10>	petro	petrus B C

TABLE 14

But both copyists also changed correct forms in [A], replacing them with incorrect case-forms; [B] did that two times, [C] did it three:

<P01>	eternam salutem	<u>eterna salute</u> B, eternam salutem C
<P03>	braccarense	bracarense B , <u>bracarensi</u> C
<P06>	filii	filii B, <u>filium</u> C
<P07>	traditore	traditore B, <u>traditorem</u> C

TABLE 15

And both failed to correct some morphosyntactic "errors" of the original:

<P02>	aliquid sue facultatibu	id. B C (pro 'aliquid suarum facultatum')
<P03>	in riuum cataui	id. B C (pro 'in riuum catauum')
<P03>	et locum	id. B C (pro 'et loco'; cf. supra 'in uilla')
<P03>	in quo dicunt paretes	id. B C (pro 'quem dicunt paretes')
<P04>	de patre nostro	de patre meo B, id. C (pro 'ex patre nostro')
<P05>	ad locum predestinatum	id. B C (pro 'loco praedestinato', cf. supra 'loco predicto')
<P07>	hunc factum nostrum	hunc nostrum factum B, id. C (pro 'hoc factum nostrum')
<P07>	ab omni cetu	id. B C (pro 'ab omne coetu')
<P07>	in quadruplum	id. B C (pro 'in quadruplo')

TABLE 16

One could say that the improvements that they made to the grammatical correctness of the original were exactly matched by the damage they inflicted. It is interesting to note that paragraph 3 was the object of more changes than any of the others. This could be because of its crucial textual importance: in that paragraph the authors and the beneficiaries of the legal act are named, and the property being donated to the See is identified. Perhaps the copyists considered it was of the utmost importance to make the terms of this section as clear and as correct as possible, and if so, both failed miserably. They failed to correct errors in spelling and in grammar, and managed to introduce some of their own.

* * *

Finally, I would like to give a precious example of Archbishop St Gerald's own writing. At the end of a judicial document of 1101, a *prazo* or pact, St Gerald added a paragraph of his own where he explained the failure of his endeavours to bring about an agreement between the conflicting parties before the King. The document survives in three copies, all contained in the *Liber Fidei*:

[B] Arquivo Distrital de Braga, *Liber Fidei* (*Liber Testamentorum* I), doc. 220, ff. 71v - 72r
[C] Arquivo Distrital de Braga, *Liber Fidei* (*Liber Testamentorum* II), doc. 652, f. 173v
[D] Arquivo Distrital de Braga, *Liber Fidei* (*Liber Testamentorum* II), doc. 674, f. 179r

I give the text of the final paragraph in lineated collation:

LINEATED COLLATION OF THE THREE VERSIONS OF THE
1101 CHARTER – FINAL PARAGRAPH

<P08>
B postea uero ego geraldus archiepiscopus uocaui fideiussorem et
C et ego geraldus archiepiscopus uocaui fideiussorem et
D postea uero ego geraldus archiepiscopus uocaui fideiussores et

B imtemptorem ut irent mecum ad regem quod habuissemus iudicium ante eum
C intentorem ut irent mecum ad regem quod abuissemus iudicium ante eum
D intemptorem ut irent mecum ad regem quod abuissemus [******] ante eum

B et noluerunt illuc ire neque ullum iudicium facere
C et noluerunt [***] ire neque [***] iudicum facere
D et noluerunt illuc ire neque ullum iudicium facere

The written language of St Gerald is different from that of the rest of the document, which presents the usual Latin-Romance traits. St Gerald wrote pure Reformed Medieval Latin, whereas the rest of the document is unmistakeably written in Notarial Latin, albeit with a fair degree of correctness (when compared with documents from the previous centuries). This is indeed a precious document, where two traditions of writing stand side by side in the same text. St Gerald must have read the original text before he added his final remark, and he clearly raised no objections to the obvious differences between his own operational models of literacy and those of the Portuguese scribe. After all, as Archbishop, he could have proof-read the text, and could have had it re-drafted in a more "Cluniac-like" fashion, before validating it, if he had wished so.

CONCLUDING REMARKS

Notarial documents, as legal acts, had a direct impact on the lives of people. It was extremely important that the texts recorded faithfully the intentions and obligations of the parties involved. Notarial documents thus encoded communicative contents that had to be delivered and received unambiguously. Reading aloud such texts went beyond the simple recognition and processing of written symbols by mapping letters into sounds: reading aloud involved the oralization of a text written with an archaic writing system in such a way that all those people attending the reading, both literate and illiterate, understood at least the dispositive sections of the documents. This was done by recognizing individual lexical items and by assigning to them a vernacular spoken form, regardless of their Latinate appearance in writing.

This strain between the traditional standards of writing and the demands for communicative realism resulted in the creation and development of alternative spellings, which co-existed as alternative operational strategies with the inherited Latin tradition. These new spelling conventions, which did not displace for several centuries the old Latin conventions, were generally more transparent and isomorphic in relation to phonemic and morphemic structure.

The gap between the Latin tradition and the everchanging Romance vernacular brought about by centuries of uninterrupted language change gave rise to a complex relationship between the written and the spoken codes, in which variation and polymorphism stand out. For the people who used and copied legal texts, variation and polymorphism were seen as normal, as part of the textual standards of the time. The changes brought about by the Gregorian Reform did not end this situation. Furthermore, in the end, the Gregorian Reform paradoxically created the conditions for extreme de-latinization in writing documents. In the early thirteenth century this process had fully unfolded and the earliest texts written in an autonomous Portuguese scriptography appear. After the the second half of that century the process was irreversible, and Portuguese writing was established as a separate system from Medieval Latin: Portuguese and Latin were finally perceived as separate languages with separate writing traditions, governed by clearly distinct representational models and used in writing with distinct operational models.

Every child in present-day Portugal groping with the first steps towards full literacy strives to, or is forced to, match its own operational models (in which variation and polymorphism abound) to the representational models enforced by the grammars, the textbooks and the teachers. Children's and young teenagers' texts remind me of medieval texts, because of the level of variation and the trend towards graphophonemic isomorphism (not because the medieval scribes were as poor spellers as children usually are, as Thomas Walsh put it in article slightly *contra* Wright [6]); these features of early literacy gradually diminish as the child

---

[6] "[...] it is worth asking why scribes who had a passing knowledge of Classical Latin morphology and syntax and who routinely used terms (albeit often misspelt) that had almost surely fallen into desuetude centuries before [...] should have been such poor spellers. Their writings leave the odd impression that the grammatical and lexical sophistication of a university student and the spelling ability of a child in the third year of elementary school have been combined in a single individual." (Walsh 1991:211).

is forced to learn the standard written language. The great difference between our culture and that of olden times is that we have acquired this peculiar and recent notion that each word and each grammatical construction has only one acceptable, correct, written form. Medieval scribes were freer and less concerned with such small things. Their literacy practices (operational models) were subject to a looser social control[7] than that which is prevalent in modern literate societies. Their representational models of literacy were not a fetter imposed on them from childhood, but merely a set of guidelines, which they freely adapted to their own communicative needs, developing their own operational models according to the textual expectations of their communities, but without wholly forsaking the centuries-old tradition that they had inherited from their predecessors.[8]

SAÚDE, RALPH!

References

Azevedo, Rui de. 1932. "O mais antigo documento latino-português." *Arquivo Histórico de Portugal* 1, 500-02.
Banniard, Michel. 1992. *Viva Voce: Communication écrite et communication orale du IVe au IXe siècle en Occident latin*, Paris: Études Augustiniennes.
Barnes, John Arundel. 1947. "The collection of genealogies." *Rhodes-Livingstone Journal: Human problems in British Central Africa*, 5 (reference transcribed from Goody & Watt [1963] 1972, *q.v. infra*).
Cardoso, Maria Adriana. 2002. *A Língua Notarial Latino-Portuguesa de Notários do Século XI. Análise de morfo-sintácticos de documentos do Mosteiro de Pendorada*

---

[7] Itkonen associates decreased social control to linguistic change: "Each *linguistic change* is characterised by the fact that the rules undergoing the change hold only approximately: when a (rule-governed) entity A is changing into, or is being replaced by, a (rule-governed) entity B, there is a period during which it is impossible to say that either A or B is definitely correct or definitely incorrect. I would say that in such cases the *social control* of rules has decreased. Where this happens, *statistical* description of factual occurrences, that is *empirical* description, is in order even at the level of grammar." (Itkonen 1978:151). This statement, although it primarily concerns language change, is in my view also relevant to the study of scriptolinguistic change and of change in literacy models and practices.

[8] I would like to thank Roger Wright for his help in drafting the English version of this article.

(1059-1100), Lisboa: Faculdade de Ciências Sociais e Humanas da Universidade Nova de Lisboa, unpublished Master's Dissertation.

Emiliano, António. 1995. "Tradicionalidad y exigencias de realismo en la lengua notarial hispánica (hasta el siglo XIII)." *Actas del I Congreso Nacional de Latín Medieval (León, 1-4 Diciembre de 1993)*, ed. by M. Pérez González, 511-18. León: Universidad de León, Secretariado de Publicaciones.

Emiliano, António. 2003. *Latim e Romance em Documentação Notarial da Segunda Metade do Século XI*, Lisboa: Fundação Calouste Gulbenkian (Textos Universitários de Ciências Sociais e Humanas).

Goody, Jack / Watt, Ian P. [1963] 1972. "The Consequences of Literacy." *Language and social context*, ed. by P.P. Giglioli, 311-57. Harmondsworth: Penguin Books; first published in *Comparative Studies in Society and History*, vol.5, 1962-63, 304-45.

Gray, William S. 1956. *The Teaching of Reading and Writing*. Paris: Unesco (Monographs on Fundamental Education 10).

Holland, Dorothy / Quinn, Naomi. 1987. "Culture and Cognition; Introduction." *Cultural models in language and thought*, ed. by D. Holland and N. Quinn, 3-43. Cambridge: Cambridge University Press.

Itkonen, Esa. 1978. *Grammatical Theory and Metascience*. Amsterdam: John Benjamins B.V. (Amsterdam Studies in the Theory and History of Linguistic Science, Series IV: Current Issues in Linguistic Theory, Volume 5).

Itkonen, Esa. 1983. *Causality in Linguistic Theory. A critical investigation into the philosophical and methodological foundations of 'non-autonomous' Linguistics*. London / Canberra: Croom Helm, Bloomington: Indiana University Press.

Labov, William. 1966. *The Social Stratification of English in New York City*. Washington: Center for Applied Linguistics.

Lloyd, Paul. 1979. "Latin-Romance phonology: prosodics and metrics. By Ernst Pulgram. (Ars grammatica, 4.) Munich: Fink, 1975. Pp. 301. DM 68.00." *Language* 55, 698-701.

Mattoso, José. [1983] 1985. "Monges e clérigos portadores da cultura francesa em Portugal (séculos XI e XII)." *Portugal Medieval. Novas interpretações*, 365-88. Lisboa: Imprensa Nacional / Casa da Moeda; first published in *Les Rapports Culturels et Littéraires entre le Portugal et la France. Actes du Colloque, Paris, 11-16 octobre, 1982*, Paris: Fondation Calouste Gulbenkian, 1983, 41-58.

Menéndez Pidal, Ramón. [1926] [1950³] 1980⁹. *Orígenes del Español: Estado lingüístico de la Península Ibérica hasta el siglo XI*, Madrid: Espasa-Calpe S. A., novena edición (según la tercera, muy corregida y adicionada).

Mohrmann, Christine. [1958] 1961. "Le Latin Médiéval." *Études sur le Latin des Chrétiens. Tome II: Latin chrétien et médiéval*, 181-232. Roma: Edizioni di Storia e Letteratura; first published in *Cahiers de Civilisation Médiévale* 1, 1958, 265-94.

Pensado, Carmen. 1991. "How was Leonese Vulgar Latin read?" *Latin and the Romance Languages in the Early Middle Ages*, ed. by R. Wright, 190-204. London/New York: Routledge.

Pérez González, Maurilio. 1991. "Restos de flexión bicasual en el latín de documentación leonesa del siglo X." *Archivos Leoneses* 89-90, 35-48.

Pérez González, Maurilio. 1993a. "El diploma del rey Silo y sus romanismos." *Cuadernos de Filología Clásica. Estudios Latinos* 5, 115-39.

Pérez González, Maurilio. 1993b. "Restes de cas oblique dans le 'roman commun' de la Péninsule Ibérique." *Actes du XXe Congrès International de Linguistique et Philologie Romanes*, 431-44. Tübingen-Basel: Francke Verlag.

Pulgram, Ernst. 1975. *Latin-Romance phonology: prosodics and metrics*. Munich: Fink (Ars Grammatica, 4).

Robinson, Peter M. W. 1994. *Collate: Interactive collation of large textual traditions, Version 2, Project Edition*, Computer Program distributed Scholarly Digital Editions, http://www.sd-editions.com.

Sabatini, Francesco. 1965. "Esigenze di realismo e dislocazione morfologica in testi preromanzi." *Rivista di Cultura Classica e Medievale*, 7, 972-98.

Stubbs, Michael. 1980. *Language and literacy: The sociolinguistics of reading and writing*. London: Routledge & Kegan Paul.

Walsh, Thomas. 1991. "Spelling lapses in Early Medieval Latin documents and the reconstruction of primitive Romance phonology." *Latin and the Romance Languages in the Early Middle Ages*, ed. by R. Wright, 205-18. London/New York: Routledge.

Wright, Roger. 1982. *Late Latin and Early Romance in Spain and Carolingian France*. Liverpool: Francis Cairns.

Wright, Roger. 1992. "La metalingüística del siglo XII español (y la *Chronica Adefonsi Imperatoris*)." *Actas del II Congreso Internacional de Historia de la Lengua Espanõla*, vol. 2, ed. by M. Ariza et al., 879-86. Madrid: Pabellón de España.

Wright, Roger. 1993. "Complex monolingualism in Early Romance." *Linguistic Perspectives on the Romance Languages: Selected Papers from the XXI Linguistic Symposium on the Romance Languages*, 377-88. Amsterdam/Philadelphia: John Benjamins Publishing Company (reprint, *Early Ibero-Romance*, Newark: Juan de la Cuesta, 1994. !-11).

Wright, Roger. 2003. "Sociophilology and Twelfth-Century Spain." *A Sociophilological Study of Late Latin*, 245-61. Turnhout: Brepols, chapter 17.

3
On the Formation of the Present Indicative Paradigm of Spanish *ir* and the Origin of *vamos* and *vais*
JOEL RINI

THE PRESENT INDICATIVE PARADIGM of Spanish *ir* presents several problems of Spanish historical grammar that have not yet been fully resolved. A comparison of Lloyd (1987) and Penny (1991, 2002) reveals that there is yet to be agreement about (1) how Latin VĀDIS, VĀDIT, VĀDUNT reduced to *vas, va, van*, (2) which forms constituted the first and second persons plural in the earliest stages of the language, and (3) the exact origin of ModSp. *vamos* and *vais*. Lloyd (1987:298) believes that *vamos* and *vais* continue the Latin present indicative forms VĀDIMUS and VĀDITIS while Penny (1991:148, 165; 2002:172, 192) prefers to derive them from the Latin present subjunctives VADĀMUS and VADĀTIS, suggesting a shift in function from subjunctive to indicative. Through both theoretical and philological analysis, the present article will explore the plausibility of Penny's unique and intriguing proposal for the origin of *vamos* and *vais*, as well as attempt to answer the other remaining questions about the formation of the present indicative paradigm of Spanish *ir*.

In accordance with the general tendencies of Spanish historical phonology, the forms of the Latin present indicative of VADERE should have evolved exactly like those of the structurally similar CADERE "to fall", shedding their stem-final /d/ and undergoing a shift in stress in the first and second persons plural, as depicted in (1):

(1) VĀDO   VĀDIMUS   *vao   *vaemos
    VĀDIS   VĀDITIS   >   *vaes   *vaedes
    VĀDIT   VĀDUNT/*VĀDENT   *vae   *vaen

like CADŌ   CADIMUS   *cao (> cayo) caemos
     CADIS   CADITIS   >   caes   caedes
     CADIT   CADUNT/*CADENT   cae   caen

That the development of CADERE may be considered the "regular" or expected one is supported by the same development found in TRAHERE after the loss of its stem-final consonant, thus: TRAHO > *trao, TRAHIS > traes, TRAHIT > trae, TRAHIMUS > traemos, TRAHITIS > traedes, *TRAHENT (< TRAHUNT) > traen. Only *vao would have led to the Old Spanish form, via loss of hiatus and subsequent mutual assimilation, thus: *[βá-o] > *[βáu̯] > *[βóu̯] > OSp. vo. Further phonetic development of the forms *vaes, *vae, *vaemos, *vaedes, *vaen would be unlikely to have resulted in vas, va, vamos, vades, van. Scholars have therefore had to seek other solutions.

Meyer-Lübke (1895:293) stated that already in Vulgar Latin the abbreviated forms VAO, VAS, VAT, VAUNT must have been employed alongside VĀDŌ, VĀDIS, VĀDIT, VĀDUNT. He believed that VAS, VAT, VAUNT were based on VAO, which itself was remodeled on *STAO (< STO), thus suggesting what one might identify in modern linguistic terms as a case of leveling from the first person singular, as depicted in (2):

VADO >	VAO	→	VA- + -O	→	VAO
	↓		↓		
	VAD- + -IS		VA- + -ØS		VAS
	VAD- + -IT	>	VA- + -ØT	→	VAT
	VAD- + -UNT		VA- + -UNT		VAUNT

He posited no such abbreviated forms for the first and second persons plural, but mentioned the existence of OSp. imos, though not of OSp. ides. Yet, he later stated that VĀDERE was fully represented in the Iberian Peninsula, citing Sp. voy, vas, va, **vamos**, **vais**, van (bold mine), as well as Portuguese vou, vas [sic], vai, vamos, vaes [sic], vão (1895:296). Thus his reconstructed paradigm provided no explanation for the origin and development of the forms vamos and vais.

Citing Meyer-Lübke (1895), Hanssen (1913:104) stated that for OSp. vo, vas, va, "se suponen formas sincopadas latinas: *vao, *vas, *vat". However, Hanssen rejected Meyer-Lübke's postulated third person plural *VAUNT, suggesting instead that van was restructured on the basis of third singular va. He also acknowledged both imos and ides as the first and second persons plural of the Old Spanish paradigm, and in fact listed them as the only forms to function in these paradigmatic slots in Old Spanish. He then stated that in place of imos and ides, the forms vamos and vais were introduced into the paradigm, but did not explain from whence they came, nor when.

Menéndez Pidal (1941:279, 306), apparently following Meyer-Lübke, posited *VAO, *VAS, *VAT, but, like Hanssen, rejected Meyer-Lübke's third person plural *VAUNT, positing instead *VANT. He further posited abbreviated *VAMUS and *VATIS from VĀ(DI)MUS and VĀ(DI)TIS respectively as the ancestral forms of *vamos* and *vades/vais*, thus filling the gaps in the paradigm left by his predecessor. However, he did not explain how the syllables -DI- and -DU- were lost from the plurals.

The paradigm handed down to Spanish philologists from Menéndez Pidal, then, is that shown in (3):

*VAO   *VAMUS (< VĀ(DI)MUS)
*VAS   *VATIS (< VĀ(DI)TIS)
*VAT   *VANT (< VĀ(DU)NT)
(based on Menéndez Pidal 1941:279, 306)

And it has been accepted by most. One finds identical postulations, for example, in García de Diego (1951:206), Lathrop (1980:130; 1984:171; 1996:165), Urrutia Cárdenas and Álvarez Álvarez (1983:246), and Liberatori (1986:154).

Alvar and Pottier (1983:229) adopted the forms *VAS, *VAT, *VANT, but rejected *VAO, claiming that "[e]n el latín vulgar debió existir *vo*." Also, in place of *VAMUS and *VATIS, they posited *VĀ(DI)MUS and *VĀ(DI)TIS, but offered no explanation for how these forms would have evolved to *vamos* and *vais*. They were aware that regular phonetic development of the Latin forms, without a shift in stress, would have led to *vemos*, *vedes*, and were therefore simply resigned to say that "[s]e perpetúan *vamos* (< VĀDIMUS) y *vais* (< *vades* < VĀDITIS), por más que sea una evolución anómala" (1983: 179). They did, however, in a footnote, consider that, perhaps in imitation of *VAS, *VAT, *VANT, "es necesario pensar en *vamus, *vates [sic]", but did not commit to these abbreviated forms.

Lloyd (1987:298) was the first to break away completely from the hypothetical paradigm bequeathed to Spanish philologists by Menéndez Pidal, attempting instead to explain the development of the Latin present indicative through a combined phonological and morphological analysis, taking as a point of departure the original, non-abbreviated Latin forms. Lloyd (1987:298) believes that the singulars VĀDŌ, VĀDIS, VĀDIT first evolved to /βao/, /βaes/, /βaet/, and that they would have continued to evolve through regular phonetic development to *vo*, **vaes*, **vae*. But VĀDIMUS and VĀDITIS, maintaining their original stress pattern, would have undergone syncope of their posttonic theme vowel, as would VĀDUNT, yielding /βamos/, /βades/, /βan/. Lloyd (1987:298) then suggests that /βaes/ and /βaet/ were reduced to monosyllabic, monophthongal *vas* and *va* on the basis of the plurals, *vamos, vades, van*, as well as "the parallelism of other single syllable verbs" like *das, da* and *(h)as, (h)a*.

Like Lloyd, Penny (1991:165, 2002:192) begins his analysis with the non-hypothetical, non-abbreviated Latin forms. With regard to VĀDŌ, VĀDIS, VĀDIT, VĀDUNT/*VĀDENT, Penny, again like Lloyd, combines phonological and morphological processes, suggesting that, after the loss of -D-, these forms were remodelled on the basis of *do, das, da, dan*, and *estó, estás, está, están*, resulting in OSp. *vo, vas, va, van*. These, together with *imos* and *ides* alone (< ĪMUS, ĪTIS), Penny proposes, made up the Old Spanish present indicative paradigm of *ir*, as shown in (4):

(4)   Pres. Ind. of OSp. *ir*
           vo   imos
           vas ides
           va   van (Penny 1991:165, 2002:192)

The implication is that VĀDIMUS and VĀDITIS were discontinued.

As for the origin of *vamos* and *vades*, Penny takes a totally different approach. As is well known, the present subjunctive paradigm of Latin VĀDERE (i.e., VADAM, VADĀS, etc.) underwent a dual development in Iberia. The loss of the intervocalic /d/ first left the two contiguous like vowels standing in hiatus, after which, these vowels either merged into one, or were kept apart through the epenthesis of an anti-hiatic yod, thus: VADAM, etc. > [βá-a] > *va/vaya*, etc. The contracted forms eventually emerged as the present subjunctive paradigm of Portuguese, while the epenthesized forms now make up the present subjunctive paradigm of Castilian. In Old Spanish, however, one finds both epenthesized and contracted forms in the first and second persons plural, such that the face of the paradigm appeared as shown in (5):

(5)   Pres. Subj. of OSp. *ir*
          vaya   *vamos/vayamos*
          vayas   *vades/vayades*
          vaya   *vayan* (Penny 1991:165, 2002:192)

In light of the Old Spanish present subjunctive paradigm, and with regard to the origin of pres. ind. *vamos, vais*, Penny first wrote and later maintained:

> Some would argue (e.g. Alvar & Pottier 1983:229) that OSp. pres. ind. *vamos, vades* similarly descend from stem-stressed VÁDIMUS, VÁDITIS. However, the phonological difficulty of explaining VÁDITIS > *vades*

makes it preferable to argue that *vamos* and *vades* were originally exclusively subjunctive forms (< VADÁMUS, VADÁTIS) which were attracted into the indicative paradigm because of their structural similarity to indicative *vas, va, van* (Penny 1991: 148).

[I]t is possible to argue that the present indicative forms *vamos, vades* are products of proparoxytonic VÁDIMUS, VÁDITIS. However, on the basis of VÁDIMUS, VÁDITIS, we would predict the outcome **vemos, **vedes, and it is more probable that *vamos, vades* are originally subjunctive forms (< VADAMUS, VADATIS), which came to compete with indicative *imos, ides* and which then displaced these forms because they were structurally better integrated with the remaining forms of the paradigm: *vo, vas, va, van* (Penny 2002:172).

Penny's hypothesis is far and away the most innovative proposed to date, and its appeal lies primarily in the problem-free phonological development of VADĀMUS, VADĀTIS > *vaamos, *vaades > *vamos, vades*. And given the structural similarity between the root morphemes of *va-s, va-Ø, va-n* on the one hand, and *va-mos, va-des* on the other, Penny's suggestion that the former may have attracted the latter into their paradigm is not totally implausible.

One wonders, however, why Penny, or Lloyd, who both invoked analogy with forms like *das, da, estás, está*, etc., for the formation of *vas, va*, and *van* did not suggest analogy for the origin of *vamos* and *vades* as well. It does not seem implausible that once VĀDŌ had reduced to *vo* through regular phonetic development an analogical change involving the forms of DARE and STARE could have ensued, with the first person singulars serving as base forms (connected by their morphological similarity), producing all of the forms of the paradigm as depicted in (6):

(6) *do*   :   *estó*   :   *vo*
    das   *estás*   X = *vas*   (replacing *vaes)
    da   *está*   X = *va*   (replacing *vae)
    damos   *estamos*   X = *vamos* (replacing *vaemos)
    dades   *estades*   X = *vades* (replacing *vaedes)
    dan   *están*   X = *van*   (replacing *vaen)

This would seem to be the simplest solution to the problem.

The present indicative paradigm of Sp. *ir*, then, may have been formed in one of the following four ways according to previous and current scholarship:

(A) Through early paradigmatic leveling of VĀDIS, VĀDIT, VĀDIMUS, VĀDITIS, VĀDUNT by the first person singular, once it had reduced to *VAO, yielding VAS, VAT, VAMUS, VATIS, VANT (combining the views of Meyer-Lübke 1895 and Menéndez Pidal 1941).
(B) Through syncope of VĀDIMUS and VĀDITIS > *vamos, vades*, and on the basis of these (and perhaps forms like *das, da*, etc.), restructuring of VADIS, VADIT, VADUNT as *vas, va, van* (Lloyd 1987).
(C) Through contraction of VĀDIS, VĀDIT, VĀDUNT to *vas, va, van* on the model of *das, da, estás*, etc., followed by a gradual attraction of pres.subj. *vamos, vades* into the indicative paradigm because of their structural similarity with *vas, va, van* (Penny 1991, 2002).
(D) Through the analogical change shown above in (6).

The reality of the foregoing hypothetical scenarios can be checked by an examination of early Old Spanish texts. If scenario (A) is correct, then one would expect to find the forms *vamos, vades* (as well as *vas, va, van*) in the earliest Old Spanish texts, perhaps in competition with *imos, ides*. If scenario (B) is correct, one would also expect to find *vamos* and *vades* in the earliest Old Spanish texts, and perhaps even earlier than *vas, va, van*. If scenario (D) is correct, then one would expect to find *vamos, vades* as early as one finds *vas, va, van*. But if scenario (C), Penny's proposal, is correct, then one should only find *imos* and *ides* in the earliest Old Spanish texts, since *vamos, vades* would have been incorporated into the present indicative paradigm later.

A search for the forms of the present indicative of *ir* in the *Auto de los reyes magos* (ca. 1150-1200), the *Poema de mio Cid*, and the Alfonsine Royal Scriptorium and non-Royal Scriptorium texts turns up the following data shown in (7) (number of occurrences of each form in parentheses):

(7) *Auto de los reyes magos*   *Poema de mio Cid*
    vo (1)   imos (2)   vo (2)   imos (1)
    X   ides (2)   X   ides (4)
    va (1)   X   va (41)   van (34)

Alfonsine Prose		Total: *Auto, Cid, Alfonso*	
vo (109)	*imos* (21)	*vo* (112)	*imos* (24)
vas (38)	*ides* (18)	*vas* (38)	*ides* (24)
va (1,226)	*van* (290)	*va* (1,268)	*van* (324)

It is truly significant, and perhaps surprising, that one finds in these early Old Spanish texts twenty-four occurrences each of *imos* and *ides*, but not a single occurrence of *vamos* or *vades*, neither as indicatives nor subjunctives. It is highly unlikely that pres.ind. *vamos* and *vades* would have been formed according to scenario (A), (B), or (D), all of which presuppose an early existence of these two forms, but would have been suppressed from the written language, while *vo*, *vas*, *va*, *van* were not. Thus it appears that Penny's hypothesis is the only viable one. Nevertheless, the textual evidence poses a couple of problems for Penny's proposal as well.

First, in a search of the Royal Spanish Academy's *Corpus diacrónico del español* (henceforth, *Corde*) one finds the following number of occurrences of the second person plural variants: *vayades* 284 times (83.5%) vs. *vades* 56 times (16.5%). As regards the number of documents in which these forms occur, one finds *vayades* in 149 documents (77.6%) vs. *vades* in 43 documents (22.4%). If these figures mirror in any way the speech habits of the time, then one may conclude that throughout the Middle Ages *vades* occurred in the speech of only 16.5% to 22.4% of the population. Thus the majority of the population (77.6% to 83.5%) would not have had the variant *vades* to pull into their present indicative paradigm. One could argue, however, that the foregoing figures represent preferences rather than the linguistic competence of the speakers, and that all speakers were familiar with both forms, as implied by Penny above in (5). Such being the case, it is quite plausible that speakers who preferred *vayades* would reallocate *vades*, originally subjunctive, to the indicative paradigm, as Penny suggests. However, the textual evidence poses a second problem.

The incorporation of subjunctive *vamos* and *vades* into the indicative paradigm would have been a gradual process, as Penny originally suggested, and later stated more specifically:

Because of their structure, *vamos*, *vades* must *increasingly* have been associated with the indicative paradigm [my emphasis]. (Penny 1991:165)

The subjunctive forms *vamos*, *vades* (< VADĀMUS, VADĀTIS) began to be used in Old Spanish as indicatives since they chimed better with the indicative paradigm (*vo*, *vas*, *va*, *van*) than with the other forms of the subjunctive paradigm (*vaya*, *vayas*, etc.). *This was a slow change...* [my emphasis]. (Penny 2002:192)

Such a gradual change would have occurred, as depicted in (8), where forms to the right of ~ represent the less frequent ones:

(8) vo   imos   vo   imos ~ *vamos*
     vas ides   >   vas ides ~ *vades*   >
     va   van   va   van

     vo   *vamos* ~ imos   vo(y) *vamos*
     vas *vades* ~ ides > vas   *vades* (> *vais*)
     va   van   va   van

However, a search of *Corde* reveals the following surprising facts: First, *vades* does not appear as a present indicative until the fifteenth century. Moreover, of the 56 occurrences of *vades* in *Corde*, only 4 occur as indicatives, appearing sporadically, one time each in the *Poema de Yosef* (1400), *Cuaderno de las Córtes celebradas en la villa de Madrid el año de 1435*, *Libro de las veynte cartas e quistiones* (1449), and *Amadís de Gaula* (1482-1492). Second, the form *vais* first appears as a present indicative in the late-15th century, when one suddenly finds 10 occurrences in 7 documents: 3 in *Amadís de Gaula* (1482-1492), 2 in the *Melosina* (1489), and one time each in the *Crónica de los Reyes Católicos* by Hernando del Pulgar (1480-1484), the *Cancionero* by Juan del Encina (1481-1496), Nebrija's *Gramática castellana* (1492), *El baladro del sabio Merlín con sus profecías* (1498) and the *Traslado de una carta de los Reyes a Bobadilla con la respuesta del Almirante* (1500). And finally, and perhaps most surprising, is the fact that *vamos*, while appearing abundantly as an imperative throughout the Middle Ages (and also as a subjunctive, sharing the load with *vayamos*), like *vais*, does not appear as a present indicative until the late-15th century, where it appears as such twice in *Letras* by Fernando de Pulgar (1470-1485), and one time each in *Amadís de Gaula* (1482-1492), *Melosina* (1489), *Crónica incompleta de los Reyes Católicos* (1469-1476), and Nebrija's *Gramática castellana* (1492).

Thus there appears to have been no gradual attraction of pres.subj. *vamos*, *vades* (> *vais*) into the indicative paradigm throughout the Middle Ages, as depicted above in (8), but rather, a more sudden appearance of *vamos*, *vais* (but not *vades*) toward the end of the Middle Ages, as shown in (9):

(9) | 1150-1400 | 1400-1470 | 1470-1500 |
|---|---|---|
| vo imos | vo(y) imos | voy imos ~ **vamos** |
| vas ides | vas ides (rarely **vades**) | vas ides ~ **vais** |
| va van | va van | va van |

It therefore remains to be explained why *vamos* and *vades* did not enter the present indicative paradigm in either the 12th, 13th, or 14th centuries, and exactly how and why they did in the late-15th century.

In order to gain an understanding of this historical linguistic event, one might consider the more general question of why some forms of ĪRE were replaced by the corresponding forms of VĀDERE. Penny (2002:192) most recently writes:

> The various present-tense forms of ĪRE suffered from the disadvantage of having no consonant in the root: EŌ, ĪS, ĪT, ĪMUS, ĪTIS, EUNT, EAM, EĀS ... This fact must have made these forms difficult to separate from adjacent words in normal speech, and which caused the majority of them to be replaced by longer forms, drawn from other verbs. The verb which most frequently provided these longer forms was VADERE 'to go, hurry', so that in the spoken Latin of Spain, the paradigms which expressed the notion of 'go' were probably VADO, VADIS, VADIT, ĪMUS, ĪTIS, VADUNT/*VADENT, VADAM, VADĀS...

Lathrop (1996:165) further suggests that regular phonetic development of the present tense forms of ĪRE would have rendered them even more problematic: "[M]ost of its forms would have been too short or too confusing: CL *ego eo* would have developed to Sp. **yo yo*, for example." However, it may not have only been a question of the forms being too short or too confusing, but also that regular phonetic development may have left a defective paradigm with almost no common element between most of the forms, as the entire present indicative of IRE may have evolved as depicted in (10):

(10) | | ĪRE | | | | ir | |
|---|---|---|---|---|---|---|
| | EŌ | ĪMUS | | | *yo | imos |
| | ĪS | ĪTIS | > | | *is | ides |
| | IT | EUNT | | | *e | *yon |

It was perhaps because of the asymmetry between the forms *yo, *is, *e, *yon that speakers came to prefer the corresponding forms of VĀDERE. The suppletive paradigm of *ir*, then, may have first appeared as shown in (11):

(11) Pre-12th century *ir*

*vao	imos
*vaes	ides
*vae	*vaen

Although Penny (2002:192) believes that after the loss of -D- from VĀDŌ, VĀDIS, VĀDIT, *VĀDENT "the root was maintained separate from the person/number marker (that is, without vowel-reduction of the type VADIS > /βáes/ > /βais/ > **/βes/, etc.)", such vowel-reduction is not inconceivable. The Portuguese forms *vou, vais, vai*, Mirandese *bai*, the forms *beis, bey* of Villaoril de Cangas de Tineo, and 13th-c. Asturian *ve* (Menéndez Pidal 1941:306) all suggest that the forms of the present indicative paradigm shown in (11) may indeed have followed the same path of development as the singular imperative from Latin to Castilian, i.e., VADE > *[βá-e] > *[βái̯] > *[βéi̯] > *ve*. Thus unlike the corresponding forms of *caer*, which acquired an antihiatic yod in the first person singular, i.e., *cao > OSp. *cayo*, and maintained hiatus in *caes, cae*, etc., the forms *vao, *vaes, *vae, *vaen, perhaps because of their higher frequency of occurrence, would first suffer a loss of hiatus, followed by mutual assimilation, and finally, monophthongization, as shown in (12a), leaving a paradigm with forms in the second person singular and third persons singular and plural which were very close in their phonetic and morphological structure to the corresponding forms of *veer* 'to see', as shown in bold in (12b):

(12) a. Pre-12th century *ir*

*vao	imos		*vau	imos		
*vaes	ides	>	*vais	ides	>	
*vae	*vaen		*vai	*vain		
*vou	imos		*vo	imos		
*veis	ides	>	*ves	ides		
*vei	*vein		*ve	*ven		

b.

	ir		*veer*	
	vo	imos	veo	veemos
	*ves	ides	**vees**	veedes
	*ve	*ven	**vee**	**veen**

The potential for *vees, vee, veen* of *veer* to be realized phonetically as monosyllabic [βés], [βé], [βén] would have rendered *ves, *ve, *ven of *ir* less useful than their precursors *veis, *vei, *vein and earlier *vais, *vai, *vain. But the potential merger of the present indicatives *ves, *ve, *ven and vees, vee, veen was avoided when monophthongization of *vou > vo led to the analogical change shown above in (6). However, the analogy only progressed as far as was necessary. That is, only the defective *ves, *ve, *ven were replaced at this time through analogy with do, das, etc., and estó, estás, etc., as shown below in (13a). The forms imos and ides, being non-problematic, indeed still well integrated with other forms of the paradigm (e.g., ir, ido, yendo, id), therefore remained. Thus the face of the paradigm changed to that found in the earliest Castilian texts, as shown in (13b):

(13) a. <u>do</u> : <u>estó</u>   : <u>vo</u>
         das   estás   X = vas (replacing *ves)
         da   está   X = va   (replacing *ve)
         dan   están   X = van (replacing *ven)

   b. Pre-13th century <u>ir</u>   13th century <u>ir</u>
        vo   imos   vo   imos
        *ves   ides   >   vas   ides
        *ve   *ven   va   van

This paradigm remained intact until the 15th century, the period in which the Old Spanish second person verbal suffixes –ades, –edes, –ides (and –odes of sodes) underwent a morphophonological reduction, resulting in two new sets of suffixes: –áis, –éis, –ís, –ois, ultimately functioning as plurals, and –ás, –és, –ís, –os, ultimately functioning as singulars. However, not all of these suffixes were reduced, nor were all lexical items affected, simultaneously. The change began in the late-14th century in a restricted grammatical context, namely, the second conjugation –edes when functioning as a future morpheme (Dworkin 1988), and from there spread slowly, eventually affecting all suffixes in all grammatical categories. As regards the third conjugation, the reduction of –ides to –ís began in the first half of the 15th century and was quickly accomplished during the second half of the same century (Rini 1999:132-33, 136). Subject to this change, the present indicative paradigm of ir would acquire the form is "you go", the reduced variant of ides. In Corde, one finds the new, reduced allomorph only sporadically in the first half of the 15th century (once in the Bursario, 1425-1450 and once in the Cancionero de Estúñiga, 1407-1463), followed by 7 occurrences in the latter part of this century (six times in Amadís de Gaula I & II, 1482-1492, and once in the Traducción de la Corónica de Aragón de fray Gauberto Fabricio de Vagad, 1499). Meanwhile, occurrences of ides declined sharply during this period. While 24 examples occur in 9 documents from 1400-1470, only 8 examples occur after 1470, 7 occur in one text (the *Istoria de las bienandanzas e fortunas*, 1471-76) and only one in *Amadís de Gaula* (1482-92). This is precisely when one suddenly finds a significant number of pres.ind. *vais*, as well as a few examples of pres.ind. *vamos*. These data suggest that throughout the course of the 15th century the paradigm underwent the changes shown in bold in (14), thus modifying slightly part of the scenario presented above in (9):

(14) <u>1400-1470</u> <u>1470-1500</u>
      vo(y)   imos   voy   imos ~ **vamos**
      vas   *ides ~ is* (rarely *vades*)   vas   ***is* ~ *vais*** (rarely *ides*)
      va   van   va   van

I would like to suggest that the appearance of pres.ind. *vais* (and subsequently pres.ind. *vamos*) in the late-15th century was a direct result of the reduction of the second person plural verbal suffixes, and in particular, the reduction of *ides* > *is*. During this process, speakers were faced with a choice between two coexisting variants, neither of which was altogether satisfactory. Speakers could continue to employ *ides*, which, while still well integrated within its own paradigm, sharing structural similarities with the forms *ir*, *ido*, *yendo*, and *id*, was now badly integrated within its own grammatical category (i.e., second person plural), where all other forms were shedding or had already shed their /-d-/. Alternatively, speakers could opt for the innovative *is* which, showing no trace of the now archaic /-d-/, was indeed well integrated within its own grammatical category, but was not so well integrated within its paradigm. Although Penny (2002:192) states that *imos* (and *ides*) "ceased to be used before the sixteenth century", *Corde* shows 45 occurrences of *imos* in 28 documents in the 16th century (followed by the last 4 examples appearing in texts from 1605, 1609, 1619, and 1622). Thus, speakers who adopted *is* by the end of the 15th century were faced with a paradigm whose first and second persons plural appeared as follows in (15):

(15)   <u>Late-15th century *ir*</u>
               voy ***imos***
               vas ***is***
               va   van

The second person plural *is* may soon have been considered by some speakers to be lacking in phonetic substance, particularly in light of its first person counterpart *imos*, i.e., *imos ~ is* (whereas earlier *imos ~ ides*), as well as its corresponding subject pronoun, whose expansion from *vos* > *vos otros* >

vosotros was completely grammaticalized by the end of the 15th century (Eberenz 2000:59), i.e., *vos ides* > *vosotros is*. Therefore, those speakers whose linguistic competence included pres.subj. *vais*, may have, at this time, pressed this form into service as a present indicative. Others, who may have only known pres.subj. *vais* passively, through contact with those speakers who indeed used it, may have reallocated this form to the present indicative paradigm. Yet others, whose linguistic competence lacked this form both actively and passively, that is, those who had only ever known *vayáis* (and earlier, *vayades*), may have created a totally new *vais* in the following manner.

The Old Spanish second person plural forms of *dar* and *estar*, i.e., *dades* and *estades*, began to undergo their reduction to *dais* and *estáis* in the first half of the 15th century, followed by a more intense reduction in the second half of that century. In *Corde*, between 1400-1450, one finds only 5 occurrences of *dais* (in 5 documents) and only 2 of *estáis* (in 2 documents). From 1451-1500, however, one finds 81 occurrences of *dais* (in 29 documents) and 28 of *estáis* (in 16 documents). This reduction set up an opposition with the corresponding singular forms, unique to these two verbs alone, in which the only difference between *tú* and *vos(otros)* was the offglide [i], which became, in effect, the morphemic marker of the latter, thus: *tú das* ~ *vos(otros) dais, tú estás* ~ *vos(otros) estáis* (all other first conjugation verbs also exhibited contrasting stress patterns, e.g., /ámas/ vs. /amáis/, etc., as well as other morphophonemic alternations, e.g., /siéntas/ vs. /sentáis/, /kwéntas/ vs. /kontáis/, etc.). I would like to suggest here, therefore, that speakers who were not at all familiar with pres.subj. *vais*, and therefore could not have pulled such a form into their present indicative paradigm, but would indeed have had this morphemic offglide as part of their linguistic competence, would have added it to singular (*tú*) *vas*, on the basis of the pattern exhibited by the structurally similar *doy, das*, etc., and *estoy, estás*, etc., as shown in (16):

(16)

<u>doy</u>	:	<u>estoy</u>	:	<u>voy</u>
das ~ *dais*		*estás* ~ *estáis*		*vas* + morphemic /i/ > *vais* (replacing *is*)

The few examples (four) of pres.ind. *vades* found in the 15th century may have similarly been formed according to the patterns *do(y)* ~ *das* ~ *dades, esto(y)* ~ *estás* ~ *estades*, hence *vo(y)* ~ *vas* ~ X = *vades* (that is, they are not necessarily examples of subjunctives functioning as indicatives). Even those speakers who may have pulled pres.subj. *vades/vais* into the present indicative paradigm may have done so, not only because of the structural similarity between these subjunctives and *vas, va, van*, as Penny has suggested, but also because of the aforementioned patterns found in *dar* and *estar*.

Once speakers began to replace *is* with *vais*, they would soon begin to replace *imos* as well, since this form now stood alone as the only inflected form of the present indicative paradigm with a root morpheme in /i-/. The replacement of the now anomalous *imos* by *vamos* probably came about in a number of ways. Those speakers whose linguistic repertoire included pres.subj. *vamos* (< VADĀMUS) may have shifted this form into the present indicative paradigm, as Penny has suggested. Others, who employed pres.subj. *vayamos* to the total exclusion of pres.subj. *vamos*, but were indeed familiar with the imperative ¡*Vamos!*, may have shifted this form into the present indicative paradigm. Yet others may have replaced *imos* through extra-paradigmatic leveling by structurally similar *dar* (and *estar*), as exemplified in (17):

(17) *doy* **damos** →   *voy* **imos**   *voy* **vamos**
     das dais   *vas vais*   >   *vas vais*
     da   dan   *va   van*   *va   van*

And finally, *vamos* may have made its appearance in the present indicative paradigm through leveling by *vais*, whereby the root morpheme *va-* would simply replace that of *imos*, as shown in (18):

(18) *voy*   *i- mos* > *va- mos* >   *voy*   **vamos**
               ↑
      vas   *va- is*   *vas*   **vais**
      va   *van*   *va*   *van*

Such leveling would have been accomplished through every-day intercourse. As long as *ides* and *is* still existed, so too would *imos*, as these forms shared the same root morpheme, e.g., *Cavalleros, ¿Dónde ides?* (and later, *Cavalleros, ¿Dónde is?*) – *Imos a Toledo*. Likewise, the natural response to *vais* would eventually have been *vamos*, not *imos* e.g., *Cavalleros, ¿Dónde vais?* – *Vamos a Toledo*. Even those who shifted present subjunctive or imperative *vamos* into the present indicative paradigm may have done so through this type of verbal exchange, or because of the patterns found in the structurally similar *dar* and *estar*. Thus the existence of pres.subj./imperative *vamos*, extra-paradigmatic leveling by *dar* and *estar*, as well as leveling by *vais* may have all been contributing factors in the replacement of *imos* by *vamos*. One may therefore conclude that the form *vamos* of the present indicative paradigm originated in part from pres.subj./imperative *vamos* because of the acts of some speakers, and in part as a paradigmatic creation on the part of others, resulting in a mere coincidence of Spanish historical morphology with *vamos* (< VADAMUS). The present understanding of the formation of the present indicative paradigm of Sp. *ir* and the origin of *vamos* and *vais* could not have been reached without a reexamination of the entire history of the paradigm and, more importantly, the intriguing proposal originally put forth in Penny (1991).

References

Alvar, Manuel and Bernard Pottier. 1983. *Morfología histórica del español*. Madrid: Gredos.
Dworkin, Steven N. 1988. "The Diffusion of a Morphological Change: The Reduction of the Old Spanish Verbal Suffixes *–ades*, *-edes*, and *–ides*." *Medioevo Romanzo* 13, 223-36.
García de Diego, Vicente. 1951. *Gramática histórica española*. Madrid: Gredos.
Hanssen, Friedrich. 1913. *Gramática histórica de la lengua castellana*. Halle: Niemeyer.
Lathrop, Thomas A. 1980. *The Evolution of Spanish*. Newark, Delaware: Juan de la Cuesta.
Lathrop, Thomas A. 1984. *Curso de gramática histórica española*. Barcelona: Ariel.
Lathrop, Thomas A. 1996. *The Evolution of Spanish*. 3rd ed. Newark, Delaware: Juan de la Cuesta.
Liberatori, Filomena and Giovanni Battista De Cesare. 1986. *Nozioni di storia della lingua e di grammatica storica spagnola*. Napoli: Edizioni Libreria Sapere.
Lloyd, Paul M. 1987. *From Latin to Spanish*. Philadelphia: American Philosophical Society.
Menéndez Pidal, Ramón. 1941. *Manual de gramática histórica española*. 6th ed. Madrid: Espasa-Calpe.
Meyer-Lübke, Wilhelm. 1895. *Grammaire des langues romanes. Tome Deuxième: Morphologie*. Paris: Welter.
Penny, Ralph J. 1991. *A History of the Spanish Language*. Cambridge: Cambridge University Press.
Penny, Ralph J. 2002. *A History of the Spanish Language*. 2nd ed. Cambridge: Cambridge University Press.
Real Academia Española. *Corpus histórico del español*. http://www.rae.es.
Rini, Joel. 1999. *Exploring the Role of Morphology in the Evolution of Spanish*. Amsterdam: John Benjamins.
Urrutia Cárdenas, Hernán and Manuela Álvarez Álvarez. 1983. *Esquema de morfosintaxis histórica del español*. Bilbao: Universidad de Deusto.

4
The Pronunciation of *h*- and *f*- in Bilingual Spanish/Arabic Treaties from the Thirteenth Century
ROBERT BLAKE

NEBRIJA MADE IT CLEAR by the end of the fifteenth century that Castilians aspirated the grapheme *h*- derived from Latin F- in the standard variety, "dándole fuerza de letra" (Nebrija 1989:133).[1] At the same time, he observed that the letter *h*- usually (or formerly) had no value—"[la *h*] ia no sirve por sí, salvo por otra letra, y llamarla emos 'he', como los judíos y moros"—his way of indicating that a phonological change had occurred with respect to earlier times when the letter *h*- ceased to be pronounced, around the first century BC according to Penny (1991:53). Nevertheless, for texts three centuries before Nebrija's remarks, determining the phonetic value of *h*—and, even more so, that of *f*—remains a thorny issue. Could it also have signaled glottal aspiration for a limited number of lexical entries with Latin F- that were leading the way to the eventual phonological split /f/:/h/ that Nebrija would explicitly talk about? Nebrija explained with great care that *h*- could function as a "true" letter with phonemic value (< F-) or as either a silent letter derived from Latin with H- (e.g. *honor, heredad, hombre*) or a silent marker for words that begin with the diphthong *ue* (e.g. *huésped, huevo, huerto*).

> La *h* entre nos otros tiene tres oficios: uno proprio, que trae consigo en las diciones latinas, mas non le damos su fuerça, como en éstas: *humano, humilde*, donde la escrivimos sin causa, pues que de ninguna cosa sirve; otro, cuando se sigue *u* después vocal, como en estas diciones: *huésped, huerto, huevo*; lo cual ia no es menester, si las dos fuerças que tiene la la *u*

---

[1] We wish to acknowledge the generous help of Professor Sam Armistead in reading the Arabic characters of the surrender treaty and helpful comments on the manuscripts. Any errors are ours alone.

distinguimos por estas dos figures: *u, v*. El tercero oficio es cuando le damos fuerça de letra haziéndola sonar, como en las primeras letras destas diciones: *hago, hijo* (133).

In this study, we seek to determine what pronunciation was given to the graphemes *h-* and *f-* around the thirteenth century, two centuries before Nebrija's more definitive comments, a period when great attention was beginning to be focused on standardizing the written language. At this time, truly phonetic writing practices were only just being introduced into Romance (Wright 1982), which suggests that not all instances of *h-* or *f-* can be interpreted in a straightforward manner. In the absence of truly phonetic—as opposed to phonemic—writing practices, we have turned to bilingual Spanish/Arabic surrender treaties from Valencia for possible clues as to the value of written *h-* and *f-*. More specifically, we examined texts gathered by R. Burns and P. Chevedden (1999) in their edition of bilingual surrender treaties between Christians and Muslims because these texts afford the next best option to having a phonetic transcription for the medieval period.

Transcriptions of Arabic into Romance or the reverse have been previously used to great advantage in order to argue for different phonological accounts of one or both languages (cf. Alarcos Llorach 1951; Catalán 1967-68; Lantolf 1974 and 1979; Torreblanca 1986 and 1994). Following this tradition, we have analyzed the surrender agreement celebrated in 1245 dealing with the Arabic stronghold at Játiva. This interlinear document with one line in Arabic alternating with its corresponding version in Castilian provides an ideal authority with which to posit *h-* rendered as [Ø] and *f-* realized either as [h] or [f], the latter alternation being the written norm for the period before Nebrija (Alarcos Llorach 1951:38). The Arabic translation is, of course, as close as possible to the Castilian text although the linguistic renditions of notions such as power (i.e. honorifics), feudalism, lineage, or time can never be seamlessly translated from one culture to another (Burns and Chevedden 1999:34).

Of crucial interest here are the Arabic and Romance toponyms and proper names because they offer some of the strongest evidence for describing the nature of the Castilian phonological system in practice two centuries before Nebrija's subsequent statements concerning the standard norms. Understandably, toponyms and proper names need to be represented literally in this type of political treaty in order to maintain good faith in bilateral negotiations, whereas the other content and functional words of Arabic and Castilian rarely have exact equivalents. In this respect, it is fortuitous that Arabic has both a labiodental fricative /f/ along with a series of aspirates (velar /x/, pharyngeal /ḥ/, and glottal /h/). We will situate the data found in the surrender treaties within a sociolinguistic historical framework that presupposes a Castilian phonemic split in progress at this time: namely, /h/ → /h/ (> [h]/[Ø]):/f/ (cf. Penny 1972, 1991, 2000:45). The historical battlefront that concerns us pits the forces of King James the Conqueror (represented here by his son Don Alfonso) and the Valencian vizier Abu 'Abd Allah ibn Hudhayl, a most clever, if not slippery, local warlord popularly known as Al-Azraq, who controlled a mini-state in and around the Ebo Valley. His name appears twice in the Romance part of the treaty: once as *Habuabdele Yvan Fudayl* and another time as *Abuabdele Yvan Fudayl*.

Also of interest is the reference in the document to the Ebo Valley itself, written in Romance as *Hebo* but in Arabic as *Abuh*. These tokens of *h-* and *f-*, along with others of interest from the document, are listed for convenience in Table 1 below, although not all the Romance terms have discrete Arabic counterparts in the treaty.

PHONETIC VALUE:	ROMANCE TEXT:	ARABIC TEXT:
h- > [Ø]	Habuabdele	Abu 'Abd Allah
	Abuabdele	Abu 'Abd Allah
	Hebo	Abuh
	Fudayl	Hudhayl
f- > [H]	Fudayl	Hudhayl
	forros (Ar. Ḥurr 'free')	*
f- > [f]	Alfonsso	Alfunsh
	Infant	alifant
	onrrado (< *HONOREM*)	*
etymological	eredat < (*HEREDITATEM*)	*
h- > [Ø]	Eredamiento	*
	ayades < (*HABEATIS*)	*

TABLE 1. TOKENS OF *H-* AND *F-* IN THE BILINGUAL SURRENDER TREATY

The Romance transcription of these names underscores the scribes' concern for phonetic accuracy. For instance, Romance *Yvan* [iban] derives from a reasonable attempt to capture phonetically Arabic *ibn* 'son of' in Castilian, a language where syllabic nasals are not allowed. Likewise, the rendition of '*Abd Allah* as [abdele] where /a/ is fronted and raised reflects the characteristic Arabic *imala* or *Ümlaut* phenomenon common in Hispano-Arabic (Corriente 1977),[2] while the syllable-final aspiration [h] is predictably ignored or not perceived. Going in the reverse direction, the Arabic voiced fricative *dh* [ð], found in *Hudhayl*, is translated into Romance only as -*d*-, because the Castilian stop would automatically be pronounced as a fricative in this intervocalic environment, again reflecting the scribes' attention to phonetic accuracy.

The obvious conclusion drawn from examining more closely these proper names and toponyms, listed below in Table 1, is that written *h*- had no phonetic value in medieval Romance. The interpretation is especially supported by the rendition of the vizier's first name *Abu*, once with an *h*- and once without. In medieval times, written *h*- was frequently used at the beginning of words beginning with vowels, perhaps to ensure that the reader would maintain hiatus with respect to the preceding determiner. In a previous study (Blake 1989a:45), we have already documented the frequent use of this written inorganic *h*- in twelfth-, thirteenth-, fourteenth-, and fifteenth-century notarial documents ranging from Leon to Aragon for such everyday words as *haldea, harcorenes, hebro, hera, herror, horden, hotros, huso, husual, huvas*. By Nebrija's day, this practice was dying out leaving only words beginning with the diphthong *ue* marked with silent *h*-. Etymological *h*- from Latin has been dropped altogether in the Romance part of this treaty as evidenced by examples such as *onrrado, eredat, eredamiento, ayades*.

In contrast, word-initial *f*- is carefully employed to capture Arabic aspiration as in the case of Romance *Fudayl* for Arabic *Hudhayl* written in the Arabic version with the symbol ه to indicate the glottal fricative /h/ in word-initial position. The Romance text also uses *f*- to write the more fully incorporated Romance adjective *forros*, as in the binominal legal expression *castielos forros y quito*, which derived from an Arabic loanword with pharyngeal /ḥ/ (< Sp. *ḥorro* < Hisp. Ar. *ḥurr* 'free').

This is not to imply that the labiodental fricative [f] is missing from the Romance text; quite the contrary, as one would expect from a document produced by Don Alfonso's heavily Aragonese-influenced chancery (Burns and Chevedden 1999:12). The Arabic version translates *Alfonsso* as *Alfunsh* and *infante* as *alifant* (see Table 1), both with Arabic *fa*, providing credible evidence for the idea that the labiodental fricative [f] was also alive and well at this time along side of an aspirated variant [h].

---

[2] Corriente (1977:22) states that "The phoneme /a/ in SpAr had a normal reflex, characterized by spontaneous fronting and raising whenever this tendency (i.e. *imala*) was not checked by inhibiting factors..."

Likewise, for words such as *fago, fer, fijo, fiel* that appear in the Romance version, a labiodental fricative [f] might still be expected in a thirteenth-century formal register. Another possibility is that speakers vary between forms with [f] and others with [h] in response to a sociolinguistic continuum. Clearly, [f] constitutes one of the Romance sounds that Arabic speakers readily accommodate with the Arabic alphabet. But unlike the orthographic system Nebrija described two centuries later, the *f-* grapheme does double-duty here by indicating aspiration for some Romance words and labiodental fricative for others; this situation is exacerbated by the phoneme split /f/:/h/ not having spread as yet to all dialects and registers, making it difficult to represent a changing spoken norm in writing. Until the split was generally accepted in all circles and writing reforms take place, writing *h-* was not a particularly good method to signal aspiration because it traditionally stood for a null value [Ø]. Written *f-*, however, stood for both the formal and the informal variants of /f/: namely, [f] and [h]; as Alarcos Llorach (1951) has already pointed out. The *f* grapheme captured the realities of the other Romance dialects as well. Again, although the grapheme *h-* appears to have no phonetic value in this document, it still performs a phonosyntactic function of signaling word boundaries in the written form.

Let us return for a moment to our previously mentioned study (Blake 1989a:42) of 900 notarial documents we examined from Old and New Castile (Sahagún, Burgos, San Millán de la Cogolla, Segovia, and Avila). These original manuscripts were all written on vellum and are presently housed in the *Archivo Histórico Nacional* (AHN) in Madrid in the *Sección de Clero*. Our scrutiny of these manuscripts turned up a small set of words from the medieval period with *h-* < F- (Blake 1989a). We have listed below only those tokens from the thirteenth century in order to serve as a basis of comparison with the Arabic/Christian surrender treaty.

 dehesados < der. DEFENSAM 'land marked off for pasture'
 haça < FASCIAM 'strip [of land]'
 halcón < FALCONEM 'falcon'
 hanbrie[n]ta < *FAMINENTUS 'hungry' der. FAMES, -IS 'hunger'
 henosa < FENOSAM 'pertaining to hay'
 Herrán < Sp. Fernán[do] < FERDINANDUM
 herrén < FERRAGINE 'fodder, land for fodder'
 herrera < FERRARIAM 'of iron'
 hondo < FUNDUM 'deep'
 hormaza < FORMACEAM 'stone wall'
 hormiella < der. FORMAM 'circular wooden button'
 hortún < der. FORTIS 'strong'

hoyales < der. FOVEA 'holes, ditches'
kahiz < Ar. Cafiz 'dry measurement'

Examples with *h-* < F- were conspicuously absent for another 750 notarial documents originating from Carrizo (León) and Montearagón (Huesca), two dialect areas where F- would not normally be aspirated. What comparison might be drawn, then, from the writing practices employed by the scribes charged with drawing up the surrender treaty and those writing notarial documents in Christian lands? Following logic or the standard writing practices of the day alone, instances of written *h-*, whatever their source, might continue to follow tradition and represent a null value [Ø]. In that case, the above notarial examples would constitute a few precious lead words for the last phase of the on-going Old Castilian sociolinguistic change of /h/ > [Ø] for words whose Latin ancestors had F-, in the same way that Menéndez Pidal argued for the existence of an ancient spoken norm F- > [Ø] in Old Castile from its origins: "Hagamos primero constar que los ejemplos de *h-*, o de pérdida de *f-*, remontan mucho más atrás de lo que se creía" (Menéndez Pidal 1964:§41.3). Coincidentally, several words we have listed above also were observed by Menéndez Pidal as occurring early on in northern Spain, without either *f-* or *h-*: namely, *Ormaza* <*Hormaza* (Burgos 1092), *Errant* < *Ferrant* (Burgos 1100), *Ortiz* < *Fortis* (Montearagón 1106)[3], *Reoio* < *Hoyo* (Oña 1212).

From a sociolinguistic viewpoint, nothing should prevent two variants for the same Castilian phoneme /h/ from happily coexisting in different registers of the same dialect, especially since we know that the null variant [Ø] or loss will eventually triumph as the standard by the sixteenth century in all of Spain. The F-> [Ø] had to manifest itself at some point in Old Castile, but the writing system would be loath to represent it unequivocally until Nebrija's orthographic reforms because it only gradually transformed itself into the prestige form.

The value of written *f-*, however, is a delicate matter. What would a scribe need to do in order to represent aspiration [h] in writing as separate from [f] or vice versa? The answer was simple: Don't! Just use *f-* until such time as /f/ reemerges as a phoneme and spelling reforms take place to capture the new /f/:/h/ contrast (i.e. during Nebrija's time). The *f-* spellings found in this thirteenth-

---

[3] Menéndez Pidal (1964:§41.5) noticed that Ortiz < FORTIS constituted the only example outside of Castile and La Rioja: "Los ejemplos más viejos de pérdida de *f* que he podido reunir pertenecen a Castilla o Rioja, salvo uno de ellos (Ortiz) que se localiza en Aragón; de León no hay ninguno, con ser la documentación leonesa muchísimo más abundante que la castellana."

century bilingual document are no more confusing than spelling practices encountered by Alarcos Llorach (1951) when tracing how labiodentals and aspirates from Arabic loanwords were accepted into Castilian: Romance *f-* can be used to represent phonetically similar Arabic *fa* as well as any one of the aspirates (/x/, /ḥ/, /h/); and the same appears to be true of *h-*, as well, making for a great deal of confusion. But Alarcos Llorach (1951:37-39) knew all too well that these loanwords were the product of both written and spoken traditions that mixed sources and dialects freely, that is to say, chaotically:[4] "la *f* era más culta, la *h* mas rústica; ambos sonidos eran, pues, variantes estilísticas de un solo fonema" (39). The passage of more time soon changed that situation and the phoneme /f/ reemerged in Castilian, as Penny (1972) has explained, leaving phonemic /h/ (> [h] ~ [Ø]) to its fate, that of oblivion [Ø].

One might muse on what factors drove the northern Castilians to prefer eventually the [Ø] variant over the aspirate pronunciation of Latin F-. Undoubtedly, their desire to set themselves apart, first by using the variant [h] as the Castilian standard and, later, the more colloquial variant [Ø]. This scenario is entirely analogous to what Labov (1972) described in his classic study of permanent residents on Martha's Vineyard: those that felt themselves truly indigenous, as opposed to others from the ranks of mere summer tourists, progressively centralized their vowels more and more to distance themselves from the "wanna be's." Pride in being distinctively Old Castilian, a theme strongly present in the society and literature, was bound to be encoded in the language as well, and might help explain the case of /h/ > [h] ~ [Ø] > [Ø].

Elsewhere (Blake 1988 and 1989b), we have suggested that the Castilian scribal practice of *ff-*doubling a common writing phenomenon that gradually builds in the thirteenth century, reaches a peak in the fourteenth century, only to end rather abruptly in the fifteenth century—represented a barometer for the spread of the /f/:/h/ phonemic split. It was never the case that scribes exclusively used *ff-* for [f] and *f-* for [h] in a phonetic sense. Rather, their increased tendency to double *ff* was symptomatic of their growing anxiety concerning the new phonemic contrast /f/:/h/ that was gaining general acceptance in the society at large. *Ff-*doubling becomes most pronounced just before the period when the society accepts /f/:/h/ in all registers. That fact that /h/ > [h] ~ [Ø] is a moving target does not make acceptance any easier, because the null variant [Ø] was undoubtedly tainted with connotations of lower-class and/or rural speech. Scribes

---

[4] Alarcos Llorach (1951:41), however, sees no difference between the capricious assignments of *f-/h-* found in Arabic loanwords and the contradictory results of two other non-loanwords such as *fiesta/hierro*.

might very well have been prone to avoid the growing colloquial preference for [Ø] by emphasizing the more prestigious [f] pronunciation using the *ff*-grapheme as a reflection of this hypercorrection.

Faced with traditional spellings and new spoken norms, Nebrija strove to reform the Castilian orthography to capture better the realities of the day: now written *h-* could either signal aspiration [h]—which represented a true spelling innovation for his day—or stand for nothing [Ø] following its traditional value, depending on the etymological source of the word. The letter *f-* was now reserved exclusively for the labiodental fricative /f/. Sound changes, of course, never cease to occur and by the next century, in Santa Teresa's day, a flood of new residents from northern Castile to Madrid soon shifted the balance in favor of the null realization and imposed it as the norm, leaving only /f/ standing with real phonetic content, a scenario that Penny (2000:42-46) has recently described most succinctly.

References

Alarcos Llorach, E. 1951. "Alternancia de *f* y *h* en los arabismos." *Archivum* 1:29-41.
Blake, R. 1988. "Ffaro, Faro, or Haro?: Doubling as a Source of Linguistic Information for the early Middle Ages." *Romance Philology* 41:267-89.
Blake, R. 1989a. "Radiografía de un cambio lingüístico de la edad media." *Revista de Filología Española* 69:39-59.
Blake, R. 1989b. "Sound Change and Linguistic Residue: The Case of f > h > Ø." *GURT '88: Synchronic and Diachronic Approaches to Linguistic Variation and Change*, ed. by Thomas Walsh, 53-62. Washington, D.C.: Georgetown University Press.
Burns, R. and P. Chevedden (eds.). 1999. *Negotiating Cultures: Bilingual surrender Treaties in Muslim-Crusader Spain under James the Conqueror*. Leiden, Brill.
Catalán, D. 1967-68. "La pronunciación [ihante] por /iffante/ en la Rioja del siglo XI. Anotaciones a una observación dialectológica de un historiador árabe." *Romance Philology* 21:410-35.
Corriente, F. 1977. *A Grammatical Sketch of the Spanish Arabic Dialect Bundle*. Madrid: Instituto Hispano-Árabe de Cultura.
Labov, W. 1972. *Sociolinguistic Patterns*. Philadelphia: University of Pennsylvania Press.
Lantolf, J. 1974. "Linguistic Change as a Socio-Cultural Phenomenon: A Study of the Old Spanish Sibilant Devoicing." Unpublished Dissertation, The Pennsylvania State University.
Lantolf, J. 1979. "Explaining Linguistic Change: The Loss of Voicing in the Old Spanish Sibilants." *Orbis* 28:290-315.
Menéndez Pidal, R. 1964. *Orígenes del español: estado lingüístico de la Península Ibérica hasta el siglo XI*. 5th edition. Madrid: Espasa-Calpe.

Nebrija, Antonio. 1989 [1492]. *Gramática de la lengua castellana*, ed. by A. Quilis. Madrid: Editorial Centro de Estudios Ramón Areces.
Penny, R. 1972. "The re-emergence of /f/ as a phoneme of Castilian." *Zeitschrift für Romanische Philologie* 88:463-82.
Penny, R. 1991. *A History of the Spanish Language*. Cambridge: Cambridge University Press.
Penny, R. 2000. *Variation and Change in Spanish*. Cambridge: Cambridge University Press.
Torreblanca, M. 1986. "Las oclusivas sordas hispanolatinas: el testimonio árabe." *Anuario de Letras* 24:5-25.
Torreblanca, M. 1994. "On Hispano-Arabic Historical Phonology: Latin and Romance Evidence." *Current Issues in Linguistic Theory: Perspectives on Arabic Linguistics*, ed. by M. Eid, V. Cantarino and K. Walters, 37-62. Amsterdam: John Benjamins Publishing Company.
Wright, R. 1982. *Late Latin and Early Romance in Spain and Carolingian France*. Liverpool: Francis Cairns.

5
Reflections on Dialect Mixing and Variation in Alfonsine Texts
DONALD N. TUTEN

TRADITIONALLY THE CORPUS OF scientific, historical and legal texts from the Alfonsine scriptorium has been seen to embody the development and use of a highly codified variety of language (particularly in later texts; cf. Lapesa 1981:239). However, in recent years, numerous scholars have chipped away at this belief by pointing out that the Alfonsine corpus is in fact characterized in its entirety by massive linguistic variation. One of the first blows to the mainstream conception of Alfonsine language came from Hartman (1974), who analyzed variation in verb forms and suggested that the famous term *castellano drecho* might not refer to the codification of grammatical norms at all but rather to lexical or stylistic aspects of language. Cano (1985) followed up on this approach in his analysis of "non-Castilian" (predominantly Leonese) forms and features in Alfonsine texts; following in part Niederehe (1987), he argued that the term *castellano derecho* must have referred primarily to the pursuit of clarity of expression and the elimination of redundancies. Cano (1989:468) explicitly rejects a specific geographic (e.g. Toledo or Burgos) base for Alfonsine language, and argues that any effort at standardization was limited to elaboration of the expressive and intellectual possibilities of the language through development of syntax and an expanded lexicon.[1] Sánchez-Prieto (1996)

---

[1] Lodares (1993-1994) limits the notion of *castellano derecho* even further to the creation and justification of appropriate technical terms according to medieval concerns for authority, custom and, especially, reason. If so, then standardization under Alfonso was focused on the sub-processes of elaboration and acceptance, with only minimal attention to codification. Given that the shift to *romance castellano* was itself stimulated by the pressing need for ease of use and comprehensibility during the expansion of Castile into Andalusia (cf. Harris-Northall 1999), it may have been counter-productive to over-emphasize codification in the early stages of use.

highlights orthographic variation and even calls into question the generally accepted Alfonsine codification of orthographic norms (although Sánchez González 2001 and Cabrera 2002 point to regular application of the phonographic principle and the development of many consistent letter-sound correspondences). It is now clear that the idea of a highly-codified "Alfonsine Standard" has been based on an unjustified projection backward of modern conceptions of standard language onto the linguistic situation of thirteenth-century Castile (cf. Niederehe 1987:128; Cárdenas 1992:54; Milroy 1992:125).

Though we have come to accept variation as a central reality of Alfonsine texts, we still have much to learn about that variation and its sources. Certainly, many of the factors affecting variation in Alfonsine scriptorium texts must be the same as those which affect other medieval texts. Such general factors are discussed in the following sections.

1. Native language variety of the scribe(s). This factor has long been recognized as influencing the final form of (Alfonsine) manuscripts (cf. Cano 1989:467-68) and continues, appropriately, to be identified by scholars as a key factor (e.g., Matute 2001). In the case of Alfonsine texts, discussion of this factor (when backed up with detailed evidence) has generally been limited to the potential impact of native speakers of Leonese, Aragonese, Galician-Portuguese or Catalan-Occitan on the language of originally "Castilian" texts. Such analyses can be used to explain away much variation in texts, but some scholars have shown scepticism. For example, in his discussion of variation between -ie- and -i- preterites, Harris-Northall makes the following observation:

> It is of course possible to attempt an explanation for the alternation, for instance, that scribes copying a previous version were sometimes able to copy a true "Castilian" form, but other times were inattentive or unable to repress their native variety. But when the variant forms appear so frequently in such close proximity, not only on the same folio side, but often several occurrences within a few lines of each other, the hypothesis that they belong to neatly distinct dialectal varieties must surely be discarded. We can therefore be sure that the textual variation reflects the situation in the Castilian of the period, without the need to look to dialect mixture [by scribes] to account for it. (Harris-Northall 2002:141)

Harris-Northall's observations include explicit or implicit reference to several key issues in the explanation of variation based on scribal alteration of Castilian originals. Of central importance is Harris-Northall's suggestion that variation in the texts may reflect real variation in verb forms in the Castilian of the time;

below I will argue that much Castilian of the period was itself characterized by dialect mixing. In addition, we should be wary of the idea that scribes were always able to distinguish forms and features of one variety from another. As Roger Wright has often argued (e.g., Wright 1994, 2002), much variation (in the north at least) was based on different frequencies of occurrence (rather than differences in kind), and, even though speakers and scribes were aware of dialect differences (particularly salient features), it is unlikely that they were able to accurately analyze different frequencies of occurrence in each variety. To this we must add that most modern scholars have tended to perceive medieval Castilian as a uniform whole (with perhaps some reference to "archaisms," vague discussions of the Burgos or Toledo norms, or the assumption that the speech of Toledo was more conservative because heavily influenced by Mozarabic), without considering in a detailed manner the possibility of geographic and socio-stylistic variation within *castellano* itself.

2. The language of source texts and earlier versions or working drafts. Even in cases where the scribe prepared a copy in his "native" language variety, it was possible that the language of the original would affect his language. This is an important factor for Alfonsine texts, for it would appear that even "final versions" of manuscripts from the Alfonsine scriptorium (= those which happen to survive today) were influenced by various kinds of prior texts. This was true of legal, historical, and even scientific texts:

> ...es muy frecuente que en la tradición textual de las obras alfonsíes convivan versiones varias, no siempre conclusas, derivadas de distintos estados de redacción, desde los borradores o cuadernos de trabajo hasta primeras o segundas redacciones. (Fernández-Ordóñez 2000:65).

Some or all of the linguistic features of source texts or of earlier versions might be copied into "final" versions. On the other hand, there is no guarantee of this, and the fact that a text was produced by particular persons (e.g. the Toledan Jewish scholar Yehudá ben Mossé and Christians who worked with him) does not guarantee that the final manuscript directly reflects those persons' use of language, since the final existing version may have actually been prepared by other scribes (see Item 3 below).[2] As with Item 1 (the scribe's native variety),

---

[2] However, Matute (2001) argues convincingly that the co-translator Johan de Aspa, of probable Gascon origin, did in fact affect the language of the manuscript of the *Libro de las cruzes*.

explanations of dialect mixing in texts based on the influence of earlier texts rely on assumptions of uniform and distinct dialects that are only mixed in the text as a result of scribal carelessness. Below I will offer an account of the Castilian of the period that sees dialect mixing as central to its nature.

3. Collaborative teams. It is well-known that Alfonsine scholars and scribes worked in teams. The scientific texts often name the teams of translators (normally one Jewish and one Christian scholar), but it may well be that the final versions of manuscripts were prepared by others. It is clear that larger teams worked on the larger scientific, legal and historical projects (Fernández Ordóñez 2000). Different scholars and scribes might prepare different sections or parts of a particular section, or work on different versions of a text. As such, both the spoken and written language of scholars and scribes were probably affected by the linguistic usage of colleagues in their teams. Since the royal scriptorium was undoubtedly characterized by the mixing of speakers of different language varieties from within (and outside) the Peninsula (cf. Romano 1996:37), it would come as little surprise to find dialect mixing in the texts. Such mixing may have been favored if dictation was used in making copies; this could lead to the influence of reader on the transcriber. Division of duties could also lead to variation within a manuscript (e.g., Diego Catalán long ago identified several different scribal hands in the *Estoria de España*). In addition, it is possible that the linguistic preferences of more important members of teams might have had an impact on language in a work. For instance, this may have been the case of the fourth part of the *General Estoria* (GE4), a long text completed in 1280 which reflects consistent use of a conservative/northern norm (see below), even though it was prepared by a team. In this case, one voice does seem to have influenced the final product, and that voice may have identified itself in the colophon: "Yo Martin perez de Maqueda escriuano de los libros del muy noble Rey don Alffonsso escriui este libro con otros mis escriuanos que tenia por su mandado."[3] Finally, and most importantly, members of the scriptorium may have altered their speech and writing as they accommodated to the speech and writing of colleagues. In this situation variation—sometimes apparently random—may well have become more accepted among the scribes.

4. The language variety or varieties used in the community where scholars and

---

[3] If this is so, then we might have to consider that at least some persons had developed a notion of codification in Castilian, even though there was no general agreement on the need for codification nor on what the prescriptive norms might be.

scribes live and work. Traditionally the scriptorium of Alfonso X has been associated with Toledo, and it is certainly likely that several translations of scientific texts, as well as the preparation of the *Tablas Alfonsíes*, were carried out by members of the Jewish scholarly community of Toledo (we do not know where the final versions of the manuscripts were made). However, we have little such evidence for other texts of the Alfonsine scriptorium. Two facts call into question a constant or necessary association between Alfonsine text production and Toledo. The first is the fact that the court often traveled, and Alfonso is well known for his personal interest in the preparation of the great scientific, historical and legal texts. It is very likely that at least some scholars and scribes working on the Alfonsine texts actually followed the court, which itself was composed of persons from across Castile and Leon. Second, if Alfonso had a preferred place of residence, then that place was not Toledo but Seville, the single city where he spent the greatest amount of time during his reign. I return to the potential impact of the traveling court and of Seville (with Andalusia) below.[4]

5. Learner language (or interlanguage). Recently, Matute (2001) has pointed out that not all the "non-Castilian" features in the *Libro de las cruzes* can be attributed to the native language variety of Johan de Aspa (the co-translator of Gascon origin who is probably responsible for the many "Eastern" features of the text). Matute points out that some of the features characterize neither Eastern/Occitan dialects nor Castilian, and seem to represent learner interlanguage forms (for example, overgeneralization of diphthongs in forms such as *helemientos, decrietos, mientira*). Given the varied origins of Alfonsine scholars and scribes, and their probable need to accommodate to speakers in a new context (be that the court, the scriptorium, the chancery or recently-colonized southern regions; see below), the introduction of interlanguage or interdialect features into texts seems very likely. Since there is no essential difference between second language learning and second dialect learning, interlanguage forms might well appear in texts prepared by "dialect speakers" from other areas nearer to Castile such as Asturias and Leon.[5] And, of course, if there were different varieties of Castilian, then similar reanalyses and overgeneralizations

---

[4] It may be best to think of the Alfonsine scriptorium not as a place but rather an activity or a community which was dependent on the mobile king and court.

[5] For example, Cano (1985:296) discusses as Occidentalisms several cases of ultradiptongación like those described by Matute, but at least one of these (*muelde*) does not seem to be either Leonese or Castilian, and could be an interlanguage overgeneralization by a speaker/scribe from a non-diphthongizing region.

(or undergeneralizations) could be expected of scribes who might otherwise be considered native speakers of Castilian. Of course, the acceptance or rejection of interlanguage forms very much depends on the specific social context and the strength or weakness of its norms and norm enforcement mechanisms. I return to this issue below.

6. Register, genre and audience. An obvious factor to consider in the analysis of linguistic variation in texts is the relation between genre, audience and register. For example, one difference that has been pointed out between the Alfonsine royal scriptorium texts and the more utilitarian legal documents produced by the Alfonsine chancery is the lesser use of apocope in the legal documents (e.g. Sánchez González 2002:144-50). Sánchez González (2002:175) also indicates that variation in chancery legal documents correlates closely with the regional destination of the documents (rather than the probable region of origin of the notary), though she also acknowledges that this may be due in part to the assignment of notaries and (unidentified) scribes to work on texts from their home regions (since, presumably, they would be familiar with those areas and their inhabitants).

These varied factors are fundamental to understanding variation in Alfonsine texts (for a more thorough and general discussion of these factors, see Fernández-Ordóñez 2001:389-98); here I would like to suggest that they must be supplemented with a more detailed analysis of the sociolinguistic context of thirteenth-century Castilian. To do so, it is important to consider the impact of dialect mixing (or koineization) on the earlier history of Castilian and its ongoing development during the reign of Alfonso X. Koineization is a process in which speakers of numerous mutually-intelligible dialects mix together in a new community, producing at first a rapid rise in variation and a rapid decline in sociolinguistic norms and norm enforcement (based on the weakening of social networks). Over the course of two or three generations, social networks resolidify and new norms are defined as children accommodate to and learn from each other, with the resulting koine showing simplification and mixing/leveling of features from different contributing dialects (cf. also Trudgill 1986 and Tuten 2003).

The potential importance of koineization to the history of Castilian was first proposed in 1986 by the honorand of this volume, when he delivered his inaugural lecture as Professor of Spanish (published as Penny 1987). In that lecture, he pointed out that Castilian had undergone a repeated process of dialect mixing, or koineization, throughout its long history. According to Penny, these stages of dialect mixing began with the "period of origins" in and around Burgos in the late ninth and tenth centuries, when settlers who spoke a range of northern varieties moved into the region. This was followed by a second great period of dialect mixing in Toledo, after the fall of that city in 1085, which saw the mixing of speakers of an even more diverse array of dialects, including Mozarab and Gallic varieties. During the thirteenth century, and throughout the lifetime of Alfonso X, a third great period of koineization took place as united Castile and Leon conquered and repopulated southern Spain, including Betic Andalusia and Murcia.

As I have argued previously (Tuten 2003), each of these periods saw significant linguistic changes. For example, the Burgos phase led to the development of the phonologized diphthongs /ie/ and /ue/ and the simplified five-phoneme vowel system of Castilian, features that would remain to characterize all varieties of Castilian. The Toledo phase led to partial simplification of the possessive system in areas around Toledo, and that change introduced (for a time) at least one significant difference between northern varieties (centered on Burgos) and central varieties (centered on Toledo). During Alfonso's lifetime, koineization in Andalusia (and most of the south) would lead to the completion of the simplification of the possessive system and the elimination of extreme apocope as a formal variant. As a result of this history of repeated koineization, certain variables of thirteenth-century Castilian can be placed on a continuum between a conservative north (Burgos), a more innovative Toledo (but which showed greater stylistic variation, with more conservative or northern variants probably characterizing a more formal style), and an extremely innovative (and, for a time, even "chaotic") Andalusia, where several conservative/northern variants were being rejected (though with much apparently random variation until the first generation of children grew up).[6]

This view of the history of Castilian acknowledges distinctions between the speech of Burgos (Old Castile) and that of Toledo (New Castile),[7] and there is

---

[6] This view contrasts with that of Lapesa (1981:241), in which the language of Toledo is seen as representing a conservative (Mozarabic?) norm and that of thirteenth-century Burgos, a more innovative norm. Of course, Burgos may have developed innovations of its own after the expansion into Toledo. For example, h-dropping may have been spreading near Burgos in the thirteenth century, and Cano (1985:295) finds a few orthographic forms in Alfonsine texts which appear to reflect this phenomenon (e.g., *ablar, echo, incado*). Nevertheless, in general Burgos represented the most conservative region for most variables.

[7] Note, however, that this is not necessarily an argument for internal uniformity within these regions. See, for example, Fernández-Ordóñez (2001) and Tuten (2003:199-202) for discussion of differing pronoun systems within New Castile.

evidence that the different norms (and styles) of these regions were known and used by Alfonsine scribes. A clear example is the use of second and third person possessive forms. In general, the texts in the *Documentos lingüísticos de España* reveal that the Burgos region retained a relatively complex set of possessive forms throughout the thirteenth century. These included a contrast between feminine *tu(s)/su(s)* and masculine *to(s)/so(s)*, as well as some interchangeable use of short and long forms (e.g., *su(y)a, sue, su(y)o*). In Toledo, short forms were reserved for use as preposed adjectives and long (disyllabic) forms for other uses. Minority variants (e.g. *sue*) were lost, and the distinction between feminine *tu/su* and masculine *to/so* was lost in all but the most conservative styles. For this feature, the Alfonsine texts can be divided between those which maintain the conservative norm, those which clearly prefer the innovative or popular norm of Toledo, and those which freely mix the two styles. This can be seen in Table 1, which provides the form counts for third person possessive forms found in a selection of Alfonsine texts (Kasten, Nitti and Jonxis-Henkemans 1997). One can see that GE4 and MOA are the most conservative texts in the group, while GE1, LEY, CRZ, and LAP prefer the innovative Toledan popular norm, and EE1 (a text which we know to have been transcribed by several different scribes) shows a mixture of the two, though with a strong preference for innovative forms.[8] Note too that the earlier texts are not necessarily more conservative than later texts, since GE4 is the latest text in the group and also one of the most conservative, and LAP is one of the earliest and most innovative. As a result, they must represent preference on the part of scribes for established and recognized dialects/registers (particularly for GE4, since the use of the conservative/northern system was already quite marked—at least in Andalusia—at the time of its completion in 1280).

---

[8] JUZ shows an interesting result: merger of *so* and *su* in the singular, but general maintenance of the gender distinction in the plural. This may reflect the history of loss of the distinction, which probably began in the singular (see Tuten 2003:204-13).

TABLE 1. FREQUENCY OF OCCURRENCE OF POSSESSIVE FORMS
IN ALFONSINE TEXTS.[9]

	so	sos	su	sus	to	tos	tu	tus	lo so	lo suyo
GE4	2454	1565	2276	1294	2	0	19	4	2	7
MOA	261	89	189	130	0	2	0	0	0	0
EE1	605	277	1979	910	28	10	180	14	2	11
GE1	225	77	4072	2534	0	1	1266	194	2	21
LEY	149	7	1076	638	2	0	19	4	3	26
CRZ	10	8	340	260	0	1	115	6	0	0
LAP	28	0	1033	377	0	2	0	0	0	1
JUZ	513	699	2745	690	4	0	34	0	0	8

The division of Alfonsine texts into conservative/northern and innovative/Toledan seems to hold up when we look at another feature: presence or absence of extreme apocope. Traditionally, the presence of extreme apocope has been attributed to eastern dialect or Gallic (foreign) influence (cf. Lapesa 1981:240), but I have argued elsewhere that by the thirteenth century it had become a native variant of Castilian that marked more formal registers (Tuten 2003:160-73). Table 2 shows the counts for apocopated and unapocopated forms of *delante* and *adelante* (forms chosen because they are frequent native forms rather than borrowings). Here again we see that MOA and GE4 are among the most conservative texts (regularly preferring apocopated forms), while LEY, LAP, and JUZ strongly prefer unapocopated forms, and EE1 shows a weak preference for unapocopated forms. The preference for conservative apocope in the otherwise innovative CRZ may seem unusual, but it corresponds to the general preference for eastern and Occitan forms in that manuscript (cf. Matute 2001). GE1 presents the only anomalous case of opposing preferences, with innovative use for possessives on the one hand and conservative use for apocope on the other (perhaps due to the conscious and easily-made association of apocopated forms and formal texts, with subsequent overgeneralization; see

---

[9] The abbreviations are those established by the Hispanic Seminary of Medieval Studies (manuscript production dates are included in parentheses): GE4 = *General Estoria IV* (1280); MOA = *Moamyn – Libro de las animalias* (1250?); EE1 = *Estoria de España I = Primera Crónica General* (1270-1274); GE1 = *General Estoria I* (1272–1275); LEY = *Libro [del fuero] de las leyes* (1256– 1265); CRZ = *Libro de las cruzes* (1259); LAP = *Lapidario de Alfonso X* (1250?–1279?). JUZ = *Libro conplido en los judizios de las estrellas* (1254).

below). Nevertheless, the high level of correlations of preferences for two different and unrelated features suggests that there existed clearly perceived differences between a set of conservative/northern/formal norms and a set of innovative/Toledan/popular norms.[10]

TABLE 2. FREQUENCY OF OCCURRENCE OF FORMS OF *(A)DELANT(E)* IN ALFONSINE TEXTS

Text	*adelant*	*delant*	*adelante*	*delante*	Other forms
GE4	332	74	3	11	13 *adeland*
					3 *deland*
					3 *delantel*
MOA	2	19	1	5	11 *adelantre*
					55 *delantre*
EE1	79	16	122	24	
GE1	437	68	196	52	1 *adelantre*
					1 *delantre*
					1 *delantel*
LEY	0	2	52	40	
CRZ	2	4	1	2	1 *delantre*
LAP	2	5	14	2	1 *delantella*
JUZ	0	1	2	3	1 *adelantre*

The above discussion is intended simply to highlight the fact that significant and consistent variation characterized Castilian even before the expansion into Andalusia and Alfonso's reign, and that a good portion of the variation in Alfonsine texts is directly attributable to it. Of course, this approach sees dialect mixing in texts only as the result of mixing of pre-existing dialect norms by

---

[10] This distinction between conservative and innovative texts finds some support in Hartman's study of past participles: "Verbs of the second conjugation (*-er*) in Alfonso may have past participles in either *-ido* or *-udo*, with the conflicting forms distributed in varying proportions among the works. Seven of the works [including GE1, GE4, EE1] prefer *-udo* in a significant majority of cases. Four works [including CRZ, JUD, LAP] clearly favor *-ido*" (Hartman 1974:52). As with the possessives and apocope, the innovative forms were those preferred during koineization in Andalusia. Sánchez González (2002:159) reports that legal documents directed to Andalusia and Murcia (and prepared by scribes living and working there?) show majority use of *-ido* forms (60 to 41), while all other regions prefer *-udo*.

individual scribes. However, one must also ask what effect contemporary dialect mixing had on the language of these texts, or rather, of the scholars and scribes who prepared them, and even the king who ordered their preparation. Even in Toledo, the scribes and scholars of the scriptorium certainly represented a mix of different language varieties. The same would be true of the court of Alfonso X, and, of course, of that area and city where Alfonso spent most time: Andalusia and Seville. The Alfonsine scriptorium and texts are commonly associated with Toledo, and this certainly seems to be a valid assumption with regard to the preparation of the scientific texts. However, for the actual copying of these texts, and for the preparation and transcription of the historical and legal texts, we cannot be sure where the work was actually done. We do know that Alfonso took direct interest in the preparation of the texts, so a safe assumption is that the activity took place close to his person.

Alfonso himself participated actively in the reconquest of Andalusia and of Seville. Indeed, the city was ceremonially surrendered to the Christians on his 27th birthday in 1248, and it was there that he acceded to the throne in 1252. Of all the cities in his kingdom, Seville was the one where he spent the greatest amount of time, the one to which he always returned, and the one where he died. It has been called the "verdadera capital" of his kingdom by González Jiménez (1999:47). In 1254 Alfonso ordered the establishment of *escuelas generales* in Seville and arranged for some former mosques to be reserved as residence and workplace for his scholars (*físicos*) and scribes (G. Menéndez Pidal 1951:366-67).[11] We even have some hard evidence of the activity of the scriptorium in the city: we know of one scholar, Bonaventura da Siena, who went to Seville in 1264 to prepare a French translation of *La escala de Mahoma* (Gil 1985:78), and the text of the *Libros de ajedrez, dados y tablas* states explicitly that it was begun and completed in Seville in 1283.

It is virtually certain that the scholars and scribes who worked on the Alfonsine texts were affected, directly or indirectly, by the sociolinguistic situation of the city of Seville and all of southern Castile (Andalusia, Murcia, Extremadura, La Mancha).[12] This may have been because the scholars and

---

[11] Alfonso X also established a similar school in Murcia (González Jiménez 1999:345).

[12] In fact, weakening of norms associated with the expansion into Andalusia and Murcia and consequent demographic mixing also seems to have been an important factor to the rapid increase in use of Romance under Fernando III: "Es precisamente desde la toma de Jaén cuando la documentación en romance adquiere un predominio casi total, y es casualmente a partir de esa fecha [1246] cuando ya el Rey Santo no volverá a salir

scribes actually lived and worked, at least some of the time, in Seville or the south, but even if they did not, they almost certainly were affected by contact with the court and the chancery, since these groups were all composed of a mix of individuals from different parts of the realm, and at least some of their members certainly resided in the south for significant periods of time.

What, then, was the sociolinguistic situation of Andalusia and Seville after the reconquest and during the reign of Alfonso? In newly-repopulated Andalusia, mixing among speakers of many different dialects certainly led first to the creation of a partly "chaotic" pre-koine. In this context, all kinds of variants can be heard, and outside their original context of use, they begin to lose the social values originally associated with them; as Robert LePage (1992) has commented, with only some exaggeration, "you can never tell where a word comes from" in a diffuse sociolinguistic context of this sort. Adults may suppress some features that are perceived as marked or minority variants, and they may also try to adopt features that they perceive as dominant or useful for social success in the new community. As a result some new norms for salient features may be negotiated early on, but most will only be defined as subsequent generations of children negotiate their own norms. In such a context, in which variation was rampant but nearly all speakers could understand each other, the concept of what constituted *lengua castellana* was probably very broad indeed, and most speakers, while aware of salient differences between dialects, probably could not have distinguished neatly or consistently between Castilian and non-Castilian features (which would consist of features of contributing dialects, including those based only on different frequency of occurrence, as well as interlanguage features). Such a diffuse sociolinguistic context may have played a key role in supporting the general acceptance of variation (by both king and scribes) in the Alfonsine texts (a more conservative homogeneous community, even one lacking any notion of a standard, might have been more effective at enforcing local community norms). Such dialect mixing in Andalusia (and in the peripatetic Castilian court) may explain a phenomenon commented on by Cano (as well as by Harris-Northall in the preceding quote). In his study of the *Libros del saber de astronomía* (Códice Complutense), Cano observes:

> ...los dialectalismos, no siempre de la misma procedencia, han de deberse a las manos de distintos redactores ...de todos modos, el dialectalismo está

---

de Andalucía, fijando su residencia en Sevilla a raíz de su conquista hasta su muerte. Es como si su alejamiento de la "burocracia" castellana le hubiese liberado de las ataduras de la tradición latinizante" (Ariza 1998:77).

difundido a lo largo de todo el Códice, con iguales o semejantes características, y no parece posible limitarlo a ciertos pasajes en los que, con la ayuda de otros criterios, podríamos aislar la presencia de un redactor concreto. (Cano 1985:305).

The apparently wild mixing of forms on even one folio can be explained by a combination of the general factors commented on above, but the fact that such mixing is so prevalent in Alfonsine texts suggests that it was favored by the mixed sociolinguistic context of Alfonso and his associates.

If many of the dialect features of Alfonsine texts were in fact associated (directly or indirectly) with koineization in Andalusia, then another frequently-noticed phenomenon might be explained: the rapid loss of many Alfonsine features immediately following the end of Alfonso's reign (e.g. past participles in -*udo*). Cano comments:

Ahora bien, si hemos de reconocer la generosidad con que Alfonso X dejaba entrar dialectalismos en las obras dirigidas y revisadas por él, también es cierto que el castellano, como tal lengua, acabó imponiendo un criterio mucho más selectivo. De esos rasgos dialectales presentes en la lengua alfonsí casi ninguno sobrevivió en etapas posteriores...los hablantes castellanos consideraron intolerable el polimorfismo reflejado en los textos reales..." (Cano 1985:306).

Of course, prototypical koineization is characterized first by a sudden rise in variation and decline in norm enforcement, to be followed within the space of one or two generations by a relatively rapid reduction in variation and definition of new sociolinguistic norms. In the case of Andalusia, the changes and heightened variation associated with koineization probably had a direct effect on the members of the court and chancery, and through them on many of the documents that survive from the period.

Still other features of Alfonsine texts might be due to the open sociolinguistic context of thirteenth-century koineization. One aspect of dialect mixing that is not always recognized is that the features in the pre-koine mix (or even in the resultant koine) are not necessarily limited to those found in pre-existing contributing dialects. This is so because child and adult dialect/language learners in the mix can produce innovative forms (in their interlanguages or interdialects) without need or even possibility of "correction," since norms and norm enforcement mechanisms (social networks) are weakened. Such innovations are generally the result of overgeneralizations or misanalyses which occur as speakers accommodate to one another. One feature that may have resulted from overgeneralization by adult learners in the koineizing context of post-conquest Andalusia (and, perhaps, in the court, chancery and scriptorium) is the sudden rise in the frequency of use of the diphthongized form *cuemo*. Sánchez González has recently studied the appearance of the forms *como/cuemo* in Castilian legal documents produced by the Alfonsine chancery:

> *Como*, adverbio y conjunción, es forma mayoritaria frente a *cuemo*, en los documentos de todas las zonas, aunque las proporciones varían de unos a otros: en los de Castilla la Vieja *como* aparece 450 veces, frente a 110 de *cuemo* [20% *cuemo*]; en los de Castilla la Nueva, 187 frente a 39 [17% *cuemo*]; en los de Andalucía, 510 frente a 275 [35% *cuemo*]; en los de Murcia, 123 frente a 30 [20% *cuemo*]; en los de León, 256 frente a 85 [25% *cuemo*], y en los de Galicia, 50 frente a 28 [39% *cuemo*]. R. M. Duncan [1950] en su estudio de *cuemo*, *como* en la obra literaria alfonsí, apuntó que *cuemo* predomina en las obras de los primeros años, mientras que *como* se impone en los últimos. En fechas más recientes M. Ariza [1998] ha señalado que efectivamente *cuemo* aparece en los primeros documentos de Alfonso X, muchas veces alternando con *como*, incluso en el mismo texto. En su opinión *cuemo* es innovación alfonsí respecto al uso fernandino, por lo que no parece razonable hablar de forma arcaizante, y, al menos en ocasiones, es evidente que depende del notario. (Sánchez González 2002: 157)

Sánchez González (2002:158) also reports that use of *cuemo* declines rapidly after the 1260s (after 1269 in Andalusia) and confirms that some scribes (e.g. Millán Pérez de Aillón) use it far more than others.

How might these patterns be explained? To begin, they cannot be explained as dialectal forms, since *cuemo* was certainly not a typical form of western dialects (Staaff 1907:206 reports regular use of *como* in all the thirteenth-century Leonese texts studied by him, with minority use of *cuemo* found only in documents from Sahagún, located near the border with Castile). Rather, what seems to have happened is that speakers and scribes from western areas (where phonological diphthongization had not taken place, or was just beginning) noticed that Castilians used a /ue/ diphthong consistently where westerners used only a monophthong or variable phonetic diphthong. Thus, such speakers would have had to change forms such as *bona, conta* to *buena, cuenta* as they accommodated to Castilian usage.[13] Likewise, having noticed that Castilians

---

[13] Cases of "ultradiptongación" are also frequently identified in texts which show

sometimes pronounced *cuemo* where westerners more consistently used *como*, western speakers/scribes could then adopt use of *cuemo*. However, not being aware of its limited frequency of occurrence in the Castilian of Burgos and Toledo (probably limited to tonic position), they overgeneralized its use in their interlanguages, in a kind of Labovian hypercorrection. This seems to have happened in Andalusia (where a significant portion of the settlers came from western areas), but also in the chancery documents prepared for Leon and Galicia (see the statistics in the preceding quote from Sánchez González). The high frequency of *cuemo* in Galician texts is particularly telling, since the rising diphthong /ue/ was not a variant in that region, and the same documents largely eliminate use of the typically western falling diphthongs /ei/ and /ou/. Apparently, chancery scribes were aiming to produce texts that looked Castilian, but sometimes they overshot the mark.

The tendency to overgeneralize *cuemo* as a marker of Castilian language was not limited to chancery texts. Scriptorium texts also show significant use of *cuemo*, but certainly not across the board. For example, the always conservative MOA and GE4 reject use of *cuemo* (MOA 644 *como* vs. 0 *cuemo*; GE4 3613 *como* vs. 108 *cuemo*), but so do CRZ (21/8), GE1 (5501/7), JUZ (247/11), and LAP (425/5). At the other extreme, EE1 prefers *cuemo* (575 *como* vs. 1021 *cuemo*), and the generally innovative LEY shows an overwhelming preference for *cuemo* (108 *como* vs. 1155 *cuemo*). Use of *cuemo* in LEY reaches an unparalleled 91%, and can only be explained as an overgeneralization by a particular scribe (or group of scholars and/or scribes). It is interesting to note that the text may actually have been prepared in Seville, since it was completed in the 1260s, when Alfonso and the court resided continuously in or near that city. Be that as it may, it is reasonably clear that use of *cuemo* in this text responds not to some established regional or sociostylistic norm, but rather to the particular interlanguage (or interdialect) of the scribe(s) who prepared it.

From the evidence provided by Ariza (1998) and Sánchez González (2002), it appears that exaggerated use of *cuemo* occurred only during the 1250s and 1260s. In the late 1260s (after 1269 in Andalusia), usage drops suddenly in chancery documents. This could mean that some person of influence in the chancery consciously rejected its use (cf. the preceding discussion of GE4), but this is also about the time that a new generation of scribes would have been entering into service—a fact which would have been of particular importance in Andalusia. Given that *como* was actually the majority form in all contributing

---

Leonese influence (e.g. *los tercieros, fueron pueblados,* from Sánchez González 2002:167, or *miete, riegla, muelde,* from Cano 1985:296).

dialects, it would have been the likely choice of children in the new koineizing communities of southern Spain. Unlike some elder scribes who may have felt a conscious need to accommodate to what they perceived as Castilian usage, the first generation of children would have considered themselves to be normal speakers of the Castilian or Romance of their region. As such, they probably overgeneralized use of *como* to the point that *cuemo* was completely lost (at least in the south).

From the above we may conclude that the history of dialect mixing in medieval Castilian must be taken into consideration as we work to understand and explain the linguistic variation that characterizes Alfonsine texts. The historical effects of earlier stages of koineization are revealed in the tendency of texts to show a preference for a set of conservative/northern norms or a set of popular Toledan norms. However, the varied effects of contemporary koineization in Andalusia and all of southern Spain were also felt, directly or indirectly, not only by the permanent inhabitants of southern regions, but also by the King, his court, the scriptorium and the chancery. These effects probably included a tendency to prefer and extend the more popular innovative usages already begun in Toledo, but also an increased acceptance to dialect mixing of all sorts, including use of interdialect features. These effects were felt during the lifetime of Alfonso X, but the continuing process of koineization which was occurring throughout the southern regions (and affecting the northern regions through weak-tie social contact) also explains the sudden decline in many variable features of Alfonsine texts following the death of the king.

References

Ariza, Manuel. 1998. "Fernando III y el castellano alfonsí." *Estudios de lingüística y filología españolas. Homenaje a Germán Colón.* Madrid: Gredos. 71-84.
Cabrera Morales, Carlos. 2002. "La ortografía de los documentos alfonsíes." In *Studia Humanitatis in Honorem Antonio Cabrera Perera*, ed. by Germán Santana Henríquez and Victoriano Santana Sanjurjo. Las Palmas de Gran Canaria: Universidad de Las Palmas de Gran Canaria. 365-412.
Cano Aguilar, Rafael. 1985. "Castellano ¿drecho?" *Verba* 12:287-306.
Cano Aguilar, Rafael. 1989. "La construcción del idioma en Alfonso X el Sabio." *Philologia Hispalensis* 4(2):463-73.
Cárdenas, Anthony. 1992. "Alfonso X nunca escribió en castellano drecho." *Actas del X Congreso de la Asociación Internacional de Hispanistas*, ed. by Antonio Vilanova, 151-59. Barcelona: PPU.
Duncan, R.M.: 1950. "*Cuemo* y *como* en la obra de Alfonso el Sabio." *Revista de Filología Española* 34: 258-68.

Fernández-Ordóñez, Inés. 2000. "El taller de las historias." *Alfonso X el Sabio y las crónicas de España*, ed. by Inés Fernández-Ordóñez, 61-82. Valladolid: Universidad de Valladolid.
Fernández-Ordóñez, Inés. 2001. "Hacia una dialectología histórica: reflexiones sobre la historia del leísmo, el laísmo y el loísmo." *Boletín de la Real Academia Española* 81:389-464.
Gil, José S. 1985. *La escuela de traductores de Toledo y los colaboradores judíos*. Toledo: Instituto Provincial de Investigaciones y Estudios Toledanos.
González Jiménez, Manuel. 1999. *Alfonso X el Sabio. Historia de un reinado: 1252-1284*. 2nd ed. Palencia: Diputación Provincial de Palencia.
Harris-Northall, Ray. 1999. "Official use of the vernacular in the thirteenth century: Medieval Spanish Language Policy?" *Advances in Hispanic Linguistics*, ed. by Javier Gutiérrez-Rexach and Fernando Martínez-Gil, 152-65. Somerville, Mass.: Cascadilla Press.
Harris-Northall, Ray. 2002. "Sources for Variation in Preterite Endings in Old Spanish." *Two Generations: A Tribute to Lloyd A. Kasten (1905-1999)*, ed. by Francisco Gago Jover, 135-146. New York: Hispanic Seminary of Medieval Studies.
Hartman, Steven Lee. 1974. "Alfonso el Sabio and the varieties of verb grammar." *Hispania* 57:48-55.
Kasten, Lloyd, John Nitti, and Wilhelmina Jonxis-Henkemans. 1997. *The Electronic Texts and Concordances of the Prose Works of Alfonso X, El Sabio*. Madison: Hispanic Seminary of Medieval Studies.
Lapesa, Rafael. 1981. *Historia de la lengua española*. Madrid: Gredos.
LePage, Robert. 1992. " 'You can never tell where a word comes from': Language contact in a diffuse setting." *Language Contact: Theoretical and Empirical Studies*, ed. by Ernst Hakon Jahr, 71-101. Berlin/New York: Mouton de Gruyter.
Lodares, Juan R. 1993-1994. "Las razones del 'castellano derecho'." *Cahiers de Linguistique Hispanique Médiévale* 18-19:313-34.
Matute Martínez, Cristina. 2001. "Interacción de sistemas lingüísticos en el *Libro de las cruzes* (1259) de Alfonso X el Sabio." *Cahiers de Linguistique et de Civilisation Hispaniques Médiévales* 24:71-99.
Menéndez Pidal, Gonzalo. 1951. "Cómo trabajaron las escuelas alfonsíes." *Nueva Revista de Filología Hispánica* 5:363-80.
Milroy, James. 1992. *Language Variation and Change: On the Historical Sociolinguistics of English*. Oxford: Blackwell.
Niederehe, Hans-J. 1987. *Alfonso X el Sabio y la lingüística de su tiempo*. Madrid: SGEL.
Penny, Ralph. 1987. *Patterns of Language-Change in Spain*. London: University of London, Westfield College.
Romano, David. 1996. "Los hispanojudíos en la traducción y redacción de las obras científicas alfonsíes." *La escuela de traductores de Toledo*, ed. by J. Samsó et al., 35-50. Toledo: Diputación Provincial de Toledo.
Sánchez González de Herrero, María Nieves. 2001. "Las grafías de la documentación alfonsí." *Nuevas aportaciones al estudio de la lengua española: investigaciones*

filológicas, ed. by J. A. Bartol Hernández, S. Crespo Matellán et al., 111-21. Salamanca: Luso-Española de Ediciones.

Sánchez González de Herrero, María Nieves. 2002. "Rasgos fonéticos y morfológicos de los documentos alfonsíes." *Revista de filología española* 82:139-77.

Sánchez-Prieto Borja, Pedro. 1996. "Sobre la configuración de la llamada 'ortografía alfonsí'." *Actas del III Congreso Internacional de la Historia de la Lengua Española.* Madrid: Arco/Libros. 1: 913-22.

Sánchez-Prieto Borja, Pedro. 1998. *Cómo editar los textos medievales.* Madrid: Arco/Libros.

Staaff, Erik. 1907. *Etude sur l'ancien dialecte léonais.* Uppsala: Almqvist and Wiksell.

Tuten, Donald N. 2003. *Koineization in Medieval Spanish.* Berlin and New York: Mouton de Gruyter.

Wright, Roger. 1994. "Sociolinguistics in Spain (8th-11th centuries)." *Early Ibero-Romance,* 155-64. Newark, Delaware: Juan de la Cuesta.

Wright, Roger. 2003. *A Sociophilological Study of Late Latin.* Utrecht Studies in Medieval Literacy 10. Turnhout: Brepols.

6
Some Phonological Features of Insular French: A Reconstruction
MARTIN J. DUFFELL

1. VARIETIES OF FRENCH AND OF ENGLISH

FOR FOUR CENTURIES AFTER the Norman Conquest the language of the victors was spoken widely in England, and by 1200 most people were to some extent bilingual. The variety of French they spoke, however, was rather different from those spoken on the European mainland and from modern French; I shall refer to it as "Insular French," but it also sometimes called "Anglo-Norman" or "the French of England." Its speakers were aware that it had many distinctive features: thus in the 1160s a nun from Barking states "un faus franceis sai d'Angleterre" (Legge 1963:63), and two centuries later Chaucer says of his prioress "Frenssh she spak ful faire and fetisly / after the scole of Stratford atte Bowe;/ the Frenssh of Parys was to hire unknowe" (Benson 1988:56).[1] In this article I shall use the following terms and abbreviations: French and English denote the modern languages and also features that are common to all varieties and periods; OE (Old English) denotes the language of texts dating from before the Norman Conquest, and ME (Middle English) for that of texts dating from between 1200 and 1500; OF (Old French) denotes varieties of French spoken in France before 1500. Because of its visual distinctiveness from the other abbreviations I shall use AN rather than *IF to denote Insular French.

We should beware of assuming that everyone in the fourteenth century regarded AN as an inferior variety: Chaucer (a royal lackey who spoke the French of Paris and his Plantagenet masters) may have done so, but his friend

---

[1] Barking Abbey was one of England's greatest seats of learning before the country had any universities; in the twelfth century it boasted among its Principals two queens, a princess, and the sister of a saint. Chaucer's model for Eglantyne was probably a nun from Barking, rather than nearby Stratford by Bow, which was needed for the rhyme.

Gower, who was landed gentry and spoke and wrote AN, certainly did not. When Gower employed French for major poems (which was long before he risked writing in the upstart language English), he made some concessions in vocabulary to mainland varieties (see Merrilees 2003), but otherwise his language was unmistakably Insular; and Legge argues that Gower's was the finest French poetry of his time (1963:71).

1.1 THE REVIVAL OF ENGLISH

AN was challenged in the fourteenth century and supplanted in the fifteenth by ME, a new English rich in words borrowed from the French lexicon. The change was gradual: in 1363 it became possible for defendants to plead "not" in English before being found "guilty" in French, and a few years later Chaucer was able to risk composing poetry in English, trusting that posterity would be able to read it. In 1399 Henry IV addressed parliament in English, its first royal public endorsement since Harold's final "ouch" a third of a millennium earlier. In 1417, two years after Agincourt, Henry V penned his first letter in the language of his troops in preference to his usual French.[2] It was the same patriotism that led to the demise of AN, and the final English defeat of the Hundred Years War was its death knell: in 1455 the battle of Remigny was lost by the English king, but won by the English language.

1.2 RECONSTRUCTING THE PHONOLOGY OF AN

Since AN is a dead language, any discussion of its phonology is an exercise in reconstruction, like W. Sidney Allen's of the Latin spoken between 200 BC and 200 AD (1973), and must depend on the same types of evidence: orthography, chronological variation, and poetic practice. All three offer valuable information on important features of AN phonology: Vising (1923:27-33) gives a concise account of the language that owes much to the study of spelling, syllable loss, and rhyme in the surviving texts. There is one aspect of those texts, however, that has led not to illumination, but to bitter altercation between scholars: most AN verse texts are extremely irregular in syllable count. The aims of the present article are: (1) to revisit the nineteenth- and twentieth-century disputes on the reasons for this, using the advances that have been made in recent years in linguistics and metrics, and (2) to gain from such an exercise new insights into AN's phonology.

---

[2] I am greatly indebted to Herbert Schendl of the University of Vienna for this information.

2. COMPARATIVE METRICS

The terms that I shall employ in re-examining AN versification were introduced by Jakobson (1960): a *verse design* consists of a pattern, or *template*, and a set of *correspondence rules*, which govern the linguistic material that may appear in individual lines or *verse instances*. A template comprises a number of *positions* containing a binary contrast that is described as *strong/weak (s/w)* by most modern metrists; older terms for it are *thesis/arsis* (see Pighi 1970) and *beat/offbeat* (see Attridge 1982). Correspondence rules can be seen as a set of *constraints*, which limit the appearance of specific features at specific points in the line, and they are subject to exceptions, or *mismatches* (between template and instance; see Kiparsky 1977:194-96), traditionally termed *tension* (Allen 1973:110-12). Generally speaking, the more constraints a metre imposes, the more tension it allows; for example, verse designs that regulate the number of both accents and syllables allow more exceptions than those that regulate only the latter. Metres usually offer a balance between regularity and variety, answering the basic human needs for *sécurité* and *surprise* (Dorchain 1919:22-23).

2.1 METRICAL PHONOLOGY

The binary contrast of positions in the template is reflected in a *prominence* contrast in the linguistic material of verse instances. Some syllables are more prominent in delivery than others; in the Romance and Germanic languages this prominence is the result of being given more stress than their neighbours. In polysyllabic words this greater stress is determined by the lexicon and is termed *strength* (thus in English *insight* is left-strong and *incite* right-strong). The relative stress of neighbouring monosyllables is not lexically determined, but depends on their position and importance in the phrase; strong syllables of polysyllables also receive extra stress when they are the most important in their phrase. The stress-profile of all utterances can thus be represented as a hierarchy (see Hayes 1995:24-31).[3] It should be noted that in languages with strong word stress, like English, all strong syllables tend to become prominent in delivery, while in languages that lack it, like modern French, only those that are phrase-final do so.

2.2 PARAMETRIC THEORY

To compare and classify the verse designs of different texts in this article I shall use the *parametric theory* of Hanson and Kiparsky (1996), which identifies five

---

[3] A tree-diagram illustrating this hierarchy is given in 4.3, below.

key features of verse design, or *parameters*: the first two describe the template in terms of: (1) *position number*, and (2) *orientation* (right-strong or left-strong, depending on whether weak positions precede strong ones or vice-versa); the remaining three parameters denote correspondence rules: (3) *position size* (the maximum amount of linguistic material that a position may contain), (4) *prominence site* (whether strong or weak positions, or both are constrained), and (5) *prominence type* (the linguistic feature that is constrained; for example, syllable length, stress, or strength).

2.3 THE PRINCIPLE OF "FIT"

Hanson and Kiparsky also put forward a hypothesis they term the *principle of fit* (1996:294), which states that metres evolve in such a way as to accommodate most of the lexicon and reflect the major phonological features of the language concerned. Although this principle confirms the insights of earlier scholars (in particular, Thompson 1961 and Jakobson 1973), there are notable exceptions to it. For example, the adoption of the Greek quantitative dactylic hexameter denied Roman poets access to a large portion of their lexicon (Raven 1965:11), and the cultivation of syllabic metres in Spanish and Russian in various periods has involved ignoring the strong word stress of those languages (Duffell 1999-2000:114-16 and Gasparov 1996:227-35). The evolution of metres is, in practice, determined partly by linguistic and partly by sociological factors (emulation, fashion, prestige). Nevertheless, most metrical systems are based on the salient phonological features of the language concerned; metres also adapt rapidly to linguistic change: the loss of vowel-length distinctions in Late Latin undoubtedly led to the decline of quantitative versifying (see Lote 1939:229-36).

3. METRIC TYPOLOGY

The most concise definition of verse is "numerically regulated texts" (Lotz 1960:135), and any of a number of linguistic features may be regulated in a verse design. The types of verse design relevant to the present article are: (1) *syllabic*, which regulates the number of syllables in the line; (2) *accentual*, which regulates only the number of stressed syllables; (3) *stress-syllabic*, which regulates both the number of syllables and the position of the prominent ones; (4) a type intermediate between accentual and stress-syllabic.

3.1 SYLLABIC VERSE

The canonical metres of French are syllabic: their verse design regulates the number of syllables in the line (or hemistich, in the case of longer, divided lines), the last of which must be accented. French versification offers a good example of the principle of fit; it employs three of the most salient features of that language's phonology: right-strength (the right-most full syllables of words is the one with a potential for stress), phrasal stress (which the loss of word stress in modern French foregrounds), and *syllable-timing* (syllables are allocated what is perceived as equal time in delivery). The combination of these three features allows French poets to create a temporal regularity, or *rhythm*, by placing a regular number of syllables between phrasal stresses (Cornulier 1995:115). As Cornulier also notes, the French syllabic method of versifying is a good fit only for languages with very weak or no word stress, and there are very few of them: he cites Japanese and, perhaps, Magyar as the only two comparable languages (1995:111).

To illustrate the relationship between design and instance in French syllabic verse, I give below four lines by Charles, Duc d'Orléans (b. 1394, d. 1464), who was a prisoner of war in England while AN was still being spoken. Charles composed in both English and French, but for the latter he used his own Francien dialect and scrupulously observed the rules of French syllabic versification.[4] The metre is the *octosyllabe*, the longest and most popular undivided French line; the lines are taken from Charles's *Balade* XXVIII (Champion 1907:56) and the line numbers are given in parentheses.[5]

(1) Pour sa-voir com-ment se por-toit (2)
(2) Qui doul-ce-ment le con-for-toit   (4)
(3) A-lors mon cueur, pour di-re voir (19)
(4) Tou-te le do-leur qu'il a-voit   (23)

In all the lines of this poem position 8 contains an accented syllable, either the strong syllable of a polysyllabic word or a lexical (tonic) monosyllable. Other than in position 8, strong syllables occur in random positions: 3 and 5 in (1), 4 in (2), 2 and 6 in (3), and 1 and 4 in (4). There is thus no rhythm in these lines other than the regularity of phrasal stress on the eighth syllable, made rhythmical by syllable-timing. The verse design may be described in terms of parametric theory as follows: position number: eight; orientation: right-strong; position size:

---

[4] For Charles's English poems see Steele 1941; for comments on their metre, which is much more like Chaucer's than Lydgate's, see Steele and Day 1946:47.

[5] I adopt the following scansion aids in all the instances quoted in this article: (1) extra space is left between words; (2) syllables occupying different positions are separated by a hyphen; (3) elided schwas are in superscript; (4) the strong syllables of polysyllabic words are in bold typeface; (5) syllables occupying strong positions (thus representing beats) are underlined; (6) void weak positions are denoted by [V].

one syllable; prominence site: position 8 (strong); prominence type: (phrasal) stress.[6] Note that, as in all Romance metres, the final position in the line may also contain an unaccented post-tonic syllable, which is not included in the syllable count and is termed *extrametrical*.

3.2 ACCENTUAL VERSE

The traditional mode of versifying in English was very different from the French. Once again it was a good fit for the language (OE) and depended upon (1) its strong word stress, (2) the predominance of polysyllables in its lexicon, (3) their left-strength, and (4) *alliteration*. Alliteration is the repetition of the left-most phoneme (onset) of each syllable, and contrasts with rhyme, which is the repetition of the syllable's right edge (nucleus and coda). OE epic metre was based on four strong stresses in each line, all but the last (and weakest) emphasized by alliteration. The rules of Old English accentual verse can be seen from the following four lines (96-99) of the *Battle of Maldon*, an anonymous poem composed soon after 991 (Scragg 1991):

(9)   **Wo**-den þa **wæl**-wul-fas   *for*   **wæ**-te-re ne **mur**-non
(10) **Wi**-cin-ga **we**-rod   **west** o-fer **Pan**-tan
(11) O-fer **scir wæ**-ter   **scyl**-de **we**-gon
(12) **Lid**-men to **lan**-de   **lin**-de **bæ**-ron

('Wolves of war, unmindful of ocean / The Viking horde surged west over Pante / Carrying their shields over shining water, / Seafarers, bearing to land the linden.' My translation.)

Note that the preposition "ofer" in (11) is *anacrusic*, like the striking-up notes in music, and the first metrical position is occupied by "scir." Anacrusis has endured as a defining feature of English verse; in most periods some poets have employed metres with optional unaccented syllables before the first beat in the line. This provides rhythmic variety (because the anacrusic lines have a rising rhythm, and those without it a falling one), and produces the syllabic irregularity that distinguishes much English poetry from its Romance equivalent. Each of the lines (9) to (12) above contains four strong stresses but the number of syllables between them varies erratically, making the line length irregular; instances (11)

---

[6] This analysis of Romance syllabic verse was first proposed by Piera (1980) and was supported by Hanson (1996). Note that the earliest OF poems (Henry 1953:7-13) seem to have had similar accentual constraints in non-final positions to those in Gower's verse (see 4.1 below).

and (12) happen to have eight syllables to the final stress, but most lines in this metre have considerably more. The verse design's parameters are: position number: eight; orientation: left-strong (any syllables before the first beat are anacrusic); position size: strong = one syllable, weak = unregulated; prominence site: strong (odd-numbered) positions; prominence type: stress (strong positions must contain it).

Although there is a dearth of textual evidence for accentual verse from between 1066 and 1350, a number of ME poems in a similar metre have survived from the second half of the fourteenth century; for example, Langland's *Piers Plowman* (Skeat 1886) and the poems of the *Pearl* manuscript (Andrew and Waldron 1987). This body of verse is usually held to be evidence of a fourteenth-century alliterative revival. We cannot be certain which, if any, OE poems its ME English authors knew; the fourteenth-century metre differs in some important respects from its predecessor (see Kennedy 1999). By that time the English language had undergone a series of changes that made the OE accentual metre a rather poor fit: English had borrowed many right-strong French words and ME phrasal stress had become right-strong; moreover, thousands of new lexical monosyllables had been created to complicate the stress profile of the language (see Strang 1980:279).

3.3 STRESS-SYLLABIC VERSE

Most verse composed in English since the early sixteenth century has been stress-syllabic: it has regulated not only the number of syllables in the line, but also the position of the prominent ones. Its evolution in English can best be explained by the principle of fit: when poets sought to regularize the number of syllables in their lines in imitation of French models, two features of English phonology stopped audiences perceiving the primary rhythm produced by the regularity of line-final stresses; the first was word stress; which made strong syllables within the line very prominent. The second was stress-timing: syllabic verse does not govern the number of strong and accented syllables within the line, and the stress-timing of lines with different numbers of stresses ensures that the line-final ones arrive at irregular intervals. The primary rhythm of syllabic verse is thus destroyed and has to be replaced by the complex secondary rhythm of stress-syllabic, produced by the regular occurrence of two types of event, stress/non-stress, beat/offbeat (Chatman 1965:29).

A good example of an English stress-syllabic verse design is that of the following stanza by John Wilmot, Earl of Rochester (b. 1647, d. 1680). Its lines (9-12) come from *The Fall* (Vieth 1968:86) and, although they are octosyllabic, their rhythm is very different from that of the French ones quoted above.

(5) But we poor slaves to hope and fear
(6) Are **ne**-ver of our joys se-**cure**
(7) They **le**-ssen still as they draw near
(8) And none but dull de-**lights** en-**dure**

In these lines the strong syllables of polysyllabic words are confined to strong positions; certain combinations of monosyllables (clitic groups) also have a fixed relationship: thus "to hope," "and fear," "and none," "but dull" are all weak/strong. As a result many of the monosyllables occupying strong positions in instances (5) to (8) are lexical and tonic. But a grammatical (atonic) monosyllable can appear in a strong position (for example, "of" in (6)) providing it is not part of such a *clitic group* (as it would be in "of joys" without the "our").

Once again, the metre is a good fit for the language. The verse captures the alternation of stronger and weaker syllables in a predominantly monosyllabic language (in modern English monosyllables make up three-quarters of all words; see Duffell 2002b:305). The iambic rhythm of this poem also mirrors the most common patterns of English speech, which contains many right-strong disyllabic verbs and left-strong nouns and adjectives preceded by an atonic article or preposition. The parameters of this metre (iambic tetrameter) are: position number: eight; orientation: right-strong; position size: one syllable; prominence site: weak positions; prominence type: strength. The last two parameters ensure that the only weak position that may contain a strong syllable is the first, an exception sanctioned by the closure principle (Smith 1968). Note that the prominence type of this verse design is not stress *per se*, because stressed monosyllables can appear in weak positions and unstressed in strong.

3.4 AN INTERMEDIATE METRE: THE *DOLNIK*

Tarlinskaja points out that many English octosyllables, unlike the poem in 3.3, are not perfectly isosyllabic (1976:86). English poets seem to find the iambic tetrameter so regular as to be monotonous, and for long poems they often prefer much rougher octosyllabics. Some treat the first weak position in the line as anacrusic and include many *headless*, trochaic lines (to French poets these would be *heptasyllabes*); for example, John Milton (b. 1608, d. 1674) in *L'Allegro* and *Il penseroso* (Jump 1964). Others combine their four-beat lines with lines in which the fourth beat is missing; for example, Oscar Wilde (b. 1854, d. 1900) in the *Ballad of Reading Gaol* (Pearson 1954). Still more give their verse variety by allowing some weak positions to contain zero or two syllables instead of one. Tarlinskaja classifies tetrameters as "strict" if 97 per cent or more of weak positions contain exactly one syllable, "loose" if between 80 and 97 per cent contain one syllable, and, if fewer than 80 per cent do so, she classifies them as "intermediate" between accentual and stress-syllabic (1976:128). This intermediate metre is very common not only in English, but also in German and Russian. In this article I shall call it by the Russian term *dolnik* (Tarlinskaja 1976), rather than her later term *strict stress-meter* (Tarlinskaja 1993).

When weak-position size is relaxed in this way, the iambic tetrameter becomes the *four-ictic dolnik*, with a variable number of syllables in each line: theoretically a line can have four syllables (all weak positions contain zero) or twelve (all contain two), but in practice almost all have between six and eleven. *The Statue and the Bust* (Williams 1954) by Robert Browning (b. 1812, d. 1889), is a four-ictic dolnik, and I give below four lines that demonstrate the variation in weak-position size, and consequently rhythm, that it contains.

(13)	There's a **pa**-lace in **Flo**-rence the world knows well	(1)
(14)	The Duke rode past in his **i**-dle way	(14)
(15)	[V] Gay he rode, with a friend as gay	(16)
(16)	[V] Hair in heaps lay **hea**-vi-ly	(19)

These lines contain eleven, nine, eight, and seven syllables respectively, and anapaests, as well as iambs, may appear anywhere in the line. Note that two of the four beats can be represented by the primary and secondary stresses of the same word (as in "heavily" (16)); some poets, including Browning, avoid making such words represent the second and third beats in the line, while others, including John Lydgate (b. ?1370, d. 1449), do not (Duffell 2000:230).

It should be noted that the dolnik was a better fit for ME than stress-syllabic verse in two ways: (1) it solved the poet's problem of variation between individuals in the syllabification of word-final schwa (see 4.3 below), and (2) it made full use of the language's tendency for stress-timing.[7] The parameters of the four-ictic dolnik are the same as those for the iambic tetrameter except that position size is: weak = one plus-or-minus one. While lines with this structure would have no rhythm at all in a syllable-timed language, they become rhythmic when delivered so as to equalize the intervals between stresses/beats.

4. VERSIFICATION IN ENGLAND, 1200-1400

The first thing that strikes a student of comparative linguistics about the verse

---

[7] See Minkova (1991) for the history of schwa deletion in English; and Roach (1982) for a discussion of the tendencies towards stress-timing and syllable-timing in delivery.

composed in AN is how similar it is to that being composed in ME between 1200 and 1400. The rhymed couplet of Chaucer's *Canterbury Tales* was the strophe design most favoured by AN poets (unlike their mainland contemporaries), and a line that is almost octosyllabic was their preferred metre. All the "octosyllabic" ME texts that have survived from before 1378 have only approximately eight syllables, and the same is true of a high proportion of AN texts, although the syllable count of both can be made more, but not completely, regular by deleting word-final schwas selectively. The verse composed in England in this period is thus quite unlike that of contemporary poets who composed in other varieties of French, and it breaks the most important rules of French metrics. Tarlinskaja analyses seven long English poems from this period and shows that in the average poem 55 per cent of lines contain eight syllables (1976:256); this is almost the same percentage as that found in my own analysis of AN verse (56 per cent; see 4.3 below). Since absolute syllabic regularity is a norm in French poetry from the eleventh century onwards, this variability might be argued to be the result of scribal error. But Johan Vising's exhaustive analysis of the scribal errors in French texts copied on both sides of the Channel in the period proves conclusively that the amount of line-length variation in AN texts is far greater than can be attributed to mistakes in copying (1884:33-50). This means that, like their English contemporaries, most AN poets did not count syllables; there are also other similarities between the line-structure of poets working in the two languages, as analysis will show.

4.1 THE ME OCTOSYLLABIC LINE

The two most regular ME poems analysed by Tarlinskaja (1976:86 and 256) are Chaucer's *Book of the Duchess* (1368), in which 84 per cent of lines have exactly eight syllables, and the anonymous *Owl and the Nightingale* (Stanley 1972), composed around 1200, in which 70 per cent of lines do so. The average for all seven, however, is 55 percent (as noted in 4 above), and I shall use an ME poem close to this average (54%) to demonstrate ME line-structure. This anonymous *Elegy for Edward I* is given by Aspin (1953:90-92) because it is an English version of an AN poem (Vising No 358a); both versions are likely to have been composed c. 1308:

(17) Wiþ four-scor^e **knyh**-tes, al of pris   (28)
(18) In **we**-rre that buen war and wys   (29)
(19) Þe **pop**^{e} of **pey**-ters stod at is **ma**sse   (57)
(20) [V] Wiþ ful gret so-**lemp**-ne-**te**   (58)

While two of these lines can be argued to have eight syllables, this is only true if a final schwa followed by a consonant is deleted in (17) but not (18). Instances (19) and (20) have nine and seven syllables respectively: in my scansion, the first has two syllables in its third weak position, and the second none in its first. All these lines, however, have four beats. Instance (20) shows that beats can be represented by either primary or secondary stressed syllables ("solempnete"), and by either atonic or tonic monosyllables ("with" and "gret").

It is clear that the metre of this poem, like those of all the poems Tarlinskaja analyses, and of all ME "octosyllabics," should be classified as a four-ictic dolnik. Its parameters are those given in 3.4 above, and it may have been chronologically transitional as well as typologically intermediate: the four-ictic dolnik may have been developed from OE four-beat verse by restricting weak-position size to a maximum of two syllables, and by making the prominence type strength not stress (thus exploiting the glut of new monosyllables in ME). The four-ictic dolnik, in its turn, became iambic tetrameter by further restricting weak-position size to one syllable. While we do not know the name of the first English poet to employ the four-ictic dolnik, we do know who first transformed it into iambic tetrameter and thus invented (iambic) stress-syllabic verse. John Gower (b. ?1330, d. 1408) first used iambic tetrameters in the AN of *Mirour de l'omme* (1375), and perfected the metre in the ME *Confessio Amantis* (Macaulay 1901), of which the first version was completed in 1390.[8]

4.2 THE AN OCTOSYLLABIC LINE

Vising shows that, while some surviving AN verse texts obey the mainland rules of syllable count, many more do not (1884:79-91).[9] The poem I have chosen to illustrate AN octosyllabic verse is not among the most irregular, but it contains all the deviant types of line that characterize the metre. The following lines are from the anonymous *Thomas Turberville* (Vising No 301, in Aspin 1953:51-53), which was probably composed between 1295 and 1297:

(21)   [V] e ju-**ré** par Seint De-**nys**   (6)
(22)   Teu ga-ri-**son** ad pur son la-**bour**   (62)
(23)   **O**-re sunt tuz, jeo **quid**ᵉ neëz   (79)

---

[8] For an analysis of Gower's metrics see Macaulay (1899:xliii-xlvi and 1901:cxx-cxxvii), Duffell and Billy (2003-04), and Billy and Duffell (2003). For the earliest iambic tetrameters composed in a Germanic language see Zonneveld (2000).

[9] Among the surviving poems in which syllables are counted correctly are the *Life of Saint Edward* (Vising No 125) and *Life of Saint Catherine* (No 11), both now believed to date from the 1160s (Legge 1963:60-72).

(24)   Ly Ducs Lo-**wys**, [V] ton pa-**rent**   (93)

All of these lines are unacceptable according to French metrics: (21) and (24) contain seven syllables, and (22) contains nine; (23) may also contain nine, but can be regularized by deleting one (but not both) of its word-final schwas, as shown here. These lines illustrate the three chief causes of syllabic irregularity in AN verse: the first syllable may be missing, as in (21), or the fifth, as in (24); an extra unaccented syllable may be present, as in (22), or the line may contain a redundant word-final schwa as in (23). The number of accented syllables in the line is also not constant (although most contain three); but, as we have seen, in ME verse any type of monosyllable can occupy a strong position and represent a beat. On this basis each of these AN lines has four beats, as do all the lines in this poem and in the other poems analysed in 4.3 below. The same correspondence rules also seem to be in operation in AN as in ME verse: an offbeat may be represented by between zero and two syllables; most beats are represented by strong syllables or tonic monosyllables, and none by weak syllables. Thus, while none of these lines is a respectable *octosyllabe*, all of them can be scanned as perfect four-ictic dolniks.

The main linguistic objection to this interpretation is that four beats can be found in any group of between seven and eleven syllables in a language with secondary stress. These four beats may thus be a property of the AN language, not of the poet's verse design. The obvious answer to this objection is that, since metre has been described as "language imitating itself" (Hanson and Kiparsky 1996:325, quoting Thompson 1961), we should not be surprised to discover that four beats is a property of both utterances and lines in AN. Some evidence that four beats are part of the poet's metrical intention is provided by the small number of lines in AN octosyllabic poems that contain only six syllables. *Thomas Turberville* contains no such lines, but there are three (65, 91, 108) in the *Lament of Edward II* (Vising No 359, in Aspin 1953:96-100), and three hexasyllabic first hemistichs (1, 3, 63) in the poem *Against the King's Taxes* (Vising No 286, in Aspin 1953:108-11). All of these lines provide four beats, as in (25), which is line 65 in the *Lament*, and none offers only three, as in (26)*, which is my construct based on line 11 (27) of the same poem.

(25)   [V] **Main**-te-**nant** [V] santz de-**lay**
(26)*   te-**rrien** a-**mur** [V] [V] es-**teint**
(27)   te-**rrien** a-**mur** [V] tost es-**teint**

The structure of such hexasyllabic lines would seem to confirm a four-beat design, but, while seven lines are sufficient to formulate a hypothesis, only an analysis based on a much larger sample of lines can confirm it.

4.3 STATISTICAL ANALYSIS OF SELECTED AN TEXTS

For my sample of octosyllabic verse I have chosen 300 lines from the mature period of AN, the hundred years before Gower's *Mirour de l'omme* (1375). The 300 lines are contained in three of the poems discussed in 4.1 and 4.2: *Thomas Turberville*, the French version of the *Elegy on Edward I*, and the *Lament for Edward II*.

I have analysed the sample on two hypotheses: (1) that their verse design is syllabic, and (2) that it is the four-ictic dolnik. The validity of the first is tested in Table 1, which shows the percentage of lines of each length.

TABLE 1. Syllabic Hypothesis
Syllable Count: No of Lines

Poem	-1	-2	+1	+2	+ -e	~8	8	8 (%)	TOTAL
T. T.	33	0	2	1	6	42	56	(57)	98
Elegy	11	0	3	0	13	27	55	(67)	82
Lament	21	3	15	0	23	62	58	(48)	120
TAL	65	3	20	1	42	131	169	(56)	300

Of the 300 lines in the sample, 216 are M (masculine), 76 are F (feminine), and 8 are T (*trans-sexual*: my term for F lines that are given as masculine in error, or for M and F lines rhymed with one another).

These figures make it clear that the syllabic hypothesis is unsatisfactory: according to the rules of OF versification almost half the lines are incorrect, and even in the most regular of the three poems, the *Elegy*, one third are incorrect. Syllabic verse does not admit void or disyllabic positions, since either would destroy its only rhythm, so we cannot attribute this irregularity to tension. There are significant differences between the proportions of lines of each length in the three poems, which is not surprising, since differences between individual poets' use of the same metre are universal.[10] *Thomas Turberville* is significantly less

---

[10] See, for example, the analyses of Tarlinskaja (1976:238-306) and Clarke (1964:5-17).

regular than the *Elegy*, and the *Lament* is the most irregular of the three and contains the only lines of six syllables in the sample (see 4.2 above). It also provides most of the trans-sexual rhymes, and its author seems to ignore more word-final schwas within the line as well as at the end of it. This may be evidence of considerable variation between individual AN speakers in the treatment of such schwas, or of deletion's increasing with time, or of both. Since most medieval poetry was composed for reading aloud (see Garcia 1978:45), inconsistent schwa deletion has serious performance implications.

Deleting word-final schwa selectively in such a way as to maximize the number of correct lines in the sample reduces the proportion of incorrect lines to 30 per cent in total, and to just under 20 per cent in the most regular poem, the *Elegy*. But, if poets intended such facultative schwa deletion, their readers would not have been able to manage it in delivery: unable to predict which schwas should be syllabified, readers would have been incapable of producing the required regularity of phrasal stress. Their audiences would thus have lost any sense of the primary rhythm on which French verse is dependent. From this it can be seen that syllabic verse is a poor fit for a language in which some people syllabify some word-final schwas, and that the ideal fit is a metre that is indifferent to them.

The dolnik is such a metre and the second hypothesis, that the metre of the sampled poems is a four-ictic dolnik, is tested in Tables 2a and 2b. The former shows the percentage of weak positions containing zero, one, and two syllables, and the latter shows the types of syllable that occur in strong positions.

TABLE 2. Dolnik Hypothesis
a. Size of Weak Positions (in syllables) as %

No of Syllables	Position 1	Position 3	Position 5	Position 7	All Weak Positions
0	33	5	20	2	15
1	60	81	70	86	74
2	7	14	10	12	11
TOTAL	100	100	100	100	100

b. Content of Strong Positions (type of syllable)

Type of Syllable	Position 2	Position 4	Position 6	Position 8	All Strong Positions
Primary Stress	35	69	26	88	54
Tonic Monosyllable	33	26	40	12	28
Total Accented	68	95	66	100	82
Atonic Monosyllable	20	4	9	0	9
Secondary Stress	12	1	25	0	9
GRAND TOTAL	100	100	100	100	100

The figures in 2b show that every line analysed provides four beats and that four out of every five beats are represented by accented syllables, the remainder being supplied by atonic monosyllables and secondary stresses. The proportion of accented syllables is more than sufficient to give the verse a pulse recognizable to any audience that speaks a language with strong word stress. The figures in 2a show that three out of four weak positions contain a single syllable, giving all three poems a predominantly iambic rhythm. The percentages of accented strong positions and of monosyllabic weak ones in my AN sample are remarkably similar to those found by Tarlinskaja in her seven ME poems (1976:258-59). My figures also show that in AN verse void positions occur mostly in positions 1 or 5, just as in ME verse, where metrists have coined the terms *headless* and *broken-backed* to describe lines that contain them.

Tables 2a and 2b also provide further confirmation that the metre of these poems is the four-ictic dolnik: measured in the proportion of accented syllables, the strongest of the strong positions are 4 and 8; and, measured in the proportion of variant size, the weakest weak ones are 1 and 5. These statistics for verse instances indicate a verse design with the hierarchical structure given below:

FIGURE 1. Dolnik Hypothesis: Stress Hierarchy

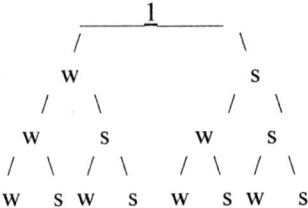

Such a hierarchical structure typifies verse designs that regulate both syllable count and accent (see Hayes 1979 and Piera 1980).

Tables 1 and 2 fully support the hypothesis that the verse design of these three poems is the four-ictic dolnik. Such an interpretation produces three important regularities: 100 per cent of lines contain four beats/offbeats; 74 per cent of weak positions contain one syllable; 82 per cent of strong ones contain an accented syllable. The regularity produced by the syllabic hypothesis is clearly much weaker: only 56 per cent of lines have eight syllables if word-final schwas are treated consistently. In the light of these figures it is not surprising that a number of writers have recognized the similarities between ME and AN versification.

5. ENGLISH INFLUENCE ON *AN*

Vising lists nine eminent scholars who "suppose that Anglo-Norman poets combined certain features of the English metrical system," and five equally eminent, including himself, who have "demonstrated the untenableness of this theory" (1923:81). In his earlier, more detailed study of AN versification, Vising argued against English influence in more detail and, since most French scholars have accepted his case, it is important to examine it here. Vising based his conclusions on two arguments (1) no ME verse had been composed when AN poets first adopted their peculiar versifying practices, and (2) poets of a high-status language are most unlikely to copy the rhythms they find in a low-status language. I shall consider these arguments separately.

5.1 THE LACK OF ENGLISH MODELS

Vising notes that the peculiarities of AN versification predate the earliest surviving Middle English texts; for the first hundred years after the Conquest there simply was no English versification to influence French-speaking poets (1884:10 n1). This argument is, however, a simplification. Some surviving AN poems are metrically correct according to French rules, but the proportion declines with time, as Vising showed (1884:68-91). He analysed all the AN poems that had been published at his time of writing, and concluded that the following proportions are metrically correct: 58 per cent of those dating from the twelfth-century, 7 per cent of those from the thirteenth, and none of those from the fourteenth. Moreover, many of the metrically incorrect poems of the early period have only one significant defect: their feminine lines have seven syllables to the final stress instead of eight (Vising 1923:82 and Legge 1963:15 and 35). The lines of these poems are obviously intended to be octosyllabic (rather than four-ictic dolniks), and they show that their poets had little difficulty in regularizing syllable count; but the equivalence 8M = 7F suggests that the poets and their audiences had difficulty counting syllables by ear, probably because AN's strong word stress interfered with their perception of the syllabic rhythm.[11]

Vising's analysis reveals that later AN verse texts are more irregular than earlier ones (1884:56), but he does not draw the obvious conclusion that the norms of versifying changed over time. Nor does he discuss the similarities between ME and AN versification, or consider whether they could be the result of the linguistic changes he deplores elsewhere (1884:57). Moreover, when Vising says that there were no ME texts early enough to influence AN poets, he is clearly thinking of written texts, but by 1200 most of the population were bilingual, and L1 speakers of AN must have encountered many oral ME texts. The most ubiquitous of such texts are proverbs and nursery rhymes, which in English are accentually based. Most English proverbs, for example, are four-ictic dolniks, like "Red in the morning, shepherds' warning." Much has been written about the influence of folk verse on literary metre in many languages and we should not underestimate the power of oral models combined with the principle of fit. Clearly, syllabic verse represented a problem for AN poets and audiences because of schwa deletion and strong word stress; if in addition AN speakers employed stress-timing, as they had to whenever they spoke ME, AN poets would have found it easier to compose dolniks than syllabic lines.[12]

---

[11] When lines of 7F and 8M are mixed in a poem, a syllable-timed delivery no longer delivers line-end (phrasal) stresses at equal time intervals. For examples of similar problems with counting syllables in other Romance languages with strong word stress see Duffell (2002a) and Parkinson (in press).

[12] In the classroom L1 speakers of English often struggle to break the habits of word stress and syllable-timing when they try to speak French for the first time.

5.2 LOW-STATUS FEATURES IN A HIGH-STATUS LANGUAGE

Vising argues that the *rhythms* of low-status languages like ME do not influence those of high-status ones like AN (1884:12), but modern readers know from the example of Afro-American music that this is untrue. While AN was undoubtedly the higher-status language in the 300 years after the Conquest, there was an interesting parallel to its possible invasion by English rhythms. The Barons' wars in the thirteenth century and the Black Death in the fourteenth enabled large numbers of L1 English speakers to occupy important positions in society (where, of course, they had to speak French). The gaps in the social hierarchy they filled can be compared with the opportunities offered English rhythms by linguistic changes in AN. This is the most likely explanation of how AN poets came to compose four-ictic dolniks in poems that contain no regularity perceptible to speakers of the mainland varieties of French.

5.3 IGNORANCE AND NEGLIGENCE

To Vising, AN versification is a disaster, and he tackles it rather like a modern air-crash investigator: he eliminates the possibility of bad communication (scribal error), and ignores that of technical (linguistic) failure, and this leaves him with only one explanation: pilot (poet) error. He attributes the syllabic irregularity of AN verse to ignorance, or negligence, or both (1884:53 and 1923:81). He lists the French scholars who agree with this diagnosis and cites a number of statements in the surviving texts consistent with it. For example, he quotes AN poets who acknowledge that their French differs from that of the mainland (1923:26-27), or that their lines are irregular (1884:54), and a copyist who disparages the metre of the lines he copies (1884:53). He also notes that one long poem (the *Life of Pope Clement*, No 110) becomes regular in the second half, and assumes that this is because the poet learned the rules of French metrics in the interval (1923:81).

Vising's examples demonstrate only that some AN poets (and copyists) were well aware that their language and metrics differed from the norms of the mainland. This is not surprising, since the poets of the Plantagenet court continued to observe those norms and, even before the accession of Henry II in 1154, there was a continuous stream of new immigrants from France. There were thus plenty of people in England who knew the rules; but, while some AN poets observed those rules, many did not. Yet regularizing the syllable count of lines does not require exceptional skill: Kastner notes that rewriting old poems in a new metre was a vogue among French clerics in the thirteenth century (1903:145), and modern editors with no poetic credentials find little difficulty in regularizing the syllable count of wildly irregular medieval Spanish texts (see

Duffell 2002a:131-34). It is difficult, therefore, to believe any AN poet could not have done the same, had he/she wished; and, as we have noted, some poets did, many on the non-canonical basis of 7F = 8M syllables.

We do not know why the syllable count of the *Life of Pope Clement* suddenly becomes regular; the author's enlightenment is only one possible explanation. But, while ignorance is unproven in this particular case, the erudition of another irregular versifier is in no doubt. The macaronic poem *Against the King's Taxes* (see 4.2 above) is composed in lines comprising a first hemistich in AN plus a second in Latin. The metre of this poem is an imitation of the medieval Latin goliardic metre, which was extremely popular across Europe among thirteenth and fourteenth-century clerics (see Raby 1934:II.190-213). The strophe of Goliardic verse *cum auctoritate* is a monorhyme quatrain in which three stress-syllabic lines of 7 + 6 syllables are followed by a quantitative one, a dactylic hexameter or pentameter quoted from classical Latin. The verse design of the stress-syllabic lines has a trochaic template, a catalectic tetrameter followed by a trimeter, but some tension is allowed in the form of variant lines with inversion. The following lines illustrate both the norm and the variant; they are lines 17 and 37 of the sixth *Moral Satire* of Gautier de Châtillon (b. 1135), as given by Raby (1934:II.96-97):

(28) Qui vir-**tu**-tes **ap**-pe-tit   **la**-bi-tur in **i**-mum
(29) Si Io-seph in **vin**-cu-lis   **Chris**-tum pre-fi-**gu**-rat

Both hemistichs in (28) match the template, as do 83 per cent of the hemistichs of the poem, in that strong syllables are constrained from appearing in weak positions; the remaining 17 per cent of hemistichs contain an inversion, as in (29), where "Ioseph" cannot be oxytonic in Latin. The author of the macaronic poem *Against the King's Taxes* successfully captures the rhythm of this Latin metre: 78 per cent of his hemistichs are trochaic, like (28), and almost all the others have the same structure as (29), in which an initial monosyllable is followed by disyllable. But the AN poet introduces a startling innovation (at least, in Medieval Latin): lines that are irregular in syllable count; this can be seen in the following lines (1, 16, 19, and 82):

(30) [V] Dieu [V] roy de ma-ges-**té**   ob per-**so**-nas **tri**-nas
(31) **U**-ne **chos**[e] est **coun**-tre foy,   un-de gens gra-**va**-tur
(32) Le **peu**-ple doit le plus do-**ner**   et sic sin-co-**pa**-tur
(33) E ceux que **pen**-sent **fer**[e] tre-**soun**   et **pa**-cis tur-ba-**to**-res

Instance (31) is perfectly regular, but in (30) two (weak) positions of the AN hemistich (2 and 4) are void. The remaining instances are also irregular: (32) has anacrusis in the French hemistich ("Le") and (33) has it in both ("E" and "et"). Such anacrusic hemistichs make up 36 per cent of the Latin and almost half of the AN ones, so there can be no doubt that the poet is applying an English rhythmic principle to his versifying in other languages. Here the work of an erudite and painstaking poet contradicts Vising's assumption that syllabic irregularity can only be the product of ignorance and/or negligence.

6. CONCLUSIONS
The foregoing analysis leads to the conclusion that the metre of the many AN poems that are only approximately octosyllabic is the four-ictic dolnik. Such a metre depends on a number of phonological features for which we find no evidence in other contemporary varieties, and which are not found in modern French. Centuries of daily contact with ME undoubtedly caused AN to diverge considerably from the language of the mainland and, as Vising points out, "il serait extraordinaire que celle-ci [la versification] eût seule echappé à la ruine générale qui fondit sur la langue" (1884:57). Although Vising describes variation and change here in judgmental terms that are unacceptable today, he is making the same point as the present article, namely that metre and language are inextricably linked. The composition of dolniks in AN is strong evidence that the language had the three features that make such a metre a perfect fit: strong word stress (including metrically significant secondary stress), variability in the deletion of word-final schwa, and stress-timing.

The refusal of so many French scholars in the late nineteenth and early twentieth centuries to recognize the similarities between ME and AN versification was only partly the result of the ethnocentrism that characterized the period; it also reflected the state of metrical theory at that time. Many metrists then believed that accentual verse requires the regular alternation of stressed and unstressed syllables, whereas we now know that a constraint on strong syllables in weak positions is a sufficient qualification.[13] Some English scholars intuitively recognized the accentual patterns in AN verse but they were unable to convince their French colleagues because they lacked sufficiently rigorous descriptions of stress-syllabic verse and of intermediate metres. Fortunately modern linguistic metrics and statistical analysis enable us to remedy this, and to resolve a controversy that divided the field for many years.

---

[13] This misunderstanding also led to a denial that accentual patterns exist in much Medieval Latin verse (see Gasparov 1987:329-30).

References

Allen, W. Sidney. 1973. *Accent and Rhythm: Prosodic Structures of Latin and Greek: A Study in Theory and Reconstruction.* Cambridge: Cambridge Univ. Press.
Andrew, Malcolm and Waldron, Ronald, ed. 1987. *The Poems of the Pearl Manuscript: "Pearl," "Patience," "Sir Gawain and the Green Knight,"* 2nd ed. Exeter: Univ. of Exeter.
Aspin, Isabel S. T. ed. 1953. *Anglo-Norman Political Songs.* Oxford: Blackwell.
Attridge, Derek. 1982. *The Rhythms of English Poetry.* London: Longman.
Benson, Larry E. ed. 1988. *The Riverside Chaucer.* Oxford: Oxford Univ. Press.
Billy, Dominique and Duffell, Martin J. 2003. "Le Décasyllabe de John Gower: le dernier mètre anglo-normand," paper prepared for publication in the Département de Lettres Modernes, Université de Nantes.
Champion, Pierre, ed. 1907. *Le Manuscrit autographe des poésies de Charles d'Orleans.* Paris: Honoré Champion.
Chatman, Seymour. 1965. *A Theory of Meter.* The Hague: Mouton.
Clarke, Dorothy Clotelle. 1964. *Morphology of Fifteenth Century Castilian Verse.* Pittsburgh: Duquesne Univ. Press; Louvain: Nauweleerts.
Cornulier, Benoît de. 1995. *Art poëtique: notions et problèmes de métrique.* Lyon: Presses Universitaires de Lyon.
Dorchain, Auguste. 1919. *L'Art des vers,* 2nd ed. Paris: Garnier. [1st ed. 1911].
Duffell, Martin J. 1999a. *Modern Metrical Theory and the "Verso de arte mayor."* London: Department of Hispanic Studies, Queen Mary and Westfield College.
Duffell, Martin J. 1999b. "The Metric Cleansing of Hispanic Verse." *Bulletin of Hispanic Studies* (Liverpool) 76, 151-68.
Duffell, Martin J. 1999-2000. "'The Craft So Long to Lerne': Chaucer's Invention of the Iambic Pentameter." *Chaucer Review* 34, 269-88.
Duffell, Martin J. 2000. "Lydgate's Metrical Inventiveness and his Debt to Chaucer." in Kennedy 2000, 227-49.
Duffell, Martin J. 2002a. "Don Rodrigo and Sir Gawain: Family Likeness or Convergent Development?'" *"Mio Cid" Studies: 'Some Problems of Diplomatic' Fifty Years On,* ed. by Alan Deyermond, David G. Pattison, and Eric Southworth, 129-50. London: Department of Hispanic Studies, Queen Mary and Westfield College.
Duffell, Martin J. 2002b. "The Italian Line in English after Chaucer." *Language and Literature* 11, 291-305.
Duffell, Martin J. and Billy, Dominique. 2003-04. "From Decasyllable to Pentameter: Gower's Contribution to English Metrics." *Chaucer Review,* 38, 383-401.
Garcia, Michel. 1978. "La versificación," in Pero López de Ayala, *Libro de poemas, o Rimado de Palacio,* I, ed. by Michel Garcia, 41-58. Madrid: Gredos.
Gasparov, M. L. 1987. "A Probability Model of Verse (English, Latin, French, Italian, Spanish, Portuguese)," translated by Marina Tarlinskaja. *Style* 21, 322-58.
Gasparov, M. L. 1996. *A History of European Versification,* translated by G. S. Smith

and Marina Tarlinskaja, ed. by G. S. Smith with L. Holford-Strevens. Oxford: Clarendon Press.

Hall, Robert A. Jr. 1965-66. "Old Spanish Stress-Timed Verse and Germanic Superstratum." *Romance Philology* 19, 227-34.

Hanson, Kristin. 1996. "From Dante to Pinsky: A Theoretical Perspective on the History of the English Iambic Pentameter." *Rivista di Linguïstica* 9, 53-97.

Hanson, Kristin and Kiparsky, Paul. 1996. "A Parametric Theory of Poetic Meter." *Language* 72, 287-335.

Hayes, Bruce. 1979. "The Prosodic Hierarchy in Meter." *Phonetics and Phonology*, I, *Rhythm and Meter*, ed. by Paul Kiparsky and Gilbert Youmans, 201-60. San Diego: Academic Press.

Hayes, Bruce. 1995. *Metrical Stress Theory: Principles and Case Studies*. Chicago: Chicago Univ. Press.

Henry, Albert, ed. 1953. *Chrestomathie de la Littérature en ancien français*, I: *Textes*, 2nd ed. Berne: Francke.

Jakobson, Roman. 1960. "Linguistics and Poetics." Sebeok 1960, 350-77.

Jakobson, Roman. 1973. "Principes de versification." *Questions de poétique*, ed. by T. Todorov, translated by Léon Robel, 40-55. Paris: Éditions du Seuil.

Jump, John D. ed., 1964. *The Complete English Poems of John Milton*. New York: Washington Square Press.

Kastner, L. E. 1903. *A History of French Versification*. Oxford: Clarendon Press.

Kennedy, Ruth. 1999. "New Theories of Constraint in the Metricality of the Strong-Stress Long Line as Applied to the Rhymed Corpus of Late Middle English Alliterative Verse." *Métriques du Moyen Âge et de la Renaissance*, ed. by D. Billy, 131-44. Paris: L'Harmattan.

Kennedy, Ruth, ed. 2000. *Medieval English Measures: Studies in Metre and Versification*, special issue of *Parergon* ns 18.1 (July).

Kiparsky, Paul. 1977. "The Rhythmic Structure of English Verse." *Linguistic Inquiry* 8, 189-247.

Legge, M. Dominica. 1963. *Anglo-Norman Literature and Its Background*. Oxford: Clarendon Press.

Lote, Georges. 1939. "Les Origines des vers français." *Annales de la Faculté des Lettres d'Aix* 21, 219-415.

Lotz, John. 1960. "Metric Typology." Sebeok 1960, 135-48.

Macaulay, G. C. ed. 1899. *The Complete Works of John Gower*, I, *The French Works*. Oxford: Clarendon Press.

Macaulay, G. C. ed. 1901. *The Complete Works of John Gower*, II and III, *The English Works*. Oxford: Clarendon Press.

Merrilees, Brian. 2003. "John Gower's French." Paper prepared for publication in the Dept of French, Univ. of Toronto.

Minkova, Donka. 1991. *History of Final Vowels in English*. Berlin and New York: Mouton de Gruyter.

Parkinson, Stephen. In press. "Concurrent Patterns of Verse Design in the Galician-Portuguese Lyric." *Proceedings of the Twelfth Colloquium*, ed. by Alan Deyermond

and Jane Whetnall. London: Department of Hispanic Studies, Queen Mary and Westfield College.
Pearson, Hesketh, ed. 1954. Oscar Wilde. *Selected Essays and Poems*. Harmondsworth: Penguin.
Piera, Carlos José. 1980. "Spanish Verse and the Theory of Meter." Doctoral thesis, Univ. of California, Los Angeles. [*DAI* 42 (1981-82) 197a]
Pighi, Giovanni Battista. 1970. *Studi di ritmica e metrica*. Turin: Bottega d'Erasmo.
Raby, J. E. 1934. *A History of Secular Latin Poetry in the Middle Ages*, 2 vols. Oxford: Clarendon Press.
Raven, D. S. 1965. *Latin Metre: An Introduction*. London: Faber and Faber.
Roach, Peter. 1982. "On the Distinction between "Stress-timed" and "Syllable-timed" Languages." *Linguistic Controversies: Essays in Honour of F.R. Palmer*, ed. by David Crystal, 73-79. London: Edward Arnold.
Scragg, Donald, ed. 1991. *The Battle of Maldon, AD 991*. Oxford: Blackwell; The Manchester Centre for Anglo-Saxon Studies.
Sebeok, Thomas A., ed. 1960. *Style in Language*. Cambridge MA: MIT Press.
Skeat, W. W., ed. 1886. William Langland. *Piers Plowman in Three Parallel Texts*, 2 vols. Oxford: Clarendon Press. [reprinted 1954]
Smith, Barbara Herrnstein. 1968. *Poetic Closure: A Study of How Poems End*. Chicago: Chicago Univ. Press.
Stanley, Eric Gerald, ed. 1972. *The Owl and the Nightingale*. Manchester: Manchester Univ. Press; New York: Barnes and Noble.
Steele, Robert, ed. 1941. *The English Poems of Charles of Orleans*. London: Oxford Univ. Press.
Steele, Robert and Day, Mabel, ed. 1946. *The English Poems of Charles of Orleans*. London: Oxford Univ.Press.
Strang, Barbara M. H. 1980. "The Ecology of the English Monosyllable." *Studies in English Language*, ed. by S. Greenbaum, Geoffrey Leech, and J. Svartvik, 277-93. London: Longman.
Tarlinskaja, Marina. 1976. *English Verse: Theory and History*, translated from the Russian by the author. The Hague: Mouton.
Tarlinskaja, Marina. 1993. *Strict Stress-Meter in English Poetry Compared with German and Russian*. Calgary: Calgary Univ. Press.
Thompson, John. 1961. *The Founding of English Metre*. London: Routledge and Kegan Paul; New York: Columbia Univ. Press.
Vieth, David M., ed. 1968. *The Complete Poems of John Wilmot Earl of Rochester*. New Haven: Yale Univ. Press.
Vising, Johan. 1884. *Sur la versification anglo-normande*. Uppsala: Almqvist and Wiksell.
Vising, Johan. 1923. *Anglo-Norman Language and Literature*. London: Oxford Univ. Press.
Williams, W. E. ed. 1954. *Browning: A Selection*. Harmondsworth: Penguin.
Zonneveld, Wim. 2000. "The *Ormulum* and the *Lutgart*: Early Germanic Iambs in Context." in Kennedy 2000, 27-52.

7
Prayers in Medieval Occitan: Critical Edition, Translation and Notes
PETER T. RICKETTS

THESE PRAYERS ARE TO be found in only one manuscript, London, British Library, Egerton 945, a volume of 328 folios, but of modest dimensions, created for personal use and belonging to the first part of the fourteenth century. The text occupies ff. 274v – 287r. As Geneviève Hasenohr has shown in a recent article (Hasenohr 2000), it is the work of a single scribe and was concocted for a widow, possibly a *béguine*, and is made up of prayers in verse and in prose, written in both French and Occitan, liturgical works and didactic writings with mystical tendencies in Latin, verse texts in French, and prose texts in Occitan.[1]

The linguistic factor is important: it supposes a competence in both vernaculars with Latin as a liturgical vehicle. Certain of the texts presented in Occitan are the translations of Old French poems, like the *Priere de Theophile* (see Ricketts 2004). But the owner of the manuscript was obviously able to read Old French, even if the texts in their original language are short and mainly popular. For more details, the reader is encouraged to go to Geneviève Hasenohr's interesting and perceptive article.

This set of prayers, accompanied by spiritual guidance, is set around an appreciation of the canonical hours. These prayers are created with the owner of the codex in mind. References to her as, for example, a miserable sinner personalize the orations at every step and are clearly intended for her particularly. While the content is sometimes repetitive, it is the cumulative effect which counts, piling clause on clause, adjective on adjective. The consequence of this is, very often, considerable syntactic complexity, and this has introduced new perspectives in the examination of Medieval Occitan syntactic structures.

---

[1] I am most grateful to Cyril Hershon and Maurizio Perugi for their help in the preparation of this article.

This edition is as conservative as possible. The fact that the poem is to be found in a single manuscript does not encourage intervention, and only those changes which are fundamental, correcting obvious omissions and the breakdown of syntactic logic, have been introduced. Notes of linguistic and biblical interest as well as those relating to emendations accompanying the text.

[f. 274v]
Oratio de mati
Al mati, quant vos auviretz los senh[s] sonar o l'auzel chantar, tantost de vostre liech levatz ses nualha, e pessatz en vostre coratge que vos auvetz aquela dossa votz qui sera dicha al Jorn del Jutgament: "Vos, mort, qui jazetz en vostres sepulcres, levatz e venetz al jutgament." E ssenhat e sseelatz vostre front e vostre cors del senhatgle de la crotz, e merceatz a Dieu del repaus que avetz agut en la nuech e d'aisso qu'el vos a gardat sas e sals del Anamic; e digatz vostre *Credo in Deum* e vostre *Pater noster*. Enapres tornatz vostre coratge a la dossa puecela debonaire Maria, maere dal dos Jesu, e de bon cor digatz li *Ave Maria*. Apres anatz al mostier e digatz vostras autras orazos, e tot vostre coratge tornatz ves Dieu, e prejat lo de cor entier, i a chascun mot metetz i vostre cor, que so que disetz de bocha vos sabore lo cor, [f. 275r] quar li angiel son aparelhat a portar vostra orazo a prezent denant Dieu. De totas aquestas chausas en redetz gracias a Dieu, e de tot vostre cor entier merceatz a vostre Creator, car nos a elescutz a estre son Filh e heretier de ssa gloria. Enapres, redetz gracias a nostre Creator d'aisso que volc estre per nos petitz effas en aquest setgle, paubres e viels e despechat de tota gent per nos, e tan vil e tan cruel e tant antosa mort per nos suffrit a nos remer[1] de mort; e d'umil cor digatz li:

Oratio
Senher Dieus, poderos e debonaire, per cui saber tota res es sostenguda, de cui forsa tota res es efforsada, per cui bontat tot quant es es be ordenat, per vostra grant gracia aujatz mi, chaetio pechador, e per vostre grant poder de vizis e de pechatz me relevatz, e gardatz me que autra vetz no·i chaia. De vostra gracia mon cor enluminatz e essenhatz me a far vostre [f. 275v] volomtat, e vos, qui los angiels qui ferm esteren, cofermetz per vostra gracia que de vos partir no poguesan, ma pessa fermatz en vostra volomtat, e daus liams de vostra amor

---

[1] *remer*. This form is not found in any of the dictionaries. Several examples are to be found in the text and support the meaning 'save'. It is also found in the same context in the *Istoria Petri & Pauli* (Guillaume 1887) and the *Istorio de Sanct Poncz* (Guillaume 1887-88).

[f. 274v]
Morning Prayer
In the morning, when you hear the bells ringing or the bird singing, straightway rise from your bed, shaking off sloth, and think in your heart that you can hear that sweet voice which will speak on the Day of Judgement: "You, the dead, who are lying in your graves, rise and come to be judged." And make the sign of the cross on your forehead and your body, and thank God for the repose you have had during the night and that he has kept you safe and sound from the Adversary; and say your Creed and your Lord's Prayer. After turn your heart to the gentle, sweet Mary, mother of gentle Jesus, and sincerely recite the *Ave Maria* to her. After, go to the church and say your other prayers, and turn your heart totally to God, and pray to him with all your heart, and make every word come from the heart, so that what comes from your lips can be savoured by your heart, [f. 275r] for then, the angels are ready to take your prayer before God. For all these things, give thanks to God, and thank your Creator with all your heart, for he has chosen us to be his child, and heir to his glory. After, give thanks to our Creator for his willingness to become, for us, a small child in the world, poor and humble and despised by all for us, and he suffered such a vile and such a cruel and shameful death for us to save us from death; and with a humble heart say to him:

Prayer
Lord God, powerful and gentle, through whose knowledge each being is sustained, through whose strength each being is given strength, through whose goodness all things which exist are ordered, through your great grace hear me, wretched sinner, and through your great power take from me my vices and sins, and prevent me from falling into them once more. Illuminate my heart by your grace and teach me to do your [f. 275v] will, and you, who by your grace confirmed in their resolve the angels who remained faithful to you, so that they could not leave you, lock my thinking into your will, and bind it closely with the bonds of your love

fermament la liatz si que de vos no puecha partir, mas en vos remanha ses fi. Amen.

Oratio
A la prima, cossiratz a tal hora s'ajusteren li preveir' e li prince deus Jujieus, e quez[er]en fals testemoni encontra Jesu Crist en la crotz [a] Caiphas, qui era princes deus preveires, i aqui fazian li e dizian escharns,[2] e ssa bela chara cruelment buferen e mot grant anta li feren, quar en sa genta chara escracheren si que lo sanc e la ordura que ilh escrachavan ensemle mesclat sobre sa bela chara endurzit, e tant que el esdevenc coma lebros; e puech meneren lo vilment apilat[3] qui fo lor jutges. Pessatz donc que tot aisso suffrit per nos, e digatz devotamen: [f. 276r] A! Senher Dieus, Jesu Crist, via de paciensa e d'umilitat, coformatz mon cor a vostra humilitat i a la paciensa de vostre cor, que c'om me diga qui·m plassa o·m despla, d'anta o de vilania, qu'io no puecha pechar mas vostra humilitat segre, e per ma paciensa l'Enamic venser, e, per los liams de vostra amor, daus liams de mos pecchatz puecha estre desliatz que seguramen puecha al jutgament devan vos apareichser et ab vos remaner ses fi. Amen.
A tercia, pessatz que a tal hora fo Jesu Crist crusifiatz de las lengas deus Jujieus, qui l'acuseren e·l dampneren davan Pilat, e dizian: "Crucifiga lo; el es colpables e dignes de mort." Puech apres, sos uelhs esbendeleren e ssa bela chara firian, e disian: "Prophetiza, qui es qui t'a firit?." Puech fo liatz a un pilar e batutz de cruels correadas tan que lo sancs li rivava per tot lo cors. Puech lo coroneren d'espinas tan que lo sancs [f. 276v] a chascuna espina en salhia. Puech lo jutgeren antosa mort. Pessatz donc que tot o sufrit per amor de nos, e digatz: Senher Dieus, Jesu Crist, qui, per vostra gran bontat a Dieu vostre Paere, per mi futz obediens duocha que a l'antosa mort de la crotz, ieo vos prec que obediensa me donetz per mi liar en vostre servizi que de liams de pechat puecha estre deliada, e qui per mi futz jutgatz a mort, de mort durabla[4] me gardetz, e qui per mi d'espinas futz coronatz, de vostra gracia me coronetz. Espandetz, dos Jesu, vostra gracia en mon cor; enserratz lo, enclavetz lo en vostra amor, qu'io puecha segre las estraessas de vostra passio, e los dalhiech de ma charn, qui son enamic

---

[2] *escharns*: MS escharnis.

[3] *apilat*: the verb *apilar* is generally given the meanings 'appuyer, élever, soutenir'. This is clearly not the sense here, which suggests the presence of a homonym. There is another example in the *Traduction de l'Evangile de Nicodème* (Suchier 1883:879-81): "Mantenen l'en a us pregatz / que la l'[la lansa] apile al costatz / de Jesu Cristz." This is the episode of Longinus, who takes the lance and pierces the side of Christ.

[4] *durabla*: MS durable.

so that it cannot separate itself from you, but rather remain in you eternally. Amen.

Prayer
At Prime, consider that at such an hour the priests and the leaders of the Jews assembled and asked Cayphas, who was the leader of the priests, to bring false witness against Jesus Christ on the cross, and they here mocked him by word and deed, and cruelly struck his beautiful face and exposed him to great shame, for they spat in his sweet face so that he suffered the blood and filth they spat mixed together on his beautiful face, and to such a degree that he looked like a leper; and then they led him away, vilely pierced, him who was their judge. Think therefore that he suffered all this for us, and say piously: [f. 276r] Ah! Lord God, Jesus Christ, way of patience and humility, make my heart at one with your humility and with the patience of your heart, whatever anyone says to me which is pleasing or displeasing to me, whether it be shame or villany, so that I may not sin but follow the example of your humility, and so that, through my patience I may vanquish the Adversary, and, through the bonds of your love, I may be freed from my sins in order to be certain of being able to appear before you at the judgement and remain with you eternally. Amen.

At Terce, think that at such an hour Jesus Christ was crucified by the tongues of the Jews, who accused him and condemned him before Pilate, and said: "Crucify him; he is guilty and deserves to die." Then afterwards, they blindfolded him and struck his beautiful face, and said: "Prophesy, who is it that struck you?" Then he was bound to a pillar and beaten with cruel whips so much so that the blood ran down his body in a flood. Then they crowned him with thorns so that [f. 276v] at each thorn blood flowed out. Then they condemned him to shameful death. Think therefore that he suffered all this for love of you, and say: Lord God, Jesus Christ, who through your great goodness to God your Father, you were for me obedient unto the painful death on the cross, I beg you to accord me obedience to bind me in your service so that I may be freed from the bonds of sin, and, you who were condemned to die for me, keep me from everlasting death, and you who were crowned with thorns for me, crown me with your grace. Spread, sweet Jesus, your grace throughout my heart; enclose it, nail it to your love, so that I may follow the paths of your passion, and put to flight the delights of my flesh, which are the enemies

a l'arma fazetz fuir. Gardatz me, dos Jesu, que,[5] per nulha aversitat qui en prosperitat me pogues venir, de vostra amor puecha flanchir, que no vos segua dessi que a la mort,[6] i ab vos en vostra dossor [f. 277r] remanha ses fi. Amen.

Oratios a miejdia
A miadia,[7] pessa[tz] que a tal hora fo nostre senher Jesu Critz pendutz en la crotz entre dos leiros, e sas mas e siei pe de gros claveus persat i a la crotz estachatz, e fors de las plajas corria lo dos sancs sobre la terra. Cossiratz donc que vos lo veetz davant vos pendre, tot son cors ensang[l]entat e a dolor de vos lhiorat, i aiatz pietat de lui, e regardatz lo dos Jesu, de cor plorant, que tant antosament pent entre dos leiros, qui fo i era Filhs de Dieu rei, e de raena qui fo maere e piocela, e tot per vos. E digatz devotament: veiatz aici qui anc mal ni pechatz no fetz, per mos pechatz es aichi pendutz, per cui dolor ieo soi garitz e de pena deliorat. E apres digatz:

Oratio a Dieu lo Paire, reis
Senher Dieus debonaere, paer omnipotens, regardatz vostre dos Filh, qui tan grant anta suefre per mi i a mi, chaetiva, per cui [atr]estals antas suefre, per mi mos pechatz perdonatz: sos pes descu[f. 277v]bers enblanchit, le[s] seos costatz plagatz; de sanc rovesit, son cors estendut, enredit,[8] la soa bela charn e·l seus beus visatges enpalvesit; li seo bel oilh la veuda i perderen, sas belas chambas vilment penden. Alas! E com li redrai de tan gran pena que per mi a sufertat: guayredo, certas, ieo, chaetiva, no sai. Apres aisso, tornatz vos al dos, si li digatz:

---

[5] *Gardatz ...que (... que)*: *que* introduces two subordinate clauses in which it governs first *puecha* (*flanchir*) and second *remanha*. Although they are at the same level of subordination, the first takes on a negative sense, 'prevent from [...]', while the second has a positive sense, 'assure the realisation of [...]'. The intervening clause, introduced by *que no vos segua*, is on a second level of subordination, being the negative consequence of the action expressed by *flanchir*. The two clauses at the first level of subordination are an illustration of a bifurcated syntactic model.

[6] For this aspect of the imitation of the life of Christ, cf. "Aichi deu quex voler morir, / nutz en la crotz" (Ricketts and Hershon 2003, *Breviari d'Amor*, 23957-58).

[7] *miadia*. I have not found this form elsewhere, but it is clearly Limousin.

[8] *enredit*. Cf. *Vie de St Alexis* (Suchier 1883: 856): "e tot son cors enregezitz." The form here is peculiar to the dialect, with loss of the intertonic syllable: *enre(ge)dit*.

of the soul. Sweet Jesus, whatever adversity may befall me in a time of prosperity, prevent me from turning away from your love, so as not to follow you to the point of death, so that I may remain eternally with you, [f. 277r] surrounded by your gentleness. Amen.

Prayer at midday
At midday, think that at such an hour Jesus Christ was hung from the cross between two robbers, and his hands and his feet were pierced by large nails and he was attached to the cross, and from his wounds his sweet blood ran onto the ground. Think then that you see him hanging before you, his entire body covered with blood and bound, to your lasting grief, and have pity on him, and look at sweet Jesus, weeping in your heart, hanging so ignominiously between two robbers, he who was ever Son of God the king and of the queen who was mother and maiden, and all for you. And say piously: See here the one who never did harm or sin, for my sins he is thus hanging, and through his pain I am healed and freed from torment. And afterwards say:

Prayer to God the Father, the king
Gentle Lord God, omnipotent Father, look on your sweet Son, who is suffering such great shame because of me and for me, wretch, for whom he is suffering such shame, pardon me my sins: his naked feet [f. 277v] white, his side wounded, reddened with blood, his body stretched out, stiffened, his beautiful flesh and his beautiful countenance pallid; his beautiful eyes thereby lost the ability to see, his beautiful legs hanging. Alas! And how shall I repay him for such great pain as he suffered for me: I, wretch that I am, I certainly know of no reward. After this, turn to the sweet one, and say to him:

Oratio ad Ihesum Christum

Senher Dieus, Jesu Crist, lavatz me en vostre sanc, e per las vostras preciosas plagas sanatz las plajas de m'arma e les pes persat de mon cor de la vostra amor. Mas volomtatz e mos desiers estachatz a la crotz de penedensa que mos cors sia ordenatz segont vostra volomtat, e li menbre de mon cors: en vostre servisi sian usat e, segont la regla de vostres comandamens, sian d'aichi avant governatz, que a vos qui etz mos Creadre puecha venir am vos e estar e viore ses fi. Amen.

[f. 278r] A ura nona,[9] cossiratz que Jesu Crist en la crotz pendia e greos penas suffria; dich qu'el avia set i hom aportet lhi a beore vinagre am fel mesclat a celui qui era fontana de dossor. Entorn hora de mengar, pessatz aisso e digatz:

Oratio ad Dominum Ihesum Christum

A! Senher Dieus, Jesu Crist, a cui neguna res mas bontatz e drechura no sabora, per vostra debonairetat perdonatz me tot quant ai pechat per desordenansa de mon gostamen, e per desordenat desier de beore e de mangar. E donatz me vertut de drecha abstinensa que per vertut d'atempransa puecha refrenar los malvatz desiers de b[e]ore e de mengar, aissi que amesuradamen[10] viore; puecha mon coratge a vos tot virar e·n vostra dossor maner e estar e repausar. Amen.

Autra Orazos a Jesu Christ

Pessatz eschamen que a tal hora Jesu Crist pendia en la crotz, e de doloirosas penas [fo] tormentatz, e dich [f. 278v] a son Paere: "Paer, en vostras mas comant mon esperit"; i aichi cel qui fo vita morit per vos qui futz mort, i a resussitar e de perdurabla mort a remer; regardatz donc vostre Creator e digatz de cor humil devotamen:

Oratio

Dieus de grant misericordia e de gran debonairetat, qui a ma lagesa volguet ressemlar que aichi ma lagesa poguessatz ostar, l'antosa mort de la croz, que jes no aviatz, d'esser vida per mi, chaetiva, suffrir, que mi de mort durabla poguessat deliorar per vostra gran pietat,[11] donatz me veraia dolor e peneden

---

[9] *a ura nona*: MS aurarona.
[10] *amesuradamen*: MS ameserudamen.
[11] *Dieus de grant* [...] *gran pietat*: this is another example of syntactic polyvalence, involving an accumulation of three constructions and a degree of interpenetration deriving from *suffrir*: 1) *suffrir* l'antosa mort; 2) *suffrir* la mort d'esser vida per mi (= *suffrir*, que la mort fos vida per mi); 3) la mort, que jes no aviatz, *suffrir*. See the

Prayer to Jesus Christ
Lord God, Jesus Christ, wash me in your blood, and through your precious wounds heal the wounds of my soul and the pierced feet of my soul with your love. Attach my wishes and my desire to the cross of penitence so that my body may be regulated according to your will, and also the limbs of my body: may they be used in your service, and according to the rule of your commandments, may they henceforth be controlled, so that I may come to you, who are my Creator, and stay and live with you eternally. Amen.

[f. 278r] At Nones, think that Jesus Christ was hanging on the cross and was suffering great torments; he said he was thirsty and he was brought vinegar mixed with gall, he who was the fount of sweetness. About the time of eating, think on this and say:

Prayer to the Lord Jesus Christ
Ah!, Lord God, Jesus Christ, who tastes of nothing but goodness and righteousness, through your gentleness forgive me for every sin I have committed through the excess of my taste, and through the excessive desire to drink and eat. And give me the the virtue of absolute abstinence so that by the virtue of temperance I may restrain the evil desires of drinking and eating, as well as living temperately; may I turn my heart totally to you and in your gentleness remain and stay and find repose. Amen.

Another Prayer to Jesus Christ
Think too that at such an hour Jesus Christ was hanging on the cross, and was tormented by grievous chagrins, and he said [f. 278v] to his Father: "Father, into your hands I commend my spirit"; and thus he who was life died for you who were dead, in order both to bring us back from the dead and also to save us from everlasting death; therefore look on your Creator and say piously with a humble heart:

Prayer
God of great mercy and great gentleness, who wished to imitate my baseness in order thereby to take away this baseness, and to suffer the shameful death of the cross, which you did not need to suffer, in order for it to be a source of life for me, wretched woman, so that you might liberate me from everlasting death by your great piety, give me the possibility of true suffering

---

translation.

sa far de mos pechatz ses fencha, e qu'io puecha far miralh de vostra dossa passio[12] a suffrir alcuna chausa per amor de vos, qui tant d'antas e de penas suffritz per mi, e qu'io puecha entendre lo pretz qui per mi fo donatz, qu'io no puecha mi mech perdre qui fui aitan char compratz com de vostre dos cors, qui maech valia que [f. 279r] totz lo mons, donatz me, dos Senher, qu'io puecha m'arma redre en vostras dossas mas, en vos i ab vos viore ses fi. Amen.

A vespras, pessatz que a tal hora fo Dieus, Jesus Cristz, abans que fos de la crotz devalatz, firitz d'una lansa duscha que al cor, per que atraiches la amor de vostre cor, aissi oratz donc e digatz:

Oratio
A! vita de mon cor, Dieus Jesus, m'amors e ma joia, perforatz privont mon cor de la lansa de vostra dossa amor qu'el de la frescha plaja de vostra passio e de vostra amor [sia] plajatz. De totas orduras e vilanias sia espurgatz qu'io, per nedes cossiers, a vos, en cui son tuch nede, puecha venir i am vos viore ses fi. Amen.

Oratio
A hora de completa devetz cossirar que a tal hora venc Joseps e Nicodemus e osteren lo cors Jesu Crist de la crotz, e mot dossament e ssuau traechen fors los clavels de las mas e da·us [f. 279v] pes, e, cum ilh ploreren tenrament, ilh baegaven los pes e las mas quant lo mesen el sepulcre. Aquesta chausa pessat e digatz devotamen:

Oratio
Mas dossors e ma vita, beus dos Jesu Cristz, talhatz de mon dur cor un lhuoc ont vos puechatz repausar, e donatz me qu'io puecha aquel estre que vos vuolhat en mi venir i ab mi estar e remaner, e qu'io puecha en la dossor de vos remaner i a vos venir, e io ja ab vos an er ses fi. Amen.

Oratio
Beos Senher Dieos, glorios Paere qui comandiest ta dossa maere a sen Joan l'Avangeliste per ta mort engoychoza e trista quant al pe de la crotz estava, e

---

[12] *donatz ...passio*: *donatz*, too, is followed by three different constructions: 1) *dolor*, direct object; 2) *[de] penedensa far*, 'give me the possibility to...'; 3) *qu'io puecha ...e qu'io puecha*, two consecutive clauses at a second level of subordination.

for my sins and of repenting honestly for them, and of mirroring your sweet passion so as to suffer something for love of you, who suffered so much shame and torment for me, and so that I may understand the debt that was paid for me in order that I may not be lost myself, I who was redeemed at such a high price as that of your sweet body, which was worth more than [f. 279r] the entire world, allow me, sweet Lord, to give up my soul into your sweet hands in order to live eternally in you and with you. Amen.

At Vespers, think that at such an hour God, Jesus Christ, before he was brought down from the cross, was struck by a lance in his heart, so that he might draw to him the love of your heart, therefore thus pray and say:

Prayer
Ah! life of my heart, God, Jesus, my love and my joy, pierce my heart deeply with the lance of your sweet love so that it be wounded by the fresh wound of your passion and of your love. May I be cleansed of all filth and baseness so that I, through pure thoughts, may come to you, in whom all thoughts are pure, and live with you eternally. Amen.

Prayer
At the hour of Compline you must think that at such an hour Joseph and Nicodemus came and took down the body of Jesus Christ from the cross, and most sweetly and gently pulled out the nails from his hands and [f. 279 v] feet and, as they wept tenderly, they kissed his feet and hands when they placed him in the sepulchre. Think on this thing and say piously:

Prayer
My sweetness and my life, beautiful sweet Jesus Christ, cut from my hard heart a place where you may take rest, and permit me to be the one you wish in order to come into me and be and remain with me, and that I may remain in your sweetness and come to you, and I may now and ever walk with you perpetually. Amen.

Prayer
Beautiful Lord God, glorious Father who entrusted your sweet mother to St John the Evangelist because of your anguished and sad death when she was at the foot of the cross, and

mot charamen te plorava quan li felo Joyeu t'aucizen en la sancta crot[z] te mezeu, en la sancta guarda de vos me coman yeo. Rey glorios, enapres sesta mortal via, me metes en ta companhia, qui nasquiest de la [f. 280r] verga maere, al regne am Dieo lo teo Paere. *Pater noster* digatz.

Oratio al Creador
Senher, de tota creatura verays Dieos totz poderos, vos crey yeo e aor e glorifi; aiatz merce de mi, si, Senher, a vos[13] a plagut que vos ayat facha la mia arma a vostra emagena e a vostra semblansa per aver los selestials bes, ni qu'e la mi'arma visques, e me regardan lo miralh de la vostra sanchta beneyta charn, de la qual beneyta charn viven li vostre beneyte angiel. A!, chars Senher, per aquela grant amor que vos avetz mostrat a la mi'arma e·l do de tant auta natura com vos m'avetz donat, da[tz] a la mi'arma, que vos fezetz quan la fezetz a vostra semblansa. A!, misericordios Senher, aparelhat la e cofortatz la de la vostra gracia, que mot es escura[14] e laga per los pechatz que yeo ay fachtz, e mot[15] es malamen chamjada[16] de tal com vos la fezet. Senher, qui es condumiers de redre be per mal, Senher, [f. 280v] no la vuolhas jutgar segon la toa drechura: Senher, ayatz ne merce segont la toa misericordia, e, Ssenher, osta ne tota lagesa de pecchat que la toa esmagena rremanha, clara e pura e resplandens d'esperital clardat. Senher, enlumina de la toa sanchta fe le meo entendemen, enbrassa de la toa sancht'amor la mia volontat, qu'eo te puecha entendre e auvir e servir a la toa honor e a la toa gloria e a profiech e a ssalvamen de la mi'arma, e que tu, Senher, te tenhas per pagat de la mia vita e de la mi'arma quan dal cor partra. Jesu Crist, Senher, veraes Dieus e veraes hom, Filh de Deo e Filh de la Verga Maria, Senher, vos lauvi e vos auri e vos glorifi e vos queri merse com al meo senhor, com al meo paere e com al meo fraere, dont a vos plac prendre companhie en la vostra natura, e volguet estre om per nos e esser com us de nos, for tan que vos fos sen pechat e si prezetz mort en vostra humanitat. A! [f. 281r], dos Jesu, per aquela grant amor que vos nos m[o]stretz quan volguet ressebre mort per amor de nos, vos queri, Senher, per la vertut de la vostra sanhta passio, que vos en aquesta vita me deffendat de pechat mortal e d'encombramen del Enamic, e la mi'arma, quan dal cor partra, guardat de mort durabla. Sanhs Esperitz, verays Dieus, larcs Senher, qui donat tota sanhtetat e tota gracia, vos

---

[13] *a vos*: MS a vos *a vos*: *a vos* expunctuated.
[14] *escura*: MS escurra: *r* expunctuated.
[15] *mot*: MS mort: *r* expunctuated.
[16] *chamjada*: MS chamnada.

wept for you very dearly when the treacherous Jews killed you yourself on the holy cross, into your holy protection I entrust myself. Glorious king, after this mortal life, place me in your company, you who were born of the [f. 280r] virgin mother, in the kingdom with God your Father. Say the Lord's Prayer.

Prayer to the Creator
Lord, true omnipotent God of every creature, I believe you and adore and glorify you; have mercy on me, if, Lord, it pleased you to have made my soul in your image and in your likeness in order to have the gifts of heaven, and so that you might dwell in my soul, looking at me as the mirror of your holy and blessed flesh, by which blessed flesh your blessed angels are sustained. Ah!, dear Lord, through that great love which you have shown my soul and the gift of such high nature as you have given me, give it to my soul, which you created when you created the soul in your likeness. Ah!, merciful Lord, provide it and comfort it with your grace, for it has become dark and ugly because of the sins which I have committed, and it is badly changed from what it was when you created it. Lord, who is wont to render good for evil, Lord, [f. 280v] do not judge it according to your justice: Lord, have mercy on it according to your mercy, and, Lord, take from it all the baseness of sin so that your image remains, bright and pure and shining with spiritual brightness. Lord, illuminate my understanding with your holy faith, embrace my will with your holy love, so that I may listen and hear and serve to your honour and to your glory and to the profit and salvation of my soul, and so that you, Lord, may consider yourself repaid by my life and my soul when it leaves the heart.

    Jesus Christ, Lord, true God and true man, Son of God and Son of the Virgin Mary, Lord, I praise you and adore you and glorify you and beg you for mercy as my lord, as my father and as my brother, I whom it pleased you to make your companion according to your nature, and wished to be a man for us and be like one of us, except that you were without sin yet you accepted death in your human form. Ah!, [f. 281r] sweet Jesus, through that great love which you showed us when you decided to receive death for love of us, I beg you, Lord, through the virtue of your holy Passion, to protect me from mortal sin and the obstacle of the Adversary, and, when it leaves my heart, keep my soul from everlasting death. Holy Spirit, true God, generous Lord, you who give all sanctity and all grace,

lauvi e aori e redi gracias e merces d'aysso que vos m'avetz donat, de la gracia que ieo ay resseubut al ssanht batisme, e m'avetz messa en cumenautat i en tot lo be de Sanhta Esglieya. Senher qui etz bontatz de totas[17] amors e de totas debonayretatz, per la vostra misericordia, si vos platz, perfazet en mi so que y avetz comensat. Honorabla chausa es a chascon obrier qu'el achabe aco qu'el a comensat. Senher, perfazetz me e fermatz lo meo cor en fe de charitat. Donatz me, Senher, per lo vostre sanht plazaer, los .vii. dos [f. 281v] de Sanht Esperit.[18] Senher, lo do de ssaviza vos queri, qu'ieo te ssapcha conoyscher coma senhor e coma paere drechurier. Senher, lo do d'entendemen vos queri, del entendemen esperital. Senher, lo do de cocelh vos queri, que tu me dones veray cocelh esperitalmen e corporalmen. Senher, lo do de fortalessa vos queri, qu'eo aya veraya forssa contra lo mon e contra l'Enamic e contra la charn. Senher, lo do de sciensa vos queri, qu'ieo sapcha governar lo meo cors e la mia arma a vostra volomtat. Senher, lo do de pietat vos queri, qu'ieo aya lo cor dos e ffranc enver vos e ver mon prueme e ves la mia arma. Senher, lo do de temor vos queri, qu'ieo vos sapcha doptar en tot quan faray ni diriey coma Dieo e coma senhor, qui avetz poder el cors e·n l'arma: en podet prendre aquela venjansa que vos plaera. Senher, plassa te per la toa misericordia que tu d'aquetz .vii. dos m'enlumines l'arma e [f. 282r] lo cors, que yeo, Senher, puecha sentir un petit d'aquela sanhta dossor que ssenten de vos li vostre privat amic, que lo cors de lor sen mielhs que la bocha no poria dire, quar, Senher, negus bes d'aquest mon amb aquel no poyria comparar. Senher, per la toa misericordia, aparelha la mia vita en estament en que la mia arma puecha sentir d'aquela sanhta dossor. Senher, ple d'umilitat, no·t desplassa si tan viels creatura ni tan pechayritz te requer tant auta chausa, que no fauc jes qu'io tropcha en mi, mas fauc o per la gran piatat c'om troba am ti — acom fay tant ostratgoza — e quar neguna arma

---

[17] *totas*: MS totos.

[18] *.vii. dos*: these are the seven gifts of the Holy Spirit, which, in the Middle Ages, were probably codified by Thomas Aquinas: wisdom (*ssaviza*), understanding (*entendemen*), counsel (*cocelh*), strength (*fortalesa*), knowledge (*sciensa*), piety (*pietat*) and fear (*temor* 25); cf. Isaias 11:2-3: "spiritus sapientiae et intellectus, spiritus consilii et fortitudinis, spiritus scientiae et pietatis, et replebit eum spiritus timoris Domini." In the Old Testament, they are referred to as different manifestations of the *spiritus*, while in the New Testament, they are gifts, *cf.*, especially, Ad Romanos 12:6: "Habentes autem donationes secundum gratiam, quae data est nobis, differentes ...," the link may have been made between these *donationes* and the seven gifts of the Holy Spirit, and confused with the *charismata*, of which there are nine, but which include wisdom and knowledge; see, for example, I Ad Corinthios 12:4-11.

I praise you and adore you and give thanks and gratitude for what you have given me, for the grace which I received at holy baptism, and you have put me in the community and in all that is good of Holy Church. Lord who are the goodness of all loves and all gentleness through your pity, if it please you, complete in me what you have begun. It is an honourable thing for each worker to complete what he has begun. Lord, make me complete and lock my heart in the faith of charity. Give me, Lord, for your holy pleasure, the seven gifts [f. 281v] of the Holy Spirit. Lord, I beg you for the gift of wisdom, so that I may learn to know you as lord and righteous father. Lord, I beg you for the gift of understanding, that of spiritual understanding. Lord, I beg you for the gift of counsel, so that you may give me true counsel spiritually amd physically. Lord, I beg you for the gift of strength, so that I may have true strength to resist the world and the Adversary and the flesh. Lord, I beg you for the gift of knowledge, so that I may control my body and my soul according to your will. Lord, I beg you for the gift of piety, so that my heart may be sweet and open towards you and towards my neighbour and towards my own soul. Lord, I beg you for the gift of fear, so that I may learn to fear you in all that I shall do and say, as God and as lord, you who have power over the body and over the soul; you may take such vengeance of them as it shall please you. Lord, may it please you through your pity to illuminate my soul and [f. 282r] my body with these seven gifts, so that I may feel, Lord, a little of that holy fragrance which your close friends sense in you, for the aroma of their bodies is better than words can say, for, Lord, no good from this world could compare with it. Lord, through your pity, put my life in such a state that my soul may smell of that holy fragrance; Lord, full of humility, do not be displeased that such a vile and sinful being should ask you for so elevated a thing, for I do not do so in order to find it in myself, but I do so through the great piety which is found in you — now I am so overweening — and because no soul no es entieramen complida ses aquestz[19] .vii. dos de la toa sanhta gracia. Sanhta Trinitatz, us sols Dieus totz poderos, Paere e Filhs e Sanhs Esperitz, tres personas, us Dieus complitz, Senher, a vos redi gracias e merces quar vos no m'avetz gurpida ni desemparada peos meos pechatz ni peos meos falhimens, ans [f. 282v] m'avetz dat trabalh a vos entendre e a vos amar aychi coma a viva forssa. Senher, qui m'avet facha tan digna e tan nobla com ieo [soy], qui soy facha a la vostra figura e[20] a la vostra semblanssa, — non ges, Senher, qu'ieo o aya desservit — mas per la t[o]a propra misericordia, Senher, plassa te, per la toa gracia, da piatat, e per la toa granda dossor, que a ti plassa que la mia arma sia escriota el libre de vita[21] davan la toa beneyta charn. Senher, per la toa misericordia, ordena los meos ans e los meos jorns e lo meo temps e la mia vita al teo servizi en aquela maniera que tu·t tenhas pro pajatz de la mi'arma quan dal cors partra. *Pater noster* digatz:[22]

Oratio
Dieus, beos Paere, ayatz merce de mi; Sanhta Trinitatz, us sols Dieus, reconciliatz mon cor en veraya fe, en veraya amor. Beos Senher Dieos, ieo vos quier cocelh en la honor, en la remenbransa d'aquel sanht aut cocelh que vos prezet de vostra propra saviza [f. 283r] quan tramezetz lo vostre sanht angiel Gabriel a la Vergena Maria dire e anomciar lo cocelh e la novela de nostra salut, que vos m'acocelhetz en aquela maniera, que sabetz que mestiers m'e[s] a l'arma e al cors, a la honor de vos e a salut de la mi'arma.

Oratio
Dieos, Senher, Paere ples de pietat, ayat pietat de la mi'arma en la honor e·n la rremenbransa d'aquela pietat que vos aguet del umanal lhinhatge quan trameset lo vostre beneyte Filh en terra per nos, e vos lo lioret en obediensa. Beos Senher Dieos, en la honor d'aquela pietat e d'aquel sanht glorios sagrament, vos queri ieo que vos aiat pietat de la mi'arma quan dal cors partra, e que m'endresset lo cors e la vita a la honor e dal vostre beneyte nom e a profiech de la mi'arma. *Pater noster* digatz.[23]

---

[19] *aquestz*: MS aquos.
[20] *a la vostra figura e*: repeated in MS
[21] This is the greeting which Jews give each other in the New Year. It may come from biblical apocryphal writings.
[22] *digatz*: MS dagatz.
[23] *digatz*: MS digath.

is quite complete without these seven gifts of your holy grace. Holy Trinity, one omnipotent God, Father and Son and Holy Spirit, three persons, one complete God, Lord, I give you thanks and gratitude for you have not abandoned or rejected me because of my sins or because of my failings, rather [f. 282v] you have given me the task of listening to you and loving you as a living force. Lord, who made me as worthy and noble as I am, I who am made in your image and in your likeness, — not, Lord, that I merited it — but through your own pity, Lord, may it please you, through your grace, by your pity, and through your great sweetness, may it please you for my soul to be inscribed in the book of life in witness of your blessed flesh. Lord, through your pity, regulate my years and my days and my time and my life to serve you in such a way that you are sufficiently recompensed by my soul when it leaves the body. Say the Lord's Prayer.

Prayer
Lord, beautiful Father, have mercy on me; Holy Trinity, one single God, reconcile my heart in true faith, in true love. Sweet Lord God, I seek counsel from you in honour and in remembrance of that holy inspired counsel that you took from your wisdom [f. 283r] when you sent your holy angel Gabriel to the Virgin Mary to tell and announce the counsel and news of our salvation, so that you counsel me accordingly, for you know that it is necessary to my soul and my body, in your honour and for the salvation of my soul.

Prayer
God, Lord, Father full of pity, have pity on my soul in honour and remembrance of that pity which you had for the human race when you sent your blessed Son on earth for us, and you bound him to obey. Beautiful Lord God, in honour of that pity and that glorious sacrament, I beg you to have pity on my soul when it leaves my body, and to make ready my body and my life in honour of your blessed Son and to the benefit of my soul. Say the Lord's Prayer.

Oratio
Dieus, Senher, Paere, ieo vos requier cocelh en la honor dal vostre beneyte Filh per la promessa qu'el fetz aus [f. 283v] seos apostols quan lor fetz nomnadamen paraula e lor dich: "Qualque chauza que vos queyrat al meo paere e nom de mi, vos l'aoret e la vos donara e la rresseb[r]et."[24] Beos Senher Dieus, aichsamen vos quier ieo que vos m'acocelhet el nom[25] dal vostre beneyte Filh en totas las mias doptansas, en totas las mias tribolatios a la honor de vos e de vostra ley e a ssalvament de la mi'arma, et quod detis mihi lumen sciencie, fervorem bone audiencie et linguam discretionis et sapiencie.

Oratio
Beos Paere, beos Senher Dieus, Filh de Dieo, ieo vos queri que vos me regardetz en veray regart e·n la honor e·n la rremenbransa d'aquel sanht regart don vos regardetz vostres sanhs dissiples quant vos dichetz: "Pater sancte, serva eos in nomine meo quos dedisti mihi." Amen.

Oratio
Beos Senher Dieus, dos Filh de Dieu, ieo vos requier que vos me regardetz en veray regart en la honor e·n la rremenbranssa d'aquel re[f. 284r]gart don vos regardetz las femnas qui vos seguian en plorant, quant vos portavatz la crotz a vostras espallas per nos e per vos; lor dichetz: "Filie Iherusalem, nolite flere super me,"[26] que, per aquel regart, me regardetz en veray cocelh a honor de vos i a salut de la mi'arma. Amen. *Pater noster*.

Oratio
Beos Senher Dieus, Paere glorios, io vos requier que vos me regardetz en la honor e·n la remenbransa d'aquel regart don[27] vos regardetz sen Peire quant el vos renejet tres vetz en una nuech e vos lo regardetz; el ac pietat e paor, e ploret am los vuelhs dal cor e am los vuelhs de l'arma, Senher, aichsi veraiament com aisso fo vers, e vos li tramezetz alegrier e cofortz de ressurectio e de la grant aparitio dal Sancht Esperit, vos requier ieo que vos me regardet en veraia salut e·n veray cocelh, a honor de vos e a salut de m'arma. *Pater noster* digatz.

---

[24] This quotation is based on Ioannem 14:12-14.
[25] *nom*: MS mom.
[26] See Lucas 23: 28.
[27] MS que.

Prayer
God, Lord, Father, I seek counsel from you in honour of your blessed Son through the promise he made to [f. 283v] his disciples when he addressed them by name and said to them: "Whatever you seek of my father in my name, you will have it and he will give it to you and you will receive it." Beautiful Lord God, equally I beg you to counsel me in the name of your blessed Son in all my fears, in all my tribulations in your honour and that of your law and for the salvation of my soul, and that you will give me the light of knowledge, the passion which comes from rapt attention and the tongue of discretion and wisdom.

Prayer
Beautiful Father, beautiful Lord God, Son of God, I beg you to look on me with the true gaze and in honour and in remembrance of that gaze with which you looked at your holy disciples when you said: "Holy Father, in my name serve them who you gave to me." Amen.

Prayer
Beautiful Lord God, sweet Son of God, I ask you to look on me with the true gaze in honour and in remembrance of that gaze [f. 284r] with which you looked on the women who were following you weeping, when you were carrying the cross on your shoulders for us and for you; you said to them: "Daughters of Jerusalem, do not weep for me," so that with that gaze, you may look on me in true counsel in honour of you and for the salvation of my soul. Amen. The Lord's Prayer.

Prayer
Beautiful Lord God, glorious Father, I ask you to look on me in honour and in remembrance of that gaze with which you looked on Saint Peter when he denied you three times in one night and you looked on him; he felt pity and fear, and wept with the eyes of the heart and with the eyes of the soul. Lord, as certainly as this was true, and you brought him the joy and comfort of resurrection and the wondrous appearance of the Holy Spirit, I ask you to look on me in true salvation and in true counsel, in your honour and for the salvation of my soul. Say the Lord's Prayer.

Oratio
Beos Senher Dieus, ples de pietat, io vos quier que vos me regar-[f. 284v]detz en aquela honor e·n aquela remenbransa d'aquel regart don nos regardem lo mont en salut, e vos regardet vostra maire e vostre disciple en gran tristeza, Senher, aichsi veraiament vos plassa gardar[28] per la vostra pietat de tot emcombrier la mi'arma e lo meo cors. Amen. *Pater noster* digatz.

Autra oratios a Jesu Christ
Senher Dieus, beos paer, ieo vos quier que vos me regardet en aquela remenbra[n]sa que vos regardet lo leiro en la crotz, quant vos li dichetz: "Amen, dico tibi, hodie mecum eris in paradiso,"[29] quant la mi'arma dal cors partra.
Beos Senher Dieus, io vos coman lo meo cors e la mi'arma, e vos pregui que vos me gardetz uei en aquest jorn de pechat e del encombrier del Enamic, e tostz los jorns que ieo vioriei, e que vos, Senher, me donetz far alcuna chauza que vos prengatz en grat e que sia a ssalut de la mi'arma.
Beos Senher Dieus, Paere, Jesu Crist [f. 285r] totz poderos, qui dal ventre de la Vergena Maria denhetz naecher per amor de nos, e rreceubetz mort en la crotz per nos e rressucitetz al tertz jorn, e vo·n pojetz lo jorn de l'Ascencio, e tramesetz lo jorn de la Pantacosta lo Sanht Esperit su·ous vostres apostols. E vendretz jutgar los bos e los mals, los mals en mort durabla, los bos en vita durabla. Senher, io vos pregi per aquela grant pietat e per aquela misericordia qui es en vos, que vos en aquel jorn aiatz pietat de la mi'arma e dal meo cors, qui en aquel jorn sara resors per auvir jutgament. Senher, en aquel jorn no vuolhas jutgar lo teo poble segon la toa drechura ni segon los lors defalhimens, ans, Senher, rregarda la toa misericordia e met nos en vita durabla. Amen.

Oratio
Beos Senher Dieus, Jesu Crist, Filh de la Vergena Maria, qui denhetz venir al seo beneite cors per la voluntat del Paere e per aministramen [f. 285v] de Sanht Esperit, Senher, qui, per ta naechensa e per la toa sanhta mort, as reduda vita e dilhiorat l'umanal linatge, Senher, delhiora me per ton sanht cors e per ta sanhta passio e per tas sanhtas plagas e per ta sanhta mort, de totz mos pechatz e de totz mos mals, e·m fai obedir a totz comandamens e no sostener, Senher, qu'io sia departida de la toa beneita gloria, ans te plassa que i trametas la mia arma, quan dal cors partra. Amen. *Pater noster*.

---

[28] MS regardar.
[29] See Luc. 23:43.

Prayer
Beautiful Lord God, full of pity, I beg you to look on me [f. 284v] in honour and remembrance of that gaze with which we looked on the world in salutation, and you looked on your mother and your disciple in great sadness, Lord, thus may it truly please you through your pity to protect my soul and my body from every obstacle. Amen. Say the Lord's Prayer.

Another prayer to Jesus Christ
Lord God, beautiful Father, I beg you to look on me in remembrance of when you looked on the robber on the cross, when you said to him: "Truly, I say to you, today you will be with me in Paradise," when my soul leaves my body.
Beautiful Lord God, I commend to you my body and my soul, and I pray to you to keep me on this day from sin and from the obstacle of the Adversary, and all the days I shall live, and, Lord, to permit me to do something which you find pleasing and which may be to the salvation of my soul.
Beautiful Lord God, Father, omnipotent Jesus Christ [f. 285r], who deigned to be born from the womb of the Virgin Mary for love of us, and underwent death on the cross for us and rose on the third day, and ascended from there on Ascension day, and sent the Holy Spirit unto your disciples on the day of Pentecost. And you will come to judge the good and the bad, the bad into everlasting death, the good into eternal life. Lord, I pray to you, through the great pity and compassion which are in you, that on that day you take pity on my soul and on my body, which on that day will be brought back to life to hear the judgment. Lord, on that day do not seek to judge your people according to your law nor according to their failings, but rather, Lord, look to your compassion and give us everlasting life. Amen.

Prayer
Beautiful Lord God, Jesus Christ, Son of the Virgin Mary, who deigned to come into her blessed body through the will of the Father and through the ministration [f. 285v] of the Holy Spirit, Lord, you who, through your birth and through your death, have given back life to the human race and freed it, Lord, free me, through your holy body and your holy passion and your holy wounds and your holy death, from all my sins and all my ills, and have me obey your commandments, and not allow me, Lord, to be separated from your blessed glory, but rather may it please you to take my soul there, when it leaves my body. Amen. The Lord's Prayer.

Oratios
Beos Senher Dieus, qui per nostre salvamen e per nos remer de la preio dal Diable, on totz lo mons era enpreijonatz, denhiest prendre charn humana de la Vergena sanhta Maria, si verament, com ieo crei, es verei c'om sagra sobre l'autar lo teo precios cors e ton precios sanc, e que la ostia esdeve la toa beneita charns, e lo vis e l'aigua lo teo sancs precios, per la vertut de las sanhtas paraulas c'om [f. 286r] i di, entre las mas del preveire. Beos Senher Dieus, aichi veraiament te queri ieo que tu·m fasas verai perdo e veraia remissio de totz los pechatz qu'io iei fachtz, en qualque maniera que fachs los aia, en cossiran o en parlan o en obran, Senher, fasetz me misericordia e perdo. Beus Senher Dieus, qui dichist que nulh hom no pogues estre salvatz si aquilh no qui mengarian la vostra carn e beorian lo vostre precios sanc, aichi veraiament com aesso es vers, e ieo o crei fermament, que aqui sia lo teus verais cors e tos verais sancs qui es entre las mas dal preveire, e negus, tan sia dignes, re no·i pot esmendar, ni negus, tan sia pechaeres, re no·i pot afolar,[30] te queri, qualque pechairitz que·m sia, que·m defendatz mon cors e m'arma e totz mos amics e totas mas amigas e totz mos befasedors d'enuoj e de mal e de pechat e dal poder al Diable. Corpus Domini nostri, Ihesu Cristi, peredu [f. 286v] catz nos sine macula ad vitam eternam.

Aquesta oraso di om al secret de la messa: ista oratio de anonyma.
Gracias ago tibi, Domine Ihesu Criste, qui grevi crucifixi voluisti pro redemptione mundi, a Iudeis reprobari, a Iuda osculo tradi, vinculis alligari et quasi agnus innocens ad victimam duci, atque[31] in conspectu Pilati offertus[32] a falsis quoque testibus accusari, flagellis et opprobriis vexari et conspui, spinis coronari, colaphis cedi, in cruce elevari atque latrones deputari,[33] clavorum quoque aculeis perforari, lancea vulnerari, felle et aceto potari. Tu, Domine, per has ferocissimas penas ab omnibus penis inferni et a temptationibus Diaboli me peccatricem libera,[34] et momenibus bonis multiplica et a criminibus conserva et semper a

---

[30] *pot afolar*: MS pot *esmendar* afolar: *esmendar* expunctuated.
[31] *atque*: MS atz.
[32] MS offerti.
[33] *latrones deputari*. This phrase mirrors Luc. 22:37, and in the Vulgate reads: "cum iniquis deputatus est." The King James version has "was reckoned with transgressors." At first glance, the structure *latrones deputari* is surprising. However, the manuscript reading has been respected, given that *deputari* may have been classed as a verb of incomplete predication.
[34] *libera*: MS liberea: *e* expunctuated.

Prayer
Beautiful Lord God, who for our salvation and to save us from the prison of the Devil, where all the world was imprisoned, deigned to take on human flesh from the holy Virgin Mary, if, truly, it is true, as I believe, that one consecrates on the altar your precious body and your precious blood, and that the host becomes your blessed flesh, and the wine and the water your precious blood, through the power of the holy words which are said there [f. 286r], in the hands of the priest. Beautiful Lord God, as truly I beg you to give me true pardon and true remission for all the sins I have committed, however I committed them, in thought or in speech or in act, Lord, show me pity and forgiveness. Beautiful Lord God, who said that no man could be saved except those who would eat your flesh and drink your precious blood, just as, indeed, this is true, and I believe it firmly, that here is your actual body and your actual blood which is in the hands of the priest, and no one, however worthy he may be, can change anything in it, and no one, however much a sinner he may be, can harm it, I beg you, however sinful I may be, to defend my body and my soul and all my friends, both men and women, and all my benefactors from grief and ills and sin and from the power of the Devil. Body of our Lord Jesus Christ, lead [f. 286v] us without a stain into eternal life.

This prayer is said in the mystery of the Mass: this prayer of an anonymous woman.
I give you thanks, Lord Jesus Christ, you who were willing to be painfully crucified for the redemption of the world, to be mocked by the Jews, to be betrayed by Judas with a kiss, to be tied by cords and led as an innocent lamb to be sacrificed, and, placed before Pilate, and also accused by false witnesses, tormented and vilified by scourges and taunts, crowned with thorns, brought down by blows, raised on the cross and reckoned among robbers, and also pierced by the points of nails, wounded with a lance, made to drink vinegar with gall. You, Lord, through these most grievous torments free me, sinner that I am, from all the pains of hell and from the temptations of the Devil, and multiply in me good impulses and keep me from criminal acts and for ever

peccatis munda et per sanctam crucem tuam salva me, tuam creaturam, semper, et custodi, et illuc perduc me, miseram peccatricem, quo perduxisti tecum [f. 287r] latronem cruci fixum et omnes tui sancti nominis confessores, qui cum Patre et Sancto Spiritu vivis et regnas Deus per omnia secula seculorum. Amen.

Oratio ad Ihesum
Domine, Ihesu Criste, fili Dei unius, rex eterne glorie qui, in cruce pendens per salute[m] mundi, virginem, matrem, Iohanni[35] discipulo comendasti, concede pro tua pietate ut ipsi me in hac vita custodiant ab omni malo, liberent Mariam tuam michi, mi plorent, ad exitum meum occurrant et in vitam eternam introducant per te, Ihesu Christe, salvator mundi, qui vivis et regnas Deus per omnia secula seculorum. Amen.

References

Guillaume, Paul, ed. 1887. *Istoria Petri & Pauli: mystère en langue provençale du XVe siècle*. Gap: Société d'Etudes des Hautes-Alpes; Paris: Maisonneuve.

Guillaume, Paul, ed. 1887-88. "Istorio de Sanct Poncz," *Revue des Langues Romanes* 31, 317-420, 461-553; 32, 5-24, 250-85.

Hasenohr, Geneviève. 2000. "Un *Donat* de dévotion en langue d'oc du XIIIe siècle: le *Liber divini amoris*." *Cahiers de Fanjeaux* 35, *Eglise et culture en France méridionale (XIIe-XIVe siècle)*, 219-43. Toulouse: Privat.

Ricketts, Peter. 2003. "A woman's poem: the *Priere de Theophile* in Occitan," *Offrande du Coeur: Medieval and Modern Studies in Honour of Glynnis Cropp*. Christchurch: Canterbury University Press.

Ricketts, Peter and Hershon, Cyril, ed. 2004. *Le Breviari d'Amor de Matfre Ermengaud*, tome IV. Turnhout: Brepols.

Suchier, H., ed. 1883. *Vie de St Alexis*, in *Denkmäler provenzalischer Literatur und Sprache*. Halle: Niemeyer, 125-55.

Suchier, H., ed. 1883. *Traduction de l'Evangile de Nicodème* in *Denkmäler provenzalischer Literatur und Sprache*, 879-81. Halle: Niemeyer.

---

[35] *Iohanni*: MS virgini. The close juxtaposition of *virginem* suggests that the scribe either misread or misunderstood the sense of the clause. The remark clearly refers to Christ, on the cross, entrusting his mother to St John; cf. Ioannem 19:26-27.

cleanse me from sins and through your holy cross save me, your creature, always, and watch over me, and take me, miserable sinner, to that place where you took with you [f. 287r] the robber nailed to the cross and all those who acknowledge your holy name, you who with the Father and the Holy Spirit live and reign God, for ever more. Amen.

Prayer to Jesus
Lord, Jesus Christ, Son of the one God, king of eternal glory, you who, hanging on the cross for the salvation of the world, entrusted the virgin, your mother, to John the disciple, grant through your pity that they themselves may protect me from every ill in this life, that they may yield your Mary to me, that they may weep for me, that they may be at hand when I die and take me into eternal life for you, Jesus Christ, saviour of the world, who live and reign God, for ever more. Amen.

8
'Confundamus ibi linguam eorum': Some Accounts of the Tower of Babel in Medieval Castilian Literature
ALAN DEYERMOND

TWO OF THE MOST remarkable transformation scenes in the Bible — scenes that have a striking typological relationship — are concerned with language: in the Tower of Babel episode (Genesis 11:1–9) mankind's single language is suddenly and catastrophically split into many languages that are mutually incomprehensible. At Pentecost (Acts 2:1–13), the apostles preach in a single language that is miraculously comprehensible to people of all nations. For an hour or so, the curse of Babel is lifted.[1] These two episodes are — and were in the Middle Ages — among the best known in the Bible.

The story of the Tower of Babel occurs early in the Old Testament, so early that, like the story of the Flood which immediately precedes it, it is perceived as one of the aftershocks of the Fall (the builders are called 'los fijos de Adam'). There are many medieval Castilian translations of the Old Testament, some made by Jews from the Hebrew text, others by Christians from the Vulgate (see Morreale 1969), so any choice of quotation must be arbitrary. I quote from an

---

[1] This typological relationship (see Auerbach 1959) was present in iconography and in literature from the early centuries of the Church: 'In the sixth century, Rusticus Helpidius composed explanatory inscriptions for a series of typological frescoes. These frescoes have disappeared, but the verses still exist. [...] the Tower of Babel and the confusion of tongues correspond to Pentecost [...]' (Mâle 1978:161). For commentary on the Tower of Babel and on Pentecost, see Guthrie and Motyer 1970:91–92 and 974–75. Hugo Gressmann presents the Tower as emblematic of Babylonian religion in opposition to that of Israel (1928). Northrop Frye points out (1982:158 and 230) that the undoing of the curse of Babel is promised in Zephaniah [in the Vulgate, Sophonias] 3:9: 'For then I will restore to the peoples a pure language, that they may all call on the name of the Lord, to serve him with one accord.'

early-fifteenth-century manuscript of a translation from the Hebrew text made in the late thirteenth or early fourteenth century (see Littlefield 1992:xx):

> E era toda la tierra de un lenguaje, and de unas palabras. [...] E dixeron: 'Dad acá, fagamos adobes and quememos los en el fuego.' E fue aellos el ladrillo por piedra, and la cal fue aellos por barro. E dixeron: 'Dad acá, hedifiquemos una cibdat, con una torre cuya cabeça sea enlos cielos, and fagamos de nós allí fama que nos derraremos por la faz de toda la tierra.' E descendió el Señor para ver la cibdat and ala torre que hedificavan los fijos de Adam. E dixo el Señor: 'Ahé, el pueblo uno and un lenguaje han todos, and esto han començado a fazer. E agora non será dellos vedado todo quanto començaron de fazer. Dad acá, descendamos and perturbemos ende sus lenguajes, que non entiendan el uno el lenguaje del otro.' E derramó los el Señor dende por la faz de toda la tierra [...]²

A noteworthy feature of this narrative is that the overweening ambition of the builders ('fagamos de nós allí fama que nos derraremos por la faz de toda la tierra') is ironically echoed in their punishment ('derramó los el Señor dende por la faz de toda la tierra'): instead of the hoped-for imperial expansion there is a helpless scattering.

The Biblical story is greatly expanded in a universal chronicle that interleaves sacred with secular history: the *General estoria*, composed at the court of Alfonso X, el Sabio. Here, the narrative is amplified from other sources (Ovid, Josephus, and Petrus Comestor are cited).³ We are told in Part I, book ii, chapters 21–22 that:

> Desí razonaron desta guisa entressí: 'Pues que éste es el acuerdo que tomamos sobresto non ay tal como que fagamos una torre muy grand e muy alta e muy fuert pora ello.' Desí dixieron se sobresto catando se unos a otros: 'Venid e labremos ladriellos, e cogamos los donde fagamos aquella torre [...] tan alta que alcance fastal cielo. [...]'
>
> Et esta torre punnavan ellos en fazer la tan alta, non tan solament pora

---

² Littlefield 1992:7. In all quotations from medieval Spanish I regularize the use of *i/j*, *u/v*, and *c/ç*. I supply accents according to modern scholarly convention (e.g. distinguishing between *a* 'to' and *á* 'has'). Obvious misprints are, with one exception, silently corrected.

³ On the relationship between Petrus Comestor and the *General estoria* see Rico 1984:48–64.

amparar se enella del diluvio, mas por llegar tanto al cielo que pudiessen alcançar por ý los saberes delas cosas celestiales. E aun, segund cuenta Ovidio enel primer libro delos quinze del su Libro Mayor que los llamava ý gigantes, su voluntad era de echar ende alos dioses, fascas alos ángeles, e seer ellos ende sennores [...] e ésta era la su grand locura.

Et dela su mala entención e mal seso, e del su mal fecho pesó a Dios; e desque los vio assí enloquecer, maguer quelo merescién, segund dize Josepho en el seseno capítulo, non quiso destroýr los todos en uno [...] Onde, assí como cuenta Moysén en el onzeno capítulo de Génesis, descendió Dios pora veer la torre e la cibdat que avién començado a fazer fijos de Adam; e dize maestre Pedro en el capítulo dela torre de Babel que descendió Dios por veer la torre, fascas por tomar cabeça en qué manera los penasse.

Desque cató Dios aquella obra dixo: 'Evat que un pueblo es éste, e uno el lenguage de todos; e comenzaron esto a fazer, de más que se non partieran de sos cuydares malos fasta que los cumplan por obra; mas venid e descendamos allá e confondamos les el lenguage que an agora todos uno, et mezclemos gele de guisa que, maguer que se oyan, que se non entiendan aun que estén muy de cerca unos dotros.'

Sobresto que dize Moysén 'venid' departe la Glosa que lo dixo la Trinidat assí mesma como en el primer capítulo del Génesis 'fagamos ell omne.' Mahestre Pedro departe enel capítulo desta torre Babel quelo dixo Dios alos ángeles. Sevilla Cassandra, segund retraye Josepho en el seseno capítulo, dize ende assí: seyendo todos los omnes de un lenguage fizieron una torre muy alta pora sobir por ella al cielo, mas los dioses enviaron vientos que trastornaron la torre e la destroyeron; e partieron a cada uno el lenguage que era antes uno comunal de todos, e diz que de guisa fue partido que ninguno de quantos se ý acertaron, non ovo ý que un lenguage todo entero retoviesse nin que sopiesse dezir nombre nin palabra de toda cosa, menos de non aprender e tomar ende alguna ayuda dell otro su vezino.

Sobresta razón fabla mahestre Pedro en este departimiento dun lenguage en muchos, e dize que non fizo ý Dios ninguna cosa de nuevo, ca las razones e las sentencias delas palabras unas fincaron en todas las gentes mas que les partió allí las maneras e las formas de dezir las, de guisa que non sopiessen los unos qué dizién los otros nin que querién, e quedarié luego la obra. [...]

Onde dize Moysén enel onzeno capítulo quelos partió Dios daquel logar por todas las tierras desta guisa: que quando ell uno demandava ladriellos ell uno le dava bitumen, et quando ell otro pidié bitumen ell otrol aduzié agua, et quando ell otro dizié agua éstel trayé una de las ferramientas que ý tenién o alguna otra cosa, de guisa que nunca ell uno dava lo que ell otrol pidié, et quedaron de fazer la cibdat e la torre. [...] (Solalinde 1930:42a–43b)

The most obvious difference is, of course, in the length of the accounts: even this extensive quotation is only part of the *General estoria*'s account, which runs to over 1000 words, as against the 200-word Biblical narrative in the Escorial manuscript (the Vulgate narrative has some 130 words). The Escorial manuscript's account is far from being perfunctory: it includes a good deal of direct speech (50 per cent, a much higher proportion than in the *General estoria* version). Nevertheless, the speeches in the *General estoria* are longer, not because they are supplemented from non-Biblical sources but because of stylistic amplification. This can be seen most clearly in God's words when he sees what men are doing: although the substance is the same in the two texts, and although there is a close correspondence in some of the words, the speech in the *General estoria* has nearly twice as many words. Another obvious cause of the difference in length of the two accounts is that the *General estoria* adds to the Biblical narrative ('como cuenta Moysén en el onzeno capítulo de Génesis') material from other sources: 'segund cuenta Ovidio [...] segund dize Josepho [...] e dize maestre Pedro', with, in each case, a fairly precise reference to the source text. The most significant difference, however, is that men's pride, which in the Biblical account is relatively harmless vanity ('fagamos de nós allí fama que nos derraremos por la faz de toda la tierra'), is presented in the *General estoria* as Promethean blasphemy: 'mas por llegar tanto al cielo que pudiessen alcançar por ý los saberes delas cosas celestiales.' This interpretation is reinforced by Ovid's words about the giants: 'su voluntad era de echar ende alos dioses, fascas alos ángeles, e seer ellos ende sennores.'[4]

A century and a half later, another universal chronicle, this time in verse – the *Siete edades del mundo* (c. 1416: see Conde 1999:22) of Pablo de Santa María –, retells the story:

---

[4] Northrop Frye, in the fifth chapter of *Words with Power*, sees the Tower as a demonic parody of the stairway to Heaven (1992:144–87), and he stresses the association with language:

> We notice that the contrast between the central image of connection between heaven and earth and its demonic parody or ironic negation is bound up with the use of language. (154)

En aqueste tiempo, primero que fuessen
éstos repartidos en tierra ninguna,
la fabla de todos e lengua era una,
antes que los lenguajes se repartiessen;
e como de tierra de oriente partiessen,
vinieron en el campo de Senaar,
adonde començaron a fabricar
la gran Babilonia do se defendiessen.
En aquel logar luego fue començada
aquesta cibdad de todos juntamente,
en uno con Cus e Nembrot el valiente,
donde su memoria fuesse celebrada;
e veyendo qu'era de todos tan loada
dixeron: 'No es bien qu'en tal cosa aya falta,
fagamos en ella una torre tan alta
que llegue al cielo después de acabada.'
Veyendo el Señor aquello que pensaron
de poner en obra los fijos de Adán,
dixo: 'Tales son ellos que non querrán
dexar de fazer lo que ya començaron.
Por ende, pues ya que tal tema tomaron,
ellos querrán la torre acabar:
vayamos e descendamos a mudar
la lengua que todo fasta aquí fablaron.'
En aquellos tiempos, quando se labrava
aquella cibdad e torre que fazían,
por sola una fabla todos se regían,
que otra ninguna nunca se fablava;
e quando quiera que alguno demandava
de encima o de baxo lo que conviniesse,
ni el uno sabía lo quel' respondiesse
ni el otro tampoco lo que le embiava.
En esta manera la torre cesó,
que non se pudo más en ella fazer
porque Dios les quiso dar a entender
el grand pecado que allí se cometió,
e por eso luego el Señor les partió
su lengua primera en diversos lenguajes,
e fueron salidos de allí los linajes
de quien todo el mundo después se pobló.[5]

---

[5] Stanzas 52–57; Conde 1999:282–83. The anonymous reworking of c.1460 is essentially unchanged for these stanzas (Conde 1999:356), but adds glosses to stanzas

This passage, which is based on Genesis 11, is unusual in its reticence about the motives of the Tower's builders: 'fagamos en ella una torre tan alta / que llegue al cielo después de acabada' (54gh), because a city as fine as theirs needs an impressive monument. The Escorial Bible's account, as we have seen, attributes the project to a desire for fame and for a power that will extend to all lands.[6] The *General estoria* ascribes a triple motive: to protection from another Flood ('pora amparar se enella del diluvio') and a desire to attain knowledge of heavenly things ('alcançar por ý los saberes delas cosas celestiales') is added, on Ovid's authority, 'su voluntad era de echar ende alos dioses, fascas alos ángeles, e seer ellos ende sennores': first a wish to evade God's vengeance, then the sin of Adam and Eve (attaining forbidden knowledge), and finally the sin of Lucifer (gaining power in Heaven).[7] In comparison with this, the civic pride mentioned in Pablo de Santa María's version of the story seems harmless enough.

Earlier than any of these texts is the *Libro de Alexandre*, written in the first years of the thirteenth century (see Arizaleta 1999). Its principal sources are from late-twelfth-century France, Gautier de Châtillon's *Alexandreis* and the *Roman d'Alexandre*. At well over 10000 lines, it is the longest as well as the earliest work of the school known as the *mester de clerecía*, and its length is in substantial measure due to the poet's fondness for digression. Thus, when Alexander's army has crossed into Asia and comes to the site of Troy, 'fizo el rey sermón / [...] enpeçó la estoria de Troya a fondón' (st.332; Cañas 1988: 202) and he gives his soldiers an extensive account of the Trojan war. This occupies 438 stanzas, or 1752 lines: at 16 per cent of the poem, it is the longest digression, but others are of impressive length. When the Greeks take Babylon, the poet gives his readers a 74-stanza excursus on the city and its history, including the Tower of Babel:

---

55 and 57.

[6] This corresponds to the words of the Vulgate: 'et celebremus nomen nostrum antequam dividamur in universas terras' (11:4).

[7] Protection against another Flood is not in the Biblical account. It is implied in Book II of the *Alexandreis*, and R. Telfryn Pritchard suggests (1986:77) that Gautier de Châtillon took it from a Latin version of Josephus, *Antiquities of the Jews*, or from Petrus Comestor's *Historia scholastica*. Both of these works are cited as sources in the *General estoria*'s Tower of Babel narrative, and it is likely that one or other of them supplied this element of the story. This motive is also found in Jewish tradition, e.g. the *Sepher hayashar*, written in Spain in the twelfth century (Bañeza Román 1994:106–07). Peter Dronke examines Dante's treatment of the giants' lust for power, and of their punishment, in the light of Patristic and medieval Latin traditions (1986: 39–54).

Creo que bien podiestes alguna vez oïr
que quisieron al cielo los gigantes sobir,
fizieron una torre — non vos cuido fallir —,
non ha quien la pudiesse mesurar nin medir.
  Vio el Criador que fazién grant locura,
metió en ellos cisma e grant mala ventura,
non conocié ningunt omne de su natura,
ovo sí a seer por su mala ventura.
  Fasta essa sazón toda la gent que era
fablava un lenguaje e por una manera,
en ebraico fablavan una lengua señera,
non sabién ál fablar nin escrivir en cera.
  Metió Dios entre ellos tamaña confusión
que olvidaron todos el natural sermón;
fablavan sendas lenguas cad' una en su son,
non sabié un del otro quel dizié o que non.
  Si uno pedié agua, el otro dava cal;
el que pediá mortero, dávanle el cordal;
lo que dizié el uno, el otro fazié ál;
ovo toda la obra por ende a ir mal.
  Non se podién por guisa ninguna acordar,
ovieron la lavor por esso a dexar,
ovieron por el mundo todos a derramar,
cad' un por su comarca ovieron a poblar.
  Assí está oy día la torre empeçada,
pero de fiera guisa sobra mucho alçada,
por la confusión que fue en ellos dada,
es toda essa tierra Babilonia llamada.
  Setenta e dos[8] fueron los onbres mayorales,
tantos son por el mundo los lenguajes cabdales,
ca est girgonz que traen, estos lenguajes tales,
sonse controbadiços entre los menestrales.
  Los unos son latinos, los otros son ebreos,
los unos dizién griegos, a los otros caldeos,
a otros dizen áraves e a otros sabeos,
a los otros egipcios, a otros avaneos.

---

[8] Cañas 1988 reads 'Sesenta e dos,' but this must be a simple misprint, since the reading in both manuscripts is 'setenta.'

> Otros dizen ingleses, otros son de Bretaña,
> escotes e irlandos, otros de Alemaña;
> los que biven en Galia fablan de otra maña,
> non es con éstos Siria en lenguaje calaña.
> Otros son los de Persia, otros son los indianos,
> otros los de Samaria, otros son los medianos,
> otros los de Panfilia e otros los yrcanos,
> otros son los de Frigia e otros los libianos.
> Otros los dizen partos, otros elamitanos,
> otros son capadocios, otros ninivitanos,
> otros son cireneos, otros cananitanos,
> otros los almoçones, e otros los citanos.
> El omne que crïado fuesse en Balilonia
> de duro entendrié la lengua de Iconia;
> más son de otros tantos que cuenta la estoria,
> mas yo pora saberlos de seso non he copia.
> (st.1505–17; Cañas 1988:399–401)[9]

Such a long quotation, most of it an enumeration, does not make for easy reading, but only if the passage is quoted in full can the difference between the *Alexandre* poet's treatment of the Tower of Babel and that of the later texts – Escorial Bible, *General estoria, Siete edades del mundo* – be fully appreciated. The difference is remarkable: the outline of the story is the same: 'quisieron al cielo los gigantes sobir, / fizieron una torre [...] Vio el Criador que fazién grant locura,/ metió en ellos cisma [...] fablavan sendas lenguas cad' una en su son, / non sabié un del otro quel dizié o que non. [...] ovieron la lavor por esso a dexar, / ovieron por el mundo todos a derramar [...].' The centre of interest, however, is very different: the confusion of tongues, rather than a substantial part of the narrative (18 per cent in the Escorial Bible, 28 in the *Siete edades del mundo*, and 38 in the *General estoria*), here dominates it, with 85 per cent of the passage. The overweening pride of the sons of Adam, the building of the Tower, its interruption, and the punitive scattering of the builders, which are central to these later accounts both thematically and in their proportion of the narrative, are, in the *Libro de Alexandre*, not much more than a frame for the splintering of language. This is reinforced by the interest shown in the languages spoken in Babylon in Alexander's time, and the poet's insistence that the diversity of

---

[9] Francisco Marcos Marín (1983) makes a detailed linguistic analysis of this passage, and César Bañeza Román studies it in relation to its sources (1994:95–109).

languages impedes communication among the inhabitants of the city, that the punishment of Babel continues many generations after the fall of the Tower:

> Qui todos los lenguages quisiesse aprender,
> allí podrié de todos certedumbre saber;
> mas ante podrié viejo desmeollado seer
> que la tercera parte pudiés' él aprender.
> Por quanto es la villa de tal buelta poblada,
> que los unos a otros non se entienden nada,
> por tanto es de nombre de confusión honrada,
> ca Babilón *confusio* es en latín llamada.
> (st.1521–22; 402)

Even more striking than the percentage of the episode devoted to language is the enumeration of the languages into which human speech was divided: of the seventy-two languages (st.1512a), thirty-two are named in the following five stanzas.[10] In the other three narratives discussed above, not one of the languages is mentioned. The idea did not, however, begin with the Spanish poet. The *Libro*'s main source at this point is the *B* version of the *Roman d'Alexandre*, which contains a list of fifty-two post-Babel languages (ll. 7806–32; see Michael 1970:202–03). The reduction in the number of languages is not surprising: Raymond S. Willis says that 'the Spanish poet [...] tended to condense digressive passages of the *Alexandreis* which contained catalogues of Biblical names' (1931:38, endorsed by Michael 1970:89), and the same could well have happened here. Willis says that 'The lists of languages are not identical, but, nevertheless, bear a distinct resemblance to one another' (1935:27), and he suggests that the difference could be explained by the fact that 'the story of the Tower of Babel enjoyed a considerable vogue, circulating in many different forms, one of which is found in manuscript *L*' (27 n. 1; see La Du 1937).

There is a striking parallel between the *Libro de Alexandre*'s list of languages and a Biblical passage, but that passage is to be found not in Genesis but in the Acts of the Apostles 2:3–11, which I quote from a Castilian translation of the Vulgate (probably of the third quarter of the thirteenth century: see Montgomery and Baldwin 1970:5):

---

[10] This number occurs elsewhere in medieval Spanish: the Donzella Teodor tells the king that 'deprendí más los setenta e dos lenguages que son por el mundo, así de cristianos como de judíos e moros' (Mettmann 1962:109).

E apparecieron les lenguas departidas assí cuemo fuego, e posó sobre cada un dellos. E fueron todos llenos de Spíritu Sancto, e compeçaron de fablar en muchas lenguas, assí cuemo el Espíritu Sancto les dava a fablar.

En Jherusalem moravan judíos, religiosos de toda nación que so el cielo es. Fecho el son desta voz, ayuntós' mucha yent, e maravillaron se, ca los oyén fablar cada uno en su lengua. Espavorecién todos e maravillavan se, diziendo: '¿No son galileos todos estos que fablan? ¿E cuemo los oýmos fablar cada uno en nuestra lengua en que naciemos? Partos e medos e elamitas, e los que moran en Mesopotamia, en Judea e Capadocia, Ponto e Asia, Frigia e Pamphilia, Egipto e tierras de Libia, que es cerca de Cirenen, e los romanos avenedizos, judíos e convertidos, cretos e árabes, oýmos los fablar en nuestras lenguas grandes cosas de Dios.

(Montgomery and Baldwin 1970:195)

This is widely recognized as the antitype of the linguistic fragmentation in Babel (see n. 1, above), and the most likely reason for adding an enumeration of languages to the Biblical account of the Tower is a wish to make the typological relationship between Babel and Pentecost even closer. I have discussed elsewhere the use made of typology by the *Alexandre* poet (Bly and Deyermond 1972), and I believe that this passage provides a further example. The probability of the poet's use of the Pentecost narrative is strengthened by the fact that nine of the sixteen languages and peoples in Acts are present in the *Libro de Alexandre*'s list, and although some of the nine are common enough (Romans, Jews), others are not (Parthians, Elamites, Cappadocians, Phrygians, Pamphylians).

It is notoriously difficult, in the absence of extensive and close textual resemblance, to know how a medieval author's composition was affected by earlier texts, even when we know that they were texts that he or she had read. Any attempt to relate a passage to two texts, operating simultaneously but in different ways, is especially difficult. All we can do is to make a guess – an informed guess, we hope–, while remembering that this is hypothesis not demonstrable fact. My guess is that the *Alexandre* poet, seeing the list of post-Babel languages in the *B* version of the *Roman d'Alexandre*, was reminded by it of the list of tongues at Pentecost, and, because of his strong typological interest, drew on the Biblical as well as the Old French account.

The typological content of much of the *Libro* is reinforced by the inclusion of the list of languages, and so is the poet's view of the importance of language (a view that is appropriate to his insistence in stanzas 1–3 on the learned nature of his poem). It is sometimes said that language is the subject of all literature. I have never understood why anyone should believe this. 'In principio erat

Verbum', but St John does not mean human language. Without language there could be no literature, either oral or written (non-verbal communication has a large part to play in life, and may be described in literature, as in the episode of the Greeks and the Romans in the *Libro de Buen Amor*), but to say that it is a necessary condition for literature is not the same as saying that literature is forever examining its own language. There are, however, some short works, and some passages in longer works, that are indeed about language. The episode of the Greeks and the Romans is one such, and the account of Babylon in the *Libro de Alexandre*, in its sharp contrast with later texts, is another. A particularly striking contrast is evident when we turn to a near-contemporary work, the anonymous *Semejança del mundo* (soon after 1222), conceived as a Castilian version of the *Imago mundi* of Honorius, which in turn draws heavily on the seventh-century *Etymologiae* of St Isidore of Seville; the *Etymologiae* and original material play an increasing part as the work progresses. The *Semejança* briefly describes Babylon and mentions a great tower and the city's foundation by a giant, but without any reference to the Babel story:

> I á luego tierra de Babilonia, e es un grand regnado rico e bien puesto. E dizen a esta tierra Babilonia del nombre de una cibdad que ha hý que dizen otrossí Babilonia. Esta cibdad fizo e pobló, de compeçamiento, .I. gigant quel dixieron Nenroth [...] En esta cibdad de Babilonia á una torre que ha en alto quanto .IIII. passos, segunt que es escripto. (Text *A*, chaps 31–32; Bull and Williams 1959:64)

I said at the outset that two of the most remarkable transformation scenes in the Bible are concerned with language, and that they have a striking typological relationship. The *Alexandre* poet has, to a far greater extent than any of the later Spanish authors studied here, understood both the role of language and that of typology, and he has organized his work in a way that brings both elements to the fore.

References

Arizaleta, Amaia, 1999. *La Translation d'Alexandre: recherches sur les structures et les significations du 'Libro de Alexandre,'* Annexes des *Cahiers de Linguistique Hispanique Médiévale*, 12. Paris: Séminaire d'Études Médiévales Hispaniques de l'Université de Paris-XIII.

Auerbach, Erich, 1959. 'Figura,' in his *Scenes from the Drama of Medieval Literature: Six Essays*, tr. Ralph Manheim. New York: Meridian Books, pp. 9–76.

Bañeza Román, Celso, 1994. *Las fuentes bíblicas, patrísticas y judaicas del 'Libro de Alexandre*. Las Palmas: the author.

Biy, P. A., and A. D. Deyermond, 1972. 'The Use of Figura in the *Libro de Alexandre*,' *Journal of Medieval and Renaissance Studies*, 2:151–81.

Bull, William E., and Harry F. Williams, ed., 1959. *'Semeiança del mundo': A Medieval Description of the World*, Univ. of California Publications in Modern Philology, 51. Berkeley: Univ. of California Press.

Cañas, Jesús, ed., 1988. *Libro de Alexandre*, Letras Hispánicas, 280. Madrid: Cátedra.

Conde, Juan Carlos, 1999. *La creación de un discurso historiográfico en el cuatrocientos castellano: 'Las siete edades del mundo' de Pablo de Santa María (estudio y edición crítica)*, Textos Recuperados, 18. Salamanca: Ediciones Universidad de Salamanca.

Dronke, Peter, 1986. *Dante and Medieval Latin Traditions*. Cambridge: UP.

Frye, Northrop, 1982. *The Great Code: The Bible and Literature*. London: Routledge and Kegan Paul.

—, 1992. *Words with Power: Being a Second Study of 'The Bible and Literature.'* New York: Harcourt Brace Jovanovich.

Gressmann, Hugo, 1928. *The Tower of Babel*, ed. Julian Obermann. New York: Jewish Institute of Religion Press.

Guthrie, D., J. A. Motyer, et al., ed., 1970. *New Bible Commentary*, 3rd ed. Leicester: Inter-Varsity Press; Grand Rapids, MI: Wm. B. Eerdmans Publishing.

La Du, M. S., 1937. *The Medieval French 'Roman d'Alexandre,'* i: *Text of the Arsenal and Venice Versions*, Elliott Monographs in the Romance Languages and Literatures, 36. Princeton: UP; Paris: Presses Universitaires de France.

Littlefield, Mark G., ed., 1992. *Escorial Bible I.ii.19*, Spanish Series, 66. Madison: HSMS.

Mâle, Émile, 1978. *Religious Art in France: The Twelfth Century: A Study of the Origins of Medieval Iconography*, tr. Marthiel Mathews, ed. Harry Bober, Bollingen Series, 90.1. Princeton: UP.

Marcos Marín, Francisco, 1983. 'La confusión de las lenguas: comentario filológico desde un fragmento del *Libro de Alexandre*,' in *El comentario de textos, 4: La poesía medieval*, Literatura y Sociedad, 32. Madrid: Castalia, pp. 149–84.

Mettmann, Walter, ed. 1962. *'La historia de la Donzella Teodor': ein spanisches*

Volksbuch arabischen Ursprungs: Unterschungen und kritische Ausgabe der ältisten bekannten Fassungen. Wiesbaden: Franz Heine.

Michael, Ian, 1970. *The Treatment of Classical Material in the 'Libro de Alexandre,'* Publications of the Faculty of Arts, 17. Manchester: UP.

Montgomery, Thomas, and Spurgeon W. Baldwin, ed., 1970. *El Nuevo Testamento según el manuscrito Escurialense I-i-6, desde el Evangelio de San Marcos hasta el Apocalipsis*, Anejos de..l *BRAE*, 22. Madrid: RAE.

Morreale, Margherita, 1969. 'Vernacular Scriptures in Spain,' in *The Cambridge History of the Bible*, ii: *The West from the Fathers to the Reformation*, ed. G. W. H. Lampe. Cambridge: UP, pp. 465–91 and 533–35.

Pritchard, R. Telfryn, tr., 1986. Walter of Châtillon, *The Alexandreis*, Mediaeval Sources in Translation, 29. Toronto: Pontifical Institute of Mediaeval Studies.

Rico, Francisco, 1984. *Alfonso el Sabio y la 'General estoria': tres lecciones*, 2nd ed. Barcelona: Ariel.

Solalinde, Antonio G., ed., 1930. Alfonso el Sabio, *General estoria: primera parte*. Madrid: Centro de Estudios Históricos.

Willis, Raymond S., 1934. *The Relationship of the Spanish 'Libro de Alexandre' to the 'Alexandreis' of Gautier de Châtillon*, Elliott Monographs in the Romance Languages and Literatures, 31. Princeton: UP; Paris: Presses Universitaires de France.

——— , 1935. *The Debt of the Spanish 'Libro de Alexandre' to the French 'Roman d'Alexandre,'* Elliott Monographs in the Romance Languages and Literatures, 33. Princeton: UP; Paris: Presses Universitaires de France.

9
The count/non-count distinction in Castilian: evidence for its place and function in the medieval language
RAY HARRIS-NORTHALL

AMONG THE MANY VALUABLE contributions made by Ralph Penny to our knowledge and understanding of Spanish, his research on the linguistic varieties of northwestern Spain over several decades stands as an excellent account of features sometimes unique to these areas and other times shared historically with Castilian, even if lost in the modern standard.[1] In fact, as our knowledge of the historical development of Spanish expands, it occasionally becomes possible to bridge gaps and make connections where they never seemed to exist or were at best tenuous and speculative. In this paper I would like to explore one of those connections and offer further evidence to suggest that Castilian in the pre-literary period shared a morphological system usually believed to be characteristic only of the local speech varieties of Asturias and Cantabria, and that this system continued to be present throughout the Middle Ages in vestigial form, and indeed may survive today, despite its virtual elimination from the written standard.[2]

---

[1] I am greatly indebted to Fernando Tejedo-Herrero and Thomas D. Cravens for their generous help and suggestions concerning this study. Any shortcomings that may remain are, of course, my own responsibility.

[2] Wright has legitimately drawn our attention to the fact that using such terms as "Castilian" to refer to linguistic varieties before the 13th century is probably an anachronism, given that the dialect continuum across the north of the Peninsula had not been chopped into individual segments centred on political units (2002:161-62, 262-65, 270-73). On the other hand, there is no evidence that the features described in this study existed outside the varieties of Ibero-Romance spoken along the Cantabrian coast east of Galicia and in the north-central areas which would eventually form the kingdoms of Castile and León. "Castilian" may thus be taken here as a geolinguistic label of convenience.

In his monograph on Pasiego, Penny described the phenomenon known as the "neutro de materia" as presented in that Cantabrian variety: a group of non-countable nouns characterized by such phonological features as the absence of metaphonic closing of the tonic caused by a final back vowel, and by triggering agreement from a class of adjectives marked differently from both masculine and feminine forms; hence the term "neuter." Such nouns included (citing by their Castilian correlates) *ganado, dinero, queso, pelo, vino, tocino, oro, humo, unto, harina, carne, leche, leña, hierba, sangre, manteca* and many more; if any of these nouns were used with countable reference (*cortar un queso, tomar este vino tan bueno*) neuter features of their morphosyntax would be replaced by the relevant feminine or masculine agreement markers (1970a:150-53). Penny also pointed out that the terminology which by that time had become commonly used was not totally appropriate, since a number of nouns which bore these characteristics did not in fact refer to non-count "material" concepts, but were simply abstracts (*miedo, odio, sueño*) or belonged to other normally non-count groups, such as the names of the months (151; see also Penny 1970b:22). The wealth of material he collected in Pas enabled Penny to specify other important details of the phenomenon: the fact that preposed adjectives did not usually exhibit neuter marking, except, arguably, in the invariable form of quantifiers (1970a:152-53); that the tonic pronoun referring to neuter nouns was *ello* (153-54); and that the atonic pronoun was *lu*, as opposed to feminine *la* and masculine *le*, the latter used with both animate and inanimate reference within a clearly *leísta* pronominal framework (154).[3] The notion that the count / non-count distinction is inextricably linked with *leísmo* has since been strengthened by the research of Klein, who has shown that in (unspecified) rural areas of the province of Valladolid, *le* and *la* are used for masculine and feminine count reference respectively, and *lo* for non-count reference (1981).

In later research, Penny was able to confirm the existence of the neuter in another Cantabrian variety, that of Tudanca, west of the Montes de Pas. Despite superficial differences (for example in the atonic pronouns, where the masculine *lu* contrasts with the neuter *lo*), it is quite clear that the underlying system acknowledges a morphological count / non-count distinction, and that the difference in pronouns reflects the non-*leísta* usage of western Cantabria (Penny 1978:79-83, 1984:136-37 and map 25). In fact, he was subsequently able to demonstrate that the count / non-count distinction was present throughout the central and western areas of Cantabria, though weakened in some spots by

---

[3] I am orthographically interpreting Penny's phonetic transcription of these pronouns.

intrusion of the Castilian standard (1984:135-37 and maps 23-25). In later studies, other researchers have identified the phenomenon in other parts of Cantabria (for example, Fernández Juncal 1989).

Since the end of the 19th century it had been known that the count / non-count distinction existed in Asturian varieties; Menéndez Pidal (1962 [1899]: 137) identified the final vowel differentiation, and the description of a clear morphological structure began to appear in Canellada (1944:31-32; here for the first time referred to as "neutro") and in Neira Martínez (1955:70-72, 1978). The excellent overview now available in García González (1989) demonstrates that the phenomenon can be traced from west-central Asturias (roughly the River Nalón) to western Vizcaya (the River Nervión), and way south of the Cantabrian mountains, possibly as far as the provinces of Valladolid, Palencia, Burgos, and Soria (García González 1981:350-52, 1989: 92-99). This geographical amplitude raises the suspicion that the neuter may not have been restricted to the most northerly varieties of Spanish: if it can still be traced, however residually, so far to the south of Asturias and Cantabria, the possibility that it once existed on a firmer basis in Castilian must surely be considered.[4]

Penny was already aware of the possibility that neuter forms might be found in Castilian too, especially in its earliest manifestations: he mentions lines 1049-50 of the *Cid*, which read "Alegre es el conde e pidió agua a las manos, / e tiénengelo delant e diérongelo privado," the pronominal forms of which had clearly puzzled Menéndez Pidal and had led him to propose that *lo* "se refiere no al agua sola, sino a todo el servicio necesario para lavarse las manos," even in the absence of any textual support for such an interpretation (quoted in Penny 1970a:154, fn. 4).

The origin of the neuter form has been the subject of some discussion.

---

[4] Romance varieties of Southern Italy have also been observed to acknowledge a neuter form; i.e., a count / non-count distinction in nouns. This was once one of the features that led some specialists to postulate Southern Italian colonization of Asturias in the Roman period (see for example Alonso 1962:125-35). Such a link, at least on the basis of this particular feature, can now be seen as implausible; apart from the proposal put forth here that the Spanish phenomenon is not unique to Asturias and Cantabria, there is the fact that the Italian distinction surfaces in a number of quite distinct ways, some of them radically different from anything found in Spain. In some areas, for example, the initial consonant of a non-count noun is geminated: thus *lu lupu* "the wolf," but *lu llatti* "the milk" (Cravens 2002:86, Rohlfs 1968:108-10). It seems more probable that the count / non-count distinction was actually present in the Latin of various parts of the Empire, and produced a number of phonetic and morphosyntactic manifestations over time, some parallel in different areas, and some divergent.

Though many non-count nouns did indeed belong to the neuter gender in Latin (LAC, MEL, VINUM, AURUM, etc.), the tripartite morphology of adjectives as preserved in some northwestern Spanish varieties is problematic. The common explanation that nominal forms in Spanish derive from the Latin accusative case is incapable of accounting for the difference between masculine endings in -*u* and neuter endings in -*o*, since in Latin the accusative of both masculine and neuter forms had the same ending, -ŪM. M. Penny proposed that the Spanish neuter forms actually descend from dative/genitive forms in -ō used as a partitive, a usage documented in Latin (1970b:25-26), and subsequently strengthened his argument by pointing out that the few documented cases of Asturian non-count feminines in -*e* (*sidre, lleñe, yedre*) might similarly descend from the Latin dative/genitive in -AE (Penny 1992-1993).⁵

In 1992, Ojeda published an important study in which he brought together the known facts of the neuter construction in its diatopic diversity, a proposal concerning its origin, and more significantly from the viewpoint of this article, evidence that an identical or at least similar phenomenon occurred in medieval Castilian. Essentially, he agrees with Penny that the distinction arose historically from Late Latin case usage, though he prefers to consider the ablative the case that surfaces as the neuter form, rather than a dative/genitive (1992:263-66; Hall (1968) had previously indicated this possible origin). Ojeda cites examples from a wide variety of early Castilian texts, literary and non-literary, which show neuter pronouns (*lo, ello*, as well as demonstratives *aquello*, etc.) referring to mass nouns which appear superficially to have masculine or feminine gender (*ganado, fierro, vino, agua, miel, salvia*) (250-52). Ojeda's study leaves no doubt that Penny's suspicion that the count / non-count distinction was not limited to Asturias and Cantabria was fully justified.

Harmon and Ojeda returned to the question of neuter pronominal reference in Castilian in a later study, which focused on one particular text: Gabriel Alonso de Herrera's *Obra de agricultura*, first published in Alcalá in 1513 (Harmon and Ojeda 1999). They found numerous cases in this text of mass nouns, both masculine and feminine, receiving pronominal reference in the atonic form *lo*, and (more significantly in the case of masculines) tonic *ello* (1999:366-70); moreover, the text differentiated countable from non-countable in the pronouns *le* and *lo* respectively (1999:374-75). The frequency of this usage in the *Obra de agricultura* is surprising, bearing in mind both the relatively late date of its

---

5 A number of other hypotheses have been proposed on the historical origin of the morphological distinction between count and non-count nouns. For a summary followed by one more proposal, see Arias Cabal (1999:117-48).

composition, and also that its author was not Asturian or Cantabrian, but born in Talavera de la Reina and had travelled widely around Spain, as well as to Italy and France (Dubler 1941:137). This raises the question of Herrera's sources, and whether some of the linguistic features of his treatise are not carried over from earlier works. This may be a significant point, and I shall return to it later.

Our knowledge of the phenomenon as it stands may thus be summarized in the following way: modern Cantabrian and (eastern and central) Asturian varieties of Ibero-Romance mark a distinction between count and non-count nouns, which in anaphoric reference takes precedence over the masculine / feminine gender distinction; it is most apparent in adjectives and pronouns in agreement with the nucleus of the noun phrase. In areas which show *leísmo*, the direct object clitics *le* and *lo* often refer to countables and non-countables, respectively, and the distinction has therefore come in recent years to be considered by some researchers as lying at the origin of Castilian *leísmo* (see, for example, García González 1978, García Menéndez 2000, Fernández-Ordóñez 2001[6]), especially since it has been revealed that similar patterns of reference spread into northern areas of modern Castile. The purpose of the present study, then, is threefold: to offer further evidence that the count / non-count distinction was broadly present in medieval Castilian; that neuter pronominal reference was structured and systemic in the language at some time, and that the phenomenon was therefore likely to have been present historically across a wide area of the north-central Peninsula; and that non-count reference was frequently semantic rather than syntactic in its reference, and linked with another structural feature of Medieval Spanish: the partitive.

Ojeda (1992) established clearly that the count / non-count distinction, with so-called neuter anaphoric reference, was present in a variety of Medieval Spanish texts, and Harmon and Ojeda (1999) presented data to suggest that the phenomenon was still active in the early 16th century. Here, in support of the position that it was a relatively common feature of Castilian varieties, two corpora of Alfonsine documents have been taken in order to examine the phenomenon. Ojeda (1992:251) gives only one example from Alfonsine

---

[6] Fernández-Ordóñez considers, in her very detailed treatment, one of the less clear aspects of the relationship between the northern varieties and Castilian: the apparent replacement of *lu* by *le* for countable reference. She concludes that the hypothesis of influence from Basque speakers of Romance is probable (2001:431-35). The origins of *leísmo* lie outside the range of the present study, though more and more scholars are willing to accept the link with the count / non-count distinction (for an important discussion, see Tuten 2003:173-203).

documents, specifically from the *Estoria de España I* (cited as the *Primera crónica general*), since his intention is to establish the existence of the count / non-count distinction over a long period of time rather than at a particular point. If we wish to broaden our awareness of the usage, however, it is necessary to consider how the structure functioned at different historical points so as to understand the way in which it eventually disappeared. Here, then, the texts searched come from the corpus of Alfonsine scriptorium documents (Kasten, Nitti and Jonxis-Henkemans 1997) and the corpus of chancery documents (Herrera, Sánchez, González de Fauve and Zabía 1999), thus ensuring a chronological focus on the second half of the thirteenth century.[7] The following examples, in the first place, demonstrate pronominal reference by *lo* made to non-count (including abstract) nouns which are feminine in gender:

> conuiene q*ue* tome*n* **carne** de palomino uolant. e q*ue* **lo** enbueluan en uino mezclado con miel MOA 24r[8]
> E la **sangre** del cabron maslo. si **lo** pusieren en un escudiella. e **lo** dexaren fasta q*ue*s esfrie un poco MOA 28v
> Ca las aues q*ue* caçan q*u*ando no*n* son much usadas a[ ]la **grosura** no **lo** pueden bien moler MOA 31v
> si comiessen la **grosura** con la carne humida no*n* **lo** podrien tan bien moler MOA 32v
> ca si les passare la **carne** al papo. o a[ ]la moliella estando humida. fazeles fastio. e no*n* **lo** pueden bien moler MOA 51r
> ceue*n*las de **carne** purgada delos neruios tanto q*ue* **lo** puedan bien moler MOA 51v
> si tomaren **pimienta** molida. e **lo** mezclaren con q*u*anto un auellana de manteca e gelo fizieren tragar MOA 54v
> despues tomen dela **carne** tierna ta*n*ta q*u*anta auran mest*er*. e fagan **lo** una

---

[7] This is not to be understood as a claim that the language of the Alfonsine corpora is in any way representative of a single variety of Medieval Castilian, either regional or stylistic: it is in fact not at all homogeneous. However, the fact that these documents were undoubtedly composed and revised with some care assures us that the morphosyntactic features they contain were acceptable, minimally, to groups of prestigious speakers.

[8] Reference to specific texts within the corpora is made here with three-letter abbreviations; see the list of Primary Sources. The status of *Moamyn - Libro de las animalias* as a scriptorium text is not certain, but its association with other Alfonsine texts and its early date make it a useful point of comparison.

taiada delgada. e escalientenlo al fuego fasta que enblanquezca MOA 56r

O tomen **carne** de cordero quanto so ceuo complido e faganlo delgado e metanlo en agua tibia e [ ] despues saquen lo e expriemanlo bien fasta que saquen dend la humidad MOA 77v

tomen **sangre** de perro e mezclenlo con orina de moça escossa. e destellengelo en los oios MOA 177r

esta piedra que es assi puesta en la pez. si despues la metieren en **agua** caliente; faz lo foyr a diestro & a siniestro. & esta uertud misma muestra; en los manadores del agua fria LAP 53r

dios que da **salut** alos Reyes & ala otra yente quando lo meresçen GE1 45v

dizen unas delas estorias que en Jersen & en ramesse o morauan los fijos de israhel. que non se danno ell **agua**. & quelos ebreos de tal sabor lo fallauan de beuer como antes GE1 152v

Tomad amos las manos llenas de **çeniza** & esparzed lo. & echelo Moysen escontral çielo GE1 154r

Essora tomaron los fijos de israhel. **farina** que tenien amassada. et fue ante ques lebdasse. & ataron lo en buenos pannos & echaron selo acuestas. et en cabo tomaron lo en los cuellos et fueron su carrera GE1 157v

& tomaua toda la **gordura** della assi como dixiemos delos sacrifficios dela paz. et quemaua lo sobrell altar otrossi GE1 229v

dela **gordura** delas aues. non les dixo nada. njn gelo uedo. njn gelo mando otrossi GE1 230r

aquella **manna** andaua el pueblo cogiendo aderredor dela huest. & unos lo molien a muela. Otros lo maiauan en morteros[9] GE1 282v

Despues desto coia toda la **ceniza** della omne que sea limpio & condese lo fuera dela huest en logar otrossi muy limpio GE1 296v

e cauaron en muchos logares a de mas. mas non pudieron sacar **agua** en ninguno. ca tod el suelo era penna & no manaua. E desque uieron que por trabaio que y leuassen que lo no aurien. crecio les la sed muy mas EE1 48r

uinie contra la cibdad un grand arroyo dond auien agua los fijos de israhel en essa cibdad de Bathalia o estauan. & era esto de parte de medio dia & fuera de la cibdad. & entendio olofernes como dalli auien **agua** los

---

[9] In the modern standard, Spanish treats *maná* as a masculine noun. In medieval texts, however, it appeared as feminine and had paroxytonic accentuation (Kasten and Nitti 2002: s.v. *maná*; Corominas and Pascual 1980-91: s.v. *maná*). The same form *la mana* has also been documented in American Spanish (for example, in Santamaría 1942).

hebreos. & que si ge **lo** tolliesse q*ue* se rendrien & darien la cibdad GE4 113v

estos q*ua*tro om*n*es bonos q*ue* uean e q*ue* cate*n* la corambr*e* por todos los menestrales de toda la villa. Et do falare*n* **corambre** falsa q*ue* **lo** taje*n* todo e al q*ue* **lo** fallare*n* peche lx. r*e*ales [...]. Et ne*n*gun menestral q*ue* comprare corambr*e* mojada cordoua*n* nj*n* vadana q*ue* peche lx r*e*ales e pierda la corambr*e*. Et ot*r*osi el q*ue* **lo** vendiere q*ue* pierda la corambr*e* e peche lx r*e*ales ACV 40r

E mando q*ue* no*n* lieue*n* de Castiella ni*n* de Leon ni*n* dotro logar ni*n*guna **corambre** pora passar a Gallicia o a Asturias. E aq*u*el q*ue* **lo** leuare si p*r*ouadol fuere q*ue* pierda lo q*ue* leuare e peche en coto al rey mill m*or*a*u*edis e numq*ua* mas pueda sacar ot*r*a corambre ALE 2v

It should be noted that the non-count marker appears only in the morphology of the pronoun: adjectives agree with the feminine gender of the noun (in the above examples *carne humida, pimienta molida, carne tierna, farina amassada, corambre falsa, corambre mojada*), and this differentiates the Castilian system from that operative in Asturian and Cantabrian varieties, in which as well as pronouns, postposed adjectives show a tripartite morphology, marked by the selection of final vowel, to distinguish masculine-count, feminine-count and non-count. Just as in the Asturian and Cantabrian varieties, however, morphological marking in these Castilian texts does extend to tonic pronouns, where *ello* is used for non-count reference, and to elliptic nuclei in the NP, which surface as *lo* under the same conditions. Given this usage, it becomes apparent that masculine nouns, whose atonic reference in *lo* is indistinguishable from the non-count pronoun in Castilian, can also be treated as non-count:

q*u*ando feruiere metan y **carne** de oueia fasta q*ue* enblanq*ue*zca. e despues saq*ue*nlo e ceuenlas con **ello** MOA 57v

o tome*n* del **çumo** delas milgranas dolces o delas agras. e remogen el ceuo en **ello**. e den gelo a comer MOA 67v

E despues tomen del buen **uino** a*n*neio e lauenles con **ello** los paladares con los cabos delos dedos MOA 101v

depues tomen **olio** de uioletas et derritan en**ello** de la cera. & remogen en**ello** un poco de algodon MOA 126r

tomen **estierco** domne q*ue* sea seco a sombra q*ue* lo no*n* tanga el sol. tanto q*u*anto entendiere*n* q*ue* auran mester. e mezclen con **ello** otro tanto de açucar blanco MOA 133v

tome*n* del **uino** anneio. e metan en **ello** del sal nidrio MOA 170v

fallan dentro en ella en manera dalgodon en sustancia & en color. & la
uertud deste **algodon** es atal que se non quema por fuego. & fila se &
fazen **dello** pannos como del otro algodon LAP 17r
ay deste **fierro** que quando lo funden meten con **ello** melezinas por que se
faze tan fuerte q*ue* taia los otros fierros LAP 18v
ca ella a por p*ro*priedat q*ue* si la allegan a alguna **carne** de qual quier
animal q*ue* sea uiuo apega se a **ello** & tira consigo toda la carne aque
se allega LAP 19r
ell abondo del **trigo** fue ta*n* gra*n*d. q*u*ela muchedumbre **dello** semeiaua alas
arenas del mar GE1 101r
yua*n* alla otrossi a comp*ra*r **pan**. ca todos los de Cananea era*n* me*n*guados
dello & murien ya muchos de fambre GE1 103r
deuen lo ungir con olio benito a q*ue* llaman **olio** de los enfermos; por q*ue*
los ungen con **ello** en la enfermedat quando se quieren morir LEY 16v
quando y llueue; assi corre alli ell agua de la lluuia assi como entra por la
puerta de orient; como si fuesse un Rio. & toma quanta **suciedad** falla
por todas las calles & da con **ello** por esta puerta q*ue* dizen dell estierco
GE4 136r
enel su sacrificio q*ue* fazie a dios. ofrecil manoios de espigas de **mies**. &
tomaualo d**e**lo de cerca las carreras GE1 3v

In many of these texts, non-count reference is not limited to a single antecedent. As Harmon and Ojeda suggest, if a non-count noun is conjoined with other nouns (countable or not), non-count reference in the pronoun appears to be the unmarked value (1999:372-73). For the modern reader it is somewhat disconcerting to find that even conjoined feminine nouns require the pronoun *lo*:

tomen duna yerua q*u*el dizen uxne*n*. e dela greda e muelan**lo**. e ciernan**lo**.
e moge**nlo** con agua calient. e ponange**lo** en aq*ue*llos logares untados
MOA 49r
tomen un poco dela fiel del osso e destemp*re*n**la** con del agua. e echenge**lo**
por las narizes MOA 107r
tomen del mestuerço e delas rayzes del espada*n*na. e muela*n***lo** e ciernan**lo**.
e de*n* les **dello** en pedaçuelos de carne MOA 108v
tomo aquella sangre. & aquellas melezinas & unto las ymagenes de los
ydolos co*n* **ello** GE4 22v
Onde mando q*ue* todos aq*ue*llos q*ue* quesieren traer pan e vino e otras
uiandas a uender a Salama*n*ca assi los de Salama*n*ca e de su t*er*mino
com*m*o los otros q*ue* **lo** tragan e **lo** uendan y ALE 41v

There are even cases in which the individual nouns belong to the countable class (as indicated by their plurality), and yet their combination will produce a non-countable mixture:[10]

> tomen de las rayzes del lilio e delas maluas montesinas. e mezclenlo en uno. e metanlo en pedaçuelos de carne e denles dello e fazer les a pro MOA 107r

In fact, it seems clear that semantic considerations could outweigh purely morphosyntactic ones in the selection of non-count reference; thus it often appears when the antecedent noun is *cosa*:

> entramos le la tierra del castiello de aroer que yaze en el ual de sobre la ribera de Arnon fasta galaat. que njnguna cosa non nos finco que non lo prisiemos GE1 321v
> si dela sangre deste sacriffi[ci]o caye alguna cosa en la uestimenta del sacerdot. lauauan la fasta que non fincasse y manziella dello GE1 229v

What these examples illustrate, therefore, is a system in which the semantic interpretation of a noun as countable or non-countable takes precedence over the morphological category of masculine or feminine, and the notion of "non-countable" extends to indefinite antecedents and to mixtures produced by a combination of ingredients, whether individually countable or not.

Another feature associated with the count / non-count distinction, not only in Medieval Spanish but also in other languages (such Romance languages as French and Italian among them), is the partitive.[11] It is inevitable then that we

---

[10] This usage is also claimed for modern Asturian varieties by de Andrés: "si el pronombre reproduce o representa a varios sustantivos de diferente género, también aparece en forma neutra: *peres, ablanes, piescos... teníalo too mecío nes caxes*" (1998:45). It is unfortunate that the example contains *too*, since Castilian, even in the modern standard, can also use *todo* to refer back to numerous antecedents; thus *peras, avellanas, melocotones ... lo tenía todo mezclado en las cajas* is also acceptable. Nevertheless, the fact that *too*, as well as *lo* and *mecío* agreeing with it, have the *-o* (rather than masculine *-u*) ending, indicates a neuter construction. For this use of *todo* in the modern standard, see for instance Martínez (1999:2754), who provides such examples as "Sirvieron marisco, carne, pescado..., todo (ello) regado con un excelente vino."

[11] The notion of the partitive is a slippery one, sometimes defined in syntactic terms and sometimes in semantic terms. Here the issue is specifically the use of *de* to indicate

should encounter the partitive in close association with non-countable notions in these thirteenth-century texts:

las carnes buenas estas son. carne de bezerro. e carne de cabron. q*u*ando les diere*n* **dello** mesurada mient MOA 28r-28v

conuiene q*ue* tomen **de carne** de culuebras e meta*n*lo en pedaçuelos dotra buena carne. enbueluanlo en bue*n* azeyt e dengelo a[ ]comer MOA 56r

q*ue* tome*n* **dela pez** e muelanlo bien co*n* uinagre fuert. e echengelo por las narizes MOA 111r

apartaron se & tomaro*n* una partida de asia. **dello** por fuerça. **dello** sin guerra & sin fuerça GE1 24r

mando les q*u*el llamassen & combrie **del pan** con ellas GE1 145v

tomara el cabrito [...] & tomara*n* **dela sangre** del. & poner lo an en amas las puertas d*e*la casa et en amos los limbrales d*e*las casas ol comiere*n* GE1 156v

departe q*ue* era todo arena seca. & q*ue* en las fue*n*tes auie ta*n* poca agua. q*ue* si om*n*e q*u*isiesse coger **dello** co*n* las manos q*ue* no*n* lo podrie fazer GE1 169r

luego q*ue* Moysen ma*n*do al pueblo q*ue* cogiessen **daq*u*ella ma*n*na**. q*ue* se metiero*n* todos a coger **dello** a ta*n* gra*n*d p*r*iessa q*ue*los flacos no*n* podie*n* y fazer nada ante los rezios GE1 170v-71r

alli la [*sc.* vaca] sacrifiq*ue* ante todos. & tinga el dedo en la sangre della. & esparza **dello** con el contra la puerta dela tienda siete uezes GE1 296v

tomo u[i]no anneio et aaguo lo con agua de pozo antigo & dexo lo posar. despues desto dio a drimiden abeuer **dello** GE4 24r

uos mando q*ue* les dexedes meter en u*ue*s*t*ra villa las huuas e el mosto e el

---

a portion of what is expressed as a non-count noun (or its pronoun). Even in Modern French, in which such partitives are widely used, accounting for variation in usage is challenging, as shown by Spence (1983); the more restricted usage in Old French is clearly parallel with what we find in Medieval Spanish, "the sphere of *noms de matière*" (1983:20). In Modern Spanish, such partitive constructions must usually be introduced by an expression of quantity, whether specific or not: *un poco de agua, algo de carne, un trozo de pan*. Alternatively, a simple quantifier such as *poco, mucho, bastante* may be used without the preposition. See below, however, for a few cases which may be remnants of the old partitive *de*. The presence of the Spanish partitive has been noted in early literary texts such as the Cid and the work of Berceo; it also appears in the Late Latin of medieval texts produced throughout the Peninsula (Bastardas Parera 1953:33-35). Despite this, the partitive *de* is rarely discussed in standard language histories; Cano Aguilar is one of the few authors who even mention it (1988:127).

vino de todas sus casas e de todas sus obediencias e cada q*ue* qu*i*siere*n* uender **dello** q*ue* vendan segu*nd* q*ue* lo husaro*n* en tie*m*po del rey don Alfonso ACV 47v

As may be seen from these examples, the partitive structure required the preposition *de* to be inserted before the noun and its article if present; if indeed the article does appear, the noun is immediately identified as masculine or feminine, regardless of its count or non-count status. On the other hand, when there is pronominal reference to the noun, the presence of the preposition requires that the pronoun be tonic, and since the noun is interpreted as non-count, that pronoun is *ello*. Thus the morphosyntactic relationship between the partitive and the count / non-count distinction was a close one. Such partitive constructions as these have been lost in the modern Spanish standard, though, significantly, the few partitive expressions that are still acceptable must be constructed with a so-called neuter adjective or pronoun: *dame de eso que llevas, sírvele de lo más tierno, compramos de lo más barato,* attesting once more to the syntactic relationship that exists between partitive and neuter (or perhaps better, partitive and non-count; it may be observed that neither adjectives nor pronouns when used in this construction are capable of pluralization).[12]

It may not be mere coincidence, therefore, that the linguistic varieties of northwestern Spain that maintain the count / non-count distinction also preserve a partitive construction like that found in thirteenth-century Castilian texts. Penny documents this usage in Pas (1970a:155), though noting that in some areas the form *dellu* has become lexicalized as an equivalent to *mucho*, which suggests the partitive notion has only a tenuous hold. Cano González reports the existence of the partitive throughout the areas where varieties of Asturian are used, though there is considerable variation in details: in some places lexicalization of the form as an indefinite is apparent, but in others it remains a true partitive of the type under discussion here, as in such examples as *nun amasóu más que dél pan, bebíu deša augua na fonte, dame delles perres, queda unu tontu con delles coses* (1982:506). In the western areas of Asturias, where the "neutro de materia" is absent, the form and functions are much closer to those of an indefinite quantifier, with forms marked for singular and plural, masculine and feminine; whereas in the central and eastern varieties where the "neutro de materia" is documented or may on firm evidence be reconstructed for earlier periods, the

---

[12] A few other constructions with *de* have sometimes been analyzed as partitives: the exclamative *qué de* as in *¡qué de gente había!*, for example (Alonso-Cortés 1999:4021-22). These are not relevant to the present discussion.

partitive form appears only as a neuter: "A la pregunta ¿*quies pan?* se responde en occidente *dame dél* (masc. sing.), y en el centro y oriente *dame dello* (neutro singular). De la misma forma, *compróu deṡa* (referido a carne), de occidente, se corresponde con *compró dello* del centro y oriente" (1982:512). These data suggest that the partitive survives in Asturias, though clearly it is threatened by grammatical reinterpretation within the system, either due to internal pressures or to the influence of standard Castilian. Moreover, they emphasize the relationship between the partitive and the count / non-count distinction, in that the shift from a true partitive toward an indefinite quantifier is associated with the lack of the "neutro de materia."

Given the linkage between the partitive and the count / non-count distinction, it seems plausible to investigate whether their disappearance from the Castilian standard took place within the same timeframe. Within the thirteenth-century Alfonsine texts under scrutiny here, there is some evidence of how the structures were breaking down, and doing so in a related fashion. The examples given above do not by any means paint the whole picture: though the outline of a count / non-count distinction is clear, there is considerable variation in usage. The first symptom of a breakdown is that feminine non-count nouns sometimes appear referred to by means of the atonic pronoun *la*, even when *lo* is clearly still available, and is used as soon as the concept of a mixture of ingredients becomes apparent or when a partitive is construed with the pronoun. Thus the notion of individual nouns as count or non-count appears to weaken earlier than the use of non-count *lo* and *ello* making reference to conjoined nouns or mixtures of materials:

> tomen de la manteca buena e pura e mezcle**nla** con seuo o con grosura. e despues po*n*ganlo en una olla sobrel fuego. e q*ue* feruiere metan y carne de oueia fasta q*ue* enblanq*ue*zca. e despues saq*ue*n**lo** e ceuenlas con **ello** MOA 57v
> tomen buena pez q*ue* sea de enebro e mezcle*n* **la** con uinagre e bata*n*lo bien en uno fasta q*ue*s faga espesso como miel. e[ ]tomen **dello** en una pe*r*nola e destellen gelo en las narizes MOA 101r
> tomen dela carne de la rabada del carnero sal presa. e alimpien**la** dela sal e den **dello** a[ ]las aues menores MOA 115v-16r
> Mas tome el sacerdot desta ceniza dela uaca. & eche **la** enell agua como dixiemos. & esparza **dello** al te*r*cer dia despues desto & al seteno sobre aq*ue*llos que ental peccado caen. & finq*ue*n limpios GE1 296v.

This overtly feminine marking for feminine nouns, even non-countable ones, turns up in a few instances in a pronominal partitive construction:

quando fuer la carne fria eles quisieren dar della. pueden la lauar con agua calient. e dexallo esfriar e despues dargelo MOA 33v
tome*n* dela leche delas asnas e alimpienla de la nata e tomen della quanto media libra. e mezclen con ella del dragragant molido e cernido peso de medio din*e*ro de plata. e ponganlo sobrel fuego. e q*u*ando feruiere tuelganlo de sobrel fuego. e remogenles en ello carne de corço MOA 131v-32r.

Thus the initial impression of agreement chaos given by the following example can in fact be accounted for:

conuiene q*ue* tomen miel de panares. e leche fresca. e mezclenlo en uno. e tomen dela carne e faganla taiadas menudas. e metanla a remoiar en ello. e dexenla en ello estar fasta q*ue* p*r*enda el sabor dello. e despues denles della MOA 140r.

Here, *la* and *ella* clearly refer to *carne*, in agreement with its feminine gender rather than its non-count semantic status; despite this shift away from the earlier type of agreement, *lo* and *ello* are still used to refer to a mixture of elements, even when the individual ingredients (*miel, leche*) belong to the feminine gender.

In this way, the original link between the count / non-count distinction and the partitive is gradually decoupled. Non-count feminine nouns are being, as it were, hypercharacterized as feminines, thus eliminating one of the triggers for non-count agreement, while other triggers, such as a combination of antecedents forming a non-countable mix, persist. Meanwhile, the possibility that non-count agreement was beginning to be felt by some speakers as anomalous might be indicated by the use of neuter forms such as *todo* to bolster it:

tomen del buen encienso. e dela clasa blanca. e del uino anneio. ta*n*to delo uno como delo al. e una poca de sal p*r*ieta e mezclenlo todo en uno. e denles dello en un pedaçuelo de carne picada MOA 174r-74v
tome*n* del uidrio bla*n*co. e del pebre blanco. tanto de lo uno como delo al. e muelanlo todo en uno MOA 176r
su uertud es atal que si la pone*n* con mil pesos de seuo dela quantia de si misma seyendo ello quaiado rite lo todo & faz lo ferbir como si lo pusiessen sobre fuego LAP 28v
Catad como daq*u*ello q*ue* leuaredes pora u*ue*s*t*ras casas. que no*n* finq*ue* y dello poco nj*n* mucho pora otro dia. ca engusanescrie & amargarie de guisa q*ue* nj*n* serie de com*e*r nj*n* t*e*rnie nj*n*gun p*r*o. & algunos dellos

nol q*u*isiero*n* creer & condesaro*n* dello. & ot*r*o dia fallaro*n* **lo todo** lleno de gusanos & podrido GE1 171r
si alguna cosa fi*n*care pora otro dia. bien pueden comer dello. Mas q*u*anto q*u*ier q*ue* sea dello. q*ue* al te*r*cer dia passare. nj*n*guno no*n* coma dello. mas q*ue*me*n* **lo todo** q*u*anto y remanesciere GE1 232r.

Thus despite the fact that the structure has not essentially changed, the pronoun *lo* can be felt to agree with *todo* rather than referring anaphorically to the ingredients involved in the mixture. In addition, *todo* can be used to refer back to strings of singular and plural non-count nouns too, so the count / non-count distinction is further weakened.

Finally, evidence that the count / non-count distinction is breaking down in thirteenth-century Castile is provided by the same texts analyzed above in which feminine non-count nouns also admit anaphorical reference by *la* and *ella*. Nevertheless, if the feminine non-count is conjoined with another substance, the anaphoric reference is still made by means of *lo*:

a esta offrenda & sacrifficio diz q*ue* llamaua*n* farina oleada. & tomaua*n* encienso con **ella** & leuauan **lo** al s*anct*uario al sacerdot GE1 226r.

There is also some evidence that the pronominal partitive was becoming lexicalized as an invariable indefinite, which is also what is found today in Asturian and Cantabrian varieties, since the superficially neuter form is in disagreement with the pronominal morphology, or the indefinite is used adjectivally:

tomasse d*e*la sangre del & metiesse **la** dentro dela tienda. & moiasse el dedo en **ella** & echasse **dello** siete uezes esq*u*antral uelo del s*anct*uario. Desi q*ue* pusiesse **dello** sobre q*u*atro cantos dell altar GE1 228r
Q*ue* tomasse el sacerdot d*e*la sangre daq*ue*l cordero. & el sacerdot tomaua **la** & fazie della como mandara dios. & poniel **dello** enel pico d*e*la oreia diestra GE1 240v.
faziendo sus maestrias **dello** por fisica **dello** por palabras de encantamientos GE4 4r
Seyendo alexandre en la cibdad de Babilonna pario una mugier una criatura en que auie **dello** omne. & **dello** como dotros bestiglos a pegado con lo del omne GE4 231v.

The interpretation I would like to offer of the data extracted from these thirteenth-century texts is as follows:

1. The count / non-count distinction widely documented in linguistic varieties spoken in Asturias and Cantabria was also present in medieval Castile; the only other possible explanation would be that a large number of scribes or composers of the Alfonsine texts were native to the northwestern areas and were allowing their speech habits to leak into the texts; given the large number of examples of the distinction in so many different texts, such a hypothesis is unacceptable.
2. As also occurs in the northwestern regions, the distinction is syntactically and semantically linked in a very close way to the regular use of a partitive construed with the preposition *de*. The use of non-count pronominal reference may also extend to semantically unspecific (though countable) antecedents such as *cosa*.
3. By the second half of the thirteenth century, this morphosyntactic feature was losing its hold in the Castilian system. Though it is not possible here to address the reasons why this decline happened in Castile at this particular time, it may well have to do with the complex sociolinguistic situation of Castile, where demographic shift had created a society in which speakers of many linguistic varieties (both from other parts of the Peninsula and from outside it) were brought together. Thus we may be seeing another consequence of the koineization of early Castilian (Penny 2000:48-50, 195-98; Tuten 2003).
4. The count / non-count distinction began to be lost in the atonic pronoun system, where feminine nouns came to require overtly feminine pronouns even when they were non-count (cp. García Menéndez 2000:60). This hypercharacterization of the feminine also affects the tonic pronoun in partitive constructions, thus in effect setting off the grammaticalization of the partitive and recategorizing its forms as indefinite pronouns and adjectives, capable of masculine and feminine agreement regardless of the count / non-count distinction.
5. Other manifestations of the distinction, where non-count pronouns are used to refer back to multiple antecedents in which a mixture of ingredients is implicit or explicit, survive in at least some styles of Castilian, and continue to appear in texts produced as late as the fifteenth and even the sixteenth centuries.

Within the context outlined here, Alonso de Herrera's *Obra de agricultura*, as analyzed by Harmond and Ojeda (1999), can be seen as containing features that are notably archaic in the Castilian of its time, except in its most northerly reaches: non-count reference appears frequently with both masculine and feminine nouns (atonic *lo* and tonic *ello*), even though such usage is not consistent throughout (1999:372), and also when count and non-count nouns are conjoined. One possible reason for this is that Alonso de Herrera was making extensive use of much earlier texts; and indeed, there is considerable evidence this was the case. Dubler demonstrates that Herrera's work relied heavily on Arabic sources, and the fact that Herrera himself acknowledges that he did not know any Arabic supports the idea that these sources were available in Castilian translation, like so many other Arabic scientific works in the thirteenth and fourteenth centuries (Dubler 1941:140-41).

Nevertheless, more research is necessary to establish Castilian usage in texts composed in the later Middle Ages. From the data presented here, it is clear that until the thirteenth century at least, Castilian shared with Cantabrian and Asturian varieties the use in close association of partitive structures and a count / non-count distinction.

Primary sources

ACV: *Documentos dirigidos a Castilla la Vieja*, in Herrera, Sánchez, González de Fauve and Zabía (1999).
ALE: *Documentos dirigidos a León*, in Herrera, Sánchez, González de Fauve and Zabía (1999).
EE1: *Estoria de España*, in Kasten, Nitti and Jonxis-Henkemans (1997).
GE1: *General estoria I*, in Kasten, Nitti and Jonxis-Henkemans (1997).
GE4: *General estoria IV*, in Kasten, Nitti and Jonxis-Henkemans (1997).
LAP: *Lapidario de Alfonso X*, in Kasten, Nitti and Jonxis-Henkemans (1997).
LEY: *Libro de las leyes*, in Kasten, Nitti and Jonxis-Henkemans (1997).
MOA: *Moamyn: Libro de las animalias*, in Kasten, Nitti and Jonxis-Henkemans (1997).

References

Alonso, Dámaso. 1962. "Metafonía, neutro de materia y colonización suditaliana en la Península Hispánica." *Enciclopedia lingüística hispánica. Tomo I Suplemento: La fragmentación fonética peninsular*, ed. by Manuel Alvar et al., 105-54. Madrid: C.S.I.C.
Alonso-Cortés, Ángel. 1999. "Las construcciones exclamativas. La interjección y las expresiones vocativas." *Gramática descriptiva de la lengua española*, ed. by Ignacio Bosque and Violeta Demonte, 3.3993-4050. Madrid: Espasa.
Andrés, Ramón de. 1998. "Concordancias y referencias neutras en asturiano." *Atti del*

XXI Congresso Internazionale di Linguistica e Filologia Romanza. Sezione 2. Morfologia e sintassi delle lingue romanze, ed. by Giovanni Ruffino, 39-47. Tübingen: Niemeyer.

Arias Cabal, Álvaro. 1999. *El morfema de "neutro de materia" en asturiano*. Santiago de Compostela: Universidade de Santiago de Compostela.

Bastardas Parera, Juan. 1953. *Particularidades sintácticas del latín medieval (Cartularios españoles de los siglos VIII al XI)*. Barcelona: Escuela de Filología.

Canellada, María Josefa. 1944. *El bable de Cabranes*. Revista de Filología Española, Anejo 31. Madrid: C.S.I.C. Reprinted 1996, Uviéu [Oviedo]: Academia de la Llingua Asturiana.

Cano Aguilar, Rafael. 1988. *El español a través de los tiempos*. Madrid: Arco.

Cano González, Ana María. 1982. "En torno al partitivo en bable." *XVIe Congrés Internacional de Lingüística i Filologia Romàniques. Actes*, ed. by Aina Moll, 499-514. Palma de Mallorca: Moll.

Corominas, Joan, and José A. Pascual. 1980-91. *Diccionario crítico etimológico castellano e hispánico*. 6 vols. Madrid: Gredos.

Cravens, Thomas D. 2002. *Comparative Historical Dialectology. Italo-Romance Clues to Ibero-Romance Sound Change*. Amsterdam: John Benjamins.

Dubler, César E. 1941. "Posibles fuentes árabes de la *Agricultura general* de Gabriel Alonso de Herrera." *Al-Andalus* 6.135-56.

Fernández Juncal, Carmen. 1989. "Neutro de materia en el Valle de Aras." *Philologica I: Homenaje a D. Antonio Llorente*, ed. by J. Borrego Nieto, J. J. Gómez Asencio, and L. Santos Río, 65-67. Salamanca: Universidad de Salamanca.

Fernández-Ordóñez, Inés. 2001. "Hacia una dialectología histórica. Reflexiones sobre la historia del leísmo, el laísmo y el loísmo." *Boletín de la Real Academia Española* 81.389-464.

García González, Francisco. 1978. "El leísmo en Santander." *Estudios ofrecidos a Emilio Alarcos Llorach III*, 87-101. Oviedo: Universidad de Oviedo.

García González, Francisco. 1981. "/le (lu), la, lo (lu)/ en el Centro-Norte de la Península." *Verba* 8.347-53.

García González, Francisco. 1989. "El neutro de materia." *Homenaje a Alonso Zamora Vicente. Vol. II: Dialectología, estudios sobre el romancero*, 91-105. Madrid: Castalia.

García Menéndez, Javier. 2000. "Leísmo no personal y neutro de materia." *Revista de filología española* 80.51-68.

Hall, Robert A. 1968. " 'Neuters,' mass-nouns, and the ablative in Romance." *Language* 44.480-86.

Harmon, Sarah, and Almerindo Ojeda. 1999. "Mass reference in 16th-century Castilian: Gabriel Alonso de Herrera's *Obra de agricultura*." *Advances in Hispanic Linguistics: Papers from the 2nd Hispanic Linguistics Symposium*, ed. by Javier Gutiérrez-Rexach and Fernando Martínez-Gil, 2.364-77. Somerville MA: Cascadilla.

Herrera, Mª Teresa, Mª Nieves Sánchez, Mª Estela González de Fauve, and Mª Purificación Zabía (ed). 1999. *Textos y concordancias electrónicos de documentos castellanos de Alfonso X*. CD-ROM. Madison: Hispanic Seminary of Medieval Studies.

Kasten, Lloyd A., and John J. Nitti. 2002. *Diccionario de la prosa castellana del Rey Alfonso X*. 3 vols. NewYork: Hispanic Seminary of Medieval Studies.

Kasten, Lloyd, John Nitti, and Wilhelmina Jonxis-Henkemans (ed). 1997. *The Electronic Texts and Concordances of the Prose Works of Alfonso X, El Sabio*. CD-ROM. Madison: Hispanic Seminary of Medieval Studies.

Klein, Flora. 1981. "Neuterality, or the semantics of gender in a dialect of Castilla." *Linguistic Symposium on Romance Languages, 9*, ed. by William W. Cressey and Donna Jo Napoli, 164-76. Washington DC: Georgetown University Press.

Martínez, José Antonio. 1999. "La concordancia." *Gramática descriptiva de la lengua española*, ed. by Ignacio Bosque and Violeta Demonte, 2.2695-786. Madrid: Espasa.

Menéndez Pidal, Ramón. 1962. "Notas acerca del bable de Lena." *El dialecto leonés*, ed. by Carmen Bobes, 119-151. Oviedo: Instituto de Estudios Asturianos. First published 1899 in *Asturias*, II, ed. by Octavio Bellmunt and Fermín Canella. Gijón.

Neira Martínez, Jesús. 1955. *El habla de Lena*. Oviedo: Instituto de Estudios Asturianos.

Neira Martínez, Jesús. 1978. "La oposición 'continuo' / 'discontinuo' en las hablas asturianas." *Estudios ofrecidos a Emilio Alarcos Llorach, III*, 255-79. Oviedo: Universidad de Oviedo.

Ojeda, Almerindo E. 1992. "The 'mass neuter' in Hispano-Romance dialects." *Hispanic Linguistics* 5.245-77.

Penny, Ralph J. 1970a. *El habla pasiega: ensayo de dialectología montañesa*. London: Tamesis.

Penny, Ralph J. 1970b. "Mass-nouns and metaphony in the dialects of north-western Spain." *Archivum Linguisticum* 1.21-30.

Penny, Ralph. 1978. *Estudio estructural del habla de Tudanca*. Beihefte zur Zeitschrift für romanische Philologie, 167. Tübingen: Niemeyer.

Penny, Ralph. 1984. "Esbozo de un atlas lingüístico de Santander." *Lingüística española actual* 6.123-81.

Penny, Ralph. 1992-93. "Final /e/ in Asturian feminine singulars: another mass-noun marker?" *Journal of Hispanic Research* 1.182-85.

Penny, Ralph. 2000. *Variation and Change in Spanish*. Cambridge: Cambridge University Press.

Rohlfs, Gerhard. 1968. *Grammatica storica della lingua italiana e dei suoi dialetti. II: Morfologia*. Turin: Einaudi.

Santamaría, Francisco J. 1942. *Diccionario general de americanismos*. 3 vols. México: Robredo.

Spence, Nicol. 1983. "Partitives and mass-nouns in French." *Romanische Forschungen* 95.1-22.

Tuten, Donald N. 2003. *Koineization in Medieval Spanish*. Berlin: Mouton de Gruyter.

Wright, Roger. 2002. *A Sociophilological Study of Late Latin*. Turnhout: Brepols.

10
Variation of the Spanish demonstratives *aqueste* and *este*[1]

DIANA L. RANSON

1. INTRODUCTION

IN HIS MOST RECENT BOOK, Ralph Penny (2000) turns his attention to the topic of variation, specifically the geographical, social, and historical variation in the Spanish-speaking world. I hope, therefore, that this study of the variation influencing the choice of the demonstratives *aqueste* or *este* in two Old Spanish texts will be a fitting tribute to his illustrious academic career.

In Spanish texts from the twelfth to the nineteenth century one finds the demonstrative adjective and pronoun *aqueste* alongside the more familiar and more frequent form *este*. Both forms derive from the Latin demonstrative *iste* 'that', but the long form contains the additional particle *accu, perhaps a variant of *ecce* 'behold' or perhaps from *atque*, which is also found in the demonstratives *aquese* from *accu ipse 'himself' and *aquel* from*accu ille 'yonder'. In the following example from the fourteenth-century prose text, *Cuento de Tristan de Leonis* (henceforth TL), one finds both *aqueste* and *este* used with the same noun, *desierto*.

(1) *Tristan se razonaua con el buen hombre, e dixole: "Señor, en* **aqueste** *desierto ¿vienen algunos caualleros andantes?"; dixo el hermitaño: "***Este** *desierto es de grandes auenturas ..."* (TL 42, 5, 189)[2]

---

[1] Preliminary versions of this study were presented at the Kentucky Foreign Language Conference in Lexington, Kentucky in April 2003 and at the Romance Linguistics Seminar at Trinity Hall in Cambridge, England in January 2004. I would like to thank Sylvia Adamson, Martin Maiden, David Pharies, Chris Pountain, Ingmar Söhrman, and Roger Wright for their helpful questions on those occasions.

[2] Citations from TL include first the number of the chapter, then the number of the

The majority of the small number of scholars who have addressed the difference between *aqueste* and *este* have suggested that the two forms have the same referential meaning, thereby implying that there is in fact no difference between them. Nebrija, for example, gives in his well-known dictionary the same Latin meaning for both forms (cited by Girón Alconchel 1998:497).

In his grammar, Nebrija (1992 [1492]) lists *este*, *esse*, and *el* as simple pronouns and *aqueste*, *aquesse*, and *aquel* as compound pronouns. He does not mention any difference of meaning between them, even though he states specifically that *mesmo* can add emphasis to these constructions. Similarly, Menéndez Pidal (1969:329) combines examples of *aqueste* and *este* in his discussion of demonstratives in the *Cantar de mio Çid* making no distinction between the two forms. Alvar and Pottier (1983:107-08) state the case for identity of meaning even more clearly when they write that the long forms, *aqueste* and *aquese*, were eliminated at the end of the Middle Ages because they coincided with the short forms, *este* and *ese*, "sin añadir ningún tipo de connotación". More recently, Sanchis Calvo (1991:397), in her study of the *Fazienda de Ultramar*, states simply that the longer forms have the same meaning as the corresponding simple forms and Girón Alconchel (1998:496) says that the synonymy of the long and short forms is obvious when they are juxtaposed in a similar linguistic context, as in (1) above.

However, the fact that two variants may have the same referential meaning does not mean that they can in fact be used interchangeably. A basic principle of variationism maintains that variants, such as *aqueste* and *este* in this case, say "'the same thing' in several different ways: that is, the variants are identical in referential or truth value, but opposed in their social and/or stylistic significance" (Labov 1972:271). Variants that are in fact synonymous on one level can then be correlated with social or stylistic factors, such as the correlation of the aspiration of Spanish /s/ with lower-class speakers or less formal styles.

However, while phonological variants, such as Spanish [s] and [h], clearly mean the same thing so that their variation may correlate with social and stylistic factors, Lavandera (1978) and Romaine (1984) long ago questioned whether this synonymy still holds for syntactic variants, and morphosyntactic variants such as *aqueste* and *este*. Silva-Corvalán (2001:129-38), in her summary of this debate, points out that while the referential meaning of two variants may be the

---

paragraph in that chapter, and finally the page number in the edition edited by Bonilla y San Martín (1912). Quotations from LBA include the number of the strophe followed by a lower case letter to indicate the line within that verse.

same, the pragmatic meanings derived from their use in discourse may be different. Furthermore, if the pragmatic meanings of two variants are different, then these pragmatic meanings will have to be determined and separated out before social and stylistic factors can be established. In other words, since it is likely that all speakers, regardless of their social characteristics and the formality of their speech, will assign the same pragmatic functions to these variants, these functions will interfere with the analysis of other social and stylistic factors.

In this article I propose that *aqueste* and *este* have the same referential meaning, but that they differ in their pragmatic functions, which derive from their use by real speakers and hearers in real situations or, in the case of written texts, from the representation of real speech acts in writing. In addition to expressing referential meaning, a linguistic form can also express pragmatic meaning by providing, for example, additional information about its interpretation in specific circumstances. An example of the pragmatic functions of syntactic variation can be found in research on the variation between pronoun and null subjects in Spanish. In addition to its referential meaning, that of the person being addressed, Stewart (2003:191) claims that subject pronoun *tú* or the use of another subject can also signal various attempts by the speaker to negotiate face in the course of a conversation. A further example of the pragmatic function of syntactic variation concerns the prenominal or postnominal position of the demonstrative adjectives, *este*, *ese* and *aquel*, in Modern Andalusian Spanish. Ranson (1999) found that postposition was used to refer to something that was known to the hearer but that had not yet been mentioned in the conversation. Therefore, the important factor in distinguishing between these two syntactic variables was not the referential meaning of the forms, but rather the informational status of their referent within discourse.

Crucial to the identification of pragmatic functions is the assumption that the speaker's choice of a marked or more informative form than is required simply to identify the referent, such as a subject pronoun or a postposed demonstrative, invites the hearer to draw an implicature (Horn 1984:22; Blackwell 1998, 2003:23; Stewart 2003:191). This means simply that a hearer, when confronted with additional information, tries to attribute a meaning to this information. For example, if someone says *yo no lo creo* rather than *no lo creo*, then the hearer assumes that some pragmatic meaning should be assigned to the additional information provided by the subject pronoun *yo*. In the same way, if someone says *I like your red shoes* rather than simply *I like your shoes*, then the hearer assumes that the shoes' being red is in some way significant.

One can extend this approach to a pragmatic analysis of *aqueste*, if one assumes that the form *aqueste* provides additional information not included in *este*, originally in the form of the deictic particle **accu*. One can then postulate that this additional information invites the hearer or reader at a time when *aqueste* was still current to make an implicature concerning the pragmatic meaning of this form. Even if one did not accept that *aqueste* provided additional information, one could still assume by virtue of its relatively low frequency of use that it was the marked form, in contrast to unmarked *este*, a condition which according to Horn (1984:22) would also invite an implicature on the part of the hearer.

I propose then that the variation between *aqueste* and *este* depends on their different pragmatic functions. More specifically, *aqueste*, by virtue of being the marked form, invites the hearer or reader to make an implicature. The analysis below will explore in greater detail the possible implicatures. In order to achieve the goal of analyzing the pragmatic functions of *aqueste* and *este*, I consider their appearance in two fourteenth-century texts, selected simply because a search of the *Corpus del español* indicated that they each contained an adequate number of tokens of *aqueste* for analysis. One is a prose text, *Cuento de Tristan de Leonis* (ed. Bonilla y San Martín 1912), and the other is a verse text, the *Libro de Buen Amor* (henceforth LBA) (ed. Blecua 1983). First I demonstrate that *aqueste* is the less frequent form in general and in the corpus for this study, then I discuss the non-pragmatic factors that may affect the variation between *aqueste* and *este*, and finally I identify and illustrate the pragmatic functions of *aqueste* to show how they differ from those of *este*.

2. OVERALL OCCURRENCE OF *AQUESTE* AND *ESTE*

The long form *aqueste* has always been very much in the minority among demonstrative adjectives and pronouns, as shown in Figure 1. A search of the masculine plural form of the various demonstratives, *estos*, *esos*, *aquellos*, *aquestos* and *aquesos*, and their orthographic variants, in the *Corpus del español* shows that *aquestos* never accounted for more than 7.5% of all demonstratives in written texts, with its highest percentage coming in the 1400s.[3] By contrast,

---

[3] It was necessary to consider only masculine plural forms in this comparison since *estos* is the only form of the demonstrative *este* that is not identical to a form of the verb *estar*, when accent marks are not taken into account, as is often the case in Old Spanish and as is always the case in the *Corpus del español*. The demonstrative *este* is identical to the third person singular form of the present subjunctive *esté*, *esta* is identical to *está*, *esto* is often identical to *esto(y)*, and *estas* is identical to *estás*. Furthermore, the search engine for the *Corpus del español* cannot distinguish among items according to their function, such as demonstrative, nor will it even show all the examples of an item with more than 2000 tokens in a single century. Since it was impossible to distinguish between the demonstrative and the forms of the verb *estar* for *este*, *esta*, *esto*, and *estas*, I decided

estos accounted for a far higher percentage of demonstratives in each century, with its greatest percentage of 63.4% occurring in the 1600s. This figure also shows that by the 1700s, and certainly the 1800s, *aquestos* had practically disappeared from use. Girón Alconchel (1998:501) claims that the long forms had died "irremediablemente" by the second decade of the seventeenth century, so by about 1610. This may or may not be true depending on whether the 413 tokens of *aquestos* found in the *Corpus del español* in the 1600s occurred in the first ten years of that century. It is interesting to note as well that the percentages of *aquestos* and *estos* are not in inverse proportion. The highest percentage of *aquestos* is occurs in the 1400s, yet the lowest percentage of *estos* occurs in the 1200s. Similarly, the highest percentage of *estos* occurs in the 1600s, while the lowest percentage of *aquestos* occurs in the 1900s. It turns out that the proportion of *estos* depends more on the relative proportions of *esos* and *aquellos* in each century, rather than on the small percentages of *aquestos*.

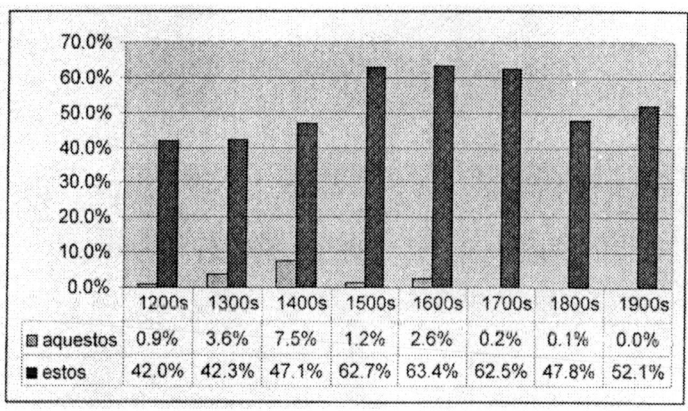

FIGURE 1: *Aquestos* and *estos* as a percentage of all demonstratives according to century

Another measure of the frequency of *aquestos* is to compare its number of tokens not to the overall number of demonstratives, since this depends on the number of tokens of *estos*, *aquesos*, *esos*, and *aquellos*, but only to the number of tokens of *estos*. Figure 2 then shows *aquestos* as a percentage of all

---

to base the comparison of the relative frequency of *aqueste* and *este* on their masculine plural forms, *aquestos* and *estos*.

occurrences of *aquestos* and *estos* combined. One sees again that *aquestos* occurs in relatively low percentages compared to its short counterpart *estos* in all centuries. At its highest point in the 1400s it still accounts for less than 14% of the total number of occurrences of the demonstratives indicating nearness to the speaker.

FIGURE 2: *Aquestos* as a percentage of total number
of occurrences of *aquestos* and *estos* according to century

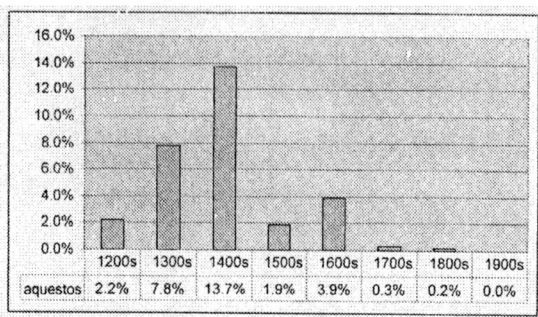

In the texts that make up the corpus for this study, *aqueste* in all of its forms, i.e. *aqueste, aquesta, aquesto, aquestos, aquestas*, also occurs in relatively low proportions, as shown in Table 1, even though I deliberately chose two texts that appeared to have a good number of examples of *aqueste*. Of the first one hundred demonstratives, *aqueste* occurs only once in TL and 17 times in LBA. When *aqueste* is compared to *este* only, one still finds only one token in TL and 20 in LBA. In the entire works, there are 63 tokens of *aqueste* versus approximately 1114 tokens of *este* in TL, so that *aqueste* accounts for only 5.4% of all demonstratives in this series. In LBA one finds 118 tokens of *aqueste* and approximately 355 tokens of *este*, so that *aqueste* accounts for about 25% of the demonstratives of the *este* series in this text.[4] It is obvious that *aqueste*, while still in the minority, occurs more often in the verse text than in the prose text.

---

[4] Rather than counting all the occurrences of *este* in each text, I identified the first 100 occurrences in each text and then extrapolated the total number by assuming that *este* would continue to occur in the same proportions throughout the texts.

	no. and % in first 100 demonstratives of all types		% in first 100 occurrences of aqueste/este		no. and % of aqueste/este in entire text	
	aqueste	*este*	*aqueste*	*este*	*aqueste*	*este*
TL	1	74	1%	99%	63 (5.4%)	1114 (94.6%)
LBA	17	66	20%	80%	118 (24.9%)	355 (75.1%)

TABLE 1: Distribution of *aqueste* and *este* in the corpus

Thus we have demonstrated that *aqueste* was far less frequent a form than *este* in every century in which it appeared. According to its appearance in the texts in the *Corpus del español*, it accounted for a maximum of 7.5% of all demonstratives in the fifteenth century and of 14% of the occurrences of both *aqueste* and *este* in the same century. In the texts which make up the corpus for this study, *aqueste* accounts for only about 5% of the demonstratives in the *este* series in *Tristan* and for about 25% of the demonstratives in this series in the *Libro de Buen Amor*. It is clear then that *aqueste* is a less frequent and therefore marked form in relation to *este*.

It is also worth mentioning that the pronoun forms of both words are less frequent in the two texts than their adjectival forms. Of the 63 tokens of *aqueste* in TL only 19 (30%) are pronouns and in LBA only 46 (39%) of the 118 tokens are pronouns. For *este*, though, pronouns account for a higher proportion of the first 100 occurrences in each text: 43 of the first 100 occurrences in TL and 53 in LBA. In the following analyses, no distinction will be made between adjectival and pronoun forms of *aqueste* and *este*, except in cases where these two grammatical classes clearly function differently in both texts.

3. NON-PRAGMATIC FACTORS AND THE VARIATION OF *AQUESTE* AND *ESTE*

In order to formulate the hypothesis that the variation between *aqueste* and *este* correlates with pragmatic factors, I first considered the possible effect of non-pragmatic factors on their variation in the corpus. Two of these factors, which had already been mentioned in the literature, are type of discourse (Girón Alconchel 1998:500) and physical presence of the referent (Montgomery 1962, cited in Girón Alconchel 1998:495). The other two factors are the function of the demonstrative, whether spatial, temporal, or referential, and its syntactic position in the sentence, whether in marked or unmarked preverbal or postverbal position. The non-pragmatic factors, since they do not depend on the possible meanings of the variants, can be defined more clearly and classified in a more mechanical way than the pragmatic factors. Therefore, they provide a first approximation of the variation between *aqueste* and *este* which can serve as useful background information to the pragmatic analysis.

3.1. DISCOURSE TYPE: CONVERSATION OR NARRATION

Girón Alconchel (1998:500), in a rare study focusing specifically on the demonstratives *aqueste* and *aquese*, indicates that the rather scarce *aqueste* was relatively more frequent in poetry and conversation than in prose narration. We have already seen in Table 1 that *aqueste* does occur more frequently in one verse text than in one prose text, since it accounts for 25% of tokens in the *este* series in the LBA yet only for 5% of such tokens in TL. In order to determine whether *aqueste* occurs more often in conversation than in narration in these two texts, I first classified all tokens of *aqueste* in each text and the first 100 tokens of *este* in each text for this factor. The classification was made quite simply by considering anything written in quotation marks to be conversation and everything else to be narration, even though the LBA has a first-person narrator. Example (2) shows *aqueste* in TL used in a direct quotation considered to be conversation, while (3) shows its appearance in narration.

(2) *E Lamarad les rogo que le dixessen que virtud auia aquel cuerno; "yo os lo dire, dixo la donzella: "**aqueste** cuerno, si alguno ha duda que su muger le haga maldad, hinchalo de vino e hagala beuer con el ..."* (TL 33, 1, 137)

(3) *E quando Tristan oyo **aquestas** palabras, começo a reyr ...* (TL 54, 1, 239)

Table 2 shows the tallies of these classifications. In both texts, when one classifies all the tokens of *aqueste* and *este* under consideration as occurring either in conversation or in narration and then calculates for each its percentage of the total number of tokens, one finds that a higher percentage of the tokens of *aqueste* occur in conversation than do the tokens of *este* (78% vs. 64% in TL and 42% vs. 32% in LBA). It appears then that conversation does favor the use of *aqueste* over *este*, but only slightly. In addition, the fact that only 14 tokens of *aqueste* occur in narration in the prose text provides support for Girón Alconchel's (1998:500) statement that *aqueste* is more frequent in poetry and conversation than in prose narration. It is interesting to note that the proportions of *aqueste* and *este* appear to depend more on the genre of the text, whether verse or prose, than on the distinction between conversation and narration. In the prose text both *aqueste* and *este* occur more often in conversation, while in the verse text they both occur more often in narration. It appears then that there may simply be more conversation in the prose text than in the verse text, or at least that demonstratives occur more often in conversation in the prose text and in narration in the text in verse. Rather than depending on the genre of the text, the differences between TL and LBA may be due to the type of narrator. The first-person narrator in LBA apparently uses these demonstratives at a higher rate than the third-person narrator in TL. We can conclude therefore that there is a tendency for *aqueste* to occur more often in verse or with a first-person narrator and in conversation.

	conversation	narration	total
TL: *aqueste*	49 (78%)	14 (22%)	63
TL: *este*	64 (64%)	36 (36%)	100
LBA: *aqueste*	50 (42%)	68 (58%)	118
LBA: *este*	32 (32%)	68 (68%)	100

TABLE 2: Variation of *aqueste* and *este* according to discourse type: conversation vs. narration[5]

3.2. PHYSICAL PRESENCE OF THE REFERENT

Montgomery (1962, cited in Girón Alconchel 1998:495) proposed that *aqueste* is generally used to refer to visible objects, a demonstration *ad oculos*, according to Girón Alconchel (1998:495). In this analysis, I propose to distinguish between a referent, whether person, object or place, that is physically present, one that is not physically present, and one that cannot be physically present, as in the case for abstract nouns, such as *amor*. The determination of physical presence is made from the point of the view of the characters within the story. To illustrate, in Example (5) the maiden referred to by *aquesta donzella* is clearly present to the characters in the story. In (6), by contrast, the woman referred to by the speaker is not present while he contemplates marriage to her.

(4) "*aquesta donzella sera vuestra que aqui veys ...*" (TL 71, 1, 303)

(5) "*Si tomo a aquesta por muger, yo saldria de gran cuyta ...*" (TL 40, 3, 173)

Something can also be considered to be physically present within narration, rather than in conversation, when the narrator is describing something present within the story, like the squire in (6) or the lawyer in (7).

(6) *E estando un dia Tristan fablando con el rey, entro un escudero por medio del palacio del rey. E **aqueste** escudero hera el que llevo el cavallo ...* (TL

---

[5] In this analysis and in all subsequent analyses, I consider the first 100 occurrences of *este* in each text and all occurrences of *aqueste* in each text for a total of 63 in TL and 118 in LBA.

13, 1, 50)

(7) *Este* gran abogado propuso de su parte: ... (LBA 333a)

Table 3 indicates that physical presence does not contribute to the variation between *aqueste* and *este* in TL, since the percentages for these two demonstratives in this text are very close in all categories. In LBA the percentages for *aqueste* are similar to those for *aqueste* and *este* in TL, but one finds far fewer examples of *este* referring to something physically present and far more examples of *este* referring to something that cannot be physically present. Since this initial classification of physical presence did not prove too revealing, I then calculated physical presence only within conversation on the assumption that physical presence might be more meaningful within the context of a real conversation rather than in a narrative where the reader is in all cases physically removed from the action. In this calculation, the use of *aqueste* with physical presence has increased overall, but it has decreased when compared to *este*. In LBA *aqueste* is now only 10 percentage points ahead of *este* rather than 19, and in TL *aqueste* now designates a referent physically present in conversation less often than *este* does. These data fail to support the contention that *aqueste* refers to something physically present. Instead, there appears to be a tendency in LBA for *este* not to refer to something physically present.

	physically present	not physically present	cannot be physically present	physically present in conversation only[6]
TL: aqueste	24 (38%)	12 (19%)	27 (43%)	21/49 (43%)
TL: este	36 (36%)	18 (18%)	46 (46%)	30/64 (47%)
LBA: aqueste	41 (35%)	20 (17%)	57 (48%)	22/50 (44%)
LBA: este	16 (16%)	17 (17%)	67 (67%)	11/32 (34%)

TABLE 3: Variation of *aqueste* and *este* according to physical presence of referent

---

[6] For this category, the percentage is the number of tokens in conversation which are physically present out of the total number of tokens in conversation.

3.3. FUNCTION OF DEMONSTRATIVE: SPATIAL, TEMPORAL, OR REFERENTIAL

In a study on the position of demonstrative adjectives in Modern Andalusian Spanish, Ranson (1999:122) proposed four possible functions for demonstratives found in the literature. Three of these, spatial, temporal, and referential function, are analysed here. The fourth function, emotional, which can co-occur with the others, is not considered.

A demonstrative with spatial function indicates the physical location of its referent in relation to a certain point of reference. Therefore, in conversation this referent is usually physically present as well. In (8), one can interpret the pronoun *aqueste* as referring to the knight facing off in the battle with the speaker by using the speaker's location as the point of reference.

(8) *aqueste no da golpes de mozo* ... (TL 8, 1, 33)

A demonstrative with temporal function serves to indicate a specific moment in time in relation to a temporal reference point. In (9) we understand that *aquesta noche* refers to the same night when Doña Endrina makes the statement because the temporal reference point is the moment of speaking.

(9) *"si vos non me descobrierdes, dezir vos é una pastija / que pensé **aquesta** noche"* (LBA 724d)

A demonstrative with referential function refers to the place of the referent within the text of the discourse. The referring expression, in this case the noun phrase containing the demonstrative adjective or pronoun, is called an anaphor when it refers to something already mentioned, as in (10), and as a cataphor when it refers to something mentioned later in the discourse, as in (11). In (10), *aquesto* refers to the crime of stealing and eating a rooster described previously, and in (11), *este acuerdo* refers to the following statement that a person's birth sign affects his or her fate and talents.

(10) *en casa de Don Cabrón ... / sacó furtando el gallo, ... / levólo e comiólo a mi pesar en tal ero. / De **aquesto** la acuso, ante vós, el buen varón /* (LBA 328a)

(11) *otros muchos maestros en **este** acuerdo son: / qual es el asçendente e la costellaçion / del que naçe, tal es su fado e su don./* (LBA 124b)

For the purposes of classification, reference is considered to be a more general

category than either spatial or temporal function. This means that an expression which refers to something mentioned elsewhere in the text is classified as having a referential function, even though it may also have a spatial or temporal function as well.

Both texts contain only a few examples of the temporal function of demonstratives, while TL has more demonstratives with a spatial function and LBA has more with a referential function. In both texts, *aqueste* occurs more often than *este* with a spatial function and *este* occurs more often with a referential function. The most noteworthy result is the 14 examples of cataphoric reference for *aqueste* in LBA. It appears that the marked form *aqueste* is preferred in this text for this less frequent type of reference. Of the 20 examples of cataphoric reference in LBA, 70% are indicated by *aqueste*.

	spatial	temporal	referential	anaphor[7]	cataphor
TL: *aqueste*	21 (33%)	0 (0%)	42 (67%)	41 (98%)	1 (2%)
TL: *este*	26 (26%)	1 (1%)	73 (73%)	71 (97%)	2 (3%)
LBA: *aqueste*	22 (18%)	2 (2%)	94 (80%)	80 (85%)	14 (15%)
LBA: *este*	12 (12%)	3 (3%)	85 (85%)	79 (93%)	6 (7%)

TABLE 4: Variation of *aqueste* and *este* according to function of the demonstrative

3.4. SYNTACTIC POSITION OF DEMONSTRATIVE:
PREVERBAL OR POSTVERBAL, MARKED OR UNMARKED

We distinguish four possible positions for demonstrative noun phrases within a sentence in order to determine whether marked or unmarked syntactic positions correlate with marked or unmarked forms of the demonstrative, that is, with *aqueste* and *este*, respectively. If we consider the typical word order in Spanish to be subject-verb-object and/or prepositional phrase, as in *vos soys culpante*

---

[7] For the categories "anaphor" and "cataphor", the percentage is the number of tokens of each type of reference out of the total number of tokens with referential function.

deste fecho e en aqueste mal (TL 32,2,142), then a demonstrative noun phrase which functions as a direct object or the object of a prepositional phrase and which precedes the verb is considered to be in preverbal marked position, as in (12) below and in (2) and (10) above. It is important to note that the object does not have to be sentence-initial to be classified as occurring in marked position; it need only be preverbal, as seen in (13) below and in (11) above.

(12)   *aquesta* batalla començamos vos e yo (TL 25, 1, 97)
(13)   yo *aqueste* don no os le daria ... (TL 76, 1, 339)

By contrast, a demonstrative noun phrase serving as subject in preverbal position is considered to be unmarked, as in examples (4), (6), (7), and (8) above. Similarly, any postverbal object is considered to be in unmarked position, as in (5) above. However, a postverbal subject is considered to be in marked postverbal position, as in (14).

(14)   *quand ella vio este mal tan grande que le hazia **aqueste** cavallero ...*
       (TL 73, 1, 317)

It is clear from Table 5 that marked syntactic position does not correlate with use of the marked demonstrative *aqueste* given that the percentages for both demonstratives are remarkably similar in all four positions. The only minor exception is unmarked preverbal position where *aqueste* occurs at a higher rate in TL.

	marked preverbal	unmarked preverbal	marked postverbal	unmarked postverbal
TL: *aqueste*	20 (32%)	14 (22%)	27 (43%)	2 (3%)
TL: *este*	33 (33%)	13 (13%)	48 (48%)	6 (6%)
LBA: *aqueste*	41 (35%)	15 (13%)	56 (47%)	6 (5%)
LBA: *este*	36 (36%)	15 (15%)	46 (46%)	3 (3%)

TABLE 5: Variation of *aqueste* and *este* according to syntactic position

3.5. SUMMARY OF NON-PRAGMATIC FACTORS
This analysis of four non-pragmatic factors has revealed the following about the factors tested:

1. *aqueste* occurs more often in the verse text than in the prose text
2. *aqueste* occurs more often in conversation than in narration;
3. *aqueste* is preferred over *este* for cataphoric reference in LBA;
4. physical presence, the function of the demonstrative and syntactic position appear not to be factors in the variation between *aqueste* and *este;*
5. Since it has been shown that non-pragmatic factors have little effect on the variation between *aqueste* and *este*, we will now consider pragmatic factors.

4. PRAGMATIC FACTORS INFLUENCING
THE VARIATION OF *AQUESTE* AND *ESTE*

Girón Alconchel (1998:498) implies that *aqueste* and *este* have the same referential meaning, but different pragmatic meanings when he says: "parece que la sinonimia de *este* y *aqueste, ese* y *aquese* es completa; sólo cabrían matices contextuales, que Correas parece reducir a la oposición 'no énfasis' vs. 'énfasis'." Girón Alconchel does not find the distinction based on emphasis to be profitable, especially since *aqueste* was such a rare form, but I believe that Correas deserves credit for providing the grain of an idea awaiting further development and for providing contemporary confirmation that the opposition *aqueste/este* may have expressed pragmatic meaning. The problem with distinguishing between *aqueste* and *este* according to emphasis is that this term has often been too widely applied and too broadly defined. If emphasis is carefully defined, however, and its components are specified, then it can be a useful concept.

A useful way of understanding what Correas might have intended by saying that *aqueste* signals emphasis is to consider *aqueste* to be a focusing device. According to Taglicht (1984:7), such focusing devices "give prominence to selected parts of sentences or utterances, and this is itself part of their meaning." This prominence is likely to be similar to what Horn (1984: 22) meant when he proposed that additional information or marked forms invite the hearer to draw an implicature to attribute meaning to this form, as discussed in the introduction. Following Halliday and Hasan (1976:26ff), Taglicht (1984:7), in a discussion of message and emphasis in English, proposes that focusing devices can have ideational, textual, or interpersonal meaning, or, in the terms preferred by Traugott (1982:247-48), propositional, textual or expressive meaning. In fact this tripartite distinction can profitably be applied to the meanings of *aqueste* in the two texts selected for analysis, and each is illustrated and discussed in greater detail below. Propositional or ideational meaning derives from the content represented, as in the case of contrast or assertion in the face of contrary expectations, while textual meaning derives from the representation of the structure of elements within a text, by indicating the cohesion between its parts. The expressive or interpersonal component "bears on the resources a language has for expressing personal attitudes to what is being talked about, to the text itself, and to others in the speech situation" (Traugott 1982:248).

Whereas in the previous section on non-pragmatic factors, we followed a variationist methodology of coding each token in the sample for every factor tested (although Varbrul was not applied nor were results tested for statistical significance), it is less common practice to apply this methodology to pragmatic factors. The typical practice in pragmatics is to offer a detailed discussion of specific examples to show how they illustrate various pragmatic meanings without any attempt at quantification. The possible meanings of each example are considered to be so nuanced that they cannot be grouped together and, therefore, they cannot be counted and quantified. Furthermore, a single example can express several different pragmatic meanings simultaneously. Since a one-to-one correspondence of token to meaning is lacking, it makes less sense to code each token for each factor (Davidson 1996, Stewart 2003). In the following analysis, I propose to adopt a middle ground between these two methods in which I discuss examples of the meaning of *aqueste* in each of the three large categories of pragmatic meaning: propositional, textual, and expressive. Then I propose to show the number of tokens of *aqueste* which probably express this meaning in each text, and, by way of contrast, I also give these numbers for *este*. I do not intend these data to imply that certain pragmatic factors favor either *aqueste* or *este*; I intend only to give an overview of the correlation between forms and meaning in the corpus. Through this process I show that it is possible to interpret almost every token of *aqueste* as giving prominence to the demonstrative noun phrase in which it occurs, but that *aqueste* is not the only means for giving prominence in these cases.

4.1. PROPOSITIONAL MEANING: CONTRAST AND
ASSERTION IN THE FACE OF CONTRARY EXPECTATIONS
One can consider that a focusing device has propositional meaning, that is, meaning related to content, when it expresses a contrast or corrects a prior contrary expectation. The most basic element of contrast, or even the more general term, 'comparison', which can include similarity as well as difference, can be seen as what Akmajian (1973:222) calls "a pairing of foci". When people are compared, for example, the foci are two or more people who are paired based on similarity or difference with respect to a certain feature or action. Specifically, I define contrast following Chafe (1976:35) and Silva-Corvalán (1982:114), who use the term 'focus of contrast,' as a person, object, or place standing in

opposition to a clearly identifiable set of candidates. Assertion in the face of contrary expectations also places something in opposition, not to other possible candidates, though, but to a contrary expectation about it.

4.1.1. CONTRAST

In classifying the examples of demonstrative noun phrases in the corpus, we distinguish between explicit and implicit forms of contrast. In an explicit contrast, both candidates standing in opposition to each other are explicitly mentioned, whereas in implicit contrast only one candidate is mentioned and the other is implied (Taglicht 1984:47). In (15), for example, we encounter an explicit contrast between two people when Tristan uses *aquesta* to refer to Yseo de las blancas manos, to whom he is contemplating marriage, and *aquella* to refer to Yseo la Brunda, his true love to whom he is bound by a love potion.

(15) Si tomo a ***aquesta*** por muger, yo saldria de gran cuyta; e, si pongo por oluido ***aquella*** dueña, no perdere nada, antes ganare honrra e dueña... (TL 40, 3, 173)

In (16), however, the contrast is implicit. When a maiden asks Tristan whether the knight with the two swords won the tournament, he replies, "not this time". His response implies a contrast to the other occasions on which this knight has won the tournament, but he does not mention these other times specifically.

(16) Dixo la donzella: "pues dezidme quien vencio el torneo; ¿venciole el cavallero de las dos espadas?" E el dixo: "No de ***aquesta*** vez" (TL 12, 2, 47)

Another type of implicit contrast can occur when something is compared not to another object, but to its former state, as in (17). On his death bed, Tristan invites Yseo to compare his changed body to what it once was like. Even though he states explicitly that death is responsible for the change, he does not ever make an explicit comparison between his arms as they are now and these same arms as they once were.

(17) "¡Ay, la mi señora reyna, Yseo! ¿que me catays?, que yo so don Tristan, el vuestro leal cavallero; ¿y son ***aquestos*** los cabellos que vos soliades catar?, ¿y son ***aquestos*** los ojos que vos soliades mirar?, ¿y son ***estos*** los braços que por vuestro servicio solian lidiar?; y agora la muerte lo ha todo tornado de su calidad y condicion". (TL 82, 1, 365)

While the identification of explicit contrast is fairly straightforward because both terms standing in contrast must be mentioned, the identification of implicit contrast is more difficult to make with any certainty. In considering whether an example expresses implicit contrast, I applied the test of adding "as opposed to others" after the demonstrative noun phrase. If I thought this addition was implied by the speaker, then I considered this example to be a case of implicit contrast. If not, then I considered the example not to express any contrast at all. In the case of a superlative, as in (18), in which Morlot declares Tristan to be the most handsome young man he has ever seen, it is uncontroversial that he meant to imply the contrast "as opposed to others I have seen". Other examples are more problematic, however, such as (19), which I classified as implicit contrast to all the other battles Tristan had fought which did not result in his death, and (20), which I classified as not expressing contrast, interpreting *aquesta batalla* as a simple reference to the battle at hand without any implied contrast to other battles.

(18)   *E Morlot paro mientes a Tristan, e dixo al rey:* "**Este** *es el mas fermoso donzel e el mas enseñado que yo nunca vi.*" (TL 4, 2, 17)

(19)   *E Tristan dixo:* "... *e* **aquesta** *batalla conozco que es de muerte*" (TL 67, 3, 291)

(20)   *E Tristan dixo:* "*no querriades que la batalla fuese empeçada de vuestra mano e que se acavase por mano de otro mientra que vos fuesedes bivo: e* **aquesta** *batalla començamos vos e yo ...*" (TL 25, 1, 97)

Part of the problem of classifying implicit contrast stems from the fact that its determination from written examples actually reverses the process used by speakers and hearers. If a speaker wishes to express contrast, then he or she will choose to apply a focusing device to the contrasting term and hearers will know to interpret this added prominence as an expression of contrast. For example, if we had already established beyond a reasonable doubt that *aqueste* was a focusing device, then we would know that one possible interpretation of the prominence indicated by *aqueste* is contrast. On the other hand, if we do not assume that *aqueste* is a focusing device then it is difficult to determine whether a speaker meant it to indicate a contrast. One can only judge from the other information available in the context whether a contrast might have been intended, but one cannot determine the speaker's intention. Along these lines it is interesting that Taglicht (1984:39) indicates that stress accent in speech is the given from which the hearer, and later the linguist, determines the newness of a linguistic item, rather than the other way around. A hearer does not guess whether the speaker would have placed an accent on an item according to whether or not it is new. He or she simply makes an interpretation based on the cues provided by the speaker.

In spite of the difficulty in determining implicit contrast, I have nevertheless classified the examples in the corpus using my best judgment. We see in Table 6 that the demonstrative *aqueste* is certainly used more often than *este* to indicate contrast, especially implicit contrast, and most especially when *aqueste* is a pronoun. This does not mean, however, that *este* is never used to express contrast, since there are 16 examples in TL of a contrast expressed by *este* and 36 examples in LBA.

	explicit contrast	implicit contrast	no contrast	explicit and implicit contrast in pronouns[8]
TL: *aqueste*	8 (13%)	29 (46%)	26 (41%)	17/19 (89%)
TL: *este*	6 (6%)	10 (10%)	84 (84%)	8/25 (32%)
LBA: *aqueste*	13 (11%)	48 (41%)	57 (48%)	24/46 (52%)
LBA: *este*	8 (8%)	28 (28%)	64 (64%)	21/53 (40%)

TABLE 6: Variation of *aqueste* and *este* according to contrast

There are several possible explanations for the choice of *este* rather than the marked form *aqueste* to express a contrast. One is that the speaker uses another focusing device, such as syntactic position, to give prominence to the items standing in contrast. One such syntactic device is to place this item in marked preverbal position. In fact, the demonstrative adjective or pronoun *este* appears in marked preverbal position in 1 of 6 cases of explicit contrast in TL and in 3 of 8 cases in LBA. For implicit contrast, 2 out of 10 are in marked preverbal position in TL and 8 out of 28 in LBA. Example (21) shows how marked syntactic position lends prominence to the first of two terms, *este* and *este otro*, standing in contrast in the same sentence.

---

[8] For the category "explicit and implicit contrast in pronouns", the percentage is the number of demonstrative pronouns which show any type of contrast out of the total number of pronouns.

(21)   El rey dixo: "el que escogistes de primer, *este* conviene que ayays, e conviene que corte la cabeça a *este otro*." (TL 5, 1, 22)

Other syntactic and lexical devices, as yet unanalysed, might also indicate contrast. Another possibility is that even though two terms stand in contrast, the speaker chooses not to give them prominence. When in the text leading up to (21) the king explains to his daughter that she will choose which man will die, he may wish not to emphasize either man so as not to influence her decision, as seen in (22).

(22)   "... ya sabeys que *este* vuestro primo a de morir, por la muerte que ha fecho, e *este* donzel deve morir, porque quiso fazer desonrra de ovs; el uno destos querria que escapase, e el otro que muera, e esto quiero que determines vos." (TL 5, 1, 22)

It also appears to be the case in some examples that once *aqueste* has been used for a referent, then subsequent references to this item or a similar one are made with *este* even though the prominence of the item continues. An example of this phenomenon can be seen clearly in (17) above when Tristan refers to his hair and eyes with *aquestos*, comparing them to how they used to be, and then uses *estos* to refer to his arms. Two other possibilities should also be mentioned. It is conceivable that in my desire to be objective and thorough I classified as implicit contrast cases where the speaker or writer would not have intended any contrast. Finally, it is also possible, given its scarcity, that *aqueste* is not always used even in cases where prominence appears to be warranted.

4.1.2. ASSERTION IN THE FACE OF CONTRARY EXPECTATIONS

Another reason for giving prominence to a demonstrative noun phrase could be the speaker's attempt to correct a contrary expectation on the part of the hearer.[9] By using a marked form in such cases, the speaker is saying in essence, "I know this is not what you expect, but this really is the case." Assertion in the face of contrary expectations, like contrast, can also be explicit when the contrary expectation is expressed, as in (23) and (24), or implicit when the expectation is only implied by the hearer or anticipated by the speaker, as in (25). In (23) the boat captain says that Galeote can't possibly want to make a certain trip because

---

[9] This category is similar to a subcategory of contrast identified for the presence of subject pronouns called refutation of a false assumption (D'Introno 1989:40).

they will all die or be taken prisoner, and Galeote replies that that is precisely why he wants to make the trip. We see that the speaker can also correct his own erroneous assumption, as in (24), when Morlot corrects his expectation that Tristan was still just a boy unworthy of battle.

(23) el maestro [de la nao] le dixo: "Bien soys vos loco, cauallero, que quereys que seamos todos muertos o presos; ... y Galeote le dixo: "por **aquesta** razon quiero yr alla." (TL 24, 1, 97)

(24) e Morlot dixo ... "Cavallero, vos soys mucho moço, por que os consejo que dexeys esta batalla" ... e desta primer batalla se dieron tan grandes golpes, que dixo Morlot entre si: "**aqueste** no da golpes de moço; antes los da como hombre de fuerça e gran coraçon." (TL 8, 1, 32-33)

Example (25) shows a case of assertion in the face of implicit contrary expectations on the part of the speaker. Galaz had not expected to find himself fighting with the devil, but his opponent, Tristan, fights so well that Galaz concludes that he must be the devil in spite of his initial expectation that he was fighting another knight.

(25) E dixo don Galaz en alta voz ...: "Santa Maria, ayuda al tu cavallero en este punto"; e dixo: "¡por Dios!, **aqueste** es el diablo, que no me a querido dezir su nombre ..." (TL 78, 1, 350-51)

One could also consider the demonstratives in (17) above to be an example of assertion in the face of implicit contrary expectations because Tristan anticipates Yseo's expectation that he would be the Tristan she remembers rather than the weakened Tristan she sees before her.

As in the case of contrast, Table 7 shows that assertion in the face of contrary expectations is more likely to be expressed by *aqueste* than by *este*, especially by the pronoun *aqueste*. There are, however, 4 cases in TL and 13 in LBA of the pronoun *este* used to correct contrary expectations. It is likely that reasons for the use of *este* similar to the ones discussed above for contrast apply in this case as well.

	explicit contrary to expectations	implicit contrary to expectations	not contrary to expectations	explicit and implicit contrary to expectations in pronouns[10]
TL: *aqueste*	10 (16%)	7 (11%)	46 (73%)	8/19 (42%)
TL: *este*	1 (1%)	3 (3%)	96 (96%)	4/25 (16%)
LBA: *aqueste*	5 (4%)	24 (20%)	89 (76%)	11/46 (24%)
LBA: *este*	3 (3%)	10 (10%)	87 (87%)	8/53 (15%)

TABLE 7: Variation of *aqueste* and *este* according to expectations

4.2. TEXTUAL MEANING: CHANGE IN INFORMATIONAL STATUS

Taglicht (1984:7), following Halliday and Hasan (1976:26ff.), stated that prominence, which can be expressed by means of a marked form such as *aqueste*, could also be used to indicate the structure of discourse to the hearer or reader. One example of this use is found in our corpus when a noun is first introduced with a definite or indefinite article and then soon after appears with the demonstrative adjective *aqueste* or *este*. The prominence of the noun phrase expressed by *aqueste* apparently signals a change in the informational status of this noun phrase from the general to the particular, as in (26), or from introductory mention with an indefinite article to topic status with *aqueste*, as in (27).

(26)   ... *e hablaron cada uno de las aventuras que les havian contescido. E Tristan le conto en como era el rey librado, e de **aquesta** aventura Lamarad fue alegre* ... (TL 47, 2, 210-11)

(27)   *E estando un dia Tristan fablando con el rey, entro un escudero por medio del palacio del rey. E **aqueste** escudero hera el que llevo el cavallo e la espada a Tristan de parte de Belisenda* ... (TL 13, 1, 50)

While few examples of this possible function of demonstratives occur in the corpus, most of these examples are expressed by *aqueste*. In fact only 6 of the 34 examples are expressed by *este*.

---

[10] For the category "explicit and implicit contrast in pronouns", the percentage is the number of pronoun forms of *aqueste* and *este* which show any type of contrast out of the total number of pronoun forms of *aqueste* and *este*.

	particularizing	topic raising
TL: *aqueste*	4 (8%)	8 (11%)
TL: *este*	0 (0%)	3 (3%)
LBA: *aqueste*	4 (3%)	12 (10%)
LBA: *este*	3 (3%)	0 (0%)

TABLE 8: Variation of *aqueste* and *este* according to change of status

4.3. EXPRESSIVE MEANING: THE SPEAKER'S ATTITUDE

This final category is the most difficult to define precisely; therefore, we will not even attempt to code all the tokens in the sample for their potential expression of the speaker's attitude or emotions. However, it is useful to consider this possible meaning, especially for the examples of *aqueste* that appear to fit into this category, whose prominence would not otherwise be explained by one of the previous meanings. When the speaker uses *aqueste* with this meaning, he or she is saying in effect: "I want to be sure you understand the importance of this for you personally or for me personally."

An example of the use of *aqueste* to indicate the importance of the noun to the speaker personally is shown in (28) where the writer is emphasizing the importance of the ideas he would like to commit to paper (and perhaps also the contrast between their importance and his lack of talent for writing).

(28) *E por **aquesto** que tengo en coraçón de escrevir, / tengo del miedo tanto quanto non puedo dezir; /* ... (LBA 1134a)

The speaker may also use *aqueste* to reinforce the importance of the item highlighted for the hearer, especially in cases of the hearer's culpability, as in (29), when Rey Mares accuses Tristan of having caused great damage by entering Yseo's room at night. It is interesting in this example that *este* occurs with *fecho* while *aqueste* occurs with *mal*; it is no doubt more important to emphasize the harm rather than the simple deed.

(29) *"vos soys culpante **deste** fecho e en **aqueste** mal, que ninguno no entro en la camara de la reyna sino vos."* (TL 33, 2, 142)

We also observe a similar example of accusation in (10) above. It is possible of course that an example would be important both to the speaker and the hearer, as in (30) when the mouse offers to free the lion from his trap.

(30) *"Señor, yo trayo buen cochillo: / con **aquestos** mis dientes rodré poco*

a poquillo, / do están vuestras manos, faré un grand portillo." (LBA 1431b-d)

In many of the other examples already cited, we can observe the personal importance of the demonstrative noun phrase to the speaker or hearer, in addition to the other meanings already mentioned. In fact (17) offers an excellent example of the multiple functions of the demonstrative *aqueste*. In the sentence, *¿y son **aquestos** los ojos que vos soliades mirar?* (TL 82, 1, 365), the demonstrative expresses contrastive meaning through the comparison with Tristan's former condition, assertion in the face of contrary expectations, since Yseo would not have expected to find him like this, and the personal importance of this condition to Tristan and to Yseo.

4.4. SUMMARY OF PRAGMATIC FACTORS

The analysis of pragmatic meanings has shown in general that *aqueste* gives prominence to its referent. This prominence can be interpreted as expressing an explicit or implicit contrast between this referent and another or an explicit or implicit assertion in the face of contrary expectations; that is, a contrast between what one might have assumed and what is actually the case. It can also signal a change in the status of the referent from generic or indefinite to specific, which sometimes also signals raising to the status of topic, or the personal importance of the referent for the speaker or the hearer or both. For all of these meanings, except for personal importance which was not quantified, *aqueste* occurred in greater proportions than *este* in the two texts serving as the corpus for this study.

It remains to see whether there are examples of *aqueste* in these two texts which do not express any of the proposed pragmatic meanings. In order to make this determination, I progressively remove from consideration the examples of *aqueste* which have been classified as expressing various meanings in a definite order, as shown in Table 9. For example, once I have removed the examples where *aqueste* expresses explicit contrast, then these examples are not considered again, even though they may express another meaning as well. At the end of this process, we find remaining 9 examples in TL and 19 examples in LBA.

	TL no. of examples for this meaning	TL remaining number out of 63	LBA no. of examples for this meaning	LBA remaining number out of 118
explicit contrast	8	55	13	105
explicit contrary to expectation	9	46	4	101
implicit contrast	18	28	46	55
implicit contrary to expectations	2	26	8	47
change in status	12	14	13	34
expressive	5	9	15	19

TABLE 9: Summary of *aqueste* according to pragmatic meanings

An examination of these remaining examples indicates that they can nevertheless be analysed as indicating the prominence of the noun phrase, but they do not fall into any of the categories already identified. The best overall term I could give to them is "specialness", yet, like personal importance, this is not a term I could define rigorously or quantify. In (31) we can conclude that a tent where some of the best knights in the world are located is a special tent, but it does not correspond clearly to any of the other proposed pragmatic meanings.

(31) "*Señores, ya podeys ver las cavallerias de Tristan, que por fuerça de armas ha preso a uno de los mejores cavalleros del mundo, ... e a tanto buen cavallero como esta en **aquesta** tienda ...*" (TL 52, 1, 229)

It is also possible that some of these remaining examples fit into some of the aforementioned categories, but that the text does not provide enough information to make this determination, at least not on my initial round of classification.

5. CONCLUSION
5.1. SUMMARY
In this analysis of the factors influencing a speaker's or writer's choice of *aqueste* or *este* in two fourteenth-century texts, one in prose and one in verse, we have seen that pragmatic factors, such as explicit and implicit contrast, explicit and implicit assertion in the face of contrary expectations, change of status of the referent, and personal importance, offer a more promising explanation of this

variation than non-pragmatic factors, such as discourse type, physical presence of the referent, function of the demonstrative, and syntactic position of the demonstrative noun phrase. Furthermore, the possible pragmatic meanings may offer an explanation for some of the non-pragmatic effects. For example, it may be that *aqueste* occurs more often in conversation than in narration because a speaker is more likely to express the pragmatic meanings associated with *aqueste* in a face-to-face conversation, or at least a written representation of one, than is a narrator, especially a third-person narrator.

5.2 FUTURE DIRECTIONS
An obvious further step in this analysis would be to continue to refine the definitions of the pragmatic functions of *aqueste* and then to apply this analysis to a larger number of texts to see whether one finds similar pragmatic functions of *aqueste* and *este* in other prose and verse texts. It would be especially interesting to analyse texts across different centuries to see whether the functions of *aqueste* changed over time.

One could also extend the analysis of the variation between *aqueste* and *este* to the related demonstratives *aquese* and *ese* to determine whether *aquese* expressed propositional, textual and expressive meanings more often than *ese* in texts in which both forms appeared. For such a study it would first be necessary to identify texts that contain a sufficient number of tokens of both *aquese* and *ese*. This would not be an easy task given their relative scarcity. In TL, for example, there is not a single occurrence of *aquese* and in LBA there are only four tokens. The calculation of *aquesos* and *esos* as a percentage of all demonstratives in the *Corpus del español*, similar to that performed for *aquestos* and *estos* in Figure 1, shows that *aquesos* accounted for only 0.15% of all demonstratives at its highest point in the sixteenth century and that *esos,* even at its pre-nineteenth century peak in this same century, accounted for less than 11% of all demonstratives.

In a larger Romance context it would be productive to compare the variation between *aqueste* and *este* in Spanish to the variation in Catalan between *aquest* and *est*, especially since the majority form in Old Catalan and the form surviving in Modern Catalan is the long form *aquest*, rather than the short form *est*. Such a comparison might make it possible to determine whether it is the infrequency of the form which makes it marked, in which case *est* would be the marked form in Catalan, or whether it is the additional information provided by the prefixed deictic particle **accu* that triggers additional pragmatic meanings, in which case *aquest* would express these meanings in Catalan. One would also like to determine why a different member of this pair of demonstratives was lost in Spanish and in Catalan.

An interesting and related question is whether any replacement developed in Spanish for the pragmatic functions formerly expressed by *aqueste* when *aqueste* fell out of use. One obvious possibility, especially for the contrastive function, is the construction *este mismo*. A quick search of all the forms of *este mismo* and *aqueste mismo* in the *Corpus del español* revealed that the percentage of *estos mismos* vs. *estos* is more or less in inverse relation to the percentage of *aquestos* vs. *estos*. In other words, there is a higher percentage of *estos mismos* after *aqueste* disappears, and in fact it reaches its highest point in the 1700s. However, *este mismo* does also occur in the same centuries as *aqueste*, so we would need to determine whether *aqueste* and *este mismo* occur in the same texts and, if so, study their variation in detail. There is even one example of *aqueste mismo* in TL, a fact which indicates clearly that *mismo* did not have the same pragmatic meanings as *aqueste*, at least at this time:

(32) *"Señor, yos mostrare como podres verlo e fallaros con el. Basteced vn torneo de aqui a veynte dias, en **aqueste lugar mismo**, e el verna."* (TL 57, 1, 250)

Another interesting topic concerning demonstratives, which is not limited to *aqueste* and *este*, is the development of demonstratives in postnominal position. An initial search of the string noun plus demonstrative in the *Corpus del español* indicates that a construction such as *el hombre este* may have begun as an appositive, such as *el hombre, éste que conoces*. Then when the relative clause *que conoces* was elided, the pronoun *éste* was reinterpreted as an adjective. This process is in fact similar to the one proposed for a similar change in Rumanian by Manoliu (1999).

The future line of research with the most promising and far-reaching results, in my opinion, is the comparison between the pragmatic meanings of *aqueste* and those of subject pronouns in Spanish. The fact that deictics, such as demonstratives and personal pronouns, could lend themselves to similar pragmatic meanings was recognized almost forty years ago by Kurylowicz (1964:245) and later developed by Traugott (1982), yet this idea has not been applied to understanding the variable expression of the subject pronoun in the abundant literature on this topic in Spanish (see, for example, the summary in Silva-Corvalán 2001:154-69). Yet many of the pragmatic functions identified here for *aqueste* are similar to the factors proposed for the variation in Spanish between a subject pronoun and a null subject. (See, for example, Davidson's 1996 discussion of pragmatic weight.) Many of the pragmatic functions proposed for subject pronouns could be better understood if they were classified as propositional, textual, or expressive. It is interesting, but perhaps not surprising, that two different deictic devices, demonstratives and subject pronouns, would have similar pragmatic functions. Both can serve as focusing devices that add prominence to parts of sentences and hearers can assign different types of meaning to this prominence. The extent of the similarities between the pragmatic meanings of *aqueste* and subject pronouns could have implications for other deictics and for the conception of emphasis, focus and prominence in general.

References

Akmajian, Adrian. 1973. "The Role of Focus in the Interpretation of Anaphoric Expressions." *A Festschrift for Morris Halle*, ed. by Stephen R. Anderson and Paul Kiparsky, 215-26. New York: Holt, Rinehart and Winston.
Alvar, Manuel, and Bernard Pottier. 1983. *Morfología histórica del español*. Madrid: Gredos.
Blackwell, Sarah E. 1998. "Constraints on Spanish NP Anaphora: The Syntactic versus the Pragmatic Domain." *Hispania* 81, 606-18.
Blackwell, Sarah E. 2003. *Implicatures in Discourse: The Case of Spanish NP Anaphora*. Amsterdam and Philadelphia: John Benjamins.
Blecua, Alberto, ed. 1983. *Juan Ruiz, Arcipreste de Hita: Libro de Buen Amor*. Madrid: Planeta.
Bonilla y San Martín, Adolfo, ed. 1912. *Libro del esforçado cauallero Don Tristan de Leonis y de sus grandes fechos en armas*. Madrid: Sociedad de bibliófilos madrileños.
Chafe, Wallace. 1976. "Givenness, Contrastiveness, Definiteness, Subjects, Topics, and Point of View." *Subject and Topic*, ed. by Charles N. Li, 27-55. New York: Academic.
Corpus del español: 100 million word corpus of Spanish texts. 2002. Ed. by Mark Davies. Brigham Young University. <www.corpusdelespanol.org>.
Correas, Gonzalo. 1954 [1626]. *Arte de la Lengua Española Castellana*, ed. by E. Alarcos García. Madrid: CSIC. (Anejo LVI de la *Revista de Filología Española*.)
Davidson, Brad. 1996. "'Pragmatic Weight' and Spanish Subject Pronouns: The Pragmatic and Discourse Uses of 'tú' and 'yo' in Spoken Madrid Spanish." *Journal of Pragmatics* 26, 543-65.
D'Introno, Francesco. 1989. "Empty and Full Pronouns in Spanish." *Hispanic Linguistics* 3, 27-47.
Girón Alconchel, José Luis. 1998. "Sobre el reajuste morfológico de los demostrativos en el español clásico." *Actas del IV Congreso Internacional de Historia de la Lengua Española*, ed. by Claudio García Turza, Fabián González Bachiller, and Javier Mangado Martínez, I:493-502. Logroño: Universidad de La Rioja.
Halliday, M. A. K., and Ruqaiya Hasan. 1976. *Cohesion in English*. London: Longman.
Horn, Lawrence R. 1984. "Toward a New Taxonomy for Pragmatic Inference: Q-based and R-based Implicature." *Meaning, Form, and Use in Context: Linguistic*

Applications, ed. by Deborah Schiffrin, 11-42. Washington, DC: Georgetown University Press.
Kurylowicz, Jerzy. 1964. *The Inflectional Categories of Indo-European.* Heidelberg: Winter.
Labov, William. 1972. *Sociolinguistic Patterns.* Philadelphia: University of Pennsylvania Press.
Lavandera, Beatriz. 1978. "Where Does the Sociolinguistic Variable Stop?" *Language in Society* 7, 171-83.
Manoliu, Maria M. 1999. "The Conversational Factor in Language Change: From Prenominal to Postnominal Demonstratives." *Historical Linguistics 1999,* ed. by Laurel J. Brinton, 187-222. Amsterdam: John Benjamins.
Menéndez Pidal, Ramón, ed. 1969. *Cantar de Mio Cid. Texto, gramática, y vocabulario.* 4th ed. Madrid: Espasa-Calpe.
Montgomery, Thomas. 1962. El Evangelio de San Mateo *según el manuscrito escurialense I.I.6. Texto, gramática, vocabulario.* Madrid: Real Academia Española. (Anejo VII del *Boletín de la Real Academia Española.*)
Nebrija, Elio Antonio de. 1992 [1492]. *Gramática castellana.* Introducción y notas por Miguel Ángel Esparza y Ramón Sarmiento. Madrid: Fundación Antonio de Nebrija.
Penny, Ralph. 2000. *Variation and Change in Spanish.* Cambridge: Cambridge University Press.
Ranson, Diana L. 1999. "Variación sintáctica del adjetivo demostrativo en español." *Estudios de variación sintáctica,* ed. by María José Serrano, 121-42. Madrid: Iberoamericana.
Romaine, Suzanne. 1984. "On the Problem of Syntactic Variation and Pragmatic Meaning in Sociolinguistic Theory." *Folia Linguistica* 18, 409-37.
Ruiz, Juan, Arcipreste de Hita. n.d. *El Libro de Buen Amor.* Edición digital basada en la edición de París, Louis-Michaud. <http://www.cervantesvirtual.com/servlet/ SirveObras/ 12582398338987512976624/index.htm>.
Sanchis Calvo, María del Carmen. 1991. *El lenguaje de la* Fazienda de Ultramar. Madrid: Real Academia Española.
Silva-Corvalán, Carmen. 1982. "Subject Expression and Placement in Mexican-American Spanish." *Spanish in the United States: Sociolinguistic Aspects,* ed. by Jon Amastae and Lucía Elías-Olivares, 93-120. Cambridge: Cambridge University Press.
Silva-Corvalán, Carmen. 2001. *Sociolingüística y pragmática del español.* Washington, DC: Georgetown University Press.
Stewart, Miranda. 2003. "'Pragmatic Weight' and Face: Pronominal Presence and the Case of the Spanish Second Person Singular Subject Pronoun *tú.*" *Journal of Pragmatics* 35, 191-206.
Taglicht, Josef. 1984. *Message and Emphasis. On Focus and Scope in English.* English Language Series 15. London and New York: Longman.
Traugott, Elizabeth Closs. 1982. "From Propositional to Textual and Expressive Meanings: Some Semantic-Pragmatic Aspects of Grammaticalization." *Perspectives on Historical Linguistics,* ed. by Winfred P. Lehmann and Yakov Malkiel, 245-71. Amsterdam and Philadelphia: John Benjamins.

11
Textual Evidence of the Development of the Sibilants of Peninsular Spain from the Eleventh to the Sixteenth Centuries
DANA L. ALLEN

THE SEVEN SIBILANT PHONEMES of thirteenth-century Peninsular Spanish as can be gleaned from the Alfonsine corpus are /tˢ/, /dᶻ/, /s/, /z/, /ʃ/, /ʒ/ and /tʃ/ (Penny 1991:86). In Northern and Central Spain, by the sixteenth century, there are /s, s̬, ʃ / and by the end of the seventeenth century, there are /θ, s, x/. By the end of the sixteenth century, in Southern Spain, there are /z̬, s̬, ʃ, ʒ/ and by the end of the seventeenth century, there are /s̬ h/. In this paper, I attempt to determine the geographical and chronological location of the origins and diffusion of these sound changes by an orthographical investigation of medieval documents and texts, in order to determine what evidence there is of the merger of the seven sibilants in any of these texts or documents.

SOURCES OF TEXTUAL EVIDENCE
The language used in historical documents often reflects a standard language rather than the vernacular spoken by the native population. It is hard to ascertain through orthography what is dialect mixing, hypercorrection or simply scribal error. There are no phonetic records of vernacular speech from the eleventh to the sixteenth centuries and it is only through second-hand evidence (e.g., information from grammarians, borrowings from foreign languages, etc.) that one can fill in the phonetic gap.

An additional difficulty in the diachronic study of medieval Spanish has been the unavailability of paleographic editions of usable texts and documents. Many surviving transcriptions cater to the historian and, more often than not, a more modern language and orthography are used to facilitate textual understanding. Consequently, there is less concern in maintaining the original orthography and graphemes, which is unhelpful to the linguist who is studying aspects of language change through orthography. Lack of faithful palaeographic editions of the limited available texts and documents that have survived has restricted the choice tremendously. With these limitations in mind, this study presents selected sources for textual evidence of the development of the Spanish sibilants. (For further information regarding the rationale for selecting each source and the folios or pages from which the data are gleaned, please consult Allen 2002.)

Part of the selection of these particular texts is based on geography and the ability to determine the place of origin of their author, as well as the date that the document or text was written. Since it is widely held that the changes involving Castilian began in the Burgos area and spread laterally and southwards, texts have been chosen whose authors originate from the northern region of the Iberian Peninsula (Ávila, Briviesca, Burgos, La Rioja, Navarra, Old Castile, Peñafiel, Quel, Santander, San Millán de la Cogolla, Santo Domingo de Silos, Soria, Treviño), the central region (Cuenca, Madrid, Guadalajara, Toledo) and the southern region (Andalusia, including Baeza, Córdoba, Jaén, Sevilla).

Some text-based, historical studies have been consulted and the works that were used by the authors in their analyses. Further data have been drawn from popular words which have a continuous oral history and follow the regular morphological and phonological processes involved in the development of Spanish (Penny 1991:32). Graphemes collected from the various texts are compared with the relatively standardized, Alfonsine late thirteenth-century orthographic representation of the phonemes in question. Where possible, paleographic editions are used which are recognized as having been faithfully edited. The following were used in this study:

1. The San Millán and Silos Glosses
2. *Auto de los Reyes Magos*
3. *Poema de mio Cid*
4. ADMYTE II
5. *Documentos lingüísticos de España*, I: *Reino de Castilla*
6. *Arcipreste de Talavera o Corbacho*
7. *Vida de Santa Teresa de Jesús*
8. *Documentos lingüísticos de la Nueva España: Altiplano Central*
9. El corpus del español, compiled by Mark Davies and found at www.corpusdelespañol. org. This database is enormous and in order to limit the search, I investigated possible evidence of *seseo* only. My initial investigation centred on a search for the following words which were found in my other data: *resare, peresa, desplaser, plaser, veses, fasen, faser, dise, rasón*. From this list, I chose sources in which these words

appeared and of which I could pinpoint the date at which it was written and the origin of the author. Then I did a search for the following word strings:

faz*, fac*, fas*, fass*
diz*, dez*, dic*, dec*, dis*, des*, diss*, dess*
raz*, rac*, ras*, rass*
rez*, rec*, res*, ress*
perez*, perec*, peres*, peress*
plaz, *plac*, *plas*, *plass*
vez*, vec*, ves*, vess*

I also looked for the following word strings for *seseo*. These include words in which one would expect the use of <ss> but find <ç> instead, and words in which one would expect the use of <s> but find <z> instead:

us*, uz* (as in *usar*)
cos*, coz* (as in *cosa*)
pass*, paç* (as in *passar*)
huess*, hueç* (as in *huesso*)
confess*, confeç* (as in *confesso*)

ETYMOLOGICAL CATEGORIES
In this section are outlined the various etymological categories into which the lexemes of each text have been placed; it shows how the various phonemes are represented orthographically. Approximately 2200 tokens have been examined. The data are arranged chronologically and, within each chronological category, geographically, beginning in the North and working southward. Then are listed the date of the text, the location (place of origin of the author) and the document or text in which the information can be found. The phoneme involved is listed and the relatively standardized, Alfonsine thirteenth-century expected orthographic representation. Then, its orthographic representation in the various texts is shown, with an example of the grapheme in several words. The number of tokens for each grapheme is calculated and a percentage out of the total number of graphemes in each etymological category given. In the data, all phonemes are in the intervocalic position unless otherwise noted. In the documents I have chosen, I look for the following graphemes: <g> (e/i), <j/i> (a,e,i,o,u), <-s->, <ss->, <-(s)ç-/-c-> (e/i), <-z-> (e/i), <-x-> and <-f-, f-> and <h-, h-> as possible indicators of shift of locus /ʃ/ > /x/.

The following have *not been included* in my samples:

a. word-initial or word-final <s> as in *santa, sangre* or *dos*, since voice is neutralized in these positions. Consequently, I have omitted the word *así*, a popular descendant of Latin AD + SIC (Penny 1991:118, 238), and words such as *asomar, assomar, asorrendar* and *assenter, consejo* and *presidente* and *presente* because the <s> or <ss> could possibly represent a phoneme perceived by speakers as word-initial after a prefix.
b. internal syllable-final sibilants, since voice was probably irrelevant (i.e., neutralization of voice occurred) in syllable-final position.
c. syllable-initial <s> when <s> is preceded by a consonant, as in *consolar* or *ensellar*.
d. <c> before <a>, <o>, <u> as in *acaba* or *comprar*.
e. words whose etymologies have proved hard to establish. Such words include *arreziado, arribança, auze* and *azémila*.
f. <ch>, since it represents /tʃ/, which passes unchanged to Modern Spanish.
g. words that, in the original text, were abbreviated but, when expanded by the editor in his edition, contained a sibilant. I do not rely on the editor's interpretation of a grapheme that was not in the original text.
h. the sibilants that show up in the past subjunctive, where the <s> and <ss> are used interchangeably. In documents in which the scribe is very careful about spelling according to the standard norms, <ss> is more often used; but, even in such documents there can be, from time to time, the use of either <s> or <ss>.
i. words which contain more than one sibilant, such as *necesario*, where there is potential confusion through metathesis, assimilation or dissimilation at the spoken level.
j. words with Latin intervocalic /tj/ and /kj/.
k. words that have traditionally been categorized as "learned" or "semi-learned". Indeed, a "learned" or "semi-learned" word could have been a part of the lexicon of vernacular speech and would have fit the phonological systems of the time. However, if one is attempting to determine a sound change in the phonology through an investigation of orthography, a study of words that do not suffer any or only some of the phonological changes would not necessarily prove productive.

EXAMPLES OF THE WORDS INVESTIGATED.
This list is not exhaustive.

1. Cases of V /k/ (e,i) > /d^z/ include:

>   FACERE > *açer, facer, faser, fazer, hazer.*
>   FACIT > *face, faze, haze.*
>   FECIT > *feço, fezo, fezot, fiço, fiso, fizo, yço.*
>   FACIUNT > *facen, façen, fasen, fazen.*
>   DICERE > *deçir, desjr, dezyr, dezir, dicere.*
>   DICIT > *dice, diçe, dize.*
>   PLACERE > *plaser, plazer.*
>   RECITARE > *rreçar, rresare.*
>   VICES > *veces, veçes, veses, vezes.*

2. Cases of /tj/ > /t^s/ include:
>   FORTIAM > *fuerza.*
>   MARTIUM > *março.*

3. Cases of C /k/ (e,i) > /t^s/ include:
>   CARCEREM > *carcere.*
>   CERTE > *certe, zerte.*

Caution is needed when considering the following words with the prefix RE-. Their categorization is problematic. If a speaker were to perceive the <C> as intervocalic, then a possible phonetic realization in Romance would be /d^z/. However, if the speaker were to perceive these words as containing the prefix re–, then the <C> could then be perceived as word-initial and a possible phonetic realization in Romance would be /t^s/. I have chosen to place these words under this category (and not under (V) /k/ (e/i) > /d^z/) because the graphemes most often found in these words in the data are <c, ç>, which could suggest that the <C> might represent /t^s/. The database which contains the complete set of texts and concordances of the Alfonsine corpus (Kasten et al. 1997; see file ALFAINDX.ALL, a merged alphabetic index of all texts with keyword alphabetically sorted with frequency counts) reveals that there are well over five hundred examples of words derived from RECĪPERE, and without exception, the grapheme used is <c>. Examples include *recebida, recebio, recibiera, recibamos, recebir.* Furthermore, Corominas and Pascual (1980-91, s.v. CONCEBIR) place these words as having a similar development as such words as *concebir* < CONCĪPERE < CĀPERE and *percibir* < PERCĪPERE. It is thus probable that *recibir* is still perceived as a prefix re- and CĪPĔRE.

    RECEPIMUS > *recebiemos, recebimos.*
    RECEPI > *reçibi.*
    Regularized Past Participle, *recibida, resçebido.*
    RECIPERE > *reçibir.*
    RECIPIO > *recibo.*
    RECIPIUNT > *resiben.*
    RECEPIMUS > *rezebimos.*

4. Cases of /sk/ (e,i) > /t^s/ include:
    Various resolutions of forms of –ESCERE, such as:
        -ESCIT > *aborrescet, acreçe, contesce, fallesce, pareçe, pareze.*
    Past Participles: *aparecidos, apareçidos, conocidas, conoçjda.*
    Forms of NASCERE, such as: *nacida, nasçe, naçen.*

5. Cases of /s/ > /z/ include:
    CASAS > *casas, cassas.*
    CAUSA > *causa, caussa, cosa.*
    *CINISIA > *cenisa, ceniza, çenjza.*
    GAUDIOSUM > *gozoso*, GAUDIOSOS > *gozossos.*
    POSUIT > *puso, pusso.*
    QUASI > *casi, quasi, quassi.*
    QUAESIT > *quiso, qujsso.*

6. Cases of /ns/ > /z/ include:
    PENSARE > *pesar, pessar.*
    REMANSIT > *remaso, remasso.*
    SENSUM > *seso, ssesso*

7. Cases of /ss/ > /s/ include:
    PASSARE > *pasar, passer, passare.*
    AD + PRESSAM > *apriessa.*
    *VASSALLOS > *basallos, vassayllos.*

Although *VASSALLOS is of Celtic origin, not Latin, Celtic "provided a number of loans to the Latin of Spain" which "became part of the word-stock of popular Latin wherever it was used, including Spain" (Penny 1991:209).

8. Cases of /ps/ > /s/ include:

DE IPSA > *desa, dessa.*

9. Cases of /rs/ > /s/ include:
   AVERSAS > *abiesas.*
   CURSUM > *cosso.*

The mainstream development of Latin /rs/ to Old Spanish is /s/, as seen in URSUM > *osso*. However, the following words most frequently appear in with <s>, which may suggest that they were assimilated to Latin /s/ ~ /ns/ words, which show Old Spanish /z/ (e.g., CASAM > *casa* and MENSAM > *mesa*). The database of the Alfonsine corpus (Kasten et al. 1997) reveals that for words derived from SŪRSUM and DEORSUM, the grapheme used in over 1200 examples is <s>, including *asuso, desuso, suso, yuso, aayuso, ayuso, deyuso* and *yuso.* The grapheme that is used in the other 12 examples is <ss>: *desusso, susso, ayusso, deyusso* and *yusso.*

10. Cases of /lj/ > /ʒ/ include:
    FILIAM > *ffija, fiia, fija.*
    FILIUM > *ffijo, fijo, hijo.*
    FILIOS > *ffijos, fijos, hijos, yjos.*
    MULIEREM > *muger, muggier, mugier.*

11. Cases of /j/ > /ʒ/ include:
    IURO > *juro.*

12. Cases of /-k'l-/ > /ʒ/ include:
    SPECULUM > *espejo.*

13. Cases of /-t'l-/ > /ʒ/ include:
    VETULAM > *vieja.*

14. Cases of /-g'l-/ > /ʒ/ include:
    TEGULATUM > *tejado.*

15. Cases of /-dj-/ > /ʒ/ include:
    *IN + ODIAT > *enoja.*

16. Cases of /ks/ > /ʃ/ include:
    DELAXAT > *delessa, deja, dexa.*

DELAXARE > *dexar, deyssar.*
EXIVERIT > *escieret.*

It appears that there are some cases in which /ps/ > /ʃ/. Note that although it appears that *eleisco* and *eleiso* would belong under a different category, namely /ps/ > /ss/ since their etymon is some combination of ILLE and IPSE, they reveal the same slightly aberrant phonological development as CAPSEAM > *caxa* > *caja* (Corominas and Pascual 1980-91, s.v. *caja*).

The word *eleiso* is seen in the Silos Glosses, *per sibi eleiso* ('por sí mismo') (Hernández Alonso et al. 1993:folio 315v).

17. Cases of /ssj/ > /ʃ/ include:
*BASSIAT > *baxa* (if the etymon existed).

SUMMARY OF THE ORTHOGRAPHIC INVESTIGATION

The graphemes in angle brackets < > in the following refer to those graphemes used in the documents and texts. In some cases, the grapheme is consistent with late-thirteenth century standard Romance orthography and, in others, it is not. I show how each phoneme is represented by a particular grapheme; the phoneme refers to the expected phonemic outcome of a certain category of Latin words that can reasonably be deduced from the relatively regular spelling of the Alfonsine texts. 'No data' means that I did not find appropriate texts or documents from which to glean data for a particular area during a given century; but it could also mean that, within a certain text or document, there is no orthographic evidence of a given phoneme.

SUMMARY CHART FOR THE 10TH / 11TH CENTURIES

	/dᶻ/	/tˢ/	/z/	/s/	/ʒ/	/ʃ/
NORTH						
San Millán de la Cogolla & Santo Domingo de Silos	<c>92% <z>4% <s>4%	<c->29.6% <z->29.6% <z>7.2% <s> 4% <sc>29.6%	<s>100%	<ss>33.3% <s>66.7%	No data	<sc>92.3% <s> 7.7%
CENTRAL						
	No data	No data	No data	No data	No data	No data
SOUTHERN						
	No data	No data	No data	No data	No data	No data

SUMMARY CHART FOR THE LATE 12ᵀᴴ CENTURY

	/dᶻ/	/tˢ/	/z/	/s/	/ʒ/	/ʃ/
NORTHERN						
	No data	No data	No data	No data	No data	No data
Central						
Toledo *Auto de los Reyes Magos*	<z>57% <c>43%	<c>76.9% <c-> 23.1%	<s>100%	No data	<i>100%	<x>100%
SOUTHERN						
	No data	No data	No data	No data	No data	No data

CONCLUSIONS FOR THE 10ᵀᴴ/11ᵀᴴ AND 12ᵀᴴ CENTURIES

Various issues regarding the language, orthographic representations and purpose of the San Millán and Silos glosses, debates over the origin of the author of, and the linguistic and dialect influences on, the *Auto de los Reyes Magos,* and a lack of consistency in the use of graphemes in the tenth, eleventh and twelfth centuries make it impossible to determine whether there were any occurrences of devoicing in the sibilants. This is not to imply, however, that the use of the graphemes is chaotic or that the lack, or apparent lack, of evidence of devoicing means that there was no devoicing in this early period. There appears to be experimentation in finding ways to represent orthographically the new phonemes of Romance. For example, the author of the *Auto de los Reyes Magos* did not consistently use the same grapheme in some of the same words (e.g., *dezid* and *decid*). It is possible that the use of <c> in *decid* is simply due to the influence from Latin orthography (DĪCĔRE), but it might have been the author's (or scribe's) attempt to represent a new phoneme by using <z> in *dezid*; and there might also have been confusion and possible merger of the phonemes /dᶻ/ and /tˢ/.

SUMMARY CHART FOR THE EARLY 13™ CENTURY – 1200 TO 1249

	/dᶻ/	/tˢ/	/z/	/s/	/ʒ/	/ʃ/
NORTHERN						
Burgos	<ç>100%	<ç>100%	<s>100%	<ss>66.7% <s>33.3%	<j,i,g>100%	<x>100%
(rest of) Old Castile	<z> 100%	<ç>100%	<s>100%	<ss>73.3% <s>26.7%	<j,i,g>100%	<x>100%
Soria	<z> 90% <ç>10%	<ç>100%	<s>100%	<ss>100%	<j,i,g>100%	No data
CENTRAL						
Toledo	<z>63.6% <c,ç>36.4%	<c> 50% <z> 50%	<s>87.5% <ss>12.5%	<ss>50% <s>50%	<j>100%	<ss>100%
SOUTHERN						
Córdoba	<c,ç>100%	<c,ç>100%	<s>100%	No data	<g> 100%	No data

SUMMARY CHART FOR THE LATE 13™ CENTURY – 1250 TO 1299

	/dᶻ/	/tˢ/	/z/	/s/	/ʒ/	/ʃ/
NORTHERN						
Briviesca	<c>100%	<c>100%	<s>100%	<ss>100%	<j>100%	<x>100%
Quel	<z>100%	No data	<s>100%	No data	<j>100%	No data
Rioja Baja	No data	No data	<s>100%	No data	<j>100%	No data
Ávila	<ç>100%	<ç>100%	<s>100%	<s>100%	<g>100%	No data
CENTRAL						
Toledo	<z>47% <ç>53%	<c>100%	<s>75% <ss>25%	No data	<j,g>100%	<x>100%
SOUTHERN						
Córdoba	<z>66.7% <c,ç>33.3%	No data	No data	<ss>50% <s>50%	<j>100%	No data
Jaén	<z>20% <ç>80%	No data	<s>33.3% <ss>66.7%	<ss>66.7% <s>33.3%	No data	No data
Seville	<ç>100% found only in syllable-initial position after a consonant	No data	<s>100%	No data	<j>100%	No data

CONCLUSIONS FOR THE 13TH CENTURY

Any comment regarding data from the thirteenth century could be misleading since full standardization of spelling had not yet occurred in the early thirteenth century, being established in the late thirteenth century. Therefore, we should be cautious in the conclusions drawn regarding the neutralization of voice in the sibilants during this century. In the northern, central and southern regions of the Iberian Peninsula the use of <ç> or <c> in the intervocalic position to represent what had hitherto been /d^z/ is widespread. This could possibly indicate that as early as the thirteenth century, neutralization of voice in the dental-alveolar sibilants is widespread throughout the northern, central and southern regions of the Iberian Peninsula. The data were gleaned from such words as *faze* 'he does/makes', *fiçiere* '(that) he did/made', *fazen/facen* 'they do/make', *facer* 'to do/make', *feçieron* 'they did/made', *dicen/dizen* 'they say'. Harris-Northall (1992) argues that deaffrication had already begun by the mid-thirteenth century. It could be argued that there was no devoicing at this early period and the use of <c, ç> was due to influence from Latin orthography. The validity of arguments regarding interference from Latin orthography depend on the century to which one is referring. It is highly possible that during the tenth, eleventh, twelfth and early thirteenth centuries, in which there was experimentation in orthography, Latin orthography could have an influence on the use of <c> from Latin -C-. However, in subsequent centuries in which the Alfonsine system became used across Castile, interference from Latin is presumably less likely. In all cases after the twelfth century, the expected /t^s/ in the intervocalic position is represented exclusively by <(s)ç, c>, the exception being one token in the data from the thirteenth century, *rezibimos*.

There is possible evidence of confusion in the /z/:/s/ contrast by the early thirteenth century. Of course, before standardization, any possible evidence of early neutralization of voice needs to be treated with caution. Some of the possible evidence of the confusion between /z/ and /s/ in the first half of the thirteenth century can be seen in the words *espeso/espessos, eso/esso, remaso/remasso* and *desa/dessa*.

Further evidence is seen in the latter part of the thirteenth century, when the Alfonsine standard was being established. This evidence includes words such as *espesso/ espesos, casas/cassas, quesieren/ quissieren* '(that) they want', *poderosos/poderossos* 'powerful', *resses* (instead of the expected *reses*) 'heads of cattle', *pasaron* (instead of the expected *passaron*).This evidence seems to confirm neutralization of voice in /z/:/s/ in Central and Southern Spain. Cano (1988), Macpherson (1975) and Penny (1991) argue that confusion in the sibilants began in the north and spread south. The data presented here indicate that neutralization of voice is seen in the south during the same period as it is seen in northern and central Spain.

The /ʒ/ is exclusively represented by <j>, <g> or <i>, which are the expected graphemes. The /ʃ/ is represented by <x>, which is the expected grapheme, or by <ss>, which is not an unexpected representation in areas to the east of Castile; Wright (1982:252) observes that the poetry of Gonzalo de Berceo (?1196-1265?) includes the use of <ss> to represent /ʃ/.

SUMMARY CHART FOR THE 14TH CENTURY – 1325 TO 1368

	/dᶻ/	/tˢ/	/z/	/s/	/ʒ/	/ʃ/
NORTHERN						
Burgos	<ç>100%	<ç>100%	<s>20% <ss>80%	No data	No data	No data
Navarra	<z>97% <ç>3%	<ç,c> 100%	<s>99% <ss>1%	<ss>4 0% <s>60%	<j,i,g> 100%	No data
Soria	<z>22% <s>78%	No data	<s>100%	<ss>100%	No data	No data
CENTRAL						
Toledo	<z>93.3% <s>6.7%	<ç>100%	<s>90% <ss>2% <z> 8%	<s>100%	<j,i,g> 100%	<x>100%
SOUTHERN						
	No data	No data	No data	No data	No data	No data

CONCLUSIONS FOR THE 14TH CENTURY
1. Merger of originally voiced and unvoiced in the dento-alveolar and alveolar sibilants and its diffusion are seen in the northern and central regions of the Iberian Peninsula.
2. There is possible evidence of *seseo* in Toledo as early as 1330 and in Soria in 1355.

During the fourteenth century, the sound that has hitherto been /dᶻ/ is regularly represented by both <z> and <ç> in the North and by <z> in the central region of the Iberian Peninsula. Evidence of this can be seen in the words *dice, perteneçen, faze, face<n>, dezir* and *deçir*. /z/ is represented by <s> in Navarra in 99% of the cases, whereas /s/ is represented by both <s> (60%) and <ss> (40%). In Burgos one sees the use of <ss> for /z/ in 80 % of instances, and in the central region of the Iberian Peninsula, the use of <s> for both /z/ and /s/ is widespread. This spelling confusion could indicate merger of voice in the north and central regions of the Iberian Peninsula. Examples include *quassi* 'almost', *cossas* 'things', *quissieren* '(that) they want', *pussieron* 'they put', *cassas* 'houses'.

There is possible evidence of *seseo* in Toledo as early as 1330 in such words as *rresare* 'I will pray' and *peresa* 'slowness, laziness'. More compelling evidence of *seseo* in Soria in 1355 is seen in such words as *faze/fase, fazes/fasen, plaze/plase* and *vezes/veses*. This evidence (and evidence seen in the fifteenth century) places deaffrication much earlier than do Alonso (1955), Cuervo (1895), Ford (1900) and Tuulio (1962), who see deaffrication as not having occurred until the sixteenth century. Alonso (1955:381) states that the <ç> represented the phoneme /t^s/ until the early seventeenth century. Penny (1991) places deaffrication in the north during the fifteenth century.

The data collected for this period offer no evidence of merger regarding /ʒ/ and /ʃ/.

SUMMARY CHART FOR THE 15TH CENTURY – 1410 TO 1465

	/d^z/	/t^s/	/z/	/s/	/ʒ/	/ʃ/
NORTHERN						
Pie de Concha, Santander	<z>58% <ç>42%	<ç>100%	<s>100%	<s>100%	<g,j>100%	No data
Peñafiel	<z>87.5% <s>12.5%	No data	No data	<ss>100%	No data	No data
CENTRAL						
Madrid	<z>36% <s>64%	No data	No data	No data	No data	No data
Toledo	<z>65% <s>31% <c,ç>4%	<ç,c>100%	<s>98% <z>2%	<ss>41% <s>59%	<g,i,j>100%	<x>100%
Cuenca	<z>98% <c>1% <s>1%	No data	No data	No data	No data	No data
SOUTHERN						
Córdoba	<z>60% <s>40%	No data	No data	<ss>100%	No data	No data
Andalusia	<z>93% <s>7%	<sç,c>10-0%	<s>76% <ss>23% <z>1%	<ss>30% <s>70%	<j,g>100%	<x>95% <j>5%

CONCLUSIONS FOR THE 15TH CENTURY

1. There is further, compelling evidence of the merger of the [+voice] and [–voice] dento-alveolar and alveolar sibilant phonemes and its diffusion in the northern, central and southern regions of the Iberian Peninsula.

2. In Central Spain, there is strong evidence of *seseo* in Madrid (1403-06), Peñafiel (1465) and Toledo (1438).
3. In Andalusia, evidence of *seseo* is seen, especially in Córdoba. The data imply that *seseo* began in the central region of the Iberian Peninsula and spread southwards during the great dialect mixing and contact that occurred in Central and Southern Spain during the thirteenth and subsequent centuries (Tuten 2003). It seems that early *seseo* is not exclusively Andalusian.
4. There is possible evidence of merger of /ʒ/ and /ʃ/.

During the fifteenth century, words hitherto pronounced with the etymologically expected /dᶻ/ are regularly represented with both <z> and <ç> in the North, indicating possible neutralization of voice. In Toledo, /dᶻ/ is represented by <z> in 65% of the cases, by <s> in 31% of the cases, as in the pairs *vezes/veses, fazer/faser, plazer/plaser* 'to please', *dize/dise* 'he says/tells' and *fazen/fasen*, and by <c, ç> in 4% of the cases, such as *decir* and *façer*. The use of the grapheme <s>, which by this time, most probably represented /s/ and not /z/, is strong evidence of *seseo* in Toledo as early as 1438. Moreover, in Peñafiel, Madrid and Cuenca, evidence of *seseo* is seen in such words as *plaser, faser, fasen, veses, rason* and *dise*. It appears from this evidence (and from evidence found in Soria and Toledo in the fourteenth century) that *seseo* is not exclusively Andalusian. There is evidence of *seseo* in Andalusia, especially in Córdoba, in such words as *desir, dise, fiso, fasen, desyr, veses, fesiste, franquesa* and *goso*. By this period, in all of the Iberian Peninsula, there is a merger of the phonemes /z/ and /s/ > /s/. It seems that the grapheme <s> is the preferred grapheme in this merger, although <ss> is also found. Examples include *trespasando~passados, cosa~cossas, casado~cassada, uso~ussan, qujso~qujsso, pusso~puso, desseo~ deseja*. The use of intervocalic <s> for /s/ can be seen as early as the eleventh century in La Rioja, in the thirteenth century in Toledo, in the northern and central regions of the Iberian Peninsula in the fourteenth century, and in all regions by the fifteenth century. /ʒ/ and /ʃ/ are almost exclusively represented by the expected graphemes <i, j, g> and <x> respectively; possible evidence of merger many be seen in the use of <j> for <x> in the word *deja* 'he leaves'.

SUMMARY CHART FOR THE 16ᵀᴴ CENTURY – 1529 TO 1532 AND 1562

	/dᶻ/	/tˢ/	/z/	/s/	/ʒ/	/ʃ/
Northern						
Avila	<c, ç> 100%	<ç>100%	<s>100%	<s>100%	<j>100%	<j>100%
Central						

Guadalajara	<z>100%	<ç>80% <z>20%	<s>100%	<s>100%	No data	<j>100%
Toledo	<z>100%	<sç,ç>100%	<s>100%	<s>100%	<j>100%	<x>100%
Southern						
Baeza	<z>100%	No data	<z>100%	No data	<g>100%	No data
Villa de Pedroso, Seville	<z>100%	<sç,ç>66.7% <s>33.3%	<s> 20% <ss>80%	No data	<j>100%	<x>100%

CONCLUSIONS FOR THE 16ᵀᴴ CENTURY
1. There is possible evidence of *zezeo* in the southern region of the Iberian Peninsula.
2. There is possible evidence of the merger of /ʒ/ and /ʃ/ in the northern and central regions of the Iberian Peninsula.

In the sixteenth century, there is continuing evidence of the merger of /dᶻ/ and /tˢ/ in the northern and central regions of the Iberian Peninsula. Examples include *pareçiere* '(that) he appeared/seemed', *parezeme* 'seems to me', *açer* 'to do/make', *doçe, pareçe*. However, in Andalusia, it appears that /dᶻ/ is still regularly represented by <z>.

Neutralization of voice between the phonemes /z/ and /s/ is evident in the exclusive use of the grapheme <s> in the northern and central regions of the Iberian Peninsula. In the southern regions of the Iberian Peninsula, there is possible evidence of *zezeo*, the abuse of the letter <z> in such cases as *caza* for *casa*. The expected /z/ is represented by <z> (and not <s>), as in *quizieren*. With such a small number of examples in the data, it is difficult to say anything conclusive regarding the development of *zezeo*.

Possible evidence of the merger of /ʒ/ and /ʃ/ can be seen in the northern and central regions of the Iberian Peninsula in the sixteenth century. Examples include *deje* 'I left' and *dejaba* 'he used to leave'.

An examination of approximately 2200 tokens and many pages of documentation offers no evidence of a shift of locus of /s̪/ > /θ/ nor of /ʃ/ > /h/, and little evidence for /ʃ/ > /x/. This is not surprising since this shift does not produce a change in the phonemic inventory of Spanish, nor unexpected developments except where /x/ merges with /h/ < Latin F-. Graphemes (e.g., <ç> and <j> and <g>) that were once used for phonemes that are no longer part of the phonemic inventory of the language (e.g., /tˢ/ and /ʒ/) can be used for the new phonemes (e.g., /θ/, /x/, /h/). Penny (1991) and Macpherson (1975) place these shifts of locus during the mid-sixteenth century, becoming the norm by the mid-seventeenth century. However, for Alonso (1976), the shift /s̪/ > /θ/ did not occur in the seventeenth, but rather sometime in the eighteenth, being the norm by the nineteenth century.

References

Allen, Dana L. 2002. "History of the Sibilants of Peninsular Spanish from the Eleventh to the Sixteenth Centuries". Unpublished doctoral thesis, Queen Mary and Westfield College, University of London.

Alonso, Amado. 1955 and 1976. *De la pronunciación medieval a la moderna en español*, I, Madrid: Gredos.

Cano Aguilar, Rafael. 1988. *El español a través de los tiempos*. Madrid: Arco/Libros.

Company Company, Concepción. 1994. *Documentos lingüísticos de la Nueva España: Altiplano Central*. Instituto de Investigaciones Filológicas. México: Universidad Nacional Autónoma de México.

Cuervo, R. J. 1895. "Disquisiciones sobre antigua ortografía y pronunciación castellanas". *Revue Hispanique* 2, 1-69.

Davies, Mark. 2002. *El corpus del español*, website: www.corpusdelespanol.org Illinois: Mark Davies at Illinois State University.

De la Fuente, Vicente. 1873. *Vida de Santa Teresa de Jesús*. Madrid: La Sociedad Foto-Tipográfico-Católica.

Ford, J. D. M. 1900. *The Old Spanish Sibilants: Studies and Notes in Philology and Literature*. Boston: Ginn.

Harris-Northall, Ray. 1992. "Devoicing, Deaffrication, and Word-Final –z in Medieval Spanish". *Hispanic Linguistics* 4, 245-74.

Hernández Alonso, César et al, eds. 1993. *Las glosas emilianenses y silenses*. Burgos: Aldecoa.

Kasten, Lloyd, Nitti, John and Jonxis-Henkemans, Wilhelmina. 1997. *The Electronic Text and Concordances of the Prose Works of Alfonso X, El Sabio*. CD-Rom Series 1. Madison: The Hispanic Seminary of Medieval Studies.

Macpherson, Ian R. 1975. *Spanish Phonology: Descriptive and Historical*. Manchester: Manchester University Press.

Martínez de Toledo, Alfonso.1970. *Arcipreste de Talavera o Corbacho*, ed. by J. González Muela. Madrid: Castalia.

Martínez de Toledo, Alfonso. 1438. *Arcipreste de Talavera*, a photostat copy (negative) from the original manuscript copy in the library of the Escorial (iii.h.10), copy obtained through the University of California at Berkeley, call number Z115.Z1 M3 Main Stack.

Martínez de Toledo, Alfonso. 1939. *Arcipreste de Talavera o sea Corbacho*, ed. by Lesley Byrd Simpson. Berkeley: University of California.

Martínez de Toledo, Alfonso. 1955. *Arcipreste de Talavera*, ed. by Mario Penna. Torino: Rosenberg and Sellier.

Menéndez Pidal, R., ed. 1964. *Cantar de mio Cid*, 3 vols, 4th edn. Madrid: Espasa-Calpe.

Menéndez Pidal, R. 1919. *Documentos lingüísticos de España*, I: *Reino de Castilla*. Madrid: Centro de Estudios Históricos.

Penny, Ralph J. 1991. *A History of the Spanish Language.* Cambridge: Cambridge University Press.
Pestana, Sebastião, ed. 1965. *Auto de los Reyes Magos.* I, *Texto Castelhano Anónimo do Século XII.* Lisboa: Edição da Revista 'Ocidente'.
Poema de mio Cid. 1988. Facsimile edition from the manuscript of Marqués de Pidal deposited in the Biblioteca Nacional. Burgos: Fournier.
Sociedad Estatal Quinto Centenario. 1999. *ADMYTE* II, ed. by Francisco Marcos Marín et al. 'CD-ROM'. Madrid: Biblioteca Nacional/ Micronet/Quinto Centenario.
Tuulio, Ovia Johannes, ed. 1962. *La gaya ciencia de P. Guillén de Segovia.* Vols I and II. Madrid: Clásicos Hispánicos.
Tuten, Donald N. 2003. *Koineization in Medieval Spanish.* Berlin: Mouton de Gruyter.
Waltman, Franklin M. 1972. *Concordance to 'Poema de mio Cid.'* Pennsylvania: Pennsylvania State University Press.
Wright, Roger. 1982. *Late Latin and Early Romance in Spain and Carolingian France.* Liverpool: Cairns.

12
Ingenio, juicio, prudencia: The Linguistic Doctrine of Juan de Valdés
THOMAS R. HART

JUAN DE VALDÉS'S *DIÁLOGO de la lengua* is the only one of his works that does not deal with religious issues. At first glance, it seems very different from the others, but this first impression is misleading. What is distinctive about the *Diálogo* is that Valdés's discussion of language rests on the use of terms usually associated with ethical choices. In this respect Valdés is a forerunner of Cervantes, for whom, as Werner Krauss notes, criticism of language is always criticism of a way of thinking: 'Kritik an die Sprache ist aber, wie immer bei Cervantes, Kritik der Gesinnung' (1966:108). He is also very much a man of his time and of his immediate circumstances, marked by the influence of Erasmus. Marcel Bataillon observes that 'seguramente, no es un azar que los más vigorosos espíritus que honran al erasmismo español [...] hayan escrito de manera tan sobria, tan viva, tan directa, y que entre ellos se haya encontrado uno que formulase esta regla del bien escribir, que coincide con la del bien hablar' (1950: II, 310). Valdés recognizes, of course, that moral decisions are much more important than linguistic ones; anyone who chooses not to accept his advice on spelling and grammar may safely disregard it, 'que no por eso se irá al infierno' (Valdés 1982:157. All citations are to this edition).

I have suggested elsewhere that 'our strongest impression of [Valdés's] personality comes from the *Diálogo de la lengua*,' perhaps because in this work 'he came closest to realizing the possibilities inherent in the dialogue as a literary genre' (2001:310). The mode of Valdés's dialogue is epideictic; it demands that the reader or listener consider not only the arguments presented but also the character (*ethos*) of the person who presents them. Aristotle notes in his *Rhetoric* that '*Ethos* involves the speaker in appearing to be good and hence worthy of trust, for "we believe good men more fully and more readily than others", and a speaker's "character may almost be called the most effective means of persuasion he possesses"' (Vickers 1990:20). It is because Valdés's interlocutors in the *Diálogo de la lengua* know his character from earlier conversations and from his letters to them that they seek his advice on linguistic matters (119-20).

Valdés and his friends know each other so well that they can adopt the tone of 'amistosa agresividad' that Isaías Lerner finds in the dialogue (1986:148) and that also characterizes Castiglione's *Libro del Cortegiano*. Valdés does not hesitate to tell his host that 'Mayor donaire es querer vos ser juez en la provincia donde no sabéis las leyes; ¿no avéis oído dezir que "Cada gallo cante en su muladar"?' (169). When he tells Coriolano that 'Maravíllome de vos que no entendáis qué cosa es *bachiller* y *bachillerías*, que lo entienden, en buena fe, en mi tierra, los niños que apenas saben andar,' Coriolano responds: 'También en la mía los niños de teta entienden algunos vocablos que vos no entendéis' and Valdés concedes that 'Tenéis razón' (185).

Although the elaborate 'deference rituals' that Wayne Rebhorn notes in Castiglione's dialogue (1978:134) are present also in the *Diálogo de la lengua*, Valdés repeatedly mocks the punctiliousness of the Italians, a tone established at the beginning of the dialogue when he declares that 'Si no adornárades esta vuestra demanda con tanta retórica, liberalmente me ofreciera a obedeceros' (118). He freely admits that 'demasiadamente soy amigo de que las cosas se hagan como yo quiero, y demasiadamente me ofendo quando una persona que yo quiero bien haze o dize alguna cosa que no me contente,' insisting only that 'es mi tacha más sufridera que las de los otros, porque la conozco, y por tanto ay esperança que me corregiré un día u otro' (261).

Cristina Barbolani remarks that 'Valdés no era un santo, sino un hombre de su tiempo' (1979:151), and above all a *cortesano*. Many of his observations warn against usage that he considers inappropriate to aristocratic circles. '*Platel* por *plato* vocablo es para entre plebeyos [...]: entre gente de corte no se usa' (205). 'Dízese entre gente baxa *vezo* por *costumbre*' (208). '*Raudo* por *rezio* es vocablo grossero, pocos le usan' (206). Valdés knows such words 'por averlos oído decir quando caminava por Castilla, porque en camino, andando por mesones, es forçado platicar con aldeanos y otras personas grosseras' (209).

Valdés's distaste for the speech of 'aldeanos y otras personas grosseras' may seem hard to reconcile with his enthusiasm for proverbs, 'los más dellos nacidos y criados entre viejas, tras del fuego hilando sus ruecas' (127), but there is no real contradiction. As Maxime Chevalier notes, 'Juan de Valdés ne dit ou n'insinue nulle part dans le *Diálogo de la lengua* que le proverbe soit proprement ou plutôt paysan' (1993:254). In this respect Valdés is very much a man of his time : 'C'est au XVIe siècle que s'édifient les monuments parémiologiques, celui de Correas mis à part. C'est au XVIe siècle que Mal Lara écrit son apologie du proverbe. C'est au XVIe siècle que fleurissent les imitations de *La Célestine*. Le

XVIe siècle est un temps où les hommes de lettres ne critiquent pas ouvertement le proverbe.' (Chevalier 1993:259).

Cristina Barbolani notes that in the *Diálogo de la lengua* Valdés 'consigue vivificar la prosa con la acogida de una auténtica invasión de refranes. Aparte los que se citan y enuncian expresamente, gran número de ellos son utilizados en la normal conversación entre los interlocutores, personas de cierta cultura' (1979:148). Valdés cautions only that the *refranes* are not reliable guides to current usage. Their language is nevertheless a model of conciseness and eloquence, unlike the language of verse; all too often the poets 'no van acomodando [...] las palabras a las cosas, sino las cosas a las palabras, y assí no dizen lo que querrían, sino lo que quieren los vocablos que tienen' (243). Small wonder that Valdés declares that 'el leer en metro no lo apruevo en castellano, ni en ninguna otra lengua, para los que son aprendices en ella' (240).

Valdés's linguistic elitism is perhaps related to his religious views, as Bataillon suggests: '¿Habrá que hablar de gusto aristocrático? Sí, si se quiere. Así como, según el *Enquiridion*, la práctica del verdadero cristianismo es obra de una minoría [...], así también la multitud de los espíritus "plebeyos y vulgares" es inmensa según Valdés, puesto que comprende "a todos los que son de bajo ingenio y poco juicio"' (1950: II, 307-08).

Ingenio and *juicio* are key terms in the *Diálogo de la lengua*. Neither is easy to define, in part because Valdés does not always use them in the same way. Sometimes he equates them with Cicero's distinction between *inventio* and *dispositio*: 'El ingenio halla qué dezir, y el juicio escoge lo mejor de lo que el ingenio halla, y pónelo en el lugar que ha de star; de manera que de las dos partes del orador, que son invención y disposición (que quiere dezir ordenación), la primera se puede atribuir al ingenio, y la segunda al juizio' (245). As a general rule Valdés uses both terms in senses close to those assigned them in the Academy's eighteenth-century *Diccionario de autoridades*, where *juicio* is defined as 'Potencia ò facilidad intellectual, que le sirve al hombre para distinguir el bien del mal, y lo verdadero de lo falso' (1734:329). This is the sense Valdés has in mind when he declares that 'más querría con mediano ingenio buen juizio, que con razonable juizio buen ingenio. [...] Porque hombres de grandes ingenios son los que se pierden en heregías y falsas opiniones, por falta de juizio' (245-46).

Juicio is thus a synonym of *prudencia*, which the Academy defines as 'Una de las quatro virtudes cardinales que enseña al hombre à discerner lo que es bueno o malo para seguirlo, ò huir de ello' (1737:418). The association of prudence with choosing between alternatives is clear when Valdés says that 'la prudencia del que scrive consiste en aprovecharse de lo que ha leído, de tal manera que tome lo que es de tomar y dexe lo que es de dexar; y el que no haze esto muestra que tiene poco juizio' (254). The *Diccionario de autoridades* lists *prudencia* as a synonym of *discreción:* 'Prudéncia, juicio y conocimiento con que se distinguen y reconocen las cosas como son, y sirve para el gobierno de las acciones y modo de proceder, eligiendo las más à propósito. Lat. *Discretio. Prudens judicium*' (1732:297). In this sense *discreción* is similar to *juicio* and quite different from *ingenio*. This is the sense Valdés has in mind when he speaks of *los discretos cortesanos*.

There is, however, another sense in which *discreción* and *ingenio* are not opposed to each other but are synonyms and are opposed to *juicio*. The Academy's definition of *discreción* goes on to say that 'Vale tambien agudéza de ingenio, abundáncia y fecundidad en la explicacion, adornada de dichos oportunos, entretenidos y gustosos' (1732:297). Its dictionary equates *discreto* with Latin *prudens* and adds that 'Se extiende figuradamente à las acciones, hechos ù dichos con prudencia, oportunidad ò agudeza' (1732:298).

In this sense *discreción* and *ingenio* need not be opposed to *juicio* and Valdés values them highly, for example when he declares that 'aunque sean quán altos y quán ricos quisieren, en mi opinión serán plebeyos si no son altos de ingenio y ricos de juizio' (172). His appreciation of *ingenio* is evident in his praise of *vocablos equívocos*: 'y más os digo que, aunque en otras lenguas sea defecto la equivocación de los vocablos, en la castellana es ornamento, porque con ellos se dizen muchas cosas *ingeniosas*, muy sutiles y galanas' (211; my emphasis). As an example Valdés cites a play on three senses of the verb *tocar*, which gives him an opportunity to attack one of his favorite targets, the friars: '*Tocar* es lo mesmo que TANGERE y que PERTINERE, y sinifica también "ataviarse la cabeça"; creo que venga de *toca*, que es lo que dizen: "Cabeça loca no sufre toca" y: "La moça loca por la lista compra la toca". Hora mirad cómo un fraile en tres palabras aludió sutilmente a las tres sinificaciones; y fue assí que, demandándole una monja le diesse una toca, el respondió: "Quando toque a mí tocaros, con más que esso os serviré"' (213). The other participants in the *Diálogo de la lengua* value Valdés's letters for their wit: 'nosotros nos concertamos desta manera: que qualquiera de nosotros que recibiesse carta vuestra la comunicasse con los otros [...] y con ello avemos tomado mucho descanso, passatiempo y plazer [...] con los chistes y donaires, de que continuamente vuestras cartas venían adornadas' (119).

Prudencia is closely allied to rhetoric; both were frequently referred to as arts of accommodation (Eden 1997:2). The prudent man adjusts his behavior to his immediate circumstances, just as the orator adapts his speech to his audience. Valdés practices accommodation when writing letters to Italians: 'voy siempre *acomodando* las palabras castellanas con las italianas, y las maneras de dezir de la una lengua con las de la otra, de manera que, sin apartarme del castellano, sea mejor entendido del italiano' (227; my emphasis). Marcio praises him for his *prudencia* in doing so (231).

Valdés's often-quoted declaration that 'el estilo que tengo me es natural, y sin afetación ninguna escrivo como hablo' (233) can be accepted at face value only if we bear in mind that he takes care to speak in a way that reflects a conscious choice among alternatives, that is, a way that corresponds to prudence, the virtue that makes moral judgment possible. His initial reluctance to talk about 'una cosa tan baxa y plebeya como es punticos y primorcicos de lengua vulgar' (122) on the ground that Spanish, unlike Latin, cannot be reduced to rules—'me queráis demandar cuenta de lo que sta fuera de toda cuenta' (121)—does not rest on the difficulty of describing his own usage but on that of justifying his choices. Sometimes, of course, he does not need to choose: he simply follows the usage he has learned 'en el reino de Toledo y en la corte de Spaña' (142). Sometimes, however, he says that he follows the practice of the best writers, 'los que se precian de scrivir bien' (158), 'los más primos en el escrivir' (160), 'los que bien escriven' (179). Here choice is involved, since one must decide for oneself which writers deserve to be imitated. Spain has no canonical authors comparable to Petrarch and Boccaccio, 'los quales, siendo buenos letrados, no solamente se preciaron de scrivir buenas cosas, pero procuraron escrivirlas con estilo muy propio y muy elegante' (123). In the absence of such authorities, Valdés falls back on the *refranes*, but their language is full of archaisms and cannot be taken as a safe guide to current courtly usage: 'no digo *ál* adonde tengo de dezir *otra cosa*, aunque se dize "So el sayal, ay ál" y "En ál va el engaño"' (194). The situation would not be very different if Spain had its own classical authors, since, as Castiglione makes Giuliano de' Medici remark in *Il libro del cortegiano*, 'molte parole si ritrovano nel Petrarca e nel Boccaccio, che or son interlassate dalla consuetudine d'oggidì; e queste io, per me, non usarei mai né parlando né scrivendo' (1987: I, xxxi, 87-88). For Castiglione, as for Valdés, the only safe guide is contemporary usage. Finally, there are cases in which Valdés is guided only by his own taste, saying 'me contenta más,' 'no me contenta dezir,' 'a mí más me contenta' (190). He distinguishes *asperar* 'to wait for' and *esperar* 'to hope,' although he recognizes that most people do not make the distinction: 'Bien sé que pocos o ninguno guarda essa diferencia, pero a mí me ha parecido guardarla por dar mejor a entender lo que scrivo' (181). Similarly, '*Luengo* por *largo*, aunque lo usan pocos, yo lo uso de buena gana' (203).

Sometimes Valdés's three criteria—the language with which he grew up, the practice of the best writers, his own taste—agree with one another. Often, however, they conflict, and he is forced to choose among them. There is an evident tension between Valdés's desire to decide everything for himself and his concern for how others will judge his decisions. This tension goes far beyond questions of language. It is reflected in the balance between seriousness and playfulness in his relationship with the other participants in the dialogue and in his awareness that he sometimes fails to live up to his own standards. If Valdés is 'tan cortés y bien criado con todo el mundo como todos dizen,' as Marcio reminds him, perhaps with a touch of irony, at the very beginning of the dialogue (118), it is the result of constant self-discipline. In all these respects, Valdés is, as Cristina Barbolani rightly notes, a man of his time and of the court circles in which he moved, though he always aspires also to be something more. He is the most *discreto* of *cortesanos*.

Juan Lope Blanch rightly insists that Valdés 'procura expresarse siempre con absoluta claridad y precisión' (1969:10). Valdés himself stresses that 'Hablar o escrivir de suerte que vuestra razón pueda tener dos entendimientos en todas lenguas es muy gran falta del que habla o escrive' (235) and that he tries to 'esplicar el conceto de mi ánimo de tal manera que, si fuere posible, qualquier persona que entienda el castellano alcance bien lo que quiero dezir' (184). But clarity and brevity, while essential, are not enough. Valdés's assertion that 'todo el bien hablar castellano consiste en que digáis lo que queréis con las menos palabras que pudiéredes' is qualified by his insistence that one must write 'de tal manera que [...] de las palabras que pusiéredes [...] no se pueda quitar ninguna sin ofender a la sentencia della, o al encarecimiento, o a la elegancia' (237).

Valdés's stress on the importance of *encarecimiento* and his evident pleasure in *palabras equívocas* and other kinds of word-play undercuts Lope Blanch's assertion that 'El celo reformista de Valdés, sus propósitos ideológicos, relegan a término muy secundario la intención artística—literaria — que pudiera haber en sus escritos' (1969:9-10).

Erich Auerbach's remark that 'what we understand and love in a work is a human existence' (1965:12) is peculiarly appropriate to the *Diálogo de la lengua*. We read Valdés's dialogue, as we read Montaigne's essays, not just to learn his conclusions but to discover how he reaches them. We read Valdés, as we read Montaigne, not just to learn what he thinks but to discover who he is.

References

Auerbach, Erich. 1965. *Literary Language and Its Public in Late Latin Antiquity and in the Middle Ages*, trans. Ralph Manheim. Bollingen Series 74. New York: Bollingen Foundation.
Barbolani, Cristina. 1979. "Los diálogos de Juan de Valdés ¿reflexión o improvisación?" *Actas del Coloquio Interdisciplinar 'Doce consideraciones sobre el mundo hispano-italiano en tiempos de Alfonso y Juan de Valdés' (Bolonia, abril de 1976)*, ed. by

Francisco Ramos Ortega. I, 135-52. Anexos de *Pliegos de Cordel*, 1. Rome: Instituto Español de Lengua y Literatura.
Bataillon, Marcel. 1950. *Erasmo y España: estudios sobre la historia espiritual del siglo XVI*, trans. by Antonio Alatorre, 2 vols. Mexico City: Fondo de Cultura Económica.
Castiglione, Baldassar. 1987. *Il libro del cortegiano*, ed. by Giulio Carnazzi. Milan: Rizzoli.
Chevalier, Maxime. 1993. "Conte, proverbe, romance: Trois formes traditionnelles en question au Siècle d'Or.' *Bulletin Hispanique* 95, 237-64.
Eden, Kathy. 1997. *Hermeneutics and the Rhetorical Tradition: Chapters in the Ancient Legacy and its Humanist Reception*. New Haven and London: Yale Univ. Press.
Hart, Thomas R. 2001. " 'Diálogo más que tratado': The Art of Juan de Valdés". *Bulletin of Hispanic Studies* (Glasgow) 78, 301-10.
Krauss, Werner. 1966. *Miguel de Cervantes: Leben und Werke*. Neuwied: Luchterhand.
Lerner, Isaías. 1986. "El discurso literario del *Diálogo de la lengua* de Juan de Valdés". *Actas del VIII Congreso de la Asociación Internacional de Hispanistas*, ed. by A. David Kossoff et al., 2 vols. Madrid: Istmo. II, 145-50.
Lope Blanch, Juan M., ed. 1969. *Diálogo de la lengua* de Juan de Valdés. Madrid: Castalia.
Real Academia Española. 1726-39. *Diccionario de la lengua castellana*, 6 vols. Madrid: Real Academia Española.
Rebhorn, Wayne A. 1978. *Courtly Performances: Masking and Festivity in Castiglione's 'Book of the Courtier.'* Detroit: Wayne State Univ. Press.
Valdés, Juan de. 1982. *Diálogo de la lengua*, ed. by Cristina Barbolani. Madrid: Cátedra.
Vickers, Brian. 1990. *In Defence of Rhetoric*. Oxford: Clarendon.

13
Vowel Prosthesis and its Maintenance in Spanish: a comparative perspective
RODNEY SAMPSON

IT HAS LONG BEEN recognised by linguists that a comparative Romance approach can yield fruitful insights when interpreting diachronic developments in one individual variety of Romance. This is especially evident when, for a given development, the varieties being considered have followed broadly similar though not identical paths of evolution with or without significant differences in the date of implementation (cf. Delattre 1946). A comparative approach might seem to be less useful, however, when a development in one language finds no evident parallel in the others considered. Yet it can be revealing to explore possible reasons for radically differing treatments of a specific characteristic in related languages, since a fuller understanding of the factors that can bring about distinct paths of change may serve to shed fresh light on the general nature of sound change.

One phonological development proves to be especially interesting when a comparative Spanish-French perspective is adopted, since we find both similarities and striking dissimilarities. It concerns the phenomenon of vowel prosthesis (or prothesis) that has affected words beginning with etymological word-initial /s/ + consonant or *s impure*, for example Latin SPERARE "to hope". In words of this type, a high front vowel /i-/ was inserted before the *s impure* sequence, as in ISPERABI "I hoped" (*CIL* X, 8189) that appears in an inscription found at Pozzuoli, near Naples. Chronologically, the earliest clear indications of the change are also epigraphical and date from the 2nd century A.D. (Prinz 1938). Thereafter, increasing numbers of speakers across the Roman Empire evidently came to use a prosthetic vowel which in many areas later developed through regular sound change to take on a mid front quality /e-/, e.g. SCALA > ISCALA > Sp., Port., Cat. *escala* "ladder", SPERARE > ISPERARE > Sp., Port, Cat. *esperar* "to hope, wait for", and French *échelle* (< OFr. *eschele*) and *espérer*. However, despite the evidently growing incidence of this phonological novelty during the Imperial period, no allusion is made to it in the writings of any Roman grammarian of the time. The delay in grammarians' calling attention to the existence of prosthesis may indicate that it remained for a several centuries a phenomenon of pronunciation that was characteristic primarily of more informal registers employed by the less favoured social classes and/or that it was typically allophonic in nature.

The data from Romance suggest that prosthesis became particularly widespread in Hispania and Gaul. Yet the surviving epigraphical evidence from the late Empire provides little evidence of this. The statistics provided by Prinz (1938:106) in fact point to Rome and North Africa as being the focal areas of prosthesis adoption, whilst the inscriptions of Gaul (including the German provinces) and Hispania offer just 5 and 7 recorded cases respectively where the presence of a prosthetic vowel is indicated. Similarly meagre results for these two areas emerge from the detailed analysis of specifically Christian inscriptions by Gaeng (1968:263-66) who reports only five examples for the Iberian peninsula and just a single example for Gaul BONE MEMORIAE ISP[ES] NOMENE. However, by the time that significant numbers of Romance texts begin to appear in which a vernacular-based orthographic representation is used (12th-13th centuries), the rule of vowel prosthesis seems fully productive in both areas. For Castilian, the 13th-century texts which are available show the rule of vowel prosthesis to be operative for forms with etymological word-initial s + consonant. For example, amongst prose writings the two texts of the *Tratado de Cabreros* of 1206, a Leonese and a Castilian version, prosthesis is general. In the Castilian version there is in fact just one case where a written prosthetic vowel is lacking, <como scpto> (with a superscript contraction diacritic on <p>). But it is significant that, if we leave aside the Latin concluding formulae, all five other instances of forms of the verb *escribir* in the text show prosthesis. The exceptional case may therefore owe itself to scribal influence from Latin (Wright 2000a). The Alfonsine corpus from later in the century offers a similar picture (Kasten and Nitti 1978, 2002). Few items written with word-initial <s> + consonant are attested and the great majority of those present represent Latin forms cited as such, e.g. *General Estoria* I (fol. 199r69) "… & por aquellos vasos dize el latin dela biblia *sciphos*. Et por aquellas maçanas. *sperulas*. ca en el latin dizen otrossi *spera* por rondeza o por çerco." Significantly, Latinisms such as *estulto, escolástico, escándalo, especificar* appear only with graphies containing a prosthetic vowel. Verse compositions are less clear indicators as the use or non-use of prosthesis clearly has metrical implications; however, it may be noted that the *Cantar de Mio Cid* contains just five lexical items with word-initial s + C- graphies. These arise from two sources: (i) etymological *s impure* forms where the expected prosthetic vowel is not written, as in <spiritual> four times (ll. 300, 372, 1102, 1651), forms of the verb *esperar* (<sperar> l. 1457,

<speró> l. 1481, <speraré> l. 1194, <sperando> l. 2239) and the place name <Spinaz de Can> (l. 393); and (ii) forms originally containing the prefix EX- which have undergone apheresis, <spidios> twice (ll. 226, 1307), <spidies> (l. 1252). The latter cases, which derive from parts of EXPETERE, would seem to owe themselves to hypercorrection, as a result of their word-initial phonetic [esp] being interpreted as containing a prosthetic vowel. It is significant that all of the lexical items in (i) occur elsewhere in the poem with a prosthetic vowel and Menéndez Pidal (1964: I, 176) plausibly concludes that "es de creer que en la generalidad de los casos esta *s* líquida no es más que una restauración meramente ortográfica de escribientes latinizantes", where "*s* líquida" designates *s impure* without prosthesis. Similarly, for the *langue d'oïl* area of N. France from which the standard French language was to emerge, the substantial corpus of vernacular texts that appears in the 12th century, literary and non-literary, prose and verse, unambiguously confirms that vowel prosthesis in *s* impure forms was already a generalised process.

Subsequently, however, a striking divergence occurs in the fortunes of the rule of vowel prosthesis in Spanish and French. In the former language, and indeed in other varieties of Ibero-Romance, the rule remains fully productive. Thus, prosthesis still systematically operates on native Spanish neologisms and loanwords, e.g. *spot* [es'pot], *snob* [ez'noβ(e)]. Indeed, in a discussion of syllabic types in contemporary Spanish, Carmen Pensado (1985:314) cites what she describes as the famous *e*-epenthesis rule as a prime example of an "exceptionless" phonological process (I reproduce her use of double inverted commas). On the other hand, a very different pattern of change can be observed in French. While the rule of vowel prosthesis continued to operate as previously in the post-medieval period in southern varieties of Gallo-Romance and is still productive in certain dialects such as that of Provence, e.g. *escrable, espoutnik, estendardisto* "switchboard operator" = St.Fr. *standardiste* (Coupier 1995), it underwent a striking loss of productivity in the northern Gallo-Romance area of the *langue d'oïl*. If we focus more particularly on the Ile-de-France zone where the norm variety of French has its roots, it is apparent that the rule of prosthesis was being abandoned here with relative rapidity, probably from the 15th century onward. In words which had already developed a prosthetic vowel such as Old French *escole* and *esp(e)rit*, the initial vowel continued to exist but it now became interpreted as simply the initial segment of the underlying lexical form. The productive pattern for new words with etymological *s impure* was for these to be lexicalised as such without prosthesis. Already in the *In linguam gallicam isagωge* [sic] by Jacques Dubois published in 1531, which was the earliest grammar of French by a Frenchman for French readers (albeit written in Latin), we find a clear presentation of the newly emerging pattern. The following three realisations are identified for words whose etyma originally contained *s* impure (the examples cited in italics are those of Dubois but some have been adapted to modern French orthography):[1]

(i) use of prosthesis of [e-] with deletion of etymological [s]: *épine, étude*, etc.
(ii) use of prosthesis of [e-] with retention of etymological [s]: *espérer, espoir*, etc.
(iii) non-use of prosthesis, with retention of etymological [s] : *scribe, station*, etc.

This arrangement points to the moribund state of the previously vigorous rule of prosthesis amongst at least certain speakers of French in the early 16th century, including presumably the educated literate classes for whom Dubois was writing. For prosthesis is only present in items of sets (i) and (ii), and both these sets exclusively contain lexical items which had long been established in the lexicon of French by the time of Dubois. However, set (iii) comprises learned forms that represent relatively recent arrivals in the language. It is this set which evidently constituted what was already establishing itself as the productive strategy for handling new (i.e. as yet non-lexicalised) forms containing etymological *s* impure, whether they were borrowings drawn from classical or contemporary languages or neologisms created from internal resources. The presentation of Dubois is, it may be emphasised, wholly in line with accounts to be found in the works of later French grammarians and orthoepists of the 16th century and thereafter. Already in 1531 therefore we have a neat characterisation of the new pattern that has continued to prevail in the standard variety up to the present day where no use is made of vowel prosthesis, as the following examples of recent lexical additions to French confirm (dates in brackets indicate earliest attestation, as cited in the DHLF):

learned forms	*strate* (1805), *spéléologie* (1893)
loans from contemporary languages	*sketch* (1879), *stress* (1950), *spoutnik* (1957)

---

[1] Dubois uses a special symbol for the initial vowel of the items in (i), namely an 'e' with an oblique line through it. This, we are told, reflects the fact that there was originally an *s* present but that it is no longer pronounced. Also, in accordance with writing habits of the time, no accent appears on the second *e* of *espérer*.

native neologisms *smicard* (1971), *sketba*[2]

The abandonment of the productive rule of vowel prosthesis in French is particularly curious in the light of its maintenance in Spanish and it prompts us to inquire more closely into the factors that could have brought about the contrasting circumstances in the two languages. Here, it would of course be helpful to be able to draw on the findings of earlier investigations but unfortunately previous work in this area has been limited. Historians of the Spanish language have, perhaps predictably, not sought to explore why a possible sound change has failed to materialise; instead, attention has focused exclusively on the original development of the rule of vowel prosthesis, cf. Menéndez Pidal (1958:§39,3), Lloyd (1987:148-50) and Penny (2002:43-44). Similarly, historians of other Ibero-Romance varieties have confined themselves to considering the rise of prosthesis; cf. Moll (1951:§134), Badía Margarit (1981:183) and Duarte and Alsina (1984:105) for Catalan, and Nunes (1960:97) and Williams (1962:65) for Portuguese. As regards the French language, somewhat more surprisingly we find that most historians of the language have likewise restricted themselves to discussing the original rise of the rule of prosthesis without consideration of the subsequent abandonment of the rule, cf. Nyrop (1935:§ 461), Fouché (1966:694-96), Price (1971:37-38) and Zink (1986:67-68). Only rarely can comments can be found on the later development and these are invariably brief, e.g. Pope (1952:§653) and Posner (1996:290-91). The present investigation therefore takes us into territory that has not been well covered and, as a result, our conclusions must remain somewhat tentative.

TOWARDS AN EXPLANATION OF THE LATER,
DIVERGENT FATE OF VOWEL PROSTHESIS

It would seem unlikely that the differing fortunes of vowel prosthesis in Spanish and French since the 15th century owe themselves to the variable action of one single factor. Such have been the similarities between the two languages since the later Middle Ages, in respect of their internal structure and the cultural forces

---

[2] A *smicard* is a recipient of the *SMIC* (*salaire minimum interprofessionnel de croissance*), i.e. someone receiving the minimum wage. The second item derives from *verlan*, a system of formally adapting words by reversing the constituent syllables (the term *verlan* itself derives from *l'envers*). Most typically used by young underprivileged inhabitants of the *banlieues* of Paris, *verlan* operates as a linguistic code that is used for group solidarity and ludic purposes. The form *sketba* derives from *basket* 'trainer (shoe)', the latter being first attested in 1898. Cf. Azra and Cheneau (1994) for data on phonological aspects of *verlan*.

that have operated on the two respective speech communities, that a sensible working hypothesis is that the divergent development in vowel prosthesis was prompted by a number of separate factors each operating with varying force in conjunction with one another. Some of the factors which can be identified were sociolinguistic in nature and others were of a more formal character. As we shall see, the former relate predominantly to prevailing patterns of usage found amongst the more favoured, educated classes of society. Such factors would have operated in a 'top-down' way. The latter type of factor relates to patterns of usage appearing amongst less educated speakers. These factors would have acted in a more 'bottom-up' fashion (cf. Labov 1994:78; 2001:272-75). In our view, it was the differing nature and effects of these various interacting forces in the two language communities that yielded the divergent results in the use of vowel prosthesis in Spanish and French.

SOCIOLINGUISTIC FACTORS
As has been mentioned, substantial numbers of vernacular texts written in a non-latinising orthography had appeared in France by the end of the 12th century. These texts ranged over literary and non-literary domains and in many instances the writers had been forced to resort to widespread lexical borrowing from Latin to meet their needs. In the following centuries, as written French was extended to a larger range of formal domains such as the law (cf. Judge 1993:7-10), the influx of Latinisms became ever greater, reaching a high point in the 14th century as Brunot (1966:566) noted, "Le XIVe siècle est véritablement l'époque où se constitue le vocabulaire savant". An important trigger for the coining of Latinisms lay in translations. 14th-century monarchs, beginning with Jean II (1350-1364) and Charles V (1364-1380), commissioned the translating of considerable numbers of Latin works into French, especially those that aimed at moral improvement or were utilitarian in character (Monfrin 1963, Marchello-Nizia 1979:358-62). Thus, for instance, Nicolas Oresme who translated a number of Latin works, introduced numerous new loanwords including *communication, négocier, scientifique, stérile, scandaleux* (Taylor 1965). Now, of considerable importance here is the mode of orthographical representation adopted for these Latinisms. Two distinct traditions of vernacular orthography developed in later medieval France. On the one hand, there was the phonemic type where spelling sought directly to represent pronunciation, and on the other hand from the later 13th century there arose a rival etymologising tradition associated with the *praticiens* or professional legal clerks whose numbers and social importance grew rapidly in the later Middle Ages. Latin had of course been the language of law and it was predictable that this should impact on French official writings for which the *praticiens* were responsible. It was the etymologising tradition that

was to prevail and its effects are clearly to be seen in modern French spelling where 'silent' letters abound, many of which are etymologically appropriate, e.g. <g> in *doigt* (< DIGITUS), but some are not, e.g. <d> in *poids* (< PENSUM and not PONDUS). The triumph of the etymologising spelling owed itself in large part to the prestige it enjoyed through its direct association with legal and royal authority. In addition, it is perhaps not irrelevant that the appropriate use of an etymologising spelling demonstrated a command of Latin that would have distinguished the learned few who were versed in *grammatica* from the rest of the population. At all events, a likely consequence of the prestige of this orthographical system, in our view, was that amongst certain of the educated French-speaking classes a tendency would have arisen to engage in spelling pronunciation, particularly with higher register words and especially Latinisms. The very use of such words in speech must have been socially marked, and assigning them a special etymology-based pronunciation would not have failed to be seen as particularly prestigious. A direct counterpart to this exists in more recent times. French speakers in the past two centuries have widely engaged in "spelling pronunciation", e.g. the final consonants of *fait* [fɛt] and *jadis* [ʒadis] and the velar plosive of *legs* [lɛg], such pronunciations doubtless being motivated in part by a desire amongst the newly literate to indicate their acquisition of literacy although other factors, particularly of a pragmatic nature, may also be relevant.

Vernacularised pronunciations of Latinisms certainly existed amongst some speakers and continued to exist into the 16th century (cf. present-day French items like *quolibet* [kolibɛ] "jibe") but these came to enjoy little prestige and became the butt of humour. Thus, the 16th-century writer Tabourot pastiches "Frenchified" pronunciations of Latin, representing DUCUM EST AMOR RUS COELI AQUILAE VITAM rather scurrilously as *Du con est amoureux celui à qui le vit tend* (1970 [1588]:45). Yet his representation of SI CUM STIPE TU ES as *Si constipé tu es* (p. 47), where no sign of a prosthetic vowel appears, indicates that such vernacular pronunciations only reflected letters that were actually present in the Latin form.

If our vision is correct, towards the end of the Middle Ages there may well have been numbers of educated speakers using a spelling-based pronunciation for Latinisms like *station, scribe* with etymological *s impure* and for which the orthographical representation was <s + consonant> word-initially. Such a pronunciation, though lexically and socially limited at first, would clearly have helped to undermine the rule of prosthesis, and its prestige and acceptability would have been considerably reinforced by the pronunciation reforms that were advocated in the 16th century by Erasmus (c.1469-1536).

The key work of Erasmus was his *De recta Latini Graecique sermonis pronuntiatione dialogus*, which was first published in 1528. This formally set out a strict spelling-based model for the correct pronunciation of the Classical languages whereby each letter corresponded directly to one sound. The Dutch scholar's work exerted an enormous influence, particularly in northern Europe including France, and it was printed thirteen times between 1528 and 1558 (Hesseling and Pernot 1919). Although initially its impact was felt most strongly on the pronunciation of Latin words, the pronunciation of Latinisms appearing in French also came to be affected. Consequently, it became ever more socially prestigious for speakers to pronounce words beginning with etymological *s* + consonant without the addition of a prosthetic vowel (which of course had no basis in Classical Latin spelling).

Few proposals have been made to explain the abandonment of prosthesis in French. Perhaps the most familiar one has been that the decisive factor was the impact of the Erasmist reforms (e.g. Pope 1952:§653). The assumption seems to be that the new prestigious pronunciation pattern using no prosthetic vowel was adopted by the educated and then spread to the *bourgeoisie* before finally reaching the mass of the population, especially in Paris and other urban environments where there was a strong cultural presence. Such a view is not easy to accept, however. Certainly, the speed of the diffusion and implementation of such a manifestly 'top-down' change would surely have been remarkable by any standards. We may recall that it was only three years after the appearance of Erasmus's work that the surgeon and scholar Jacques Dubois published his grammar of French in which, as far as the use of vowel prosthesis was concerned, the Erasmist principles had seemingly already been fully accepted and integrated. Furthermore, by a little over a century later, i.e. the mid-17th century, there are no longer any apparent signs of vowel prosthesis being used in Paris and its environs, even amongst the least educated members of society (cf. the absence of any indications of prosthetic vowels in pastiches of uneducated speech in 17th-century texts such as the *Mazarinades* and the plays of Molière and Guez de Balzac).

Although intellectual life in France did make dramatic advances under François I (1509-1547) from the scholarly backwardness in which the nation had been languishing at the outset of the century (cf. Gadoffre 1997), it is difficult to believe that the educated classes in 16th-century France could alone have shaped linguistic habits in this particular context with such extraordinary speed, even allowing for their increasing socio-political influence and the impact of printing which enabled their ideas to be diffused rapidly and cheaply. This is especially so if we accept the claim of Glatigny (1989:18) that in the 16th century about 90% of the population of France was illiterate (although it is not entirely clear whether this figure relates to individuals able just to read or those able both to read and write). In view of the circumstances, a safer conclusion would perhaps be that already in the 15th century, and perhaps earlier for some speakers, a pattern of spelling-based pronunciation was established amongst certain sections of the educated, literate minority whereby learnèd words beginning with *s impure* were realised with no prosthetic vowel. This usage then received powerful support from the work of Erasmus and, during the course of the 16th century, became increasingly generalised as the only socially acceptable mode of pronouncing all neologisms with etymological word-initial *s* + consonant in the crystallising norm variety of French.

A different situation existed in Castile. Here, the establishment of a comparable written vernacular tradition including prose is associated particularly with the court of Alfonso X (1252-1284) in Toledo. Once again, Latin provided a fundamental lexical (and syntactic) resource when extending the vernacular language to new, formal domains of expression. However, unlike in France, an etymological spelling system was never systematically exploited in the Alfonsine works or those that came later. One reason for this may be connected with the special position that Castilian occupied as a linguistic code in later medieval Castile in relation to Arabic, Hebrew and Latin. As our honorand has noted (2002:20-21), whereas the latter three had strong religious connotations associated with their use, Castilian operated as a more neutral, secular linguistic variety, thereby ensuring its acceptability for speakers of different religious and cultural backgrounds. The result was that in Castile there "had not developed the exclusive deference towards Latin which was reserved for it in other countries" (Tavoni 1998:17). The adoption of latinising orthographical representations for vernacular words, particularly if these conflicted with the normal phonetic habits of native speakers, would not therefore have been compatible with this sociolinguistic role. A further possible reason that has been proposed is that Alfonso's use of Castilian with a spelling directly reflecting its pronunciation was motivated by nationalistic feelings as a means of asserting the "independent value of Castile" (Wright 2000b:236-37). In this vision of things, the new vernacular writing system was a deliberate reaction to the long dominant use of Latin; the use of a latinising orthography would have undermined the impact of the politico-linguistic statement being made by Alfonso. In fact, both these considerations would have yielded the same outcome, ensuring that spellings such as *escriba, estaçion, especulaçion* appeared as the norm in later medieval Castilian texts. Thus the conditions that might have promoted the adoption of a Latin-based spelling pronunciation were not really present for Castilian as they were for French.

Despite the unpromising circumstances in Castilian, it might perhaps be expected even so that the linguistic recommendations associated with the name of Erasmus would have exercised some (negative) effect on the continued use of prosthesis. However, it seems that their impact in Spain, and indeed the Iberian Peninsula as a whole, was limited even though the religious ideas of the Dutchman created considerable interest and controversy (Bataillon 1966). One possible explanation for the failure of his linguistic views to exercise a significant effect may lie in the lack of a strong Latinate tradition amongst the educated classes, reflecting a university system which was "very backward even with regard to its elementary knowledge of Latin" (Tavoni 1998:7). Significant moves toward restoring a more solid Latin tradition came with the reforming work of Antonio Nebrija (1464-1512) who had received his training in Italy from the eminent Humanist scholar Lorenzo Valla. However, it was to take much of the first half of the sixteenth century for Humanist Latin to triumph. In his various publications on the Latin language, Nebrija addresses the question of pronunciation in some detail and in effect sets out the Erasmist model *avant la lettre*. Thus, the *Introductiones latinae* (especially the 1510 edition) contains a discussion that clearly prefigures Erasmus's views. Central here is the Quintilian principle that speech should reflect writing and vice versa, the ideal being the use of a 1 letter - 1 sound arrangement. In his writings on Castilian pronunciation, Nebrija likewise applies the Quintilian principle, emphasising "Que así tenemos descreuir como hablamos y hablar como escriuimos" (*Ortographía* [1517] 1977: *Principio segundo*, f. 3v.; cf. *Gramática española* 1492: I, ch.5 and 10). This leads him simply to accept that, unlike in Latin, etymologically *s impure* forms show the regular insertion of [e-] in Spanish pronunciation. There is no suggestion that the non-use of prosthesis in Latin was somehow more prestigious and that a more 'authentic' Latin-style pronunciation without prosthesis should be adopted in Castilian in the case of *cultismos* derived from *s impure* forms.

FORMAL FACTORS
Little attention has been paid to the possibility that structural factors may also have played a role in either promoting or discouraging the retention of the rule of vowel prosthesis, even though structural considerations have long since been accepted to have been crucial in the initial establishment of the rule of vowel prosthesis in Roman times (cf. Fouché 1966:694-95, Lausberg 1963:§94, Tekavčić 1972:§297). In our view, however, an appeal to factors of this type is essential if we hope to be able to explain the abandonment of prosthesis in French. For it is not clear that the 'top-down' culturally-based factors outlined above would alone have been sufficient to cause the uneducated mass of speakers from Paris and beyond in northern France to lose the well-established rule of prosthesis so completely and so rapidly. Other, 'bottom up' factors relating to the changing patterns of everyday pronunciation would surely have

played a role too, helping to predispose such speakers to the abandonment of prosthesis as a productive process. One such factor, relating to complexity of syllable structure, appears to be of special relevance. However, before this is examined, reference may briefly be made to another formal factor which has been identified as a possible trigger to prosthesis abandonment in French.

LOSS OF PRE-CONSONANTAL /S/
In a brief remark, Posner (1996:290-91) suggests that French prosthesis may have ceased to be productive as a result of the regular deletion of pre-consonantal /s/ in the *langue d'oïl* during the later medieval period, whereby OFr. forms like *escu, espi* were transformed into [eky epi]. The contention is that such a change would have meant that the resulting word-initial sequence [eC-] (where 'C' represents any consonant) was now in some sense 'stranded' from etymological [sC-] so that the formerly productive rule of prosthesis became demotivated. The implication would thus be that whereas the adaptation of [sC-] to [esC-] involves a relatively transparent process (as is confirmed by the normal practice of Spanish speakers today), the adaptation of [sC-] to [eC-] would be less psychologically transparent. Consequently, the previous habit of phonetic accommodation through prosthesis was undermined and was progressively abandoned. In contrast, pre-consonantal /s/ has been preserved in Spanish, at least in northern and central Peninsular varieties, and this has ensured the maintenance of prosthesis as in previous centuries.

The proposal is an interesting one although not without problems. One of these relates to chronology. The loss of pre-consonantal /s/ is generally recognised to have occurred in Old French during the period from the later 11th century to the later 12th or early 13th century (Pope 1952:§377, Fouché 1966:696, Zink 1986:122-23). At first sight therefore there seems to be a significant time-lag between the completion of /s/ deletion and the abandonment of vowel prosthesis. However, if we accept that attested learnèd forms such as <scrupule>, <spectateur> and <statut> with no written prosthetic vowel (the *FEW* gives as the earliest date of attestation for these forms 1375, 1375 and 1282, respectively) may also have been realised phonetically without prosthesis by certain highly educated (and affected?) speakers, then the chronological link is of course better. However, it is debatable just how far a sound change affecting "popular" words (i.e. pre-consonantal /s/ deletion) would have impacted on the pronunciation of highly specialised learnèd words. From at least the 1930s, linguists have been careful to distinguish formally between the phonology of native lexis and "synchronistic foreignisms", as the Prague School scholar V. Mathesius described them. The latter are "identified in language by some formal feature or features" in their structure and are accepted "as a specific stratum of their vocabulary" (Vachek 1966:70-71). It seems very likely that the high register Latinisms entering French in growing numbers in the later Middle Ages would have been interpreted at first as synchronistic foreignisms. If so, they would have formed a separate lexical subclass like French words *contretemps* and *restaurant* in RP English. In that case, the suggestion that the deletion of pre-consonantal /s/ was the direct cause of the loss of the rule of prosthesis would be difficult to sustain.

Further, the rationale of the supposed link between the two changes is not immediately obvious as it stands. If native French speakers were becoming unused to articulating /s/ before a consonant, it might be expected that they would adapt a neologism with initial etymological [sC-] in some way rather than simply maintaining the initial consonant sequence unchanged. The only exception would be the highly educated few who might articulate Latinisms with [sC-], as we have seen; for the mass of other speakers, there would surely be adaptation. One obvious possibility is [sC-] > [eC-] especially during the period when variation must have existed between more or less 'advanced' realisations that can be inferred from surviving documentary evidence, [esC- , e^sC-, e^hC-, $e^{(h)}C$-, eC-]. The presence of such a range of variants would have enabled a readily identifiable link of association to be created between ([sC-] >) [esC-] and [eC-], so that adaptation to [eC-] could have become a fairly psychologically transparent process. However, appeals to psychological transparency can only be speculative as, clearly, we have no possibility of entering the mind of a late medieval French speaker to establish what was or was not transparent. Some helpful light might be sought in this connection from comparable cases found elsewhere in Romance. The nearest parallel would seem to occur in Andalusian and Latin American varieties of Spanish where /s/ deletion pre-consonantally and, more generally, syllable-finally is well-advanced and in some instances complete. Unfortunately, the present writer is not aware of any studies formally exploring the accommodation of loanwords with etymological *s impure* within such varieties, although the likelihood of speakers maintaining an initial /s/ + consonant sequence without adaptation would seem to be slight.

In sum, it might perhaps be safest to view pre-consonantal /s/ deletion as having acted as at most a significant contributory factor in undermining the original basic phonological rule of vowel prosthesis (sC- > esC-). Given that the only possible new rule preserving prosthesis (sC- > eC-) would now involve both /e/ insertion and /s/ deletion, native speakers might have come to find it formally somewhat complex. This might have rendered it in some sense less 'transparent' and hence less desirable.

Syllabic developments

Whilst the deletion of pre-consonantal /s/ has been of arguably lesser importance in determining the fate of prosthesis, we can identify another internal development which appears to have been more significant. This relates to the general evolution of syllable structure in medieval Spanish and French. The diverse patterns of internal phonological change in the two languages created marked differences in syllabic complexity and this, in our view, may well have exercised a major influence on the predisposition of speakers to preserve, or not, the use of vowel prosthesis in *s impure* forms.

To set the scene, we may briefly outline the internal structure of the Latin syllable (cf. Marotta 1999 for a more detailed presentation). Onset sequences typically contained at most two consonants. Medially, the two consonant sequences were of the form obstruent + liquid, as in PA-TRES, DU-PLEX. However, in word-initial position the range of onsets was greater. Latin could not only have two-consonant sequences made up of obstruent + liquid (PLENUS, GRANDIS) but also sequences of /s/ + plosive (STARE, SPERARE). Also, it was possible to have word-initial onsets of three consonants, the pattern of which was always /s/ + voiceless plosive + liquid (SCRIBO, SPLENDERE). Syllable codas contained at most two consonants word-medially, but three-consonants codas could be found in word-final position, as in CONS-TARE, PERS-PICAX and STIRPS, ARX, respectively. The final consonant of such maximal coda sequences was always /s/ which word-finally almost always acted as the exponent of an inflection, marking grammatical number, person or case.

From this relatively uncomplex starting point in Latin, the subsequent evolution of syllable structure has been varied. In Central and Western Ibero-Romance, it has shown simplification notably in respect of the consonantal margins (onsets and codas). In contemporary Spanish, according to Harris (1983:9) "syllables contain at most five segments" and examples cited for the maximum total include *cliente* and *triunfo*, from which it might appear that there has been little overall syllabic simplification from Latin. However, if glides are interpreted as not being true consonants but rather as forming part of the vowel nucleus of syllables (cf. Harris 1983:10), the resulting consonant margins in syllables and especially those located at *word* edges give clear evidence of severe reductions having taken place. Spanish words other than proper nouns and loanwords may not end in a sequence of more than one consonant. Word-medially, there are examples of codas containing two consonants, e.g. *obs-curo, exponer* [eɣs-po'ner], *texto* ['teɣs-to]. In such cases, the second consonant is always /s/ (cf. Latin above) but more significantly these complex codas only arise in more recent and learned styles of pronunciation. Thus, Navarro Tomás (1968:§129) notes in connection with Spanish forms spelt with <x> "su pronunciación sólo se ajusta al valor literal que este grupo representa en casos muy marcados de dicción culta y enfática"; in ordinary conversation, forms like *exponer* are realised as [esp-]. Similarly, items like *obscuro* in ordinary usage have typically been realised over the centuries as *oscuro* with the addition of a further coda consonant [β] occurring only more recently in formal styles of articulation (cf. Navarro Tomás 1968:§79; Schmitt 1984: esp. 419-21). In these forms with complex codas, the effects of growing literacy on the pronunciation patterns of the educated can readily be detected. Prior to this development which relates to social patterns of only the past century or two, Spanish can be seen to be characterised by a simple syllable structure of the form C(C)VC, where the only permissible complex onset clusters contain obstruent + liquid, such clusters being widely treated by phonologists as comparable in status to single consonants, e.g. in Government Phonology (Kaye et al. 1990). Against this syllabic backcloth, the maintenance of vowel prosthesis amongst speakers is comprehensible as its abandonment would have resulted in a substantial complication of syllabic structure in Spanish through the creation of new, more complex onsets of the form /s/ + consonant.

Turning to French, a less clear picture emerges. On the one hand, a number of sound changes in the later Middle Ages appear to have promoted a simpler syllabic structure, e.g. the deletion of pre-consonantal /s/ (which was subsequently generalised to the deletion of syllable-final /s/) and the loss in popular speech of syllable-final /r/, /k/, /t/ in the 15th and 16th centuries. Such changes clearly tie in with a more general Romance tendency to unblock syllables through the weakening of coda consonants (cf. Granda 1964, Sala 1976:21-50). However, counterbalancing these changes were a number of developments that served to create a more complex surface syllable structure. Loanwords such as *est, ouest* (first att. 12th century) from English, *lest* from Dutch (13th century) and *laps* (14th century) from Latin entered popular usage and restored greater complexity to codas. This in turn suggests the possibility that speakers might be open to accepting and using onsets of greater complexity.

A factor that also appears to have promoted the acceptability of more complex onsets and codas was the gradual abandonment of schwa. Fouché (1969:509-27) describes in some detail the stages of this process which, depending on phonetic context, extended from preliterary times to the late 17th century when word-final schwa, as in *la port(e)*, 'ne se prononce en aucun cas dans la conversation.' But schwa deletion represented a feature originating in popular speech so that it seems likely that in informal usage amongst the less educated it may well have already enjoyed some currency before the 16th and 17th centuries and given rise to more complex syllable structures. Thurot (1881-1883: I, 162-64) notes the observations of various 16th-century grammarians who indicate the weakened realisation of word-final schwa, so that the 15th century may well be the period when the change is beginning to gain ground in the informal speech of the uneducated. As a result of schwa deletion, a range of more complex codas would have developed, as in words like *pacte, basque, farce*, and more complex onsets too. According to Fouché (1969:526), word-initial sequences of fricative + schwa + consonant were especially susceptible to deletion of the second element, this being borne out by numerous observations by grammarians of the 16th and 17th centuries. The appearance of items such as *stier* "a measure of grain", *squenie* "a smock", *c't, c'tte, c'tui* in 16th-century writings for *setier, sequenie* (mod.Fr. *souquenille*), *cet, cette, cestui* is of special interest, as the deletion of schwa gave rise to onsets which presumably enjoyed some currency amongst less educated speakers, particularly the high frequency demonstrative forms. Indeed, *c't* and *c'tte* went on to establish themselves as acceptable variants for use in informal conversation by educated speakers of the 17th and 18th centuries, as is noted by the influential grammarians Thomas Corneille (1625-1709) and Pierre Restaut (1696-1764); cf. Thurot (1881-1883: I, 210).

In this way, French of the later Middle Ages displays a complex pattern of syllabic structure change wherein forces are operating that led to syllabic simplification but where other countervailing forces are also at work. The latter are of particular interest because, as we have seen, they can serve to create the structural conditions for licensing the systematic incorporation of *s impure* forms in the language without their being subject to the rule of vowel prosthesis.

CONCLUSION

The divergent treatment of the rule of vowel prosthesis in Spanish and French over the past five hundred years or so poses many interesting problems for the Romance linguist. Although our attention appears to have been drawn to negatives (the abandonment of prosthesis in French and the failure of this to happen in Spanish), the investigation has yielded some positive insights on factors, sociolinguistic and structural, that have helped to shape important phonological characteristics of these languages today. It is not clear whether the various factors identified, and these factors alone, have been decisive in determining the more recent fate of vowel prosthesis in Spanish and French or whether others have intervened. This offers an intriguing focus for further investigation.

References

Azra, Jean-Luc and Cheneau, Véronique. 1994. 'Jeux de langage et théorie phonologique. Verlan et structure syllabique du français.' *JFLS* 4:147-70.
Badía Margarit, Antoni. 1981. *Gramàtica històrica catalana*. Barcelona: Climent.
Bataillon, Marcel. 1966. *Erasmo y España*. 2nd ed. Mexico City-Buenos Aires: Fondo de Cultura Económica.
Brunot. Ferdinand. 1966. *Histoire de la langue française des origines à nos jours*. Vol. 1. New.ed. Paris: Armand Colin.
CIL: *Corpus Inscriptionum Latinarum*. 1868-. 17 vols. Berlin: Wiedmann-De Gruyter.
Coupier, Jules. 1995. *Dictionnaire Français-Provençal. Diciounàri Francés-Prouvençau*. Aix-en-Provence: Diffusion Edisud.
DHLF: *Le Robert dictionnaire historique de la langue française*, ed. by A. Rey. 1998. 3 vols. Paris: Robert.
Delattre, Pierre. 1946. "Stages of Old French phonetic changes observed in Modern Spanish." *Publications of the Modern Language Association* 61, 7-41.
Duarte i Montserrat, Carles and Alsina i Keith Alex. 1984. *Gramàtica històrica del català*. Vol.1. Barcelona: Curial.
Dubois, Jacques (= Iacobus Sylvius Ambianus). 1531. *In linguam gallicam isagωge, unà cum eiusdem Grammatica Latinogallica, ex Hebræis, Græcis, & Latinis authoribus*. Paris: R. Estienne. [Facs. Geneva: Slatkine 1971].
Erasmus, D. [1528] 1978. *De recta Latini Graecique sermonis pronuntiatione dialogus*, ed. by J. Kramer. Meisenheim am Glan: Anton Hain.
FEW: Wartburg, Walther von. (ed.) 1922 -. *Französisches etymologisches Wörterbuch*. 25 vols. Leipzig-Basel: Klopp-Zbinden.
Fouché, Pierre. 1966. *Phonétique historique du français. III. Les consonnes*. 2nd ed. Paris: Klincksieck.
Fouché, Pierre. 1969. *Phonétique historique du français. II. Les voyelles*. 2nd ed. Paris: Klincksieck.
Gadoffre, Gilbert. 1997. *La révolution culturelle dans la France des humanistes*. Geneva: Droz.
Gaeng, Paul. 1968. *An Inquiry into Local Variations in Vulgar Latin as reflected in the Vocalism of Christian Inscriptions*.Chapel Hill: Univ. of North Carolina Press.
Glatigny, Michel. 1989. "Norme et usage dans le français du XVIe siècle." *La langue française au XVIe siècle: usage, enseignement et approches descriptives*, ed. by P. Swiggers & W. van Hoecke, 7-31. Louvain: Leuven Univ. Press - Peeters.
Granda Gutiérrez, Germán de. 1966. *La estructura silábica*. Madrid: RFE Anejo LXXXI.
Harris, James W. 1983. *Syllable Structure and Stress in Spanish*. Cambridge, Mass.: MIT Press.
Hesseling, D.C. and Pernot, H. 1919. "Erasme et les origines de la prononciation érasmienne." *Revue des Etudes Grecques* 32, 278-301.

Hope, T.E. 1971. *Lexical Borrowing in the Romance Languages*. 2 vols. New York: New York University Press.
Judge, Anne. 1993. "French: a planned language?" *French today*, ed. by C. Sanders, 7-26. Cambridge: CUP.
Kasten, Lloyd A. and Nitti, John J. (eds). 1978. *Concordances and Texts of the Royal Scriptorium Manuscripts of Alfonso X, El Sabio*. Madison: Hispanic Seminary of Medieval Studies.
Kasten, Lloyd A. and Nitti, John J. (eds). 2002. *Diccionario de la prosa castellana del Rey Alfonso X*. 3 vols. New York: Hispanic Seminary of Medieval Studies.
Kaye, J., Lowenstamm, J. and Vergnaud, J.-R. 1990. "Constituent structure and government in phonology." *Phonology* 7, 193-231.
Labov, William. 1994. *Principles of Linguistic Change. I. Internal Factors*. Oxford: Blackwell.
Labov, William. 2001. *Principles of Linguistic Change. II. Social Factors*. Oxford: Blackwell.
Lausberg, Heinrich. 1963. *Romanische Sprachwissenschaft. I. Einleitung und Vokalismus*. 2nd ed. Berlin: De Gruyter.
Lausberg, Heinrich. 1967. *Romanische Sprachwissenschaft. II. Konsonantismus*. 2nd ed. Berlin: De Gruyter
Lloyd, Paul M. 1987. *From Latin to Spanish. I. Historical Phonology and Morphology of the Spanish Language*. Philadelphia: American Philosophical Society.
Marchello-Nizia, Christiane. 1979. *Histoire de la langue française aux XIVe et XVe siècles*. Paris: Bordas.
Marotta, Giovanna. 1999. "The Latin syllable." *The Syllable: views and facts*, ed. by H. van der Hulst and N.A. Ritter, 285-310. Berlin: Mouton de Gruyter.
Menéndez Pidal, Ramón. 1958. *Manual de gramática histórica española*. 10th ed. Madrid: Espasa-Calpe.
Menéndez Pidal, Ramón. 1964-69. *Cantar de Mio Cid*. 3 vols. Madrid: Espasa-Calpe.
Moll, Francisco B. de. 1952. *Gramática histórica catalana*. Madrid: Gredos.
Monfrin, Jacques. 1963. "Humanisme et traductions au Moyen-Age." *Journal des Savants*, 161-90. Also in Monfrin, Jacques. 2001. *Etudes de philologie romane*. Geneva: Droz, 757-85.
Navarro Tomás, T. 1968. *Manual de pronunciación española*. 14th ed. Madrid: CSIC.
Nebrija, Antonio de. [1481] 1981. *Introductiones Latinae*, ed. by E. de Bustos. Salamanca: Universidad de Salamanca.
Nebrija, Antonio de. [1492] 1946. *Gramatica Castellana*, ed. by Galindo Romeo and L. Ortiz Muñoz. 2 vols [Critical edition and facsimile]. Madrid: Ed. de la Junta del Centenario.
Nebrija, Antonio de. [1517] 1977. *Reglas de orthographia en la lengua castellana*, ed. by A. de Quilis. Bogotá: Publicaciones del Instituto Caro y Cuervo.
Nunes, José. 1960. *Compêndio de gramática histórica portuguesa*. 6th ed. Lisbon: Livraria Clássica.
Nyrop, Kristoffer. 1935. *Grammaire historique de la langue française*. Vol. 1. 4th ed. Copenhagen: Gyldendalske Boghandel.

Penny, Ralph. 2002. *A History of the Spanish Language*. 2nd ed. Cambridge: CUP.
Pensado, Carmen. 1985. "On the interpretation of the non-existent: non-occurring syllable types in Spanish phonology." *Folia Linguistica* 19, 313-20.
Pope, Mildred K. 1952. *From Latin to Modern French*. 2nd ed. Manchester: Manchester University Press.
Posner, Rebecca. 1996. *The Romance Languages*. Cambridge: CUP.
Price, Glanville. 1971. *The French Language: Present and Past*. London: Arnold.
Prinz, Otto. 1938. "Zur Entstehung des Prothese vor *s*-impurum im Lateinischen." *Glotta* 26, 97-115.
Sala, Marius, 1976. *Contributions à la phonétique historique du roumain*. Paris: Klincksieck.
Schmitt, Christian. 1984. "Variété et développement linguistiques. Sur les tendances évolutives en français moderne et en espagnol." *RLiR* 48, 397-437.
Tabourot, Etienne. 1588 [1970]. *Les bigarrures du Seigneur des Accords*. Geneva: Slatkine.
Tavoni, Mirko. 1998. "Renaissance Linguistics. Western Europe." *History of Linguistics. III. Renaissance and early Modern Linguistics*, ed. by G. Lepschy, 2-108. London: Longman.
Taylor, Robert. 1965. "Les néologismes chez Nicole Oresme traducteur du XIVe siècle." *Actes du Xe Congrès International de Linguistique et Philologie Romanes (Strasbourg 1962)*. Vol. 2, 727-36. Paris: Klincksieck.
Tekavčić, Pavao. 1972. *Grammatica storica dell'italiano. I: Fonematica*. Bologna: Il Mulino.
Thurot I, II: Thurot, Charles. 1881-1883. *De la prononciation française depuis le commencement du XVIe siècle*. 2 vols. Paris: Welter. [Repr. Geneva: Slatkine, 1966].
Vachek, Josef. 1966. *The Linguistic School of Prague*. Bloomington: Indiana University Press.
Williams, Edwin B. 1962. *From Latin to Portuguese*. 2nd ed. Philadelphia: Univ. of Philadelphia Press.
Wright, Roger. 2000a. *El Tratado de Cabreros (1206): estudio sociofilológico de una reforma ortográfica*. Papers of the Medieval Hispanic Research Seminar 19. London: Department of Hispanic Studies, Queen Mary and Westfield College.
Wright, Roger. 2000b. "The assertion of Ibero-Romance." *Forum for Modern Language Studies* 36, 230-40.
Zink, Gaston. 1986. *Phonétique historique du français*. Paris: PUF.

14
Ambiguitas and the Secret Language of the Glossed *mote*
IAN MACPHERSON

> Guiada por una visión esencialmente simplista y un tanto puritana de la concepción del amor en los cancioneros, durante mucho tiempo la crítica venía repitiendo que se presuponía siempre una relación casta, platónica, entre el galán y la dama. Se suprimió, así, toda una corriente erótica y hasta obscena que se manifiesta en los cancioneros y que se remonta ininterrumpidamente hasta la poesía provenzal.
> GERLI 1994:17

THE THIRD QUARTER OF the twentieth century was a time for major reappraisal of critical attitudes towards Courtly Love in general and Spanish *cancionero* poetry in particular (Le Gentil 1949–52, Lazar 1964, Dronke 1968, Martin 1972, Boase 1977, Bowden 1979). In the nineteen-eighties Alexander A. Parker and Keith Whinnom typify two very different approaches. Parker, while prepared to recognize the general laxity of the society in which many *cancionero* poets composed, and equally conscious of the frequent absence of chastity in the poets' own lives, none the less felt constrained to defend the corpus of *cancionero* poetry in traditional terms as a demonstration of human love idealized and a sublimation of baser human instincts:

> If fifteenth-century poets found satisfaction in posing as suffering martyrs of love are we not justified in concluding that they would have liked to be such? In other words, that this convention was a kind of wish-fulfilment, an attempt to envisage a pure and perfect love by conceiving it as a self-sacrificing and therefore ennobling devotion? (Parker 1985:17).

At the opposite end of the spectrum, Keith Whinnom, basing himself on close reading of a number of texts which did not seem to conform to this pattern, had begun to suspect that much of Courtly love poetry is little more than

sensuality in disguise:

> Estamos ante una poesía cargada de un velado y ambiguo erotismo y he tratado de insinuar, si no demostrar, que muchos versos se pueden calificar de picantes más bien que de insulsos [...] La sutileza y la ingeniosidad conceptista de algunos poetas son tales que exigen muchísima más atención de la que han recibido, y estos versos nos plantean, por su lenguaje especializado y por su ambigüedad, gravísimos problemas de interpretación (1981:88).

The philosopher and the linguist found themselves fundamentally at odds.

Central to the debate has been the question of language. As the fifteenth century progressed, a conscious—almost self-conscious—ambition can be observed among practitioners of the courtly love-lyric in Spain to formalize the structures of popular forms such as the *villancico* and the *canción*, to express themselves more succinctly within those structures, and to achieve a conscious reduction and refinement in the nature and range of vocabulary which they choose to deploy (Whinnom 1970). With imagery at a premium, the immediate appeal of most *cancionero* poetry is to the head rather than to the heart. Abstraction is the keynote and this, coupled with a rhetoric which places a high premium on ellipsis, paradox and wordplay, results in a way of writing which is not immediately accessible and which, with a small number of recent exceptions, has tended to discourage close reading.[1]

If Whinnom was right to describe Courtly love poetry as 'el arte de la miniatura' (1981:50–51) then the fashion for the glossed *mote* must represent the ultimate example of the *brevitas* considered so fundamental to good poetic composition during the third quarter of the fifteenth century and the early part of the sixteenth. The literary *mote* in this period is formalized as a single octosyllable, generally in the form of an aphorism, maxim or paradox, and presented to be briefly glossed by a practising poet or poets. There are examples of the *mote* glossed by a single stanza, among them the unattributed 'Olvidé y desconocí' (ID 2077), self-consciously elucidated in a single anonymous *quintilla* preserved in Biblioteca de Palacio MS 617:[2]

---

[1] Whinnom (1970), Rico (1970 and 1990), Casas Rigall (1995), Moreno (2001), and Kennedy (2002) are among notable exceptions.

[2] Brief references, including an identity number and the abbreviation by which the manuscript or early printed work is most commonly known, are to Dutton (1990-91).

> Hasse de entender anssí:
> que yo, siendo enamorado,
> desd'el día que la vi
> olvidé y desconocí
> todas quantas e mirado.
>
> (MP2-261)

Nevertheless, the *canción*, with its most common form settling as four rhymes deployed in three stanzas and incorporating a return to the *mote* in the reprise, quickly becomes the preferred vehicle for the gloss. Practitioners of this genre aim in general at developing a theme or enigma provided for them by a single octosyllable, while voluntarily restricting themselves to the highly-formalized constraints of a further three short stanzas (Beltrán 1998:129–56). At the same time the poet would be expected to please, instruct, and above all entertain a sophisticated Courtly audience.

The ludic possibilities are considerable. One prime resource available to all is the rhetorical device of *ambiguitas*, the 'significar a dos luces' so admired by Gracián (1969:53). A paradoxical *mote*, for example, may provide a poet with a golden opportunity to exercise his *agudeza* in the form of deliberate wordplay within the glossing *canción*. The *obscuritas* of such a *mote* becomes simultaneously a springboard and a word base with development potential, allowing a gloss to be constructed which allows for multiple interpretation or for a coherent and consistent option between two possible meanings. The result is a form of secret language much to the taste of courtly circles in the late fifteenth century (Macpherson 1985).

There are occasions, now fully documented, when wordplay may involve erotic innuendo. A number of key terms, among them *pasión, gloria, medio, remedio, muerte, vida*, well represented in the scatological poetry of the period, may or may not retain their secondary sense in poems less demonstrably obscene.[3] Roy Jones and Carolyn Lee, aware of the suggestive possibilities of some of Juan del Encina's writing, but also alert to the pitfalls of fanciful interpretation, provided an early warning for the over-enthusiastic seeker after innuendo:

---

[3] The possibilities are illustrated, among others, by Cropp (1975), Alzieu, Jammes, and Lissorgues (1975, passim); Alonso Hernández (1976); Whinnom (1981:34–46); Macpherson (1984: esp. 99–105; 1985: esp. 54 and 59–61); Macpherson and Mackay (1994: esp. 32-33); Moreno (2001: esp. 473-84).

> El lenguaje de los cancioneros, del mismo modo que todo sistema de convenciones—verbales o cualesquiera—es una cifra que cumple descifrar, aunque hay que guardarse de las interpretaciones doctrinarias o caprichosas. (1975:28)

The most innocent of statements in any language may be vulnerable to the extraction of a suggestive meaning, but there is always the danger that any secondary innuendo detected derives from the fancies of the listener rather than the intention of the speaker. Context is therefore critical. For example, the terms *lanza, escudo* and *muerte* might reasonably be expected to refer in an epic to the accoutrements and consequences of warfare. In a 'Justa de amor,' based on the battle of the sexes, the same words appear routinely as euphemisms for the organs employed in reaching sexual climax, and the moment of climax itself (Macpherson and MacKay 1994).

For the court poet, the glossed *mote* provides a linguistic and social context ideally designed for the exploitation of the literary possibilities of wordplay. Particularly in the south of the peninsula during and after the Wars of Granada, courtiers and their ladies gathered together regularly with professional poets attached to the courts in order to make their own entertainment with song, dance, poetry and games.[4] Love of words and the games which can be played with them is a characteristic of a social group more renowned for its verbal ingenuity than the profundity of its learning. One of the most fashionable and popular diversions is that in which a lady or gentleman of the court is encouraged to bring forward in octosyllabic form, as a kind of literary challenge, a one-line aphorism, quotation, maxim, or paradox (the *mote*), for the attention of any poet in the group who may care to develop it with a succinct paraphrase, commentary, or interpretation in the form of a *canción* (the *glosa*). Because the *mote* comes without an immediate framework, its sense, like that of the gloss, may not be immediately self-evident: 'La glosa de motes [...] carece de un contexto rígido, y, así, es facilmente moldeable en un marco verbal mayor' (Casas Rigall 1995:57). A typical circumstance is spelled out in the rubric to Juan Álvarez Gato's gloss 'Gentil dama, ell alto muro' (ID 3085):

> A un mote que traíe una dama que dizíe 'si nunca fuese solía' que, sentiendo que no queríe que se pasase aquello que amava y algunos galanes no entendíen el mote, rogóle que dixiese cómo s'entendíe. (MH2–19)

---

[4] Le Gentil (1949–52: I, 214); Beltrán (1988:129–30).

Juan Álvarez Gato does respond to the request, but on this occasion the baffled *galanes* might have been well advised to consult his earlier 'O, cuán dichosa sería' (ID 1970), an explanatory gloss on the *mote* 'Si nunca fuese solía' (ID3044), attributed to Mencía Fajardo and recorded in MP2–136.

If wordplay is to be found in any aspect of *cancionero* poetry, then this must be one of the most fruitful potential sources for it. In her study of the language of the troubadour poets, D. R. Sutherland observes that:

> On the question of pure love eschewing intercourse but allowing everything short of possession, it is true that the poets do not mention possession, but it is difficult to see how they could in a poetry meant for public recital in circles with pretensions to delicacy and refinement, and often in the presence of the *donna* herself; they ask for the favours it is decent to ask for publicly, and they go as far as decency allows. (1956:212)

In fifteenth-century Spain the glosser of a *mote*, should he choose to do so, would be in a position to entertain, flatter, amuse, or gently tease his audience by offering an interpretation which could be received on either an innocent or a suggestive level. This aim could be achieved by the establishment of an appropriate context and underpinned in practice by the deployment of a vocabulary in no way tasteless or taboo. With these considerations in mind, I should now like to consider nine glosses recorded in Spanish *cancioneros*, along with the *motes* which generate them, as examples of the genre which, on the basis of the internal evidence suggested by author, vocabulary and treatment of theme, might invite interpretation on more than the obvious surface level. All of these have appeared in print at some time. None, to the best of my knowledge, has been considered in detail or in context.

1. *PASIÓN*

Mote: ES IMPOSSIBLE SUFRIRSE
(Anon, ID 6794)

Glosa del maestre Juan el Trepador.
Mi passión es de tal suerte
que no consiente dezirse
ni callarse, qu'es tan fuerte
que sin menos mal que muerte
es impossible sufrirse.
Si se descubre mi mal,

> mayor mal es que ser muerto,
> y, si se tiene encubierto,
> mucho más es que mortal.
> Porqu'es passión de tal suerte
> que no consiente dezirse
> ni callarse, qu'es tan fuerte
> que sin menos mal que muerte
> es impossible sufrirse.

Erich Auerbach's seminal study of the complex etymology of the Latin term *passio* (1965:67–81) brings out the *ambiguitas* implied historically by its two principal meanings: 'suffering' and 'ecstatic love'. Jane Tillier (1985) develops this for Spanish *cancionero* poetry, demonstrating that what *pasión* might mean in any given context would depend on the circumstances of that appearance: its connotations might be religious, or courtly, or erotic, or any combination of the three. The immediate setting for this gloss is that an obscure poet, Juan el Trepador, chooses to develop an open-ended *mote*, 'Es impossible sufrirse,' within the context of a passion which can neither be articulated in public nor left unexpressed.

The name of Maestre Juan el Trepador stands out in the section of the *Cancionero general* (fols 143^v–46^v) devoted to *motes* and their glosses. Maestre Juan's social standing is very different from that of the other poets represented here, and his only other recorded verse, satirical and scabrous, consists of two compositions—'Pues que no soy socorrido' (ID 6774) and 'Por navidad la rosada' (ID 6777)—which appear in the 'Obras de burlas provocantes a risa' gathered together by Hernando del Castillo at the end of the *Cancionero general*. Juan's trade as a haberdasher and outfitter involved the provision of decorative trimmings and accessories for gentlemen's clothing and the accoutrements of their animals. This calling is one which has been known to attract those drawn towards their own sex. In 'Por Navidad la rosada' (11GC-1009) he ridicules the red tunic with non-matching accessories selected as appropriate Christmas costume by a middle-aged gentleman customer. 'Pues que no soy socorrido' (11CG–1006) is devoted to explicit and earthy abuse of a customer unprepared to pay him in the agreed form for some saddle trimmings:

> Pues que no soy socorrido,
> señor, cagarm'e en la silla;
> vós, cagáos en la capilla
> del capuz, pues no es venido.
> Que si no me socorréis,

> viéndome cagar de frío,
> cágom'en vós, señor mío;
> vós, cagáos donde querréis.
> Y si la copla es cagada,
> vuestras mercedes son más,
> porque lo que viene atrás
> cerca está de la rabada.
> Pues librea no me dais,
> digo c'os caguéis en ella,
> y yo, pues qu'estoy sin ella,
> cágom'en quanto mandáis.

These would appear to be circumstances, therefore, which invite a reading of 'Mi passión es de tal suerte' in a specialized environment. The poem could be interpreted coherently, but unexceptionally, as a reflection by a tradesman on the tensions between the need to maintain discretion in order to protect the honour of a lady and the innate desire to articulate one's love for such a lady. It reads more vividly, and in context more plausibly, as a reflection on a passion felt for a member of the same sex. Juan's initial dilemma is the fear of discovery. He cannot speak openly of his passion: 'Mi passión es de tal suerte / que no consiente dezirse / ni callarse.' His is the love that dare not speak its name. Nor can he conceal his passion, since either to articulate his feelings or to remain silent would be a fate worse than death. The first would betray and dishonour his lover. The second would lead to a suffering more intolerable than death itself. Both prime meanings of *pasión*, 'suffering' and 'ecstatic love,' are exploited to the full within a three-stanza gloss for which the circumstances encourage a reading at other than surface level.

2. GLORIA

Mote: AYA LA PENA POR GLORIA	*Mote*: QUALQUIER PENA POR MÁS GLORIA
(Anon, ID 6330)	(Salazar, ID 6606)
Glosa de Sacedo	*Glosa de Luis de Salazar*

Por vuestra gran perfectión
os amo y tengo en memoria
y, aunque os falta compassión,
pues lo quiere la razón,
aya la pena por gloria.
   Y, aunque penado, vencido
soy d'amores y aquexado;
mi morir de mal d'olvido,
por gran merescer sofrido,
cierto está bien empleado.
   Y por la gran perfectión
dev'os tamaña memoria;
aunque os falte compassión,
pues lo quiere la razón
aya la pena por gloria
Cancionero general
(ID 6415,11CG–611)

Por poder mejor gozar
mayor bien de tal victoria
aunqu'es grave comportar,
siempre deve dessear
qualquier pena por más gloria.
   Porque, según de quien viene
el remedio desseado,
por largo tiempo que pene,
es más plazer el que tiene
que todo'l mal c'a pasado.
   Assí que, para dexar
de amar, biva memoria;
es forçado de [es]forçar
y morir por comportar
qualquier pena por más gloria.
Cancionero general
(ID 6422,11CG–618)

    These two glosses, on what are very similar variations of the same *mote*, demonstrate the diversity of approach and technical range of two contemporary poets. The chosen *mote* allows each glosser to exploit, should he elect to do so, the semantic potential of *gloria*: always the joy of love reciprocated but, depending on context, reciprocated on either a spiritual or a physical level. Sacedo's *vuelta* repeats the *estribillo*, and he incorporates within the constrictions of the fifteen lines of verse at his disposal references to the perfection, the merit, the lack of compassion of the one loved, the impossibility of putting the lady out of mind, the exercise of reason to justify suffering. Although his gloss is technically sound, the sentiments expressed show little hint of individuality and remain at the level of topos. Sacedo provides a context which defines *gloria* firmly in its prime sense: for the lover spurned suffering is to be welcomed as a route to spiritual ennoblement.
    On the other hand, and given the capacity for *annominatio* of the key terms *gloria, pena, victoria, remedio, forçar*, and *morir*, their concentration in the gloss

by Luis de Salazar actively encourages a reading at both courtly and erotic levels. Pain and suffering enhance the pleasure of final success in love because, depending always on the lover involved, eventual relief and reward outweigh the long process of suffering which precedes them. He who wishes not to love can have recourse to memory. But he who is prepared to go through a degree of suffering in order to achieve final glory has no choice but to strive and 'die' (live a living death / achieve a sexual climax). Salazar's gloss operates coherently at both the courtly and the erotic level, suggesting that both interpretations are likely to be invited and legitimate.

Mote: NUNCA MÁS GLORIA QUE PASE
(Anon, ID 3552)

Glosa de Juan Fernández de Heredia	*Glosa de Alexandre*
Después que perdí mi gloria s'ha perdido, ansí la siento, que de sólo el escarmiento no me dexa la memoria tomar nuevo pensamiento.	Quiero agora aborrecella tanto quanto quise amalla a mi gloria, pues se halla ser más el mal de perdella que ha sido el bien de gozalla.
Mas si, con desseo d'ella, por bentura otra tomase, dado que pudiese havella, si ha de ser para perdella nunca más gloria que pase.	Y aunque otra pudiese haver, y no perdella pensase, el temor de la perder me haría no querer nunca más gloria que pase.
Cancionero de Gallardo (ID 2884, MN17–85)	*Cancionero de Gallardo* (ID 2844, MN17–34)

The unattributed *mote* here presents a challenge taken up by two contemporary poets. Each resolves the hyperbaton and the slightly faulty syntax of the *mote* in the same way: 'Que [no] pase nunca más gloria,' 'May I never experience such bliss again.' Both Heredia and Alexandre allow for the circumstance of love won, celebrated, and subsequently lost to be interpreted in the Parkerian sense as an ennobling experience, a cautionary lesson against the dangers of falling in love once more and failing to reach heights previously experienced.

The vocabulary used by both poets, however, opens other possibilities. Juan Fernández de Heredia repeats *gloria* in the first line, associating it immediately with *perder*: past bliss has been lost. In the second stanza, with *perder* now associated with *deseo, tomar, aver*, and then *gloria* again, there is an open invitation to reassess the context and to interpret both *perder* and the stanza accordingly: 'But if I were fortunate enough for my lust to lead me to another woman, and I could enjoy her physically, then even should I have my way with her, I hope never to experience such bliss again.' In his first *quintilla*, Alexandre provides a rather more overt invitation to a secondary reading: alongside *gloria*, he introduces the concepts of *el mal de perdella* and *el bien de gozalla*. Within the suggestive context of *gozar* the *aver* and *perder* of the second *quintilla* fall into place. Thus he is able to conclude neatly with the reflection that the fear of consuming his love (less satisfactorily) with another would make him want never to experience a greater ecstasy again. The two glossers take similar lines, with the trigger of *gloria*, provided by the *mote*, actively encouraging wordplay on *perder* and *aver*. Each gloss can be read coherently on either or both of two possible levels.

3. *MEDIO, REMEDIO, REMEDIAR*

Mote: DAÑOSO M'ES EL REMEDIO
(Anon, ID 4768)
Glosa de Pedro Manuel de Urrea

Sino sólo en olvidaros
no puedo hallar otro medio,
inposible es desamaros.
Pues remedio es no miraros,
dañoso m'es el remedio.
   Tan lexos voy de apartarme,
pues no puedo despedirme;
tanto quanto vais de amarme
que el triste galardonarme
feneciendo se confirme.
   E por malo el olvidaros
no puedo hallar otro medio,
inposible es desamaros;
pues remedio es no miraros,
dañoso m'es el remedio.
Cancionero de Pedro Manuel de Urrea,
(ID 4769, 13UC–55)

Mote: NO SÉ NI PUEDO NI QUIERO
(Anon, ID 4480)
Glosa de Juan del Encina

Es la causa bien amar
de la vida con que muero
que sólo por os mirar
a mí, triste, remediar
no sé, ni puedo, ni quiero.
   Vós sola tenéis poder
de remediar mi tormento,
vós sóla podéis hazer
de mi tristura plazer,
y escusar mi perdimiento.
   Y con todo mi penar
vós sois mi bien verdadero,
vós me podéis remediar;
yo, sin vós, de mí gozar
no sé ni puedo ni quiero.
Cancionero de Juan del Encina,
(ID 3688, 96JE–81)

The widespread practice of erotic wordplay on *medio, remedio, remediar* has recently been convincingly demonstrated by Manuel Moreno (2001:473–82). In courtly poetry, *remedio* represents the 'remedy' for the suffering of the courtly lover. In a spiritual sense, this would require acceptance of a situation in which the lover is destined to worship from afar, but must resign himself to the fact that the need to preserve the honour of the lady or the fact that she is not in a position to reciprocate his advances means that his love will never be consummated. At the physical level—a solution recommended by well informed medical opinion of the time—the most straightforward remedy for the suffering of unrequited passion would be the physical consummation of that passion (Lowes 1913–14: 496–507, Whinnom 1972:13–15, Martínez Crespo 1995:254). Given that the recognized secondary acceptance for *medio* in a framework established as erotic is *cunnus*, the means (*medio*) by which one or other of these solutions could be achieved would be open to interpretation. The verb *remediar*, while always defining a possible resolution for the suffering of the lover, could thus refer to a cure paradoxically achieved either by abstention or by consummation, depending totally on the context established by an individual author.

Pedro Manuel de Urrea chooses to gloss an anonymous *mote*, 'Dañoso m'es el remedio,' in which the key term *remedio* might be expected to alert the contemporary reader to the possibility of forthcoming *ambiguitas*, allowing for an option between two possible meanings. *Amphibolia obscena* might or might not ensue. In practice it does not. Pedro Manuel de Urrea devotes the first *quintilla* to ensuring that there is no possibility of ambiguity: he is incapable of ceasing to love the lady, and since the remedy for his suffering would be never to see her again and to put her existence out of mind, such a remedy could only cause him pain. The next ten lines confirm and develop this single interpretation: he cannot stay away from the lady, forget her, or cease to love her. There is, then, no other *medio* (defined in context as 'means') of achieving a *remedio* (defined in context as 'cure') for his suffering, and the only possible but unthinkable solution—never to look upon the lady again—could lead only to further suffering. The gloss is devoted to developing the *mote* as a paradox.

In contrast, Juan del Encina chooses to develop a *mote* which has no intrinsic meaning unless provided with a context. He supplies this at once. The depth of his love is like a living death, but finds that the mere contemplation of the object of his affections is a less than sufficient remedy for his suffering. And he does not know how to, nor can he, nor does he want to find a remedy merely by looking upon his loved one. The *mudanza* now exploits the possibilities opened up by the *estribillo*. Given that contemplation of the lady is an insufficient antidote to the poet's suffering and unhappiness, only the lady can provide a more sufficient outcome. The immediate recipient of the verses and the reader may now feel free to speculate whether this 'remedy' might be spiritual or physical. And the *vuelta* does nothing to resolve the double-entendre: 'yo, sin vós, de mi gozar / no sé ni puedo ni quiero.' The suggestive verb *gozar*, noticeably absent in Pedro Manuel de Urrea's gloss, sustains the ambiguity to the end: the lady's consent and cooperation will be required if Juan del Encina is to 'enjoy' the resolution of his problem. All the internal evidence suggests that this is a gloss designed to be read on a choice of two possible levels, not the least of which is as a codified entreaty to the lady in question to respond physically to the advances of her suitor.

4. *MUERTE, VIDA*

Mote: EN LA MUERTE ESTÁ LA VIDA
   (Anon, ID 6986)
Glosa del Comendador Ávila

Es un peligro tan fuerte
adonde amor me combida,
qu'es el remedio la muerte
y en la muerte está la vida.
   Porque, quando a mi dolor
pongo fuerças de valerme,
es ell esfuerço temor,
es la victoria perderme.
   Es mi mal mi mejor suerte
es mi bien pena crescida,
es el remedio la muerte,
pues en ella está la vida.
   Cancionero general
      (ID 6986, 11CG–604)

Mote: NO HAY LUGAR TENIENDO VIDA
   (Gabriel, ID 6747)
Glosa de Quirós

La fe, de amor encendida,
me tiene tan encendido,
que al remedio que se h'avido
no ay lugar teniendo vida.
   Pues ved agora siquiera
qué tan mal por vós me quiero,
que ni con morir espero
lo qu'en la vida no s'espera.
   Assí que con tal herida
me tenéis tan mal herido
que al remedio que se h'avido
no ay lugar teniendo vida.
   Cancionero general
      (ID 6427, 11CG-623)

At a first reading, Comendador Ávila's gloss develops the paradox suggested by the *mote* in a courtly context. For the lover who serves his lady without hope of reward life represents a living death from which the only escape is physical death. He fears to pluck up his courage to make an approach, since victory, leading to the loss of the lady's honour, would represent defeat. He consents to his present suffering: a living death is his only remedy. The linguistic context provided by Comendador Ávila, nevertheless, provides a structured invitation to a secondary reading. Alongside *remedio*, the sexual act, *muerte* invites interpretation as a euphemism for the climax of that act.[5] The two terms are introduced into the *estribillo* and reprised in the *vuelta*; within this context, *perderse*, 'to achieve physical union' reinforces in the *mudanza* any suspicions which might have been aroused earlier. As in Jorge Manrique's 'Justa fue mi perdición' (ID 1955)—Es victoria conosçida / quien de vós queda vençido, / qu'en perder por vós la vida / es ganado el qu'es perdido (MP4a–27:6-9)—what is celebrated as a victory is the consummation of the union (Macpherson 1985).

In these circumstances the *pena crescida* of line 10, with its invitation to consider possible wordplay on *pena/pene*, now falls under suspicion, in the same way as the first line of Juan del Encina's flagrantly erotic *Justa de amores* (ID 4469): Pues por vós crece mi pena / quiero, señora, rogaros / que queráis aparejaros / a la justa que se ordena, / y abrir luego la cadena / donde está mi libertad (96JE-72:1–6).[6] Given the context, Comendador Ávila's vocabulary is sufficiently concentrated to encourage a reading at this level (Macpherson 1985:60–61, Moreno 2001:475–76): the conclusion, based on a *mote* which offers the possibility of two very different developments, becomes a proposal that the most effective cure for the pains of love is the physical consummation of that love.

The *mote* attributed to the musician Gabriel Mena can be read at the level of a generalization—'In a lifetime, there is no place / no way'—and then

---

[5] Comendador Escrivá's *canción*: 'Vós me matáis de tal suerte' illustrates the double-entendres at the disposal of the poet who chooses to deploy *muerte* and the related verb *matar*: 'Vós me matáis de tal suerte / con pena tan gloriosa, / que no sé más dulce cosa / que los trances de la muerte. / Y d'ella só tan ufano, / tan penado y tan contento / que no trocaré un tormento / por mil bienes de otra mano. / Y pues que quiso mi suerte / darme pena gloriosa, / no quiero más dulce cosa / que los trances de muerte' (ID 6846, 14CG–445). The possible semantic implications of the 'pena tan gloriosa,' in line 2 and repeated in line 10, are discussed in n. 6.

[6] This is a situation where the taboo word to be supplied by the reader—*pene*—needs to be phonetically similar to but differing in one small respect from the form which appears in the text. The possible *annominatio* of *pena / pene* must, however, be treated with great circumspection, since the Spanish term *pene* <Latin *penis*) is not formally documented until the eighteenth century (Cela 1974:184; Corominas 1980–91, sv. *pincel*). In the fifteenth century any *annominatio* involving the two terms would be dependent on the existence of a closed circle sufficiently familiar with the Latin terminology to be linguistically equipped to engage in such wordplay. A passing familiarity with the nature of the joke would be all that was required, however, and in court circles experienced practitioners such as Comendador Ávila, Comendador Escrivá, and Juan del Encina could reasonably expect to find such an audience.

interpreted as a courtly expression of the hopelessness of love: Quirós ostensibly applies this to himself, and develops the theme: 'My burning love for you is such that there is no place for the cure which you provided. I love you so deeply that not even death can offer what cannot be hoped for in life. You have wounded me so deeply that there is no place for the cure which you provided.' Quirós's gloss, with its repetition in the *vuelta* of the last two lines of the opening statement, its severely restricted metrical pattern, and its dense vocabulary of abstract terms, has caused it to be described as one of the *canciones* which most perfectly represent the aesthetic ideal of the period (Whinnom 1981:62). The technical perfection of the gloss is also striking. Within the three conventional *redondillas*, the *canción* is composed in *arte de macho y fembra*, with the second and third lines of each quatrain providing the masculine counterparts of the words with feminine endings used in the first and fourth lines. The consistency of the vocabulary used, coupled with the fact that the logic of the gloss does not quite convince at the courtly level, nevertheless suggests that Quirós may be offering this *canción* as an extended set of double-entendres. It would be remarkable if a poet of Quirós's talent and experience were unaware of the secondary meanings of the key vocabulary which he uses throughout. The reader is inevitably drawn to interpret the vocabulary of the gloss in a more erotic context. If this is so, then *encendido* ('aroused'), *herida* ('consummation') and *lugar* ('sexual organ'), introduced alongside *remedio* and *morir*, take on the all the connotations associated with them and well documented in the erotic poetry of the late-fifteenth and sixteenth centuries. At this level, the gloss can be read: 'I find myself so aroused by you that as long as I live I can envisage no place for the love's cure which you provided. And my desire for you is so deep that I do not expect, even in the sexual act, to realize my hopes. Making love to you has left such a mark on me that I cannot imagine experiencing the same thing again as long as I live.' The poem becomes a coded message to the lady, a celebration of physical love mutually experienced.

5. CONCLUSION

Secondary meanings may be implied by the *mote* or elaborated by the gloss, but the basic test for any critic who wishes to see the possibilities of a secondary reading must be the internal consistency of the development. There can be little doubt that in the fifteenth century the great majority of glossed *motes* do not depend on erotic wordplay. Consequently the occurrence of one or two suspect terms in a gloss which could allow for a suggestive implication in a specialized context should be treated with extreme caution. On the other hand, I hope to have shown that there are a number of glosses which hold together coherently on more than one level, with *ambiguitas*, *annominatio*, and *traductio* clearly detectable in the key terminology, and that these need to be seen in perspective, treated with due respect and judged according to their own terms. The concept of key terminology is critical. For a reader or listener to be encouraged to detect a secondary meaning in any situation a trigger is required. That stimulus may be the expectations which an audience might have of a particular poet, the nature of the subject matter, governed frequently by its key vocabulary, or the circumstances of the literary experience—for example a social gathering in which men and women are gathered together for their mutual diversion. Or it could be a combination of any two or all three of these components. The springboard for the glossed *mote* is love, idealized or otherwise. By the last quarter of the fifteenth century the evidence is that many poets who practised this genre were not only well versed in rhetoric but also had become keenly aware of the multiple semantic implications of the terminology at their disposal. They were alert to the possibilities inherent in and the expectations which could be generated by the use of key abstractions such as *gozar, gloria, medio, muerte, pasión, pena, perder, remedio,* and *vida.* All of these might have one semantic connotation in a spiritual context and quite another, often erotically suggestive, when deployed in a courtly milieu by imaginative poets with a real love of words and the games which those words might be encouraged to play.

References

Alzieu, Pierre, Robert Jammes, and Yvan Lissorgues, ed. 1975. *Poesía erótica del Siglo de Oro.* Barcelona: Crítica.
Alonso Hernández, José. 1976. *Léxico del marginalismo del Siglo de Oro.* Salamanca: Universidad.
Auerbach, Erich. 1965. *Literary Language and its Public in Late Latin Antiquity and in the Middle Ages,* trans. Ralph Manheim. London: Routledge and Kegan Paul.
Beltrán Pepió, Vicente. 1988. *La canción de amor en el otoño de la Edad Media.* Barcelona: PPU.
Boase, Roger. 1977. *The Origin and Meaning of Courtly Love: A Critical Study of European Scholarship.* Manchester: University Press.
Bowden, Betsy. 1979. "The Art of Courtly Copulation." *Medievalia et Humanistica* ns. 9:67–85.
Casas Rigall, Juan. 1995. *Agudeza y retórica en la poesía amorosa de cancionero.* Santiago de Compostela: Universidade.
Cela, Camilo José. 1974. *Diccionario secreto,* 2nd ed. Madrid: Alianza.
Corominas, Joan, and José A. Pascual. 1980–91. *Diccionario crítico etimológico castellano e hispánico.* 6 vols. Madrid: Gredos.
Cropp, Glynnis. 1975. *Le Vocabulaire courtois des troubadours de l'époque classique.*

Manchester: University Press.
Dronke, Peter. 1968. *The Medieval Lyric.* London: Hutchinson.
Dutton, Brian, with Jineen Krogstad. 1990–91. *El cancionero del siglo XV, c. 1300–1520.* Salamanca, Universidad.
Gerli, Michael. 1994. *Poesía cancioneril castellana.* Madrid: Akal.
Gracián, Baltasar. 1969. *Agudeza y arte de ingenio*, ed. de Evarista Correa Calderón. Madrid: Castalia.
Jones, R. O., and Carolyn R. Lee, ed. 1975. Juan del Encina, *Poesía lírica y cancionero musical.* Madrid: Castalia.
Kennedy, Kirstin. 2002. "Inventing the Wheel: Diego López de Haro and his *invenciones.*" *Bulletin of Hispanic Studies* 79:159–74.
Lazar, Moshé. 1964. *Amour Courtois et fin'amor dans la littérature du Xiième siècle.* Paris: C. Klincksieck.
Le Gentil, Pierre. 1949–52. *La Poésie lyrique espagnole et portugaise à la fin du Moyen Âge.* 2 vols. Rennes: Plihon.
Lowes, John Livingstone. 1913–14. "The Loveres Maladye of Hereos." *Modern Philology* 11:491–546.
Macpherson, Ian. 1984. "Conceptos e indirectas en la poesía cancioneril." *Estudios dedicados a James Leslie Brooks*, ed. by J. M. Ruiz Veintemilla, 91–105. Durham: University of Durham.
Macpherson, Ian. 1985. "Secret Language in the *Cancioneros*: Some Courtly Codes." *Bulletin of Hispanic Studies* 62:51–63.
Macpherson, Ian. 2004. '*Motes y glosas*' in the Cancionero General.' PMHRS, 46. London: Department of Hispanic Studies, Wueen Mary.
Macpherson, Ian, and Angus MacKay. 1994. "*Manteniendo la tela*: el erotismo del vocabulario caballeresco-textil en la época de los Reyes Católicos." *Actas del Primer Congreso Anglo-Hispano*, I:5-36. Madrid: Castalia.
Martin, June Hall. 1972. *Love's Fools: Aucassin, Troilus, Calisto, and the Parody of the Courtly Lover.* London: Tamesis.
Martínez Crespo, Alicia. 1995. "Amor y medicina en dos composiciones cancioneriles del siglo XV." *Medioevo y Literatura: Actas del V Congreso de la Asociación de Literatura Medieval*, ed. de Juan Paredes, I:253–60. Granada: Universidad.
Moreno, Manuel. 2001. "El dulce placer de significar agudamente lo que se quiere decir: sobre una invención en LB1." *Bulletin of Hispanic Studies* (Liverpool) 78:465–87.
Parker, Alexander A. 1985. *The Philosophy of Love in Spanish Literature, 1480–1680.* Edinburgh: University Press.
Rico, Francisco. 1970. *El pequeño mundo del hombre: varia fortuna de una idea en las letras españolas.* Madrid: Castalia.
Rico, Francisco. 1990. *Texto y contextos: estudios sobre la poesía española del siglo XV.* Barcelona: Crítica.
Sutherland, D. R. 1956. "The Language of the Troubadours and the Problem of Origins." *French Studies* 10:199–215.
Tillier, Jane Yvonne. 1985. "Passion Poetry in the *Cancioneros.*" *Bulletin of Hispanic Studies* 62:65–78.

Whinnom, Keith. 1970. "Hacia una interpretación y apreciación de las *canciones* del *Cancionero general.*" *Filología* 13:361-81.

Whinnom, Keith. 1972. Diego de San Pedro, *Obras completas* II. *Cárcel de Amor*. Madrid: Castalia.

Whinnom, Keith. 1981. *La poesía amatoria de la época de los Reyes Católicos*. Durham: University of Durham.

15
A Study of Intra-Personal Linguistic Variation in Cervantes (Grapho-Phonology)
K. ANIPA

1. INTRODUCTION

'TRADITIONAL DIALECTOLOGY STUDIES THE fact that different people [in different regional conglomerates] do not speak in the same way. Contemporary dialectology adds to this study the fact that the same person does not speak in the same way all the time. Individuals vary in their pronunciation, grammar and vocabulary' (Crystal 1994:32). Whether focused on regional variants or on such variables as social class, age, sex, education and profession, the study of variability in languages has been one of the major advances in linguistics over the decades; across many languages, countless works have been produced on variation (and change). The vast majority of those works, however, concentrate on the macro-sociolinguistic dimensions of social variables, with relatively few systematic works on intra-personal variation (i.e. 'the fact that the same person does not speak in the same way all the time') across all levels of linguistic enquiry. This state of affairs is worse for historical linguistics, where one is often haunted by the pessimistic insistence on the serious limitations on written data for variation studies. This is how it was recently reiterated by Penny (2000:8), words which are representative of historical linguists' general conviction about their subject:

> Written evidence is incapable of showing more than a small fraction of the range of variation we assume to have existed. In particular, each piece of written evidence will typically reflect the formal register (because written) of a particular user of the language concerned, a user who must, of course, reflect the variants in use only at one place, in one social milieu, at one moment.

Whilst it may be true that a pessimist is an informed optimist, this observation tilts too heavily on the pessimistic side. In the first place, part of the statement is not exclusive to historical data. Secondly, not every written piece (or every part of it) typically reflects formal register. Another point is that language use is such a complex human behaviour that the writing of an individual cannot be so firmly caged in 'variants in use at one place, in one social milieu,' let alone 'at one moment.' And there is also the crucial fact that communication is never a one-way affair; it involves a locutor or locutors and an interlocutor or interlocutors, the two parts of which make up the complete picture of a communication process. This being the case, features used by one writer must have been recognized by others who lived around the same period and who read, or were potential readers of, his writing. This is not a contentious argument, hence it has not been overlooked in the conception of this study.

In the light of these considerations, it can be hoped that with patience and application, a great deal more can be discovered using written data from the past than has hitherto been believed. Milroy and Milroy (1985b:381) have observed a methodological shortcoming in modern sociolinguistics, which they state in these words:

> Present-day sociolinguistics (although sensitive to social phenomena) is in fact strongly oriented to a system approach and has often not made a sufficiently sharp distinction between the linguistic behaviour of speakers and the effect of that behaviour on the language system.

There is no evidence so far of any significant shift on such a fundamental question. For the historical linguist, however, the issue is not to be ignored, as taking care of it ensures better productivity from problematic data. In this article, therefore, my primary concern is the linguistic behaviour of Cervantes.

Another methodological problem, closely related to the system approach, is that of the overwhelming focus on *change*, to the detriment of continuity, although, in reality, linguistic continuity far outweighs change (see Milroy and Milroy 1985b, Milroy 1992, and Anipa 2001).

To focus on linguistic behaviour of speakers involves some shift from large-scale social variables to finer levels of language use. Referring to general linguistic behaviour in written material, Harre (1991:96) has this word of caution for historical linguists:

> Some writers will be more forward-looking in their use of language, and others will be more conservative. We must remember this when using textual evidence, and should be wary of throwing together examples of the

construction taken from different authors, even when they are from the same period.

Harre is pointing out how syncretism can stifle variation based on written material. But we could go a few steps further than what she alludes to by considering (a) variation in two or more works of the same author, and (b) variation within the same work of the same author. This article, therefore, takes care of this word of caution and transcends it in testing linguistic variability.

2. DATA

When we consider Cervantes's language within the context of the sixteenth- and seventeenth-century standard ideology, it is not difficult to see his position as one of the 'authorities' on his mother tongue, as embedded in the title of the first Academy dictionary. The source of data for this study is one of his short narratives, *Novela de Rinconete y Cortadillo*, first published in the collection *Novelas ejemplares* (1613), but with evidence of an earlier date of composition, probably by 1601, as some modern critics believe (Cervantes mentioned the story in Part I of his *Quijote* (1605)). A full draft version of the text has survived, known as the Porras manuscript. The edition being used for this study is that of the Real Academia Española (1905) by Francisco Rodríguez Marín, which, amongst other qualities, has a two-column format displaying the two versions of the text side by side.

The term 'standard' will be employed rather loosely in this study. Strictly speaking, it is difficult to think of a standard form of Castilian prior to the works of the Royal Academy from the eighteenth century (first dictionary in 1726–37; first grammar in 1771). Nonetheless, since the concept of standard is an issue of linguistic value judgement, just another form of the correct-incorrect language dichotomy, it may be incorrect to think that the concept was non-existent in the sixteenth and seventeenth centuries.

The arguments amongst intellectuals at the time all showed consciousness of some underlying standard to aim for. For instance, Valdés would acknowledge where his personal taste deviated from expectation, before defending his preference. Herrera later ridiculed that sort of defence. He also believed that the claims by some northern intellectuals about lack of a broad standard, and that the correct form of the language only existed within the province of Castile at the time, were unjustified. He intimated that the problem was largely in their imagination: 'Pero dezid por vuestra vida,' he challenged, '¿que son diciones cortesanas? ¿Son de otra naturaleza que las que se usan en todo el reyno? ¿Tienen maior preuilegio, ó son las que todos savemos i nos sirven para el uso de hablar y escriuir?' Valdés for his part (although writing several decades before Herrera, and in spite of being a staunch advocate of the linguistic superiority of Castile) expressed a similar conviction, as can be seen in the following words: 'la lengua castellana se habla no solamente por toda Castilla, pero en el reino de Aragón, en el de Murcia con toda el Andaluzía, y en Galizia, Asturias y Navarra, y esto aun hasta entre la gente vulgar, porque entre la gente noble tanto bien se habla en todo el resto de Spaña.'

Further, printing contributed towards the notion of standard. The fact that publishers in the sixteenth century would frequently apologize for incorrigible errors always committed by incorrigible printers and then appeal to readers to correct them themselves as they read the books (see José Díaz 1983) points to the awareness of some standard or norm to aim for at the time, however vague that might have been, looking back from today. It is that broad concept—which was to become the basis of the Academy's standardization processes and, eventually, the modern perspective, as can be seen in modern works on the history of the language—that I shall be referring to as 'standard' (and 'non-standard') throughout. This loose concept is necessary in order to have a rough yardstick against which to view Cervantes's use of the language. In the same vein, since the concept of phoneme equally involves the choice of one phone usually over other contenders, the phoneme-based column of variables in the table on page 5 and elsewhere in the article should also be understood as a loose but necessary use of the term.

Below are the grapho-phonological variables that have been extracted from the material. The search was done electronically; the scanned text was searched by computer for the occurrences of the variables. Text A is the definitive version whilst Text B refers to the draft. The indication 'etc.' in the fourth column implies that for the variables concerned examples other than those in the table have been counted. Details of those other examples are provided under section 4.1.

Variable	'Standard'	Variants	Examples	Text A Counts	Text B Counts
Vowels					
1. /a/	a	a	casi	3	0
		ua	cuasi	0	4
2. /de+e/	de+e	de e	de este, etc.	29	2
		de	deste, etc.	0	27
3. /e-/	e-	e	esecutor	6	3
		ø	secutor	0	3
4. /e/	e	e	ver, etc.	30	26
		ee	veer, etc.	3	0
5. /e/	e	e	cuestión	1	0
		i	quistión	0	1
6. /eo/	eo	eo	anteojos, etc.	0	2
		o	antojos, etc.	2	0
7. /ié/	ié	ié	riéronse, etc.	4	2
		iyé	riyéronse, etc.	1	0
8. /o/	o	o	Repolido, etc.	21	2
		u	Repulido, etc.	0	17
Consonants					
9. /ø/	ø	ø	san	7	0
		t	sant	0	11
10. /kt/	-ct-	ct	efecto, etc.	1	13
		t	efeto, etc.	19	12
11. /θ/	c	c	parecer, etc.	43	26
		sc	parescer, etc.	0	15
12. /d, t/	-d-, -t-	d, t	duda, etc.	8	2
		bd, bt	dubda, etc.	0	6
13. /ø/	h-	h	hoja	4	2
		f	foja	0	4
14. /ø/	-h-	h	ahora	2	7
		g	agora	5	2
15. /k/	c-	c	camuza	1	0
		g	gamuza	0	1
16. /l/	-l	l	mil	7	2
		ll	mill	0	7
17. /mp/	mp	mp	sumptuosidad	1	0
		n	suntuosidad	0	1
18. /mp/	mp	mp	pompa	1	1
		p	popa	2	0
19. /rl/	rl	rl	decirlo, etc.	27	18

CONSONANTS, Cont'd.

20. /s/	-s-	ll	decillo, etc.	5	9
		s	tiseras, etc.	1	1
		ø	tisera, etc.	2	1
21. /t/	-t-	t	escrito, etc.	3	0
		pt	escripto, etc.	1	2
22. /u/	u	u	mucho	26	12
		un	muncho	0	11
23. /x/	-x-	j	ejecutor, etc.	1	7
		s	esecutor, etc.	5	3

3. APPROACH

This study is not faithful to research parameters for data from present states of languages, particularly that of the quantitative approach, in which features whose counts fall below a certain number are generally treated as peripheral and given little attention or discarded. 'In diachronic linguistics,' argues Harre (1991:2), 'the "awkward" cases shunned by the synchronic linguists are frequently the most useful,' as they provide clues to the past states of the language and indicate the possible course of future development. The following methodological issues have been addressed in the conception of this work:

- a. No strong prejudgements about the usage status of the variables in Renaissance Spain.
- b. Qualitative discussion is given prominence, with little attention to quantitative analysis. Only in the counting of variants will quantification be used so that the usage patterns in the texts can be easily compared.
- c. Nothing in the data will be ruled out; even single occurrences are accorded equal importance.

A few fundamental assumptions have been deemed useful for this study:

- d. Language is primarily speech and although not a great deal of colloquial features in language can readily be seen in writing, the majority of written features have the potential to be spoken, particularly in a language like Spanish with a largely homographic writing system.
- e. Assigning usage in literature exclusively to the author rather than to fictional characters.[1]

---

[1] The logic for this treatment is that when in linguistics we refer to the language of fictional characters such as Quijote, Sancho, Monipodio, Repolido, etc., we are pushing

The methodological framework for this work is designed to be thorough and self-sufficient. The study is largely synchronic, with attention focused on variation, not change—i.e. alternative forms of features available to Cervantes at the time and how he made use of them. The qualitative approach adopted—specifically structured to test the range of variation attested in the data source—will consist of the following levels of analysis:

f. Overall variation in both texts.
g. Variation within Text A only.
h. Variation within Text B only.
i. Levels of variation: overall structure, unidirectionality or bidirectionality.

Given that the features that define the variables on which this study is based have been studied over the decades, I shall not be repeating references to experts all over the article, for that would be too repetitive (see section (4.5) below and References for this information).

4. Description and Analysis
4.1 Overall Variation in Both Texts

In this section, I shall cite one example of the occurrence of the variants from the data source, with a brief description of the variable to which they belong. The examples are taken from both versions of the text, because it is impossible to exemplify all the variables from just one version. This in itself is an early signal of potential complexity of the structure of variation in the data.

It would be ideal to provide parallel examples of the same sentence in each case, but that has proved to be impossible, because in the process of rewriting, Cervantes, naturally, changed words and phrases around, modified sentences and deleted entire paragraphs, etc. Consequently, the data do not lend themselves to the desirability of comparing like with like from the two versions of the text all the time. But this state of affairs is an integral part of linguistic reality, whereby not everything should be expected to fall in well-defined patterns and neatly take perfect shape. Accommodating the apparently chaotic dimensions of language can be seen to be analogous with what happened in the natural sciences with the move from the theory of relativity to accommodate the realm of quantum physics.

The lack of perfect correspondence of features in the two versions of the

---

ourselves into a corner that constrains us to call the language in most of Cervantes's *El coloquio de los perros*, for example, 'the language of dogs,' which would, evidently, be inappropriate.

text, as just reported, also accounts for another interesting picture, which is the fact that numerically, there is no perfect correspondence between the sum of both variants in Text A and that of Text B in every variable. In 16 out of the 23 variables the sums do not add up. Hence we have, for example, a total of 33 variants of variable (4) in Text A, but only 26 in Text B, or 7 variants of variable (9) in Text A, whilst in Text B the total is 11. The examples and brief descriptions follow:

1. *a/ua*

Traía cubierta una capa de bayeta **casi** *hasta los pies, en los cuales traía unos zapatos enchancletados* (Text A, p.276)

Llegaron luego, **cuasi** *de los postreros, dos bravos y bizarros mancebos, de bigotes largos y engomados, sombreros de falda grande* (Text B, pp.274–75)

This variation concerns the difference between a simple vowel and a diphthong in the word in question. However, there may be a possible connection between the orthographic form *cuasi* and the *cu-qu* variation, representing the phoneme /k/ (see example (5) below), which persisted for a long time in pre-modern Castilian (and of which Juan de Valdés could only say 'en esto no tengo regla ninguna que daros' (p.90)).

2. *de+e/de+ø-*

Que después pareció ser un cuello almidonado **de estos** *que llaman valones* (Text B, p.246)

No es mi corte **desa** *manera, respondió el menor* (Text A, p.248)

This variation is about the elimination or retention of hiatus involving the preposition *de* immediately followed by determinants with initial /e/. The pronouns that are used in the text in this context are *ella*(*s*), *ello*(*s*), *esta*(*s*), *este*, *esto*(*s*), *esa*(*s*), *ese*, and *eso*(*s*).

3. e/ø

No se lea la casa, que ya yo sé dónde es, respondió Monipodio, y yo soy el tuáutem y **esecutor** *de esa niñería* (Text A, p.320)

"La primera, al mercader de la encrucijada: vale cincuenta escudos; están recebidos treinta á buena cuenta. **Secutor***, Chiquiznaque"* (Text A, p.317)

The variation in this case concerns the use of aphaeresis of /e/ in the lexeme in question. To the examples highlighted can be added *ejecutor*, *ejecución* and *ejecutaba*, which also occur in the texts.

4. e/ee
> *Y si vuesa merced es versado en este juego,* **verá** *cuánta ventaja lleva el que sabe que tiene cierto un as á la primera carta* (Text A, p.251)

> *Y aunque vuesa merced los* **vee** *tan astrosos y maltratados, usan de una maravillosa virtud con quien los entiende* (Text A, p.251)

In this variable we are dealing with either the retention or elimination of hiatus in the verb *ver*. The verb has been considered in its infinitive form as well as all its conjugated forms that occur in the texts.

5. e/i
> *Cese toda* **cuestión**, *mis señores; que ésta es la bolsa, sin faltarle nada de lo que el alguacil manifiesta* (Text A, p.287)

> *Cese toda* **quistión**; *que ésta es la bolsa sin faltarle nada de todo aquello que el alguacil dice* (Text B, p.287)

This case presents two different types of variation, both in the initial syllables of the words in question. One involves the spelling *q+u* and *c+u* whilst the other involves the switching between the atonic mid-high and high front vowel alternatives, another well-known variation feature in pre-modern Castilian.

6. eo/o
> *Señores, yo no me meto en* **teologías**; *lo que sé decir es que cada uno en su oficio puede alabar á Dios* (Text B, p.269)

> *Señor, yo no me meto en* **tologías**, *lo que sé es que cada uno en su oficio puede alabar á Dios* (Text A, p.269)

This is another case of the choice between the retention and elimination of hiatus in this lexical item. Another occurrence of the variable that has been counted comes from the pair *anteojos/antojos*.

7. ié/iyé

Riéronse *á esto Chiquiznaque y Maniferro, de lo cual se enojó Repulido* (Text B, p.306)

Riyéronse *desto Chiquiznaque y Maniferro, de lo cual se enojó tanto el Repolido* (Text A, p.306)

This variable involves a morpho-phonological feature, but has been included under grapho-phonology, because its phonological component is relevant. The issue at stake is the choice between a diphthong and the epenthetized variant of the feature, which eliminates the diphthong. The simple past and the future subjunctive are the tenses in which the variable occurs in the texts.

8. u/o
Desta manera, prosiguió, me ha parado aquel ingrato del **Repolido**, *debiéndome más que á la madre que le parió* (Text A, p.297)

Mirad, señores, cuál me ha parado aquel ladrón del **Repulido**; *aquel que me debe más á mí que á la madre que lo parió* (Text B, p.297)

This example is a proper noun and one cannot say for certain how the name would have been usually said at the time. However, it makes linguistic sense to count it, since the basic feature in question is that of pronunciation and that the variation is between the two back vowel phonemes /o/ and /u/. The pair *rodillas/rudillas* have also been counted.

9. ø/-t
Avisóles su adalid de los puestos donde habían de acudir: por las mañanas, á la Carnicería y á la plaza de **San** *Salvador* (Text A, p.259)

Avisóles también el gallego de los puestos donde habían de acudir, que fueron: por la mañana, á la Carnecería y plaza de **Sant** *Salvador* (Text B, p.259)

This variable concerns a Latinate form against a more Castilianized variant of this particular word.

10. t/ct
Y me hicieron salir de la ciudad más que de paso, y por este **respecto** *no tuve lugar de acomodarme de cabalgadura ó carro, ó de algún coche de retorno* (Text B, p.253)

*En **efeto**, él representaba el más rústico y disforme bárbaro del mundo*
(Text A, p.276)

The case here involves the choice between a Latinate consonant cluster /kt/ and its Castilianized counterpart in which the cluster is simplified to /t/. Other lexical items in the texts, which have this variable and have been counted, are *fruto, rectitud, santo, victoria,* and the proper name *Héctor*. It has been ascertained from the contexts in which *respectar/respetar* are used that the semantic fields that the variant orthographic forms correspond to in modern Castilian had not been fully established by the time Cervantes wrote his *Rinconete*. It has, thus, been counted as the same lexical item.

11. *c/sc*
*No les **pareció** mal á los dos amigos la relación del asturianillo, ni les descontentó el oficio, por **parecer**les que venía como de molde para poder usar el suyo con cubierta y seguridad* (Text A, p.258)

*No les **paresció** mal la relación del galleguillo, antes les **paresció** oficio tan á propósito para el suyo, por la comodidad que se les ofrecía de entrar en todas las casas de la ciudad* (Text B, p.258)

This is an exclusively orthographic variation between a Latinate form against a Castilianized spelling. Other lexical items in this category that have been attested and counted are *agradecer, conciencia, conocer, desaparecer* and *obedecer*.

12. *d/bd, t/bt*
*Sin **duda**, dijo Rincón, debe de ser buena y santa, pues hace que los ladrones sirvan á Dios* (Text A, p.269)

*Sin **dubda** debe ser tan buena y santa como decís, pues hace que los ladrones sirvan á Dios, dijo Rincón* (Text B, p.269)

We have here another instance of alternation between a form with a consonant cluster /bd/ and the simplified form /d/. The other items also counted are derivatives of *sutil*.

13. *f/h*
*Abrióle Rinconete, y vido en la primera **foja** las partidas siguientes* (Text B, p.317)

Abrióle Rinconete, y en la primera **hoja** *vió que decía* (Text A, p.317)

In this variable, the alternation is between the Latinate *f* and the more Castilian form with *h*.

14. *h/g*

Hasta **ahora** *tengo hechas hartas hartas [sic] experiencias, y, bendito, sea Dios, jamás he sido cogido entre puertas* (Text B, p.253)

Renta la puta que me parió. Y ¡estoy yo **agora** *para decir lo que renta!, respondió el sacristán con algún tanto de demasiada cólera* (Text A, p.264)

The choice in this variable is between *h*, silent in Castilian, and phoneme /g/ (in the form of its allophonic approximant realization [ɣ]).

15. *c/g*
Á la espalda y ceñida por los pechos, traía el uno una camisa de color de **camuza**, *encerada, y recogida toda en una manga* (Text A, p.246)

Á las espaldas y ceñida por el pecho, traía el uno una camisa de color de **gamuza**, *metida toda en la una manga* (Text B, p.246)

The variation in this case has to do with allophonic realizations ([k] and [g]) of the initial velar phoneme /k/ in the word.

16. *l/ll*
Y en menos de media hora le ganaron doce reales y veinte y dos maravedís, que fué darle doce lanzadas y veinte y dos **mil** *pesadumbres* (Text A, p.254)

Y me puso galana á las **mill** *maravillas, y me llevó á dormir con un bretón que hedía á vino y brea á tiro de arcabuz* (Text B, p.297)

This is another purely orthographic variation between a single and a double final consonant *l*.

17. *n/mp*
Hecho esto, se fueron á ver la ciudad, y admiróles la grandeza y **sumptuosidad** *de su mayor Iglesia* (Text A, p.257)

Y, despidiéndose de los caballeros, se dieron á pasear la ciudad cuya grandeza los admiró juntamente con la **suntuosidad** *de la Iglesia Mayor y el gran concurso de gente que acude al río* (Text B, p.257)

This variable involves the choice between the Latinate consonant cluster /mp/ and its simplified, castilianized equivalent of /n/.

18. *mp/p*
Por todos los cuales hacemos decir cada año su adversario en cierto hospital de esta ciudad, con la mayor devoción y **pompa** *que podemos* (Text B, p.279)

Y por todos estos que he dicho hace nuestra hermandad cada año su adversario, con la mayor **popa** *y soledad que podemos* (Text A, p.279)

Somewhat similar to variable (17), the variation in this case involves the simplification of the Latinate consonant cluster /mp/, which results in the elimination of the nasal element, presumably a largely colloquial feature in the language at the time.

19. *rl/ll*
Venían en él envueltos y guardados unos naipes de figura ovada, porque de **ejercitarlos** *se les habían gastado las puntas* (Text A, p.246)

Pues cargue vuesa merced á su gusto; que ánimo tengo y fuerzas para llevarme toda esta plaza, y aun si fuere menester que ayude á **guisallo***, lo haré de muy buena voluntad* (Text A, p.260)

This variable has both phonological and syntactic aspects, as it involves the enclitic use of atonic pronouns, in the first instance, and their effect on the final segment of the infinitives with which they are combined, on the other hand. Only the phonological aspect is of interest in this study. A number of other verbs in the texts have the phenomenon, all of which have been counted.

20. *-ø/-s*
Del corte de las **tiseras** *en las medias salté con mi buen ingenio en cortar bolsas y cordones* (Text B, p.252)

Mi padre es sastre; enseñóme su oficio, y de corte de **tisera***, con mi buen ingenio, salté á cortar bolsas* (Text A, p.252)

The alternation in this case is, in principle, morphological, with the use or not of the plural morpheme {s}. Its inclusion here is, however, for only the orthographic value.

21. *t/pt*
Así es la verdad, dijo Rinconete; que todo eso está aquí **escrito***; y aun más abajo dice: "Clavazón de cuernos"* (Text A, p.320)

Así es la verdad, dijo Rinconete; que todo eso está aquí **escripto** *al pie de la letra, y más abajo dice así: "Item: Se debe poner una colgadura de cuernos ...."* (Text B, p.320)

This is variation between Latinate cluster /pt/ and its simplified variant /t/. The other item in the texts that falls within this category is *excepto*.

22. *u/un*
No tardó **mucho** *cuando entraron dos viejos de bayeta, con antojos, que los hacían graves y dignos de ser respetados, con sendos rosarios de sonadoras cuentas en las manos* (Text A, p.274)

No tardó **muncho** *cuando entraron dos viejos vestidos de bayeta, con* **muncha** *gravedad, cada uno con sendos rosarios en la mano* (Text B, p. 274)

The variable in this case concerns the choice between an open first syllable in the lexical item in question and a syllable closed with the nasal /n/. It is, to a large extent, typical to this lexeme.

23. *j/s*
No se lea la casa, que ya yo sé dónde es, dijo Monipodio, y tengo de ser el **ejecutor***, y están dados á buena cuenta cuatro ducados* (Text B, p.320)

No se lea la casa, que ya yo sé dónde es, respondio Monipodio, y yo soy el tuáutem *y* **esecutor** *de esa niñería* (Text A, p.320)

This is a case of alternation between *s* and *j*, that is, the alveolar /s/ and the velar /x/ fricative phonemes, acting as allophones [s] and [x] in this lexical item. We can add the pair *tijera/tisera*, which are also attested in the material. This alternation used to be very common in Early Modern Castilian. In addition to the examples displayed, different forms of the words have also been counted.

4.2 Variation within the Definitive Text (Text A)

In the last section it was shown that between the two versions of the text under examination 23 variables have been identified as having more than one variant, which are duly displayed in the table on pages 281-82. Within that broad variation framework, evidence has been discovered of intra-textual variation in a number of variables, which also can be deciphered from the same table.

In the definitive version of the text there is variation in 9 out of the 23 variables. They correspond to numbers (4), (7), (10), (14), (18), (19), (20), (21) and (23) in the table (and in the corresponding descriptions of the examples in the previous section). The structure of the variations could be summarized, thus, based on the perceived standard at the time:

(4) In this variable, there are more occurrences of the standard variant (with a single vowel, *e*) than the non-standard one (with *ee*).

(7) With the 5 occurrences of this variable counted, 4 are in the standard form with a diphthong in their radical parts (*riéron*) whilst the other occurrence is epenthesized (*riyéron*).

(10) In this case the simplified variant (*efeto*) is favoured over the Latinate one (*efecto*).

(14) Here, Cervantes uses more variants with a velar element (*agora*) than the form *ahora*.

(18) With the 3 occurrences of this variable, 2 are in the form without the labial nasal (*popa*) as against 1 with it (*pompa*).

(19) For this variable, there is an overwhelming use of the form that retains the infinitive form of the verb (*decirlo*) in 27 occurrences against 5 in the fused form.

(20) Of the 3 examples counted for this variable, 2 are in the form without the plural morpheme {s} (*tisera*) as against 1 which has it (*tiseras*).

(21) There are 4 occurrences of this variable in the definitive text, with more instances of the simplified variant (*escrito*) than the Latinate counterpart (*escripto*).

(23) A total of 6 occurrences of this variable have been counted, 1 of which uses the velar element (*ejecutor*) whilst the other 5 have the alveolar element (*esecutor*).

4.3 Variation within Draft Text (Text B)

Intra-textual variation has equally been attested in the draft version of the text. There is variation in 13 of the total of 23 variables. These correspond to numbers (2), (3), (8), (10), (11), (12), (13), (14), (16), (19), (20), (22) and (23) in the table (and the descriptions under 4.1). As in the previous section, the structure of the variations could be summarized, thus, on the basis of the generally perceived standard variants at the time:

(2) The orthographic fusion that characterizes this variable is the favourite choice of Cervantes in this text: 27 occurrences (*deste*), with only 2 of the other variant (*de este*).

(3) The variation picture in this case is perfectly balanced, with 3 occurrences each of the fuller form of the word (*esecutor*) and the aphaeresized counterpart (*secutor*).

(8) In this variable, the choice between the variants leans heavily in favour of the higher back vowel (*rudillas, Repulido*): 17 occurrences have been counted against 2 of the other variant.

(10) Variation in the usage picture here is fairly balanced between the two variants: 13 cases of the Latinate form (*efecto*) against 12 occurrences of the simplified counterpart (*efeto*).

(11) The favoured variant in this case is the simpler one, with 26 counts (*parecer*) against 15 occurrences of the other variant (*parescer*).

(12) In this case, the form (*dubda*) predominates with 6 counts whilst the simplified variant (*duda*) occurs twice.

(13) Of the 6 occurrences of this variable, 4 have the earlier, Latinate, form with an initial labio-dental element (*foja*) whilst the other 2 are in the later form with the silent initial *h* (*hoja*).

(14) The variation in this case, which is between *h* and *g*, is tilted in favour of the former (*ahora*), with 6 counts against 2 occurrences in the other variant (*agora*).

(16) Here Cervantes favours the variant with the double final consonant (*mill*), with 7 occurrences, compared with 2 counts of the other form (*mil*).

(19) In this variable the form that preserves the infinitive ending of the verb (*decirlo*) predominates with 18 counts whilst the other form (*decillo*) occurs 9 times.

(20) There are 2 occurrences of this variable, one in the form without the plural morpheme {s} (*tisera*), the other with it (*tiseras*).

(22) Between the simple vowel variant (*mucho*) of this lexical item and the form extended with a nasal (*muncho*), the usage picture is fairly balanced, with 12 occurrences of the former against 11 of the latter.

(23) This is the second variable present in the text in the same lexical item, the first one presented under variable (3) above. In this case the variation is between a velar fricative and an alveolar fricative. The

usage distribution tilts in favour of the former (*ejecutor*) with 7 counts, against 3 occurrences of its counterpart (*esecutor*).

4.4 LEVELS OF VARIATION: OVERALL STRUCTURE, UNIDIRECTIONALITY AND BIDIRECTIONALITY

Since this study concentrates on a snapshot of Renaissance Castilian as captured in a given piece of work, that is a synchronic analysis of historical data for variation, in which the less favoured variants are viewed against their more favoured counterparts, this section reports different levels of variation attested in the texts. This degree of detail is designed to minimize the rather confusing nature of the variation picture, compounded by the fact that a great deal of comparing and contrasting has become necessary, both between the two texts and within each one.

4.4.1 OVERALL STRUCTURE

This section is designed to report on the degree of usage balance between the variants that has been attested in the material as a whole. The following levels of variation will be considered:

> Level A. For a given variable, Text A, or B, or both stick exclusively to just one variant with no switching from one variant to the other.
> Level B. Both texts switch between variants, but with *inter-textual* usage total tilted on the more generally favoured variant (i.e. switching in favour of the standard).
> Level C. Both texts switch between variants, but with *inter-textual* total tilted on the less-favoured variant (i.e. switching away from the standard).
> Level D. *Intra-textual* perfect balance in Text A only.
> Level E. *Intra-textual* perfect balance in Text B only.

All these levels of variation, except Level D, have been attested in the material, as follows:

> **Level A** *Text A*: (1), (2), (3), (4), (6), (7), (8), (9), (11), (12), (13), (16), (21) and (22).
> **Level A** *Text B*: (1), (4), (5), (6), (7), (9), (15), (17), (18) and (21).
> **Level B**: (14) and (19).
> **Level C**: (10) and (20)
> **Level D**: No perfect balance in the choice of variants in Text A.
> **Level E**: (3) and (20).

4.4.2 UNIDIRECTIONALITY

The variation picture here involves the usage pattern of variables in both versions of the text taken together. When, for a given variable, both texts give preference to the same variant, the variation is described as unidirectional. This means that despite the demands of the rewriting process, Cervantes maintains a single direction in his choice of variants from the variables in question. Under this category fall variables (4), (7), (11), (19) and (22). It can be seen from the table on pages 281-82 that in all of these variables, the usage favours the standard variant in both versions of the text. For example, in variable (4), Text A uses forms corresponding to *ver* 30 times and those that correspond to *veer* 3 times. In a similar vein, Text B uses variants relating to *ver* 26 times with no occurrences corresponding to *veer*. One is tempted to think that for analyses of a diachronic kind, it is the variables that fall in this category that would be of particular interest. It must be noted, however, that a glance at usage in *Don Quijote* indicates that the unidirectional status established for these variables based on *Rinconete* may not necessarily hold elsewhere for the same author.

4.4.3 BIDIRECTIONALITY

In this category of variation also, the features involve the usage pattern of variables in both versions of the text, but in contrast with each other. When, for a given variable, one version of the text gives preference to the standard form whilst the other prefers the non-standard variant, the variation is described as *bidirectional*. In other words, Cervantes leans in one direction in his draft, for a given variable, but then in the process of rewriting switches to the other direction on the same variable. For example, in variable (2), he uses the form *de este* twice in his draft and 27 times of *deste*, but then in his definitive text he changes direction and uses *de este* throughout, 29 times, with no *deste* at all. Under this category fall variables (1), (2), (3), (5), (6), (8), (9), (10), (12), (13), (14), (15), (16), (17), (18), (20), (21) and (23).[2] The directions attested in each variable in this category are shown below by the arrow against each text:

(1) Text A → standard   Text B → non-standard
(2) Text A → standard;   Text B → non-standard
(3) Text A → standard;   Text B → balanced
(5) Text A → standard;   Text B → non-standard

---

[2] Variables (3) and (20), treated 4.4.1, Level E, have been included here, because their balanced distribution in the draft text changed to preference of one form over the other in the final text.

(6) Text A →	non-standard;	Text B →	standard
(8) Text A →	standard;	Text B →	non-standard
(9) Text A →	standard;	Text B →	non-standard
(10) Text A →	non-standard;	Text B →	standard
(12) Text A →	standard;	Text B →	non-standard
(13) Text A →	standard;	Text B →	non-standard
(14) Text A →	non-standard;	Text B →	standard
(15) Text A →	standard;	Text B →	non-standard
(16) Text A →	standard;	Text B →	non-standard
(17) Text A →	standard;	Text B →	non-standard
(18) Text A →	non-standard;	Text B →	standard
(20) Text A →	non-standard;	Text B →	balanced
(21) Text A →	standard;	Text B →	non-standard
(23) Text A →	non-standard;	Text B →	standard

From the usage directions of the variables just displayed, it can be seen that within the category of bidirectionality, Cervantes changes direction in variables (6), (10), (14), (18) and (23) of Text A in favour of the non-standard forms, whilst in Text B the picture is the reverse for the same variables. With the exception of (10), (14) and (23), the variables in this category coincide with those of Level A in section 4.4.1, based on contrastive parameters. This state of affairs introduces into the variation picture a slight modification of the contrastive basis of bidirectionality. We are dealing with cases of *absolute contrast*, on the one hand, and what may be called *relative contrast*, on the other. An example of each phenomenon may be helpful here:

i. In variable (9) we have a case of absolute contrast, for Text A sticks to the standard variant, and Text B sticks to the non-standard form.
ii. In variable (2) there is a case of relative contrast, for Text B switches from one variant to the other, but favours the non-standard form, whilst Text A uses exclusively the standard variant.

Therefore, whilst, in considering both texts, we are dealing with a case of bidirectionality in the examples in (i) and (ii), the comparative/contrastive parameters that establish it are slightly different, hence the dual characterization adopted.

4.5 BRIEF OVERVIEW

Given the large number of variables examined in this study, it is impossible, within the limited space, to make any comprehensive overview of the implications of its findings for how Renaissance Castilian is generally perceived. I shall only draw attention to the fact that in the table of variables, the forms recorded under the first two columns—i.e. under 'Variable' and 'Standard'—are based on the perceived more favoured variants at the time. My main sources of reference in this respect are Lapesa's (1981) *Historia de la lengua española*, Alvar and Pottier's (1983) *Morfología histórica del español* and Penny's (2000) *Variation and Change in Spanish*. I have complemented these modern sources with Valdés's (1535) *Diálogo de la lengua*, which, despite preceding Cervantes's text by several decades, has been a major primary source of reference to many modern Hispanists. I have also consulted the RAE's *Diccionario de Autoridades* (1726–37), which, in spite of having been produced in the eighteenth century, was primarily based on writers from several centuries back (from 1200 to 1700). Below is a sample of statements more or less about some of the features studied in this article, from the main primary source (Valdés's *Diálogo*):[3]

(a) *o*/*u*: 'En todos essos yo siempre scrivo la *u*, porque la tengo por mejor; creo hazen assí los más.' (p.87)

(b) *de* + *e*: 'Para conservar la gentileza de mi lengua, hazer desta manera: que si el vocablo que precede acaba en *e*, no la pongo en el que se sigue […] y si el vocablo precedente no acaba en *e*, póngola en el que se sigue.' (p.79)

(c) *e*/*i*: 'Pongo yo siempre *i* y no *e*, porque me parece mejor y porque siempre lo he usado assí y veo que los más primos en el escrivir hazen lo mesmo. Los que hazen el contrario, por ventura es por descuido.' (p.80)

(d) *cu*/*qu*: '(Marcio) Siempre que scrivo algún vocablo que comience en *c* o en *q* y después se siga *u*, estoy en dubda si tengo de poner *c* o *q*, y mirando el vocabulario de Librixa, hallo que los escrive casi todos con *c*; mirando vuestras cartas, hallo muchos más escritos con *q* que con *c* […] (Valdés) Pareciéndome que conviene assí a todos los nombres que sinifican número, como *quatro*, *quarenta*, pongo *q*, y también a los pronombres, como *qual*, y de verdad son muy pocos los que me parece se deven escrivir con *c*.' (pp.89–90)

(e) *ié*/*iyé*: '(Marcio) ¿Quál os contenta más, escrivir *rígase* o *ríyase*? (Valdés) Yo por mejor tengo *ríyase*, con tanto que la primera *i* sea pequeña, porque es vocal, y la segunda sea griega, porque es consonante.' (p.96)

---

[3] Citing of these sample statements from Valdés does not imply a whole-hearted belief in his authority, from a sociolinguistic point of view.

(f) Valdés does not discuss the *ee/e* variation feature, but in his own language uses *veen* on several occasions throughout the *Diálogo* (and some of his other writings).

It is apparent from the above quotes that not all of Valdés's recommended options coincide with the eventual standard features. Similarly, a quick glance at the table shows that the choices that Cervantes made from the linguistic variants available to him at the time are far from perfectly coinciding with the standard ideology (in the context of the loose employment of the term as defined above). These pictures only confirm the fact that what we label Castilian, English, Japanese, etc., are just abstractions of variable linguistic phenomena rather than tangible entities in reality.

4.6 CONCLUSIONS

Written evidence from the past is capable of showing a great deal of variation, at diverse levels that are rather challenging to find clear patterns in, as has been shown in this study. The status of Miguel de Cervantes as a celebrated writer in Golden-Age Spain does not need any special presentation. But what, in precise terms, is 'Cervantes's language'? Two possible responses may be provided for this question, which are: (a) an *abstraction* of everything that is known to exist in his writings; and (b) haphazard portions of his writings that may be found to coincide with the standard variant of the language of his time or as we perceive it from our modern perspectives today. The Academy, in calling the main writers in the language, including Cervantes, 'authorities,' was operating in the sphere of response (b) ('se han puesto los Autores que ha parecido à la Académia han tratado la Lengua Española con la mayor propriedád y elegáncia'), but it is evident that response (a) is most objective and linguistically apt, whilst (b) is less objective, ideologically driven and removed from linguistic reality.

The usage characteristics found in this study reflect what sociolinguists acknowledge, in principle, and should often expect to see: pervasive variability. Cervantes does not uniformly switch from non-standard features in his draft text to standard ones in the final text. In his choice of variants, he moves *back and forth* not only between the two versions of the text, but equally within each of them, in line with the sociolinguistic truism that even the same speaker does not use language in the same way all the time.

To the above points can be added, in reiteration, the fact that notwithstanding the designations 'Cervantes's language' or 'Cervantes's linguistic behaviour,' his contemporaries would read, identify with and understand him—the other side of any communicative process. It is, therefore, quite reasonable to believe that the variation that characterized his writing must be a reflection of the usage variation in the Castilian language at the time.

Whenever we read such statements as 'y aunque muchos escriben *aóra* y *agora*, es más propio *ahora*' (*Autoridades*: s.v. *ahora*), or 'dezid de dónde viene que algunos españoles en muchos vocablos, que por el ordinario escrivís con *z* ellos ni la pronuncian ni la escriven' (Valdés 1535:108), we are inclined to associate automatically those 'muchos' and 'algunos españoles' with the low-class, rustic end of the speech community, and hardly with intellectuals and top writers, such as the great Cervantes. Preconceptions, therefore, constitute part of the sociolinguistic problem.

This study has substantially expanded how to search for variation in a written historical source and offers a reflection on linguistic behaviour rather than the system. It is hoped that with more investigations of this kind, the prevailing level of pessimism about the relative impotence of written (historical) material for variation studies can be effectively called into question in order to enhance knowledge about the state of Renaissance Castilian.

References

Alvar, Manuel and Bernard Pottier. 1983. *Morfología histórica del español*. Madrid: Gredos.
Anipa, K. 2001. *A Critical Examination of Linguistic Variation in Golden-Age Spanish*. New York: Peter Lang.
Cervantes, Miguel de. 1613. *Novela de Rinconete y Cortadillo*. Edición crítica por Francisco Rodríguez Marín (1905). Sevilla: Real Academia Española.
Crystal, David. 1994. *The Cambridge Encyclopaedia of Language*. Cambridge: Cambridge University Press.
Harre, Catherine E. 1991. *Tener + Past Participle. A case study in linguistic description*. London: Routledge.
Lapesa, Rafael. 1981. *Historia de la lengua española*. Madrid: Gredos.
Milroy, James, and Lesley Milroy. 'Linguistic change, social network and speaker innovation.' *Journal of Linguistics* 21, 339–84.
Penny, Ralph. 2000. *Variation and Change in Spanish*. Cambridge: Cambridge University Press.
Real Academia Española. 1726–1737. *Diccionario de Autoridades*. Facsimile directed by Dámaso Alonso. Madrid: Gredos, 1963.
Valdés, Juan de. 1535. *Diálogo de la lengua*. Madrid: Clásicos Castalia.

16
Analogical Feminines: Uniformity and Variety in Golden Age Spanish
JOHN ENGLAND

THE MOST IMPORTANT DEVELOPMENT in the gender system as Latin evolved into Romance was the reduction of a three-gender system (masculine, feminine, neuter) to a two-gender system (masculine, feminine), via the designation of neuter nouns as either masculine or feminine. The principal development in medieval Castilian, though not of the same magnitude as the loss of the neuter gender, was the creation and increasing standardization of a number of analogical feminines, particularly in the case of adjectives and animate nouns: -*or*(m./f.) > -*or*(m.)/-*ora*(f.); -*ón*(m./f.) > -*ón*(m.)/-*ona*(f); -*és*(m./f.) > -*és*(m.)/-*esa*(f.) (England 1984 and 1987; Malkiel 1957). By the end of the fifteenth century these innovative forms had become the norm, and the following system for animate nouns and adjectives (other than comparatives such as *mejor*, *peor*, etc.) showed a high level of consistency:

1. words ending in -*o* = masculine, -*a* = feminine
2. words ending in -*or* = masculine, -*ora* = feminine
3. words ending in -*és* = masculine, -*esa* = feminine
4. words ending in -*ón* = masculine, -*ona* = feminine
5. words ending in -*e* = masculine or feminine; a few had separate feminine forms in -*a* (e.g. *pariente*/-*a*; *monje*/-*a*)
6. words ending in consonants (other than -*or*, -*és*, -*ón*) = masculine or feminine; a few had separate feminine forms in -*a* (e.g. *huésped*/-*a*).

Clearly there was a strong sense of the ending -*a* = feminine (nouns such as *espía* and *guarda* were often feminine, even when referring to male human beings), and in the light of the clear direction in which the language had evolved in the Middle Ages it would have been reasonable to anticipate further developments in types 5 and 6 above to make explicit in form the features masculine and feminine through the creation of further analogical feminines in -*a*.

However, other factors could be expected to work against substantial further developments. Firstly, the impact of print culture and of overt pressures to promote and fix Castilian usage on reducing variation at the levels of orthography, morphology and syntax has been demonstrated convincingly by Harris-Northall 1996-97; similar points are made by Anipa (2001:53-54), although he also gives a timely reminder that some local variations and innovations were disseminated in print, and this could have given people a greater awareness of variation.[1] And secondly during the Golden Age there do not appear to have been major social changes in terms of increasing roles for women; whilst the reality was obviously more complex than that described in treatises of the time, there were limitations on the number of roles which women played:

> ...en los siglos XVI y XVII, los libros de doctrina destinados a mujeres incluían normalmente cuatro estados: doncella, casada, viuda, y monja. Establecían una diferenciación entre los estados civiles y el religioso, y los estados civiles se configuraban según la posición de las mujeres dentro de la familia. Lo que significa que, desde el punto de vista de la ideología dominante, no se concebía más posiciones femeninas que aquellas que cercaban a las mujeres dentro del ámbito de lo familiar. (Vigil 1986:11)

A large number of words associated with roles within the convent continued to be used (*capellana, celadora, clavaria, lectora, perlada, portera, priora, receptora, rectora, sacristana, superiora*, etc.), and it is possible to find nouns which refer to women performing functions outside the home or convent (*bercera, carcelera, castañera, frutera, mondonguera, limera, toquera, verdulera*, etc.), but there is no indication of developments similar to those in the latter part of the twentieth century, when the rapid expansion of roles for women created strong pressures for linguistic change (England 1999).

The focus of this study will be on variation in the forms of feminine animate nouns, with a brief glance at adjectives, through an analysis of a large number of peninsular texts published between 1500 and 1700, together with extensive consultation of the historical data-base (CORDE) of the Real Academia de la Lengua Española, accessed at www.rae.es.

---

[1] On the broader question of variation in the Spanish-speaking world, the key work is Penny 2000; the current article seeks to make a small contribution to our knowledge of variation in Spanish.

1. NOUNS IN -O/-A

The Old Spanish system of the alternation of -*o*(m.)/-*a*(f.) for animate nouns was well established, with the grammatical markers -*o*/-*a* corresponding to male/female. The following lists indicate in which form(s) the feminine nouns are found.[2]

List 1a: Feminine nouns ending only in -*a*
abacera (*havaçera*)*; abridera; abuela; académica; adufera; adúltera; albendera; aldeana; ama; amiga; andadera; arquitecta; asturiana; aya; bailadera; ballestera; bandolera; barbera; barrendera; beata; bellaca; bercera; bodegonera; borracha; boticaria; bruja; bujarra; burra; caballera; cabrera; camarera; camisera; candelera; canonesa/canoniguesa; cantonera; captiva; carbonera; carcelera; carnicera; casada; casamentera; casera; castañera; castañetera; catedrática; caudilla; cautiva; cicatricera; cierva; cirujana; clavaria; cocinera; cochina; compañera; comunera; confederada; confesa; contraria; consejera; copera; corsaria; cortesana; costurera; cotorrera; criada; cristiana; cuñada; daifa* (*daifises*?); *descosida; despabiladera; despensera; desposada; deuda; dieciochera/deciochena); dueña; discípula; embustera; enamorada; enbaydera; encantadera; enfermera; escalentada; esclava; escolástica; escribana; escuchadera; espigadera; espingardera; esposa; establera; estaçionera; estrellera; fantesca; farmacéutica; farandulera; favorida; filósofa; física; florera; forastera; frutera; fulana/fulanica; gaitera; gallofa; garitera; gata; gitana; gritadera; guerrera; guisandera; habladera; hada; handorra; harpía; hebrea; hechicera; heredera; herética; hermana; hija; hilandera;* (*h*)*iza; hornera; hospitalera; hostalera/hostelera; huérfana; india; indiana; ingeniera; invencionera; jornalera; joyera; judía; labrandera; lacayu, lamparera; lavandera; lega; licenciada; limera; loba; llavera; macha; madona; madrastra; madrina; maestra/maesa; maga; mágica; malaventurada; manceba; mandadera; mangonera; mahometana; mayordoma; maya; medianera; médica; meguera; melecinera; mendiga; menina; mensajera; mesonera; mondonguera; molinera; mona; mora; morisca; moza; muchacha; mula; mulata; musa; música; napolitana; negra; nicromántica; nieta; ninfa; niña; novelera; novia; novicia; nuera; nuncia; obispa; Orfea; osa; padrina; paloma; panadera; papagaya; parroquiana; partera;*

---

[2] This list does not include nouns ending only in -*a* which, when referring to male human beings, were either variable in gender (*guarda, centinela,* etc.), or which, in the case of nouns in -*ista*, tended to be masculine (*alquimista, jurista,* etc.). A detailed study based on the CORDE database will provide a more accurate picture of such nouns.

pastelera; pazpuerca; pelotera; perdonera; peregrina; perlada; perra; pícara/picaronaza; piltraca; piltrafa; piltrophera; pilletera; placera; portera; pregonera; prelada; prima; prisionera; profesa; prostituta; propietaria; puerca; puta; ramera; randera; rapandera; raposa; ratera; reina; religiosa; rogidera; romancera; romana; romera; ropera; rravanera; rregatera; saltadera; saludadera; santa; santera; sargenta; secretaria; serrana; sevillana; sibila; sierva; sirena; sobrina; soltera; solla; sortílega; sotadera; súbdita; suegra; sufragánea; sustituta; tabernera; tarasca; tendera; teóloga; tercera; terciaria; tesorera; tía; tirana; toledana; tontóloga; toquera; torda; tornera; tramoyera; trastendera; tripera; tronga; turronera; valenciana; vasalla; vecina; vellaca; vendedera; ventanera; ventera; verdulera; vicaria; villana; vinatera; viuda; xabonera; zingara; zurcidera

List 1b: Feminine nouns ending in both -*o*/-*a*
    abogado(?)/-a; cordero/-a (corderilla); demonio/-a; diablo/-a (diablesa); enemigo(?)/-a; hidalga/hijadalgo/hijodalga; ministro(?)/-a; reo(?)/-a

List 1c: Feminine nouns ending only in -*o*
    miembro(?); oíslo; piloto(?); sujeto; testigo; trotalotodo; verdugo(?); virgo

ANALYSIS

Many of the nouns listed in 1a occur frequently (*hija, hermana*, etc.), to such an extent that the lists above understate the consistency of this pattern; comparison with the analysis of similar nouns in modern Spanish (England 1999:416-26) shows a much higher level of consistency in Golden Age Spanish, which was not subjected to the pressures of strong social change which have affected the modern language. The following observations on selected words from the lists above create a more accurate picture:

i) A large number of the forms in -*a* refer to women carrying out jobs or professions, but they are in a restricted number of areas, with no discernible increase over the period analysed: *abacera, bercera, camarera, camisera, carcelera, castañera, costurera, frutera*, etc.

ii) At first glance it is surprising to see the feminine form of nouns which refer to traditionally male roles used consistently in -*a*: *académica, arquitecta, catedrática, cirujana, ingeniera, nuncia, obispa, sargenta*, etc. Closer scrutiny of such words, which have been problematical in modern Spanish, reveals that

their use in Golden Age Spanish was either metaphorical or playful: typical examples are that Gerarda is a 'catedrática de amor' (Lope de Vega 1980:493), that a female character's hand gesture provokes the observation 'Obispa te vea yo,/ que con tal mano bendices' (Fernández Gómez 1971:II, 1934), and that Tirso creates the form *sargenta*, punning on *capitana*, 'flagship' (Tirso de Molina 1982:164). Such innovations reveal the potential for analogical creations, but at this stage in the history of the language they are marked forms, used in limited ways.

Writers clearly felt free to create such feminine forms:

..aquellos villanos que me tenían por médica... (Delicado 1975:322)

In contrast, however, the masculine form was widely used generically:

No lo sentía así la hermosa reina, que como más acertado médico había entendido de qué accidentes nacía la enfermedad de Federico... (Zayas 1983:414)

iii) The use of the feminine form in the sense of 'wife of...' was well-established; examples of this are *barbera* (Timoneda 1973:96) and *ventera* (Cervantes 1998:168). Further instances of this can be found in the lists of different types of noun below: *alcaidesa, alcaldesa, autora, capitana, comendadora, corregidora, gobernadora, huéspeda, regenta, sastra, tenienta*. It is not uncommon for the form *mujer de* to be used first, presumably to avoid ambiguity; for example, the *barbera* in *El patrañuelo* is referred to first as *la mujer del barbero* (Timoneda 1973:94), and in the *Novelas ejemplares*, *la señora tenienta* is initially introduced as *la mujer del señor teniente* (Cervantes 1980:I, 77). The longer forms not only make explicit that the woman is not the person performing the job or holding office (in many cases improbable in the sixteenth and seventeenth centuries); they also ensure that the exact relationship of the man and woman is clear, as the feminine nouns can indicate other relationships: *molinera* = 'miller's daughter' (Fernández Gómez 1971:III, 1837), *açipresta* is used in colloquial dialogue by Juan de Luna with the meaning 'archpriest's mistress' (Anónimo 1988:305), and *obispa* 'bishop's mistress' occurs in *La pícara Justina* (López de Úbeda 1974:98).

iv) *dueña/dueño*

Dueña was a standard feminine noun, with a variety of meanings: 'married woman', 'nun', 'widow', 'servant of noble family', etc. In certain contexts, however, the masculine noun, with full agreement of articles, adjectives, etc.,

was used to refer to women; this was explained in the *Diccionario de Autoridades* as follows:

> ...y también se suele llamar assí [*dueño*] a la muger y a las demás cosas del género femenino que tienen dominio en algo, por no llamarlas Dueñas, voz que ya comunmente se entiende de las dueñas de honor: y en este caso si a la voz Dueño se añade algún adjetivo, es siempre con la terminación masculina. (II, 348)[3]

The use of *dueño* (m.) to refer to a woman who was the object of a man's love was frequent, and occurred in both prose and verse; its origins possibly lie in a metaphorical extension of *dueño* as a legal term (= 'owner'). The two senses are present simultaneously in the following:

> ...antes de muchos días me hice dueño de su voluntad y casa... (Zayas 1983:154)
> Ya estamos en nuestra casa, su dueño y mío has de ser... (Lope de Vega 1963:I, 397)

In the first example, Isabel is speaking of herself, as the owner of her lover's house and will; in the second example, Peribáñez explains to Casilda that he sees her in the same dual role. In the following example, failure to recognise the metaphorical sense is comic:

> LISEO ...considerando que os quiero
> por mi dueño para siempre.
> FINEA ¡Por mi dueña, majadero!
> (Lope de Vega 1963:252)

Dueño is one of several instances from the register of legal terminology, which is often conservative, of the form in -*o* referring to women (cf. *reo*, *testigo*). Its use as a metaphor for a beloved woman was no doubt also supported by the meaning of *dueña* 'woman who has lost her virginity'; in *Amadís de Gaula* (1983:19) Helisena comes out of her first sexual encounter with a man 'quedando de allí en adelante dueña', and the expression *dueña ni donzella* is used regularly to mean 'no woman' (51, 113, etc.). In the context of the idealized rituals of

---

[3] Menéndez Pidal (1941:53) points to similarities with Arabic and Provençal, but sees this use of *dueño* in Spanish as motivated by the undesirable association of *dueña* with old age and grumpiness.

courtship, *dueña* would have been a tainted word.

v) The small number of nouns listed in 1c are mainly infrequently used special cases, and several of them are probably not feminine nouns. *Miembro, piloto, sujeto,* and *verdugo* are used as metaphors to refer to women, and the examples found either contain no indication of gender or are masculine:

> ...una malvada doncella, miembro del diablo... (Molloy Carpenter 2000: 197)
> ...gran piloto de los rumbos más secretos de Sevilla...(Vélez de Guevara 1968: 193)
> ...[Marfisa] fue el primer sujeto de mi amor en la primauera de mis años... (Lope de Vega 1980: 407)
> ...y pues Poncia es el verdugo, razón es de pagalle sus derechos... (Silva 1988: 577)

Oíslo and *trotalotodo* are compound nouns in which the *-o* of one of the component words (*lo, todo*) remains unadjusted, whilst *la virgo* 'virgin' (Delicado 1975:245) is a latinism. The case of *testigo* is more complex; although Nebrija (1998:35r) in 1492 used the alternation *el testigo/la testiga* to illustrate masculine and feminine gender, I found no examples of *testiga* in Golden Age texts. In a large number of cases *testigo*, when referring to a woman, is used without article or adjective, and it is impossible to know the gender of the noun; when the gender is explicit, it is feminine, as in a large number of legal texts which use *la/una/esta testigo* (Sánchez Ortega 1992:12-13; San Jerónimo and Valle de la Cerda:218-19 and 264).

vi) The words in list 1b are worthy of individual comment:

abogado(?)/*-a*
There are many examples of the form *abogada* 'intercessor' (Real Academia Española 1960-96:I, 108-10). In the sense of 'advocate', the two examples which refer to women are masculine in gender:

> ...a la fe que no tenía Heraclio por acá en mí mal auogado... (I, 109)
> ¡Ah Dios mío, lo que hace un buen abogado! (I, 109)

cordero
The usual feminine form is *cordera*; I noted one example of *una mujer cordero* (Lope de Vega 1963:248), in which *cordero* has a quasi-adjectival function.

demonio/-a; diablo/-a
Demonio and *diablo* are masculine nouns; in Christian theology the devil, as a fallen angel, does not have male or female sex. In the popular imagination, however, devils could be of either sex, and the analogical feminines were used:

> ...pase a vna galeria donde estaua Luzifer çercado de diablas, que tanbien ay henbras como machos. (Quevedo y Villegas 1993:188)

The analogical forms *demonia* and *diabla* are also used frequently to refer to women:

> Mejor fuera llamarla demonia que Serafina... (Fernández Gómez 1971:I, 822)
> ...se encendió en amores de ella.
> Gozó a la diabla... (Calderón de la Barca 1976:147)

At the same time the forms *demonio* and *diablo* were also used in similar contexts, sometimes with masculine gender (e.g. *esse demonio*, in Lope de Vega 1980:127; *un diablo*, in Corfis 2001:79), and sometimes with feminine gender (e.g. *la diablo*, in López de Úbeda 1974:274). All three possibilities (*diabla/demonia*; *diablo/demonio*[f.]; *diablo/demonio*[m.]) were current in referring to women; the contrast with the much more consistent use of *diosa* in parallel contexts is clear from examples such as the reference to a female character as 'Diosa en años, diablo en gesto' in Lope de Vega 1977:164.

enemigo(?)/-a
The feminine form *enemiga* is used frequently, in a range of texts. I noted three examples of *enemigo* referring to a woman: *el enemigo* (Cervantes 1998:390), *su enemigo* (Cervantes 1980:II, 55), and *fuerte enemigo* (Zayas 1983:449). The gender of the noun in the last two cases is not explicit, but they are probably examples of the masculine used generically; all three texts also use *enemiga*.

hidalga/hijadalgo/hijodalga
The shortening of the compound noun *fijodalgo > hidalgo* was a lengthy process, and in the case of the feminine form also involved transferring the gender-marker *-a* from word-interior to word-final position (*fijadalgo > hidalga*). The data in CORDE provides 16 examples of the longer form *hijadalgo/fijadalgo* in texts from 1535 to 1626; the shortened form *hidalga* occurs 17 times, in texts from 1528 to 1648. I also noted one example of *hijodalga*, not documented in CORDE (Rojas Zorrilla 1926:192).

ministro(?)/-a
The CORDE database provides 42 examples of *ministra*; I found one example of *ministros* referring to women:

> ...halló traza por los medios de una buena dueña de tocas largas reverendas, que suelen ser las tales ministros de Satanás, con que mina y prostra las fuertes torres de las más castas mujeres. (Alemán 1987:I, 145)

There is also one example of *una ministro* in CORDE (from Alonso de Villegas' *Fructus sanctorum*), but the context makes clear that this is an erratum; the full phrase is *una ministro suyo*, and the individual is thereafter referred to as *él*.

reo(?)/-a
The *Diccionario de Autoridades* defines *reo* as follows:

> El que ha cometido algun delito, porque se hizo digno de castigo. Hablando de muger suelen algunos decir rea. (V, 576)

In spite of the above comment, and the fact that hesitations over *reo/rea* have continued into the modern language, *rea* is the dominant form in Golden Age texts. There are six examples documented in CORDE, and in legal texts there are nine seventeenth-century examples (Sánchez Ortega 1992:137, 199, 201, 209, 212). I noted only one example of *reo* referring to a woman, with the gender of the noun unclear:

> Sólo que me hagáis testigo
> Falta, después de haberme hecho
> Juez y reo. (Leiva Ramírez de Arellano 1924:366)

vi) The pattern *-o/-a* is so strong that sometimes it is a new masculine form in *-o* which is created on the basis of a feminine word:

> !Tomá! ¿No dezía yo que se andaba
> ya mueso amo hecho galançete y damo? (Hernando de Ávila 1995:fol. 149v)

The context for the form *damo* is clearly informal and playful. Fichter (see Lope de Vega 1944:226) points to further examples in Lope (*damo*), Cervantes (*muso*) and Calderón (*sombro*), emphasising the colloquial and/or humorous nature of such creations.

2. Nouns in -OR/-ORA

In the case of animate nouns the innovative opposition -or(m.)/-ora(f.) had become firmly established in the fifteenth century, and was matched by a similar structure with adjectives in -or/-ora; this high level of consistency remained throughout the sixteenth and seventeenth centuries.[4]

List 2a: Feminine nouns ending only in -ora
abridora; acariciadora; acarreadora; acrecentadora; actora; aduladora; advogadora; agresora; allegadora; amadora; antecesora; anunciadora; asadora; augmentadora; autora; ayudadora; avisadora; ayudadora; bailadora; beneficiadora; bienhechora; burladora; cantadora; cantimplora; cantonera; cantora; capeadora; causadora; cazadora; celadora; cercenadora; colectora; comedora; comendadora; cometedora; competidora; compradora; conchabadora; condenadora; confesora; conqueridora; contaminadora; consultora; correctora; corredora; curadora; danzadora; decididora; defensora(defensatriz); derramadora; descubridora; desengañadora; despertadora; destruidora; deudora; dezidora; dezidora; embaidora; embajadora (embajatriz); empadronadora; empanadora; emperadora (emperatriz); encandiladora; encantadora; encubridora; endechadora; enflautadora; engañadora; engazadora; engendradora; entendedora; entrenedora; escanciadora; escritora; escupidora; eslabonadora; espigadora; estornudadora; fautora; fundadora; gastadora; gobernadora; guardadora; habitadora; habladora; historiadora; hospedadora; imitadora; infamadora; inquietadora; inspiradora; intercesora; introductora; inventora; jodedora; jugadora; labradora/labradorcita; lectora; legisladora; libertadora; madrugadora; malhechora; mandadora; matadora; medidora; mesonera; moradora; mullidora; murmuradora; negociadora; obradora; ofensora; opositora; pastora; pecadora; perdonadora; perturbadora; pescadora; pesquisidora; pintora; ponedora; poseedora; preceptora; precursora; predicadora; preguntadora; pretensora; priora/prioresa; procuradora; progenitora; protectora/protectriz; provisora; quitadora; recaudadora; receptora; rectora; redentora; reformadora; remediadora; revendedora; rezadora; rogadora; ruiseñora; salteadora; saludadora; servidora; sucesora; sufridora; superiora; tejedora; tenedora; trabajadora; traidora; trasegadora; trazadora; tundidora; turbadora; tutora(tutriz); vendedora; vendimiadora; vencedora; vengadora;

---

[4] See England 1984 and 1987; there continued to be hesitation over the gender of a few abstract nouns in -or, particularly *color* and *calor*, and over the form of the name *Leonor/Leonora* (no equivalent man's name existed to provide a contrasting pair).

volteadora

List 2b: Feminine nouns ending in both *-or/-ora*
acreedor/-a; acusador/-a; asesor/-a; corregidor/-a; fiador(?)*/-a; señor*(?)*/-a*(*sora*)*; soliçitador/-a*

List 2c: Feminine nouns ending only in *-or*
sor

ANALYSIS

As is clearly shown by list 2a, the *-ora* suffix continued to be productive, particularly in its post-verbal function. It was under some pressure from the latinate *-iz* (<-ICEM), and Lope de Vega was moved to defend himself against criticism of his use of *emperadora* and *tutora* rather than *emperatriz* and *tutriz*, and to contemplate with horror the creation of *cantatriz, hablatriz*, etc.; he views such forms in *-iz* as nonsensical *bachillería* (Cotarelo 1928:567-68). In his plays, however, he did use words such as *defensatriz* and *tutriz* (see Fernández Gómez 1971:I, 810 and III, 2814), and perhaps surprisingly Fernández Gómez records three examples of *emperadora* and six of *emperatriz* (II, 1014); nevertheless in CORDE the preference for *emperatriz* over *emperadora* is much stronger (349 to 6).

The majority of the words in list 2b can be dealt with together: *acreedor/-a, acusador/-a, asesor/-a, fiador/-a, soliçitador/-a*. The feature which they share is that they are often used in legal language, and as has already been observed in the analysis of *abogado, reo* and *testigo*, it appears that legal terminology included a higher incidence of non-analogical feminines:

i) *acreedor/-a*
There are 11 examples of *acreedora* in CORDE, and I noted one example of *acreedor* referring to a woman:

> Essa acción es para mí
> de recatarme de vos,
> pues sois acreedor, por Dios,
> de mis honras...
> (Calderón de la Barca 1956:114; addressed to Leonor)

Even if the requirements of versification played a part in the choice of *acreedor*, its use indicates that this form continued to be a possibility.

ii) *acusador/-a*
There are two examples of *acusadora* in the *Diccionario histórico*, pp. 621-22, and one example from Santa Teresa of *acusadores* referring to women:

> Las mesmas más amigas suyas quiere Dios sean sus acusadores... (San José 1965:621)

iii) *asesor/-a*
The *Diccionario de Autoridades* (I, 444) distinguishes between *assessor, ra*, 'La persona que persuade y aconseja', and *assessor*(m.), 'El que assiste juntamente con otro juez para juzgar y sentenciar algunas causas'. CORDE has one example from Quevedo's poetry of *asesora*, in a non-legal sense, and I note one example of *asesor* referring to a woman in Quevedo's prose:

> Asistíale como asesor de cachivaches una dueña...(Quevedo Villegas 1945:294)

iv) *fiador/-a*
Fiadora is used many times in Golden Age texts, including in a legal text cited in the *Diccionario de Autoridades*:

> La muger no se pueda obligar por fiadora de su marido, aunque se diga y alegue que se convirtió la tal deuda en provecho de la muger. (*Autoridades*, III, 742; from *La nueva Recopilación de las leyes del Reino*)

I note one example of *fiador*, used by Celestina in reference to herself:

> ¿Soy yo obligada a ser su fiador y traella de traílla? (Silva 1988:528)

In similar contexts Celestina uses *fiadora* three times (pp. 400, 512, 516); it is possible that the inconsistency is intended to reflect the variation which is a feature of informal speech.

v) *soliçitador/-a*
I noted two examples of *soliçitadora* (Delicado 1975:78; San Jerónimo and Valle de la Cerda 1991:75), and one example of *soliçitador* referring to a woman:

> Más parecéis juez que solicitador. (Lope de Vega 1980:160; Dorotea speaking to Marfisa)

It may be significant that the simile uses another vocabulary item (*juez*) associated with the law.

The only other words in list 2b are *corregidor/-a* and *señor*(?)/*-a*. The single occurrence of *señores*(f.) is probably the result of a printing error. It occurs in Silva 1988:244, but as the editor, Consolación Baranda, points out (p. 93), there are many cases of misprints in the original text of *e* for *a* (e.g. *he* for *ha*) which cannot be explained as archaic or dialectal; in view of the huge number of examples of *señora*(*s*) in the text, it is best regarded as an erratum. *Corregidora* is a standard feminine form (= 'la mujer del corregidor'), with one example noted of *la dama corregidor*, in Leiva Ramírez Arellano 1924:375, in reference to Ángela acting as *corregidor* disguised as a man.

The one word in list 2c is *sor* ('nun, sister'), a latinism possibly borrowed from Catalan; the absence of a masculine counterpart to *sor* reduces pressure to add an analogical -*a*.

It is clear from the preceding analysis that this linguistic development was all but complete; in the early stages of the evolution of Castilian the form in -*ora*(f.) had been the marked form, with -*or*(f.) the norm, but by the Golden Age the situation had been reversed with -*ora*(f.) the norm, and -*or*(f.) the marked form.

3. Nouns in -ÓN/-ONA

List 3a: Feminine nouns ending only in -*ona*
  alquilona; amazona; baratona; bordiona; bufona; bujarrona; buscona; Calderona; capona; çinturiona; comadrona; cronicona; chillona; esclavona; faraona; fregona(fregatriz); Galeona; glotona; gorrona; juntona; lechona; leona/leonesa; matrona; mirona; Nerona; patrona; peona; picarona; poltrona; porcona; Postillona; remendona; reñona; setentona; soplona; temblona; tragona; trotona; tusona; varona/varonesa

List 3b: Feminine nouns ending in both -*ón*/-*ona*
  ladrón/-a

List 3c: Feminine nouns ending only in -*ón*
No examples

Analysis
Although not as numerous as the words in -*or*/-*ora*, words in -*ón*/-*ona* show a similarly high level of consistency in favour of the analogical feminines which were innovative in Old Spanish and had become firmly established by the end of the fifteenth century. The pattern was so secure that it could be used to create

nicknames, as in *Nerona* 'a female Nero' (Lope de Vega 1980:77), *la Galeona* and *la Postillona* (Vélez de Guevara 1968:216), as well as nonsense words such as *capona*:

> ...no deues de ser muger,
> y deues de ser capona. (Solís 1984:I, 441)

Castillo Solórzano (1943:1334) uses *capona* pejoratively with the meaning 'woman in love with a eunuch'.

The single exception to this pattern occurs in *Don Quijote*:

> Una cosa quiero que se entienda: que no soy ladrón ni persona facinorosa, sino una doncella desdichada... (Cervantes 1998:1030)

There are 34 examples of *ladrona* in CORDE, and it is difficult to account for the use of *ladrón* in preference to *ladrona* here; it does not appear to be significant that it occurs in direct speech, as the character, *la doncella curiosa*, uses very formal language. In a similar context, Preciosa uses the analogical feminine:

> ¡Pues en verdad no somos ladronas ni rogamos a nadie! (Cervantes 1980:I, 95)

4. NOUNS IN *-ÉS/-ESA*

List 4a: Feminine nouns ending only in *-esa*
    albanesa; aragonesa; cordobesa; feligresa; ferraresa; francesa/francesita/francesilla; ginovesa; inglesa; irlandesa; marquesa; montañesa; pavesa; portuguesa; senesa

List 4b: Feminine nouns ending in both *-és/-esa*
    No examples

List 4c: Feminine nouns ending only in *-és*
    No examples

ANALYSIS

I found no examples of feminine nouns in *-és*. The majority of the words are gentilics, and as will be seen in the analysis of List 7, the situation was somewhat different in the case of adjectives. The consistency of *-és/-esa* possibly supported the productive use of the *-esa* suffix independent of *-és*, as in, for example, *juglaresa* (*Autoridades*, IV, 329) and *papesa* (Cervantes 1998:1042), and the addition of -*a* in the borrowing *metresa* (Spadaccini and Zahareas 1978:II, 467).

5. Nouns in -*E*/-*A*

List 5a: Feminine nouns ending only in -*a*
alcahueta; alcaida/alcaidesa; alcaldesa; arcipresta; almiranta/almirantesa; archiduquesa; cisna; comedianta; conda/condesa; danzanta; duquesa; durandarta(?); *estudianta; farsanta; fraila/freila; governanta; monja/monjuela; negocianta*(?);*oyenta; platicanta; pleiteanta; pobreta; preguntanta; priosta; representanta; salvaja; sastra*(*sastresa*)

List 5b: Feminine nouns ending in both -*e*/-*a*
amante/-*a; cacique*(?)/-*a; consorte*/-*a; duende*/-*a; envergonzante*/-*a; gigante*/-*a/gigantesa; hereje*/-*a; héroe/heroína; infante*/-*a*(*ynfantesca*); *mercadante*/-*a*(?); *pariente*/-*a; pobre*/-*a; presidente*/-*a; pretendiente*/-*a; principiante*/-*a; regente*/-*a; sacerdote*/-*a/sacerdotisa; sirviente*/-*a; teniente*/-*a; tigre*/-*a; tratante*/-*a; zape*/-*a*(?)

List 5c: Feminine nouns ending only in -*e*
agente; asistente; ayudante; comadre; cómplice; concurrente; confidente; delincuente; demandante; descendiente; doncellaponiente; escuchante; ignorante; inocente; intérprete; judaizante; maleante; marchante; mendigante; náyade; paciente; parturiente; penitente; predicante; rebelde; residente; superintendente; suplicante; vergonzante; vigilante

Analysis

Animate nouns which end in -*e* in the masculine show greater variation than any other type with regard to the corresponding feminine noun. There were inconsistencies both in the system and in individual words in Old Spanish right up to the end of the fifteenth century, and even in cases where the momentum was building up in favour of the analogical form, as with *infante*/-*a*, Nebrija was still recommending the etymological feminine *la infante* 'segund el uso cortesano' (England 1987:211). A small number of words of this type had developed the analogical feminine in the Middle Ages, a few occurring consistently (e.g. *monje*/-*a, pariente*/-*a*), and others inconsistently (e.g. *infante*/-*a, sirviente*/-*a*), whilst others had resisted change (e.g. *amante, descendiente*). There appears to have been an increase in nouns ending in -*e*, largely as a result of increasing use of the participial endings -*ante*/-*ente* with a nominal function; many such words were innovative (e.g. *comediante, preguntante*), were being added to a group of nouns prone to variation *(la infante* vs *la infanta, la sirviente* vs *la sirvienta)*, and in many cases would only infrequently be used in the feminine (e.g. *presidente/-a*). In a different context Penny (2000:37 and 55-57) shows that features displayed by a relatively small number of words are prone to irregularity, and it is likely that in some of these cases it was the lack of familiarity with the word which allowed speakers and writers to bring their creativity into play when needing to use a feminine form.

I deal first with nouns ending in *-ante/-ente*, as they constitute the largest single group. There are 12 such words in List 5a:

> *almiranta* (*Diccionario histórico*, II, 510, ='mujer del almirante' [1614])
> *comedianta* (CORDE, 8 examples, 1613-64)
> *danzanta* (López de Úbeda 1974:137)
> *estudianta* (CORDE, Francisco Santos [1663])
> *farsanta* (CORDE, 8 examples, 1613-64)
> *gobernanta* (CORDE, *Estebanillo González* [1646])
> *negocianta* (?) (Fernández Gómez 1971)[5]
> *oyenta* (Solís; see Bello and Cuervo 1945:410)
> *platicanta* (CORDE, Quevedo)
> *pleiteanta* (López de Úbeda 1974:264)
> *preguntanta* (Cervantes 1998:1139)
> *representanta* (CORDE, 10 examples, 1620-72)

There are 13 such words in List 5b:

amante/-a
Diccionario histórico, II, 733-34, has one example of *amanta* from Lope de Vega, rhyming with *infanta*; *amante*(f.) is the norm.

envergonzante/-a
López de Úbeda (1974:180-84) has 5 examples of *envergonzanta* and 3 examples of *envergonzante*(f.) (180, 182, 188), possibly reproducing the variation found in informal speech.

gigante/-a
There are 9 examples of *giganta(s)* in CORDE (1549-1629); I noted one example of *gigante*(f.), in Valbuena 1905:189, probably used for reasons of rhyme.

---

[5] A single example of *negocianta* is given in Fernández Gómez 1971:II, 1,899; it is taken from *Porfiando vence amor*, but must be regarded as doubtful as it breaks the *a-e* assonance, which the feminine form *negociante* would preserve.

infante/-a
There are 1,257 examples of *infanta(s)* in CORDE, whilst I found only 4 examples of *infante*(f.).[6]

mercadante/-a
The correct reading of the single example is unclear. CORDE gives *mercadanta*, from *La vida y hechos de Estebanillo González* (Carreira and Cid 1990:II, 28). However, the reading in Spadaccini and Zahareas (1978:II, 321) is *mercadante*, and an earlier edition by Carreira and Cid (1971:277) reads *mercadanta*, but in the footnote to the word cites it as *mercadante*.

pariente/-a
There are 167 examples of *parienta(s)* in CORDE; I found just three examples of *pariente(s)*(f.), one in CORDE (Biblia de Ferrara, 1553), one in Place 1959:20, and one in Castillo Solórzano 1943:1346, a text which also uses *parientas*.

presidente/-a
As part of the background to his excellent study of an eighteenth-century debate on the word *presidenta*, Álvarez de Miranda (forthcoming) provides examples of variation in Golden Age Spanish. He notes four examples of *presidente*(f.) (1512, 1543, 1555, 1657) and five of *presidenta* (1589, 1596, 1611, 1647, 1657), as well as the critical comments made by Lorenzo Matheu y Sanz on Gracián's use of *presidenta* rather than *presidente*. In CORDE there are a further seven examples of *presidente*(f.) from 1636, to which five examples can be added from the writings of Santa Teresa (San José 1965:137, 152, 157, 186, 334), along with three examples of *presidenta* from the letters (1626-38) of Teresa Valle de la Cerda, pp. 203, 216, 225. Both forms were clearly available, with a predominance of *presidente* in the sixteenth century and *presidenta* in the seventeenth.

pretendiente/-a
CORDE records eight examples of *pretendienta* (Rodríguez de Villaviciosa 1661), and one example of *pretendiente*(f.) (Santos 1661).

---

[6] Alcina Franch and Blecua (1975:579) quote one example from Vélez de Guevara; Fernández Gómez 1971:II, 1514, gives one example from Lope's *Jerusalén conquistada*; there are two examples in CORDE, from Ercilla (1578) and Gabriel del Corral (1632). The first two are used for purposes of rhyme. The statement of Alcina Franch and Blecua that *infante* was 'invariable todavía en el siglo XVII' (p. 579) shows the danger of generalizing on the basis of a single example.

principiante/-a
CORDE has one example of *principiante*(f.) (Juan Rodríguez Florián 1554) and one of *principianta* (Lope de Vega, *Caballero de Olmedo*).

regente/-a
In CORDE there is one example of *la regente* 'Queen Regent' (Alfonso de Valdés 1529), and three of *regenta* 'mujer del regente' (*Don Quijote*); Álvarez de Miranda (forthcoming) adds *la regenta* [de Francia] (Prudencio de Sandoval 1606), which rather muddies the water over claims that there was a separation between *la regente* (='la reina regente') and *la regenta* (='la mujer del regente').

sirviente/-a
There are 17 examples of *sirvienta(s)* in CORDE, and six of *sirviente*(f.) (1500-1629); *sirvienta* had become the preferred form in the fifteenth century, but *sirviente* has continued to be used as a variant into modern times.

teniente/-a
The examples from CORDE support the division of meanings of *-a* ('wife of') and *-e* ('woman office-holder'); *tenienta* occurs twice in Cervantes (='la mujer del teniente'), and *la teniente de aya de la Infanta* occurs once (Luis Cabrera de Córdoba 1614).

tratante/-a
There is one example of each form in CORDE: *tratante* (Quevedo 1620) vs *tratanta* (Santos 1663); both refer to women performing a job.

Many of the words in List 5c occur infrequently (e.g. *confidente* (f.) is recorded twice in CORDE, 1614 and 1633), and a number of them are predominantly adjectives used occasionally as nouns (*ignorante*, *inocente*, etc.).

Several conclusions can be drawn by looking at the words ending in *-ante/-a* and *-ente/-a* in Lists 5a, 5b, and 5c as a whole:

1. A significant number of the words which end consistently in *-a* are from the world of the performing arts (*comedianta*, *danzanta*, *farsanta*, *representanta*), and it seems reasonable to suggest that women's increasing presence in this sphere promoted the creation and use of distinct feminine forms.[7]

---

[7] Women's participation in the theatre increased in the late sixteenth century, and continued through the following century; see chapter 18 of Shergold 1967.

2. The forms in -*a* are often used in a pejorative or ironical way:

> A poco rato plantan la mesa sobre sus pecadoras basquiñas para merendar, y el pobre estudiante en Escoto apenas puede alcanzar, con que las estudiantas tomistas engullen a cuenta del escotista. (Francisco Santos: CORDE, s.v. *estudiantas*)

> ...estaban de rodillas sobre sus chapines con un moñazo imperial en las dos manos y a su lado una doncellita platicanta de botes... (Quevedo: CORDE, s.v. *platicanta*)

3. There is no clear division of functions according to the form (e.g. -*a* = 'wife of', -*e* = 'woman office-holder').

4. Phonetic factors may have contributed in some measure to the different behaviour of nouns in -*ante* and -*ente*; 11 of the 12 nouns in List 5a end in -*anta*, as do 7 of the 13 words in List 5b; only 12 out of 25 of the words in List 5c end in -*ante*. This suggests that a contributory factor in the creation of the forms in -*a* could have been assimilation of the final [-e] to the preceding [-á-]; this would account for the predominance of -*anta* and -*ente* over -*ante* and -*enta*.

The remaining words in -*e*/(-*a*) are difficult to deal with as a single group, but the following points can be made:

1. The suffix in -*esa* was widely used as a means of creating a separate feminine form, often with the function 'wife of' (e.g. *alcaidesa* [*Diccionario histórico*, II, 156-58]; *alcaldesa* [*Diccionario histórico*, II, 160-66]). Lesser used suffixes occur in *pobre*/*pobreta* and *héroe*/*heroína*. The form *heroína* is a Romance innovation; Juana de Contreras in a letter of 1504 wishes to refer to herself in Latin as *heroina*, but her tutor, Lucio Marioneo Sículo, insists that she use the correct Latin *herois*. As a figure of linguistic authority, he rejects linguistic change; see Rivera Garretas 1997:88-90.

2. There are cases of analogical feminines created to refer to female animals: CORDE gives examples of *cisna* (1528, 1636), and as an infrequent alternative to *la tigre*, the form *tigra* was used (Jáuregui 1973:159). Further analogical creations could be envisaged:

> 'Señor Ingeniero, en esta aldea hay muchos zapes, porque es muy abundante de gatos; zapas, si no son las hembras de este linaje, no hay otras

ningunas...'(Spadaccini and Zahareas 1978:II, 478)

3. A number of words are humorous, playful creations:

conda
The *gracioso* Bras in *Del rey abajo ninguno* uses (in rhyming position) the highly unusual form *conda*:

> Pero si vos sois la Conda
> Tendréis muy mala ventura. (Rojas Zorrilla 1926:6)

consorta
The standard feminine form was *consorte*, documented nine times in CORDE; it also documents two examples from Quevedo of *consorta*, in the comic speech of an Italian attempting to speak Castilian.

durandarta
The form *durandarta* 'a female Durandarte' is used with strong irony in *La pícara Justina*:

> —Señora hermosa— aunque sea una lamparera más pesada que higo duñigal se huelga de que la llamen hermosa, y se derrite aunque sea durandarta... (López de Úbeda 1974:181)

pobra
The standard feminine form was *pobre*, whether in its adjectival or (less frequent) nominal function. CORDE documents six examples of *pobra(s)* as a noun in Golden Age texts, five occurring in *El diablo cojuelo* and one in Quevedo. CORDE also records a handful of examples from medieval texts, mainly from the east of the Peninsula, which suggests that *pobra* was a dialectal, non-standard form which continued to surface occasionally in the written language. Three of the examples from *El diablo cojuelo* occur in the form *los pobres y las pobras*; similar pairings of masculine and feminine forms, often with one of the forms being unusual, were used from time to time as intensifiers.[8]

salvaja
When there are few documented examples of a word, it can be difficult to

---

[8] Gillett (1943-61:III, 236-37) gives examples such as '¡Qué nidos ni qué nidas!', 'Algo ni alga', 'ni ínsulos ni ínsulas'.

estimate its stylistic impact. CORDE contains lots of examples of *salvaje* as a feminine adjective, but the only two examples of the word occurring as a feminine noun take the form *salvaja* (Calderón, *El golfo de las sirenas*); both occur in the speech of a comic character who uses non-standard language (*habrando, empreando,* etc.), but in the absence of documentation of *salvaje* as a feminine noun it is not possible to be absolutely certain that *salvaja* is a marked form, part of the comic rustic language.

4. Documentation of some forms is uncertain. *Cacica* is well documented in CORDE, but the context of the only example of *las caciques* (Pedro Cieza de León) suggests that the correct reading should be *los caciques*.

In this category, then, there was considerable innovation in the sixteenth and seventeenth centuries, and a high level of variation. Comparison with the situation in the modern language suggests that the momentum for change has not continued; although there have been changes in recent years, the preference is still for feminine nouns in *-e*, and there are only a few words such as *infanta, parturienta* and *sirvienta* which have all but lost the feminine form in *-e*.[9] Linguistic evolution is rarely smooth and consistent.

6. NOUNS ENDING IN CONSONANTS (OTHER THAN *-OR/-ÓN/-ÉS*), AND *-í*
List 6a: Feminine nouns ending only in *-a*
   abadessa; alcatraça; alemana; andaluza; atuna/atunesa; bachillera; bailarina; botillera; capellana; coronela; diosa; doncella (doncelleja; doncellica); doña; española; fiscala; guardiana; holgazana; jayana; juglaresa; mercadera; nodriza; oficiala; poncella; provinciala; rapaza/rapazeja; rufiana; sacristana; sultana; sumillera; truhana; trujamana; zagala/zagaleja; zahorina

List 6b: Feminine nouns ending in both -cons./*-a*
   capitán/-a; galán/-a; huésped/-a; torcaz/-a

List 6c: Feminine nouns ending only in -cons.
   alférez; alguazil; ángel/angelito(?); *aprendiz; badaluquas; capataz; desvirgaviejos; juez; mártir; matacandiles; mayoral; mentecaptas; meretriz; natural; nutriz; roesantos; seglar; servicial; tragaavemarías; virgen*

---

[9] See England 1999. The adjective *parturiente* (f.) has also given way to *parturienta*.

Analysis

The words listed above form a heterogeneous group, within which some patterns can be identified (e.g. *-án/-ana*), whilst others are more isolated (e.g. *zahorí/zahorina*). As is the case with the words from Lists 5a-c, analogical feminines had a stronger presence in Golden Age Spanish than in modern Spanish, although the different types of words included here make exact comparisons difficult.

List 6a contains a number of patterns with a high level of consistency; for example, the forms of the suffixes *-esa* and *-ina* were not prone to variation. Also consistent is the ending *-a* added to masculine nouns in *-er*: *bachillera, botillera, mercadera, sumillera*; such forms are often pejorative or playful (as in Lope de Vega 1980:66), but I did not note a single example of *-er*(f.). It is reasonable to assume that the frequency of the *-era* suffix as the feminine counterpart to *-ero* will have strengthened *-era* as the feminine counterpart to *-er*.

A large number of the words in List 6a show the alternation *-án*(m.)/*-ana*(f.): *capellana, guardiana, holgazana, jayana, rufiana, sacristana, sultana, truhana, trujamana*. Only two words show some inconsistency: *capitán/-a* and *galán/-a*. There are seven examples in CORDE of *capitana* as an animate noun, with meanings as diverse as 'female military leader', 'leader (of wet-nurses)', and 'lover of captain'; the one exception is *La dama capitán*, a play by the Figueroa brothers, which uses the not uncommon structure of *la dama* + masculine form of the noun, with the meaning 'lady performing the function of...'(McKendrick 1974:197). The feminine noun *galana* also appears in a wide variety of Golden Age texts, whilst there are three references in the *Retrato de la loçana andaluza* to a character known as *la Galan portuguesa* (Delicado 1975:122, 337, 339); elsewhere Delicado uses *-ana*, as in *capellana* (284), *rufiana* (188), and *trujamana* (249).

By the Golden Age *nodriza* (< NUTRICEM) had acquired an analogical *-a* (examples in CORDE [*nodriça*, 1598] and *Autoridades*, IV, 675), but other words in *-iz* such as *aprendiz* and *meretriz* had not (the earliest example of *aprendiza* in CORDE is from 1878). *Nutriz* is a latinism, with examples given in *Autoridades*, IV, 695. There is greater variation in words ending in *-al*: *fiscala, oficiala, provinciala* and *zagala* contrast with the feminine nouns *mayoral, natural* and *servicial*. The use of *fiscala* is clearly playful:

BEATRIZ	Y tú, si me oyeres
	frase negada a bárbaras mujeres,
	por ver si en esto topa,
	tírame de la manga de la ropa.
INÉS	La concesión aceto,

y ser fiscala de tu voz prometo.

(CORDE: Calderón, *No hay burlas con el amor*)

Examples of *zagala* appear frequently in texts in CORDE from 1500 to 1700, and *oficiala* is recorded with a number of meanings: 'seamstress' (CORDE, 1577), 'cook' (CORDE, 1614), 'female prison officer' (San Jerónimo 1991:81, 86), and was extended to the performing arts ('una volteadora, gran oficiala de todas vueltas' [López de Úbeda 1974:29]; 'buena oficiala de tañer' [id., 84]); *provinciala* belongs to the register of religious organisations (San José 1965:1115). Both *mayoral* and *servicial* refer to women in working roles, but CORDE does not document either with -*a*.

Nouns in -*az*, which are fewer in number, also show variation. A woman is described by Remiro de Navarra as 'amiga de coches y meriendas, la capataz del río' (CORDE, 1646), whereas the noun *rapaza* is documented 31 times (the feminine adjective is usually *rapaz*). There are three cases of the animate noun *torcaza*(*s*), and six of *torcaz*/*torcaces*(f.). And the unique example of *alcatraça* 'whore' (< *alcatraz* 'pelican') in Delicado 1975:269, again shows the potential for creativity.

Two other nouns are worthy of comment. The feminine form *huéspeda* was the norm, with eight examples documented in CORDE, and many more examples noted in texts not included in that corpus; I found just one example of *huésped* (f.), from Calderón's *La protestación de la fe* (Flasche and Hoffmann 1980-83:III, 3085). The dominance of *huéspeda* has not, however, continued into modern Spanish. On the other hand, *ángel* probably should not be classified as a feminine noun; although it was frequently used to refer to a woman, the gender, when made explicit, is masculine, and when a diminutive is used, it has the overtly masculine -*o* ending (*angelito*, in Lope de Vega 1980:166).

7. ADJECTIVES

andaluz/-*a*; *aragonés*/-*a*; *cartaginés*/-*a*; *común*/-*a*; *cortés*/-*a*; *francés*/-*a*; *galán*/-*a*; *gigante*/-*a*; *guzmán*/-*a*; *hereje*/-*a*; *hidalga*/*hijadalgo*; *montañés*/-*a*; *montés*/-*a*; *necio*/-*a*; *pobre*/-*a*; *rapaz*/-*a*; *simple*/-*a*; *torcaz*/-*a*; *traidor*(?)/-*a*; *triste*/-*a*

Although the focus of this study is on animate nouns, the overlap between adjectives and nouns in Spanish means that a brief glance at adjectives will give a more complete picture. The gender structure for adjectives by the end of the fifteenth century was a clear one, with separate feminine forms for adjectives ending in -*o*, -*or*, -*ón*, and -*és*, and shared masculine and feminine forms for those ending in any other consonant or -*e*. List 7 contains the adjectives which exhibited some variation in Golden Age Spanish.

The sharpest contrast between nouns and adjectives involves words in *-és*: nouns consistently have the feminine form in *-esa*, but this was not always the case with adjectives. *Cortés* was the standard feminine form (no examples of *cortesa* are documented in CORDE), and the adverbial form was normally *cortésmente*; I note one example from Torres Naharro of *cortesament* (Gillett 1943-61:II, 107), in the speech of a Valencian character. Elsewhere, he uses *(des)cortés* (e.g. II, 94, 301). There is greater inconsistency in the case of *montesa(s)* (14 examples in CORDE) and *montés(es)*(f.) (18 examples). Gentilics in *-és* also show some variation: *aragonés*(f.) is documented once in CORDE (1624), against 18 examples of *aragonesa*; *cartaginesa* is documented once in CORDE (1644), and I noted one example of *cartaginés*(f.) (Mariana 1912:3). *Francesa* was the dominant feminine form (219 examples in CORDE), with *francés* (f.) a rare variant (CORDE, 1624); *montañesa* is documented seven times in CORDE, with one example of *montañés*(f.) (1624). Other feminine gentilics are found consistently in *-esa* (e.g. *holandesa, inglesa, leonesa*).

The most inconsistent gentilic was *andaluz/-a*. CORDE documents *andaluza* six times, and *andaluz/andaluces*(f.) eight times; the only sixteenth-century examples of *andaluza* in CORDE are from *La loçana andaluza* (there are also 2 examples from 1589 cited in the *Diccionario histórico*, I, 997-98), and it is possible that this was an innovative, marked form when the work appeared in 1528; see Anipa 2001:10.

Adjectives ending in *-o, -or*, and *-ón* show a high level of consistency in the use of the feminine marker *-a*. Adjectives in *-ón* consistently add *-a* (e.g. *glotona*), and those ending in *-o* and *-or* are more consistent than their noun counterparts; the only example of *-or*(f.) which I found is almost certainly an error of transcription or printing,[10] and I noted a single example of an adjective in *-o* referring to a woman: 'ella es loca sobre necio', in Lope de Vega 1963:253. The ending in *-o* preserves the *-é-o* assonance, and may result from an incomplete adjustment of a set phrase *loco sobre necio*. There are also a few examples in Lope de Vega of *hija(s)dalgo* as a feminine adjective (see Fernández Gómez 1971:II, 1417), although he does more frequently use the shortened form *hidalga* (*ib.*), a form which I noted in seven other texts.

Adjectives ending in *-e*, normally unmarked for gender, were occasionally used with analogical *-a*. I recorded five adjectives which show such variation: *giganta, hereja, pobra, simpla, trista*; in no case is the form in *-a* the norm. *Giganta* and *gigante*(f.) are each recorded twice in CORDE; *hereje*(f.) is recorded

---

[10] The example is 'tan traidores centinelas', in Calderón 1969:I, 1725; the reading given in CORDE is *traydoras*.

four times in CORDE, and I note one example of *hereja* (López de Úbeda 1974:25); there is just one example of *pobra* in CORDE (1500), two examples of *simpla* (1586, 1636), and 13 examples of *trista*, mainly from the sixteenth century, several of them occurring in stretches of texts in Italian, Valencian or African Spanish, or written by Catalans (e.g. Boscán). This variant also provided a convenient rhyme (*trista* rhymes twice with *vista* in Luis Milán's *El cortesano* [CORDE, 1561]); there are no examples of *trista* in prose written by a Castilian.[11]

There are minor inconsistencies in three other types of adjective. Those ending in *-án* normally have the corresponding feminine in *-ana*; however, *galán* appears as an occasional variant of *galana* (see Lope de Vega 1980:150; Corfis 2001:517), whilst Lope used both *guzmana* and *guzmán*(f.) (Fernández Gómez 1971:II, 1376), the latter form seemingly used for purposes of rhyme. Of adjectives ending in *-az*, there was hesitation over *torcaza* (nine examples in CORDE) and *torcaz*(f.) (15 times in CORDE), with the last example of *torcaza* dated 1607; and CORDE documents a single example of the adjective *rapaza*, in informal dialogue written by Torres Naharro. The norm is *rapaz*. Similarly, there is a single example of *comuna* (1507; in rhyme), a variant of the standard feminine *común*.

CONCLUSIONS
The preceding analysis shows that the formal expression of gender in Golden Age Spanish followed predominantly a standardized system, particularly in the case of nouns ending in *-o*, *-or*, *-ón*, and *-és*. There were no major shifts discernible in the system similar to those which occurred in Old Spanish. However, there were categories of words which did not conform to a regular pattern (especially nouns ending in *-e*), and just as there were several words with variable gender in Golden Age Spanish (*calor, color, puente*, etc.), so there were large numbers of individual words with unstable feminine forms; as is to be expected (see Penny 2000:37), a significant proportion of these are words which occur with low frequency.

This variation resulted in part from a process of standardization which was incomplete; indeed it continues in modern Spanish. Examination of written texts allows us to see two further reasons for the variation. The first, the greater variation natural to informal speech, is harder to detect, but it does bubble up to the surface in written texts from time to time; it is not surprising that many of the

---

[11] Penny (1991:115) points out that this type of adjective was subject to analogical pressure in spoken Latin; indeed two of the adjectives just discussed appear in the *Appendix Probi* (PAUPER MULIER NON PAUPERA MULIER; TRISTIS NON TRISTUS). Such developments were stronger in many other varieties of Romance than in Castilian.

examples come from texts like *La loçana andaluza* and *La pícara Justina*, which contain much informal dialogue, or from attempts to reproduce language varieties such as black African Spanish.[12] The other reason underlying variation is the creativity which writers exercised in coining new forms, parallel to what often happens in informal speech. The clear structure of the basic gender system meant that writers could extend or play with it in several ways, all of which would be transparent. In addition to the analogical feminines examined in this study, one can also point to doublets such as *algo ni alga* and *ínsulos ni ínsulas*; playful masculines such as *damo, muso, sombro* and *soneto*, of which there are many in Golden Age texts (see Lope de Vega 1944:226); and the creation of personal names, as in the following:

> Y como si aquéstos fueran
> patriarcas o prelados
> confirman a sus pastoras
> en unos nombres soñados:
> Hay Riselas por Riselos,
> Belardas por los Belardos;
> hay Damonas por Damones,
> Menalias por los Menalios,
> Lucindas por los Lucindos,
> Filardas por los Filardos(...)
> hay Amarilis, Belisas,
> y Silvanas de Silvanos(...)
> Verrugas hay por Verrugos,
> Panzonas por Panzonazos,
> y por Tripones, Triponas,
> y Gazpachas por Gazpachos.
>   (Lope de Vega 1980:76, note 37)

The standardized system, then, was constantly being put under pressure from various sources, and analysis of surviving texts allows us glimpses of several of these: informal speech, regional variations, archaisms, and creative use of language by producers of written texts and, one supposes, by many speakers

---

[12] See, for example, Luis de Góngora y Argote, *En la fiesta del santísimo sacramento*, in Góngora 1967:342-44. The analogical *-a* appears not only in words such as *trista*, but also *la procesiona* (p. 343). Such hypercharacterization is also typical of Judeo-Spanish, which has been little affected by peninsular standardization; see Penny 2000:189.

whose words cannot be recovered.

References

1. TEXTS CITED

Alemán, Mateo. 1987. *Guzmán de Alfarache*, ed. by José María Micó. Madrid: Cátedra.
Anónimo, and Juan de Luna. 1988. *Segunda parte del Lazarillo*, ed. by Pedro M. Piñero. Madrid: Cátedra.
Ávila, Hernando de. 1995. *Colloquio de Moisés*, ed. by Julio Alonso Asenjo. Valencia: UNED.
Calderón de la Barca, Pedro. 1956. *Dramas de honor. II. El medico de su honra. El pintor de su deshonra*, ed. by Ángel Valbuena Briones. Madrid: Espasa-Calpe.
Calderón de la Barca, Pedro. 1969. *El golfo de las sirenas*, in *Obras completas*, ed. by A. Valbuena Briones, vol I, 1723-38. Madrid: Aguilar.
Carreira, Antonio, and Jesús Antonio Cid, eds. 1971. *La vida y hechos de Estebanillo González*. Madrid: Narcea.
Carreira, Antonio, and Jesús Antonio Cid, eds. 1990. *La vida y hechos de Estebanillo González*. 2 vols. Madrid: Cátedra.
Castillo Solórzano, Alonso de. 1943. *La niña de los embustes*, in *La novela picaresca española*, ed. by Ángel Valbuena Prat, 1294-1384. Madrid: Aguilar.
Cervantes Saavedra, Miguel de. 1980. *Novelas ejemplares*, ed. by Harry Sieber. 2 vols. Madrid: Cátedra.
Cervantes Saavedra, Miguel de. 1998. *Don Quijote de la Mancha*, ed. by Francisco Rico et al. Barcelona: Instituto Cervantes.
Corfis, Ivy A., ed. 2001. *Libro del noble y esforçado & inuencible cauallero Renaldos de Montaluan*. New York: Hispanic Seminary of Medieval Studies.
Delicado, Francisco. 1975. *Retrato de la loçana andaluza*, ed. by Bruno M. Damiani and Giovanni Allegra. Madrid: Porrúa Toranzas.
Gillett, J. E. 1943-61. *'Propalladia' and Other Works of Bartolomé de Torres Naharro*. 4 vols. Bryn Mawr: University of Pennsylvania.
Góngora y Argote, Luis de. 1967. *Obras completas*, ed. by Juan Millé Giménez and Isabel Millé González. Madrid: Aguilar.
Jáuregui, Juan de. 1973. *Obras*, ed. by Inmaculada Ferrer de Alba. Madrid: Clásicos Castellanos.
Leiva Ramírez de Arellano, Francisco. 1924. *La dama presidente*, in *Dramáticos posteriores a Lope de Vega*, ed. by Ramón de Mesonero Romanos. Biblioteca de Autores Españoles, 47, 361-84. Madrid: Librería de los Sucesores de Hernando.
Lope de Vega Carpio. 1944. *El sembrar en buena tierra*, ed. by William L. Fichter. London-New York: M.L.L.A.
Lope de Vega Carpio. 1963. *Peribáñez y el Comendador de Ocaña. La dama boba*, ed. by A. Zamora Vicente. Madrid: Espasa-Calpe.
Lope de Vega Carpio. 1977. *La viuda valenciana*, ed. by José-Luis Aguirre. Barcelona:

Duki.
Lope de Vega Carpio. 1980. *La Dorotea*, ed. by Edwin S. Morby. Madrid: Castalia.
López de Úbeda, Francisco. 1974. *La pícara Justina*. Geneva: Ferni.
Mariana, Juan de. 1912. *Obras*, ed. by Francisco Pi y Maragall. Biblioteca de Autores Españoles, 30-31. Madrid: Imprenta de Hernando y Compañía.
Molloy Carpenter, Dorothy, ed. 2000. *Arderique (Valencia, Juan Viñao, 1517)*. Alcalá de Henares: Centro de Estudios Cervantinos.
Nebrija, Antonio de. 1998. *Gramática*, ed. by John O'Neill. Madison: Hispanic Seminary of Medieval Studies.
Place, Edwin B., ed. 1959. *Amadís de Gaula*, vol. I. Madrid: CSIC.
Quevedo Villegas, Francisco de. 1945. *Obras completas en prosa*, ed. by Luis Astrana Marín. Madrid: Aguilar.
Quevedo y Villegas, Francisco de. 1993. *Sueños del infierno*, ed. by James O. Crosby. Madrid: Castalia.
Rojas Zorrilla, Francisco de. 1926. *Comedias escogidas*, ed. by Ramón de Mesonero Romanos. Biblioteca de Autores Españoles, 54. Madrid: Librería de los Sucesores de Hernández.
Sánchez Ortega, Mª Helena. 1992. *La mujer y la sexualidad en el antiguo régimen. La perspectiva inquisitorial*. Madrid: Akal.
San Jerónimo, Magdalena de, and Teresa Valle de la Cerda. 1991. *Cárceles y mujeres en el siglo XVII*, ed. by Isabel Barbeito. Madrid: Castalia.
Silva, Feliciano de. 1988. *Segunda Celestina*, ed. by Consolación Baranda. Madrid: Cátedra.
Solís, Antonio. 1984. *Comedias de Antonio Solís*, ed. by Manuela Sánchez Regueira. Vol. I. Madrid: CSIC.
Spadaccini, Nicholas, and Anthony N. Zahareas, eds. 1978. *Vida y hechos de Estebanillo González*. 2 vols. Madrid: Castalia.
Timoneda, Juan. 1973. *El patrañuelo*, ed. by Federico Ruiz Morcuende. Madrid: 1973.
Tirso de Molina. 1982. *La huerta de Juan Fernández*, ed. by Berta Pallares. Madrid: Castalia.
Valbuena, Bernardo de. 1905. *El Bernardo*, in *Poemas épicos*, ed. by Cayetano Rosell. Biblioteca de Autores Españoles, 17, 143-399. Madrid: Imprenta de Hernando y Compañía.
Vélez de Guevara, Luis. 1968. *El diablo cojuelo*, ed. by Enrique R. Cepeda and Enrique Rull. Madrid: Ediciones Alcalá.
Zayas, María de. 1983. *Desengaños amorosos*, ed. by Alicia Yllera. Madrid: Cátedra.

2. LINGUISTIC AND LITERARY STUDIES
Alcina Franch, Juan, and José Manuel Blecua. 1975. *Gramática española*. Barcelona: Ariel.
Álvarez de Miranda, Pedro. Forthcoming. "Gramática y promoción de la mujer: la polémica sobre la voz *presidenta* en 1787". *Claves de la Ilustración. Josefa Amar y Borbón, la figura y la obra*. Zaragoza: Diputación General de Aragón.
Anipa, Kormi. 2001. *A Critical Examination of Linguistic Variation in Golden-Age*

Spanish. New York: Peter Lang.
Bello, Andrés, and Rufino J. Cuervo. 1945. *Gramática de la lengua castellana*, ed. by Nicolás Alcalá-Zamora y Torres. Buenos Aires: Ariel.
Cotarelo, E. 1928. "Un pasaje de Lope de Vega sobre la formación de algunos femeninos castellanos". *Boletín de la Real Academia Española* 15: 567-68.
England, John. 1984. "Observaciones sobre las nuevas formas femeninas en el castellano del siglo XIII". *Estudios dedicados a James Leslie Brooks*, ed. by J. M. Ruiz, 29-44. Barcelona: Puvill.
England, John. 1987. "New Feminine Forms in Old Spanish: The Fourteenth and Fifteenth Centuries". *Bulletin of Hispanic Studies* 64, 205-14.
England, John. 1999. "Analogical Feminines in Modern Spanish: Pressures on the Peninsular Standard". *Bulletin of Hispanic Studies (Liverpool)* 76, 415-39.
Fernández Gómez, Carlos. 1971. *Vocabulario completo de Lope de Vega*. 3 vols. Madrid: Real Academia Española.
Flasche, Hans, and Gerd Hoffmann. 1980-83. *Konkordanz zu Calderón*. 5 vols. Hildesheim-New York: Olms.
Harris-Northall, Ray. 1996-97. "Printed Books and Linguistic Standardization in Spain: The 1503 *Gran Conquista de Ultramar*". *Romance Philology* 50, 123-46.
Malkiel, Yakov. 1957. "Diachronic Hypercharacterization in Romance". *Archivum Linguisticum* 9, 79-113.
McKendrick, Melveena. 1974. *Women and Society in the Spanish Drama of the Golden Age. A Study of the 'Mujer Varonil'*. Cambridge: Cambridge Univ. Press.
Menéndez Pidal, Ramón. 1941. *Poesía árabe y poesía europea*. Buenos Aires: Espasa-Calpe.
Penny, Ralph. 1991. *A History of the Spanish Language*. Cambridge: Cambridge Univ. Press.
Penny, Ralph. 2000. *Variation and Change in Spanish*. Cambridge and New York: Cambridge Univ. Press.
Real Academia Española. 1963. *Diccionario de autoridades*. Facs. ed. 6 vols. Madrid: Gredos.
Real Academia Española. 1960-96. *Diccionario histórico de la lengua española*. 4 vols. Madrid: Espasa-Calpe.
Rivera Garretas, María-Milagros. 1997. "Las prosistas del humanismo y del Renacimiento (1400-1550)". *Breve historia feminista de la literatura española (en lengua castellana). IV. La literatura escrita por mujeres desde la Edad Media al s. XVIII*, ed. by Iris M. Zavala, 83-129. Barcelona: Anthropos.
San José, Fr. Luis de. 1965. *Concordancias de las obras y escritos de Santa Teresa de Jesús*. Burgos: El Monte Carmelo.
Shergold, N. D. 1967. *A History of the Spanish Stage From Medieval Times Until the End of the Seventeenth Century*. Oxford: Clarendon.
Vigil, Mariló. 1986. *La vida de las mujeres en los siglos XVI y XVII*. Madrid: Akal.

17
Gender without Sex: the semantic exploitation of the masculine/feminine opposition in the history of Spanish

CHRISTOPHER J. POUNTAIN

1 INTRODUCTION

In Pountain (2000a:295) I hypothesised that some linguistic changes might be seen as the product of a process I labelled 'capitalisation'; by which 'a linguistic feature which already exists in a language comes to be substantially exploited for wider purposes, sometimes simply making overt distinctions which were previously covert, but sometimes apparently creating new expressive possibilities.' In this paper I want to examine the history of gender contrasts in Spanish in this light, and to suggest that capitalisation is responsible, at least in part, for some of the developments observable in this area. It would surely not be surprising *prima facie* if this were so. Grammatical gender in Indo-European languages is often held to be a functionally redundant morphological category except insofar as it correlates with reference to the sex of animate beings, masculine gender corresponding to male sex and feminine gender to female sex. Yet in Spanish, as in many other languages, all nouns obligatorily belong to one of the genders. From the point of view of cost-effectiveness, it would clearly pay to put gender to other uses — gender, that is to say, for other reasons apart from sex. And since grammatical gender has some very obvious morphological exponents (in Spanish the inflections *-o* and *-a* are the clearest examples), one particular way in which gender might be exploited economically would be to use the same noun stem with different gender inflections. At the same time, it is also possible that productive use of this device might lead to new coinings and hence the 'new expressive possibilities' which I have seen as a feature of capitalisation.

Gender is also interesting to me because of another theme I have been concerned with in connection with historical syntax, that is, the importance of pragmatic factors in linguistic change. In Pountain (2000b) I argued (in simple terms and amongst other things) that the extensive use of the reflexive in the Romance languages is facilitated by the impossibility of its being understood literally when the subject of a verb is inanimate. In a similar way, we might expect that gender can be used in nouns which inherently refer to inanimates to encode semantic contrasts relating to features other than sex precisely because there is no risk of such nouns having an animate reading.

Gender has been the subject of many copiously-exemplified studies by Spanish historical linguists, and it may seem otiose to be pursuing it once again. Yet to my mind, although much of the basic data is well known, scholars have not looked sufficiently at the chronological trajectory of the changes which can be observed with a view to explaining why the chronology is as it is, and what it might tell us about the nature of language change.[1] That is my aim in the present rather preliminary article, the preparation of which has often been frustrated by the many gaps in the information available for such research. For example, while the Corominas and Pascual (1980–91) etymological dictionary is thorough on the first textual attestations of words, it often does not chart in the same detail the appearance of new, or different, meanings of words; dictionaries in general are often undiscriminating about the currency of particular meanings, and do not provide the statistical information which might help trace the diffusion of new words and their meanings; finding out if and how a language expresses a particular notion (as opposed to finding out which words were used and with what meaning) is a wellnigh impossible task before the existence of glossaries and (especially) bilingual dictionaries.

2.1 TREES AND FRUITS

I will begin with what I think is a very clear example of the utilisation of gender opposition in a non-animate area of reference, the distinction between the names of trees and their fruits. This is an opposition which was embryonic, in type if not in detail, in Classical Latin, where we have the following clearly attested relations, a tree typically being a feminine noun of the second declension and its fruit a corresponding neuter noun of the second declension:

---

[1] Malkiel (1983:171) sets this as an important agenda for the resolution of the 'augmentative feminine' problem.

	tree	fruit
apple	MĀLUS (f.)	MĀLUM (n.)
pear	PIRUS (f.)	PIRUM (n.)
cherry	CERĂSUS (f.)	CERĂSUM (n.)
plum	PRŪNUS (f.)	PRŪNUM (n.)

However, it would seem that the contrast was far from systematic or clearcut. According to Lewis & Short (1879), though PŌMUS (f.) has the primary meaning 'fruit tree' and PŌMUM (n.) that of 'fruit', there are also attested examples of each word also having the other meaning. Both ĀMYGDĂLA (f.) and ĀMYGDĂLUM (n.) are glossed as both 'almond' and 'almond tree', though ĀMYGDĂLUS (f.) was exclusively 'almond-tree.' OLĪVA (f.) had the meaning of 'olive' or 'olive-tree' (OLĪVUM (n.) is 'olive oil'); FĪCUS (f.) was similarly 'fig' or 'fig tree'. Another kind of opposition (the one which eventually prospered in Romance with the analogical change of gender of nouns in -US from feminine to masculine) can be observed between SPĪNA (f.) 'blackthorn, sloe' and SPĪNUS (f.) 'blackthorn (tree)' (cf. *espino* (m.) 'hawthorn' in modern Spanish). In a number of Romance languages, including Castilian, the fruit/tree distinction is now marked in a significant number of cases by feminine/masculine formal counterparts: Sp. *manzana/manzano* and It. *mela/melo*, 'apple'/'apple tree', Rom. *cireașa/cireș* 'sweet cherry'/'sweet cherry tree', so preserving the gender basis of the opposition whilst adapting the detail to associate the tree with the masculine and the fruit with the feminine and encoding this with a more transparent match between gender and gender-inflection.[2] In Castilian, this pattern has become very highly productive, and there can be no doubt that this gender-based contrast is systematic. Latin adjectives have provided a source of such oppositions, e.g. CĒREOLUS, a diminutive form of CĒREUS 'wax-coloured', originally qualifying PRŪNUS/-UM, yielded *ciruela/ciruelo* 'plum'/'plum tree'; another adjective, ATRĪNUS 'blackish', also used to qualify *PRŪNUS/-UM,

---

[2] Italian and Romanian appear to be like Spanish in this respect: cf. It. *arancia/arancio, banana/banano, cilegia/cilegio, oliva/olivo, pera/pero, pesca/pesco, prugna/prugno, prugnola/prugnolo, susina/susino*; Rom. *banana/banan, cireașă/cireș, goldană/goldan, măslină/măslin, pară/păr, piersică/piersic, portocală/portocal, prună/prun*. But other discriminatory strategies are adopted by Romance: French and Portuguese use the formerly adjectival -ĀRĪU inflection to distinguish the tree: Fr. *pomme/pommier*, Ptg. *maçã/macieira*, 'apple'/'apple-tree', This suffix is also used in Spanish, though less systematically than gender: *albaricoquero* (m.) 'apricot-tree', *higuera* (f.) 'fig-tree', *limero* (m.) 'lime-tree', *limonero* (m.) 'lemon-tree'.

yielded *endrina/endrino* 'sloe'/'blackthorn'. A significant measure of the productivity of the gender opposition in Castilian is that foreign borrowings have also followed this model: from Arabic, we have *aceituna/aceituno* 'olive'/'olive-tree' and *algarroba/algarrobo* 'carob bean'/'carob tree'; from Amerindian languages *lúcuma/lúcumo* 'eggfruit'/'eggfruit tree'. *palta/palto* (in parts of the Southern Cone) 'avocado'/'avocado tree'; from French *frambuesa/frambueso* 'raspberry'/'raspberry cane'; from an Indian source *chirimoya/chirimoyo* 'custard apple'/'custard apple tree'. In this case, then, the evidence that Spanish and other Romance languages have capitalised on gender oppositions for the purpose of encoding a distinction which is nothing to do semantically with sex seems overwhelming.

2.2 'ACCIDENTAL' GENDER PAIRINGS

Let us contrast this situation with what we might call 'accidental' gender pairings. By this I mean gender pairs which have evolved through etymological coincidence. One example of the very many in Spanish is *acera* 'pavement' / *acero* 'steel'. The latter derives from the Latin adjective *ACIĀRIU(M) (from ACIĒS 'sharp point') as applied to FERRUM 'iron'. since steel was the iron-based alloy from which sharp blades were made. The former is from *facera*, a derivative of *faz* 'face', which underwent a number of metonymic developments: 'façade' → 'row of houses' → 'pavement in front of houses'. So while *acero* and *acera* conveniently occupy parallel gender 'slots', it is impossible to see in this state of affairs any principled exploitation of the gender contrast, since there is no semantic relatedness of any kind between the two words, either synchronically or historically.

The absence of synchronic semantic relatedness in the modern language, however, is not necessarily a diagnostic of such 'accidental' gender pairing, since pairs which were once semantically related may have evolved in meaning subsequently; a clear example of this is *braza* 'fathom; breaststroke', originally 'two arms' length' and hence historically related to *brazo* 'arm'.

2.3 SEMI-PRODUCTIVE PAIRINGS

Between these two extremes are a number of intriguing cases in which the semantic basis for gender distinction appears to be principled, though not as productive or thoroughgoing as either the male/female or the tree/fruit distinction. It is these that for our present purposes need to be analysed in more detail.

The Latin opposition between singular -UM and plural -A in neuter nouns of the second declension appears to have been reanalysed in Romance to provide the basis for two kinds of semantic distinction encoded by gender: first, that between an individual and a collective notion, and, secondly, distinctions based on size.

2.3.1 INDIVIDUAL AND COLLECTIVE

The first is much less extensive than the second. We can see direct descendants of Latin nouns in the following Spanish pairs:[3]

INDIVIDUAL	COLLECTIVE
fruto 'piece of fruit' < Lat. FRŪCTU(M) (past participle of FRŬOR 'to enjoy')	*fruta* 'fruit (in general)'
huevo 'egg' < Lat. OVU(M) 'egg'	*hueva* 'spawn'
leño 'log' < Lat. LIGNU(M) 'wood that is gathered'	*leña* '(fire)wood'

We might add to these the feminine *grana* 'cochineal', which perhaps passed through the stage of 'seed (collective)' corresponding to *grano* 'seed (individual)' < Lat. GRĀNU(M), and the pair *labio* 'lip' / *labia* 'gift of the gab' < Lat. LABIU(M) (the plural LABIA was already used in Latin to denote the lips as a pair). Spanish *tormento* 'torment' and *tormenta* 'storm', though in all probability learned words, perhaps reflect an early stage of this process (Lat. TORMENTA was already used as a singular in post-Classical Latin according to Cor. V, 554). By what we might perhaps regard as an analogical development in Spanish, we have the following. On the basis of *madera* 'timber' < Lat. MĀTERIA (sg.) 'matter, timber' we also have *madero* 'piece of timber'. *Grito* 'cry', a postverbal derivative of *gritar* 'to cry', has a (now infrequent) counterpart in *grita* 'shouting' which could be regarded as a collective notion, and similarly *grado* < Lat. GRĂDU(M) (4th declension) 'step, position' has a corresponding *grada*, two of the meanings of which given by the *DRAE* are 'conjunto de asientos [a manera de escalón corrido] en los teatros y otros lugares públicos' and 'conjunto de escalones que suelen tener los grandes edificios delante de su pórtico o fachada', though *gradería* and *gradas* are more common representations of these concepts today. On the basis of *corcho* 'cork (individual object or substance)' the feminine noun *corcha* 'cork (substance)' is attested in

---

[3] Corominas and Pascual (1980–91: II, 967) derive *fruto* from the post-Classical noun FRŪCTUM (the Classical form was the 4th declension noun FRŪCTUS, the plural of which was FRŪCTŪS), but the past participle FRŪCTUS would have provided a plausible model.

the Nebrija dictionary and continues to be included with the mass meaning of 'corcho arrancado del alcornoque y en disposición de labrarse' in the *DRAE*. There are also one or two cases of what we might call inverse analogy: the masculine *guijo* 'gravel, shingle' has a collective meaning by comparison with *guija* 'pebble' (the *DRAE* glosses it as 'conjunto de guijas'), and formerly *mato* was 'conjunto de matas' (*mata* 'bush, shrub').

2.3.2 SIZE
It is natural to think that association of the feminine with larger dimensions than a corresponding masculine was an extension of the plural or collective notion encoded by the reanalysed Latin neuter plural -A just discussed. It indeed seems impossible to trace any such gender pairs of this kind back to Classical Latin. The use of gender to encode differences in size must have been a peculiarly Romance development, and can certainly be viewed as an important instance of capitalisation on gender contrast. There are examples both of the creation of feminines on the basis of masculines and of the converse process. On the basis of *huerto* < Lat. HORTU(M) 'garden', the feminine form *huerta* '(large) garden, market garden' is formed (note that HORTUS in Latin was masculine and its plural was therefore HORTĪ, not HORTA); similarly *ramo* < Lat. RĀMU(M) 'branch' has given rise to *rama* 'branch, bough'. *Cesta* '(large) hand basket' < Lat. CISTA now has the parallel masculine *cesto* '(smaller) basket', and *cuenco* 'bowl, hollow', is formed from *cuenca* '(geographical) basin' < Lat. CONCHA.

Again, the productivity of this opposition can be measured by the sheer number of examples and the fact that there are similar creations on the basis of non-Latin sources. From *jarra* 'pitcher, jug with two handles' < Ar. *ỳarra* there develops the masculine *jarro* 'jug with one handle'. What is in all probability an onomatopoeic creation *tiritar* 'to shiver, tremble' has two morphological derivatives, *tiritón* '(single) shiver', and *tiritona* 'fit of shivering'. Sometimes in these cases it is of course difficult to establish which is the primary term and which the secondary. The source of the pair *charco* 'pool, puddle' / *charca* 'basin, pond' is unknown, possibly pre-Latin; similarly *gorro* 'cap, bonnet' / *gorra* 'peaked cap' and (though more widely adopted in Romance) *zapato* 'shoe' / *zapata* 'half boot' (cf. It. *ciabatta*).

It is interesting to note that the number of size-based gender distinctions available in Spanish is much increased if regional varieties and different diachronic stages of the language are taken into account. That is to say, those pairs which are actively known by most speakers of modern Spanish represent only a part of the overall creativity of the device; though conversely that might also suggest that the structural importance of the opposition is not so great as might at first be thought. To *dedo* 'finger, toe' (< Lat. DIGITU(M)) there corresponds a form *deda* 'big toe' in Asturias and León (Kahane and Kahane 1948–9:150); *guitarra* 'guitar' (< Ar. *kīāra*, from Gk. κιθάρα) has a corresponding *guitarro* 'small guitar'. The form *mosco*, corresponding to *mosca* 'fly' (< Lat. MUSCA), is defined as 'mosquito, insecto' in one of its meanings by the *DRAE* (cf. Bergen 1980:53, Kahane 1948-49:151), yet this use seems to be not at all general, and in some areas it even substitutes *mosca*. *Lora* is recorded as denoting a large species of parrot (*loro*) in Honduras (Bergen 1980:53, Kahane and Kahane 1948–49:151).

So far we have been considering cases in which the feminine member of the pair represents a 'larger' notion than the masculine, whether because a masculine is created on the basis of the feminine or the feminine on the basis of the masculine; but the size distinction can also be reversed, with the masculine representing a larger notion than the feminine. On the basis of *barca* < Lat. BARCA 'small boat' (contrasting with Lat. NĀVIS 'boat, ship') a corresponding masculine *barco* visibly comes into play, first also with the meaning of 'small boat' in opposition to *navío*, but then broadening in meaning to be the generic word for boat, not restricted in size. *Mampara* 'screen, partition', and presumably the older word, is a less substantial notion than *mamparo* 'bulkhead, partition on a ship', which according to Cor. IV, 395 first appeared in use only in the late 17th century.

It seems not implausible to regard such a movement, which is subsequent to the general association of feminine with 'large' and masculine with 'small', as a further exploitation of gender as an icon of difference in meaning, even though in so doing the definition of the opposition is blurred.

2.4 UNPRINCIPLED DISCRIMINATIVE DIFFERENCE IN MEANING

A further step in the use of gender oppositions seems to take place with their exploitation for what are apparently 'unprincipled', that is, simply discriminative, differences in meaning between masculine and feminine (though note we are still examining cases in which there is common semantic ground and where one gender form seems to have been created on the basis of the other).[4]

---

[4] Kahane and Kahane (1948-49:175) regard the development of a purely discriminative meaning as crucial to the vitality of the *-a* inflection generally, the diminutive value of *-a* being only one of its many functions (a position followed by Bergen 1980:54). García (1986:20) is also of the opinion that the meaning of gender is primarily contrastive: 'the "switch" in gender [from primitive to derivative] may serve to counterbalance the identity of the root, and point up the specialisation of the derivative in its reference to a diverse kind of object.'

Sometimes what has in later stages of the language become a purely discriminative meaning distinction has been produced by the metonymic extension of one of the members of an existing 'principled' gender pair (in this, the greater strength of the tree/fruit contrast is again revealed, since there are very few, if any, movements away from that opposition). Thus from *caña* (< Lat. CANNA 'reed') the masculine *caño* is formed; this has a variety of meanings in Old Castilian ('tube (of a wind instrument)', 'underground passage', 'drain, sewer') which pre-date the modern general meaning of 'pipe' (Cor. I, 821). *Caño* is clearly related to *caña* in that both represent long, hollow objects, *caño* generally denoting larger concepts than *caña*: we may suspect that it was precisely this that motivated the coining of the word in the first place. However, the semantic link between *caña* and *caño* in Old Castilian has already moved a long way towards being 'unprincipled'. The same kind of situation is observable in the development of *cuchilla*, a feminine formation from *cuchillo* < Lat. CULTEL-LU(M) 'knife': the most common Peninsular meaning is '(razor) blade' (originally a 'smaller' notion than 'knife'?), but the 'larger' meaning of 'cleaver', 'kitchen knife', 'blade (of a machine)' is also attested in the modern language; in Latin America, there has been metonymic extension to such meanings as 'ridge (of mountains)', 'slavedriver', 'old hag', the semantic relation of which to 'knife' is far from transparent.

The availability of 'unprincipled' discriminative gender oppositions is therefore not inconsistent with 'principled' discriminative oppositions. There is some evidence that Latin already a number of instances of the former. A well-known example is the distinction between Lat. ANIMA 'wind, breath (physical)' and ANIMUS 'life, soul (spiritual and intellectual)'; another is PORTA 'gate' and PORTUS 'harbour'. The latter pair survive popularly in Spanish as *puerta/puerto* with broadly the same meanings as in Latin (*puerto* has extended its meaning to that of 'mountain pass') and the former have been taken into Spanish as a result of learned borrowing, with *ánima* a high register equivalent for *alma* 'soul' and *ánimo* undergoing downwards diffusion as 'courage, encouragement, intention'. We can also see some movements towards the exploitation of such 'unprincipled' gender distinctions in post-classical Latin: CŪPUS 'bucket' is formed on the basis of CŪPA 'tub, cask', perhaps because a bucket, originally made in the same way as a cask (Cor. II, 261–2), is conceived of as a smaller kind of cask; from these sources we have Sp. *cuba/cubo*. Another pair which are both nominalised forms of the past participle of PUNGO 'to prick, puncture' are PUNCTUS 'point (in time)' and PUNCTA 'prick, puncture'. In the Classical language PUNCTA is rare, but we may surmise that it gained currency to yield Spanish *punta* 'tip, point, sharp extremity' as opposed to *punto* 'point, dot'. However, it is easy to overstate the productivity of such gender neologisms within Latin itself on the basis of later Romance descendants. In Spanish we have the pair *cinta* 'ribbon, tape' and *cinto* 'belt', which Cor. II, 87 derives from Lat. CINCTA 'that which is bound', the past participle of CINGO, and CINCTUS (a fourth declension noun postclassically attested as the second declension neuter CINCTUM) 'girdle, belt'. From this, however, it will be seen that there was no gender opposition as such in Latin itself; in fact, *cinto* is attested relatively late in Spanish (1490) and may well be a learned borrowing. A similar story might be told about CONDUCTA, the feminine past participle of CONDŪCO 'to conduct, lead forth' (amongst many other meanings), and the fourth declension verbal noun CONDUCTUS: Spanish *conducta* 'conduct, behaviour' and *conducto* 'duct', with their specific meanings, are learned borrowings which do not demonstrate the existence of such a gender pair previously. We shall return to the importance of such postverbal derivations shortly.

We must look carefully at cases of apparently simple 'discriminative' gender distinctions in Spanish, because, as we have seen, the role of semantic evolution from the 'principled' distinction based on size is important, and we do not always have ready access to the intermediate stages of such evolutionary processes. The difference between *cabeza* 'head' and *cabezo* 'hillock; reef' might at first sight seem to be nothing to do with a 'principled' distinction. However, though we cannot be certain about these stages, the semantic trajectory through which *CAPITIA passed is most likely to have involved, as a plural of CAPITIUM, the collective notion of 'head(-count)', while CAPITIUM, originally 'covering for the head' or 'opening in a garment for the head', reached the meanings of 'hillock' and 'reef' by metaphorical association. The discriminative difference observable from early in the textual record of Castilian is therefore likely to have been a collective/individual difference in origin.

In fact, sources of 'unprincipled' gender pairs in Spanish seem to fall into a number of categories. Some are the result of calques or borrowings which the availability of a gender distinction seems to propitiate. *Modo* 'way, manner' is a learned borrowing from Lat. MODU(M) (same meaning), while *moda* 'manner of dress, fashion' is in fact the result of a later borrowing from French *mode* (f.); *banca* 'banking (system)' as opposed to *banco* 'bank', is probably a borrowing from It. *banca* or Fr. *banque*, although *banca* and *banco* existed previously in Spanish with contrasting meanings, *banco* as 'bench' and *banca* as the later discriminated meaning of 'seat without a back'. It is interesting, however, that in both these cases the feminine noun does in a certain way represent a collective notion: *moda* as a cumulative set of 'ways' and *banca* as the collectivity of individual banks.

Spanish has also exploited learned borrowings in making discriminative gender distinctions. Amongst such cases is *acto* 'act' as opposed to *acta* 'minutes, certificate, agreement', the latter corresponding well to Lat. ACTA but not sharing its plurality. Furthermore, there are a number of examples of discriminative gender distinction of learned words without concomitant suffixal marking, presumably in order to achieve finer semantic nuances. *Cólera* (f.) 'bile', later 'rage', adds as a masculine the more technical meaning 'cholera' in the 19th century. *Margen* (Lat. MARGO varied in gender as masculine or feminine) developed the discriminated meanings of 'bank of a river' (feminine) and 'margin of page' (masculine); this distinction is relatively recent, since it is still treated as a feminine in both meanings down to the 18th century.[5] *Orden* (Lat. ŌRDO was masculine in all its meanings) is discriminated between 'order, arrangement' (masculine) and 'order, command' (feminine).

2.5 MORE TRANSPARENT MOTIVATIONS
FOR GENDER OPPOSITIONS:
ELLIPSIS AND METONYMY

The stock of gender distinctions is further increased by a rather different creative means from the ones we have been examining so far, namely, through ellipsis and metonymy. Ellipsis of a noun with an originally adjectival form creates such nominal pairs as *derecho* 'law, right' / *(mano/ala) derecha* 'right (hand/wing)' and *capital* (m.) 'capital (monetary)' / *(ciudad) capital* (f.) 'capital (city)' (Rosenblat 1952:2). An interesting case of reanalysis of a noun as an adjective can be seen in *mayo* 'May' / *(canción) maya* 'May song'. Metonymy accounts for such creations as *mañana* (f.) 'morning' / *mañana* (m.) 'tomorrow, the future', *caza* (f.) 'hunt' / *(avión de) caza* (m.) 'fighter plane', and, we may note in passing, many figurative usages of (usually feminine) concrete nouns with reference to (male) humans: *bala* (f.) 'bullet' / *bala (perdida)* (m.) 'wastrel', *cura* (f.) 'cure' / *cura* (m.) 'parish priest, one who has the cure of souls'. It is worth pointing out again that these are Romance creations and that, so far as we can tell, Latin did not exploit gender extensively in this way. Even the most obvious case of ellipsis which is paralleled in Latin, (MĀNUS) DEXTERA 'right hand', does not have a corresponding noun DEXTER or DEXTERUM. At the very least we must conclude that the ellipsis and metonymy we observe in Romance were compatible with, and were very possibly encouraged by, the more systematic exploitation of gender pairs for semantic distinctions other than sexual.

---

[5] It is still treated as feminine in the *Diccionario de autoridades*, where there are 17th-century examples.

2.6 SUFFIXAL GENDER OPPOSITIONS

Another area of gender opposition which merits attention is that of suffixal derivation. I have looked at a number of suffixes for their productivity in this respect. While what we might regard as the primary semantic opposition is the animate-referring one of male/female, there is at the same time a more limited range of oppositions based on non-sexual, or only partly sexual, distinctions. One typical pattern is that the masculine form is animate-referring while the feminine form is not; historically, no doubt, this is because of the absence of female counterparts to a noun which typically denoted a job or function most frequently carried out by a male, e.g. *cazador* '(male) hunter' but *cazadora* 'jacket' (also 'female hunter'), *cartero* 'postman' but *cartera* 'wallet' (now also 'postlady'). But this is not the only basis for such gender distinctions: we also find examples such as *planeador* 'glider' / *planeadora* 'speedboat'; *partido* 'party (political)'; 'match (one game)'; 'advantage' / *partida* 'departure', 'quantity', 'certificate', 'match (several games)', 'detachment, e.g. of troops'; *pago* 'payment' / *paga* 'pay, instalment of salary or wage'. I will examine each of these suffixes in turn.

2.6.1 -DOR/-DORA[6]

The most productive source of gender oppositions is clearly based on the male/female animate contrast. However, there is a very strong association between the feminine *-dora* suffix and the names of machines, no doubt originally because of the ellipsis of *máquina* and the substantivisation of the adjectival *-dora* form, e.g. *fotocopiadora*. Most of these words are relatively recent creations in the language, the consequence of the Industrial Revolution and the plethora of modern gadgets and gizmos: *(silla) mecedora* 'rocking chair', *cosedora* 'sewing machine', *calculadora* 'calculator', *fotocopiadora* 'photocopier' give a fair chronological range. However, the *-dor* suffix is also used for a number of instrumental devices over a rather more general semantic range, a number of examples of which are of longer standing in the language than the *-dora* forms: tools such as *soldador* 'soldering iron' and *desatascador* 'plunger'; rooms designated for certain functions, e.g. *comedor* 'dining room', *probador* 'fitting room', *tocador* 'powder room', *cambiador* 'changing mat; dressing table', devices such as *amplificador* 'amplifier', *remolcador* 'tugboat', *radiador* 'radiator', *andador* 'zimmer frame'; materials such as *bronceador* 'suncream', *moldeador* 'perm', *betabloqueador* 'beta-blocker'; more abstract

---

[6] The behaviour of nouns in *-dor(a)* is examined in greater detail in Pountain (forthcoming).

functions such as *cuantificador* 'quantifier', *multiplicador* 'multiplier'.

We can surely hypothesise a pragmatically-based diachronic trajectory for these developments. The agentive suffix *-dor* is available to indicate a notion associated with agentive functions (device, location, substance) in precisely those cases where there is normally no human agent. (Note my use of the word 'normally': it is not that there could not be occupations associated with the functions just illustrated, but such functions as powdering, trying on clothes, changing babies, etc., are not under normal circumstances trades or professions, because they are too specific or too personal. In a very few cases, ambiguity is encountered, such as *soldador* 'soldering iron; solderer', and I would suggest the appearance of *soldador* in the sense of 'solderer' is due to relatively recent specialisation of trades.) The suffix *-dora*, motivated more recently by ellipsis, originally distinguished machine and operator at a time when the operator was most likely to be male: thus *segador* 'reaper, one who reaps' as opposed to *segadora* 'harvester (machine)'. This is where the first basis for a productive gender contrast between *-dor* and *-dora* which is not based exclusively on sex originates, although in the modern language multivalency of the *-dora* form is much more possible; for example, *segadora* also means 'female reaper'. Since it is possible for nouns in both *-dor* and *-dora* to refer to inanimates, it is in principle possible to have a gender contrast which involves no reference to sex at all, although this seems to happen in relatively few cases, and again perhaps for pragmatic reasons: a particular function, if not carried out by a person, is either associated with a tool, location or substance (masculine) or carried out by a piece of machinery (increasingly feminine); it is difficult to imagine two different inanimate agentive functions for stapling, sewing, silencing, etc. In the light of this, the opposition mentioned at the outset, *planeador* 'glider' / *planeadora* 'speedboat', is actually atypical, though it does seem to be an example of the use of gender to carry out semantic discrimination of vehicles which operate in a similar way, i.e. by the action of *planear* 'to glide, to plane'. Another contrast of a similar kind is the Peninsular Spanish distinction between *secador* 'hairdryer' and *secadora* 'tumble-dryer', which is consistent with the general notions of 'tool' and 'machine' respectively.

2.6.2 *-ERO/-ERA*

The same kind of interaction between animate reference on the one hand and reference to a range of related inanimate functions on the other is evident also in this suffixal pair. However, in this case both the masculine and feminine forms are associated with characteristic inanimate meanings. The Latin postnominal suffix -ĀRIUM was associated with the notion of 'store', 'container', e.g. GRĀNĀRIUM 'granary', PLANTĀRIUM 'nursery garden', and this is continued quite productively in Romance (cf. *azucarero* 'sugar bowl', *escobero* 'broom cupboard', *cenicero* 'ashtray', the latter appearing as late as the early 17th century). Simultaneously, the *-ero* suffix was also the inheritor of Latin -ŌR U(M), which was associated with the postverbal notion of 'place where something happens', e.g. LĀVĀTŌRIUM 'place for washing' (cf. Spanish *lavadero*), a use which was also highly productive: *invernadero* 'greenhouse, place where plants spend the winter (*invernar*)', *embarcadero* 'jetty, place of embarkation (*embarcar*)', *secadero* 'drying (*secar*) shed'. The *-era* suffix owes some of its functions to the elliptical use of Latin adjectives in -ĀRIA evident in what are now independent nouns: *ribera* 'river-bank' < RĪPĀRIA 'frequenting the banks of rivers', *carrera* < VĪA *CARRĀRIA 'road for carts'; in more recent times the same process may be observable in such creations as *(parte) delantera* 'front (part)' and in a number of garments worn for a particular purpose, e.g. *(chaqueta) guerrera* 'army jacket', *(zapatilla) playera* 'beach shoe', as well as *rinconera* 'cornerpiece' and *enredadera* 'climbing plant' (for which however there are no corresponding adjectives *rinconero and *enredadero). *-era* has developed a number of more specific values in postnominal formations: 'container, receptacle' (*cafetera* 'coffee-pot', *carbonera* 'coal bunker', *cartelera* 'billboard'), 'garment covering a particular part of the body' (*rodillera* 'knee bandage', *pechera* 'front of shirt', *espinillera* 'shinpad'), 'place where an animal is kept' (*leonera* 'lion's cage', *pecera* 'goldfish bowl', *aguilera* 'eyrie'). It also has a collective or augmentative value (which may be the result of occasional derivation from a Latin plural, cf. *escalera* < Lat. SCALĀRIA (neuter plural) 'a flight of stairs'): *cabellera* 'hair, flowing locks', *ladera* 'hillside', *pradera* 'large meadow'. We have already noted its occasional use as the designation of a tree name. In postverbal formations it has the meaning of 'instrument', and in this function in fact complements the *-dor* suffix: *abrazadera* 'clamp', *bañera* 'bathtub', *regadera* 'watering can'. In derivations from adjectives it serves as a nominalisation: *sordera* 'deafness', *borrachera* 'drunkenness', *cojera* 'limp'.

Here again, and no doubt for similar reasons, despite the more varied semantic range of these suffixes, contrasts between *-ero* and *-era* are largely restricted to cases where the *-ero* suffix denotes a person and the *-era* suffix an inanimate notion and more recently the corresponding female reference. Thus *cristalero* is '(male) glazier' but *cristalera* 'window pane, glass case' (as well as '(female) glazier'). The specific meanings of the postnominal suffixes are also largely pragmatically predictable on the basis of the stem noun. However, there is an interesting area of semantic overlap between *-ero* and *-era* in their function of 'container'. This seems to be permitted by the fact that if a noun in *-ero* could be construed as animate-referring (e.g. *papelero* 'worker in the paper industry'), then the receptacle is feminine rather than masculine (*papelera* 'waste paper basket'); this perhaps is what encourages the use of *-era* in this function in the first place. Another case in which we find gender contrast is when the *-ero* suffix denotes a container and the *-era* suffix an establishment (maybe an ellipsis with *fábrica*): thus *salero* 'salt cellar' / *salera* 'salt mine', *azucarero* 'sugar bowl' / *azucarera* 'sugar refinery'.

On the whole, however, this is an ill-defined contrast in semantic terms, and perhaps this is reflected in the greater possibility of synonymy: thus both *mosquitero* and *mosquitera* are used for 'mosquito net', *cabecero* and *cabecera* for 'headboard'.

2.6.3 *-DO / -DA*

The various functions of these suffixes in Old Castilian are summarised in Pattison (1975:29–40). They are characteristic of past participles, though *-da* is also used postnominally. I shall not be interested in their substantivised adjectival use as past participles but in their function as a semiproductive nominalising suffix with a lexical meaning that is different from that of the past participle. As a postverbal, *-do* denotes the result of the verbal action rather than the action in progress: *moldeado* 'moulding', *decorado* 'decoration', *tecleado* 'keyboarding'; as a postnominal, it expresses an office (*papado* 'papacy', *principado* 'principality') and very occasionally a 'load' (*puñado* 'handful'). *-da* can also denote as a postverbal the result of an action (*nevada* 'snowfall', *callada* 'silence', *herida* 'wound'), or the action itself (*llegada* 'arrival', *acogida* 'welcome'); what distinguishes the two genders here, interestingly, appears to be that the feminine is associated principally with verbs which are inherently punctual in lexical aspect. As a postnominal, *-da* bears the meanings of 'blow' (*puñada* 'blow with the fist', *martillada* 'blow with a hammer') and 'load' (*camionada* 'lorryload', *hornada* 'batch (of baking)'). As with the other suffixes we have examined, some gender contrasts involve animate / inanimate distinctions, such as *parado* 'unemployed man' / *parada* 'stop (for bus, etc.); unemployed woman'. But in this case there are quite a number of gender oppositions which do not involve animates at all. The postverbal possibilities of both suffixes are often exploited: thus *planchado* 'ironing (as task)' / *planchada* 'a single application of the iron', *peinado* 'hairstyle' / *peinada* 'quick combing', *pisado* 'treading (of grapes)' / *pisada* 'footstep, footprint'. As in the last example, the feminine may render a more concrete notion: *picada* 'bite, sting' (as opposed to *picado* 'act of grinding, mincing or chopping'), *tostada* 'slice of toast' (as opposed to *tostado* 'toasting'), although there are also converse examples: *puesto* 'position, stall' / *puesta* 'act of placing'. And there are more idiosyncratic distinctions: *pasado* 'past' / *pasada* 'wipe (effect of passing a cloth over something)'. This surely is an area in which gender contrasts have come to be substantially exploited. It is interesting in this connection that there are few such gender contrasts evidenced in Pattison's glossary: this may be accidental, but it is more likely to indicate that the use of both -*do* and -*da* was not in the first place motivated by the creation of gender oppositions but that such 'slots' came to be exploited more systematically at a later date.

2.6.4 POSTVERBALS IN -O/-A

The last area of derivational morphology I want to consider is that of postverbal formations in -*o* and -*a*. The most substantial investigation of this topic is Martín Baldonado (1981), who was struck by the scarcity of such formations in Classical Latin but nevertheless hypothesises that such examples as there were provided an analogical model for the general tendency in early Castilian to create postverbals from simple verb stems in -*a* (on the analogy of LUCTA, PUGNA, etc.) and postverbals from affixed verb stems in -*o* (on the analogy of COMPŬTUS). Although Old Castilian shows some lapses in this pattern (one might surmise because of the opaque nature of such an analogical motivation) and indeed evidences a number of doublet and even triplet creations, the fact is that by the modern language the number of such gender contrasts is extremely limited. One of the few surviving examples is the triplet *costa*, *costo* and *coste*, which appear in that chronological order according to Corominas. *Costa(s)* is nowadays restricted to the notion of 'legal costs', though it had a wider meaning, corresponding to modern *coste* and *costo*, in Old Castilian: even Covarrubias says that *costa* is 'el precio de una cosa... Otros dizen Coste, que es todo uno'. Nowadays, -*o* is the commonest suffix encountered: *abandonar* → *abandono*, *brillar* → *brillo*, etc. But -*a* (and also -*e*) are used in some cases: *hablar* → *habla*, *buscar* → *busca*; *cesar* → *cese*, *cerrar* → *cierre*, etc.[7] Maybe the fact that some infinitives are postnominal derivations provides a reverse analogical model (*brote* → *brotar*, *ansia* → *ansiar*); it may be that homonymic clash in some cases encourages a particular choice (*cortar* yields *corte* because of the existence of *corto* and *corta* as adjectives), or because the pattern was already established in Latin (*habla* < Lat. FABŬLA).[8] At any rate, the variation provides at first sight

---

[7] The topic clearly warrants further study: Alvar and Pottier (1983:42-3), having written off the choice between -*o*, -*a* and -*e* as arbitrary, point to one or two cases of semantic contrast: *roce* (m.) 'rubbing' / *roza* 'clearing of ground', *toque* (m.) 'signal with a bugle or bell' / *toca* 'female garment', *cante* (m.) 'popular song' / *canta* 'copla, refrain' (the latter not in the *DRAE* and apparently limited to Aragón).

[8] It is interesting to note that this variation is constant throughout the history of the language. Despite the clear preference for -*o*, *conserva*, *consulta* and *charla* make their

a gender distinction that in principle might be exploited. In fact, however, on the whole it is not.

Here, then, we have a case of a rich potential source of gender pairs which was not fully exploited, so we must ask the question why. We may surmise that the reason for the absence of gender pairs is the lack of potential semantic distinction in nominalisations of verbal activities, especially since there is a wealth of other nominalising devices available (e.g. the suffixes *-ción*, *-miento*, the *-do/a* forms already mentioned, and indeed the infinitive itself). The various vocalic suffixes are accordingly further variant nominalisers which all have different degrees of productivity. Only in cases where semantic distinctiveness could be established, or was even desirable because of heavy functional load, did gender pairs survive. Martín Baldonado entertains the possibility of a semantic motivation for cases of 'gender-switching' such as the formation of *cuenta* in addition to *cuento*, speaking (p.75) of the meanings respectively of 'story' and 'narrative, account' as having 'enough semantic distance between them to allow for peaceful coexistence'.

3 CONCLUSION

What we have seen in the above detailed discussion is evidence that the exploitation of gender when not referring to sex in Spanish has taken place in different degrees during the language's evolution. Such exploitation is not to be confused with, though it is complemented by, the accidental development of gender pairs through coincidental phonetic development (at the same time, the latter might be seen as a useful antidote to potential homonymy). At the top end of the scale we have the masculine/feminine = tree/fruit contrast, which is systematically exploited in a way which suggests that this opposition is still productive today. Gender distinctions based on collectivity and size are also numerous, though less systematic, while what I have called 'unprincipled' gender differences appear to be completely idiosyncratic, as are the many gender contrasts occasioned by ellipsis and metonymy. These distinctions are correspondingly less productive, though there is some evidence that they continue to be exploited from time to time. In Pountain (2001:208) I called attention to cases of neologistic gender contrast to achieve distinction in the rural Chilean use of *puebla* 'worker's dwelling on an estate' and *rancha* 'hovel' as opposed to *pueblo* 'village, settlement' and *rancho* 'ranch, estate'. The data reported in Pountain (forthcoming) suggests that the *-or/-ora* opposition is

---

appearance in the late 15th / 16th centuries, according to Cor. II, 178, 180 and 339, and *condena* is first attested in the 1791 Academy Dictionary.

exploited to a greater extent than has hitherto been supposed, and such modern examples as *terminal* (f.) '(transport) terminal' / *terminal* (m.) '(computer) terminal' suggest similarly opportunistic exploitation. It seems that the more clearcut the basis for the gender opposition is, the more propensity it has to undergo analogical extension and therefore to become more systematic and productive. At the same time, however, it is at the less well-defined, and hence less systematic, end of the scale that the rather more random extension of gender oppositions appears to create new kinds of semantic contrast.

What is especially interesting about such creativity in the use of gender oppositions is that the process of the creation of new semantic contrasts is constrained by pragmatic and structural need. This, I surmise, is what explains the lack of take up of oppositional possibilities within the derivational morphology of Spanish. From the pragmatic point of view, neologisms do not proliferate beyond conceptual necessity. Lack of pragmatic motivation may also account for a number of cases where we can see that gender contrasts, even if established, have been abandoned. Both *emiendo* and *e(n)mienda* are attested in Berceo, but only *enmienda* survives into modern Spanish; similarly of Old Castilian *quexo* and *quexa*, and of *afruento* and *afruenta*, only the latter of each pair survives today (Martín Baldonado 1981-82:71–72). Although both *cayado* and *cayada* 'crook, crozier' are given in Nebrija and in the *DRAE*, *cayado* is much the commoner term today. From the structural point of view, gender oppositions are not the only source of neologism, and are merely one of the strategies available in Spanish for the labelling of new concepts and the making of finer semantic distinctions. The creation of a gender distinction may possibly be inhibited by homonymic clash (note that I am not thinking of homonymic clash teleologically here, but rather as the preempting of an otherwise potentially available category). It seems possible, for example, that the development of a more distinctive feminine in /a/ in Latin for the names of fruits was inhibited in some cases as a result of preemption by a homonym: MĀLA 'cheekbone', PRŪNA 'live coal' (though it is ultimately the fruit names which prosper in Romance). The potential distinction based on size bewéen *rata* 'rat' and *rato* 'mouse' which is evidenced in Galician according to Cor. IV, 792 (see also Kahane and Kahane 1948–49: 151) is rendered in Castilian by the use of the otherwise rather odd augmentative suffix *-ón* in the masculine *ratón*, maybe because in Castilian *rato* (< RAPTU(M)) was already used as in the meaning it still has of 'short space of time'. Conversely, gender is used to make semantic distinctions in cases of heavy polysemy (e.g. *orden*).

Returning to my own concern about the nature of capitalisation (Pountain 2000a), I have to conclude that the exploitation of gender does not have the same systematic nature as I claimed for the exploitation of the *ser/estar* distinction. That is surely in the nature of things: in the latter case we are dealing with very generalised syntactic constructions and the grammaticalisation of the individual lexical verbs on which they are based, while gender is essentially a non-lexical nominal feature. Another difference is that while I was able to trace what I called the collateral consequences of the capitalisation on the *ser/estar* distinction (the extension of the range of inceptive verbs of Spanish, with which copulas are closely related semantically, and features of the expression of adjective negation), I cannot perceive any such collateral consequences of capitalisation on gender in Spanish. However, in many other respects there are similarities. The range of the masculine/feminine gender opposition in Spanish quite clearly extends in the course of the historical development of the language without any abandoning of the original meaning-differences which the opposition encoded: thus, as in the case of *ser* and *estar*, we see an expansion, not a transfer, of functions. Another similarity is that gender distinctions sometimes make covert distinctions overt, as we have seen especially in the collective/individual opposition and in the 'aspectual' opposition between *-do* and *-da*. As with the *ser/estar* distinction, expansion in the semantic range of gender tends to go against isomorphism between form and meaning, though this view must be heavily qualified in the case of gender, since, unlike the 'original' values of *ser* and *estar*, 'original' gender in inanimate-referring nouns was largely meaningless. Another similarity with the *ser/estar* contrast is that gender may be exploited to reiconise certain semantic distinctions, the feature noted by the Kahanes and Malkiel.

In looking at the development of *ser* and *estar* I was able to establish that each successive stage of their evolution could be understood in associational terms in much the same way as many changes in lexical meaning. However, in the case of gender, the basis of associational change is far from obvious. Assuming that the fundamental meaning of masculine is 'male' and that of feminine is 'female', there seems to be nothing inherently 'male' about trees: indeed, one would think that the tree as the producer of fruit was more likely to be female; and biologically, trees can be 'male' or 'female', both male and female bearing fruit. The 'psychological' theories which attempted to relate the notion of 'female' to that of relatively larger size are now largely discredited.[9] The picture I have given in the above account of gender in Spanish is rather that

---

[9] See Kahane and Kahane (1948-9), Echaide (1969) and Malkiel (1983). The resolution of this interesting question may now be expected to come from comparative evidence of the kind offered by Corbett (1991:32).

of somewhat arbitrary exploitation of the opposition, motivated by semantic differentiation of a number of quite different kinds.

Is the exploitation of gender more likely to be an instance of exaptation, the reutilisation of redundant features in the sense of Lass (1990), a possibility which I was at pains to discount for the history of *ser* and *estar*? I have an ambivalent answer to this question. On the one hand, gender is not a redundant feature as far as discrimination between male and female goes in human-referring nouns. Yet on the other hand, it is strictly speaking semantically redundant in inanimate-referring nouns. This is plainly different from the use of *ser* and *estar* where the question of 'redundant' usage simply does not apply. What we are in fact saying about gender is that it is partly redundant and partly not, and that it (a) retains the functions it already has, extending them further (capitalisation) and (b) utilises some of its redundancy for new purposes. This, then, is a type of change which lies somewhere in between capitalisation and exaptation, or perhaps contains elements of both. However it may be, I think that the further investigation of these two processes may yield interesting insights into some of the traditional areas of investigation of Romance linguistics, on which the last word has surely not yet been spoken.

References

Alvar, Manuel and Bernard Pottier, 1983. *Morfología histórica del español* (Madrid: Gredos).
Corbett, Greville, 1991. *Gender* (Cambridge: University Press).
Cor: Corominas, Joan and José A. Pascual, 1980-91. *Diccionario crítico etimológico castellano e hispánico*, 6 vols (Madrid: Gredos).
Echaide, Ana María, 1969. 'El género del sustantivo en español: evolución y estructura.' *Iberoromania* 1, 89-124.
García, Erica C., 1986. 'The case of Spanish gender: referential strategies in language change.' *Neophilologische Mitteilungen* 87, 165-84.
Kahane, Henry and Renée, 1948-9. 'The augmentative feminine in the Romance Languages.' *Romance Philology* 2, 135-75.
Lass, Roger, 1990. 'How to do things with junk: exaptation in language evolution.' *Journal of Linguistics* 26, 79-102.
Lewis, Charlton T. and Charles Short, 1879. *A Latin Dictionary* (Oxford: Clarendon Press).
Malkiel, Yakov, 1983. 'Gender, sex, and size, as reflected in the Romance languages.' In *From Particular to General Linguistics. Selected Essays 1965-1978* (Amsterdam/Philadelphia: Benjamins), pp.155-75.
Martín Baldonado, Joanne, 1981-82. 'Affixation and gender desinence in the Old

Spanish postverbal nouns.' *Romance Philology* 35, 64-79.
Pattison, David G., 1975. *Early Spanish Suffixes* (Oxford: Blackwell).
Pountain, Christopher J., 2000a. 'Capitalization.' In John Charles Smith and Delia Bentley (eds), *Historical Linguistics 1995, Volume 1: General Issues and non-Germanic Languages* (Amsterdam: Benjamins), pp.295-309.
Pountain, Christopher J., 2000b. 'Pragmatic Factors in the Evolution of the Romance Reflexive (with special reference to Spanish).' *Hispanic Research Journal* 1.1, 5-25.
Pountain, Christopher J., 2001. *A History of the Spanish Language through Texts* (London: Routledge).
Pountain, Christopher J., forthcoming. 'Gender and Spanish agentive suffixes: where the motivated meets the arbitrary,' to appear in a homage volume for John Butt.
Rosenblat, Ángel, 1952. 'Género de los sustantivos en *-e* y en consonante.' In *Estudios dedicados a Menéndez Pidal* (Madrid: CSIC), Vol.3, pp.159-202.

18
Template Formation in Western Hispano-Romance
DAVID PHARIES

INTRODUCTION AND DEDICATION

I have only twice had the opportunity to return to the subject of template formation since the publication in 1986 of my book *Structure and Analogy in the Playful Lexicon of Spanish*, which, incidentally, was reviewed in 1989 by Ralph Penny, our honoree, in *Romance Philology*. In 1990, I forayed into difficult territory in order to investigate the significant correspondences in this respect between Basque and Spanish, in an article entitled "A Structural Correspondence in the Lexicons of Basque and Spanish." Most recently, in 1999, I returned to the issue of the quiquiriquí template in my article "Additional Evidence of Template Formation in Spanish," in which I presented data collected from recently published dictionaries covering a wide range of Hispanic dialects. In the present study, which I am pleased to offer in honor of Ralph Penny, I will limit my purview to a single template—the one I have labeled chiquirritico—and also to the dialects of western Hispano-Romance, viz., Asturian, Leonese, and Extremeño.

TEMPLATE FORMATION

The term "template" is used in manufacturing to designate a pattern or gauge used to produce a standard object from a variety of input materials. A stencil, for example, is a template, in that it can be used to create structurally identical forms (e.g., numbers or letters) from materials of varying sizes and shapes. A word-formation template, it follows, produces structurally identical words from a whole array of input forms, by performing whatever changes are needed in order to bring them into compliance with its own parameters.

To illustrate, I will briefly describe the "repetitive" template in Spanish, which may be abstractly represented by the formula "X X," indicative of the fact that such words contain a repeated segment. One of the operations that leads to this form is (1) reduplication, where X is simply repeated, as in Cub. *corre-corre* 'rush of people', from *corre* 'he/she runs'. However, the form "X X" can be arrived at in a number of other ways, including (2) clipping, followed by reduplication (Cub. *zunzún* 'hummingbird', from the first syllable of *zumbar* 'to buzz, hum', remodeled to Spanish phonotactics), (3) apheresis (*chacha* 'babysitter', from *muchacha* 'girl'), (4) vowel change (Amer. *lele* 'stupid', from *lelo* 'id.'), and (5) consonant change (Amer. *yaya* 'sore, hurt', from *llaga* 'id.'), among others. The template may thus be understood as the moving force behind a series of changes which appear arbitrary when viewed individually, but which viewed as a group represent a "conspiracy" whose common goal is to produce words of the type "X X".

Template formation also has a semantic side, in that its products must be marked with what I have called a "playful" connotation, i.e., a signal that the word is a kind of verbal plaything, serving to evoke laughter, merriment, and gaiety on the one hand, or derision, facetiousness, and ridicule on the other. In English, the absence / presence of this connotation is illustrated on the positive side by the pairs *small / teeny-weeny*, *quick / lickety-split*, *device / thingamabob*, and on the negative side by *fool / nincompoop*, *nonsense / mumbo-jumbo*, *hesitate / shilly-shally*. Parallel Spanish examples would include the child-like *aguzanieves / chichiribía* 'wagtail', *columpio / bimba-bamba* 'swing', and *perinola / pimpirinola* 'toy top', beside the more caustic *astroso / ropilindango* 'shabby', *pretextos / chánchurras máncharras* 'excuses for not doing something', and *cojeando / cojín-cojeando* 'limping'. The playful connotation appears most commonly in onomatopoeias, infantile words, names of bright flowers and common animals, characterizations of human foibles, both physical and mental, and in what I have called "diagrammatic" words, which describe repeated, continuous, or intensified actions, intensified qualities, visual alternations, and disorder.

THE *CHIQUIRRITICO* TEMPLATE

I refer above to the quiquiriquí template, the most complex of the many I describe in Pharies (1986). Its parameters are shown below in the form of a consonant-vowel skeleton (where L = liquid consonant, and subscripts denote identity within a single lexical item), together with two examples of the convergence, mapped out according to these parameters.

	C_i	V_j	(C)	C_i	V_j	L	V_j	(C)	C	
	[k	i		k	i	r	i		k	í]
[re	p	o	m	p	o	l	o		nísimo]	

Since this precise form is also represented in several western Romance languages, I have concluded that it originated in an early Pan-Western-Romance imitation of the cock's crow, an ancestor to Sp., Port. *quiquiriquí*, Cat. *quiquiriquic*, Gasc. *cacaracá*, Ital. *chicchirichì*.

The chiquirritico template is similar to quiquiriquí in that they both begin with a dactyl, i.e, an embedded proparoxytone, and contain a sequence -V_j L V_j- spanning the second and third syllables. However, it is less complex in that the requirement that the first two syllables be largely identical is removed:

```
...  C    V    (C)  C    V_j   L    V_j   (C)  C    ...
     [tʃ  i         k    i     r    i          tíko]
     [m   o         k    a     l    a     n    drán]
```

It is highly likely, in my opinion, that chiquirritico derives from quiquiriquí, since otherwise it would be difficult to imagine how a template of such complexity could have evolved.

I observed in Pharies (1999:108) that chiquirritico is the most productive of the templates, speculating that the total for the Peninsula could reach over 200 new items in addition to the 63 cited in Pharies (1986). This explains why I have opted to limit the dialectal scope of the present study. The choice of the western Hispanic dialects for the study is particularly significant, since, to judge from the original selection in Pharies (1986), the presence of the template is weaker here than in any other part of the Peninsula; only five of the original items were western, compared to ten each from both the northeast and Andalusia, and 14 from Castilian. Thanks to the work of contemporary lexicographers, I have been able to compile a list of 46 new items from these regions.

My objectives in this study are as follows: (1) to present additional evidence of template formation in Spanish, specifically of the chiquirritico type, (2) to show the extent to which this type of formation has affected western Hispano-Romance dialects, (3) to identify the input forms of the items presented, (4) to categorize the items according to the changes that these input forms underwent in order to be brought into compliance with the parameters of the template, and (5) to comment on the frequency with which this form occurs in words which exist outside of the formal/semantic convergence which constitutes chiquirritico.

Objectives 1 - 4 are addressed in the following section, in which the various members of the convergence are divided into categories according to the types of changes they underwent, then described lexicologically and etymologically. In Pharies (1986) I cited ten such categories, which largely parallel the nine shown here.

CHANGE CATEGORIES

In order to simplify documentation in this section, I have established the following default references: Asturian (Neira and Piñeiro 1989), Leonese (Miguélez 1993), Extremeño (Murga Bohigas 1979), Navarrese (Iribarren 1984), Aragonese (Andolz 1984), Andalusian (Alcalá Venceslada 1980), Castilian (Academia 1984). All other references are specifically marked in the text.

1. -L V_j- EPENTHESIS. The sequence -V_j L V_j- is the most characteristic marker of playful words in Spanish. In the great majority of cases it is unstressed, occurring either in the first and second syllables, as in *perendengue* 'bauble', or, more typically, in the second and third syllables, where it may be word-final, as in *trápala* 'hubbub', or internal, as in *chiquirritico* and *quiquiriquí*. In a few words, such as *bomborón* 'feast', it is stressed, but one suspects that also in these cases the sequence is unstressed in the underlying structure (*bómboro-* + *-ón*). Among the template examples cited both in Pharies (1986) and in the present study the insertion of -L V_j-, what I have called -L V_j- epenthesis, is the most common individual change contributing to the stock of template items.

dinguirindainas Leon. f. pl. 'mimos, arrumacos' < Ast. *diguindainas* 'juego de niños que consiste en acertar las chinas que se guarda en un puño o en ambas manos sobrepuestas y ahuecadas', a word which I surmise is based on the phrase "diga (cuántas son)." The nasal epenthesis evidenced in the longer variant is extremely common in playful words in Spanish (cf. Pharies 1986:224-38).

lingualateiro Leon. adj. 'charlatán', cf. Ast. *šinguateiru, yinguateiru* 'deslenguado, atrevido en el hablar' (Cano González 1982) < Ast. *šingua* 'lengua', also present in the North-West in the following forms: *lingua, llengua, llingua, tsingua, dingua, yingua*.

mastarazuelo Leon. m. 'hierbabuena de burro' < salm. *mastazuelo* 'id.'. Additional Asturian reflexes of Lat. *mentastrum* (Cast. *mastuerzo*) include *mastuericiu, mastuírzanu, mastuérzanos, mastuirzu* and *mastuerzos*.

mataladura Ast. f. 'matadura, llaga' < *matadura* 'id.'.

miajirrinina Extr. f. 'rediminutivo cariñoso de *miajinina*, parte mínima de algo' < Extr. *miajinina, miajina* 'id.', cf. Nav., Arag. *miajitina*, Arag. *miajica*.

mozarangón Extr. m. 'mozo grande y desgarbado' (Viudas 1980), whose etymon is attested in Andalusian, viz., *mozangón*, the local equivalent of Cast. *mozancón* 'persona moza, alta y fornida'.

patilifuso Leon. adj. 'estupefacto' < Leon. *patifuso* 'patidifuso'. *Pata* figures in several compounds of this type, cf. Cast. *patituerto, patizambo, paticojo*, this last word having served as input for a similar enlargement in Sant.

andar a la patilicoja (Penny 1969:345), a parallel which suggests that *patilifuso* is an enlargement of *patifuso* rather than an example of a consonant change [d] >[l] from the Castilian form *patidifuso*.

rascalarrabia Leon. m. 'cascarrabias' < *rascarrabias* 'id.' < *rascar* + *rabia*.

rebiribuelta Extr. f. 'revuelta' (Viudas) < *revuelta*, cf. the interesting variant collected by Murga Bohigas, Extr. *revirigüerta* 'persona sin ideas fijas', which is both formally and semantically different enough to be etymologically opaque when viewed apart from *rebiribuelta*.

tambarrascada Ast. f. 'emboscada, lluvia repentina y fuerte' < Ast. *tambascada* 'lluvia que alterna con tiempo despejado'. *Tambascada* appears to be a blend of two words, of which the second is its synonym *emboscada*. The first element is possibly *tambascazu* 'golpe dado con una tambasca' < *tambasca* 'rama, ramasco'.

zapalarrastru Ast. adj. 'zarrapastroso' < Leon. *zaparrastru* 'id.'

In two cases the precise input form is not attested, but there is sufficient evidence to assume its existence:

chiquirrinino Extr. adj. 'extremadamente pequeño', cf. Arag. *chiquinín* 'id.', rather than the required *chiquinino. Parallel formations: Cast. *chiquirritico*, *chiquirritín*, And. *chiquirrín* 'pequeño'.

picarranchón Ast. m. 'pico carpintero, pájaro carpintero', which appears to derive from a word for 'pick-axe' similar to Ast. *picachón* 'pico grande, usado para remover piedras y tierra', cf. additional Asturian words for the woodpecker: *picorrinchón, picurrinchón*.

2. -L V_j- EPENTHESIS AND ADDITION OF WORD-ENDING MATERIAL

This category is a variant of the first. It differs in that, in these cases, in order to insert the -L V_j- sequence into the right rhythmic context, it was necessary to add additional syllables at the end of the word. These are sometimes recognizable as some combination of interfixes and suffixes, as in *pozo* + *-aco* + *-ín* > *puzaraquín*, though more often one or more of the elements is unrecognizable, as in *poco* + *-istr-* + *-ín* > *puquirristrín*. The latent western raising of atonic [o] to [u] is apparent in several of these examples.

mandurruteo Extr. m. 'mangoneo, acción de mangonear y entremeterse'. This word seems to be an elaboration on an unattested *mandotear 'to boss people around' (< *mandote 'bossy person'), whose existence is more strongly suggested by Nav. *mandorrotear* 'mandar, entrometerse en cosas

que no le afectan', 'tratar de imponer su voluntad a todos'.

mangalachón Extr. adj. 'desastrao, destartalao, esmanguillao; que deja las cosas a medio hacer; que no las termina ni las completa, y en el mismo vestir es un adefesio'. As the gloss *esmanguillado* suggests, this word probably derives ultimately from *manga* 'sleeve' (accompanied by *-acho* and *-ón*), a word associated with slovenliness in the phrase *andar manga por hombro* 'andar en total abandono y desorden'.

mocalandrán Leon. m. 'persona atolondrada'. The Leonese vocabulary offers two possible etyma for this word, viz., *mocalán* 'que hace muecas', 'burlón', 'que tiene cara de tonto o tiene algún defecto en el rostro', a derivative of *mueca* 'funny face', and *mocalón* 'mocoso', 'simple, fatuo, necio', 'hablador', from *moco* 'snot'. The rest of the word was probably modeled on compounds such as *chupalandrina*, for which see below.

pinguilixín Ast. adj. 'colgante', an elaboration, with change of atonic vowel, on Ast. *pingaxo* 'pingajo', plus *-ín*, cf. *pingar* 'colgar, pender'.

puquirristrín Ast. adj. 'muy poco', one of many reflexes of Ast. *poucu, pucu* 'poco', cf. also *poqueñín, poquerrichín, puquinín, pouquitsín, pouquinín*, plus Leon. *puquitín, puquirritín*. The sequence *-str-*, here combined with the diminutive *-ín*, is of unknown origin.

puzaraquín Ast. m. 'diminutivo de *pozo*; dícese principalmente del hoyo que se hace en el cuechu ['gachas'] o papas etc., una vez servido en el plato, para echar en él un poco de leche, manteca, chorizo, etc.' (Cano González 1982), an elaboration on Ast. *pozu* 'pozo' together with *-aco* and *-ín*.

voltoronario Leon. adj. 'loco, botarate', an adjective based on Leon. *volta* 'vuelta', combined with *-ón* and *-ario*.

xugaratiar Ast. v. 'jugar poco o mal', an elaboration on Ast. *xugar* 'jugar' which presupposes an intermediate form **xugatiar*.

3. STRESS SHIFT

Although the sequence $-V_j \, L \, V_j-$ appears in several Spanish templates in a variety of rhythmic positions (see above), I have never postulated one that would change *bocada* to *bocarada* or *nevada* to *nevarada*. Actually, a change from *bocada* to **borocada* would have been less surprising, so much so that, were these examples not so numerous, I would be tempted to posit a back-formation from *bucaradón* to *bucarada*. In any case, the examples in this category differ from those in the previous section in that here, it is an already existent $-V_j \, L \, V_j-$ sequence that is moved into the correct position by the addition of word-final material.

bucaradón Ast. m. 'bocado' < *bucarada* 'bocanada' + *-ón*, cf. Ast. *bucaráu*

'bocado', 'la parte del aparejo que va metida en la boca del burro', also *búcara* 'jarro alto de barro', *bocalada* 'bocanada', *bocarada* 'bocanada', 'fanfarronería'.

cucharapáu Ast. m. 'pequeña cantidad de una cosa, principalmente de comida' (Cano González 1982) < Ast. *cucharapa* 'renacuajo' (Cano González 1982), cf. Cast. *gusarapa* 'bicho'. The semantic influence of the near-homonym *cucharada* 'spoonful' is especially evident here.

cuvaratina Ast. f. 'cueva pequeña' (Cano González 1982) < Ast. *cuvarata* 'cueva mal formada' (Cano González 1982) + *-ina*, cf. three additional Asturian diminutives, *cuviquina*, *covarachu*, *cuvaracha*, the latter two reminiscent of the Castilian diminutive *covacha*.

nevaradona Ast. f. 'nevada grande' (Cano González 1982) < Ast., Leon. *nevarada* 'id.' + *-ona*, cf. Leon. *nevarar* 'nevar con frecuencia'.

timbirimbao Extr. m. 'derrumbamiento de cosas poco seguras' (Viudas 1980) < Extr., Leon. *timbirimba* 'tablado sencillo y mal construido, que se derrumba fácilmente' (Viudas 1980), also appearing in Leon. as *timbiramba* 'pendencia, reyerta'.

4. VOWEL EPENTHESIS

In these examples, a former sequence -C L- is remodeled to -C V_j L- and placed, through the addition of final material, into the correct rhythmic context.

chinguiliar Leon. v. 'sonar cualquier instrumento metálico' < Leon. *chinglar* 'id.', cf. Leon. *chingar* 'id.'.

umbiligueira Leon. f. 'ombligo' < *ombligo* + *-eira*. This is just one of many variants of this body-part name, cf. Leonese *ombrigo*, *menigro*, *embligo*, *embeligo*, and Asturian *embelilgu*, *imiligu*, *meligu*, *miligu*, *embenigru*, *embilingueira*, *umbiligu*, *menigu*, *embeligu*, *menigro*, *umbligu*, *umbrigo*, *embligo*, *imbidigu*, *imidigu*.

chocolotear Leon. v. 'bazucar [revolver moviendo la vasija en que está] un líquido' < Leon. *choclear* 'chocar moviéndose cosas que no están bien sujetas', 'producir un ruido un instrumento que tiene un sonido parecido a un cencerro' + interfixal *-ote*, cf. the Leonese synonyms *chocolatear* and *chocolear* as well as Ast. *choclar* 'producir ruido al andar con las madreñas en el agua'.

5. VOWEL HARMONY

Here a sequence -V L V- is altered to -V_j L V_j-.

monfaradiña Leon. f. 'hierba parecida a la albahaca' < Leon. *monforadiña* 'id.'

ribilicoque Ast. m. 'rebelicoque, adorno' < *rebelicoque* 'id.' (Cano González).

Neira and Piñeiro also list a variant *reblicoque*, which, if taken as the input form, would presuppose a category 4 change (vowel epenthesis). There is one more Asturian variant, *rublicoque* (Cano González 1982), plus Salm. *bicoque* 'recipiente muy pequeño' (Lamano 1915) and Cast. *bicoca* 'cosa de poca estima o precio'.

titaratero Leon., Extr. m. 'titiritero' (Lamano 1915) < Leon., Extr. *títare* 'títere' + *-ero*.

6. BLEND

pitarrañoso Leon. adj. 'pitarroso', a blend of the synonyms *pitarroso* and *pitañoso*.

7. COMPOUNDING

chupalandrina Leon. f. 'adivinanza', 'golosina', 'cosa baladí, pero de mucha apariencia' (Lamano) < *chupa(r)* + *andrina*, where Leon., Ast. *andrín* and Ast. *andrina* are local variants of *endrina* 'sloe', cf. the similar compound Mont. *cascandrinas* 'persona inútil, cascaviruelas' (García-Lomas 1949).

chipilindrín Leon. m. 'niño pequeño', a word modeled probably on *chupalandrina* but based on Basque *txipi* 'pequeño' (Azkue 1905), a word which has penetrated into various Spanish dialects, cf. Nav. *chipi* 'pequeño', Mex. 'niño llorón', Mex., Col. *chipilín, chipilingo* 'niño de corta edad' (Alonso 1958).

pixalandrín Ast. m. 'hombre de poco carácter', again modeled on *chupalandrina* but probably based on Ast. *pixa, pixo* 'pene'.

vivalapepa Leon. m. 'voz expresiva aplicada a la persona indiferente, a quien todo da igual' < *vivir* + *Pepa*, according to Miguélez (1993).

8. COMPLEX AND ISOLATED CHANGES

The template changes brought to bear in these two cases are unclassifiable, since they are essentially arbitrary.

cipiripanda Extr. f. 'alboroto' < Extr. *ciripanda* 'id.', var. *zuripanda*. The mysterious form *panda* also occurs in Cast. *cuchipanda* 'francachela', Nav. *curripanda* 'cuchipanda, juerga, parranda', and Extr. *sapalipanda* 'alboroto', *guarripanda* 'persona puerca, sucia', *tulipanda* 'prostituta' (Viudas 1980).

ujurubáu Leon. adj 'jorobado' < *jorobado*, cf. the Asturian synonyms *gorrumbéu, agorrumbéu, agorrumbáu, ajurrumbáu, jorrumbu, gorrumbo*.

9. ONOMATOPOEIA

The direct imitation of natural sounds provides a unique opportunity to create words in a template mold. Not infrequently, though, such words are based on already existing imitative root words, as here, *chóquele chóquele*, evidently based on *chocar*. The fact that some of these items are orthographically represented as two words is irrelevant to their template status, since apparently their constituent parts cannot stand alone.

chápele chápele Ast. 'voz onomatopéyica del ruido al caminar sobre terreno empapado de agua', an imitation reminiscent of Cast. *chapalear* and *chapotear* 'golpear el agua de manera que salpique'.
cháquele cháquele Ast. 'voz onomatopéyica del ruido al caminar con almadreñas herradas', cf. Leon. *chacarrachaca* 'ruido de las castañuelas u otro objeto parecido'.
chin-pi-rin-chin Ast. 'voz onomatopéyica usada en algunas rimas infantiles' (Vigón 1955), cf. *chinchirinchín*, also from infantile rhymes (Pharies 1986:93). It is not clear what is being imitated here.
chóquele chóquele Ast. 'voz onomatopéyica del ruido de las madreñas herradas', similar both in form and meaning to *cháquele cháquele*, but based on *chocar* 'to strike'.
pazpallareda Leon. f. 'codorniz', cf. Cast. *parpar* 'to quack', which portrays a similar sound. *Pazpallareda* is only one of many Asturian words for the quail, cf. *parpayuela, parpayar, parpayara, parapayada, parpabajar, parpachara, pazpachar, farpayar, falpachar, falpayar, zalpayara, zalpapar, palpariegues*.
trocolotró Ast. 'voz imitativa del caminar haciendo ruido o del hervir a borbotones', cf. Arag. *trocolonazo, trocolón* 'golpe, coscorrón dado con la cabeza en la pared'.
(andar) tumba la tumba Leon.'(andar) tambaleándose', based on *tumbar* 'to fall', cf. the Leonese synonym *tramba la tramba*, perhaps related to *trambullón* 'vaivén'.

10. UNKNOWN ORIGIN
Although I can provide clues to the origins of some of the following words, I do not feel confident enough to place them in any of the change categories.

chiviricante Ast. m. 'bogavante'. Additional Asturian variants of this word include *llocantu, llocántaru, llobicante, tsibricante*, and *lobagante*.
equilicuatro Extr. adv. 'así es'. Formally, this word is reminiscent of Cast. *chiquilicuatro* and murc. *chivilicuatro*, both meaning 'chisgarabís' (García Soriano 1932). In Spanish argot, the word *équili* also means 'así es' (Oliver 1985), as do *equilicuá* in Navarrese and Murcian and *equilicué* in Andalusian (Cepas 1985). One suspects some sort of Macarronic Latin origin,

perhaps based on *ecce*.
gamarranchón Leon. m. 'cerdo al destete'. A word reminiscent of Nav. *marrancho* 'marrano, puerco', Cast. *marranchón* 'marrano o lechón'.
jabalangorra Leon. f. 'cierto juego', var. *jabajingorra*. Without further information about the game, it is impossible to tell whether it involves, for example, beans (cf. Leon. *jaba* 'haba, judía', Ast. *jabalín* 'haba'). The ending of this word is reminiscent of Basque *gorri* 'red' (Azkue 1905), which appears in numerous Navarrese borrowings, cf. *anchagorri* 'pájaro de papo rojo', *bichingorri* 'amapola', *bustanangorri* 'pájaro de cola roja'.
misquiligrillo Extr. m. 'juego infantil' (Viudas 1980), *misquiligriyo* 'juego de naipes para niños' (Viudas 1980, Murga Bohigas). Again, more information about the nature of the game is needed. There could be a connection with *mezquino*, cf. Nav. *misquiñoso* 'egoísta', Murc. *misquino* 'mezquino', 'melindroso en comer' (García Soriano 1932).
salsarapico Ast. 'voz usual en una rima popular infantil' (Vigón 1955). This word looks tantalizingly transparent, but without additional information, I will not hazard a guess about its origins.
tambarachina Leon. f. 'caída, percance, accidente'. Among the words that may elucidate the origin of this word are Leon. *tambarón* 'tumbo', *tumbo* 'voltereta que da el carro que voltea y se sale del camino', *tumbaeru* 'lugar en que vuelca un carro', and *andar tumba la tumba* 'andar tambaleándose', all of which suggest some kind of connection with *tumbar* 'to fall', with an unexplained vowel change. Another possible source: Cast. *tambalear* 'menearse una cosa a uno y otro lado, como que se va a caer por falta de fuerza o de equilibrio'.
trampalandán Ast. adj. 'entrometido', *trampalandrán* 'persona o animal desmedrado o flaco' (Cano González). All additional words in *tramp-* that I have been able to identify fit into one of two semantic categories that are difficult to connect with those of shyness and thinness, viz., (1) puddles of water, cf. Ast. *trampal* 'charco', *trampaloso* 'dícese del terreno encharcado, barrizoso', and (2) traps and lies, cf. *trampa* 'artificio de caza', *trampear* 'engañar', *tramposo* 'embustero', etc.

FURTHER CONSIDERATIONS
Having hopefully laid to rest any residual doubts about the reality of the chiquirritico template with the 46 etymologically identified examples cited here, in addition to the 50 analyzed in Pharies (1986), I would like to continue with discussion of the fifth objective mentioned above: the degree to which words which conform to the template's structural parameters may nevertheless lie outside the formal/semantic "convergence" which defines this lexical entity.

Below I identify two groups of words that fall into this category.

The first type comprises the numerous western Hispanic verbs and verbal derivatives whose stems begin with the sequence $C\ V_j\ L\ V_j$-, and which therefore match the consonant-vowel skeleton of the <u>chiquirritico</u> template when combined with a monosyllabic prefix. Among the derivatives of this type whose meanings might be construed as playful in nature are the following:

Leon., Ast. adj. *aberreado* 'enfadado', cf. Cast. *berrear* 'id.'
Ast. *aburuyar* v. 'aborujar', 'embrollar' < Ast. *buruyar* 'hacer borujos'
Leon. *acallantar* v. 'hacer callar' (Lamano), cf. Cast. *callantar* 'id.'
Ast. *acuruxar* v. 'cantar la curuxa [lechuza]' < Ast. *curuxar* 'id.'
Ast. *ajalagar* 'halagar', cf. Cast. *halagar* 'id.'
Leon. *agarradeiras* m. 'persona poderosa e influyente', *agarradizu* 'camorrista', Extr. *agarraéra*, Ast. *agarraíru* 'agarradero', cf. Cast. *agarrar*
Ast. *amarradiella* f. 'pelea, pendencia', *amarrador* 'que tiene propensión a pelearse' < Ast. *amarrarse* 'pelearse'
Extr. *emperrearse* v. 'encolerizarse', cf. Cast. *emperrarse* 'id.'
Ast. *encuruxase* v. 'acuclillarse', 'encogerse', cf. Arag. *currucarse* 'arrugarse los frutos al secarse'
Leon. *esjorobase* v. 'estropearse', cf. Cast. *jorobar* 'fastidiar', 'estropear'

I do not believe that the prefixation which has taken place in each of these cases was motivated by the <u>chiquirritico</u> template. Instead, I would attribute it to the process of parasynthetic derivation, which combines a prefix with a verbal suffix in certain combinations, such as *a...ar, em...ar, en...ar,* and *es...ar*. In other words, I believe that the motivating factor in these cases is morphological rather than aesthetic.

The second type comprises words which do not qualify for semantic reasons, i.e., because they do not have playful meanings. This applies to many verbal derivatives similar to those cited above, viz., Leon. *acorralar* 'recoger la hierba en el prado', a parasynthetic derivative of *corral*, Leon. *desarratar* 'soltar las trabas que impiden moverse a un animal' < Leon. *arratar* 'poner la "rata" a los animales para que no corran, trabarlos para que no corran', Leon. *emperecer* 'amanecer y anochecer', cf. Cast. *perecer (un día)*, Ast. *esbarallar* 'esparcir', cf. Arag. *barallar* 'barajar los naipes', Leon. *esgarranchar* 'desgajar una rama' < Ast. *garranchar* 'enganchar', Ast. *esmerecer* 'desmerecer', cf. Cast. *merecer*, and many others. This objection also applies to the few learned words which conform to the consonant-vowel skeleton, such as Greek compounds in *-olo-*, e.g., *apología, astrología, teología,* and learned Latin derivatives in *-ili-*, e.g., *agilidad, facilidad, debilitar* y *comilitón*.

There is a second factor which may be construed as eliminating both of these types of words from membership in the chiquirritico convergence, viz., their syllable-accentual arrangement, or rhythm. While it is true that Navarro Tomás (1957:196) stipulates that all four- and five-syllable words in Spanish are pronounced with an initial dactyl, i.e., èm-pe-ra-dór, rè-con-qui-stár, I have on many occasions heard an alternative accentuation pattern in words such as these, namely the iambic, as in em-pè-ra-dór, re-còn-quis-tár. The iambic pattern would be most likely in verbal derivatives such as those cited above, since they are iambic in their unprefixed form: fà-la-gár, cà-llan-tár. Since I do not believe that this alternative pattern would be acceptable in examples of either quiquiriquí or chiquirritico—entities for which the dactylic pattern is an essential, quasi-musical element—it would follow that the mere possibility that a given lexical item might be pronounced with the iambic rhythmic pattern could be taken as grounds for its exclusion from the convergence.

References

Academia de la Lengua Española. 1984. *Diccionario de la lengua castellana*. 20th ed. 2 vols. Madrid: Espasa Calpe.
Alcalá Venceslada, Antonio. 1980. *Vocabulario andaluz*. 2nd ed. Madrid: Gredos.
Alonso, Martín. 1958. *Enciclopedia del idioma*. Madrid: Aguilar.
Andolz, Rafael. 1984. *Diccionario aragonés*. 2nd ed. Zaragoza: Librería General.
Azkue, Resurrección María de. 1905. *Diccionario vasco-español-francés*. Bilbao: author.
Cano González, Ana María. 1982. *Vocabulario del bable de Somiedo*. Oviedo: Instituto de Estudios Asturianos.
Cepas González, Juan. 1985. *Vocabulario popular malagueño*. Barcelona: Plaza y Janes.
Corominas, Joan. 1980-91. *Diccionario crítico etimológico castellano e hispánico*, with the collaboration of José Antonio Pascual. 6 vols. Madrid: Gredos.
García-Lomas, G. Adriano. 1949. *El lenguaje popular de las montañas de Santander*. Santander: Centro de Estudios Montañeses.
García Soriano, Justo. 1932. *Vocabulario del dialecto murciano*. Madrid: Bermejo.
Goicoechea, Cesáreo. 1961. *Vocabulario Riojano*. Madrid: Aguirre Torre.
Iribarren, José María. 1984. *Vocabulario navarro*. 2nd ed. by Ricardo Ollaquindia. Pamplona: Comunidad Foral.
Lamano y Beneite, José de. 1915. *El dialecto vulgar salmantino*. Salamanca: Tipografía Popular.
Miguélez Rodríguez, Eugenio. 1993. *Diccionario de las hablas leonesas (León, Salamanca, Zamora)*. León: Eugenio Miguélez-Rodríguez.
Murga Bohigas, Antonio. 1979. *El habla popular de Extremadura: vocabulario*. Madrid: Quirós.
Navarro Tomás, Tomás. 1957. *Manual de pronunciación española*. 5th ed. New York:

Hafner.
Neira Martínez, Jesús and María R. Piñeiro. 1989. *Diccionario de los bables de Asturias*. Oviedo: Instituto de Estudios Asturianos.
Oliver, Juan Manuel. 1985. *Diccionario de argot*. Madrid: Sena.
Penny, Ralph J. 1969. *El habla pasiega: ensayo de dialectología montañesa* (Tamesis: London).
Penny, Ralph J. 1989. Review of Pharies (1986). *Romance Philology* 42, 472-75.
Pharies, David. 1986. *Structure and Analogy in the Playful Lexicon of Spanish*. Beihefte zur *Zeitschrift für romanische Philologie*, 210. Tübingen: Niemeyer.
Pharies, David. 1990. "A Structural Correspondence in the Lexicons of Basque and Spanish," *Neuphilologische Mitteilungen* 91, 107-21.
Pharies, David. 1999. "Additional Evidence of Template Formation in Spanish." In *Essays in Hispanic Linguistics Dedicated to Paul M. Lloyd*, ed. by Robert J. Blake, et al., 95-110. Newark, Delaware: Juan de la Cuesta.
Vigón, Braulio. 1955. *Vocabulario dialectológico del concejo de Colunga*. Madrid: CSIC.
Viudas Camarasa, Antonio. 1980. *Diccionario extremeño*. Cáceres: Univ. de Extremadura.

19
From 'Thinking' to 'Caring': The Semantic Evolution of Lat. COGITARE and CURARE in Hispano-Romance
STEVEN N. DWORKIN

ALTHOUGH ORIGINALLY FORMULATED AS a reaction to the Neogrammarian concept of sound change, the adage traditionally attributed to Jules Gilliéron, "Each word has its own history," is equally applicable to traditional diachronic Romance semantics. Until fairly recently, most studies in this area examined the development of the selected lexical item's meaning without attempting to place its semantic evolution in a wider cross-linguistic context. Over the last two decades, linguists working within the theoretical framework of diachronic cognitive semantics have provided new insights into the nature and processes of semantic change (cf. Traugott and Dasher 2002). Peter Koch, his late student Andreas Blank and his current collaborators in Tübingen are the leading proponents of the application of the principles of diachronic cognitive semantics to Romance data (see especially Blank 1997, 2001, the essays collected in Blank and Koch 1999, 2003, and Gévaudan, Koch and Neu 2003; cf. the overview in Dworkin in press a, b). The proponents of this approach have reminded linguists of the crosslinguistic nature of numerous instances of semantic evolution, many of which may reflect the linguistic manifestation of human cognitive processes. Such an approach bids fair to throw new light on individual changes that, viewed in isolation, at first glance seem baffling.

Such a case is offered by the descendants in Spanish and Portuguese of Lat. COGITARE 'to think', namely *cuidar*. Whereas Old Spanish and Old Portuguese *cuidar* retained the meaning of its parent, it has come to signify in the modern languages 'to take care of, to care for'. In no other Romance language has COGITARE shown a similar semantic evolution. This contribution in honor of Ralph J. Penny, who has ably described semantic change in Chapter 4 of his excellent *A History of the Spanish Language*, seeks to describe and analyze the semantic history of Sp. *cuidar* in the wider context of the history of verbs denoting 'to care (for, about)' in the Romance languages.

In many languages, the word equivalent to the English *care* means both 'serious mental attention' and 'mental distress, anxiety, preoccupation'. Often the latter is historically the earlier meaning of the word (as is the case for E. *care*, G. *Sorge*, a cognate of E. *sorrow*, and of Sp. *cuidado*, discussed below). Also, cross-linguistically, many of the words meaning 'care', be they nouns or verbs, derive from terms originally meaning 'thought' or 'to think' or some other form of mental action (Buck 1949:1091-93). In many Indo-European languages the word for 'cure' represents a medical specialization of the general term 'care for, attend to' (Buck 1949:306). The semantic shift at issue undergone by *cuidar* seems to have happened in what we may label early modern Spanish (the language of the sixteenth century). The concept of 'care' (in all the senses of the English verb, i.e., 'to care for, about, to be concerned, to be preoccupied, anxious about, to pay attention to') was reserved in medieval Hispano- and Luso-Romance languages for descendants of the Latin word family headed by the noun CURA and the verb CURARE, namely OSp., OPtg. *cura, aver cura de, curar*.

The reader can find a general overview of the semantic range and uses in Latin of *cura* and its family with abundant textual documentation in Hauser (1954) and Palma (1980). Scholars have devoted much attention to this noun; Hiltbrunner 1992: 327-41 provides 222 references to studies or notes in editions of Latin texts that discuss some aspect of the history and use of *cura*. This noun is documented early and frequently in funerary inscriptions with reference to the cares of everyday life. It also acquired fairly early the notion 'care, preparations'. The family of *cura* had numerous ideological connotations in both the political and religious spheres for pagans and Christians. Tertullian spoke of *cura in deum* as the most important requirement of the religious life. The Church also used *cura* in both its spiritual and administrative senses in the phrase *cura animarum* 'the care and guidance or governance of souls'.

The semantic range of *cura* in attested Latinity is wide-ranging: Lewis and Short gloss the noun as 'care, solicitude, carefulness, thought, concern, attention, pains; management, administration, charge; management of state administration, affairs, oversight, command; guardianship, trusteeship (of a minor); medical attention, cure; anxiety, trouble, grief, sorrow, concern; care, pain, anxiety of love' (whence 'the loved one, mistress'). It is well known that in Latin many abstract nouns originally had a narrow concrete meaning reflecting the rural agricultural nature of early Rome. I have found no evidence that would allow us to determine the original meaning of *cura* (earlier documented *coira*), for which no cognate in other Indo-European languages has been identified. In many of the

Romance languages (see below) the descendants of the verb *curare* have acquired concrete meanings such as can be seen in Fr. *(é)curer* 'cleanse, flush out, clear (land); dredge (a river)', meanings for which Ernout-Meillet (s.v. *cura*) see as the starting point the expression *corpus curare*. Indeed, could this use of *curare* with such a concrete object as the human body reflect its original sense and use? Latin *cura* constituted the center of a multi-pronged word family that includes the verb *curare*, itself the source of the deverbal nouns *curatio*, *curator*, *curatura*, *curamen* , the adjectives *curabilis*, *curiosus* (whose stem final –*i* seems to presuppose an intermediate adj. *curius; cf. the late compound *domicurius*) and its nominal derivative *curiositas*.

The family of *cura/curare* clearly formed part of the vocabulary of Spoken Latin as it survived with the meaning 'care' in all the Romance languages, except Rumanian where the word for 'care' is *grija*, of Slavic origin. Lat. *curare* lives on in Rumanian as *cura* 'to clear land' (Meyer-Lübke 1935: #2412, Cioranescu 1959: s.v. *cura*). The descendants of CURA continued to display much of its semantic range inherited from Latin in the medieval stages of the various Romance languages. However, in modern French, Spanish and Portuguese, *cure/cura*, and the corresponding verbs no longer function as the basic term to express the notion '(to) care'.

The meaning 'care, preoccupation, concern' of OFr. *cure* survives only in the set phrase *n'avoir cure de* 'to take no notice, to pay no heed'. In modern French *cure* is limited to the medical meaning 'cure' especially with reference to treatments involving baths (thermal hot springs). In the ecclesiastical sphere *cure* acquired the meaning 'spiritual direction, guidance of a parish' and thence the parish itself and the priest's residence (Rey 1992:s.v. *cure*).

The verb *curer* quickly yielded in the medieval period to *guérir* (originally *guarir*, a verb which entered Hispano-Romance: *guarir > guarecer*) and *soigner*, both of Germanic origin. The former verb originally meant 'protect, defend' (cf. German *wehren* 'to defend'). *Soigner* derives from a Germanic base *SUNNJON meaning 's'occuper de' (cognate to Ger. *sehnen* 'to long for'). The use of the verb itself seems to be later than the phrase *avoir soign de*; *soigner* meant in Old French 'être préoccupé, veiller à'; *soigner de* 's'occuper avec attention de qqch, avoir soin de qqch' and developed the extended meaning of 'conseiller, avertir, s'occuper de, tenir propre'. Only in the seventeenth century did it acquire its current meaning 's'occuper de, rétablir la santé de quelqu'un' (Rey 1992:s.vv. *guérir*, *soigner*). In modern French *curer* expresses the notion of 'clean out, cleanse, flush, dredge (a river)'; note *se curer les dents* 'to pick one's teeth', *se curer les ongles* ' to clean one's fingernails', and 'to cure leather'.

Although *cura* and *curare* are the primary terms for 'care' in standard Italian, *curare* is used with specialized concrete meanings in the domain of rural life, e.g. Abruzzese *curà le ciammajiche* 'to wash and purge edible snails in brine'. In Venetian the verb came to mean 'to shuck peas, beans, to shell nuts, to clean poultry, to weed gardens, to clean out irrigation ditches' (Edward F. Tuttle, personal communication). Note also It. *curadenti* 'toothpick', *curaorecchi* 'earpick', *curacessi* 'cleaner of septic systems', as well as facetious *curagoti* 'heavy drinker' and *curapiatti* 'glutton'.

In contrast to the situation in Modern Spanish, the family headed by the noun *cura* is the basic (and for all intents and purposes) sole signifier in Medieval Spanish for the notion 'care' in all senses of the word. The *Tentative Dictionary of Medieval Spanish* (Kasten and Cody 2001) gives the following meanings for OSp. *cura*: 1 'cuidado, preocupación'; 2 'cargo de cuidar a sus feligreses'; 3 'sacerdote'; 4 'curación': That same dictionary gives the following glosses for the verb *curar*: 1 'remediar, curar'; 2 'preocuparse con'; 3 'curar o lavar paños, blanquear paños'; 4 'guardar, mantener un día santo'; 5 'preocuparse, tener codicia de'; 6 'tener cuidado o carga de'; 7 'preocuparse, hacer caso de'. In other words, the Spanish noun and verb *cura/curar* correspond to the various senses of the English noun and verb 'care' and 'cure', and retained the 'care' meaning into the early modern language (16th-c.). Whereas the verb *cuidar* continued in the medieval language the meaning inherited from its Latin starting point COGITARE, 'to think', the noun *cuidado*, originally a substantivized past participle of *cuidar*, appears from the time of the earliest Spanish texts with the meaning 'care' in the sense of 'preoccupation, worry, concern' (alongside the meanings 'thought, desire, judgment') and in that particular meaning functioned as a synonym of *cura*; both, for example, occur with the verb *aver* in the phrases *aver cura/cuidado de*, 'to have concern, care for'. In all likelihood, the semantic split between the verb *cuidar* and its substantivized participle was a major factor (if not the starting point) in the semantic evolution ('to think' > 'to care for') undergone later by *cuidar* itself. A possible factor overlooked to date in the seemingly independent semantic evolution of *cuidado* may have been its near-homonymy with the adjective *cuitado* 'afflicted, worried, concerned', a point to which I shall return below.

The formal variant that dominates by far in the thirteenth century is *curiar* (which, to judge by the data in Cunha 1988, does not turn up in Old Portuguese). The *-i-* of *curiar* has not been satisfactorily explained. Corominas and Pascual (1980-1991) suggest that *curiar* is a denominal verb based on the rare noun *curia*. However, given the frequency of *curiar* and the rarity of the noun, it seems likely that *curia* mirrors the influence of *curiar*. Typologically, the formation of *curiar* is reminiscent of the formation in Latin of the adjective *curiosus* vis-à-vis *cura*. It is doubtful that the rare OSp. *curioso* (alongside *curoso/curosamente* 'careful[ly]' ~ *cura*) is the source of the frequently attested verb *curiar*. It is essential to note that this verb has the basic meaning 'guard, protect, watch over, observe' rather than 'to care (for, about), display mental concern'. The verb *curar* seems to be distinctly rare in all the meanings of Lat. *curare* in thirteenth-century sources. This verb turns up once in Berceo's *Milagros de Nuestra Señora* ("A los que la dessierven sabelos mal *curar*", 73*d*) and twice in the *Calila e Digna*, both texts dating from approximately the midpoint of the thirteenth century. Since the texts at issue are preserved in manuscripts from the late fourteenth and fifteenth centuries, these scattered examples of *curar* may be alterations by the later copyists of original *curiar*, a form which is found in other Berceo texts (*Vida de San Millán* 277*b*; *Vida de Santo Domingo de Silos*, 350*c*). Two instances of *curiar* 'to protect' in the phrase "Dios te *curie* de mal", "Dios de mal me *curia*" (*Libro de Alexandre* P, 455*d*, 1887*b*) are matched by forms of *curar* in the corresponding passages in MS O. The immense Alfonsine corpus, preserved in great part in thirteenth-century manuscripts produced in the Royal Scriptorium of Alfonso X (1252-1284) offers only seven examples of forms reflecting the presence of the verb *curar* (alongside more dominant *curiar*). However the meanings of the verb in these passages is 'to cure (medically)'; 'to cure skins and hides' and 'to observe, keep a religious observance', not 'to care (for, about)'. Speakers/writers in the thirteenth century preferred the phrase *aver cura* de to express the notion 'to care' in all its senses. The presence of the noun *curador* 'protector, guardian' in thirteenth-century (legal) texts may well bespeak the presence of *curar*, although the noun could also be the local reflex of Lat. CURATOR. Thirteenth-century texts also show *cura* used in the ecclesiastical expression *cura de almas* 'power and responsibility of the care of souls'. Fourteenth-century sources offer the first examples of *cura* 'priest': e.g., *Libro de buen amor* 386*a*, 1155*b*, 1158*c*.

Starting with the beginning of the fourteenth century *curiar* gives way rapidly to *curar*. It seems reasonable to suggest that the presence and high frequency of the noun *cura* (and the model provided by Lat. *curare*) facilitated the integration of *curar* at the expense of *curiar*. I have found 5 examples of *curar* in the version of the *Castigos y documentos* as preserved in BN MS 6603 and 8 examples of *curar* (*de*) in the *Crónica de 1344* (as in O'Neill 1999). Throughout the rest of the medieval period *curar* and the verbal periphrasis *aver cura (de)* were the sole signifiers of the notion 'to care (for, about)'. The verb *curar* also cast off a small number of derivatives: *curador, curamiento, curación*; cf. the larger number of derivatives attested in Medieval French. The *Altfranzösisches Wörterbuch* lists the following items: *curable, curacion* 'Kur, Behandlung, Heilung', *curage* 'Reinigung, Bleichen', *curaille* 'Spreu, Abfall, Kehricht', *curatif, curator, curie, curiete* 'Sorge'. Serradilla Castaño (1996:61-63, 1997: *passim*) and Cano Aguilar (1977-78:365) offer examples of the different syntactic constructions into which *curar* entered in Old Spanish.

A major restructuring of the semantic field at issue occurred in the late medieval and early modern language. By the end of the sixteenth century the family of *cura/curar* was beginning to fall into disuse as the principal signifier for the concept 'care' and was being replaced by the family of *cuidar/cuidado* in the sense 'to care for, take care (of)'. The first monolingual dictionary of Spanish, Sebastián de Covarrubias, *Tesoro de la lengua castellana o española* (1611) gives as the first definition of *curar*: "Medicinar al que está enfermo o llagado por el *cuidado* que se debe tener con él" (note the use here of the noun *cuidado* with the sense 'care, attention to'). The entry goes on to state: "*A veces* (my emphasis) vale tener *cuidado* en común." With the meaning 'to think, consider, judge, intend, propose' OSp. *cuidar* co-existed with *asmar* and *pensar*. In the medieval language *pensar* seems to have had a narrower semantic range than *cuidar* and occurs with less frequency in the Alfonsine corpus. Kasten and Nitti (2002: s.v. *pensar*) distinguish for this verb the following three meanings: 'imaginar, considerar o discurrir; intentar o formar ánimo de hacer una cosa; cuidar de'. Used as a noun, *cuidar* meant 'opinion, thought, consideration'. Kasten and Cody (2001: s.v. *cuidar*) offer the following translation equivalents of the verb: 'pensar, creer; meditar, considerar; tener la mente en; proyectar, inventar; proponer, tener intención; esperar; entender, juzgar; mirar, atender', all verbs relating to mental and intellectual activity. The following passage from the fifteenth-century *Morales de Ovidio* seems to point to a distinction between *cuydar* and *pensar*: "ca el mal *cuydar* e el mal *pensar* no se pueden de ligero apartar" (fol. 92v, ed. Carr as in O'Neill 1999). As is the case in all instances of semantic change, the shift to the modern meaning of *cuidar* must have been a gradual process, during which *cuidar* displayed for a period of time both its original and its new meaning (cf. Cano González 1988).

There seem to be scattered cases of OSp. *cuidar* where the verb displays a meaning that may be on the borderline between the meanings 'think' and 'take care to do something', i.e., to put thought into carrying out an action, conceivably the first step in the semantic evolution of *cuidar*. Kasten and Nitti (2002: s.v. *cuidar*[2]) offer two examples of *cuidar* taken from the 13th-c. Royal Scriptorium MSS that they gloss as 'poner atención, diligencia y solicitud en la ejecución de una cosa': "...todos los pueblos del mundo & todos los sos príncipes sopieron & prouaron la grandeza de los godos. & por ventura esfuerça se paulo & *cueda* auer ayuda de los franceses" (*EEI*, fol. 177v85); "amas las partes se auiuauan a lidiar fiera mientre & de comienço cada una dellas *cuedaua* uençer" (*GE I*, fol. 76r9). Note the following passage from *GE IV* (cited at p. 547a): "& diziendo a los simples oreias de los príncipes que de su buena natura an de *cuedar* de los otros que tales son como ellos." Here the verb seems to be

on the line between to 'think of' and 'to care about, for'. The compilers of the dictionary employ the gloss 'ocuparse, dedicarse o atenderse a'. The following example appears in *Castigos y documentos*, a late-thirteenth-century text preserved in various 14th-c. MSS (ed. Bizarri, p. 205): "¿ cómmo *cuydas* tú mío fijo, que Dios guíe la tu fazienda ... quando tú le quieres fazer pesar con mugeres de otra creencia mala?" To me, this passage is right on the borderline. Even looking at it in the broader context of its place in the text, it could mean 'How do you think that God will guide your actions...?' or 'How are you taking care that God will guide ...?'. The use of the subjunctive verb form *guíe* may (but not necessarily) tip the scales in favor of the latter interpretation.

The first traces of *cuidar* with the meanings 'to worry about, care for, care about' turn up in the fifteenth century. The following passage appears in the *Tratado de las fiebres* (as in Herrera and González de Fauve 1997) : "Ca las almas enflaquescen & enferman por el mucho cuydar & por el mucho pesar." Herrera (1996: s.v. *cuidar*) provides examples from 15th-c. medical texts of forms of *cuidar* with the meaning 'poner diligencia, atención y solicitud en la ejecución de algo', i.e., 'to take care in carrying out an action or task'. Note the following example from the fifteenth-century *Tesoro de los remedios* (as in Herrera and González de Fauve 1997), in which *cuidar* seems close to having its modern meaning: "deue el físico departir e *cuydar* la virtud del hombre sano o enfermo." Although Nebrija's Spanish-Latin dictionary (ca. 1495) does not provide an entry for a head word *cuidar*, it glosses *descuidar* with Lat. *negligo*. In that dictionary the headword *curar* is followed by a Romance equivalent "tener *cuidado*" rather than *cuidar*. The use by Nebrija of a Romance synonym of the headword before giving the Latin gloss may well indicate that he felt that *curar* may have been unfamiliar to his readers. In his Latin-Spanish dictionary (1492) Nebrija chooses *pensar* as the Spanish gloss in the entry COGITARE.

By the end of the third quarter of the sixteenth century *cuidar* seems to have no longer had 'to think' as its primary meaning; in the glossary of antiquated words and expressions appended to his edition (1575) of *El Conde Lucanor* (1335), the Seville humanist Argote de Molina included the entry "*cuidar* 'pensar'". Cristóbal de las Casas did not record *cuidar* as a headword in the Spanish-Italian section of his *Vocabulario de las dos lenguas toscana y castellana* (1570; ed. Kossoff 1988). In the first decade of the following century the bidirectional Spanish-French dictionaries of A. Palet (1604) and César Oudin (1607) glossed *cuidar* as 'soigner, avoir soign' and 'se soucier, se chagriner, soigner, cuyder ou penser' respectively (Gili Gaya 1960-:s.v. *cuidar*). However, Covarrubias's *Tesoro* glosses *cuidar* as 'pensar, advertir', describes it as "término antiguo" and declares the verb to be the Castilian adaptation of Fr. *cuidier*. Cuervo (1954:685a) provides examples from the writings of Fray Luis

de León in which *cuidar* is clearly used with its modern 'care' meaning: "Y si *cuida* mas de nosotros y a las aves y a los animales, de quien *cuida* menos, provee tan largamente, como por los ojos lo vemos, cierto es que no nos fallará a nosotros ..." (*Exposición de Job*); "Son con razón inútiles para *cuidar* por su casa, porque son como cosas pintadas, asentadas para no más de ser vistas, y no hechas para ser caseras cuidadosas" (*La perfecta casada*); additional examples can be found in Mark Davies, *Corpus del español*. The object is usually linked to *cuidar* by the preposition *de* (less frequently, by *en, por*). According to Cano Aguilar (1984:235) *cuidar* was not used transitively in its modern senses until the eighteenth century. Serradilla Castaño (1996:56-8, 1997:*passim*) and Cano Aguilar (1977-78:364) offer examples of the different syntactic constructions into which *cuidar* entered in Old Spanish. Boyd-Bowman (1971:s.v. *cuidar*) provides the following examples from late sixteenth-century Caracas: "por ser onbre ynpedido y ocupado en *cuidarse*", as well as instances of *cuidado* used with the meaning 'care, attention'.

A series of circumstances may have combined to bring about the gradual change in meaning of *cuidar*. Although the basic sense of the verb in Old Spanish is 'to think', the corresponding noun *cuidado*, originally 'thought judgement', is used in the earliest texts with the sense 'care, concern, preoccupation, worry'; note *aver cuidado de* 'to care, worry, be concerned about', i.e., 'have in one's thoughts, have on one's mind', in essence a synonym of *aver cura de* which, as noted above, also meant 'to care for, about'. An eloquent example of the close semantic overlap between the nouns *cura* and *cuidado* can be seen in the following passage from the Alfonsine *Estoria de Espanna*: "et traye la cura, esto es el *cuedado* y la guardia de todas las eglesias de espanna" (EE2,179v36). Might the essential synonymy of *cura* and *cuidado* have spilled over into the verb *cuidar*, thus making it essentially a synonym of *curar*? Such a situation could have led speakers to attempt to differentiate the two verbs by assigning them distinct semantic spheres in the early modern language, so that *curar* retained its medical sense (alongside rivalry from *sanar, remediar, guarecer*). To judge by the entry *curar* in the *Vocabulario de Cervantes* (Fernández Gómez 1962) and in the *Diccionario de construcción y régimen* (Cuervo 1954), *curar* was used with its full gamut of medieval meanings in the writings of Cervantes (1547-1616) and in numerous other Golden Age writers.

To what extent is the growth of this semantic aspect of *cuidar* the result of near-homonymy with the family of OSp. *cuitar (se)* 'to afflict, be afflicted with cares or worries'? Both word families display notable similarities in their formal structure: *cuitar, cuitado, cuitamiento, cuitoso* alongside *cuidar, cuidado, cuidoso*. The parallelism is not perfect: whereas *cuidado* is a substantive, *cuitado* functions solely as an adjective. Scattered instances of *cuidoso/cuedoso* used with the meanings 'afligido, acuitado, desventurado, infeliz' turn up in medieval sources: e.g., " E la fambre de que sodes *cuedosos* se uos apegara en Egypto" (*GE* IV, fol. 95v, ed. Kasten et al). Herrera et al. (1996) document additional instances of *cuidoso* so used in various fifteenth-century medical treatises: *Menor daño de medicina, Tratado de las fiebres, Tratado de cirugía* and *Compendio de cirugía*. The adjectives *cuitado* and *cuidoso* are used as synonyms in the following passage from Polo de Grimaldo's 1516 elegy on the death of Fernando de Aragón: "Y estando por esto *cuitado* y *cuidoso*" (v. 161, ed. Mazzochi 1999). At least two instances of *cuyto* ~ *cuytar* turn up with the meaning 'to think' in the 1503 edition (Salamanca) of the *Gran conquista de Ultramar*: "mas aqueste *cuyto* que es algún cavallero suyo de su mesnada" (ed. Cooper 1979, I:77vb22) and "e bien *cuyto* que antes que la hayades ganado, será muy caramente vendida" (I:779vb19). It seems reasonable to propose that the near formal identity between *cuidado* and *cuitado* may have been the initial point of contact between the two word families. Both display similar root variants *cuid-* ~ *cued- coid-*; *cuit-* ~ *cuet- coit-*. A not unimportant role may have been played by the verb *descuidar* 'to neglect' and its family, *descuidado* and *descuido*. *Descuidado* has always meant 'careless, negligent'.

Buck notes that cross-linguistically verbs that mean 'to care for, about, to take care of' often go back to verbs that originally meant 'to think'. Thus the evolution in Spanish of the local descendant of COGITARE, *cuidar*, does not represent a semantic anomaly. Similarly, in the medieval language the verb *pensar de* also acquired uses which would qualify it for inclusion in a list of Old Spanish 'care' verbs. According to Kasten and Nitti 2002 (s.v. *pensar*), examples of *pensar de* with the meaning 'cuidar de' abound in Alfonsine texts and represent the most frequent use of that verb, a vestige of which survives in the phrase *pensar los caballos* 'feed the horses' and the noun *pienso* 'feed'. Such developments need not happen; OFr. *cuidier* (<COGITARE), which fell into disuse by the seventeenth century, never came to mean 'to care'. The same is true of Old Italian *coitare*. However in Salentino the local reflex of COGITARE, *cuscitare*, acquired the meaning 'to worry about'; note also the noun *cúscwetu* 'preoccupation, care' (Rohlfs 1956, 195). Rumanian *a cugeta*, which never had to contend with a rival descended from Lat. PENSARE, retained its original meaning. A parallel from Gallo-Romance is the history of the verb *panser* 'to bandage (a wound)', which is a semantically-specialized doublet of *penser* 'to think'. In Middle and Early Modern French *penser* and *penser de* could mean 's'occuper de, soigner', as did *pensar de* in Old Spanish. In modern French *penser* and *panser* are homophones. A striking parallel occurs in English with the use of the verb *to mind* (a cognate of German *meinen* 'to think') in such phrases "I am minding the children"; "Mind your manners", and the announce-

ment heard in certain London underground stations "Mind the gap!"

A summary of this paper's findings is in order. This paper has sought to examine the semantic evolution of the Spanish reflexes of COGITARE in the wider context of the history of verbs expressing the notion 'to care (for, about)'. Although the first clear examples of *cuidar* in the meaning 'to care for, to take care of' turn up in the sixteenth century, the semantic shift 'to think' > 'to care (for, about)' has its origin in the medieval language. This process seem to have begun with the noun *cuidado* which from the earliest texts displayed the meaning 'care, concern, preoccupation' alongside 'thought, judgement'. Both at the level of Latin and Romance the relevant nouns (*cura, cuidado*) played a more central role than the corresponding verb in expressions denoting 'care' (in all its senses). With regard to Spanish (and Portuguese), the formal near-homonymy between the families of *cuidado* and *cuitado* may have been decisive in the semantic history of *cuidado*, a noun which eventually acted on its related verb, from which it had been following an independent semantic course for centuries. This entire semantic development falls within two crosslinguistic patterns: the evolutions 'to think' > 'to care' and 'care' (i.e., preoccupation, anxiety, concern) > 'care' (attention to).

References

Bizarri, Hugo, ed. 2001. *Castigos del rey don Sancho IV*. Madrid: Iberoamericana and Frankfurt am Main: Vervuert.

Blank, Andreas. 1997. *Prinzipien des lexikalischen Bedeutungswandels am Beispiel der romanischen Sprachen*. Beihefte zur *Zeitschrift für romanische Philologie* 285. Tübingen: Max Niemeyer.

Blank, Andreas. 2001. *Einführung in die lexikalische Semantik für Romanisten*. Tübingen: Max Niemeyer.

Blank, Andreas and Peter Koch. 1999. *Historical Semantics and Cognition*. Berlin and New York: Mouton de Gruyter.

Blank, Andreas and Peter Koch, eds. 2003. *Kognitive romanische Onomasiologie und Semasiologie*. Linguistiche Arbeiten 467. Tübingen: Max Niemeyer.

Boyd-Bowman, Peter. 1971. *Léxico hispanoamericano del siglo XVI*. London: Tamesis.

Buck, Carl Darling. 1949. *A Dictionary of Selected Synonyms in the Principal Indo-European Languages: A Contribution to the History of Ideas*. Chicago: University of Chicago Press.

Cano Aguilar, Rafael. 1977-78. "Cambios en la construcción de los verbos en castellano medieval." *Archivum* 27-28:335-79

Cano Aguilar, Rafael. 1984. "Cambios de construcción verbal en español clásico". *Boletín de la Real Academia Española* 64:203-55.

Cano González, Ana María. 1988. "Resultados romances de COGITARE y PENSARE en la Península Ibérica." *Actas del I Congreso Internacional de Historia de la Lengua Española*, ed. by M. Ariza, A. Salvador, and A. Viudas, I, 731-47. Madrid: Arco/Libros.
Cioranescu, Alejandro. 1959. *Diccionario etimológico rumano*. Fasc. 2. La Laguna: Universidad de la Laguna.
Cooper, Louis, ed. 1979. *La Gran Conquista de Ultramar. Edición crítica con introducción, notas y glosario*. 4 vols. Bogotá: Instituto Caro y Cuervo.
Corominas Joan and José Antonio Pascual. 1980-1991. *Diccionario crítico etimológico castellano e hispánico*. 6 vols. Madrid: Gredos.
Cuervo, Rufino José. 1954. *Diccionario de construcción y régimen de la lengua castellana*. II. Bogotá: Instituto Caro y Cuervo.
Cunha, Antônio Geraldo da. 1988. *Indice do vocabulário do português medieval. Vol. 2:B-C*. Rio de Janeiro: Fundação Casa de Rui Barbosa.
Davies, Mark. 2000. Corpus del español. [http:// www.corpusdelespanol.org].
Dworkin, Steven N. In press a. "Lexical Change." To appear in *The Cambridge History of the Romance Languages*.
Dworkin, Steven N. In press b. "La naturaleza del cambio léxico." To appear in *Actas del VI Congreso Internacional de Historia de la Lengua Española*.
Ernout, Alfred and Antoine Meillet. 1966. *Dictionnaire étymologique de la langue latine*. 4th ed. Paris: Klincksieck.
Fernández Gómez, Carlos. 1962. *Vocabulario de Cervantes*. Madrid: Real Academia Española.
Gévaudan, Paul, Peter Koch and Antonia Neu. 2003. "Hundert Jahre nach Zauner: Die romanischen Namen der Körperteile in DECOLAR." *Romanische Forschungen* 115:1-27.
Gili Gaya, Samuel. 1960. *Tesoro lexicográfico 1492-1726*. Madrid: C.S.I.C.
Hauser, Manfred. 1954. *Der römische Begriff 'cura'*. Winterthur: P. G. Keller.
Herrera, María Teresa et al. 1996. *Diccionario español de textos médicos antiguos*. 2 vols. Madrid: Arco/Libros.
Herrera, María Teresa and María Estela González de Fauve. 1997. *Textos y concordancias electrónicas del Corpus Médico Español*. Madison: Hispanic Seminary of Medieval Studies. 1 CD-ROM.
Hiltbrunner, Otto, ed. 1981. *Bibliographie zur lateinischen Wortforschung*. Vol 4: *Censeo – Cura*. Bern: Francke.
Kasten, Lloyd and Florian J. Cody. 2001. *Tentative Dictionary of Medieval Spanish*. 2d ed. New York: Hispanic Seminary of Medieval Studies.
Kasten, Lloyd and John Nitti. 2002. *Diccionario de la prosa castellana del rey Alfonso X*. 3 vols. New York: Hispanic Seminary of Medieval Studies.
Kossoff, David A., ed. 1988. *Vocabulario de las dos lenguas toscana y castellana de Cristóbal de las Casas, Sevilla 1570*. Madrid: Istmo.
Lewis, Charlton T. and Charles Short. 1966 [1879]. *A Latin Dictionary Founded on Andrew's Edition of Freund's Latin Dictionary*. Oxford: Clarendon Press.
Mazzochi, Giuseppe, ed. 1999. *Elegía sobre la muerte del muy alto et muy católico*

príncipe et rey nuestro señor don Fernando. Zaragoza: Institución "Fernando el Católico".

Meyer-Lübke, Wilhelm. 1935. *Romanisches etymologisches Wörterbuch*. 3d ed. Heidelberg: Winter.

O'Neill, John, comp. 1999. *Electronic Texts and Concordances of the Madison Corpus of Early Spanish Manuscripts and Printings*. Madison and New York: Hispanic Seminary of Medieval Studies. 1 CD-ROM.

Palma, Antonio. 1980. *Le 'Curae' pubbliche. Studi sulle strutture amministrative romane*. Naples: Eugenio Jovene.

Rey, Alain. 1992. *Dictionnaire historique de la langue française*. Paris: Dictionnaires Le Robert.

Rohlfs, Gerhard. 1956. *Vocabolario dei dialetti salentini*. Munich: Akademie der Wissenschaften.

Serradilla Castaño, Ana María. 1996. *Diccionario sintáctico del español medieval: Verbos de entendimiento y lengua*. Madrid: Gredos.

Serradilla Castaño, Ana María. 1997. *El régimen de los verbos de "entendimiento" y "lengua" en español medieval*. Madrid: Ediciones UAM.

Traugott, Elizabeth Closs and Richard B. Dascher. 2002. *Regularity in Semantic Change*. Cambridge Studies in Linguistics 96. Cambridge University Press.

20
Achievement Verbs in Medieval and Modern Spanish
IAN MACKENZIE

1. INTRODUCTION

A NUMBER OF INTRANSITIVE verbs in Spanish are noteworthy in that in the medieval language they selected *ser* as an embryonic perfect auxiliary (*venidos/muertos/entrados son* etc.), while in modern Spanish they are compatible with subject NPs that have object-like properties, in particular the ability to be bare: *Entraban hormigas en la tienda, Morían soldados como moscas, Sale agua* etc. The implication of Perlmutter's (1978) unaccusativity hypothesis, recast within a Chomskyan framework in Burzio (1986), is that this coincidence is not fortuitous, because the verbs in question are all said to belong to the class of unaccusative verbs (Perlmutter's term) or ergative verbs (Burzio's term). An ergative verb (only Burzio's term is used in this paper) is one whose superficial subject NP is regarded as having a patient-like role and so is said to be a direct object at a deeper level of analysis. It is now widely thought that the development in Romance of a "be"-verb as a perfect auxiliary is related to the distinction between ergative verbs and unergative verbs (i.e. ordinary intransitives), with the former gravitating towards ESSE and the latter towards HABERE (see Posner 1996:19-20, for example). It is also assumed that the group of verbs that are in general associated with "be"-verb selection are also associated with object-like subjects and that in fact both phenomena are different syntactic manifestations of a single underlying phenomenon, i.e. ergativity.

However, using data from Old and Modern Spanish, it will be argued in this paper that the phenomena in question have separate causes, but that many of the affected verbs turn out to be achievement terms (i.e. they are aspectually punctual) and it is perhaps this coincidence that gives the impression that there is a fundamental link between "be"-verb selection and object-like subjects.

2. THE THEORETICAL AND CROSS-LINGUISTIC BACKGROUND

Intransitive verbs of movement and change of state, together with verbs expressing notions such as "die", "be born", "(dis)appear" and "remain", are associated with a cluster of properties across the Romance languages, the most important of which are:

(i) Selection of a "be"-verb as the perfect auxiliary: modern Italian *Giovanni è arrivato* "Giovanni has arrived", Old Spanish *Salidos son de Valençia* "They have left Valencia" (*PMC* 1821).[1]

(ii) Compatibility with post-verbal bare subjects (in those languages that allow them): Spanish *Entraban hormigas en la tienda, Salía humo del motor.*

(iii) Compatibility with subjects that construe with an adnominal clitic reflex of Latin INDE (these construe more commonly with object NPs): Italian *Ne arriveranno molti* "Many of them will arrive", Catalan *En passen alguns* "Some of them pass through", French *Il en est mort trois* "Three of them have died" (syntactically, *il* occupies subject position here, but *trois* remains the "notional" subject).

Not all of the relevant verbs exhibit all of the above properties (for example, Spanish does not have an adnominal clitic like Italian *ne*), but there are enough cross-linguistic similarities to enable a group of intransitive verbs to be identified as special in some way.

Following Burzio, many linguists have argued that this group of intransitive verbs can be assimilated to the category of ergative verbs. An ergative verb, in the prototypical case, has as its apparent subject an NP that appears as the direct object when the same verb is used transitively. Thus Italian *affondare* "sink" is said to be ergative in (1) but transitive in (2):

(1)   Affondarono due navi.
      "Two ships sank."

(2)   L'artiglieria affondò due navi.

---

[1] The abbreviations that will be used to refer to Old Spanish texts are as follows. *PMC*: *Poema de mio Cid* (Smith 1972); *Cal*: *Calila e Dimna* (Cacho Blecua and Lacarra 1984); *Ult*: *La Gran Conquista de Ultramar* (Gayangos 1951); *Millan*: *La vida de San Millan de Cogolla* (Dutton 1967); *Alex*: *El libro de Alexandre* (Willis 1934); *SD*: *Vida de Santo Domingo de Silos* (Labarta de Chaves 1972); *LBA*: *Libro de buen amor* (Gybbon-Monypenny 1988); *Milagros*: *Los milagros de Nuestra Señora* (Dutton 1971).

"The artillery sank two ships."

It is widely (though not universally) assumed that the apparent subject of a verb used ergatively is actually the verb's direct object at the theoretical level of D-structure (formerly called Deep-structure). This is said to follow from the fact that the superficial subject in the ergative construction has the same theta role (i.e. theme or patient) as the direct object in the transitive counterpart.

Burzio and others argue that verbs of the sort under consideration in this paper are like *affondare*, except for the fact that they "lack a transitive counterpart" (Burzio 1986:29), e.g. there is no sentence **Giovanni arriva molti esperti*. The original motivation for this rapprochement was the fact that in Italian both types of verb select *essere* as the perfect auxiliary and both types admit *ne*-cliticization (Burzio 1986:23-27, 53-54), as illustrated in (3) and (4):

(3)   Ne sono arrivati molti.
       "Many of them have arrived."

(4)   Ne sono affondate due.
       "Two of them have sunk."

These and/or other supposed "diagnostics" are now also used to identify ergative verbs in the other Romance languages (see, for example, Zagona 2002:153-54). There is also a semantic dimension to the hypothesis, because it is claimed that, like traditional ergative verbs, those that lack a transitive counterpart assign the theta role patient/theme to the superficial subject. In this respect, the connection that is made between "be"-verb selection and ergativity parallels the thesis put forward in Vincent (1982), viz. that the "be"-auxiliary in Romance requires a "neutral" (an equivalent term to "theme") as subject.

3. AUXILIARY SELECTION IN OLD SPANISH

If the widespread view linking "be"-verb selection in Romance and ergativity is correct, then one would expect that linkage to apply also to the use of *ser* as a perfect auxiliary in Old Spanish. It is true that Spanish *ser* + intransitive past participle (henceforth: "PP") began to disappear before it became fully grammaticalized as an exponent of the perfect tense. However this is perhaps an advantage, as it implies that the body of data is relatively rich in examples in which the original meaning of the periphrastic perfect is preserved and which can therefore cast light on the issue of why particular verbs gravitate towards a "be"-verb rather than a "have"-verb. With this in mind, I will not impose on the data a strict distinction between *ser* qua copula and *ser* qua perfect auxiliary, although I accept that in some cases *ser* is more obviously a copula than an auxiliary, e.g. *es folgado* (compare modern *está descansado/recuperado*) and *es errado* (compare *está equivocado*). Thus the method adopted here differs from the more usual practice of segmenting *ser* + PP usage in Old Spanish into categories suggested by modern Spanish (see, for example, Pountain 1985).

In his extensive work on the subject, Benzing (1931) identifies the following intransitive verbs as having been capable of being construed with *ser* in Old Spanish:

> *acabar, acae(s)cer, adormecer, adormir, amanecer, anochecer, apare(s)cer, arribar, avenir/abenir, caer, caminar, cenar, correr, crecer, cuntir, deçir, de(r)ramar, descender, despertar, desviar, entrar, errar, escapar, exir, falle(s)cer, fallir, fenecer, finar, fincar, holgar/folgar, huir/fuir, ir, llegar, morir, na(s)cer, partir, pas(s)ar, quedar, r(r)astar, salir, subir, tornar, transir, venir, (u)viar, volver, yantar.*

This list obviously is not exhaustive (for example, *descavalgar* "dismount" is missing) but given the number of texts used in Benzing's survey, it can be assumed that it gives a very clear idea of the types of verbs that selected *ser*. What I will argue is that what characterizes these verbs as a group has more to do with aspectual class than with ergativity.

To demonstrate this, I will follow Vendler's four-way classification of verbs and predicates into achievements, accomplishments, activities and states (see Vendler 1967:97-121). Achievements (e.g. dying, arriving) and accomplishments (e.g. repairing a computer, flying to Madrid) imply completion and so differ from states (e.g. liking, hating) and activities (e.g. running, riding a bike), both of which are inherently unbounded in time. Achievements differ from accomplishments in that the former are momentary events, while the latter are essentially activities that culminate in an achievement. For example, running home (an accomplishment) involves an activity (running) but finalizes in an achievement (arriving home). The difference between achievements, accomplishments and activities (we ignore states for the moment) is nicely brought out by the types of questions that are pertinent in each case:

At what time/moment did the bomb explode? (achievement)
How long did it take you to write your book? (accomplishment)[2]

---

[2] Note that cases like *How long did it take you to reach the summit?* are deceptive,

For how long did you ride your bike? (activity)

In this paper I will be primarily concerned with achievement terms and, to a lesser extent, accomplishment terms. As a rule, achievement terms are lexical (*aparecer, aterrizar* etc.), whereas accomplishments are often syntactic, consisting frequently in an activity verb plus a noun phrase or prepositional phrase, e.g. *cantar + una copla, correr + a casa*. The category of achievement terms comprises verbs of arriving and departing (*llegar, salir, irse*), change of state verbs (*morir, romperse, aumentar*), verbs of acquisition and loss (*perder, encontrar, vender*), certain psychological or perceptual verbs (*reconocer, acordarse, avistar*) and aspectual verbs (*empezar, terminar*). The category of accomplishment terms comprises certain verbs of movement when used with a directional complement (*caminar a casa, volar a París*), verb phrases of execution (*leer un libro, pintar una pared*) and verb phrases of creation and destruction (*construir una casa, demolir un edificio*)—see also Russinovich Solé (1990:59). In the first part of this paper, I will argue that only achievements and, to a lesser extent, accomplishments selected *ser* as a perfect auxiliary in Old Spanish.

If we take the verbs of movement first, these can be categorized as follows: (i) verbs that denote reaching or moving away from a determinate position: *arribar, escapar, fuir/huir, llegar, partir, tornar* (and also *volver* when this acquires the sense of *regresar*);[3] (ii) verbs of exiting and entering: *entrar, exir, salir*; (iii) verbs of passage: *ir, venir, passar* (in the sense illustrated by *de Marruecos es passada*, PMC 1789), *caminar*; (iv) verbs of ascent and descent: *deçir, descender, subir*; (v) manner of movement verbs: *correr*.

Apart from *fuir/huir*, the verbs in categories (i) and (ii) seem uncontroversially to be achievement terms, as they denote events that have no extension in time and in respect of which questions of the form ¿A qué hora? or ¿En qué momento? are likely to be appropriate. The verb *fuir/huir* is difficult to classify, as it seems to oscillate between an achievement sense that reduces to the mere notion of taking flight and an accomplishment sense that involves an additional implicit reference to some activity such as running.

---

as the question in this instance does not refer to the event of reaching the summit, which is an achievement, but to the accomplishment that culminates in reaching the summit.

[3] *Uviar* [= *llegar/acudir*] presumably also belongs in this group; likewise *desviar*, in the sense illustrated by *el ladrón cató ora que el religioso fuese desviado* "the thief waited until the monk had gone away", *Cal* p. 138 (assuming this is intransitive and not reflexive).

The verbs of passage (category (iii)) are in principle accomplishment terms, as in this case it is appropriate to enquire how long the journey took rather than at what moment it occurred. On the other hand, *ir*, *venir* and *passar* have additional uses in which they function as achievement terms. For example, *ir* is often used in Old Spanish without a directional complement to mean *marcharse*, while *venir* and *passar* can be used to indicate the beginning or end of a period of time (e.g. *Passada es la noche, venida es la mañana*, PMC 1540). *Passar* was also commonly synonymous with the achievement verb *morir* (for which, see below).

The verbs of ascent and descent (category (iv)) can be either activity terms (compare *Subimos durante media hora*) or accomplishment terms (compare *Tardamos media hora en subir*), but it is the accomplishment sense that is activated in the *ser* + PP construction. In particular *deçir* and *descender* often come to mean *apearse*:

(5)   la meitad de ellos eran decendidos á pié (*Ult* p. 158)
        "half of them had dismounted"

Manner of movement verbs (category (v)) are similar to *subir* etc. in that in their most basic sense they are activity terms (compare *Corrimos durante media hora*) but they become accomplishment terms when used with a directional complement (or when a directional complement is implicit). Now most of Benzing's examples with *correr* turn out to be unreliable, often because the verb is in fact being used transitively (e.g. *fueron corridos los moros aquel dia*, Ult p. 209). On the other hand, it would not be surprising to find that, when used in reference to an accomplishment, *correr* did construe with *ser*. Compare, for example, modern Italian *Sono corso a Roma* (with *correre* as an accomplishment term) and *Ho corso* (with *correre* as an activity term).[4]

Moving on to the verbs that broadly speaking signal the beginning or end of a state, these all appear to be clear-cut achievement terms. This category includes the birth and death verbs (*nascer, morir, transir*), verbs meaning "come to an end" (*acabar, fenecer, finar*), the dawn and dusk verbs (*amanecer, anochecer*), verbs of going to sleep and awakening (*adormir, adormecer,*

---

[4] The verb *der(r)amar*, as in *las yentes de fuera todas son deramadas* (PMC 463) "the people have spilled out [of the city]", is not an obvious candidate for any of the main categories of movement verb. Concerning its aspectual class, it seems to be an accomplishment term, given that it appears to describe an event consisting in multiple actions.

despertar),[5] verbs of apparition (*parescer, aparescer*), and inceptive *caer* as in (6) below:

(6) era conna vejez en flaqeza caído (*Millan* 260b)
    "he had with old age become weakened"

The other common use of *ser caido* involves *caer* as a synonym for the achievement term *morir*, as in *quando Etor fue caydo* (*Alex* [Paris ms.] 717c).

In the beginning/end of a state category we can also include *crecer*, which is systematically ambiguous between a state sense, as in *Creció durante unos meses*, and an achievement sense that arises when the verb is used to refer to the fact that someone or something has crossed the threshold between the state of being size X and the state of exceeding size X. The sense associated with Old Spanish *es creçido* is always the latter sense.

As used in the *ser* + PP configuration, *folgar* too can be assimilated to the change of state category. This verb can be likened to *dormir*, in that although it is normally an activity term, the past participle as used with *ser* is essentially an adjective expressing the state resulting from an achievement. Thus just as *es dormido* could only mean, in modern terms, *está dormido* (i.e. "is gone to sleep") and never *ha dormido* (i.e. "has engaged in the activity of sleeping")—see Lapesa (2000:784)—so *es folgado* amounts to *está descansado* (or *recuperado*) and not to *ha descansado*:

(7) sólo que y plegasse luego serié folgado (*SD* 599d)
    "just getting there would bring him respite"

This use of *folgado* can be compared to the use with *haber* illustrated in (8):

(8) desque ahí hobieron morado é folgado algunos dias (*Ult* p.87)
    "after they had stayed and rested there for a few days"

Here *hobieron folgado* means "had engaged in the activity of resting" (not "had become rested") and so *folgar* has its normal activity sense.

---

[5] Perhaps, *pace* Benzing, *adormir* and *adormecer* more commonly were transitive verbs that were capable of being used ergative-reflexively, like *dormir* (*a una persona*) and *dormirse* (*una persona*). The sequence *es/era adorm(ec)ido* itself gives no clue in this respect, given the routine absence of any reflexive pronoun in the *ser* + PP construction.

I now turn to the verbs of failure, namely *errar, fallir* and *fallescer*. The latter two can be taken together, as they have overlapping, though not identical, ranges of meanings. Although they could be used like modern *faltar* in the stative sense of "to be lacking", they are achievement terms when used in the *ser* + PP construction, where they mean *acabarse/desaparecer* or, in the case of *fallir* at least, *frustrar la expectativa* or *dejar de cumplir*:

(9) a poco tienpo es la su lus fallida (*Alex* 1487d)
     "soon its light has died away"

(10) todas [las artes/salidas] me son fallidas (*LBA* 882d)
     "they have all proved useless"

(11) Cantabria era a Dios fallida (*Millan* 281b)
     "Cantabria had turned away from God"

Particularly in the case of *fallescer* there are also the senses *morir* and *desfallecer/quedarse sin fuerza*, which again can be assigned to the achievement category (for a similar view of *desfallecer*, see Russinovich Solé 1990:59, although it may be that she has in mind *desfallecer* in the sense of *desmayarse*). The verb *errar* also appears to be exclusively an achievement term when used with *ser*, conveying the inceptive notion of *caer en el error*:

(12) Duenna—disso—mercet, ca mucho so errado (*Milagros* 571c)
     " 'My lady,' he said, 'forgive me, as I have committed a grave error' "

It is tempting to see a resemblance between *errar* and the *folgar/dormir* type of case, with *errar* being capable of meaning "engage in the activity of erring", just as *pecar*, for example, can mean "engage in the activity of sinning" (compare *Durante mi vida he pecado mucho*). However, no examples of *errar* as an activity term are forthcoming. In particular, Benzing did not find any examples of *errar* with *haber*, which would be likely to have illustrated any putative activity sense.

The range of meanings associated with the verbs of remaining, *fincar, quedar* and *r(r)astar*, is quite broad. These are plainly state terms when they mean *permanecer* (compare *Permaneció en el país durante un mes*) or *quedar* as used in, e.g., *Quedan cinco ejemplares*. When used in the *ser* + PP construction, however, the usual meanings of *fincar* and *r(r)astar* at least are *encontrarse* (example (13) below) or *no irse* (example (14))—examples like *Fincadas son las tiendas* (*PMC* 1657) can be excluded, as *fincar* seems there to be transitive, with the meaning *montar*, harking back to line 1631 *fincaron las tiendas*. In addition *quedar(se)* has its original sense of *quedarse quieto/callado* or *terminar*, as in example (15):

(13)   Los amigos leales solos eran fincados (*Alex* 2016a)
        "The loyal friends had found themselves alone"

(14)   el Çid e sos hyernos en Valençia son rastados (*PMC* 2270)
        "the Cid and his sons-in-law have remained in Valencia"

(15)   Maguer era el planto e el duelo quedado (*Alex* [Paris ms.] 652a)
        "Although the lamenting and mourning had ended"

In all of these cases, the event referred to is momentary, hence an achievement. This may not be immediately obvious in the case of *en Valençia son rastados*, but a comparison with modern *quedarse*, as in *Me quedé en la cama* (*cuando los otros se levantaron*), is instructive. *Me quedé en la cama* refers to my failure (or refusal) to get out of bed and this instantaneous non-event is not something that can endure through time. The achievement status of *me quedé en la cama* is evidenced also by the fact that in *Me quedé en la cama cuando los otros se levantaron*, it is asserted to be simultaneous with *los otros se levantaron*, and *levantarse* is an uncontroversial achievement term. My contention is that *r(r)astar* in the favoured sense (as well as *fincar* when used similarly, as in *non valien çinco sueldos los que eran fincados, Alex* 2039b) corresponds to *quedarse* in the staying in bed example.

Turning now to the verbs *acae(s)cer* and *cuntir*, these can mean *suceder* but perhaps the commoner meaning in the *ser* + PP construction is *tocar*:

(16)   Hya vos sabedes la ondra que es cuntida a nos (*PMC* 2941)
        "You already know of the honour that has befallen us"

In the sense illustrated, which embodies the concept of abstract arrival, the verbs *acae(s)cer* and *cuntir* are clearly achievement terms. It also seems reasonable to classify them as achievement terms when they mean *suceder*, because in this sense the only subject NPs with which they are compatible are those that refer to momentary occurrences such as *su muerte, el accidente* (but not, e.g., *la guerra, la conferencia* etc.). In other words, the concept of occurrence cannot be reconciled with the notion of extension in time.

The verb *abenir* can also mean *suceder* but, to judge from Benzing's examples (if we exclude the adjectival locution *ser bien avenido* meaning "get on well" or "be satisfied"), the usual sense in the *ser* + PP construction is *llegar a un acuerdo*, which is uncontroversially an achievement sense:

(17) quando fueron en todo abenidos (*Alex* 746c)
      "when they had agreed on all matters"

Note that in this case, as in others, it is unclear whether the corresponding infinitive is an intransitive verb or a reflexive, as both possibilities seem to have been available.

The two verbs of consumption, viz. *cenar* and *yantar*, are accomplishment terms, referring respectively to having supper and having a midday meal, rather than to the mere activity of eating. The accomplishment sense of *cenar* is nicely brought out in the following example:

(18) dellos seyen en çena dellos eran çenados (*Alex* 1201b)
      "some of them were having supper, some of them had had supper"

4. *SER*-SELECTION IN OLD SPANISH AND ACHIEVEMENTS/ACCOMPLISHMENTS

What we see then is that in Old Spanish the *ser* + PP construction is compatible, as far as intransitive verbs are concerned, only with achievement and accomplishment terms, and primarily with achievement terms. The reason for the bias towards achievement terms probably stems from the fact that the class of intransitive verbs contains few accomplishment terms. Apart from the relatively limited group of accomplishment terms formed from intransitive activity verbs plus a directional complement (e.g. *caminar a* + NP), accomplishment terms typically consist in a transitive verb plus its direct object, as in *pelar una naranja*.

On the other hand, it is difficult to argue that all the intransitive verbs that select *ser* in Old Spanish take subjects that are non-agents, which would be the case if they were indeed ergative (assuming agents are never encoded as direct objects). One test for agency (due to Vendler 1967:106) involves seeing whether adverbs meaning "deliberately" or "carefully" can be used with the verb in question. This shows that verbs like *caer, morir, nacer*, for example, do not take agentive subjects (?*murieron a propósito*, ?*nació con cuidado* etc.). If this is our criterion, a number of the verbs discussed or mentioned in section 3 above appear to take agentive subjects and so cannot, on semantic grounds at least, be regarded as ergative. For example, the verbs meaning *apearse* (e.g. *descavalgar* and *deçir*) would presumably have been capable of occurring with an adverb meaning "carefully" (compare modern *Se apeó con cuidado*), as would the verbs of entering and exiting (compare modern *Entró/Salió con cuidado*). Similarly, verbs meaning to "return" would presumably have been compatible with an adverb meaning "deliberately" (compare modern *Volvió a propósito*). Another possible test for agency involves inserting a phrase meaning "decided to" between the subject and the verb in question. According to this test, the verbs *cenar* and *yantar*, for example, together with *correr* and *caminar*, select clearly agentive subjects. Indeed, being primarily an activity term, *correr* is a prototypical example of a verb that takes an agentive subject. Results from other tests for agency, such as seeing whether the appropriate question is "What did X do?" as opposed to "What happened to X?" (due to Lyons 1968:356), will also indicate that not all the *ser*-selecting verbs are ergative.

In addition, a correlation between *ser*-selection and achievements /accomplishments accords naturally with the commonly held view that the *ser* + PP construction originated as a resultative construction. Already Latin ESSE + PP was often implicitly resultative, both when used as a passive (e.g. ROMA A ROMULO CONDITA EST "Rome was founded by Romulus") and as used with at least some of the deponent verbs (NATUS/MORTUUS EST etc.). The resultative meaning was more prominent in Old Spanish, and was localized primarily to the case in which the present or imperfect of *ser* was used with the past participle. This is evident both in examples involving intransitive verbs, such as *Hido es Minaya, Salidos son de Valençia* (*PMC* 1391, 1821), *los unos eran muertos e los otros fuydos* (*Alex* [Paris ms.] 1415b), and also in examples in which the past participle is from a verb that was normally reflexive, such as *en pie es levantado, non era puesto el sol, todos juntados son* (*PMC* 2219, 416, 291). The preterite of *ser* + PP, in contrast, was inceptive and indicated entrance into the resultant state, as in *cayóle a los piedes luego que fue llegada* (*SD* 320d) and the many examples involving *nado* (e.g. *en ora buena fuestes nado*, *PMC* 266). This inceptive use of *ser* with past participles can be compared to its use in, for example, modern Spanish *en cuanto fue de noche*.

Now in a resultative construction, the past participle functions as an adjective that assigns to the subject the property of having undergone or carried out whatever it is that the verb denotes. Achievement and accomplishment terms, with their implication of completion or execution, supply past participles that can sensibly be predicated of a subject. States and activities, in contrast, lack a "built-in" objective or natural climax. Thus state and activity terms typically supply past participles that it would be pointless to predicate of a subject and so one would not expect them to be available for use in the *ser* + PP construction (apparent exceptions, such as Old Spanish *es folgado*, are not really exceptions, as in those cases the meaning of the past participle does not replicate that of the finite verb).

5. BARE SUBJECTS IN MODERN SPANISH

Turning now to the data from modern Spanish, we find that many of the verbs that selected *ser* in Old Spanish are compatible with bare subjects in modern Spanish. A number of researchers have argued that this compatibility indicates they have ergative status. Torrego (1989:255), for example, states that "in Spanish, unaccusative [i.e. ergative] verbs allow their single argument to appear as a bare plural in postverbal position, but unergatives [i.e. ordinary intransitives] do not". In contrast, as with *ser*-selection in Old Spanish, the claim advanced here will be that ergativity is not in fact the trigger for the phenomenon highlighted.

In the first place, it can be noted that a subject NP introduced by *unos* or *unas* typically is distributive in its reference:

(19)   Dimitieron unos ministros.

Here, what is asserted in the predicate applies separately to each individual indicated by the subject phrase, i.e. the plural verb *dimitieron* indicates that the corresponding singular form *dimitió* applies to two or more ministers taken individually. On the other hand, in other instances the reference is not intended to be distributive, a case in point being when a verb with a plural subject is used to describe a recurring event, as in (20) below:

(20)   Dimitían ministros cada semana.

If the subject was distributive, the above sentence would entail that *dimitía cada semana* was true of individual ministers. But obviously that is not what is meant. What (20) says is that there was a general state of affairs consisting in the weekly resignation of ministers, with no reference to individual ministers. Now in this type of case, i.e. the non-distributive case, the verb typically calls for a bare subject. Thus the insertion of *unos* would produce an anomalous result:

(21)   ?Dimitían unos ministros cada semana.

This makes the unlikely claim that each of several ministers resigned on a weekly basis, i.e. ?*Hay unos ministros que dimitian cada semana*.

What I want to suggest is that the examples that allegedly demonstrate a link between ergativity and bare subjects are always instances of a verb with a non-distributive subject and it is this circumstance that explains why the subject is bare:

(22) Salen alumnos de la escuela. (Schroten 2002:79)[6]
(23) Entran alumnos en la escuela. (Schroten 2002:79)
(24) Pasan vacas. (Garrido 1996:303)
(25) Caen gotas. (Garrido 1996:303)
(26) Crecen flores. (Torrego 1989:254)

Before any comment is made on these sentences, it should be noted that, in the Iberian Peninsula at least, (22) and (23) are likely to be regarded as being slightly anomalous as they stand. However, perfectly acceptable versions can be constructed using time adverbials and/or different tenses:

(27) Salen alumnos continuamente de la escuela.
(28) Estuvieron entrando alumnos en la escuela durante media hora.

On the other hand, sentences (24), (25) and (26) are perfectly normal if suitably contextualized, e.g. [*Por aquí*] *Pasan vacas*; [*Hay que cambiar el grifo,*] *Caen gotas*; *Crecen flores* [*en los campos recién labrados*]—this last piece of contextualization is inspired by an example from Green (1976:22).

Even if we include the slightly problematic examples (22) and (23), it seems that all of the sentences above illustrate the same basic pattern as the *dimitian ministros* case (example (20)), i.e. a verb with a plural but non-distributive subject is used to describe a recurring event. For instance, (27) does not entail that *sale continuamente de la escuela* is true of individual pupils and (25), to take another example, does not entail that iterative *cae* is true of individual drops. Even sentences (22) and (23), if we ignore their problematic status, can be explained in this way. In both cases, the verb can only be iterative and so neither sentence entails that the corresponding singular predicate, i.e. *sale de la escuela* and *entra en la escuela* (with *salir* and *entrar* understood as indicating recurrence), is true of individual pupils.

A slightly different case is presented by example (29) below, from Zagona (2002:153):

(29) Faltan tomates.

In the use illustrated above, *faltar* is a state term and so the concept of recurrence is not relevant. However, as in the previous examples with bare subjects, it is not the case that the subject noun designates a group of individuals

---

[6] Schroten himself is sceptical about the link between ergativity and bare subjects.

to whom the predicate applies separately. In other words, it is not being said that each of several tomatoes is missing (compare *Faltan unos niños*, which does say that each of several boys is missing), merely that there are no tomatoes. Therefore the subject in (29) is non-distributive and so the example as a whole, despite the state term *faltar*, can be thought of as instantiating the same general schema as examples (22) to (28), i.e. verb plus non-distributive subject.

Thus what emerges from the discussion in this section is that bare subjects are called for whenever the presence of the appropriate form of the indefinite article would imply a distributive reference that is not intended. This principle, incidentally, is actually enshrined in the grammar of mass nouns, which by definition refer cumulatively rather than distributively and which never appear with the indefinite article (unless they are modified by an adjective or other item): [*Por aquí*] *pasa gente, Sale agua* [*de la cisterna*]. Note also that the link between bare subjects and non-distributive reference is not undermined by the apparent interchangeability, in certain instances, of a bare plural subject and its counterpart introduced by *unos/unas*, as in *Han pasado camiones* (Torrego 1989:254) and *Han pasado unos camiones*. In such cases, the sentence with the bare subject may imply the corresponding sentence with the determined subject (thus *Han pasado camiones* implies *Han pasado unos camiones*), but it does not have exactly the same semantic content. This can be seen if we extract from each sentence the untensed "radical" (a term borrowed from Herweg 1991:369), namely *pasar camiones* and *pasar unos camiones*, and inflect it for different tenses, particularly for tenses implying recurrence, which as we have seen are likely to be sensitive to the distributive versus non-distributive distinction. For example, *Pasaban/Pasan camiones* (i.e. "Lorries [habitually] passed/pass through") would be unproblematic, but ?*Pasaban/Pasan unos camiones* (again with an intended habitual meaning) would be anomalous.

Finally, it is important to observe that there is an indirect connection between bare subjects and achievement verbs. *Dimitir* in my own example (20) is an achievement term (resignation itself occupies no time, although the attendant actions obviously do), as are verbs such as *salir* and *entrar*, together with, in certain applications at least, *caer* and *pasar*. In fact, out of Vendler's four aspectual classes, it is the achievement terms that are most likely to have bare subjects. For, given their punctual nature, achievement terms will almost always be iterative when used with a plural subject in the imperfect or present tense or in the progressive aspect, and in many cases the subject will be non-distributive: *Morían soldados como moscas, Están entrando hormigas en la tienda* etc. Thus achievement terms are linked, for separate reasons, not just to "be"-verb selection (as was highlighted in section 4) but also to bare subjects. What I want to suggest is that this dual coincidence has been mistaken for evidence that "be"-

verb selection and bare subjects are different diagnostics for a single phenomenon, viz. ergativity.

6. CONCLUSION

In this paper I have examined whether the theory linking "be"-verb selection and ergativity, which is widely applied to modern Italian and French, can be supported by a representative sample of data from Old Spanish. The principal finding in this respect was that *ser*-selection in Old Spanish is better accounted for in terms of aspectual class, as there is a natural relationship between the resultative meaning expressed by *ser* + PP and the implication of completion that is associated with accomplishments and, above all, achievements. A corresponding linkage in modern French and Italian is perhaps obscured because the original resultative meaning of the perfect has become less prominent within the range of meanings associated with that tense (particularly in French).

I also examined the alleged link between ergative verbs and bare subjects in Spanish and again found that ergativity is incidental to the phenomenon in question. For the basic principle turns out to be as follows: subjects in Spanish are bare when they do not have distributive reference. This circumstance arises commonly when the main verb is an achievement term, as a consequence of the punctual meaning of such verbs. Thus many of the verbs that are likely to select a bare subject in modern Spanish also belong to the group of verbs that at previous phases in the language's history selected *ser* as an embryonic perfect auxiliary, but this coincidence is not in principle dependent on the verbs in question being ergative. As far as Spanish goes, then, any relationship between these alleged diagnostics for ergativity is essentially fortuitous.

References

Benzing, Joseph. 1931. "Zur Geschichte von *ser* als Hilfszweitwort bei den intransitiven Verben im Spanischen." *Zeitschrift für Romanische Philologie* 51, 385-460.

Burzio, Luigi. 1986. *Italian syntax*. Dordrecht: Reidel.

Cacho Blecua, Juan Manuel and Lacarra, María Jesús, eds. 1984. *Calila e Dimna*. Madrid: Clásicos Castalia.

Dutton, Brian, ed. 1971. Gonzalo de Berceo: *Los milagros de Nuestra Señora*. London: Tamesis.

—— 1967. Gonzalo de Berceo: *La vida de San Millan de Cogolla*. London: Tamesis.

Garrido, Joaquín. 1996. "Sintagmas nominales escuetos." *El sustantivo sin determinación. La ausencia de determinante en la lengua española*, ed. by I. Bosque, 269-338. Madrid: Visor.

Gayangos, Pascual de, ed. 1951. *La Gran Conquista de Ultramar*. Biblioteca de Autores

Españoles. Madrid: Atlas.
Green, John. 1976. "How free is word order in Spanish?" *Romance syntax:synchronic and diachronic perspectives*, ed. by M. B. Harris, 7-32. Salford: University of Salford Press.
Gybbon-Monypenny, G.B., ed. 1988. Arcipreste de Hita: *Libro de buen amor*. Madrid: Clásicos Castalia.
Herweg, Michael. 1991. "A Critical Examination of Two Classical Approaches to Aspect." *Journal of Semantics* 8:4, 363-402.
Labarta de Chaves, Teresa, ed. 1972. Gonzalo de Berceo: *Vida de Santo Domingo de Silos*. Madrid: Clásicos Castalia.
Lapesa, Rafael. 2000. *Estudios de morfosintaxis histórica del español*. Madrid: Gredos.
Lyons, John. 1968. *Introduction to Theoretical Linguistics*. Cambridge: Cambridge University Press.
Perlmutter, David M. 1978. "Impersonal passives and the unaccusative hypothesis." *Proceedings of the Fourth Annual Meeting of the Berkeley Linguistics Society*, 157-89. Berkeley, California.
Posner, Rebecca. 1996. *The Romance Languages*. Cambridge: Cambridge University.
Pountain, Christopher J. , 1985. "Copulas, Verbs of Possession and Auxiliaries in Old Spanish: The Evidence for Structurally Interdependent Changes." *Bulletin of Hispanic Studies* 62, 337-55.
Russinovich Solé, Yolanda. 1990. "Valores aspectuales en el español." *Hispanic Linguistics* 4:1, 57-86.
Schroten, Jan, 2002. "Sobre la ausencia de determinante y su interpretación." *La oración y sus constituyentes: Estudios de sintaxis generativa (Foro Hispánico 21)*, ed. by R. Bok-Bennema, 71-86. Amsterdam: Rodopi.
Smith, Colin, ed. 1972. *Poema de mio Cid*. Oxford: Oxford University Press.
Torrego, Esther. 1989. "Unergative-unaccusative alternations in Spanish." *Functional Heads and Clause Structure (MIT Working Papers in Linguistics Volume 10)*, ed. by I. Laka and A. Mahajan, 254-72. Cambridge, MA.
Vendler, Zeno. 1967. *Linguistics in Philosophy*. Ithaca: Cornell University Press.
Vincent, Nigel. 1982. "The development of the auxiliaries HABERE and ESSE in Romance." *Studies in the Romance Verb*, ed. by N. Vincent and M. Harris, 71-96. London: Croom Helm.
Willis, Raymond S., ed. 1934. *El libro de Alexandre*. Princeton: Princeton University Press.
Zagona, Karen. 2002. *The Syntax of Spanish*. Cambridge: Cambridge University Press.

21
La lengua, patria común: Política lingüística, política exterior y el post-nacionalismo hispánico
JOSÉ DEL VALLE

LA LENGUA ESPAÑOLA ES muchas cosas. Para algunos ni español es; es castellano. Y lo es, en cada caso, por muy distintas razones. Se habla esta lengua en lugares lejanos y de maneras diferentes. Vive en comunidades muy dispares y en todas ellas asume valores materiales y simbólicos peculiares. Coexiste con otras en mundos plurilingües que, con frecuencia, los hablantes saben negociar con mucha más serenidad, con mucha menos estridencia que los guardianes del lenguaje y la cultura. A lo largo de su historia, de la historia lingüística de las comunidades hispánicas, han surgido múltiples discursos sobre la lengua y el habla cuyo análisis casi siempre (y me inclino a pensar que el "casi" sobra) nos revela su imbricación en fenómenos que pertenecen a otros órdenes: económico, político ... Los últimos treinta años no han sido excepcionales; es probable incluso que de haberlo sido su desvío de la tradición haya ocurrido por exceso y no por defecto. Efectivamente, en las últimas décadas parece haberse sentido con especial intensidad la necesidad de intervenir en la protección y promoción de lenguas (del español, del gallego, del quechua), y así han proliferado políticas destinadas al ordenamiento de la vida lingüística, y con ellas, ideologías (algunas de las cuales se remontan a tiempos bien lejanos en la historia de la humanidad) al servicio de su triunfo en el complejo mercado de la opinión pública.

En este ensayo me propongo discutir precisamente algunos de los rasgos de las políticas e ideologías lingüísticas que, en nombre del español, han saltado a la palestra, dando nueva vida, en unos casos, a visiones de antaño sobre el papel de esta lengua en España y en el resto del mundo, y produciendo, en otros, nuevas visiones propias de las necesidades y conflictos contemporáneos de las sociedades en las que el español cumple una función comunicativa, económica y política importante. Empezaremos por la misma España para, poco a poco, irnos acercando a los campos discursivos internacionales que la globalización ha engendrado.

1978: LA ARTICULACIÓN DE ESPAÑA Y LA POLÍTICA LINGÜÍSTICA DOMÉSTICA

La aprobación de la Constitución Española de 1978 marcó un hito en la historia reciente del país. De entre los múltiples objetivos que se planteaban los padres de la carta magna, adquiría relevancia especial el intento de resolver el histórico contencioso sobre la problemática definición de España como estado-nación y, consecuentemente, de adoptar un modelo apropiado para la organización administrativa del Estado. Así, y como respuesta a estos desafíos, nacía, en 1978, el Estado de las Autonomías, un marco legal y político que aspiraba a acomodar, por un lado, las reivindicaciones sobre la unidad cultural y política de España, y por otro, las demandas de los nacionalismos catalán, gallego y vasco.[1]

Por supuesto, tan ambicioso y complicado proyecto de modernización y construcción nacional habría de tener que enfrentarse a también complejos problemas lingüísticos: desde el establecimiento del español o castellano[2] como "la" lengua de España hasta el reconocimiento oficial de su carácter plurilingüe. A pesar de la instauración de la Constitución (que en su artículo 3 trata de responder a los retos lingüísticos),[3] de la puesta en vigor de los Estatutos de Autonomía y de la aprobación de las respectivas Leyes de Normalización Lingüística en las Comunidades que las consideraron necesarias, aquellas disputas de los años setenta y ochenta sobre quién ha de hablar qué, cuándo, dónde y por qué aún persisten: todavía se oyen de vez en cuando expresiones de

---

[1] La bibliografía sobre estos temas es extensísima. En lugar de intentar en vano crear una lista "representativa" me limitaré a dar tres referencias que están entre mis lecturas más recientes y que por ello habrán influido más (en la dirección que sea) mi actual percepción de estos asuntos. En relación con la elaboración de la Constitución, de Esteban (1987). Sobre el nacionalismo español, especialmente en el siglo diecinueve, el estudio de Álvarez Junco (2001). Para una visión más contemporánea y polémica del nacionalismo vasco y del nacionalismo español actual, el libro de Edurne Uriarte (2003).

[2] Para saber más (aunque no necesariamente mejor) sobre el embrollo de la nomenclatura, véase el libro de Gregorio Salvador (1987) o la revisión que, en tono muy distinto, hace Mar-Molinero (2000:35-37).

[3] "1. El castellano es la lengua española oficial del Estado. Todos los españoles tienen el deber de conocerla y el derecho a usarla. 2. Las demás lenguas españolas serán también oficiales en las respectivas Comunidades Autónomas de acuerdo con sus Estatutos. 3. La riqueza de las distintas modalidades lingüísticas de España es un patrimonio cultural que será objeto de especial respeto y protección."

alarma ante el hecho de que la sustitución del catalán, gallego o vasco por el español sigue su curso; aún surgen a veces acusaciones de discriminación contra hablantes de una u otra lengua; saltan todavía a las noticias discusiones sobre el tiempo que en las escuelas se dedica o se ha de dedicar a la enseñanza del castellano. Es incuestionable la actualidad y relevancia política de estos y otros temas aún en 2004 y de ahí que hayan recibido una atención especial de los investigadores de la vida social del lenguaje.[4]

LA PLANIFICACIÓN LINGÜÍSTICA Y SU ESTUDIO
En efecto la mayoría de los estudios de política lingüística desarrollados en España y sobre España se han centrado en las múltiples dimensiones de los llamados procesos de normativización y normalización en las comunidades con "lengua propia." Si asumimos la perspectiva tradicionalmente adoptada por la sociología del lenguaje en relación con el estudio de la vida lingüística de una comunidad, el volumen y naturaleza de la atención prestada a estos procesos no nos sorprende, pues son ellos precisamente los que constituyen el principal objeto de observación y análisis para los estudios de política lingüística. Partamos de la definición canónica de planificación que nos ofrecen Robert B. Kaplan y Richard B. Baldauf en su visión panorámica del campo: "Language planning is a body of ideas, laws and regulations (language policy), change rules, beliefs, and practices intended to achieve a planned change (or to stop change from happening) in the language use in one or more communities. To put it differently, language planning involves *deliberate*, although not always overt, *future oriented* change in systems of language code and/or speaking in a societal context" (1997:3).

Nótese la diferencia entre la definición de planificación lingüística que proponen Kaplan y Baldauf y mis propias palabras en las líneas que sirven de prefacio a la misma. Si los autores de *Language Planning* hablan de "ideas, reglas y normas," yo me refiero a su estudio crítico. Conviene subrayar la distinción, pues al hablar de planificación lingüística y de estudios de política lingüística estamos ante actividades profesionales e intelectuales claramente diferenciadas que, si bien son prácticas compatibles ligadas por una relación simbiótica, responden a motivaciones dispares y derivan su legitimidad de fuentes distintas. La planificación o política lingüística (como se observa en la definición arriba reproducida) es un campo eminentemente práctico, una suerte de ingeniería social con sus ramas teóricas y aplicadas. Debido a la aparente

---

[4] Entre las visiones panorámicas se encuentran Bossong y Báez de Aguilar González (2000), Etxebarria (2002), Mar-Molinero (2000), Siguan (1992), Söhrman (1993), Turell (2001).

voluntad de esta disciplina de proyectar una imagen eminentemente técnica—con lo que ello conlleva de presunción de objetividad y neutralidad ideológica—se hace necesario su estudio crítico, es decir, una reflexión metadisciplinaria que permita entender mejor los planteamientos de los planificadores situándolos en el contexto político de su emergencia y analizando las prácticas discursivas que producen.[5]

Pues bien, con esta distinción en mente, volvamos a las políticas lingüísticas catalana, gallega y vasca. En los años setenta, los planificadores partían de un escenario en el cual, sostenían ellos, la lengua de la Comunidad estaba siendo sustituida por el español. Su objetivo iba a ser frenar este proceso e incluso invertirlo, es decir, como señalan Kaplan y Baldauf, condicionar las prácticas lingüísticas de modo tal que aumentara el uso de la lengua que los textos legales habían etiquetado como "propia." Los procesos que se pusieron en marcha para llevar a cabo tal transformación se proponían, por un lado, fijar la norma lingüística y que ésta fuera aceptada por la población (sería la llamada "normativización"), y por otro, garantizar su presencia en todas las esferas de la vida pública y privada de la comunidad (la llamada "normalización").[6] Estos dos

---

[5] No establecer esta distinción con claridad puede llevar a que se produzcan preocupantes equívocos y a que se caiga en un error metonímico que confunda "sociolingüística" con "planificación lingüística." A los planificadores puede venirles de perlas tal confusión al quedar automáticamente impregnados del halo de prestigio que les conferiría verse inmersos en una práctica académica reconocida como es la sociolingüística. Esta confusión podría a su vez llevar a que los adversarios de políticas lingüísticas concretas descalifiquen sin más la disciplina sociolingüística. Algo de esto (y mucho más) hay en las siguientes palabras de Gregorio Salvador, procedentes de su libro *Política lingüística y sentido común*: "Ahora bien, la mayor parte de los verdaderos lectores de ese libro [*Lengua española y lenguas de España*], acostumbrados al camelo sociolingüístico, a las estadísticas amañadas, a las afirmaciones inconsistentes, al falseamiento de la historia y al escamoteo de lo real en el cotidiano discurso ideológico-idiomático que se practicaba y se practica, lo que vieron en él fue una ventana abierta a la realidad, que les permitía afirmarse en sus personales experiencias y encontrarse en sus propias opiniones" (Salvador 1992:11).

[6] Aunque tenga sólo una relevancia tangencial para el propósito de este ensayo, merece la pena apuntar algunas de las trampas que pueda encerrar el concepto de normalización. ¿Es la normalidad una noción estadística o ética? ¿Qué es la normalidad en materia lingüística? ¿En qué sentido serían "anormales," por ejemplo, las comunidades criollas? ¿Es verdaderamente anormal, en el sentido estadístico, el carácter cambiante de la personalidad lingüística de un grupo humano? ¿En qué sentido es anormal la coexistencia en un territorio de distintas lenguas o normas de conducta lingüística distribuidas desigualmente por los dominios de uso? Me conformaré, por ahora, con plantear estas preguntas retóricas; pero en relación con este asunto aún hay mucha tela

procesos se corresponden con las dos grandes categorías en que se suele organizar la planificación lingüística: planificación del *corpus* y planificación del *estatus*.[7] La primera de ellas incluye a su vez dos procesos: la *codificación*—establecimiento de un sistema de escritura, una gramática y un léxico—y la *elaboración*—creación de mecanismos que mantengan la lengua siempre a punto, siempre al día, velando, por ejemplo, por su modernización léxica. La planificación del estatus se compone a su vez de dos proyectos: la *selección* de la variedad o variedades que han de servir como base para la norma y la *implementación* de la misma, es decir, el diseño y puesta en práctica de medidas que lleven a su uso generalizado en los contextos deseados. Volveré enseguida sobre la implementación. Pero subrayemos de nuevo que los programas de planificación lingüística catalanes, gallegos y vascos han ocupado un espacio prominente en la política de las respectivas Comunidades, y asimismo han sido y son observados de cerca, analizados críticamente y frecuentemente debatidos tanto en foros científicos y universitarios como en espacios de mayor impacto en la formación de la opinión pública tales como la prensa.

NUEVAS POLÍTICAS LINGÜÍSTICAS PARA UNA ESPAÑA GLOBALIZADA
Contrariamente, ha recibido poca atención crítica la también intensa, pero quizás menos estridente, política lingüística orientada hacia la planificación del corpus y estatus del español. Por lo que a la planificación del corpus se refiere, el trabajo de las agencias lingüísticas pertinentes (principalmente la Real Academia Española, pero sin olvidar la importante intervención de la prensa escrita por medio de sus libros de estilo y de los corsarios de la estandarización con sus manuales de urbanidad y buena conducta lingüística[8]) ha sido intenso, y desde principios de los noventa han proliferado proyectos de codificación y elaboración de entre los cuales se destacan el *Diccionario*, la *Gramática* y la *Ortografía*

---

que cortar.

[7] Esta es una clasificación convencional propuesta ya por el pionero de la disciplina Einar Haugen (1972). Para una visión más contemporánea del asunto véase de nuevo a Kaplan y Baldauf (1997:28-58).

[8] Se podría hablar aquí de Álex Grijelmo y sus apasionadas defensas del idioma español (1998). Sin embargo, el que verdaderamente merece ser mencionado es Fernando Lázaro Carreter, quien, con sus dardos en la palabra ha jugado un papel central en la difusión de un tipo de cultura lingüística que fomenta esa paranoia del mal hablar que tan bien sirve a los guardianes de la corrección lingüística. Cuando repaso estas líneas muere Lázaro. Me doy cuenta de que en mi simple ironía, en el espíritu irreverente que la inspira, hay un mucho de admiración. Sirva mi humilde dardo como saludo y modestísimo homenaje al erudito filólogo, sabio lingüista, astuto político del lenguaje y celoso defensor de una lengua, que como él sabía mejor que nadie, se defiende muy bien sola.

académicas. Si los esfuerzos de planificación de corpus han sido abundantes, no lo ha sido el análisis de la naturaleza y significado de los mismos; como tampoco lo ha sido el estudio de las estrategias de planificación del estatus del español, especialmente el interés manifiesto en el mismo período por dotar al idioma de una determinada imagen pública—a la que enseguida me referiré—y por promocionar su estatus más allá de las fronteras de la propia España. En términos concretos estas estrategias se canalizaron a través de la creación del Instituto Cervantes en 1991, con el objeto de promover el español internacionalmente, y de la renovación y modernización de la Academia, que, distanciándose del viejo lema "limpia, fija y da esplendor," asumía ahora como objetivo prioritario el de salvaguardar la unidad de un idioma que se habla en tantos y tan distantes países.[9]

Curiosamente, el significado de esta reorientación ha despertado escaso interés entre los investigadores, y no digamos entre la población general, que parece incluso inconsciente de la existencia de una política lingüística española fuera del ámbito que les corresponde a los gobiernos de las Comunidades Autónomas con lengua propia. Un aspecto estratégicamente central de la política lingüística a la que me voy a referir en este ensayo es precisamente su invisibilidad. No pretendo sugerir, por supuesto, que la implementación de la misma tenga lugar a espaldas de la población. Muy al contrario, gran número de actos públicos asociados con la puesta en práctica de esta política se caracterizan precisamente por su espectacularidad y por su amplia proyección mediática. No son, por lo tanto, los conceptos y prácticas culturales y lingüísticas en sí lo que es objeto de una suerte de ocultamiento, sino el carácter político y económico de las mismas, es decir, su estrecha conexión, tanto en lo que se refiere a su formulación como a sus consecuencias, con intereses y proyectos que nacen en ámbitos más "prosaicos" de la vida nacional.[10] Me refería, al abrir esta sección, a la menor "estridencia" de la planificación del corpus y el estatus del español, es decir, a la escasa aparición de crispadas disputas sobre el asunto en foros de

---

[9] Además de la Academia y del Cervantes, entre los agentes de la política lingüística exterior española se podrían incluir instituciones tales como el Instituto de Comercio Exterior (ICEX), la Sociedad Española para la Acción Cultural Exterior (SEACEX) o la Fundación Siglo de la Junta de Castilla y León, así como grupos mediáticos y corporaciones (Telefónica, por ejemplo) que, al menos en parte, financian y apoyan la implementación de la política en cuestión.

[10] Al hablar aquí de ocultamiento pienso en el concepto de *erasure* propuesto por Judith T. Irvine y Susan Gal: "[T]he process in which ideology, in simplifying the sociolinguistic field, renders some persons or activities (or sociolinguistic phenomena) invisible. Facts that are inconsistent with the ideological scheme either go unnoticed or get explained away" (2000:38).

amplia difusión tales como la prensa. Esto pudiera ser precisamente producto del éxito con que se ha llevado a cabo el ocultamiento de la dimensión política e ideológica de la promoción de la lengua española desde las instituciones ya mencionadas. El destape de esta dimensión es justamente uno de los objetivos que los estudios de política lingüística deben plantearse. Porque si es cierto que los proyectos de planificación catalanes, gallegos y vascos son parte de la acción de los gobiernos autonómicos y han de ser entendidos y evaluados en el contexto de la dinámica política de cada Comunidad, también lo es que al profundizar en el análisis de la política lingüística de España en relación con el español nos encontramos con instituciones y acciones que no se circunscriben al terreno de lo asépticamente cultural sino que se inscriben en el más amplio contexto de las relaciones y transacciones que caracterizan el ejercicio del poder político y económico.

El mencionado giro en el interés y en la acción lingüística y cultural del ámbito de lo doméstico al de los asuntos exteriores está conectado con otro de los importantes desafíos a los que hubieron de enfrentarse los agentes de la reforma política de los años setenta una vez superada la transición legal e institucional. El telón de fondo frente al cual se deben interpretar las nuevas estrategias de planificación es la creciente participación española en los principales foros de la política internacional y en la pugna por los tesoros del mercado económico global. A principios de los ochenta, el Partido Socialista se enfrentó al reto de conducir el país hacia las autopistas de la modernidad. A lo largo de aquella década, España pasó a formar parte de la OTAN y la Unión Europea, logros que acercaron al país a los centros de decisión del mundo occidental. En 1992, los Juegos Olímpicos de Barcelona y la Exposición Universal de Sevilla sirvieron como plataformas de exhibición de la preparación y capacidad organizativa de España. También en los noventa, se asistió al despegue de las multinacionales españolas, muchas de las cuales aterrizaron en Latinoamérica. Estos y otros procesos parecían probar de una vez por todas la superación de la excepcionalidad de España y su ascenso al rango de oficial en los ejércitos de la globalización.

Cambios tan radicales en el sistema político, vida cultural, actividad económica y prestigio internacional del país no podían tener lugar sin dejar su impronta en la vida lingüística: a medida que el Estado de las Autonomías pugnaba por asentarse en un incómodo espacio nacional, a medida que España se modernizaba y a medida que gobierno y empresas jugaban o anhelaban jugar un papel mayor en la vida internacional, desde las instancias del poder se forjaban nuevas ideologías lingüísticas. Por un lado, los nacionalismos catalán, gallego y vasco, en el espacio de poder que les correspondía, pretendían naturalizar la condición nacional de sus comunidades y legitimar así su reivindicación de autogobierno a través de la lengua: de su instalación en la administración, en el sistema educativo, en los medios de comunicación y en todos los espacios de la vida pública; de su consolidación como símbolo nacional; y sobre todo, de la difusión de prácticas y creencias lingüísticas que distinguieran la verdadera y legítima ciudadanía (catalana, gallega o vasca, según el caso) tal como estos movimientos políticos la concebían. Asimismo, desde el gobierno de Madrid y desde las instituciones investidas de poder lingüístico se iba sintiendo la necesidad de proyectar una imagen del español—de su relación con la propia España, con los países hispánicos y con el resto del mundo—que complementara los esfuerzos de construcción nacional y los planes de modernización, crecimiento económico y ampliación de la presencia política y económica del país en el mercado global.

EL ESTUDIO DE LAS IDEOLOGÍAS LINGÜÍSTICAS

Acabo de utilizar el concepto de "ideologías lingüísticas" para referirme a ciertos aspectos de las políticas diseñadas e implementadas tanto en las Comunidades Autónomas en relación con la lengua propia como en España en relación con el español. Dada su centralidad en el análisis que aquí propongo, detengámonos brevemente en este concepto y en las disciplinas que se han ocupado de su estudio.[11] La emergencia, desarrollo y reconocimiento de un campo del saber destinado al estudio de las ideologías lingüísticas es, al menos en parte, consecuencia de la redefinición del lenguaje como objeto de reflexión científica e intelectual que va cristalizando tras el giro social de la lingüística[12] y el giro lingüístico de las ciencias sociales y de la filosofía.[13] La nueva prominencia de estas aproximaciones en círculos de actividad intelectual dio lugar a que se vieran más claras las funciones no-referenciales del mismo y a que se reconociera la centralidad de las actitudes y creencias lingüísticas de los hablantes, ya fueran estas explícitas o implícitas.[14] El estudio de las ideologías lingüísticas se distanciaba, por lo tanto, de las aproximaciones formalistas y radicalmente despolitizadas al lenguaje que había producido el paradigma

---

[11] Las distintas manifestaciones de los estudios de ideologías lingüísticas están representadas en los siguientes libros: Joseph y Taylor (1990); Kroskrity (2000); Schieffelin, Woolard y Kroskrity (1998).

[12] Representado por la obra de figuras tales como Basil Bernstein, John Gumperz, Dell Hymes y William Labov.

[13] Aquí se podría mencionar a Pierre Bourdieu, Jacques Derrida o Michel Foucault.

[14] Sigo aquí, en términos generales y tomándome algunas libertades, a Paul V. Kroskrity (2000).

neogramático/saussureano (del cual es máximo exponente en la actualidad el generativismo de corte chomskyano).[15] Los protagonistas del desarrollo de esta nueva área de conocimiento se han mostrado más bien reacios a delimitarla, exhibiendo así la irritante resistencia postmoderna a la definición; una resistencia que si bien, y muy acertadamente, reconoce el resbaladizo carácter de los procesos de significación, también permite al investigador eludir los desafíos de la síntesis y las responsabilidades de la explicación. Aun así, a partir de los textos que van marcando la trayectoria del campo se puede deducir que las ideologías lingüísticas son entendidas como sistemas de ideas que integran nociones generales del lenguaje, el habla o la comunicación con visiones y acciones concretas que afectan la identidad lingüística de una determinada comunidad. En su análisis, el funcionamiento de estos sistemas de ideas se analiza siempre en el contexto de las estructuras sociales, relaciones de poder y actividades políticas y económicas relevantes para el colectivo humano estudiado. Paul V. Kroskrity ha señalado cuatro rasgos que pueden servirnos para completar la caracterización de este campo: "language ideologies represent the perception of language and discourse that is constructed in the interest of a specific social or cultural group" (8); "language ideologies are profitably conceived as multiple because of the multiplicity of meaningful social divisions (class, gender, clan, elites, generations, and so on) within sociocultural groups that have the potential to produce divergent perspectives expressed as indices of group membership" (12); "members may display different degrees of awareness of local language ideologies" (18); "members' language ideologies mediate between social structures and forms of talk" (21).

Arriba, al referirme a la planificación de corpus y de estatus prometí volver a los procesos de implementación, y este punto, tras la introducción del concepto de ideologías lingüísticas, es el oportuno. Kaplan y Baldauf ofrecen la siguiente definición de este proceso: "The implementation of a language plan focuses on the adoption and spread of the language form that has been selected and codified. This is often done through the educational system and through other laws and regulations which encourage and/or require the use of the standard and

---

[15] La ruptura con este paradigma da lugar también, por ejemplo, a la reconfiguración de la lingüística histórica por medio de la inclusión de los hallazgos de la sociolingüística variacionista y de la sociología del lenguaje. En este cambio de orientación intervienen de una manera fundamental Roger Wright, con su propuesta sociofilológica (1989, 2000), y Ralph Penny, con su texto, clásico al nacer, *Variation and Change in Spanish* (2000). Piénsese simplemente en los muy distintos ecos que produce el título de esta historia del español de Penny comparada con su primera y más convencional *A History of the Spanish Language* (1991).

perhaps discourage the use of other languages or dialects" (36). Como se desprende de esta definición, la implementación consiste en la proyección del plan lingüístico diseñado sobre la comunidad afectada, es decir, se refiere a las múltiples estrategias que los agentes de la política lingüística deben diseñar para persuadir a la población de la bondad y conveniencia del plan. Una vez seleccionada la lengua o dialecto que ha de servir como base para el desarrollo de la norma, una vez completada la codificación y una vez dispuestos los mecanismos de elaboración, es imprescindible conseguir que los hablantes acepten la visión de la comunidad lingüística que se les propone y la legitimidad de las instituciones a las cuales se encomienda formular la política lingüística.[16] Cierto es que, como señalan Kaplan y Baldauf, el sistema educativo suele jugar un papel protagónico como instrumento al servicio de la implementación. Ahora bien, no hay que olvidar la relevancia de otros campos discursivos, así como de las instituciones que los producen, en la difusión de ideas que, una vez arraigadas en la opinión pública y en el llamado sentido común, faciliten la puesta en práctica de proyectos políticos. Esta fase de implementación, que podríamos también llamar de persuasión, en la que se pretende condicionar las ideas y prácticas lingüísticas de los hablantes, es obviamente trascendental y el concepto de ideologías lingüísticas nos ofrece un valioso soporte teórico para su análisis.

La complejidad lingüística de España, derivada tanto de su plurilingüismo como de la enrevesada (y con frecuencia envenenada) negociación política de éste, ha dado lugar a la emergencia de múltiples ideologías lingüísticas y a la utilización de numerosas estrategias para la difusión social de cada una de ellas. Ya se ha hecho referencia, si bien de pasada, a las ideologías que se han desarrollado tanto en las comunidades autónomas con lengua propia[17] como en España en relación con el español. En torno a estas últimas girará el resto del ensayo.

Como ya queda dicho, desde las agencias a cargo de la política lingüística española se ha ido mucho más allá de la simple elaboración de la norma culta del español. La preservación de la unidad del idioma, es decir, la garantía de la lealtad de los hispanohablantes a la norma culta y a sus guardianes, y la promoción del español internacionalmente, es decir, el estímulo y explotación

---

[16] Hay que puntualizar que la planificación lingüística puede por supuesto promover la normativización y uso de dos o incluso más lenguas. De hecho es frecuente que una política lingüística intervenga para diseñar un marco legal que gestione la coexistencia de varias lenguas.

[17] Para mi análisis de la naturaleza de los conflictos entre ideologías lingüísticas aparentemente contrapuestas en Galicia véase mi artículo, del Valle (1999).

de un interés por la lengua española en el mundo, han sido declarados objetivos prioritarios por la Academia y el Cervantes respectivamente. Se ha desarrollado una visión del español y de su relación con España, con la comunidad hispánica y con el mundo; y se han puesto en marcha medidas para alcanzar su aceptación y extensión. Se ha producido, en suma, un sistema de ideas formado por nociones lingüísticas y visiones de la identidad colectiva (española o hispánica) cuyo funcionamiento ha de ser entendido en el contexto del desarrollo político y económico de la España contemporánea.

LA NUEVA IMAGEN DEL ESPAÑOL:
CONCORDIA, INTERNACIONALISMO Y RENTABILIDAD
Como ya he señalado en trabajos anteriores realizados en colaboración con Luis Gabriel-Stheeman (del Valle y Gabriel-Stheeman 2002),[18] al analizar la imagen del español desarrollada por las mencionadas instituciones, nos encontramos, en primer lugar, con que aparece insistentemente caracterizado como lengua de encuentro, como instrumento de comunicación que posibilita un diálogo y una convivencia armónica propios, aparentemente, de una patria común. Este principio lo formulaba así, de forma concisa pero extraordinariamente elocuente, Víctor García de la Concha, Profesor de la Universidad de Salamanca y actual Director de la Academia: "Es realmente emocionante cómo la lengua está sirviendo de lugar de encuentro y no sólo como canal de comunicación. La lengua nos hace patria común en una concordia superior" (citado en *EL PAÍS*, 9 de julio de 2000). La idea del español como lugar de encuentro está directamente relacionada con la voluntad de promover la cooperación pan-hispánica. No en vano el Director de la Española y muchos otros agentes de las políticas lingüísticas con ella asociadas insisten en señalar que el mayor peso del español se encuentra en América, y que la Academia, siguiendo las recomendaciones del Rey de España, no da un paso sin consultar con las otras Academias de la Lengua Española. El "encuentro" hizo su más sonada aparición en un muy controvertido discurso pronunciado por Juan Carlos I: "Nunca fue la nuestra lengua de imposición, sino de encuentro; a nadie se le obligó nunca a hablar en castellano: fueron los pueblos más diversos quienes hicieron suyo por voluntad

---

[18] Es aquí donde quiero expresar mi agradecimiento y reconocimiento a Luis Gabriel-Stheeman, amigo y colaborador desde hace ya varios años. El estudio de la política lingüística española lo hemos hecho juntos, recabando datos y armando argumentos en largas conversaciones a distancia. Esta sección ("La nueva imagen...") procede fundamentalmente de los capítulos 9 y 10 de la edición española de nuestro libro publicado bajo el título *La batalla del idioma: la intelectualidad hispánica ante la lengua*.

libérrima, el idioma de Cervantes" (Juan Carlos I, ceremonia de entrega del Premio Cervantes, 23 de abril de 2001).[19] La segunda idea que perfila la imagen del español en la política lingüística a la que aquí me refiero afirma el carácter internacional del mismo. Esta proyección global del idioma se deriva no sólo de su presencia en los países que constituyen el mundo hispánico sino, y muy especialmente, de su capacidad de expansión. La prensa española ha insistido en esta propiedad y los siguientes titulares resultan reveladores de la euforia que acompaña la promoción internacional de la lengua: "Los expertos llaman a los hispanohablantes a conquistar el ciberespacio" (*EL PAÍS*, 11 de abril de 1997); "El español conquista Brasil" (*EL PAÍS*, 8 de mayo de 2000); "El Instituto Cervantes a la conquista de América" (*EL MUNDO*, 12 de octubre de 2000). A pesar del marcado tono militarista que las opciones léxicas de la prensa dan al asunto, hay que señalar que la expansión del idioma se suele justificar más bien invocando los valores universales que se le atribuyen, tanto político-culturales, como hemos visto en el párrafo anterior, como económicos, como veremos en el que sigue.

Las virtudes conquistadoras de la lengua son buenas compañeras de la tercera y muy valiosa propiedad que se le asigna: su condición de recurso económico. En octubre de 2001, por ejemplo, la RAE y el Instituto Cervantes organizaron en Valladolid el II Congreso Internacional de la Lengua Española con el título "El español en la Sociedad de la Información." Patrocinado por Telefónica, Iberia y Caja Duero, el congreso fue dividido en cuatro secciones, una de las cuales recibió el título "El activo del español." La conferencia plenaria, pronunciada por el Sr. D. Enrique V. Iglesias, Presidente del Banco Interamericano de Desarrollo en Washington D.C., fue "El potencial económico del español."[20] Por su parte, el Instituto Cervantes a través de sus Anuarios ha mostrado igualmente enorme interés por analizar y enfatizar la relación entre la lengua española y la actividad económica. Algunos de los títulos incluidos en el Anuario 2001 resultan indicativos: "Econometría de la lengua española" (Martín Municio), "El libro y la imagen de marca de la lengua española" (Ávila Álvarez), "Una década de inversiones españolas en Iberoamérica (1990-2000)"

---

[19] Nótese la coincidencia en la aparición de la noción de lengua-encuentro en el lenguaje del Director de la RAE y en el discurso Real. Volveré más adelante brevemente sobre este episodio. El Discurso se puede encontrar en http: www.casareal.es/casareal/ home -Discursos y Mensajes: 23/4/01.

[20] La subsección titulada "La industria del español como lengua extranjera" incluyó comunicaciones tales como las siguientes: "El español como recurso económico: anatomía de un nuevo sector" de Óscar Berdugo, "El español como recurso económico en Francia (una aproximación desde el marketing)" de José María Davó Cabra. Se puede acceder a las ponencias a través de http://cvc.cervantes. es/ obref /congresos/valladolid/.

(Casilda Béjar), "El mercado de las lenguas: la demanda del español como lengua extranjera en Francia y Alemania" (Lamo de Espinosa y J. Noya).[21] Aunque no faltan en estos ensayos concesiones retóricas a la lengua como depósito de un legado histórico y cultural y a su condición de lazo unificador de la comunidad hispánica, su objetivo primario es la identificación y ordenamiento de los factores que inciden sobre el potencial productivo del español: el español como producto anhelado por extranjeros ansiosos de aprenderlo y con ello incrementar su capital cultural; el español como instrumento publicitario, como imagen de marca que hace un producto más apetecible; y el español como basamento de la identidad panhispánica que invita y legitima las inversiones e intervenciones españolas en las Américas.

Mención especial merece la discusión de la presencia del español en Estados Unidos. En líneas generales, el tratamiento del asunto que en estos textos encontramos parte de tres hechos: el creciente número y porcentaje de estudiantes de español a todos los niveles de enseñanza, el creciente número y porcentaje de hispanos que forman parte de la población del país norteamericano, y la moda de "lo latino." La aproximación que prima es cuantitativa, y la presentación de los datos suele estar arropada por comentarios como los siguientes (tomados de la mencionada ponencia plenaria de Valladolid a cargo de Enrique V. Iglesias "El potencial económico del español"): "La población hispana ha venido incrementando el promedio de ingresos individuales de su población económica activa"; "la población hispana de los Estados Unidos constituye la tercera entidad económica del mundo latino"; "el español tiene una importante y creciente impronta en la cultura, las comunicaciones y en el volumen del consumo de los Estados Unidos." Vemos pues que prima el interés por el hispano estadounidense como consumidor, en tanto que constituye un mercado en cuya configuración y explotación la lengua española desempeña un papel central. La misión de las agencias e instituciones que articulan y financian la política lingüística aquí discutida la dejaba clara Óscar Berdugo—Director de la Asociación Español Recurso Económico—en la comunicación por él presentada en Valladolid ("El español como recurso económico: anatomía de un sector"): "Si España se consigue colocar como referente de identidad o como proveedor de señas de identidad culturales con respecto a la comunidad hispanohablante de Estados Unidos, estaremos en una inmejorable situación para mejorar *nuestras* posiciones en aquel país" (énfasis mío). En otras palabras, España debe pugnar por convertirse en una fuente de identidad para los hispanos estadounidenses y así crear un vínculo comunitario, una lealtad al colectivo, que

---

[21] El Anuario se puede consultar en http://cvc.cervantes.es/obref/anuario/ anua rio_ 01/.

sólo puede ser beneficiosa para las compañías españolas que aspiran a acceder y a seducir al mercado hispano.

LA IDEOLOGÍA DEL NACIONALISMO LINGÜÍSTICO

Hemos repasado hasta ahora tres de las propiedades que, desde las instituciones investidas con poder lingüístico, se le atribuyen al español: concordia, internacionalismo y rentabilidad. Se trata de propiedades que se le asignan para que, operando conjuntamente, contribuyan a articular su significado y determinar su valor en varios frentes: España, la comunidad hispánica y los mercados lingüísticos internacionales. En lo que resta de ensayo, quiero sugerir la existencia de un cuarto elemento en la ideología que sirve de apoyo a la implementación de la política lingüística española: me refiero a la construcción de una imagen del español basada en el rechazo, explícito en muchos casos, de las premisas del nacionalismo lingüístico. La relevancia de este cuarto componente se pone de manifiesto al analizar su presencia tanto en los terrenos político y económico como en los ámbitos geográficos español e hispánico.[22]

Los modos de concebir la relación entre lengua e identidad colectiva son ciertamente complejos y probablemente por eso han recibido—y aún reciben—gran atención de parte de antropólogos, historiadores, lingüistas, sociólogos, etc. El nacionalismo lingüístico es precisamente uno de los discursos que articulan lengua e identidad grupal, y si nos fijamos en la ideología que yace bajo la mayoría de los proyectos de planificación lingüística, quizás el que más haya influido las políticas del lenguaje tanto gubernamentales como no gubernamentales en los últimos dos siglos. Los movimientos políticos nacionalistas se definen a partir de la afirmación de la existencia de una entidad nacional y de la reivindicación para la misma del derecho a ejercer el nivel de autogobierno que sus miembros deseen. En otras palabras, asumen como pieza central de su ideario el principio o doctrina de las nacionalidades, de acuerdo con el cual, en palabras de Álvarez Junco, "cada pueblo o nación tiene el derecho a ejercer el poder soberano sobre el territorio en que habita" (2001:12). El modo concreto de definir la nación (en base a criterios políticos o étnicos, por ejemplo) y las funciones que su defensa desempeñe (separatismo, expansionis-

---

[22] Igual que ocurre con el nacionalismo en general, la literatura sobre el nacionalismo lingüístico es inabarcable. Mencionaré aquí, siguiendo el mismo criterio que seguí arriba, una serie de libros y artículos que constituyen mis lecturas más recientes sobre el tema y que por consiguiente deben de estar más presentes en las ideas y en la armazón argumental de este ensayo: Barbour y Carmichael (2000); Blommaert y Verschueren (1998); Coulmas (1988); Edwards (1985:23-46); Errington (1999); Fishman (1989:97-367); Haugen (1972:237-54).

mo, reforma política) son parámetros que permiten distinguir unos movimientos nacionalistas de otros.

Al examinar la fijación del primero de estos parámetros en diversos discursos nacionalistas encontramos que algunos tienden a señalar el carácter subjetivo de la nación, como un contrato social de convivencia diariamente renovado en un metafórico plebiscito que confirma la lealtad de la ciudadanía al proyecto político común (se oirán aquí los ecos de la doctrina de Jean-Jacques Rousseau y de la idea de la nación como plebiscito cotidiano que planteó Ernest Renan en su famoso discurso de 1882). Otros movimientos nacionalistas han afirmado en cambio la existencia objetiva de la nación, colectivo humano que una serie de circunstancias históricas cualesquiera ha dotado de una cultura propia y uniforme, entendida ésta como modo de racionalizar la experiencia vital en el cual se realiza el individuo (se oirá aquí quizás resonar el pensamiento de Johann G. Herder o Johann G. Fichte).[23] Si bien esta clasificación dicotómica presenta ventajas analíticas, advierte A. D. Smith (2000) que elementos propios de las concepciones cívicas de la nación se cuelan frecuentemente en discursos etnicistas y que, del mismo modo, rasgos de éstos aparecen en diseños predominantemente políticos de la nación. Teniendo en cuenta esta importante matización, podemos afirmar que las naciones se definen discursivamente a partir de una lista de elementos potencialmente constitutivos de la misma, un menú de propiedades nacionales (lengua, religión, tradiciones folclóricas, tradiciones sociales, narraciones históricas, instituciones políticas, sistemas de leyes, etc.) del cual cada movimiento nacionalista seleccionará los que le convengan según las necesidades específicas del contexto político concreto en que se desenvuelva. Si una colectividad humana percibe que para la consecución de unos objetivos (culturales, económicos o políticos) ha de definirse como una nación, utilizará con tal fin los elementos que mejor sirvan al cumplimiento de aquellos objetivos. Finalmente, añadamos un último elemento que no falta en los discursos nacionalistas, ya tiendan éstos hacia el lado cívico o hacia el lado étnico del espectro: la *territorialidad*, "el principal requisito—y el control del territorio el principal objetivo—de las naciones" (Álvarez Junco 2001:13).

Sean cuales sean los elementos que se seleccionan para la construcción discursiva de la nación, todo movimiento político que se define como nacionalista afirma la existencia de una identidad grupal que legitima el ejercicio de la soberanía y las instituciones que la ejercen. Lo que distingue a los nacionalismos lingüísticos (frente a otros de carácter religioso o político, por ejemplo) es el situar la lengua en el mismo centro de la identidad. De nuevo, encontraremos

---

[23] Véase, por ejemplo, Álvarez Junco (2001:31-62), de Blas Guerrero (1994:38-46), Mar-Molinero (2000:3-17).

diferencias al observar el papel que distintos movimientos nacionalistas asignan a la lengua, el modo en que la integran en el proyecto de construcción identitaria. En versiones predominantemente étnicas/culturales/primordialistas de la nación, se tiende a asumir un determinismo lingüístico que implica la identificación de lengua y cultura y sugiere la existencia de un isomorfismo entre la estructura gramatical de la lengua en cuestión y la percepción de la experiencia en forma de categorías que constituye la cultura. Para este tipo de nacionalismo lingüístico, la pérdida de la lengua supone la desaparición de una forma de ver el mundo, un peligroso e irreparable trastorno de la ecología cultural de la Tierra. Por ejemplo, el 10 de mayo de 2001 se celebraba en Galicia el "CorreLingua 2001," carrera pedestre popular organizada (como acto simbólico en defensa de la lengua) por departamentos de gallego y equipos de normalización lingüística de los institutos de la Comunidad. Al final de la misma se leyó un manifiesto a los jóvenes participantes que decía lo siguiente: "Somos a voz dos sen-voz, a vangarda dos que rexeitan usar falas prestadas para non ficaren orfos de pensamentos... Nós somos o futuro de Galiza. Somos galegas e galegos e falamos galego. Porque só falando galego somos galegas, somos galegos." No podría quedar expresada con mayor claridad y contundencia la conexión que se supone entre pensamiento, lengua e identidad grupal.

En cambio, en versiones predominantemente cívicas/políticas/voluntaristas, la lengua tiende a ser concebida como instrumento de comunicación propio de la comunidad, instrumento que posibilita la vida en común y la articulación de la vida económica y social del colectivo. Con todo, y aun cuando se acepte el carácter relativamente arbitrario de la relación entre gramática y cultura, la lengua suele verse investida de un carácter simbólico que la convierte en elemento representativo de la nación. En un contexto histórico y geográfico en que la vida cotidiana de los miembros de dos naciones distintas no presente mayores diferencias salvo las lingüísticas, serán justamente éstas las que legitimen la existencia de las entidades nacionales diferenciadas (al margen, por supuesto, de la existencia de hecho de estructuras administrativas y políticas separadas) y sería precisamente a éstas a las que se recurriría para aunar al pueblo si se diera, pongamos por caso, un conflicto con la nación vecina. En estas situaciones, la desaparición de la lengua supone la eliminación de la marca diferenciadora y con ella de la frontera étnica que constituye la base de la soberanía nacional.

A modo de síntesis, la estructura conceptual básica del nacionalismo lingüístico está formada por tres elementos: una identidad (a) grupal, o *cultura* (cívica o étnica) compartida, (b) posibilitada o determinada por una *lengua* común, (c) y circunscrita a un *territorio*.

EL NUEVO RÉGIMEN LINGÜÍSTICO:
LA LENGUA Y EL POST-NACIONALISMO HISPÁNICO
Pues bien, los portavoces de la nueva política lingüística española así como los autores de discursos ideológicamente afines han rechazado de plano el nacionalismo lingüístico y con él la que ha tendido a ser su premisa fundamental: la visión de la lengua como encarnación de la cultura de un pueblo, como singularísimo modo de interpretar la experiencia vital humana. En este sentido, en 2001, Francisco Marcos Marín, por aquel entonces Director Académico del Instituto Cervantes, afirmaba en el suplemento cultural del diario madrileño *ABC* la separación conceptual entre lengua y cultura: "Frente a toda idea de mente colectiva o de propiedad de la comunidad de hablantes, la lengua debe estudiarse como propiedad individual... la identidad lingüística no implica identidad cultural" (*ABC Cultural* junio 2001). Una vez disociada del concepto de cultura, la lengua queda neutralizada como elemento potencialmente constitutivo de la nación, al menos en las formulaciones románticas de ésta. Sin embargo, aún se podría afirmar, desde nacionalismos más cívicos, el valor de la lengua como marca, como símbolo arbitrario de la nación. Pero esta posibilidad ha sido también rechazada. En 1995, Gregorio Salvador, distinguido miembro de la Academia, hacía la siguiente afirmación: "El español no es seña de identidad ni emblema ni bandera... La vieja lengua de mil años y miles de caminos no es vernácula ya en ninguna parte, ni siquiera en la vieja Castilla donde nació... [ha] devenido en pura esencia lingüística, es decir, en un valiosísimo instrumento de comunicación entre pueblos y gentes, en un idioma plurinacional y multiétnico" (citado en *EL PAÍS*, 7 de noviembre de 1995). En el mismo sentido, y en términos más firmes aún, rechaza Juan Ramón Lodares la visión nacionalista de la relación entre lengua y cultura: "El integrismo lingüístico se presenta como un eficaz elemento nacionalizador, basándose en la idea—falsa, por lo demás—de que la comunidad de lenguas es trasunto de la comunidad racial y de la comunidad de ideas, creencias, sentimientos, así como un bastión de fidelidad a los valores patrióticos" (2002: 21).[24]

---

[24] La intervención del Profesor de la Universidad Autónoma de Madrid Juan Ramón Lodares en la confección de una ideología de apoyo a la implementación de la política lingüística española es notable y merece un estudio detenido para el cual no hay aquí espacio pero que se ha de producir. A través de su "trilogía de la lengua," publicada en Taurus y reseñada en los principales periódicos españoles, Lodares desarrolla, con un admirable e impresionante despliegue de erudición, accesibilidad estilística y gracejo, varios de los pilares que sustentan la ideología lingüística dominante: la crítica al nacionalismo lingüístico, la inevitabilidad de la sustitución de unas lenguas por otras y la superioridad de aquellas cuyo conocimiento y uso puede más fácilmente traducirse en dinero (la trilogía aparece en la lista de referencias, Lodares 2000, 2001, 2002).

Vemos pues que estos filólogos y lingüistas, directamente vinculados o cercanos a las instituciones de implementación de la política lingüística de promoción del español, abrazan una concepción de la lengua—una ideología lingüística—que parece situarlos en el polo opuesto del nacionalismo lingüístico clásico que utilizaba aquélla como pieza central de la construcción nacional, ya fuera por la vía estructural-semántica-cultural (como materialización del espíritu del pueblo) o por la vía simbólica-arbitraria (como tótem en torno al cual se agrupan los miembros de la nación). Frente a esta visión, se promueve en España una ideología lingüística que libera al español de sus ataduras culturales y nacionales para que se convierta en lengua panhispánica, para que salga de las fronteras físicas que delimitan un territorio nacional específico, y para que asuma un carácter expansivo e internacional.

Volvamos brevemente a la imagen del español dibujada por el Director de la Academia: "Es realmente <u>emocionante</u> cómo la lengua está sirviendo de lugar de <u>encuentro</u> y no sólo como canal de <u>comunicación</u>. La lengua nos hace <u>patria común</u> en una <u>concordia</u> superior" (citado en *EL PAÍS*, 9 de julio de 2000, subrayado mío). En el fondo de esta imagen, se sitúa el rasgo básico que caracteriza a cualquier lengua: su poder comunicativo. Se asume, por supuesto, que el español, al ser una lengua altamente codificada y elaborada, está dotado de una especial transparencia significativa. Pero más sobresaliente aún es el hecho de que al referirse a la lengua el Director de la Academia no se limita a señalar su utilidad: el español es más—debe ser más—que un simple instrumento al servicio del diálogo eficiente. Como canal de comunicación que es, produce el "encuentro" de todos aquellos que lo hablan y el establecimiento de una comunidad caracterizada por la "concordia." Por medio de estas figuras del lenguaje, García de la Concha asocia el español con un valor superior, ya no sólo limitado a la utilidad administrativa o a la rentabilidad económica, sino estrechamente vinculado a un orden moral y cívico.[25] Fernando Lázaro Carreter, antiguo Director de la RAE y uno de los principales impulsores de su renovación, daba un paso más y, en una entrevista celebrada con motivo de la publicación de su *El nuevo dardo en la palabra* (2003), asociaba la lengua con uno de los valores supremos de la sociedad moderna: "La lengua es un

---

[25] Al igual que ocurre con la idea de lengua-encuentro, como ya hemos señalado Gabriel-Stheeman y yo (2002 y 2004, capítulo 9), el español como instrumento de la concordia aparece también en otros autores: "No puede haber mayor concordia que el diálogo, el entendimiento, la comprensión para el respeto y la paz, y el instrumento fundamental, esencial, es la lengua, y las entidades que representan la lengua desde una perspectiva digamos oficial son las academias" (Ignacio Chávez citado en *EL PAÍS*, 7 de septiembre de 2000).

instrumento esencial de la democracia" (citado en *EL PAÍS*, 21 de enero de 2003). Este tipo de retrato del español, realizado en foros de gran visibilidad (los cursos de verano de El Escorial con la amplia cobertura mediática que reciben o las páginas del diario *EL PAÍS*) y por figuras de extraordinaria relevancia cultural (como el Profesor de Salamanca y Director de la RAE Víctor García de la Concha o el popularísimo Lázaro), es herramienta fundamental en el proceso de implementación de la política lingüística española por medio de la difusión de la ideología lingüística en que esta política se basa. La difusión de esta ideología, por supuesto, es sólo posible si los miembros de la comunidad a quien va dirigida—la hispánica en este caso—la aceptan como propia. Ya el relativo fracaso del nacionalismo liberal decimonónico puso de manifiesto el hecho de que la superioridad práctica de una lengua no basta para vencer el poder de lealtades lingüísticas establecidas de un modo, digamos, más primordial.[26] De ahí que en la actualidad se insista no sólo en la utilidad del español sino también en su asociación con valores universales superiores, tales como la concordia y la democracia, que estimulen la formación de vínculos más "emocionantes" entre la lengua y los individuos que integran o que se aspira a que integren la comunidad.[27]

Por supuesto, como ha quedado claro, los agentes de la política lingüística española han superado la concepción de la lengua como depósito de una cultura asociada a un territorio, como valor superior en tanto que garante de la existencia de un pueblo, de una forma de ver el mundo. Parecería, por lo tanto, que ante la comunidad hispanohablante, española y latinoamericana, no se puede apelar explícitamente a una hermandad de tipo nacional. ¿O sí? A fin de cuentas la lengua "nos hace patria común," dice García de la Concha recurriendo al tópico de Camus ("Oui, j'ai une patrie, la langue française"). Efectivamente, en el elogio del español desnacionalizado se produce un distanciamiento retórico del nacionalismo lingüístico, pero no se abandona completamente el esquema conceptual en que éste se asienta. En la imagen que nos traza el Director de la RAE, se expande el ámbito de significación del concepto "lengua," que pasa ahora, en el triángulo en que se aloja la ideología del nacionalismo lingüístico (lengua, cultura y territorio), a ocupar los espacios vacíos desalojados por el

---

[26] Véase la presentación que hace E. J. Hobsbawm de la irrupción del nuevo nacionalismo de base étnica a partir de 1870 (especialmente en el capítulo 4 de la Segunda edición su libro de 1992), o la discusión del tema en el capítulo 1 de del Valle y Gabriel-Stheeman (2002 o 2004).

[27] Esto separa, al menos a nivel retórico, el discurso del Director de la RAE de visiones más puramente prácticas de la superioridad del español, tales como la ultraeconomicista del profesor Lodares.

descarte de las nociones de cultura y territorio. El código, el instrumento de comunicación, se desdobla convirtiéndose en lugar de armonioso encuentro. Queda así espacializado, e investido con el valor de la "concordia superior" que naturaliza y posibilita la coexistencia de todos los que la hablan. El propio español sustituye al territorio (lugar de encuentro) y a la cultura nacional (concordia superior) convirtiéndose en la "patria común," en la imaginada comunidad panhispánica post-nacional, a la cual, por razón de sus virtudes (concordia, internacionalismo y rentabilidad), entregaremos nuestra lealtad.

Por un lado, la coexistencia del español con otras lenguas en España se ha vivido, en el período que aquí nos ocupa, en términos conflictivos. Ya se señaló antes que las políticas lingüísticas de las Comunidades con lengua propia fueron diseñadas a partir de la idea de la preocupante sustitución de ésta por el español, el cual tiende a ser percibido como una lengua de fuera, "prestada" (aun cuando la mayoría de los miembros de la comunidad la hablen y la hayan hablado a lo largo de muchas generaciones) que amenaza la supervivencia de la "propia" y con ella de la singularidad cultural de la comunidad. Pero en el ámbito español, en círculos próximos a la política lingüística española, también se ha visto el actual bilingüismo como fuente de conflicto, del cual se hace responsables a las agresivas políticas regionales de inversión de la mencionada sustitución. En la nota de advertencia que abre su libro *La lengua española y sus problemas*,[28] Juan M. Lope Blanch afirma: "No me referiré aquí a los problemas con que tropieza actualmente la lengua española en su solar originario, debido al acoso de otros idiomas peninsulares, como el catalán, el vascuence, el gallego y aun el bable" (1997:5). Como respuesta, en parte, a las políticas de las Comunidades Autónomas han de entenderse también los trabajos ya citados de Gregorio Salvador y Juan Ramón Lodares. El discurso de oposición a aquéllas, por lo tanto, existe, pero rara vez se genera en las instituciones que de un modo más explícito se encargan de la promoción del estatus del español. En este sentido, la política parece ser más bien de hechos consumados. En el terreno económico de los mercados lingüísticos, catalán, gallego y euskera tienen poco que hacer ante el español.[29] En el terreno político, frente a la instrumentalización de

---

[28] Curiosamente, a pesar del título, *La lengua española y sus problemas*, la conclusión que uno saca de la lectura del trabajo del profesor Lope Blanch es que el español no tiene problemas.

[29] El 19 de agosto de 2003 se publicaban en *ABC* unas declaraciones de Jon Juaristi, en ese momento Director del Cervantes, en las cuales indicaba el poco interés en el mundo por el estudio del gallego y el vasco (al catalán le va un poco mejor): "... se están dando bastantes clases de catalán... Ahora bien, la demanda disminuye... En el Instituto hemos sido extraordinariamente generosos en la estimación de la demanda. Hemos llegado a dar clases de euskera con dos alumnos. La rentabilidad económica no se

aquellas lenguas por parte de los nacionalismos para cuestionar la entidad nacional de España, se presenta el español como símbolo de la concordia, de la democracia, del progreso económico, como instrumento al servicio de una post-nación, de una comunidad internacional pan-hispánica que deja reducidas al atavismo y al particularismo reaccionario al catalán, gallego y euskera.[30]

Por otro lado, la relación con América Latina ha sido y es uno de los frentes que definen la política exterior de España. A lo largo de los años noventa, crecieron las inversiones españolas en aquel continente, y con ellas, los programas y esfuerzos puntuales de cooperación cultural. La nueva presencia española en las antiguas colonias ha dado lugar a una suerte de reedición del "movimiento hispanista,"[31] es decir, al rescate del concepto de una comunidad hispánica de intereses basada en la existencia de una afinidad cultural. Por supuesto, el rescate de este concepto no es fácil, sobre todo porque la comunidad hispánica, por muy armónica y coherente que se quiera que sea, por muy unida que se quiera que esté, ha de enfrentarse al hecho de que esa voluntad de unidad carga con el peso de la conquista y colonización que se encuentran en su mismo origen. Este lastre es, para algunos, irrelevante en el presente, especialmente ante lo que perciben como el prometedor futuro de la comunidad panhispánica. Otros, en cambio, ven en el rescate de ese desgraciado pasado compartido una condición fundamental para la construcción verdaderamente democrática y justa de proyectos culturales, económicos y políticos igualmente beneficiosos para españoles y latinoamericanos.

El hecho es que en los últimos años se han producido situaciones que han perturbado el armonioso encuentro entre España y sus antiguas colonias. Ya se mencionó arriba el discurso en el que el Rey Juan Carlos I afirmaba que el español no fue nunca "lengua de imposición sino de encuentro" y la consecuente controversia que la metáfora del encuentro provocó al ser interpretada como un intento de esquivar la políticamente incorrecta simbología del "descubrimiento"

---

sostiene." El día 22 de agosto, quizás algo herida en su orgullo e imbuida de la misma ideología que pretende valorar una lengua en términos rigurosamente cuantitativos, el diario coruñés *La Voz de Galicia* publicaba, en un ejercicio de enternecedora ingenuidad, un artículo con el siguiente titular: "Arredor de 6000 personas [sic] aprenderon galego no estranxeiro no curso pasado."

[30] En este contexto encaja un titular con que *EL PAÍS* introducía una noticia sobre un viaje del ex-Presidente del Gobierno José M. Aznar López a Estados Unidos: "Aznar pone a los hispanos de EEUU como ejemplo frente al nacionalismo" (12 de junio de 2003).

[31] Sobre el contenido y emergencia histórica del movimiento hispanista véase el clásico estudio de Pike (1971) o algunos de los ensayos incluidos en Pérez de Mendiola (1996).

y por ocultar la incómoda historia de conquista y colonización.[32] Pero ese componente de la historia común sigue vivo en el recuerdo de muchos y retorna como instrumento de lectura de hechos presentes. ¿Cómo si no interpretar el título del libro *Los nuevos conquistadores* de los periodistas argentinos Daniel Cecchini y Jorge Zicolillo sobre la inmoral (si no ilegal) penetración en su país de algunas de las multinacionales españolas? ¿Cómo interpretar si no la codificación en términos neocoloniales de conflictos laborales que han enfrentado a trabajadores latinoamericanos con empresas españolas? Así se expresaba, por ejemplo, el presidente del sindicato de trabajadores de la banca en Chile: "Cada vez que prendo la luz, llamo por teléfono, hago efectivo un cheque o tomo un vaso de agua, estoy poniendo dinero en los bolsillos de alguien en Madrid . . . Es como si fuéramos una colonia de nuevo, pagando impuestos a la Corona española" (citado en *The Washington Post*, 14 de febrero de 2000). Y de un modo similar, con una "ola de antiespañolismo" (*EL PAÍS*, 21 de junio de 2001), reaccionaban los trabajadores argentinos en junio de 2001 ante la posición del gobierno español en relación con la crisis de Aerolíneas Argentinas.

Por todo ello no cabe sino reconocer que la configuración actual de la comunidad hispánica es un proceso disputado en una dinámica dialéctica que enfrenta visiones discrepantes sobre la naturaleza de la relación, pasada, presente y futura, entre las distintas naciones del mundo hispánico. Y en esta dialéctica ha intervenido con gran presencia y apoyo institucional la política lingüística española orientada hacia la promoción del estatus del español como pilar central que sostiene a la comunidad panhispánica, una comunidad basada en la "pura esencia lingüística" de la que hablaba Gregorio Salvador, y que, según el análisis que he venido proponiendo en este ensayo, viene a cumplir una función análoga a la desempeñada por la ya clásica nación.

En realidad, las discusiones sobre la legitimidad de las reivindicaciones nacionalistas esconden pugnas sobre las fuentes legítimas de autoridad, es decir, sobre la supuesta naturalidad de los grupos poblacionales que, al ser aceptados como sujetos activos del derecho a la soberanía, autorizan la ostentación y el ejercicio del poder, ya sea éste cultural, económico o político. La nación es una unidad de acción política, un mercado, una esfera legítima de influencia y de sentir colectivo. Es el garante de la lealtad a los poderes establecidos. ¿Podría ser que el panhispanismo post-nacionalista de base lingüística sea también—al menos en parte—una cuestión de poder y lealtad? Ya recordábamos Gabriel-Stheeman y yo, en nuestro mencionado estudio, que en 1995, Jesús de Polanco,

---

[32] Esta estrategia nos remite a las pugnas simbólicas que tuvieron lugar durante las celebraciones en 1992 del Quinto Centenario.

Presidente del conglomerado mediático PRISA, afirmaba: "Iberoamérica es un objetivo político, económico y empresarial legítimo para los españoles... Estamos mucho menos lejos de América Latina de lo que nadie puede pensar" (citado en *EL PAÍS* 24 de julio de 1995). Pocos años más tarde, Carlos Gasco, funcionario de alto nivel en el Ministerio de Economía español declaraba a un reportero del *The Washington Post*: "España entiende a Latinoamérica como ningún otro país fuera de Latinoamérica podría hacerlo... Hemos usado esto a nuestro favor para construir lo que percibimos como una conexión económica a largo plazo que seguirá acercándonos más y más a Latinoamérica" (*The Washington Post* 14 de febrero de 2000).

Permítanme enfatizarlo: "España *entiende* a Latinoamérica." ¿Qué hace ese entendimiento posible si no el instrumento de comunicación que es la lengua? ¿Cómo se establece esa proximidad entre España y Latinoamérica a la que se refería Polanco si no en el lugar de encuentro que ofrece el español? ¿Qué legitima la proyección política, económica y empresarial de España—por usar los mismos términos que Polanco—sobre las naciones americanas si no la patria común del idioma? ¿Qué mejor garantía de esa legitimidad que la emocionada lealtad de todos los hispanos a la post-nación lingüística? ¿Quién podrá, en definitiva, resistir el atractivo de una patria/lengua como el español, conciliadora, universal y rentable?

Referencias

Álvarez Junco, José. 2001. *Mater Dolorosa: la idea de España en el siglo XIX*. Madrid: Taurus.
Barbour, Stephen y Cathie Carmichael (eds.). 2000. *Language and Nationalism in Europe*. Oxford: Oxford University Press.
Blommaert, Jan y Jef Verschueren. 1998. "The role of language in European nationalist ideologies." En Schieffelin, Woolard y Kroskrity (eds.), 189-210.
Bossong, Georg y Francisco Báez de Aguilar González (eds.). 2000. *Identidades lingüísticas en la España autonómica*. Frankfurt/Madrid: Vervuert/Iberoamericana.
Cecchini, Daniel y Zicolillo, Jorge. 2002. *Los nuevos conquistadores*. Madrid: Ediciones Foca.
Coulmas, Florian. 1988. "What is a national language good for?." En Florian Coulmas (ed.), *With Forked Tongues: what are National Languages good for?* Singapore: Karoma. 1-24.
De Blas Guerrero, Andrés. 1994. *Nacionalismos y naciones en Europa*. Madrid: Alianza Editorial.
De Esteban, Jorge. 1987. *Por la senda constitucional*. Madrid: Ediciones El País.
Del Valle, José. 1999. "Monoglossic policies for a heteroglossic culture: misinterpreted

multilingualism in Modern Galicia." *Language and Communication* 20:105-32.
Del Valle, José y Luis Gabriel-Stheeman (eds.). 2002. *The Battle over Spanish between 1800 and 2000: Language Ideologies and Hispanic Intellectuals*. London/New York: Routledge.
Del Valle, José y Luis Gabriel-Stheeman (eds.). 2004. *La batalla del idioma: la intelectualidad hispánica ante la lengua*. Frankfurt/Madrid: Vervuert/Iberoamericana.
Edwards, John. 1985. *Language, Society and Identity*. Oxford: Basil Blackwell.
Errington, Joseph. 1999. "Indonesian('s) authority." En Kroskrity (ed), 205-27.
Etxebarria, Maitena. 2002. *La diversidad de lenguas en España*. Madrid: Espasa.
Fishman, Joshua. 1989. *Language and Ethnicity in Minority Sociolinguistic Perspective*. Clevedon/Philadelphia: Multilingual Matters.
Grijelmo, Álex. 1998. *Defensa apasionada del idioma español*. Madrid: Taurus.
Haugen, Einar. 1972. *The Ecology of Language*. Stanford (CA): Stanford University Press.
Hobsbawm, E. J. 1992. *Nations and Nationalism Since 1780*. 2ª ed. Cambridge: Cambridge University Press.
Irvine, Judith T. y Susan Gal. 2000. "Language Ideology and Linguistic Differentiation." En Kroskrity (ed.), 35-83.
Joseph, John E. y Talbot J. Taylor (eds.). 1990. *Ideologies of Language*. Londres/Nueva York: Routledge.
Kaplan, Robert B. y Richard B. Baldauf Jr. 1997. *Language Planning: from Practice to Theory*. Clevedon: Multilingual Matters.
Kroskrity, Paul V. 2000. "Regimenting Languages: Language Ideological Perspectives." En Kroskrity (ed.), 1-34.
Kroskrity, Paul V. (ed.). 2000. *Regimes of Language: Ideologies, Polities, and Identities*. Sante Fe (NM)/Oxford: School of American Research Press/James Currey.
Lodares, Juan Ramón. 2000. *El paraíso políglota*. Madrid: Taurus.
Lodares, Juan Ramón. 2001. *Gente de Cervantes*. Madrid: Taurus.
Lodares, Juan Ramón. 2002. *Lengua y patria*. Madrid: Taurus.
Lope Blanch, Juan M. 1997. *La lengua española y sus problemas*. México: UNAM.
Mar-Molinero, Clare. 2000. *The Politics of Language in the Spanish-Speaking World*. Londres/Nueva York: Routledge.
Penny, Ralph. 1991. *A History of the Spanish Language*. Cambridge: Cambridge University Press.
Penny, Ralph. 2000. *Variation and Change in Spanish*. Cambridge: Cambridge University Press.
Pérez de Mendiola, Marina (ed.). 1996. *Bridging the Atlantic*. Albany (NY): State University of New York Press.
Pike, Fredrick. 1971. *Hispanismo, 1898-1936*. Notre Dame/Londres: University of Notre Dame Press.
Real Academia Española. 1992. *Diccionario de la Lengua española*. 21ª edición. Madrid: Espasa.
Real Academia Española. 1999. *Ortografía de la Lengua Española*. Madrid: Espasa.

Renan, Ernest. 1987. *¿Qué es una nación? Cartas a Strauss*. Madrid: Alianza Editorial.
Salvador, Gregorio. 1987. *Lengua española y lenguas de España*. Barcelona: Ariel.
Salvador, Gregorio. 1992. *Política lingüística y sentido común*. Madrid: Istmo.
Schieffelin, Bambi B., Kathryn A. Woolard y Paul V. Kroskrity (eds.). 1998. *Language Ideologies : Practice and Theory*. New York/Oxford: Oxford University Press.
Siguan, Miquel. 1992. *España plurilingüe*. Madrid: Alianza Editorial.
Smith, A. D. 2000. *The Nation in History*. Hanover: University Press of New England.
Söhrman, Ingmar. 1993. *Ethnic Pluralism in Spain*. Uppsala: Centre for Multiethnic Research, Uppsala University.
Turell, Teresa. 2001. *Multilingualism in Spain*. Clevedon: Multilingual Matters.
Uriarte, Edurne. 2003. *España, Patriotismo y Nación*. Madrid: Espasa Calpe.
Wright, Roger. 1989. *Latín tardío y romance temprano*. Madrid: Gredos.
Wright, Roger. 2000. *El Tratado de Cabreros (1206): Estudio sociofilológico de una reforma ortográfica*. London: Queen Mary and Westfield College.

22
El Atlas de Paraguay y la distinción [s]/[θ]
FRANCISCO MORENO FERNÁNDEZ

1. INTRODUCCIÓN

LA GEOGRAFÍA LINGÜÍSTICA DE Hispanoamérica ha dado un salto gigantesco, cualitativo y cuantitativo, a partir de la publicación de los primeros volúmenes del proyecto denominado "Atlas Lingüístico de Hispanoamérica." Las casi mil quinientas preguntas del cuestionario general, planteadas del mismo modo en numerosísimos puntos de encuesta de toda la América hispanohablante, garantizan la comparabilidad de los datos y la compilación de una ingente cantidad de materiales.

Estas páginas tienen la intención de detenerse en uno de los volúmenes del proyecto hispanoamericano, de entre los varios que la Universidad de Alcalá ya ha editado, todos ellos de la autoría de Manuel Alvar. Se trata de la obra *El español en Paraguay. Estudios, encuestas, textos*. Al margen de su valor científico, la publicación de este trabajo tiene un valor sentimental, por ser el primer tomo póstumo de los atlas de Alvar; en la imprenta quedan México, Argentina y Uruguay y Chile, ya preparados por su autor, para completar la serie alcalaína.

El español de Paraguay no es de los mejor conocidos de Hispanoamérica, ni mucho menos. Muy pocos son los trabajos de campo que se han practicado, como muy pocas son las investigaciones históricas. Pero, de todo lo publicado sobre este territorio, sin duda ha sido la obra de Germán de Granda la que más información y luz ha arrojado. Granda lleva muchos años prestando atención e interés a la situación lingüística de Paraguay y a la descripción de su perfil dialectal, sociolingüístico e histórico. La obra de Alvar viene a dar continuidad a esa preocupación por el español paraguayo y a aportar datos que permitirán un mejor conocimiento de la realidad.

Como muestra de hasta qué punto *El español en Paraguay* ha de ser útil a la dialectología paraguaya e hispanoamericana, ofrecemos en estas líneas un análisis cuantitativo realizado sobre los textos en transcripción fonética que acompañan a los materiales de encuesta. Concretamente, analizaremos el comportamiento del sonido [θ] en los hablantes paraguayos cuyo discurso fue grabado y transcrito para el atlas. Además de conocer los usos de [θ] en el español de Paraguay, nuestro análisis nos pondrá en condiciones de situar lo que ocurre en esta tierra respecto a las manifestaciones de ese sonido localizadas en otros territorios hispánicos.

Ralph Penny ha dedicado muchas horas de estudio a la historia de las sibilantes del español. Sobre el origen y la expansión del seseo en Hispanoamérica su postura es clara: "There are many features of American Spanish which demonstrate that southern Peninsular tendencies have successfully gained the upper hand in all or most of Spanish America. Such features include *seseo*" (2002:25). Ojalá que estas páginas, dedicadas a un aspecto de ese proceso general, sean de utilidad para su interpretación, a la vez que de modesto homenaje al trabajo y la inteligencia de Penny, hispanista modélico.

2. EL ESPAÑOL DE PARAGUAY

Paraguay es la nación del mundo hispanoamericano en la que el bilingüismo se hace más patente (Corvalán 1981; Corvalán y Granda 1982). Las lenguas que coexisten son el español y el guaraní, éste con diversas modalidades, incluidos los usos más hispanizados que dan lugar a la denominación *jopará* [jopará] 'mezcla'. También el español ha recibido la influencia del guaraní (Granda 1994), como se puede comprender fácilmente si pensamos, no solo que ha habido contacto de lenguas, sino que el guaraní tiene un prestigio y un uso derivados de su consideración de lengua nacional. Ello no es óbice para que la presencia del guaraní se detecte más en el campo que en la ciudad, o para que sea como la lengua de las relaciones de "solidaridad," familiaridad o cercanía.

Aparte del patente bilingüismo, se viene caracterizando la situación lingüística de Paraguay como una situación de marginación, de conservadurismo o de tradicionalismo. Esta característica se fraguó desde la dictadura de José Gaspar de Francia (1817-1840), que llevó al país a un aislamiento extremo y al rechazo de lo externo, incluidas las pautas lingüísticas circundantes, sobre todo argentinas, cuando el contacto entre ellas podía producirse.

El carácter conservador al que aludimos ya fue señalado por Bertil Malmberg, quien apunta matices interesantes. Según el ilustre hispanista sueco (1970:276-77), el español paraguayo ofrece rasgos conservadores motivados por la preocupación por la corrección que tan frecuentemente se da en las personas bilingües, por inseguridad ante la posible influencia de una lengua sobre la otra y por el deseo de mantener entre ellas una clara diferencia. No se olvida Malmberg del aislamiento como elemento favorecedor del conservadurismo ni de los contextos en los que se espera el uso del español: las situaciones más solemnes, oficiales o, simplemente, formales.

En lo que se refiere a la caracterización lingüística del español de Paraguay (Granda 1994; Alvar 1996), encontramos un vocalismo que no ofrece rasgos dispares de lo que es habitual en el vocalismo panhispánico, incluidos los usos populares o vulgares, como las traslaciones acentuales en formas verbales (*véngamos*), aunque no en *raíz, baúl* o *país*. En el consonantismo, apreciamos un tratamiento diverso de la *s* en posición implosiva, con un índice de elisión alto, una *s* que, cuando se articula, suele ser de carácter predorsodental. También es destacable la asibilación tanto del grupo -*tr*- (*tripa, tres, cuatro*) como de *r* simple en posición inicial de palabra. Pero, sin duda, los rasgos más interesantes afectan a las palatales paraguayas: por un lado, se aprecia un uso en retraimiento de la africada sorda; por otro, suele darse una realización africada para la palatal central /j/; pero, sin duda, destaca el mantenimiento de la palatal lateral sonora. Es este un rasgo que merece un detenido análisis estadístico, puesto que una de las noticias que sustentan los datos más recientes apuntan al inicio del resquebrajamiento de la distinción fonológica a favor del yeísmo. Esa distinción puede deberse a diversas causas, pero tanto el carácter conservador del área, como la presencia de hablantes distinguidores desde los primeros tiempos de la colonia, ayudan a comprenderlo fácilmente.

En el ámbito gramatical es interesante destacar la existencia de voseo, abundante en las áreas circundantes de Uruguay y Argentina y de leísmo, así como de un plural que pierde los morfemas específicos, como en *dame dos pan* 'dame dos panes', fenómeno que también se encuentra en el portugués de Brasil, por ejemplo. Las características más particulares del léxico del español de Paraguay se desprenden del perfil de la situación lingüística esbozada más arriba. Por un lado, siempre ha llamado la atención el uso de formas léxicas arcaizantes, aunque, si se analizan las listas aportadas en la bibliografía, no se incluyen muchas formas diferentes de otras de regiones hispánicas (*frazada, pollera, refrigerio*). Por otro lado están los indigenismos, entre los que destacan, por su particularidad, las voces de origen guaraní, como no podía ser de otra manera: *agatí* 'libélula', *cama* 'ubre', *pehagüé* 'hijo tardío', *guaraná* 'bebida', *jauarundí* 'felino'. Ahora bien, si consultamos la edición de 2001 del *Diccionario* de la Real Academia Española, en la que se han revisado con especial cuidado los americanismos, y buscamos las voces marcadas de forma específica y exclusiva con la etiqueta "Paraguay," sin ninguna otra marca geográfica, comprobaremos que entre ellas destacan palabras comunes a otras zonas, pero de desarrollo semántico propio (*cancha* 'cantidad que cobra el dueño de una casa de juego'; *forrado* 'aperado'; *mariscar* 'cazar animales silvestres que viven a la orilla del río') y bastantes formas ligadas a la vida ganadera más característica (*pireca* 'piel que cubre la carne asada'; *zoquete* 'pedazo grande de carne vacuna'; *chura* 'víscera comestible'; *castizo* 'prolífico'; *novillear* 'rondar a una mujer'). Finalmente, el *Diccionario* académico nos descubre muchas voces compartidas en su especificidad con Argentina y con Uruguay, sobre todo con la primera, y entre ellas las hay de clara influencia portuguesa (*cacho* 'racimo de bananas', *urubú* 'zopilote'). En total se recogen 356 paraguayismos, incluidas voces y acepciones, de los cuales 32, salvo error u omisión, no se comparten con ningún otro territorio.[1]

Los investigadores que más atención le han prestado a la situación lingüística de Paraguay han sido, en relación con la historia y la caracterización del español, Germán de Granda y, en relación con el bilingüismo, Graziella Corvalán, al margen de estudios particulares, de mayor o menor importancia, que han sido muy influyentes en los últimos cincuenta años y que han permitido conocer mejor determinados aspectos lingüísticos de Paraguay; pensamos en estudios como los de Bertil Malmberg (1947, 1970) o Joan Rubin (1968).

Vista la producción bibliográfica con que contamos hoy sobre Paraguay, tal vez pueda hablarse de cuatro ámbitos que necesitan actualmente una profundización y una actualización de conocimientos: el de la sociología del lenguaje, el de la situación de lenguas en contacto, el de la sociolingüística y el de las variedades geolectales del español paraguayo. Los dos primeros ya se han tratado en la bibliografía anterior, pero, por su propia dinámica, requieren atención periódica y regular, con actualizaciones permanentes. La sociolingüística del español de Paraguay está pendiente y cada día se hace más necesario un estudio pormenorizado del español de Asunción. El ámbito de las variedades geolectales es el que más impulso ha recibido recientemente, si bien queda abordar de modo pormenorizado todas las posibilidades abiertas o reabiertas con tal impulso. Naturalmente, con ello nos referimos a la publicación del volumen *El español en Paraguay*, de Manuel Alvar. De estos materiales recibimos un anticipo en el *Manual de dialectología hispánica* de 1996, pero ahora, con el atlas, el caudal de datos es sencillamente abrumador.

---

[1] Estos son los que faltan por citar: *aperado* 'intrigante', *argel* (caballo) 'de mala suerte', *boleado* 'aturullado', *bolear* 'decir muchas mentiras', *bolicho* 'tiendecita', *churero* 'persona que vende vísceras', *dúo* 'colega', *galerón* 'sombrero de copa', *garandumba* 'especia de balsa', *mariscador* 'hombre que marisca', *palito* 'barra de pan pequeña', *pancho* 'bocadillo de chorizo', *plaguear* 'refunfuñar', *plagueo* 'acción de plaguear', *proporción* 'medio para enviar una carta o un paquete', *sustancia* 'alimento de huevo, leche y azúcar', *taquicuela* 'juego de los cantillos', *trincha* 'conjunto de seis bollos de pan', *vaquero* 'fiambre', *zoquete* 'cargo público', *zoqueterismo* 'reparto interesado de cargos públicos' *zoquetero* 'que desempeña un cargo público en beneficio propio'.

3. EL ATLAS DE PARAGUAY

El español en Paraguay es una obra dividida, como reza su propio subtítulo, en tres partes. La primera de ellas reúne dos trabajos de Manuel Alvar ya publicados previamente: una caracterización del español paraguayo y un estudio sobre las voces guaraníes recogidas en las encuestas. Se añade, como complemento del primero, el análisis acústico de algunas palabras grabadas *in situ*, que permiten tener una idea más precisa de la fonética paraguaya. Este análisis fue realizado por María Jesús Redondo en el Laboratorio de Fonética de la Universidad de Alcalá.

La segunda parte del volumen, la más larga y rica en datos, ofrece las respuestas obtenidas en 18 puntos de encuesta a propósito de 1415 aspectos léxicos, fonéticos y gramaticales. Dada la dimensión geográfica de que se trata y dado que el número de localidades encuestadas no es muy grande, para la presentación de los materiales se ha optado por el formato de listas de datos y no por el cartografiado. Esas listas aparecen acompañadas de un pequeño mapa de Paraguay en el que se reflejan los puntos de encuesta para facilitar una más rápida localización por parte del lector.

La tercera parte reproduce las transcripciones y los textos en ortografía ordinaria de fragmentos de grabaciones realizadas en varias comunidades de Paraguay con hablantes de diversas características sociales. El contenido de los textos versa sobre temas variados, como la mitología guaraní, cuentos tradicionales, historias locales, aspectos etnográficos de Paraguay y alguna historia de vida. La obra se cierra con un índice de voces que facilita enormemente la localización de cualquier rasgo lingüístico a lo largo de toda la obra.

Lejos de nuestra intención está hacer de menos la información de este volumen procedente de las encuestas propiamente dichas, pero nos permitimos llamar la atención, en esta ocasión, sobre la importancia de los textos en transcripción fonética que se ofrecen en la tercera parte. Estos textos son la llave para conocer el comportamiento de muchos rasgos lingüísticos en discurso continuo, frente a las restricciones que conlleva la respuesta breve y directa de un cuestionario. Es cierto que el número de textos es relativamente corto para poder desarrollar análisis muy completos; es cierto que la representatividad sociológica de los hablantes cuyo discurso se ha transcrito también ofrece limitaciones; pero no menos cierto es que estamos ante una información lo suficientemente valiosa como para abordar aspectos muy poco tratados hasta ahora o con procedimientos que no se han podido aplicar con anterioridad. Las bases están puestas para, a partir de esta información, proceder a más pormenorizados estudios sociolingüísticos y etnográficos.

Una de las ventajas que presenta la transcripción de discurso continuo es la posibilidad de utilizar procedimientos cuantitativos con menos inconvenientes que con otro tipo de materiales: ya no se trata de saber cómo es un rasgo o si aparece o no lo hace; se trata de conocer cómo se distribuye cuantitativamente. Eso es lo que hemos hecho a propósito de las manifestaciones de [θ] en estos textos paraguayos. Los resultados de este tipo de investigaciones suelen ser satisfactorios si se trabaja con un número suficiente de casos, lo que ocurre cuando el elemento analizado es muy recurrente en la lengua. Tuvimos la oportunidad de aplicar este modo de trabajo sobre los *Textos andaluces en transcripción fonética* (Alvar, Llorente, Salvador 1995) y el resultado fue interesante (Moreno Fernández 1996-1997). Una de las ventajas que aporta esta cuantificación es la posibilidad de incluir las localidades de origen como variable explicativa o independiente, llevando la cuantificación al terreno de la geolingüística, de modo semejante a como se hace con las variables de naturaleza social (Moreno Fernández 1993).

4. ANÁLISIS DE LA PRESENCIA DE [θ]
Germán de Granda ha explicado en varias ocasiones, desde los años ochenta, que el fonema /s/ del español paraguayo tiene distintas modalidades articulatorias: predorsal convexa, coronal plana y, en hablantes ancianos, interdental ciceante (Granda 1982:164; 1991:24; 1994:302).[2] Esta es la principal referencia a la aparición de elementos de timbre ciceante en el español paraguayo, referencia que ha sido repetida por diversos autores (Vaquero; Aleza y Enguita). Antes, Bertil Malmberg (1947) había hecho alusión a su existencia, sin muchos más datos. Después, Alvar, a partir de los materiales del atlas, volvió a dar fe de la abundante existencia del sonido y a ponerlo en relación, someramente, con los datos equiparables de otros lugares de Hispanoamérica (1996:202-03). Así pues, no son muchos más los detalles de que disponemos sobre la realización [θ] en Paraguay, sobre su distribución o su origen, ni hasta ahora se han practicado cuantificaciones.

Dentro de la obra *El español en Paraguay*, son numerosas las láminas de formas léxicas en las que aparece un elemento [θ] interdental o postdental,[3] pero lo más importante es que a esas formas se suman las incluidas en 20 textos de lengua hablada transcrita, que permite proceder a un análisis cuantitativo más detallado que los que se han practicado hasta el momento. Eso es lo que hemos hecho.

Los textos proceden de 13 informantes, hombres y mujeres, con edades

---

[2] Bertil Malmberg (1947) también hace referencia a ello.
[3] Véanse, por ejemplo, las respuestas relacionadas en 139, *zapatillas*; 185, *pavesa*; 399, *lucero del alba*; 937, *inyección*.

comprendidas entre los 31 y los 57 años y con diversos niveles de estudios.[4] Los hablantes eran originarios de las siguientes localidades: Asunción (4), Villarrica (2), San Ignacio (2), Caacupé (1), Encarnación (1), Florida (1), Colonia Independencia (1), Pedro Juan Caballero (1). La mayor parte de estas localidades se localizan en el Sur de Paraguay, excepto Florida (Noroeste) y Pedro Juan Caballero (Nordeste).

Para proceder al análisis, localizamos todos los casos de las distribuciones correspondientes a lo que en las zonas distinguidoras son /s/ y /θ/ (Caravedo habla de formas canónicas), para anotar detalladamente la naturaleza de la realización fonética encontrada en cada caso. La realización de la zeta en Paraguay es postdental, mientras que la de la ese, según afirma Alvar, es predorsal. Al revisar uno a uno los contextos de cada una de las sibilantes de las descripciones, observamos que no había ningún caso correspondiente a la distribución de /s/ en zonas distinguidoras que no fuera realizado mediante una sibilante predorsal: no se anotó, pues, ningún caso de [θ] para /s/ canónica, es decir, ningún caso de ceceo o de timbre ciceante.

Sí se registró variación, en cambio, en las realizaciones correspondientes a la distribución de /θ/ en zonas distinguidoras. En concreto, los textos arrojaban 406 casos de lo que Caravedo llamaría zeta canónica (por ejemplo, en *zapato, rapaz, veces*). De ellos, 199 (49%) se manifestaron con realización [s] (seseante) y 207 (51%) se manifestaron con realización zeta postdental. La probabilidad de aparición de una u otra variante en esta distribución fue de 0,514, lo que es característico de un fenómeno prototípicamente variable. Esto nos lleva a unos índices de presencia de [θ] similares a los encontrados en algunos lugares de Perú y de Argentina (Caravedo 1992; Alvar 1995).

Pero esta cuantificación no es suficiente. La sociolingüística ha demostrado que no podemos dar por satisfactoria una estadística de pan y chocolate, como dicen los sociólogos, cuando tenemos a mano recursos estadísticos e informáticos muy poderosos. Por este motivo decidimos someter los 406 casos de realizaciones correspondientes a la distribución de /θ/ en zonas distinguidoras a un análisis probabilístico en el que se tuvieran en cuenta diversas variables explicativas, lingüísticas y extralingüísticas, en un intento de entender mejor la variable dependiente, que a su vez incluía dos variantes: realización [θ] o realización [s].

Para el estudio estadístico de esos usos paraguayos realizamos un análisis probabilístico de regresión a través del programa GOLDVARB, en su versión para PC adaptada en la Universidad de New Hampshire (http://www.unh.edu/linguistics/lab/goldvarb.html). El análisis consiste en determinar la probabilidad

---

[4] No había analfabetos. Muchos de ellos tenían formación superior.

de aparición de cada una de las variantes de la variable independiente cuando concurren variables explicativas de distinta naturaleza (Moreno Fernández 1994). En nuestro caso, las variables analizadas son las siguientes:

VARIABLE DEPENDIENTE
Realizaciones de las unidades correspondientes a la distribución de /θ/ en las zonas conservadoras:

Realización [s]
Realización [θ]

VARIABLES INDEPENDIENTES O EXPLICATIVAS
Informante (con indicación de sexo, nivel de estudios y edad, según las pautas de Alvar):

1 Mujer – Licenciada - 55
2 Hombre – Culto - 57
3 Mujer – Periodista - 55
4 Hombre – Estudios primarios - 47
5 Mujer – Bachillerato - 55
6 Hombre – Estudios primarios - 48
7 Mujer – Estudios primarios - 55
8 Hombre – Estudios primarios - 38
9 Mujer – Universitarios - 32
10 Mujer – Estudios primarios - 31
11 Mujer – Maestra - 36
12 Hombre – Licenciado - 36
13 Mujer – Maestra - 55

Localidad: Asunción, Villarrica, San Ignacio, Caacupé, Encarnación, Florida, Colonia Independencia, Pedro Juan Caballero.
Contexto fónico siguiente: e, i, a, o, u, semivocal palatal, pausa, consonante.
Contexto fónico anterior: nasal, no nasal.
Tonicidad: en sílaba átona, en sílaba tónica.
Categoría de la palabra: sustantivo, adjetivo, verbo, adverbio, preposición, conjunción, numeral.

Una vez introducidos todos los datos en el programa estadístico, se procedió a practicar un análisis binomial, tanto de un nivel como escalonado, tomando como valor de aplicación la variante [θ]. El resultado fue que solo las variables "informante" y "localidad" arrojaban un valor de significación por debajo del 0,05, que es el que se toma habitualmente como referencia en las Ciencias Sociales. Esto quiere decir que ninguna de las variables explicativas de naturaleza lingüística se reveló significativa o determinante respecto de la aparición de las variantes [θ] o [s] en la distribución ya comentada. Y, en efecto, al ojear las probabilidades de aparición de la variante [θ] cuando se dan cada una de las variantes de las variables lingüísticas independientes, se observa que rara vez bajan de 0,4 y casi nunca están por encima de 0,6, lo que quiere decir que la aparición de una variante u otra en cualquier circunstancia lingüística de las previstas es una cuestión de cara o cruz, sin que ningún rasgo lingüístico haga que la balanza se incline hacia un lado o hacia otro.

Es muy importante llamar la atención sobre el hecho de que las dos únicas variables significativas (informante y localidad) sean de naturaleza extralingüística. Esto obliga, sin ningún género de dudas, a buscar explicaciones ajenas a la lengua misma para entender el porqué de la aparición de [θ]. Así, en cuanto a las localidades, existen dos en las que parece verse favorecida esa variante, aunque no con valores incontestables: se trata de Caacupé y de Colonia Independencia. Si está en el carácter rural y tradicionalista la causa de que se tienda a usar la zeta en algunos lugares, habría que comprobar si efectivamente estas características son reconocibles en ambas comunidades, como puede parecer. Asunción, por su parte, se muestra más tradicionalista que innovadora o favorecedora de la solución plenamente seseante: la probabilidad de aparición de [θ] en la capital es de 0,53.

En cuanto a los hablantes, variable especialmente significativa, se aprecian las siguientes probabilidades de uso de la variante [θ]:

1: 0,56	2: 0,71	3: 0,47
4: 0,60	5: 0,67	6: 0,86
7: 0,31	8: 0,62	9: 0,34
10: 0,44	11: 0,46	12: 0,39
13: 0,30		

Probabilidad de aparición de [θ]
en los 13 informantes paraguayos

Los datos más destacados del cuadro son las probabilidades que muestran los hablantes con los números 2 y 6. Estos son los que más favorecen la aparición de la variante [θ]. En el polo opuesto se encuentran los hablantes con los números 7, 9 y 13, en los que se favorece más la variante [s]. El siguiente paso es averiguar qué características tienen en común unos y otros, de modo que se puedan deducir las condiciones sociales que propician cada variante. Al comprobar el perfil social de los hablantes, anotado más arriba, apreciamos que los hablantes 2 y 6 son hombres y que, de ellos, quien muestra una más alta probabilidad de uso de [θ] (0,86) es el de menor instrucción. Por su lado, las hablantes 7, 9 y 13 son mujeres, de distintas edades y diferente nivel de instrucción.

Las conclusiones que se desprenden de este análisis son bastante clarificadoras. La aparición de [θ] está condicionada por factores extralingüísticos, de los cuales el sexo se revela como el de más destacado poder de determinación: las mujeres favorecen las realizaciones de timbre siseante y los hombres favorecen el uso de [θ], especialmente cuando es menor la instrucción recibida. Asimismo no parece que la edad sea determinante para la aparición de ninguna de las variantes, lo que contrasta con la afirmación de Germán de Granda, que restringe los usos de la interdental a los hablantes ancianos. Los materiales de Alvar en Argentina atestiguan el uso de [θ] en hablantes de diversas edades, incluidos los de instrucción universitaria (1995), y algo similar se encuentra en los datos de Caravedo, procedentes de Cajamarca y Cuzco, en el Perú (1992).

Al poner en relación los resultados de los análisis de Paraguay con los aportados por Alvar para Argentina y por Caravedo para Perú, lo primero que se observa es que en todos estos casos se trata de usos de [θ] en contextos que se corresponden con los de /θ/ en las áreas que son distinguidoras. En esas hablas, la frecuencia del sonido interdental (o post-dental) es tan notable que hace pensar en la posibilidad de que estemos, no ante un deslizamiento articulatorio (de timbre seseante a timbre ceceante), sino ante un resto de la distinción fonológica de /s/ y /θ/, lo que hemos denominado una "falsa distinción residual" (Moreno Fernández en prensa). Como ya hemos explicado en otro lugar, se trata de una falsa distinción porque en la actualidad no puede hablarse para la fonología del español de América del mantenimiento de dos espacios funcionales, de modo que la distinción no es real, sino falsa; y hablamos de residual porque la consideramos resto de un estadio distinguidor que durante siglos debió de estar vivo en una parte de la sociedad americana (Caravedo 1992:654; Guitarte 1983).

Las causas externas que explican tal manifestación residual pueden estar en la naturaleza marginal de los territorios en que aparece y en el carácter más tradicionalista o conservador de los grupos donde es más frecuente, entendiendo la marginación y el tradicionalismo no como factor *sine qua non*: simplemente, las probabilidades de encontrar la falsa distinción aumentan cuanto más aislado, periférico, conservador o tradicionalista sea un territorio o un grupo social de una comunidad.

5. CONCLUSIONES

Sin escamotear un ápice de la importancia que han tenido y tienen los estudios de Malmberg y muy especialmente de Germán de Granda, *El español en Paraguay*, de Alvar, ha abierto una nueva etapa en el conocimiento de la realidad lingüística paraguaya, dentro de sus fronteras y en relación con las hablas americanas que las circundan. El nuevo atlas, que forma parte de la serie del "Atlas Lingüístico de Hispanoamérica," ofrece materiales de encuestas y una valiosa muestra de discurso hablado en transcripción fonética que da más posibilidades para la investigación, incluida la cuantitativa.

Sobre esos textos hemos tenido la oportunidad de practicar un análisis estadístico de regresión de todos los casos de uso de [θ]. En general, la bibliografía se refería a ellos como usos marginales y característicos de ancianos, pero los textos aportados por Alvar dejan ver que el rasgo aparece también en hablantes más jóvenes y de instrucción superior. El análisis estadístico revela que los factores lingüísticos no tienen capacidad de determinación sobre la aparición de las variantes [s] o [θ]; son más bien extralingüísticos los factores que la explican. Esos factores son la localidad de origen y las características de los hablantes. De este modo, la interdental, pronunciada a menudo como post-dental, se ve favorecida, sobre todo, por los hombres, mientras que la variante de timbre siseante es claramente la preferida por las mujeres cultas.

Desde un punto de vista lingüístico, los casos de [θ] aparecen siempre en contextos que se corresponden con los de /θ/ en las áreas distinguidoras, mientras que en los contextos correspondientes a /s/ no aparece el sonido interdental o post-dental. Debido a este reparto distribucional y a las estadísticas de uso de las variantes implicadas, nos inclinamos a interpretar el rasgo como una falsa distinción residual de /s/ y /θ/, es decir, como una fase intermedia entre la distinción fonológica, que debió existir en determinados momentos a lo largo la historia del español paraguayo, y la tendencia general al seseo de timbre seseante, con *s* predorsodental, que es la solución mayoritaria tanto en Paraguay como en todo el español de América.

Referencias

Aleza, Milagros y José María Enguita. 2002. *El español de América: aproximación sincrónica.* Valencia: Tirant lo Blanch.

Alonso, Amado. 1967. *Estudios lingüísticos. Temas hispanoamericanos.* 3ª. ed., Madrid: Gredos.

Alvar, Manuel. 1990. *Norma lingüística sevillana y español de América.* Madrid: Cultura Hispánica.

Alvar, Manuel. 1995. "Muestras de polimorfismo en el español de Argentina." *La lengua y su expansión en la época del Tratado de Tordesillas*. Valladolid: Junta de Castilla y León 125-45.

Recogido en *América, la lengua*, Valladolid: Universidad de Valladolid, 2000, 315-47.

Alvar, Manuel (dir.). 1996. *Manual de dialectología hispánica. El Español de América*. Barcelona: Ariel.

Alvar, Manuel. 2000. *El español en el Sur de Estados Unidos. Estudios, encuestas, textos*. Alcalá de Henares: Universidad de Alcalá-La Goleta.

Alvar, Manuel. 2000. *El español en la República Dominicana. Estudios, encuestas, textos*. Alcalá de Henares: Universidad de Alcalá-La Goleta.

Alvar, Manuel. 2001a. *El español en Venezuela. Estudios, mapas, textos*. Alcalá de Henares: Universidad de Alcalá-La Goleta-AECI.

Alvar, Manuel. 2001b. *El español en Paraguay. Estudios, encuestas, textos*. Alcalá de Henares: Universidad de Alcalá-La Goleta- AECI.

Alvar, Manuel, Antonio Llorente y Gregorio Salvador. 1995. *Textos andaluces en transcripción fonética*. Madrid: Gredos.

Caravedo, Rocío. 1990. *Sociolingüística del español de Lima*. Lima: Pontificia Universidad Católica del Perú.

Caravedo, Rocío. 1992. "¿Restos de la distinción /s/ / /θ/ en el español de Perú?" *Revista de Filología Española* 72, 639-54.

Corvalán, Graziella. 1981. *Paraguay, nación bilingüe*. 2ª. ed. Asunción: Centro Paraguayo de Estudios Sociológicos.

Corvalán, Graziella y Germán de Granda (eds.) 1982. *Sociedad y lengua. Bilingüismo en el Paraguay*, Asunción: Centro Paraguayo de Estudios Sociológicos.

Fontanella de Weinberg, María Beatriz. 1992. *El español de América*. Madrid: Mapfre.

Frago Gracia, Juan Antonio. 1989. "El seseo entre Andalucía y América." *Revista de Filología Española* 69, 277-310.

Frago Gracia, Juan Antonio. 1999. *Historia del español de América*, Madrid: Gredos.

Granda, Germán de. 1982. "Observaciones sobre la fonética del español de Paraguay." *Anuario de Letras* 20, 145-94.

Granda, Germán de. 1988. *Sociedad, historia y lengua en el Paraguay*. Bogotá: Instituto Caro y Cuervo.

Granda, Germán de. 1991. *El español en tres mundos. Retenciones y contactos lingüísticos en América y África*. Valladolid: Universidad de Valladolid.

Granda, Germán de. 1992. "Hacia la historia de la lengua en el Paraguay. Un esquema interpretativo." *Historia y presente del español de América*, ed. por César Hernández, 649-74. Valladolid: Junta de Castilla y León.

Granda, Germán de. 1994. *Español de América, Español de África y hablas criollas hispánicas*. Madrid: Gredos.

Guitarte, Guillermo. 1983. *Siete estudios sobre el español de América*. México: UNAM.

Lapesa, Rafael. 1964. "El andaluz y el español de América." *Presente y futuro de la lengua española* II, 173-82. Madrid: OFINES.

Lapesa, Rafael. 1981. *Historia de la lengua española*. 9ª. ed. Madrid: Gredos.

Malmberg, Bertil. 1947. *Notas sobre la fonética del español en el Paraguay.* Lund: C. W. K. Gleerup.

Malmberg, Bertil. 1970. *La América hispanohablante. Unidad y diferenciación del castellano.* Madrid: Istmo.

Moreno de Alba, José Guadalupe. 1988. *El español en América.* México: FCE.

Moreno Fernández, Francisco. 1993. "Geolingüística y cuantificación." *Actas del III Congreso de Hispanistas de Asia* 289-300. Tokio: Asociación Asiática de Hispanistas.

Moreno Fernández, Francisco. 1994. "Sociolingüística, estadística e informática." *Lingüística* 6, 95-154.

Moreno Fernández, Francisco. 1996-1997. "La variación de /s/ implosiva en las hablas andaluzas: análisis cuantitativo." *Studia Hispanica in honorem Germán de Granda. Anuario de Lingüística Hispánica* 12-13, 939-57.

Moreno Fernández, Francisco. En prensa. "Sobre la existencia de [θ] en América," *Homenaje a Antonio Quilis.*

Navarro Tomás, Tomás. 1974. *El español en Puerto Rico.* Río Piedras: Universidad de Puerto Rico.

Penny, Ralph. 2002. *A History of Spanish Language.* 2a. ed. Cambridge: Cambridge University Press.

Rubin, Joan. 1968. *National Bilingualism in Paraguay.* The Hague: Mouton.

Sánchez Méndez, Juan. 2003. *Historia de la lengua española en América.* Valencia: Tirant lo Blanch.

Vaquero, María. 1998. *El español de América I. Pronunciación.* Madrid: Arco/Libros.

23
A Forbidding Agenda: The Morphosyntax, Semantics and Pragmatics of Forbidding in Spanish
JOHN N. GREEN

1. INTRODUCTION

This paper examines the form and pragmatic intent of expressions of prohibition in modern Castilian Spanish. The analysis is based on a corpus of public notices forbidding certain activities, contrasted with reported prohibitions and some types of negative request. The corpus has been assembled by observation and jotting over many years and is believed to be typical, though not statistically rigorous or necessarily exhaustive. Provisionally, we define a 'public' notice as one displayed in an open-access space where it could be seen and read by anyone. We begin by considering the grammatical form and lexical content of public prohibitions. We then consider the pragmatics of forbidding in contexts where the addressees are unknown and their reactions literally incalculable. In the concluding section we ask whether the form of Spanish public prohibitions is actively constrained or just conventionally formulaic.

2. DESCRIPTIVE ANALYSIS

Although the examples in the corpus evince quite a narrow range of syntactic frames, they could still be subclassified in various competing ways. We shall make a primary split on semantic grounds between those that convey a direct prohibition and those whose prohibition is either attenuated or indirect. The first group then subdivides conveniently into those instances that include an explicit verb of forbidding and are all ostensibly positive, and the remainder, which all rely on negation.

This first group of explicit prohibitions is by far the most common, and represents patterns that can be found on public notices in diverse contexts all over Spain. Typical attestations would be:

(1) Se prohibe la venta ambulante
(2) Se prohibe hacer aguas contra esta fachada
(3) Se prohibe terminantemente sujetar las puertas
(4) Prohibido el paso a peatones
(5) Prohibido el paso a toda persona ajena a la obra
(6) Prohibida la estancia en zonas sin alumbrado
(7) Prohibida la venta ambulante en toda la ciudad
(8) Rigurosamente prohibida la entrada a visitantes de menos de 14 años
(9) Prohibido jugar a la pelota
(10) Prohibido fijar carteles – responsable la empresa anunciadora
(11) Prohibido fumar o llevar el cigarro encendido bajo multa de mil pesetas
(12) Está terminantemente prohibido utilizar aparatos eléctricos salvo las máquinas de afeitar.

As can readily be seen, these direct prohibitions are very restricted in their lexis and only slightly more variegated in their morphosyntactic structure. Two basic syntactic frames account for all the examples. The first relies on the reflexive–mediopassive *se prohibe*, resulting in a short but fully grammatical sentence in the present indicative (as in 1-3). The second employs a non-finite participial construction akin to a Latin ablative absolute or to certain types of modern newspaper headline (4-11).[1] Complete sentences with an auxiliary (as in 12) are rare as direct prohibitions. The injunction may be strengthened by a suitable adverb: *rigurosamente* (8) and *terminantemente* (3, 12) are now most common, though an earlier generation of signs in the Madrid Metro used *tajantemente* for activities judged to be conspicuously dangerous.

Invariably, the prohibition is the first constituent and in most cases literally the first word. Assuming that no major type has been overlooked, only a strengthening adverb or an auxiliary may precede the verb of forbidding (8, 12).[2] The second, and often final, constituent specifies the undesirable activity. Without exception, it takes the form of a nominalization, morphologically either an infinitive or a noun, usually abstract. The infinitive is clearly preferred in transitive contexts where an object is mentioned (2, 3, 10-12). The abstract noun is favoured (but not categorical) in intransitive contexts, substituting for monovalent verbs like *estacionar* and *entrar*, bivalents like *pasar*, and intransitivized transitives such as *vender* (as in 6, 8, 5, 7 respectively). Both

---

[1] Compare *Desconvocada la huelga en el servicio de basuras* (*Diario de Sevilla*, 5 June 2002), which is a decent syntactic match for (6) but could not function as an instruction. For a discussion of the pragmatics of headlines, see Dor (2003).

[2] The *se* is treated as an affix and therefore integral to the verb.

infinitives and abstract nouns accept various types of adjunct phrase (2, 4-9, 11), ostensibly datives of the persons affected (4, 5, 8), locatives (2, 6, 7), concessives (12) and what might be termed 'minatory conditionals' (10, 11). Whether the type of adjunct interacts in any way with the first constituent (that is, the choice between a finite reflexive-mediopassive and a participle) cannot be determined on a small corpus, but we should note that the affected dative construction does not seem to occur with a finite verb.[3]

It is worth examining the adjunct phrases in greater detail, since their grammatical status is not always self-evident, and the effect of the limiting phrase is sometimes, perversely, to turn a prohibition into a partial invitation. In examples (4), (5) and (8), the constituents beginning with *a* are probably best treated as indirect objects of the matrix verb which, for reasons of sentence focus or the lightness of the intervening nominal, have been fixed in utterance-final position. Semantically, they are exception statements. In (4) and (5) the way is not blocked, but it is only authorized for vehicles or company employees. Prohibition (8), seen at the entrance to a cinema of dubious repute, only excludes young clients; to all others, it is almost an invitation (and maybe a challenge to the young too). The locatives differ in their scope, with (7) acting as a reinforcement of what is already an absolute injunction, whereas in (2) and (6) the location is an inherent part of the prohibition: like admission to the cinema, parking is not forbidden, just parking in districts with no street lighting, and *hacer aguas* presumably cannot be forbidden, just when directed against a façade that calls for greater reverence. Formally a concessive, injunction (12) appears to be a swingeing general prohibition on the use of electrical appliances, but its physical location, as a printed sign above a hotel shaver socket, may have meant only that the socket was specialized for shavers and hazardous for any other purpose. Unlike the other examples with adjuncts, (11) is an absolute prohibition: the phrase that specifies the penalty for infringement is grammatically attached but not integral or semantically limiting. Finally, example (10) sidesteps grammatical integration and merely juxtaposes a paratactic phrase identifying a target for reprisals as yet unspecified.

The next group to be discussed consists of prohibitions dependent on overt negation:

(13) No se admite la propina (El Corte Inglés)

---

[3] It would not necessarily be ungrammatical but might have undesirable pragmatic effects. So, a version of (11) like *Prohibido a todo transeúnte fumar o llevar el cigarro encendido* may be understood to implicate that there is no danger from smoking by non-passengers, such as employees of the Metro.

(14) No está admitida la propina (Galerías Preciados)
(15) Una vez efectuado el pago del alquiler de la almohadilla no se admite su devolución
(16) No está permitido sacar la almohadilla fuera de la plaza (both Ventas)
(17) No se permite vender en los coches (Metro)
(18) Peatón, no cruce con luz roja
(19) Peatón, no cruzar con luz roja
(20) No pisar la césped
(21) Carteles no.

Despite their more heterogenous appearance, the direct prohibitions relying on negation in fact share some of the salient characteristics that we have identified for the first group. The two most common patterns are both passive, either mediopassives with *se* (13, 15, 17), or stative passives selecting *estar* as their auxiliary (14, 16). The verbs are either generic presents if finite (13-18), or timeless (19-20). There is very little syntactic freedom within the prohibiting clause: the prohibition is almost invariably expressed before the name of the activity (the sole exception is the gnomic ellipsis in (21), which is susceptible of various analyses). The exponent of the undesirable activity is again apparently restricted to a nominalization, either an infinitive or an abstract noun, with the infinitive preferred in transitive contexts (16, 18). It does, however, seem that complete sentences are more acceptable here than in the first group of prohibitions and that sentences of almost pedantic length do occasionally occur on public notices (as in 15-16, both observed inscribed on individual plaques at Ventas, Madrid). The reason may be that the absolute participial construction illustrated in (4-11) is apparently incompatible with negation, at least for the purposes of prohibition.

Indirect prohibitions may be exemplified as follows:

(22) Reservado el derecho de admisión
(23) Reservado para los mutilados
(24) Reservado autobuses parque sindical
(25) Coto privado de caza
(26) Vedado de pesca.

These tokens bear some resemblance to those of our two earlier groups, notably in their timelessness and the location of the implied prohibition at the start, followed by the more specific new information. The participial constructions in (22-24) are obviously akin to those frequently attested among our direct prohibitions (4-11) and similarly incomplete as sentences. The veneer of similarity, however, masks some significant differences, with only the participial absolute in (22) offering a comfortable match for one of the earlier productive patterns. (23) is an ellipsis, with *el asiento* or a similar noun omitted, and (24) is a kind of telegraphese which requires a non-verbal context to be fully interpretable. The last two examples, (25) and (26), frequently observed in rural settings, are both complex noun phrases and derivationally unproductive. It is arguable that (26), regardless of the ellipsis of its head noun, is a more explicit prohibition than (25) and does not belong in the 'indirect' group; it has been included because, like (25), it denotes a place where restrictions apply, rather than a direct instruction to potential anglers.

All of our attestations share two features that may not be typical of other kinds of public notice, or indeed of other kinds of prohibition. In no case is any mention made of the agent of prohibition or of the authority for the instruction. Moreover, though any prohibition is clearly intended for a comprehending person, direct interpellation and imperative verb-forms are both extremely rare in this context. The only ones found, (18) and (19), are variants of flashing warning signs observed on pedestrian crossings, and may be expressed in this way to mark the imminence of the danger. It is noteworthy, even so, that (19) is defocused from an imperative to an infinitive, as also in (20), where there is no imminent danger.

The scant incidence of imperative verbs in the corpus has the obvious consequence that the vocabulary used for direct prohibition in public notices is very small. By far the most common lexical item is – not surprisingly – *prohibir*, followed by *no admitir* and *no permitir*, with *reservar* as the most frequent verb in indirect prohibitions. *Vedar*, though technically available as a synonym of *prohibir*, has not been observed on any public notice except in the set phrase *vedado de pesca* (26) where *vedado* is a substantivized past participle rather than a finite verb. We return to the semantic relations among these verbs in modern Spanish after a brief excursus into their historical development.

3. LEXICO-HISTORICAL INTERLUDE

By their spelling and phonology, *prohibir*, *admitir* and *permitir* are all marked out as not belonging to the continuous inherited vocabulary of Spanish. Corominas and Pascual (*DCECH*) explicitly define them as learned forms, while Penny (2002:158) draws attention to the irregular high pretonic vowel surviving in *permitir* and congeners. *DCECH* dates *admitir* to the fifteenth century, with *permitir* emerging some time later, and gives a first attestation for *prohibir* of 1515, noting that the word must have been in use earlier, since its abstract nominalization *prohibición* has a prior attestation. It is interesting that the most frequent item in the corpus expressing indirect prohibition, namely *reservar*, is also classed as learned and appeared in the language at about the same date.

Before that, direct prohibition had been expressed by *vedar*, the continuator of Latin V TARE, which appears in the Silos Glosses, *Mio Cid* and Nebrija's dictionary, though originally with the expected stem diphthong. The evidence of *Mio Cid* is that *vedar* had a broad range of functions: witness line 667, *El agua nos han vedada, exir nos ha el pan*, where the meaning is that 'they have cut off our water supply' rather than forbidden us access. *DCECH* notes that *vedar* remains functional in written registers of modern Spanish, while in speech it has been progressively narrowed to collocations involving hunting. Indeed, *vedado de pesca* is the only instance in our corpus though, like its analogue *coto privado de caza*, it has been observed in numerous locations.[4] In quite a long entry on *vedar* (*DCECH*, V, 1983:752), the authors do not venture an opinion on the dramatic decline in popularity of the verb, or the somewhat Pyrrhic victory of its monophthongal variant. Conversely, they do discuss the complex polysemous history of *privar* (*privado*, similar in age to *vedado*, should not be assumed to be a Romance past participle but may derive directly from Latin PRIVĀTUS), and they do mention the tendency in popular Spanish for *privar* to function as a near-synonym of *prohibir*, as in *le han privado fumar*.[5]

Why, then, should Spanish have replaced its inherited vocabulary of prohibition? It cannot be a simple case of attrition and therapeutics *à la Gilliéron*. That explanation might be satisfactory in French, where *veër* barely reached the fifteenth century, struggling amid multiple homonymies. In Ibero-Romance, by contrast, *vedar* could have remained as vigorous as *vietare* in Italy, where on public signs *(è) vietato fumare* is the most natural modern equivalent of Spanish *prohibido fumar*. The dating of the lexical replacements suggests a sociocultural explanation. By its nature, prohibition is a formal act, requiring (or

---

[4] The hunting connotations are reinforced by the deverbal noun *veda*, 'closed season'. I am grateful to my colleague Rafael Sala for this observation and the following music-hall song, which again plays on the hunting theme, albeit metaphorically:

De amor no hablar
que es juego arriesgado
en la caza el amor.
Para los amantes
siempre en veda,
has de ir con cuidado
por el monte, cazador.

[5] Compare colloquial English *They've stopped him smoking*. This use of *privar* is not unlike that of *vedar* in the line quoted from *Mio Cid* above.

assuming) authority and perhaps a certain solemnity. It is, of course, not confined to public notices and may be found in numerous legal and administrative documents, almost certainly of a high and technical register. It cannot be coincidental that so many new terms are attested in the busy sixteenth century, with its flurry of administrative and regulatory activity at home and in the new colonies. The remark in *DCECH* that *prohibir* became frequent from the end of the sixteenth century leads naturally to the speculation that this Latinate newcomer was favoured over the established term not only because of its phonological robustness but also because *vedar* seemed too low in register, too lacking in authority, for its new contexts.

4. SEMANTICS AND PRAGMATICS

Returning now to modern Spanish, two lines of approach suggest themselves. The first, which we shall not explore in great detail, would be to formalize the semantics of *prohibir* ~ *vedar* versus *no admitir* ~ *no permitir* beyond the etymological sketch presented above. Though *prohibir* and *vedar* technically remain denotational synonyms, their sharp divergence in frequency and patterns of collocation is very likely to lead to a mismatch of associative readings and register. Substituting *vedar* in some of the public notices quoted above produces an odd, if not bizarre, effect:

(4a) ? Vedado el paso a peatones
(8a) ?? Rigurosamente vedada la entrada a visitantes de menos de 14 años
(1a) ?* Se veda la venta ambulante.

Similarly, the substantial denotational overlap of *admitir* and *permitir* does not entail full grammatical equivalence, as can be seen if we reverse the occurrences in our examples (13-17). This small sample appears to show that *admitir* is preferred with a postposed nominal subject, whereas *permitir* favours an infinitive, possibly with its own direct object. Contrast (13a) below with the original (13) and (16a) with (16).

(13a) ? No se permite la propina
(16a) ? No está admitido sacar la almohadilla.

Whereas in (13) gratuities merely cannot 'be accepted', *permitir* in (13a) requires a human experiencer and so forces an inappropriate reading in which *la propina* seems to be personified and thereby loses its generic value. Conversely, (16) merely forbids taking the cushion outside, while (16a) suggests that it is inconceivable and morally reprehensible to do so.

If there is not perfect synonymy between verbs of overlapping denotation used positively, we should probably be suspicious of positive-negative pairs like *prohibir* and *no permitir*. At first sight, and for the purpose of public notices, they do seem to function as referentially equivalent deontics; compare (17) above with an invented (17a):

(17a)   Se prohibe vender en los coches.

Closer examination, however, reveals that the relationship may not be amenable to treatment as neutralized antonymy, since it is well known that negated antonyms do not necessarily result in syntagmatic equivalence (saying that my house is 'not small' is not the same as asserting that it is 'big'). If, for instance, we follow the model of examples (3) and (12) and try to strengthen the prohibition, the resulting (17b) is perfectly acceptable while (17c) is incoherent:

(17b) Se prohibe terminantemente vender en los coches
(17c) * No se permite terminantemente vender en los coches.

Conversely, substituting a different adverbial may rescue (17c) while invalidating (17b):

(17c^1) No se permite en absoluto vender en los coches
(17b^1) *Se prohibe en absoluto vender en los coches.

Though there are obvious questions of lexical compatibility between verb and adverb in these examples, the negation itself does not seem to be problematic, witness:

(17b^2) No se prohibe terminantemente vender en los coches.

This is grammatical if not very plausible. It denies the truth of the assertion in (17b) and might, for instance, be used by a hawker as an emphatic denial to a passenger who uttered (17b) in the hope that it would make the hawker go away.

We could multiply the tests of collocational acceptability, but it seems that the difference between *prohibir* and *no permitir* and similar pairs, at least in the context of public notices, cannot be reduced to formal sense relations. Functionally, another dimension is involved, that of 'face' and the pragmatics of politeness. We suggest, therefore, that a second, and more fruitful, approach to public prohibitions lies via speech act theory. First, however, some justification is required for applying speech act theory to linguistic sequences that are patently not speech. The application may be intuitively satisfying but, as we shall see, it is not formally straightforward.

Most of the examples we have collected could fall comfortably within the class originally termed 'exercitives' by Austin (1962:150, 154-56) and later reanalysed as 'directives' by Searle (1976). Essentially, they are orders, having illocutionary force based on authority or power. Yet they fail the very first diagnostic test proposed by Austin for performatives. Performatives should normally have a first-person subject and a verb in the present tense, conditions with which exercitives can readily comply, as in *I require you not to do that*. Though our public notices are all expressed in the present tense or are timeless, they conspicuously fail to show first-person subjects, or personal subjects of any kind. Austin did allow for the possibility of non-first-person performatives, including passivized forms, but our examples do not fit these templates either. Nor is it manifest that they comply with Austin's felicity conditions requiring completeness and adequate authority.

Let us argue back. True, not all our examples are syntactically complete, as we specifically noted in the case of (4-11) and (21-26). Even so, Austin's condition refers not to grammaticality but to the presence of all the semantic elements necessary to make the exercitive fully interpretable; here, our attestations do comply, save perhaps for the telegraphese (24). Also true, our examples fail to make explicit the authority on which they are based or even to allude to its existence; none matches an utterance like *In the name of the Law, I require you to surrender*. In public prohibitions, however, the absence of explicit agency is compensated, or at least mitigated, by context and format. Someone has chosen a form of words, commissioned the production of a sign and caused it to be erected in a conspicuous position, where its appearance might invite comparison with other regulatory symbols of modern life such as mandatory traffic signs. Presumably, the 'someone' had authority to do this and to enforce compliance. We are unlikely to query the instruction unless it is patently absurd rather than merely irksome.

These are interesting, but not the most telling arguments. For Austin, the crucial distinction between performatives and ordinary declaratives ('constatives' in his terminology) is that some utterances have two readings: they may be illocutionary acts with intended perlocutionary effects, or merely reports of illocutionary acts. He proposes the 'hereby' test as a diagnostic: an utterance that accepts the word *hereby* (as in *I hereby promise to...*, *I hereby absolve you...*, *You are hereby required to...*) is performative in nature and explicitly claims the competence to perform its meaning. Most of the examples of public signs in our corpus have a similar property, though it is implicit in the context rather than specified by a word corresponding to *hereby*. Consider (1), repeated here for convenience:

(1) Se prohibe la venta ambulante.

When read on a public sign, (1) becomes a performative, requiring any readers who are engaging in activities covered by *venta ambulante* to desist. Such readers interpret the prohibition as specific to them, though they may of course refuse to comply. Other readers interpret the sign as a report of a public decision. We can illustrate the difference by adding a locative phrase to (1) or embedding it as a subordinate clause:

(1b) En Cartaya, se prohibe la venta ambulante
(1c) El alcalde acaba de declarar que se prohibe la venta ambulante.

Neither is likely to appear as a public sign, and neither has illocutionary force under normal conditions.[6] We could therefore argue that, in instances like (1), where the message is certainly intended as an injunction, the public sign itself is acting as the proxy for the *hereby* of the performative utterance.

These provisional conclusions about the performative nature of prohibitions like (1) have implications for the subgrouping of the corpus. We made the primary cut on the grounds that the prohibition was explicit (1-21) or indirect (22-26). From a semantic standpoint, this remains true. Considering the examples as speech acts, however, raises the question whether the prohibitions that rely on negated permissives (13-17) are true performatives or 'only' reports that, under special conditions, can be invested with illocutionary force. The same stricture may apply to (12), the only instance of an explicit prohibition couched as a fully grammatical passive sentence with *estar*. An *estar*-passive is automatically stative, and often resultative, neither of which is compatible with performative status.

The examples affected might be described as semantically attenuated, not because they necessarily forbid the undesirable activity less categorically, or because they are overtly polite, but because they present the instruction in a generalized way that defocuses the addressee. In other words, they save the addressee's face. In classic politeness theory (Brown and Levinson 1987), those prohibitions that we have argued to be performatives must be ranked as 'bald, on the record', the highest grade of Face Threatening Act. Prohibitives like (4),

---

[6] At best, (1b) or (1c) might function as indirect prohibitives if uttered rather archly by a passer-by who disapproved of the activity but wished to avoid an altercation by deflecting the source of the instruction.

(9) and impositives[7] like (20) and (21) brook no opposition and make no concessions to gentler feelings. The reason that they are defused and do not normally provoke rage is precisely that they are so general. By contrast, (18) and (19) court disaster by combining a bald demand with an identifiable addressee, but are condoned because they can be interpreted as safeguarding the wellbeing of the same addressee. The strategy is nevertheless risky, and the fact that this benign interpretation cannot be guaranteed may explain the scarcity of such examples in our corpus. Those instances of prohibitions that we have now deemed non-performative, mainly (13-17), lacking a specific addressee and defocusing instruction into a statement, contrive a double saving of face: readers are not obliged to cast themselves as addressees and may feel able to endorse the writer's sentiments once they have decided that they are not the intended target.[8]

Finally in this section, we should note that neither the strength of the prohibition nor the degree of pragmatic attenuation necessarily correlates with the seriousness of the potential offence or its likely repercussions. The bald demands in (3-5) and (18-19) are mitigated if interpreted as safety precautions, and the reinforcement in (3) is the more acceptable as the danger is perceived to be more imminent. The attested prohibition in (17) is phrased in a more conciliatory way than its counterpart (17a), though the phrasing would presumably make no difference to any penalty. The non-performative prohibitions (13-16) are directed towards paying customers and it is not clear that any penalty could be exacted for non-compliance. Examples (13-14), indeed, could be interpreted not as prohibitions but as indirect requests to comply with company policy on gratuities. As requests, they are very firmly articulated, probably in tacit recognition of the fact that the only effective sanctions can be visited on the hapless employee, not on the offending customer. Nor are polite requests in general necessarily free from sanctions. Consider such explicit requests as –

(27) Se ruega a los señores clientes respetar las normas del día hotelero.[9]

---

[7] Impositive is a useful concept pioneered by Haverkate (1979) taking in a wider group of utterances than imperatives alone, but it seems to have been little used in recent years.

[8] For an exploration of the means available for distancing the speaker from the message, see Vaquero (2000), which also points up differences between written Spanish and the colloquial usage of young speakers, and between European and Latin American usage. The criss-crossing patterns vividly illustrate the difficulty of predicting with certainty the pragmatic effect of any one strategy.

[9] In the context of our earlier discussion of the historical discontinuity of the vocabulary of prohibition, it is noteworthy that *rogar* has had a continuous history in

Being decoded, (27) is a polite reminder to leave the accommodation by 12.00 noon or face the bill for an extra night's stay. The sanction is not stated and no linguistic reinforcement is used, but it is probably more effective than heavily emphasized bans like (8). Indeed, the only generalization we can draw from the prohibitions that are explicitly reinforced is that they reveal the apprehensiveness of the prohibitor about the consequences of any infringement.

5. CONCLUDING REMARKS

We have argued that public prohibitions constitute a defined pragmatic domain in which only a narrow range of morphosyntactic structures is acceptable. Typically, they are short, non-specific in time reference, have neither addressee nor agent, and serialize the mark of prohibition before the forbidden activity.[10] The great majority are passives or mediopassive impersonals, passivization being a prime device for focusing on the underlying 'theme' (here, the forbidden activity) at the expense of the human participants. Passives are well known to have deontic modality, sometimes explicit, more often inferred, since the suppression of the agent leaves *what is not done* susceptible to reinterpretation as *what must not be done*.[11] A public prohibition, fitted into the limited space of a conventional sign, must be succinct, readable, and not tax the average attention span. As such, it will probably be formulaic, including (as Wray 2002 contends) sequences that we recognize as wholes and do not process internally. In syntactic terms, most of our examples are formulaic to some extent.

We have also claimed that there are pragmatic characteristics that justify treating prohibitions as a subset of directives within speech-act theory.[12] A narrowly semantic analysis, though a necessary precursor, does not offer a satisfying account of usage. We have provided evidence, through the scope and compatibility of adverbials and negation, against the generative semanticist temptation to analyse *prohibir* as the surface realization of some such underlying

---

Spanish, is morphophonologically regular, and is attested in the earliest texts with much the same meaning as it has in the modern language.

[10] For a discussion and useful taxonomy of word order constraints in two-constituent utterances, see Ocampo (1995). Although the data are drawn from River Plate Spanish and no claims are made about European usage, the main findings seem intuitively comparable.

[11] See Green (1987) for discussion of deontic modality in passives, and Sánchez-López (2002) for good coverage of the uses of *se*-constructions.

[12] In reaching these conclusions, I have benefited from a close reading of Mackenzie (2000), Placencia and Bravo (2002), and Stewart (1999: especially 169-76; and 2003). These items, however, are discussing related phenomena rather than directly comparable data, and their authors are not responsible for any use I have made of their insights.

structure as [AFFIRM [NOT [ALLOW [*allow X*]]]], so denying the possibility that *prohibir* and *no permitir* might not be synonymous. Their non-congruence can be illustrated by the difficulty of creating analogues for the participial absolute frame (4-11); ?* *no admitida la venta ambulante* and ?* *inadmitidos los aparatos eléctricos* fail whether the negation is freestanding or incorporated. These and other divergences point to different subgroupings within our corpus, depending less on the direct semantic marking of prohibition and more on the illocutionary force of the 'utterance' in its context.

Finally, we have tried to demonstrate that the cline running from *se prohibe*, via *no está permitido*, to *se ruega* does not correlate directly either with the force of the prohibition or the severity of the consequences of infringement. It corresponds much better to the attenuation of threats to the face of the recipient. Bald, on-the-record prohibitives achieve social acceptability by focusing on the undesirable activity and offering the let-out that the reader may not belong to the class of potential infringers. For this reason, second-person prohibitives are very rare: as with second-person requests, they risk reciprocal loss of face if the addressee accepts the challenge of a direct refusal. Our corpus has also shown that the distinction between directives and requests is not always clear cut: the non-performative prohibitions in (13-16) could be analysed as disguised requests, with the negative politeness serving to strengthen what would otherwise be more obviously a prohibition without sanctions. Our general conclusion must be that public prohibitions are always to an extent negotiated and negotiable. Minimal politeness turns out to be the precondition of acceptability.

References

Austin, J. L. 1962. *How To Do Things With Words*, ed. by J. Urmston. Oxford: Clarendon Press.
Brown, Penelope and Stephen C. Levinson. 1987. *Politeness. Some Universals in Language Usage*. Cambridge: Cambridge Unversity Press. Revised and extended edition.
DCECH = Corominas, Juan – J. A. Pascual. 1980-91. *Diccionario crítico etimológico castellano e hispánico*. Madrid: Gredos. 6 vols.
Dor, Daniel. 2003. "On newspaper headlines as relevance optimizers." *Journal of Pragmatics* 35, 695-721.
Green, John N. 1987. "The evolution of Romance auxiliaries: criteria and chronology". *Historical Development of Auxiliaries*, ed. by Martin Harris and Paolo Ramat, 257-67. Berlin: Mouton de Gruyter.
Haverkate, Henk. 1979. *Impositive Sentences in Spanish*. Amsterdam: North Holland.

Mackenzie, Ian E. 2000. "Marginal codification in Spanish". *Hispanic Research Journal* 1, 215-27.
Ocampo, Francisco. 1995. "The word order of two-constituent constructions in spoken Spanish". *Word Order in Discourse*, ed. by P. Downing and M. Noonan, 425-47. Amsterdam: Benjamins.
Penny, Ralph J. 2002. *A History of the Spanish Language*. Cambridge: Cambridge University Press. Second edition.
Placencia, María E. and Diana Bravo. 2002. "Panorámica sobre el estudio de los actos de habla y cortesía lingüística". *Actos de habla y cortesía en español*, ed. by María E. Placencia and Diana Bravo, 1-19. Munich: LinCom Europa.
Sánchez-López, Cristina. 2002. (ed.) *La construcciones con SE*. Madrid: Visor Libros.
Searle, J. R. 1976. "A classification of illocutionary acts". *Language in Society* 5, 1-23.
Stewart, Miranda. 1999. *The Spanish Language Today*. London: Routledge.
Stewart, Miranda. 2003. "'Pragmatic weight' and face: pronominal presence and the case of the Spanish second person singular subject pronoun *tú*". *Journal of Pragmatics* 35, 191-206.
Vaquero, María. 2000. "Impersonalidad y distanciamiento". *Introducción a la lingüística española*, ed. by Manuel Alvar, 491-500. Barcelona: Ariel.
Wray, Alison. 2002. *Formulaic Language and the Lexicon*. Cambridge: Cambridge University Press.

24
Convergence and Divergence in World Languages: Spanish, Latin and English
ROGER WRIGHT

IN THE SECOND EDITION of his *History of the Spanish Language* (2002), Ralph Penny included a brief new section (319-20) entitled "Convergence and Divergence," which he introduced with the question: "Will Spanish remain a single language, or will it fragment into a number of mutually unintelligible languages?" Following this train of thought, this chapter considers the validity of the language name *Spanish*, how it arose in the past as the result of the linguistic divergence of Latin, and for how long it is likely to seem applicable in the future, whether that involves divergence or convergence.

THE START OF SPANISH: WHEN DID SPANISH BEGIN?
The question of how and when Spanish actually began concerns the changes in the language's name as much as it concerns actual changes in the language itself. The study of how language names are chosen, and why they change, seems at first glance to be a minor area of research interest. And yet the fact that a language has changed its name can lead to misunderstandings, since it is natural to assume that a new name must refer to a new language. But in a case such as the change of name from Latin to Romance, and then to Spanish, inevitably there are also major continuities, and it is not easy for a subsequent investigator to see what the change of name did and did not involve.

In the case of Spanish, nobody would deny that there has been an unbroken line of direct diachronic descent for at least ten thousand years, and probably much longer, without there having ever been an obvious chronological point at which the speakers stopped speaking one language and started speaking another. There has always been continuity; and yet we, the modern historical linguists, are happy to call its ancestor language of eight thousand years ago *Proto-Indo-European*; we call the intervening stage of five thousand years ago *Italic*; and the language of two thousand years ago *Latin*, which happens in this case to correspond to the name that the speakers gave to it themselves (*lingua latina*). And now Latin as it is spoken in the Iberian Peninsula is called (in English) *Spanish*.

From a strictly linguistic point of view, none of these changes of name have been inevitable or necessary. And they are essentially independent of changes in the language itself. Language change happens all the time, but we do not need for that reason to give the language a different name every week. Linguists realize this; and yet studies of the History of the Spanish Language rarely take in the whole chronological sweep of the last ten thousand years, in order to begin at the earliest reconstructable point in the language's diachronic line of descent.

This reluctance is natural, and largely explicable by the derivation of the name *Spanish* itself from the area of Spain. It could never seem appropriate to apply this name to any variety of Latin before 206 B.C., which was when the Romans took over from the Carthaginians in the Iberian Peninsula; whereas specialists in Italian seem much happier to delve into their language's prehistory, given their geographical continuity; see for example Pulgram (1958), and several studies in Herman and Marinetti (2000). The end of the Punic war coincides with no easily reconstructable internal development, but it is still a natural turning point within both the History of Latin and the linguistic history of the Peninsula, in that it completely changed the Peninsula's sociolinguistic nature. Punic had been the language with power and prestige, but suddenly it was replaced in that role by the Latin spoken by their victorious conquerors. The Romans gradually extended their domination over the whole Peninsula, and after a couple of centuries Roman power covered also the North and West. This was the first time that the whole Peninsula had ever had a common language; even though the earlier ones also survived for some time alongside it, the Celtic, Punic and Iberian spoken there eventually died out. We cannot be sure exactly when. Basque, of course, has survived, although it too has naturally evolved considerably in the last two thousand years. As has Latin; and even though, unlike Basque, Latin has changed its name, it makes sense to say that the language of the Romans is the one spoken in the whole Peninsula still.

The Iberian Peninsula had never before been a single or coherent cultural unit, rather than the contingentially collective home for a large variety of separate groups, states and languages, so the name "Spanish" (*lingua hispanica*, or anything similar), intended to refer to the language spoken by all in the Peninsula, could never have seemed appropriate for any of the languages that existed there before the arrival of the Romans. It is true that modern historical linguists have no inhibitions about applying names to language stages of the past which the speakers did not or could not have used, but even so the earliest possible date at which we can envisage calling any language *Spanish* can only be when the contemporary ancestral stage of Ibero-Romance and modern Spanish was first introduced into the Peninsula, as a language of indigenous prestige, in 206 B.C.. Thus even though the most ambitious of the Romance reconstructionists might wish to envisage the relevant Ibero-Romance node on their tree diagrams as existing from the arrival of the Romans in the Iberian Peninsula (e.g. De Dardel 1996), it is difficult to see how any modern scholar could justify calling that node *Ibero-Romance* if they wished to locate it at a time when effectively none of the speakers were in the Peninsula. But a speech community speaking the ancestral form of what we now call Spanish has indeed been resident in the Peninsula ever since 206 B.C., so there is a possible argument for dating the start of *Spanish* to 206 B.C., even though nobody called it by that name at that time. There is an unbroken line of internal linguistic descent in the Peninsula from then until now; that is why University courses and handbooks in the History of the Spanish Language all start at that chronological point, rather than discussing the earlier history of Latin's development in Italy from Italic and Proto-Indo-European, or considering the history of Celtic, Punic, Iberian and Basque, which have the relevant geographical rights but no such line of direct descent. I know of only one modern scholar who has used the word *Spanish* to refer to pre-Roman languages in the Peninsula, Balsdon (1979); this usage is at best confusing. Adams, though (2003:279-83), calls them collectively "Hispanic Languages," in the same way as Roman writers could refer to words borrowed from them into Latin as *Hispanus* (Adams refers [2003:458] to Martial's *Epigram* 12.57.9, *illinc balucis malleator Hispanae*, although this comment is not necessarily metalinguistic).

The speakers of Peninsular Latin (Romance) did eventually change their language's name, of course; some fourteen centuries later. The reasons why languages change their name have not been studied much, although Tore Janson has written acutely on the topic (Janson 2002). We need from the start to distinguish between the labels which modern historical linguists give to language states of the past, and the names which the speakers involved gave their native language at the time (cp. in the Romance context, Wright 2003a: chapters 3 and 13). Other things being equal, it is not natural for speakers ever to want to change the name of their language; but if they do, the new name chosen tends to be geographical, typically the nominalization of a toponymic adjective. Latin had been one such name, since *latinus* is the nominalization of the adjective derived from *Latium*, the area around Rome where Latin came from. What the ancestral stage of that language was called by its own speakers before the speech community arrived in Latium is lost in time (if indeed it was called anything at all, since many communities have no specific name for their own language) but we can assume that they did not themselves call it by the name of *Proto-Indo-European*, which is what we call it now. That name has been chosen from a modern perspective, in that we now know that its descendant languages spread geographically from Europe to India, and it is not intended to help clarify the metalinguistic consciousness of the speakers of this language at the time concerned.

Latin, the *lingua latina*, was taken by its speakers to geographical areas far from the Latium area that had given rise to its name. The geographical connection thereby lost its morphological transparency. If it had not travelled to so many other places, maybe the language of the Lazio area would still now be called *latino* (in the same way as Greek is still called Greek, *elliniki glossa*; Janson 2002:85, as it was in Aristotle's day). As it was, the link with Latium was attenuated; and in due course, for reasons that were essentially political rather than linguistic, the whole wide Latin-speaking community came to be thought of as being several different speech-communities rather than just one, and new language names had to be devised to distinguish between them. At first, the new entities, and more specifically the new written forms, were called *romance* (variously spelt); but Romance soon came to be thought of as being several languages, so they needed new names as labels for their separate conceptual status. These names too were geographical adjectives in origin, such as *françois*, *proenzal*, *castellano*, and so on; and in these cases the change of name was made by the speakers, not just by the modern historical linguist. These developments date to the late twelfth and thirteenth centuries.

Yet there was almost certainly no single great break in the spoken language's internal development which coincided chronologically with the changes in the language's name. Most of the internal changes which we see now as distinguishing diagnostically between Latin and the Romance Languages had taken place long before this time. The names of *romance*, *romance castellano* and *castellano* were used by speakers in the thirteenth century; the name *Old Spanish* was chosen by modern scholars, as the label for the Medieval Ibero-Romance spoken in the North-central areas of the Peninsula, because that was the way people spoke the evolved Latin in the area whose local speech variety later came to be used as the standard throughout Spain. They could not foresee that future development at the time. The decision taken by the modern investigator to call that variety *Old Spanish* implies that *Spanish* started when the language of Castile was no longer called *Latin*, since that name, borrowed from French as *latin*, was used from the late twelfth century to refer to the newly standardized Medieval Latin.

Labels such as *castellano* were chosen for geographical reasons, but were needed mainly as a consequence of a second line of reasoning which only applies in literate communities; in general, when there is a reform in the writing system of a language, it seems natural for people to come to believe that the new writing system is a different language from the old one, rather than just being the same language written in a different way. This metalinguistic instinct applies to the speakers of the time, but even more so to the subsequent philologists and historical linguists. Thus the earliest emergence of a Romance language has often been thought by philologists and historical linguists to be effectively the same phenomenon as the earliest emergence of a Romance text. These historical linguists and philologists have often instinctively (or sometimes even explicitly) believed this at the same time as ostensibly following the general line taken within General Linguistics to the effect that the written form is merely a parasitic phenomenon, the true linguistic reality lying in speech. But their instincts, and those of the contemporary speakers, have a genuine point; the identity of a language is often more closely bound up with its manner of written representation than the theoretical linguists would usually like to believe. This perspective has recently been nuanced into even greater plausibility by Tore Janson, who has shown that the advent of new language names tends to follow the adoption of new writing systems rather than pre-date or coincide with them (as the philologists might prefer).

There was thus a serious point in the traditional dating by subsequent Romanists of the start of *Spanish* to the advent of texts deliberately written in the North Central Peninsula in a new way. Such Romance texts were first written at different times in different places; in the Iberian Peninsula, the first Spanish texts have traditionally been said to be the Glosses of San Millán (*Glosas emilianenses*), which Menéndez Pidal (in 1926) dated to the second half of the tenth century; this is the dating which came to be integrally connected with the phrase he used as the title of his major work, *Orígenes del español*. So *Spanish* has often been said to have begun in the late tenth century, with these Glosses. For this reason there was a meeting held in San Millán in 1977 to celebrate one thousand years of Spanish, and in the same vein, Alatorre's book (1979), *Los 1001 años de la lengua española*, explicitly calculated that figure as from the start of the year 975 A.D.. Those mathematics are unusable now, because since then the Glosses have been convincingly re-dated to about one hundred years later than that (see Hernández Alonso and Ruiz Asencio 1993); but the general view, that a new way of writing naturally coincides with the arrival of a new language, is still widely accepted.

Even so, some Romanists now feel that these Glosses, and the earliest Romance texts in France (the *Strasbourg Oaths* and the *Cantilène de Eulalie* from Valenciennes) are very special cases, probably best characterized as being the Late Latin of the time and place written in an experimental way, rather than being the representation of a different language (e.g. Banniard 2003 and Wright 2003b, in the same volume). Subsequently, the eleventh and twelfth centuries see the lasting advent of more independent and coherent methods for writing texts in Romance mode in both France and Provence, although even in France the new written mode needed to wait until the very end of the twelfth century, or even the thirteenth, to acquire any sociolinguistic prestige and official status, rather than merely being used for relatively unimportant literary genres.

The upshot of this traditional perspective, allying the advent of a new language with the advent of a new writing system, is that the earliest date at which we might want to envisage the contemporary conceptual existence of separate Romance languages, rather than of different varieties of a monolingual Romance, is the twelfth century. As regards the Iberian Peninsula, this is the date for the presence of the concept of a distinctive peninsula-wide kind of Romance, which subsequent scholars identify as Ibero-Romance, as opposed to Italo-Romance and Gallo-Romance, or as *Spanish*; *Spanish* here gains its semantic content from its opposition to the other twelfth-century Romance languages, rather than from the new geographical situation which would underlie its use for the speech of the second century B.C. in the eyes of the reconstructionists.

Linguists might also decide that *Spanish* should be said to have started at the point where this label first came to be applied by the language's speakers. Unfortunately, in the Spanish case this is not straightforward. The language now called *Spanish* by English-speakers was not called *español* by its own speakers until the existence of a political unit called *España*, and that only came about with the federation of Castile and Aragón in 1479. But the reasoning is valid enough, and underlines the conclusion that the adoption of a new name, both by speakers and by subsequent linguists, is not necessarily a clear-cut event.

These three criteria, the geographical (which gives us 206 B.C., the date when a stage of the language first acquired a sociolinguistic standing in the Peninsula), the graphemic (which gives us whatever date we wish to assign to the earliest texts deliberately written in a new way), and the first use of the name by the speakers (after 1479, once "Spain" existed), are not the only possible methods that have been used for deciding when the language label *Spanish* might be first applicable. A new method of dating the time at which *Spanish* began has recently been applied by Quilis Merín, in her book whose title is a conscious updating of Menéndez Pidal's as seen from a historical-political viewpoint: *Orígenes históricos de la lengua española* (1999). Quilis located the origin of Spanish at the emergence of the Peninsula as a whole separate integral cultural community, rather than just being a part of wider Romania; that is, to 589 A.D., when the Visigoths established their political supremacy in the whole

Peninsula (but nowhere else). The Peninsula had never before been a single political unit with borders at the Pyrenees, and it is this combination of internal coherence and the subsequent borders which led to Quilis's decision. There is no reconstructable internal linguistic development which coincides directly with the events of 589, any more than with those of 206 B.C. or 1479, so as ever the change of name, even under this perspective, misleads the unwary investigator who might assume that the change of name implies a change of language.

The conclusion from this survey is that languages can change names for a variety of reasons, none of them usually linguistic reasons; and in addition that we need to be clear about whether we are referring to changes of name undertaken by speakers of the time, or by subsequent linguists. In any event, the names applied to the languages that developed divergently from Latin deserve to be studied with some care. For if the new names had not been generally adopted, and the whole were still called Latin (which would not have been an impossible sequence of events), the present Romance-speaking world would not be seen as a case of divergence so much as of wide internal variability, much as Chinese still is (by Chinese speakers, if not by linguists).

POSSIBLE DIVERGENCE; WHEN WILL SPANISH END?
There may be an analogy we can turn to when considering the future limit to the applicability of the language name *Spanish*. It has often been suggested that the export of Castilian Spanish to the New World, and the development of emigrant dialects in America, might be a parallel for the export of Latin to the Iberian Peninsula and the development of an emigrant dialect there. This was a fashionable topic in the nineteenth century (see Del Valle 1999; the arguments have been reconsidered in an updated context in Wright 1999, 2000, and 2003a:ch.2). The worry in the nineteenth century was that Spanish in Latin America might diverge and fragment into different languages in the same way as Latin fragmented into Romance languages. If that happens, it seems almost inevitable that as soon as the concepts of these newly fragmented separate languages exist, the language-name *Spanish* will no longer be able to be used any more to refer to a living spoken language. This is what happened to the language-name *Latin* in the Iberian Peninsula from the late twelfth century; after that, the name *Latin* became largely confined to use for both what we now think of as "Classical" Latin and to the quasi-dead but standardized mode which we now call "Medieval" Latin; after the foreseen future divergence the label *Spanish* might similarly only be used to refer with hindsight to the pre-divergent whole and possible antiquarian imitations.

Fragmentation, rather than divergence, is the word normally used by Romanists for the splitting of Latin into separate Romance languages; specialists in other fields do not usually use this term, and Trask's superb *Dictionary of Historical and Comparative Linguistics* (2000) has no entry for the word. In itself, however, it has become a deep-rooted concept, appearing to be not far off a universal. There seems to have arisen a common assumption in Historical Linguistics that it is the default case; that is, that over a long time languages are likely to diverge and fragment. In such cases, language-internal variation increases continually until the whole turns into several different languages rather than merely remaining as several varieties of the same language. This is certainly what happened to the prime example of the academic discipline, Proto-Indo-European. Indeed, it has seemed a reasonable generalization to say that such divergence may be inevitable. Not just that language change is inevitable, which is probably true; and that for a language to be changing in different ways in different places is the norm, which is also probably true; but also that fragmentation is a natural consequence of this increasing variability.

Yet this cannot really be a universal truth. If the speakers of a language do not become geographically separated from each other, as did the Romans who crossed to the Iberian Peninsula and the Spaniards who crossed the Atlantic, and instead they stay more or less in the same geographical area, then fragmentation, as opposed to normal internal variation, is probably unlikely. The Indo-European case was a very special one, for it involved travel over huge distances, during very long periods of time, by small groups of people who were no longer in regular contact with each other, and with no standard or written form to maintain unity through being the target for style-shifting. The fragmentation of Latin into the Romance languages occurred in quite different circumstances; through the relevant period the geographical extension of Romance became smaller than it had been in the Empire, rather than greater; the numbers of speakers were not small, and the different communitites remained in constant contact; there continued to be the same centripetal pull of the inherited written standard. At the very least, Romance fragmentation was not inevitable, even if it is explicable.

Any future fragmentation of Spanish into different languages with, therefore, necessarily different names, will also not be inevitable, since here too, unlike in the case of the Proto-Indo-European speakers, the odds are overwhelmingly that the different communities concerned will remain in regular contact with each other and maintain a single written form. The written Spanish standard might be generally updated in some details from time to time, but it will almost certainly still be the same over the whole area; after the generally unsettling experience of the reforms which Chile alone decreed for written Spanish between 1860 and 1927, all the separate national Academies in the Spanish-speaking world seem to have agreed on the need to maintain written unity (see Del Valle and Gabriel-Stheeman 2002). In the same way as *La*

Francophonie is and will probably remain a single variable unit, what we could analogically call *La Hispanofonía* is likely to remain a single variable speech community; in the same way as what we could call the "*Romanophonie*," the wide community of Romance speakers, was collectively for many centuries a single speech community, with a single written norm inherited from the Roman Empire. Unless we accept the very early dating for the nodes on the tree-diagrams of the Romance reconstructionists as having ontological validity---as Penny (1996) and I (1995:ch.3) both prefer not to do---we may have to accept that in the minds of the speakers this single state of complex monolingualism ("*Romanophonie*") lasted until the Latin written system was backgrounded in favour of the new written systems invented in the central Middle Ages, different in different places. There were thirteen or fourteen centuries between the initial Roman invasion and this metalinguistic fragmentation; so if there is some kind of universal analogical principle at work here, and divergence is inevitable to the point of fragmentation, *Spanish*, as the name of a living language, will only even then cease to be applicable some fourteen centuries after Columbus; that is, towards the end of the present millennium.

POSSIBLE CONVERGENCE
But that divergence scenario is unlikely to happen, unless there is some kind of global catastrophe which separates the different Spanish-speaking communities as effectively as simple distance separated the Proto-Indo-European communities. Such a catastrophe is entirely possible, of course, as Janson (2000) points out when speculating on the future of language and languages. If this happens, this would be a paradigm case where an understanding of sociocultural circumstances will be essential to the subsequent analyses of historical linguists.

Historical Linguistics is an odd discipline at best, and one of the odd things about it is the fact that some of its practitioners have thought that it ought be "predictive" (e.g. Lass 1980). But this perspective has usually taken the form of claiming that changes which we know now to have happened could have been predicted at an earlier stage; which is a somewhat circular argument, since that earlier stage in the past has usually been reconstructed to some extent by us, by means of assuming the same kind of logical principles of development which we are hoping to discover in operation. This desire for predictiveness has not usually taken the form of actively predicting the distant future. But if we do for once try to predict the future, in cases of widespread world languages such as Spanish, we may well want to ignore the ancient precedent of Proto-Indo-European and foresee convergence rather than divergence. Ralph Penny does just this, and he is probably right to do so.

There are historical precedents for convergence as well. Indeed, it seems likely that the later stages of the Roman Empire itself experienced the many linguistic changes that were happening as tending towards convergence rather than divergence; that is, despite all the changes that Latin had undergone, the nature of the Latin-speaking community as a whole was probably more homogeneous in 410 A.D. than it had been four hundred years before. József Herman (2000) on the whole favours this view. There were a number of reasons for this tendency towards convergence, if that is indeed what happened, several of which would have continued to be effective for long after the political end of the Empire; they include the loss of many of the pre-Roman languages and therefore the weakening of substratum influences, the incorporation of many previously bilingual communities into the status of native speakers, the general use of the fourth-century Grammar of Aelius Donatus (*Ars Minor*) as the arbiter of the written standard, the uniting and even levelling influence of army units which normally contained recruits from every province, and more significantly in the long term the levelling influence of Christian church usage, as recently studied by Banniard (2001), a phenomenon which certainly continued long after the end of the Empire itself. That is, linguistic evolutions occurred, but several of these tended for several centuries towards similar results in different places rather than towards fragmentation. This is the phenomenon of convergence, which the traditional tree-diagrams might lead historical linguists to regard instinctively as weird or even inherently impossible (given that the branches of trees tend not to converge in this way).

And yet convergence, slow and gradual but detectable, has been shown to apply to the development of Medieval Castilian as well, not just by Ralph Penny but more recently and in illuminating detail by Donald Tuten (2003); it happened to the Hispanic dialects transported to the Americas after 1492 (see e.g. Lüdtke 1994); and it is also what seems to be happening within the modern "world languages." This includes the modern English-speaking world, which is unexpectedly homogeneous for all its amazing variety, as best evidenced in the fascinating *Oxford Guide to World English* (McArthur 2002). It is also happening in the modern Spanish-speaking world, at least as seen from a diatopic perspective. Thus most informed Hispanists no longer fret about the possible geographical fragmentation of Castilian as their forebears did a century and a half ago. On the other hand, several linguists in Spain itself worry about the effects of the rise in sociolinguistic prestige of their territorial competitors, such as in particular Catalan (e.g. Lodares 1999), which may perhaps some time lead to the applicability being questioned of the label *Spanish* (*español*) for a language spoken in only a part of Spain.

Penny (2002:319-20) predicts that convergence in World Spanish is likely to continue, without adducing detailed evidence. But there is compelling evidence in his support. Dialectal variation is becoming increasingly less marked in Spain itself, as it is in Britain. For example, Navarrese is gradually getting ever more like Castilian, either because it happens to be evolving that way anyway or because of Castilian influence, as González Ollé (1983) has tried valiantly to disentangle. Many people in Asturias speak a kind of mixture of Bable and Castilian, a mixture which may be likely to become the most usual speech mode in future. In Galicia, the linguists distinguish clearly between Galician and Castilian, but many of the actual speakers operate commonly in *castrapo* (which is Galician heavily influenced by Castilian) or *picheleiro* (which is Castilian heavily influenced by Galician), two categories which in turn may be becoming none too easy to distinguish from each other; over forthcoming centuries the future in Galicia may well involve convergence of the four. Hernando de Larramendi recently startled a Valencia conference audience by suggesting in all seriousness that over the next two centuries Spanish and Portuguese could and indeed ought to merge (Hernando de Larramendi 1995); indeed they could, and it is probably only trivially political rather than serious linguistic circumstances that will be able to prevent it. And this process might continue after that; since on the whole it is the case even now that speakers of different Romance languages can often understand each other, in several hundred years most, or even all, of the present separated Romance speech-communities could even be reconverging, both conceptually and in practice, as one single variable one. There are already half-serious movements in the European Community consciously intended to lead to this outcome. Arthur C. Clarke seems to envisage something like this as having happened by the year 3001 (in his book *3001: The Final Odyssey*: Clarke 1997), where he sees only four languages as having survived the present millennium; and although he calls the sole Romance survivor in 3001 *French*, it may be more likely to be a convergent koine developed from several Romance tributaries, and thus almost necessarily have a different name from all the geographical labels in existence now. It could be called *Romance*, even. If Spanish and Portuguese and others of the Romance family merge in some distant future century, and that merged language acquires a new separate written form either before (as Janson would envisage) or after (as Banniard would envisage) the merging of the concepts, then that merged language will need a new and different label to distinguish it from all the previously spoken and written languages endowed with the labels that emerged in the minds of speakers during the 1200s. This convergence process is likely to take several centuries; thus towards the end of the present millennium, under this convergence scenario just as under the divergence scenario previously considered, the language-label of *Spanish* will have outlived its usefulness, both for the speakers of that age and the historical linguists of an even later one.

CONCLUSION

Thus, whether the future for Spanish is divergence or convergence, it seems possible to predict that the lifespan of the validity of the *Spanish* language label will only last to the later part of the present millennium. Even so, its continuing status as a World Language, as Latin once was and English also is, means that it comes into a special category. Janson (2000) warns us in effect that the past may be no guide to the future in such cases. McArthur (2002:416) was right to say that: "we cannot know, however, what a world language of the long-term future will be like, or what it might be called"; it is still interesting to speculate.

References

Adams, James N. 2003. *Bilingualism and the Latin Language*. Cambridge: University Press.
Alatorre, Antonio. 1979. *Los 1,001 años de la lengua española*. Mexico: Tezontle.
Balsdon, J. P. V. D. 1979. *Romans and Aliens*. London: Duckworth.
Banniard, Michel. 2001. "Action et réaction de la parole latinophone: démocratisation et unification (IIIe - Ve siècles)." *An Tard* 9, 115-29.
Banniard, Michel. 2003. "Latinophones, romanophones, germanophones: interactions identitaires et construction langagière (VIIIe - Xe siècles)." *Médiévales* 45, 25-42.
Clarke, Arthur C. 1997. *3001: The Final Odyssey*. London: HarperCollins.
De Dardel, Robert. 1996. *A la recherche du protoroman*. Tübingen: Niemeyer.
Del Valle, José. 1999. "Lingüística histórica e historia cultural: notas sobre la polémica entre Rufino José Cuervo y Juan Valera." *Essays in Hispanic Linguistics dedicated to Paul M. Lloyd*, ed. by Robert Blake et al., 173-87. Newark: Juan de la Cuesta.
Del Valle, José and Luis Gabriel-Stheeman, eds. 2002. *The Battle over Spanish between 1800 and 2000*. London: Routledge.
González Ollé, Fernando. 1983. "Evolución y castellanización del romance navarro." *Príncipe de Viana* 44, 173-80.
Herman, József. 2000. *Vulgar Latin*. University Park: Penn State Press.
Herman, József and Anna Marinetti, eds. 2000. *La preistoria dell'italiano*. Tübingen: Niemeyer.
Hernández Alonso, César and J. M. Ruiz Asencio, eds. 1993. *Las Glosas Emilianenses y Silenses. Edición crítica y facsímil*. Burgos: Ayuntamiento.
Hernando de Larramendi, Ignacio. 1995. "Geopolítica del idioma castellano para el siglo XXI." *Historia de la Lengua Española en América y España*, ed. by M. T. Echenique Elizondo et al, 543-59. Valencia: University Press.
Janson, Tore. 2002. *Speak: A Short History of Languages*. Oxford: University Press.
Lass, Roger. 1980. *On Explaining Language Change*. Cambridge: University Press.

Lodares, Juan Ramón. 1999. *El paraíso políglota*. Madrid: Taurus.
Lüdtke, Jens, ed. 1994. *El español de América en el siglo XVI*. Frankfurt: Vervuert.
McArthur, Tom. 2002. *The Oxford Guide to World English*. Oxford: University Press.
Menéndez Pidal, Ramón. 1926; 7th ed. 1972. *Orígenes del español*. Madrid: Espasa-Calpe.
Penny, Ralph. 1996. "El árbol genealógico: ¿modelo lingüístico desfasado?" *Actas del III Congreso Internacional de Historia de la Lengua Española* 827-39. Madrid: Arco.
Penny, Ralph. 2002. *A History of the Spanish Language* (2nd ed.). Cambridge: University Press.
Pulgram, Ernst. 1958. *The Tongues of Italy: prehistory and history*. Cambridge (Mass.): Harvard University Press.
Quilis Merín, Mercedes. 1999. *Orígenes históricos de la lengua española*. Valencia: University Press.
Trask, R. Larry. 2000. *The Dictionary of Historical and Comparative Linguistics*. Edinburgh: University Press.
Wright, Roger. 1995. *Early Ibero-Romance*. Newark: Juan de la Cuesta.
Wright, Roger. 1999. "Expansión y divergencia: el latín en el viejo mundo, el español en el nuevo." *Actas del XI Congreso Internacional de la Asociación de Lingüística y Filología de la América Latina*, ed. by J. A. Samper Padilla et al., 107-22. Las Palmas: University Press.
Wright, Roger. 2000. "The Future of Spanish: Divergence or Convergence?" *La Marca Hispánica* 11, 1-19.
Wright, Roger. 2003a. *A Sociophilological Study of Late Latin*. Turnhout: Brepols.
Wright, Roger. 2003b. "La Période de transition du latin, de la *lingua romana* et du français." *Médiévales* 45, 11-24.

Notes on Contributors

ANTÓNIO EMILIANO is Assistant Professor (with tenure) in the Departamento de Linguística, Faculdade de Ciências Sociais e Humanas, Universidade Nova de Lisboa, Av. de Berna 26-C, 1069-061 Lisboa, Portugal (ah.emiliano@fcsh.unl. pt); his publications include "O mais antigo documento latino-português (882 a.D.): edição e estudo grafémico", *Verba. Anuario Galego de Filoloxía* 26, 2000:7-42; and (with Susana Pedro), "De noticia de torto: aspectos paleográficos e scriptográficos e edição do mais antigo documento particular português conhecido", *Zeitschrift für Romanische Philologie* 120/1, 2004:1-85. His main research interests are in Historical Linguistics, Ibero-Romance Linguistics, Medieval Philology and the Phonology of Portuguese.

JOEL RINI is Professor of Spanish Linguistics in the Department of Spanish, Italian & Portuguese, 115 Wilson Hall, University of Virginia, Charlottesville, Virginia 22903, USA (jr6b@virginia.edu): his publications include *Motives for Linguistic Change in the Formation of the Spanish Object Pronouns* (Juan de la Cuesta, 1992) and *Exploring the Role of Morphology in the Evolution of Spanish* (John Benjamins, 1999). His research interests are in the area of Spanish historical grammar.

ROBERT J. BLAKE is Professor of Spanish at the University of California, Davis, and founding Director of the UC Consortium for Language Learning and Teaching, One Shields Avenue, Voorhies 220, UC Davis, CA 95616 (rjblake@ ucdavis.edu). He was the academic consultant for *Nuevos Destinos* (Annenberg/ CPB Project, WGBH, and McGraw-Hill Companies) and co-author for *Tesoros* (BeM, McGraw-Hill Companies), a five-disk multimedia CD-ROM program for introductory Spanish; his articles include "Radiografía de un cambio lingüístico" and "Squeezing the Spanish Turnip Dry: Latinate documents from the Early Middle Ages". His research interests are in Spanish linguistics, second language acquisition, and computer-assisted language learning.

DONALD N. TUTEN is Associate Professor of Spanish in the Department of Spanish and Portuguese, Emory University, Atlanta, Georgia 30322, USA (dtuten@emory.edu); he is the author of *Koineization in Medieval Spanish*

(Berlin and New York: Mouton de Gruyter, 2003). His research interests are in historical linguistics and sociolinguistics, and questions of language and dialect contact.

MARTIN J. DUFFELL is Honorary Fellow and Research Fellow in the Department of Hispanic Studies, Queen Mary, University of London, Mile End Road, London E1 4NS, England (m.j.duffell@qmul.ac.uk); his publications include *Modern Metrical Theory and the "Verso de arte mayor"* (London, 1999) and "The Metric Cleansing of Hispanic Verse", *Bulletin of Hispanic Studies* (Liverpool), 76, 1999, 151-68. His research interests are in comparative, historical, and linguistic metrics.

PETER T. RICKETTS is Honorary Professor in the Department of French, University of Birmingham, Birmingham, B15 2TT, England (p.t.ricketts@bham.ac.uk), and Emeritus Professor of Romance Philology at Queen Mary, University of London; his publications include *Le Breviari d'Amor de Matfre Ermengaud* (to be six vols in all, with the collaboration of Cyril Hershon, Turnhout, 1989-) and *The Concordance of Medieval Occitan* (to be four vols in all, Turnhout, 2001-). His research interests are in Romance philology, Medieval Occitan language and literature, and textual editing.

ALAN DEYERMOND is Research Professor in the Department of Hispanic Studies, Queen Mary, University of London, Mile End Road, London E1 4NS. He taught in the Department from 1955 until his retirement in 1977. He is a fellow of the British Academy. His main research area is medieval Spanish literature, and he has also worked on comparative medieval literature. His books include *A Literary History of Spain: The Middle Ages* (1971) and the first volume of *La literatura perdida de la Edad Media castellana; catálogo y estudio* (1995).

RAY HARRIS-NORTHALL is Professor of Hispanic Linguistics in the Department of Spanish and Portuguese, 1018 Van Hise Hall, 1220 Linden Drive, University of Wisconsin, Madison, Wisconsin 53706, USA (rharris1@facstaff.wisc.edu). His publications include *Weakening Processes in the History of Spanish Consonants* (London, 1990) and (with John J. Nitti) the edition of Peter Boyd-Bowman's *Léxico hispanoamericano 1493-1993* on CD-ROM (New York, 2003). His research interests are in all aspects of the history of Spanish, dialectology, and the application of sociolinguistic theory to language change.

DIANA L. RANSON is Associate Professor of Romance Linguistics in the Department of Romance Languages, Gilbert Hall, University of Georgia,

Athens, Georgia 30602-1815, USA (dranson@uga.edu); her publications include *Change and Compensation: Parallel Weakening of /s/ in Italian, French, and Spanish* (New York, 1989), and, as co-editor, *Essays in Hispanic Linguistics Dedicated to Paul M. Lloyd* (Juan de la Cuesta, 1999). Her research interests are in language change and variation in the Romance languages.

DANA L. ALLEN is a lecturer at the University of Hertfordshire, Hatfield, Hertfordshire, AL10 9AB, England (d.l.allen@herts.ac.uk). In 2002 she completed a doctorate under the supervision of Ralph Penny, entitled *History of the Sibilants of Peninsular Spanish from the Eleventh to the Sixteenth Centuries*. Her research interests are in Spanish phonetics and phonology.

THOMAS R. HART is Professor Emeritus of Comparative Literature and Romance Languages at the University of Oregon; his home address is 2580 Spring Boulevard, Eugene, Oregon 97403, USA (trhart@darkwing.uoregon.edu); his publications include *Cervantes and Ariosto: Renewing Fiction* (Princeton, 1989) and *'En Maneira de proençal': The Medieval Galician-Portuguese Lyric* (London, 1998). His research interests are in Spanish, Portuguese and Catalan literature of the Middle Ages and Renaissance.

RODNEY SAMPSON is Professor of Romance Philology in the Department of French, The University of Bristol, BS8 1TE, England (rodney.sampson@bristol. ac.uk). His publications include *Nasal Vowel Evolution in Romance* (Oxford, 1999) and *Early Romance Texts. An Anthology* (Cambridge, 1980). His research interests are in historical Romance phonology.

IAN MACPHERSON is Research Fellow in the Department of Hispanic Studies, Queen Mary, University of London, E1 4NS, England (ianmac@debrett.net); his publications include *Spanish Phonology* (Manchester, 1975) and (as co-editor with Brian Tate) Juan Manuel's *Libro de los estados* (Oxford, 1974; Madrid, 1991). His research interests are in historical linguistics and medieval literature.

K. ANIPA is Lecturer in Spanish in the Department of Spanish, University of St Andrews, KY16 9AL, Scotland (ka17@st-andrews.ac.uk): his publications include *A Critical Examination of Linguistic Variation in Golden-Age Spanish* (New York, 2001), "*Devría y debería*: el conflicto homonímico y la fusión léxica en el español premoderno", *ALPHA* 15, 1999: 157-172, and "A Study of the Analytical Future/Conditional in Golden-Age Spanish", *Bulletin of Hispanic Studies* (Liverpool), 77, 2000, 325-37. His research interests are in the historical sociolinguistics of Renaissance Castilian and the history of linguistic thought in

Spain.

JOHN ENGLAND is Senior Lecturer in the Department of Hispanic Studies, University of Sheffield, S10 2TN, England (j.p.england@sheffield.ac.uk). The article published in the current volume is one of a series on analogical feminines in Spanish. His principal research interests are in medieval Spanish literature, especially Don Juan Manuel, and the history of the Spanish language, principally morphology and syntax.

CHRISTOPHER J. POUNTAIN is Professor of Spanish at Queen Mary, University of London, Mile End Road, London E1 4NS, England (c.j.pountain@qmul.ac.uk) and a Life Fellow of Queens' College at the University of Cambridge, CB3 9ET, England; his publications include *A History of the Spanish Language through Texts* (London, 2001) and *Exploring the Spanish Language* (London, 2003). His research interests are in the historical syntax of the Romance languages, especially Spanish.

DAVID PHARIES is Professor of Spanish and Chair of the Department of Romance Languages and Literatures at the University of Florida, P.O. Box 117405, Gainesville, Florida 32611, USA (pharies@rll.ufl.edu); his publications include the *Diccionario etimológico de los sufijos españoles* (Madrid, 2002) and the *University of Chicago Spanish Dictionary, 5th ed.* (Chicago, 2002). His research interests are in Spanish lexicology, especially word-formation.

STEVEN N. DWORKIN is Professor of Romance Linguistics in the Department of Romance Languages, University of Michigan, Ann Arbor, Michigan 48109-1275, USA (dworkin@umich.edu). He has recently published a series of papers dealing with the linguistic circumstances underlying the introduction of *cultismos* in late Medieval Spanish. His principal research interest is in diachronic Romance lexicology (with emphasis on Medieval Spanish); his current project involves an examination the nature of lexical and semantic change and the roles played by cognitive and cultural conditions.

IAN MACKENZIE is Senior Lecturer in Spanish in the School of Modern Languages, Old Library, University of Newcastle upon Tyne, NE1 7RU, England (i.e.mackenzie@ncl.ac.uk); his publications include *Introduction to Linguistic Philosophy* (Thousand Oaks, 1997), *The Semantics of Spanish Verbal Categories* (Berne, 1999), and *A Linguistic Introduction to Spanish* (Munich, 2001). His research interests are in Spanish syntax and semantics, together with the philosophy of language.

JOSÉ DEL VALLE is Associate Professor of Hispanic Linguistics at the Graduate Center of the City University of New York, 365 Fifth Avenue, New York 10016, USA (jdelvalle@gc.cuny.edu); his publications include *El trueque s/x en español antiguo: aproximaciones teóricas* (Tübingen, 1996) and, as co-editor, *The Battle over Spanish between 1800 and 2000: language ideologies and Hispanic intellectuals* (London, 2002) and its Spanish edition *La batalla del idioma: la intelectualidad hispánica ante la lengua* (Frankfurt and Madrid, 2004). His research interests are in language ideologies in the recent linguistic history of Spain and Latin America.

FRANCISCO MORENO FERNÁNDEZ is professor of Spanish Language in the Departamento de Filología. Universidad de Alcalá, 28801 Alcalá de Henares, Madrid, Spain (francisco.moreno@uah.es), and currently Director of the Instituto Cervantes of Chicago. His publications include *Principios de sociolingüística y sociología del lenguaje* (1998), *Qué español enseñar* (2000) and (as co-director) *Atlas Lingüístico (y etnográfico) de Castilla La Mancha* (2003). His research interests are in Sociolinguistics, Hispanic Dialectology and Applied Linguistics.

JOHN N. GREEN is Professor of Romance Linguistics in the Department of Languages at the University of Bradford, BD7 1DP, England (j.n.green@bradford.ac.uk). His publications include (as co-editor) *Trends in Romance Linguistics and Philology* (Berlin, 1980-93); he is currently co-editing the *Journal of French Language Studies* (Cambridge) and the revision of the *Lexicon Grammaticorum* (Tübingen). His research interests are in Spanish, French and comparative Romance linguistics, including the Romance Creoles.

ROGER WRIGHT is Professor of Spanish in the Department of Hispanic Studies, University of Liverpool, L69 3BX, England (rhpwri@liv.ac.uk); his publications include *Late Latin and Early Romance* (Liverpool, 1982), *Early Ibero-Romance* (Newark, Delaware, 1995), *El Tratado de Cabreros (1206)* (London, 2000) and *A Sociophilological Study of Late Latin* (Turnhout, 2003). His main research interest is in how Latin turned into several different languages.

Tabula Gratulatoria

Dana L. Allen
K. Anipa
Iris Bachmann
Francisco Bautista
Juan Carlos Bayo
Barbara Bisegna
Robert Blake
Jenny Cheshire
Thomas D. Cravens
Alan Deyermond
José Manuel Díaz de Bustamante
Martin J. Duffell
Steven M. Dworkin
María Teresa Echenique Elizondo
Antonio Emiliano
~~John England~~
Roegiest Eugeen
Peter Evans
Paloma García-Bellido García de Diego
Alfonso García Leal
David George
Jean Gilkison
Robert Gillett
Anthony Gooch
John M. Green
Ray Harris-Northall
Stephen Hart
Thomas R. Hart
Louise M. Haywood.
Ann Henderson
David Henn
Leo Hickey
Marian Hobson
F. W. Hodcroft
Guenter Holtus
David Hook

Rosaleen Howard
Lynn Ingamells
Patricia James
Laurence Keates
Tom. Lathrop
Martti Leiwo
Paul Lewis-Smith
Ann L. Mackenzie
Ian Mackenzie
Ian Macpherson
Ian Michael
Laura Minervini
Francisco Moreno Fernández
Michael Moriarty
Brian Mott
Carol Overton
Stephen Parkinson
Mair Parry
David G. Pattison
René Pellen
Sheldon Penn
David Pharies
Bernard Pottier
Christopher J. Pountain
Ian Press
Idoya Puig
Diana L. Ranson
Peter T. Ricketts
Joel Rini
Ian G. Roberts
Rebecca Frances Rogers
Rafael Sala
Rodney Sampson
Fernando Sánchez Miret
Kim Schulte
Dorothy Sherman Severin
Verity Smith
Clive R. Sneddon
Ingmar Söhrman
Philip Swanson
Barry Taylor
Isabel Torres

David Trotter
Donald M. Tuten
Edward F. Tuttle
José del Valle
Nigel Vincent
Dieter Wanner
Geoffrey West
Max W. Wheeler
Jane Whetnall
Roger Wright
Stephen Young
Departamento de Filología Hispánica, Universidad de León
Sydney Jones Library, University of Liverpool
Taylor Institution Library, Oxford
Caroline Skeel Library, Queen Mary, Universiy of London
University of Wales Aberystwyth

Printed in the United States
38763LVS00005B/37